I dedicate this book to my wife, Becky, who became a temporary author's widow and to the many methodologists and language developers whose advances influenced and contributed to the work presented here.

# Object-Oriented Requirements Analysis and Logical Design

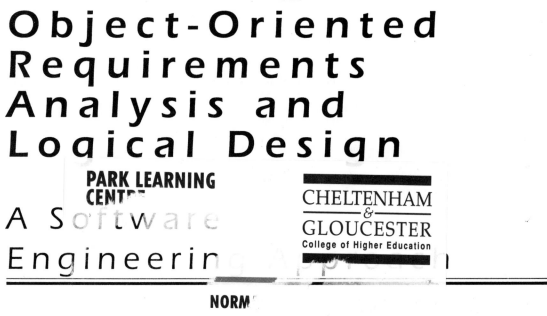

A Software

Engineering

NORM

Donald G. Firesmith

Advanced Software Technology Specialists

John Wiley & Sons, Inc.

New York • Chichester • Brisbane • Toronto • Singapore

In recognition of the importance of preserving what has been written, it is a policy
of John Wiley & Sons, Inc., to have books of enduring value published in the
United States printed on acid-free paper, and we exert our best efforts to that end.

**Library of Congress Cataloging-in-Publication Data:**

Firesmith, Donald G.
      Object-oriented requirements analysis and logical design  :  a
    software engineering approach / Donald G. Firesmith.
            p.    cm.
      Includes bibliographical references and index.
        ISBN 0-471-57806-1 (alk. paper).—ISBN 0-471-57807-X (pbk. : alk. paper)
        1. Object-oriented programming (Computer science)   2. Software
    engineering.   I. Title.
    QA76.64.F57   1992
    005.1'1—dc20                                                    92-15453
                                                                       CIP

Printed in the United States of America

10   9   8   7   6   5   4   3   2   1

# Contents

# Preface

## GOALS

The overall objective of this book is to provide the professional software engineer with the necessary concepts, models, notations, method, and knowledge needed to effectively and efficiently develop large, complex software applications using a practical, yet state-of-the-art, object-oriented method. Specifically, this book:

- Provides a solid understanding of the underlying concepts of Object-Oriented Development (OOD).
- Provides a detailed description of a comprehensive graphical and textual notation for use during Object-Oriented Requirements Analysis and Logical Design (OORALD).
- Teaches the ASTS Development Method 3 (ADM3), a state-of-the-art, third generation object-oriented development method.
- Provides a balanced handling of static architecture and dynamic behavior (including concurrency) issues during requirements analysis and logical design.
- Provides numerous practical examples of object-oriented software and how it can be effectively documented.
- Provides important guidance on how to effectively manage object-oriented developement.
- Points out that there is far more to object-orientation than Object-Oriented Programming (OOP). While important, programming is only a small part of the development of non-trivial applications. The most "bang for the buck" can be achieved by concentrating on the analysis and design aspects of the software.

## AUDIENCE

This book is primarily intended for professional software engineers wishing to learn the basics of object-oriented analysis and logical design. This book also offers the technical manager useful insights into the impact of object-orientation upon software management. It provides much of the material necessary for the development of project proposals, plans, standards, procedures, and training materials. For the CASE tool user and builder, this book provides a detailed description of the ADM3 object-oriented graphics notation and the OOSDL object-oriented specification and design language. It includes both syntax and semantics as a basis for graphical tools (such as ObjectMaker and Paradigm Plus) as well as future language sensitive editors, automatic documentation and code generators, etc. For trainers, professors, and students, this book provides the information necessary to begin to develop good Object-Oriented Software Engineering (OOSE) skills. It can be used for individual study or in undergraduate, graduate, and corporate courses.

## STRUCTURE OF THIS BOOK

This book is divided into nine chapters that build on and reinforce one another. The first chapter, Introduction, provides the justification for the subject-matter of the book. The second chapter, Fundamental Concepts, defines and discusses the fundamental concepts of OOD including different development activities, iteration and recursion, software engineering, objects, classes, subassemblies, assemblies, frameworks, attributes, operations, exceptions, messages, inheritance, polymorphism, etc. The third chapter, Object-Oriented Models, discusses the Assembly, Object, Class, State, Control, and Timing Models and their associated graphical notations. The fourth chapter, Identifying Objects, Classes, and Subassemblies, discusses numerous practical approaches to the identification of objects, classes, and subassemblies including their strengths and limitations. The fifth chapter, The ASTS Development Method 3, emphasizes the requirements analysis and logical design steps of the ADM3 method, but also discusses those activities that take place both before analysis and after logical design. The sixth chapter, Object-Oriented Specification and Design Language, provides the complete syntax and an overview of the semantics of the OOSDL. The seventh chapter, Documenting Object-Oriented Requirements Specifications and Logical Designs, provides content and format guidelines for adequately documenting requirements and designs in an object-oriented manner. The eighth chapter, Automotive Dashboard Application, provides a complete example developed using the ADM3 method. The ninth chapter, Development Cycles and Major Reviews, discusses the benefits and risks associated with various object-oriented development cycles, provides guidelines for when the traditional waterfall development cycle must be used (e.g., for contractual reasons), and discusses the types of major reviews best suited for object-oriented development cycles. The appendicies include an abbreviations list, a complete glossary, a detailed index, a definition of the syntax and semantics of the diagrams, a general bibliography, and an appendix that should prove useful on military projects using DOD-STD-2167A.

The ASTS Development Method 3 (ADM3), its associated notation, and the OOSDL specification and design language described in this book are in the public domain, and their use is encouraged.  Please acknowledge their source and send all recommendations and problem reports to Mr. Donald Firesmith at the following address:

> Advanced Software Technology Specialists (ASTS)
> 17124 Lutz Road
> Ossian, Indiana 46777
> (219) 639-6305 (voice)
> (219) 747-9389 (fax)

Dedicated to bringing both developers and customers the most modern cost-effective solutions to their critical software problems, ASTS delivers high quality state-of-the-art services and products in the following areas:

- Consulting and training at both the management and technical levels.
- Evaluation and independent verification and validation (IV8V) of software products and activities.
- Development of transition and development plans, request for proposals (RFPs) and proposals, standards and procedures, and reports.

## ACKNOWLEDGMENTS

I would like to acknowledge the important work of Ed Berard, Grady Booch, Peter Coad, Ed Colbert, Jean Ichbiah, Bertrand Meyer, Stephen Mellor, Sally Shlaer, and Ken Shumate who have most influenced my ideas.  I would also like to thank (in alphabetical order) Roy Bell, Grady Booch, David Brookman, David Brownbridge, Tim Fujita-Yuhas, Dale Gaumer, Peggy Halavi,  Ken van der Loo, Don Reifer, Ken Shumate, and Dan Sivertson who reviewed this book for their numerous helpful suggestions and criticisms that greatly improved its quality. I am also indebted to Dale Gaumer, who provided significant support in the production of many of the graphics of this book. I would also like to take this opportunity to thank Magnavox Electronics Systems Company for their generous support, first when I was an employee and later as a consultant.  I would also like to thank the over 2500 students who have attended my seminars and tutorials in the US, Canada, Western Europe, Australia, and New Zealand over the last five years and who have significantly improved the material presented in this book through their rigorous questioning;  you never really know anything until you have had to teach it over and over to professionals.  Finally, I would also like to acknowledge the support of Herm Fisher, President of Mark V Systems, who was the first CASE tool vendor to support the method and notation of this book.

# Chapter 1

# Introduction

## 1.1 WHY WE NEED SOFTWARE ENGINEERING

The size, complexity, criticality, and long life of many of today's software applications far exceed the ability of any single developer to understand, not to mention develop, regardless of how experienced or clever the developer. Whereas the rare excellent hacker may be able to generate significant amounts of functioning prototype code, such an approach is clearly inappropriate for safety- or business-critical software. Hacking certainly does not scale up to projects that employ tens or hundreds of developers working over several years on the same software. On such significant projects, it is crucial that the software be well engineered, and software engineering has much to offer the individual analyst and designer. Despite this need, most universities do not yet teach software engineering, as opposed to computer science, and many developers first encounter software engineering on the job.

A representative of a major software buyer [Strassmann 1992] characterized the need for modern software engineering as follows:

> [The primary agents of resistance to modern software engineering] are the creative loner-programmers. You can easily identify them. Every computer installation survives only by having a few such individuals. They are committed to solving complex malfunctions. They are immersed in their craft, but find it difficult to explain or document it. They usually work late into the night, trying to fix a problem caused by low-quality and frequently repaired incomprehensible software. They treat their work as a challenging artistic experience. They place little reliance on assistance from others and most likely disregard orderly documentation and business practices that do not concern their work. The computer code they write is unique, elegant, and usually incomprehensible to others—which explains why they are highly valued as indispensable staff.
>
> I am sure that you can recognize here the analogy with the highly skilled medieval craftsman, who guards the privileges of his guild against the onslaught of low-cost, mass produced merchandise that consumers can purchase at a fraction of the cost of individually produced creations. The craftsman-programmer is like the small-town shoemaker a few hundred years ago, who fashions shoes from custom-produced materials, custom-fitted

1

to the preferences of an individual customer. The only problem with this craft-mode of production is that it usually took a very long time to get a single pair of shoes, and they cost 10-20 times more than their mass produced modern equivalent.

The age of individually crafted software code, custom-fitted to a customer's temporary needs, has passed. . . . The old mode of production and trouble-shooting is financially not affordable as budgets are cut. Programming, as a personalized art form, is intolerable because systems interoperability across applications, functions, and [organizations] is now mandatory.

Software engineering is not the same as computer science. *Software engineering* is the practical application of the results of modern computer science to the timely and cost-effective development, reuse, and maintenance of high-quality software. It is concerned with the establishment and application of current, sound engineering concepts, principles, processes (with associated activities and development cycles), methods, techniques, models, metrics, and environments including tools and languages. These in turn must be supported and enforced by the appropriate policies, standards, procedures, guidelines, practices, evaluations, and tools. The primary goal of software engineering is to produce software that is correct, efficient, extensible, flexible, maintainable, modifiable, portable, reliable, reusable, safe, testable, validatible, verifiable, and understandable.

## 1.2  WHY WE NEED A NEW PARADIGM AND METHODS

Most developers have learned the software engineering paradigms and methods of the 1970s: top-down functional decomposition and the classic waterfall development cycle. Unfortunately, many have not been able to keep up with the advances of the 1980s and 1990s associated with object orientation because of schedule deadlines and other pressures. As software technology has advanced, so have its paradigms, methods, principles, and concepts. Some concepts (e.g., modularity) have evolved and are being applied in new ways. Other concepts (e.g., inheritance) are relatively new to many developers and have led to a major paradigm shift in how software is developed.

When new software technology is introduced, this question is often asked: "Why change the tried and true method [or paradigm or language] we're using now? After all, if it ain't broke, don't fix it." I have even heard one so-called software engineer say that "good engineering is timeless."

There are many obvious answers to this position. First of all, all technology evolves, and software technology is evolving extremely rapidly. Computer hardware engineers certainly recognize the need for and the advantages of new technology. Even the long-established disciplines—such as civil engineering or architecture, which have been around for thousands of years and are relatively stable—are constantly evolving and improving though much more slowly than software technology.

Software engineering is a human activity, and human activities are always subject to improvement. Engineers have a professional responsibility to use the best available technology for the application, and to do this, they must keep current by studying and evaluating new technology. Technologies are made to be superseded.

Most important, if someone thinks that traditional software development paradigms and methods are not broken, they have not been very observant. Older paradigms (e.g., functional decomposition, the waterfall development cycle) and their associated methods have numerous well-known problems and limitations that need to be fixed. Methods that are appropriate for small, simple tasks tend to be inappropriate for larger, more complex tasks. Thus, the older methods are proving less suitable as the size and complexity of today's applications increase. Older software development paradigms tend not to be uniform in that they use different methods and notations during different software activities (e.g., Structured Analysis and data-flow diagrams during requirements analysis, Structured Design and structure charts during design). This in turn has led to transitions between activities that are more difficult than would otherwise be necessary.

By concentrating heavily on only a single type of abstraction (i.e., functional), many older approaches have produced incomplete specifications and designs. Important information fell through the cracks. By forcing the analyst and the designer to use the paradigm of the machine (i.e., by concentrating on algorithms), the mapping to the real world and the problem domain has been obscured, and understanding has been lost. As Ed Seidewitz [1989] has noted, "Functional analysis and specification techniques actually sacrifice closeness to the problem domain in order to allow a smooth transition to functional design methods." By localizing the software around the requirements most likely to change (i.e., around functionality rather than around objects or attributes), extensibility has been sacrificed, and different parts of the objects have been scattered to the four winds. As Peter Coad and Ed Yourdon [1990] have noted, "Function/sub-function breakdowns are difficult to construct (because of the indirect mapping) and highly volatile (because of the continual change of functional capability which may be successfully delivered within budget and schedule constraints). For these reasons, we feel that the overall analysis approach should *not* be based on function/subfunction" (emphasis in original).

Functional-decomposition analysis methods have greatly limited software reuse and have led to the redundant development of numerous partial versions of the same objects, thereby lowering productivity and creating configuration management nightmares. By being based on the obsolete waterfall development cycle [Agresti 1986], such software is typically not available for testing until late in the development process, when errors are far more costly to fix [Boehm 1981]. Ultimately, the resulting delivered software is often of suboptimal quality in terms of correctness, extensibility, maintainability, reliability, reusability, safety, and understandability. Software is typically more expensive than it should be and takes too long to develop. Finally, productivity using the older paradigms and methods is not increasing as rapidly as the demand for new software, and the disparity is widening every year.

Clearly, these problems are endemic to the way we develop software, and something major must be done to address them. Significant improvement requires significant change. After all, it is a law of the universe that if we keep doing the same things in the same way, we will obtain the same unacceptable result. As Peter Coad [1991] has noted, what is needed is a paradigm shift, a revolution built upon yet superseding the older methods, rather than a minor evolutionary enhancement of them.

## 1.3 WHY WE NEED OBJECT-ORIENTED DEVELOPMENT

Despite the clear need for new methods, the fact that a method is new does not mean that it will solve the existing problems. It may even create more problems than it solves. What then is Object-Oriented Development, and why should software engineers master it?

**Object-Oriented Development** (OOD) is not a single method. It is the name given to a set of related development methods, based on the concept of an **object**: an abstraction or model of a single application-domain entity that has structure, state, and behavior. Instead of being based on functional decomposition or event partitioning, software applications that are developed using object-oriented methods are analyzed, designed, implemented, and tested in terms of their component objects, classes of related objects, and subassemblies and frameworks of related objects and classes. Instead of being restricted to the obsolete waterfall development cycle, object-oriented software is incrementally developed, using recursion and iteration.

Because of the significance of these differences compared with older methods, OOD requires a fundamental paradigm shift. Unfortunately, paradigm shifts are inherently difficult to achieve. As Niccolo Machiavelli noted in *The Prince* as early as 1513, "There is nothing more difficult to take in hand, more perilous to conduct, or more uncertain in its success, than to take the lead in the introduction of a new order of things. For the reformer has enemies in all those who profit by the old order, and only lukewarm defenders in all those who would profit by the new order, this lukewarmness arising partly from . . . the incredulity of mankind, who do not truly believe in anything new until they have had actual experience with it." Similarly, Ben Franklin noted in 1781 that "to get the bad customs of a country changed and the new ones, though better, introduced, it is necessary to first remove the prejudices of the people, enlighten their ignorance, and convince them that their interests will be promoted by the proposed changes; and this is not the work of a day." Finally, Tolstoy wrote, "I know that most men, including those at ease with problems of the greatest complexity, can seldom accept even the simplest and most obvious truth if it is such as would oblige them to admit the falsity of conclusions which they have delighted in explaining to colleagues, which they have proudly taught to others, and which they have woven, thread by thread, into the fabric of their lives."

Unfortunately, these same factors are at work today in many software development organizations, and the shift to object orientation is often difficult and slow. Many of us have practiced older paradigms, methods, models, and concepts for many years, and a certain amount of "hardening of the neurons" seems inevitable once something is mastered. Eventually, however, the advantages of the new overcome the orthodoxy of the old, and progress occurs. *Object-oriented* has become the buzzword of the 1990s, as *structured* was to the 1980s.

What are the advantages of object-oriented methods? Although not a panacea, modern object-oriented methods address many of the problems plaguing today's software manager and engineer. The major advantages of object-oriented methods are addressed in more detail later in this book but can be summarized here. Object-oriented methods can

- Address the problems that increasing size and complexity cause, by (a) using all major types of abstraction, (b) localizing around larger abstractions (i.e., object and class abstractions rather than functional abstractions), and (c) using recursion to divide software into small, manageable subassemblies (a.k.a. "subsystems")
- Produce more complete and understandable specifications and designs by using all types of abstraction and objects that directly model entities in the application domain
- Ease the transitions between development activities by better applying the software-engineering principle of uniformity (i.e., by using the same paradigm, concepts, models, and notation throughout analysis and design)
- Improve the extensibility, maintainability, reusability, and configuration management of the specifications, designs, and code, by localizing around objects and classes rather than around operations (i.e., functions), which are much more subject to change
- Improve the software engineering principles of modularity and information hiding by forming more cohesive modules with fewer and more abstract interfaces
- Facilitate the transition to implementation with object-oriented programming languages (OOPLs) and object-oriented database management systems (OODBMSs)
- Bring major benefits in terms of code size, efficiency, and reuse, due to the use of OOPLs and OODBMSs
- Make developers' jobs easier and improve the resulting software and documentation
- Increase the quality of the specifications, designs, and code, as well as increase the productivity of the software engineers by relying on global recursion and iteration to incrementally develop, verify, and validate these critical products
- Produce relatively higher quality software in terms of extensibility, maintainability, reuse, and understandability and relatively less expensive software in terms of cost and schedule, when such methods are properly managed and applied

Considering both the importance of software and today's economy, using obsolete paradigms and methods is dangerous at best and may even be professionally and organizationally suicidal.

## 1.4  AN ILLUSTRATION OF THE BASIC CONCEPTS, USING BASEBALL

The game of baseball is used herein to illustrate some of the basic concepts of OOD. Those concepts that are printed in boldface in the following sentences may also be found in the glossary; other key concepts are highlighted in italic type. Figure 1-1 shows the relevant roles (e.g., players), devices (e.g., balls), systems (e.g., teams), and conceptual entities (e.g., rules). An object-oriented software simulation of the baseball game would consist of corresponding **objects**—that is, models of individual players, coaches, managers, umpires, balls, bats, bases, stadiums, and rules. Notice that some of the objects are **concurrent**, with their own thread of control (e.g., the players, coaches, managers, and umpires), whereas other objects are **sequential** (e.g., the balls and bats). Some objects are *tangible* (e.g., players and balls), whereas others are *intangible* (e.g., the rules). Objects (e.g., players) have **attributes** (e.g., batting average and salary), **operations** (e.g., pitch, catch, run bases), and **exceptions** (e.g., pull hamstring). Notice also that data and functionality are localized within objects rather than being scattered, as with functional decomposition. This produces a higher, more powerful form of **modularity**. Objects are **black boxes** with a visible **specification**

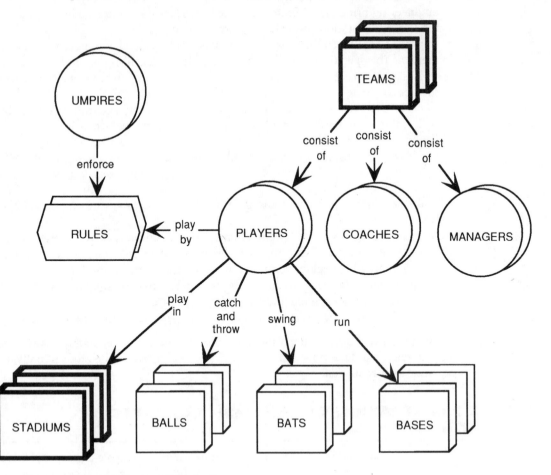

**Figure 1-1: Object-Oriented Baseball**

detailing both the object's *responsibilities* (e.g., show up, play well) and a hidden **body** (i.e., fans are not concerned with the player's biology of the nerves, muscles, and bones as long as they play well, though a sports physiologist may be very concerned with how a player can play well). The attributes and operations are **encapsulated** together, meaning that the way in which they are implemented and interact is irrelevant (i.e., information hiding) to the outside observer.

Because no object or class is an island, both objects and classes are **associated** with each other in various ways. They *collaborate* with one another, often as equal partners, to accomplish their goals (e.g., win the game). Object-oriented software therefore has fewer strict control hierarchies than does functionally decomposed software. For example, the pitcher throws the ball to the catcher, and the catcher throws the ball back to the pitcher without each toss being directed by the coach.

Objects interact by sending **messages** to one another (e.g., the catcher suggests the type of pitch with a hand signal; the umpire yells "You're out!"). Figure 1-2 shows the messages sent from two concurrent objects to two sequential objects.

Some objects are **aggregates** of others (e.g., each team is composed of a specific manager and a specific set of players, coaches, and trainers). Figure 1-3 shows an example aggregation hierarchy of sequential objects.

Objects naturally fall into **classes** of related objects, and when describing the object in general terms, the speaker naturally talks in terms of the classes of objects rather than of individual **instances** of the classes. Classes typically exist in **classification hierarchies** of **superclasses** and **subclasses** that **inherit** the properties of their superclasses (e.g., pitchers and catchers are subclasses of the superclass baseball players, and they inherit the superclass's attributes, operations, and exceptions). Figure 1-4 shows an example classification hierarchy of concurrent classes. One reason that classification is difficult is that there are different ways to classify the same objects (e.g., baseball players also could have been classified as either rookies or old

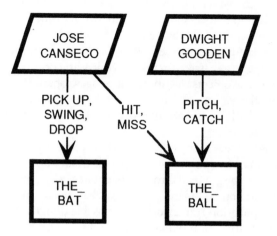

**Figure 1-2: Example Message Passing**

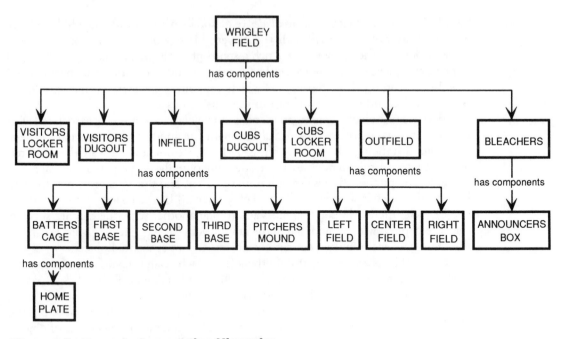

**Figure 1-3: Example Aggregation Hierarchy**

timers). **Single inheritance** occurs when subclasses only inherit from a single super-class, whereas **multiple inheritance** occurs when subclasses inherit from multiple superclasses. *Single classification* describes objects that are instances of only one class, whereas **multiple classification** describes objects that are instances of more than one class (e.g., Dwight Gooden is a member of the class "pitchers" and a member of the class "athletes," which also includes race horses). *Dynamic classification* occurs when the class that an object belongs to changes over time (e.g., as an infant, Jose Conseco was not a member of the baseball-players class).

Just as the umpires can send both pitchers and outfielders to the bench with the same message (e.g., "strike three!"), **overloading** occurs when the same name is given to the different objects, attributes, messages, operations, or exceptions in different scopes. Similarly, just as batters and pitchers respond differently when they hear the phrase "Play ball!" **polymorphism** occurs when different objects respond differently to the same message.

Because a great many objects and classes exist in any nontrivial application, the developers must find some way to organize them into manageable collections. Objects and classes can be grouped into **subassemblies**, which can be grouped into **assemblies**, just as players can be organized into baseball teams and teams can be organized into leagues. Application **frameworks** are reusable designs that occur over and over again in the same application domain, just as the basic structure of baseball teams occurs over and over in various leagues around the world.

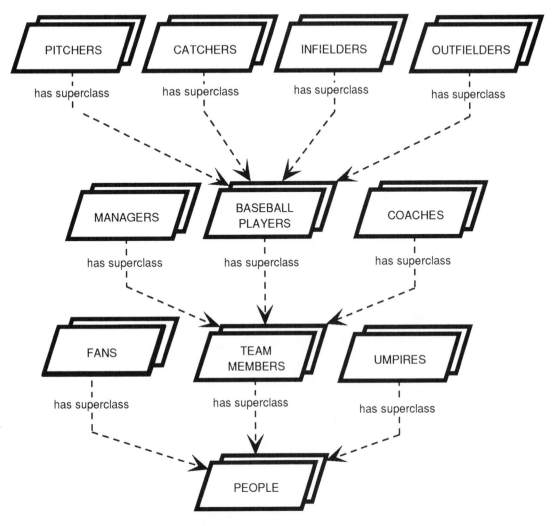

**Figure 1-4: Example Classification Hierarchy**

## 1.5 CHAPTER REFERENCES

[Agresti 1986] William W. Agresti, Ed., *New Paradigms for Software Development*, Washington, D.C., IEEE Computer Society Press, 1986.

[Boehm 1981] Barry W. Boehm, *Software Engineering Economics*, Englewood Cliffs, NJ, Prentice-Hall, 1981.

[Coad 1991] Peter Coad, "Paradigm Change," *The Coad Letter: New Advances in Object-Oriented Analysis & Design*, 3202 W. Anderson Lane, Suite 208-724, Austin, Texas 78757-9974: Object International Inc., 3 January 1991.

[Coad and Yourdon 1990] Peter Coad and Edward Yourdon, *Object-Oriented Analysis*, Englewood Cliffs, NJ, Prentice-Hall, 1990.

[Seidewitz 1989] Ed Seidewitz, "Notes on Object-Oriented Analysis and Specification," Greenbelt, MD, NASA Goddard Space Flight Center (unpublished), December 1988.

[Strassman 1992] Paul A. Strassman, "From Craft to an Industry," a speech presented at George Mason University and quoted in full in *CrossTalk*, the monthly technical report of the U.S. Air Force Software Technology Support Center, 14 January 1992.

# Chapter 2

# Fundamental Concepts

As with other areas of software engineering, Object-Oriented Development (OOD) has its own set of fundamental concepts and associated technical jargon. These must be mastered if the software engineer is to successfully develop and communicate object-oriented specifications and designs. This is especially true because OOD is a relatively young discipline, and many of its concepts are new to the beginning developer or even to the experienced developer coming from the world of procedural languages, functional decomposition, and the classic waterfall development cycle. This task of learning new ideas is also made difficult because the terminology has not yet stabilized, and many object-oriented methodologists either use the same word for different concepts or use different words for the same concept.

This chapter presents the most important concepts and terms used in object-oriented domain analysis (OODA), requirements analysis (OORA), and logical design (OOLD). Concepts and terms from object-oriented programming (OOP) are only introduced where relevant, and any differences among meanings are emphasized.

## 2.1  SOFTWARE DEVELOPMENT

### 2.1.1   Traditional Development

Traditional software development methods (e.g., Structured Analysis [DeMarco 1978], Structured Design [Yourdon and Constantine 1979], Structured Analysis and Design Technique (SADT) [SofTech 1978], Structured Development for Real-Time Systems [Ward and Mellor 1985]) were typically based on functional decomposition or event partitioning and the now obsolete waterfall development cycle. Although these offered a vast improvement over the undisciplined hacking that they have largely replaced on nontrivial projects, these methods have since grown past maturity and exhibit significant limitations and signs of obsolescence. They were created for traditional implementation languages (e.g., C, COBOL, FORTRAN, Pascal), were limited to functional building blocks (e.g., subroutines), and had limited ability to model application-domain entities. Such software tends to be both difficult to understand and expensive to develop and maintain, and it offers limited potential for significant reuse. While a great deal of good (and far more bad) software has been developed using these methods and languages, software developers have long sought improved methods and languages that would better support software-engineering principles and goals. OOD, as both an evolutionary (and revolutionary) advance, has proven to be the next great paradigm for software development and is to the 1990s what structured development was to the late 1970s and early 1980s.

## 2.1.2    Object-Oriented Development

*OOD* is a set of related development methods based on the concept of an **object**—an abstraction or model of a single application domain entity with structure, state, and behavior. Instead of being based on functional decomposition or event partitioning, software applications developed using OOD methods are incrementally analyzed, designed, implemented, and tested in terms of their component objects, classes of related objects, and subassemblies and frameworks of related objects and classes.

The scope of OOD can either be an entire application domain (i.e., object-oriented domain development) or an individual application (i.e., object-oriented application development). The first approach supports massive software reuse, whereas the second supports the development of a specific product. (See Figure 2-1: Classes of Object-Oriented Methods.)

*Object-oriented domain development (OODD)* is the development of common reusable objects, classes, subassemblies, and frameworks within a specific application domain. **Object-oriented domain analysis (OODA)** is the identification, analysis, and specification of common, reusable capabilities within a specific application domain, in terms of common objects, classes, subassemblies, and frameworks. **Object-oriented domain design (OODDes)** is the design of common reusable objects, classes, subassemblies, and frameworks within a specific application domain. *Object-oriented domain programming (OODP)* is the programming of common reusable, objects, classes, subassemblies, and frameworks within a specific application domain.

*Object-oriented application development (OOAD)* is the development of application-specific objects, classes, subassemblies, and frameworks. *Object-oriented requirements analysis (OORA)* is the identification, analysis, and specification of capabilities in terms of application-specific objects, classes, subassemblies, and frameworks. **Object-oriented logical design (OOLD)** is the language-independent design of application-specific objects, classes, subassemblies, and frameworks. *Object-oriented implementation design (OOID)* is the language-dependent design of application-specific objects, classes, subassemblies, and frameworks. **Object-oriented programming (OOP)** is the programming of application-specific objects, classes, subassem-

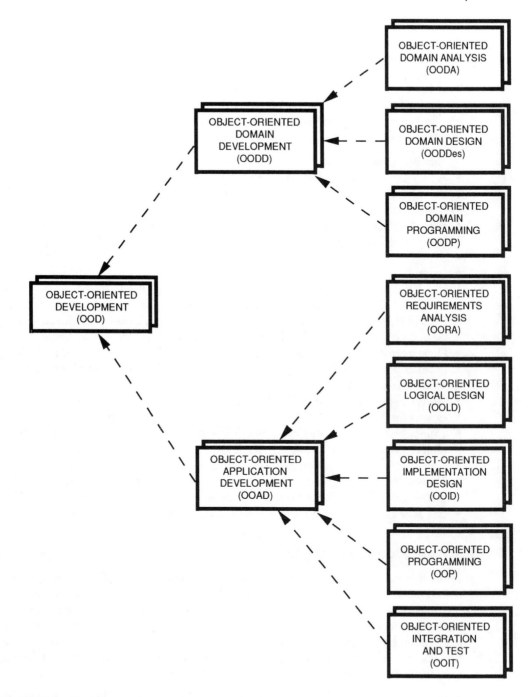

**Figure 2-1: Classes of Object-Oriented Methods**

blies, and frameworks. *Object-oriented integration and test (OOIT)* is the integration and testing of application-specific objects, classes, subassemblies, and frameworks.

Optimally, OOD methods should cover all relevant development activities in a uniform, relatively seamless manner, using the same concepts, models, and notations. This book is primarily restricted to one such method, the ASTS Development Method 3 (ADM3). As one can see from the following list, there are many object-oriented development methods to choose from, and others are constantly being developed and extended:

| | |
|---|---|
| • Ada box structures method | [Comer 1989] |
| • ASTS Development Method 3 (ADM3) | [Firesmith 1993] |
| • Bailin's object-oriented requirements analysis | [Bailin 1989] |
| • Berard's object-oriented design | [Berard 1991a] |
| • Berard's object-oriented domain analysis | [Berard 1991b] |
| • Berard's object-oriented requirements analysis | [Berard 1991c] |
| • Booch's object-oriented design | [Booch 1983, 1991] |
| • Bulman's model-based object-oriented design | [Bulman 1987] |
| • Coad and Yourdon's object-oriented analysis | [Coad and Yourdon 1989] |
| • Coad and Yourdon's object-oriented design | [Coad and Yourdon 1991] |
| • Extended Buhr design method | [Vidale and Hayden 1986] |
| • General object-oriented development (GOOD) | [Seidewitz and Stark 1986] |
| • Hierarchical object-oriented design (HOOD) | [HTG 1991] |
| • Layered virtual machines/object-oriented design | [Nielsen and Shumate 1988] |
| • Model-driven object-oriented systems analysis | [Embley et al., 1992] |
| • Object behavior analysis (OBA) | [Gibson 1990] |
| • Object modeling technique (OMT) | [Rumbaugh et al., 1991] |
| • Object-oriented software development (OOSD) | [Colbert 1989] |
| • Object-oriented systems analysis (OOA) | [Shlaer and Mellor 1988] |
| • Object-oriented (OOO) systems development | [Henderson-Sellers 1992] |
| • ObjectOry | [Jacobson and Linstrøm 1991] |
| • Seidewitz's object-oriented systems analysis | [Seidewitz 1989] |
| • Software construction through object-oriented pictures | [Cherry 1988] |

## 2.1.3    Software Domain Analysis

*Software domain analysis* is the identification, analysis, and specification of common requirements from a specific application domain, typically for reuse on multiple projects within that application domain, such as avionics; banking; command, control, and communications (C3); telecommunications; etc. *OODA* (the identification, analysis, and specification of common, reusable capabilities within a specific application domain, in terms of common objects, classes, subassemblies, and frameworks) has the following objectives:

• Capture application-domain expertise in a consistent, verifiable, understandable format, appropriate for further analysis

- Identify commonly occurring objects, classes, subassemblies, and frameworks
- Analyze and abstract their common capabilities in terms of attributes (including state), operations, and exceptions, using appropriate object-oriented models
- Analyze their common relationships, including aggregation, association, inheritance, and message passing
- Specify and document these capabilities in a form that is useful as input to
  —domain-specific OODDes
  —project-specific OORA

Although OODA is most cost-effective when performed at the organizational level, in order to support multiple projects within the same application domain, many organizations perform either inadequate domain analysis or none at all prior to project inception. If the project is large enough to justify the effort, project-specific OODA can also be performed with the purpose of identifying, analyzing, and documenting common objects, classes, subassemblies, and frameworks for reuse within the project.

## 2.1.4    Application Development

### 2.1.4.1  Software Requirements Analysis

*Software requirements analysis* is the identification, analysis, and specification of requirements for a specific application. OORA (software requirements analysis in terms of the essential objects, classes, and subassemblies and their required capabilities within a specific application) has the following objectives:

- Identify all essential objects, classes, and subassemblies within the application
- Analyze and abstract the essential capabilities of these elements, in terms of attributes (including state), operations, and exceptions, using appropriate object-oriented models
- Analyze the essential relationships among these elements, including aggregation, association, inheritance, and message passing
- Specify and document these requirements in a form that is useful as input to OOLD

OORA specifies only the essential, required capabilities (i.e., the *what* rather than the *how*) of the essential objects and classes, and their essential attributes, operations, and exceptions within the application software. If the analyst can determine multiple, fundamentally different ways of specifying something, then any chosen way represents a design decision rather than requirements. If specified in this way, the chosen way becomes a design constraint rather than a pure requirement.

### 2.1.4.2  Software Logical Design

*Software logical design* is the determination and development of a *language-independent* architecture and behavior for the software of a specific application. OOLD (the software logical design of the architecture and behavior of both essential and nonessential objects, classes, and subassemblies within a specific application) has the following objectives:

- Identify all nonessential objects, classes, and subassemblies within the application
- Design the architecture and behavior of all objects and classes in terms of attributes (including state), operations, and exceptions, using appropriate object-oriented models
- Design the relevant relationships among these elements, including aggregation, association, inheritance, and message passing
- Document these design decisions in a form that is useful as input to OOID

Software logical design covers both essential and nonessential objects, classes, and subassemblies. It is concerned with answering the question "how?" rather than "what?" If there exists only one way of designing something, it is a requirement rather than a design decision. Whereas analysis involves discovery, design requires invention.

## 2.2  ITERATION AND RECURSION

### 2.2.1    Iteration

No software engineer is perfect, and mistakes during analysis and design are all too common. As Grady Booch remarked on February 19, 1992 at the CASEWorld Conference, "I have never seen a class that was developed correctly the first time." While prevention is clearly preferable to cure, and developers should therefore strive to avoid all errors, no complex piece of software can be safely assumed to be bug free. Software engineers must actively search for, find, understand, and fix as many errors as is practical in software specifications and designs, as well as in the resulting software itself.

Iteration is the main process that software engineers use to repair known bugs and to make incremental improvements. With regard to a software-development method, **iteration** is the repetition of the method's relevant steps to modify existing product(s), typically at the same level of abstraction, to correct errors prior to product release. When a bug is found, the software engineer(s) iterate back to fix it by repeating the relevant steps of the method (this time correctly), including both development and verification steps. Iteration is also used to modify specifications and designs as requirements change over time and as improvements are identified. *Iteration* is often confused with *recursion*, which is discussed in the following paragraphs. OOD methods recognize the need for continual improvement and are naturally iterative.

Some software developers (and OOD methods) rely very heavily on iteration to continually improve the software. They start with the first design that comes to mind and continually iterate it like a dog worrying a bone until they are satisfied, or more likely, they run out of time and money. Managers sometimes refer to this as having to "shoot the engineers in order to get the product out the door." This approach might also be called "object-oriented hacking" and should be limited to where practical in terms of cost, schedule, and risk. Software engineering demands a more methodical approach and a reasonable mix of controlled iteration and recursion.

## 2.2.2    Recursion

It is not at all uncommon to find large software applications that contain dozens, if not hundreds or thousands, of objects and classes. No single software engineer can simultaneously understand so many entities at once, and certainly no single developer can easily develop them simultaneously. One loses track of the forest for the trees, and things fall through the cracks. Software engineers need to attack the problem in small, manageable bite-sized pieces.

Recursion is the main technique developers use to solve the size and complexity problem. With regard to software-development methods, **recursion** is the repetition of the method's steps to generate new product(s) at the next lower-level of abstraction. In other words, the developers follow the steps of some method to generate an increment of some products (e.g., specifications, designs, software, and test plans, data, and code), and then repeat the steps of the method at the next lower level of abstraction to generate new increments. Thus, recursion and iteration are related, but quite different:

iteration    ->    same steps and *preexisting* product(s)
recursion    ->    same steps and *new* product(s)

Recursion has long been a fundamental aspect of software-development methods, and software engineers should be quite familiar with it. For example, software engineers using Structured Analysis (SA) do not produce a single giant data flow diagram (DFD) that shows all transforms, data stores, and data flows for an entire project. Such a DFD would typically cover all of the walls of a large room, would be beyond human comprehension, and would be relatively useless. Instead, they develop one or more small, manageable, top-level DFDs and then recurse to produce child DFDs at the next lower-level of abstraction by expanding complex transforms. Similarly, large projects may be incrementally developed in terms of multiple builds or releases, with the software-development method repeated for each increment. This is sometimes referred to as "design a little, code a little." Because builds and releases are often larger than some small projects, this might better be referred to as "design a lot, code a lot."

OOD methods are naturally recursive, although many OOD methodologists have underemphasized the recursive nature of OOD. Recursion has been an important part of OOD since the first OOD method, in which Booch [1983] stated that his "process is not quite complete since, as we begin to implement the operations, we shall certainly uncover other objects and operations that form part of the current [*sic*] level of implementation. Thus, we must repeat the process, at this different level, and again identify objects and operations applicable at this point in the design."

OOD methods can be either locally or globally recursive. **Locally recursive** methods (by definition) repeat the steps of the specific method within a single development activity, such as a phase of the traditional waterfall development cycle

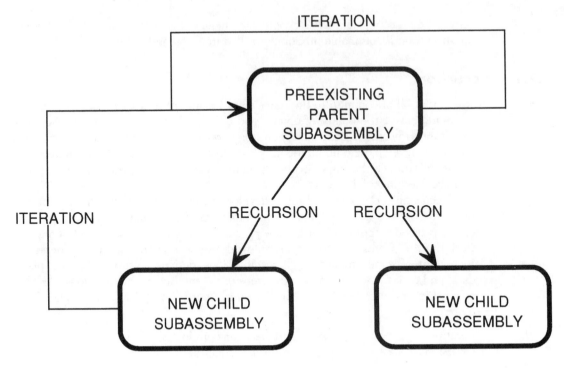

**Figure 2-2: Iteration and Recursion**

or an activity of *Defense System Software Development* (i.e., DOD-STD-2167A)[1] [DOD 1986]. On the other hand, **globally recursive** methods (by definition) span multiple phases of the traditional waterfall development cycle or activities of DOD-STD-2167A. Globally recursive development methods therefore "design a little, code a little." They may even be used to "analyze a little, design a little, code a little, test a little, and integrate a little." On OOD projects, "a little" typically means only the small number (i.e., 3 to 7) of objects and classes making up the relevant subassembly of the current level of abstraction. The difference between iteration and recursion can be seen in Figure 2-2: Iteration and Recursion.

The ADM3 method documented in this book is both globally and locally recursive. Developers repeat the steps of the method numerous times to develop the software in increments of subassemblies at lower and lower levels of abstraction.

*Understanding global recursion is critical to software development.* Globally recursive methods are significantly more efficient and cost-effective because fewer mistakes are made, the resulting analysis and design can be verified as you go, and any mistakes are

---

[1]DOD-STD-2167A is an ANSI and U.S. military standard for developing software that is very popular in the United States, Canada, Western Europe, and Australia for large, complex projects. It is also used for air-traffic control, aerospace, and commercial projects.

found sooner, when they are typically much easier and less expensive to fix. Globally recursive methods also require new (nonwaterfall) development cycles with major impacts on the contract, cost, schedules, staffing, and major reviews involving customer/user personnel.

## 2.3  SOFTWARE ENGINEERING GOALS AND PRINCIPLES

The primary goal of software engineering is high-quality software. Specifically, this means software that is appropriately compatible, correct, correctable, efficient, extensible, maintainable, modifiable, portable, reliable, reusable, robust, safe, secure, testable, understandable, user-friendly, validatible, and verifiable [Meyer 1988; Ross, Goodenough, and Irvine 1975].

**Compatibility** is the ease with which the software may be combined with other software.

**Correctness** is the degree to which software meets its specified requirements and that the requirements meet their associated needs.

**Correctability** is the ease with which latent errors can be found and corrected in the software.

**Efficiency** is the degree to which the software uses hardware resources effectively; efficiency is often overemphasized at the expense of the other goals.

**Extensibility** (a.k.a. *extendibility, flexibility*) is the ease with which the software can be modified to meet changes in requirements.

**Maintainability** is a combination of correctability and extensibility.

**Modifiability** is the ease with which the software can be changed.

**Portability** is the ease with which software can be transitioned to another hardware or software environment.

**Reliability** is the degree to which the software functions correctly over time.

**Reusability** is the ease with which the software may be used for purposes other than those originally intended.

**Robustness** is the degree to which the software continues to function correctly under abnormal circumstances.

**Safety** is the degree to which the software functions without accidental harm to life or property.

**Security** (a.k.a. *integrity*) is the degree to which the software protects itself from unauthorized access or modification.

**Testability** is the degree to which and ease with which the software can be tested for correctness, efficiency, reliability, and robustness.

**Understandability** is the ease with which humans can comprehend the software and its documentation.

**User-friendliness** is the ease with which humans can use the software.

**Validatability** is the ease with which the software can be demonstrated to be correct.

**Verifiability** is the ease with which the software can be demonstrated to meet development standards and procedures.

In order to achieve the aforementioned goals of software engineering, sound engineering principles must be applied. Specifically, software engineers must properly use the principles of abstraction, encapsulation (i.e., localization, modularity, and information hiding), completeness, confirmability, independence, and uniformity. These principles, as they apply to object-oriented requirements analysis and logical design, are discussed in the following paragraphs.

## 2.3.1    Abstraction

While trivial object-oriented applications may consist of 10 or fewer objects and classes, it is not at all unusual for large applications to consist of hundreds, if not thousands, of objects and classes distributed across several processors. Similarly, while many objects and classes contain only a few attributes, attribute types, messages, exceptions, and operations, it is not unusual for some to contain dozens. The potential number of interactions among these objects, classes, and their resources can be staggering. No software engineer can comprehend, at any one time, all aspects of a complex system; nor should one try. Psychologist George A. Miller [Miller 1956] and others have determined that the human mind can only grasp about seven—plus or minus two—units of information at any one time. As Miller observed, "The span of absolute judgment and the span of immediate memory impose severe limitations on the amount of information that we are able to receive, process, and remember." Beyond this inherent human limitation, one loses track of the forest for the trees. Above this limit, a software developer's productivity decreases while the number of errors increases dramatically. Like a juggler with too many balls in the air, software engineers begin to make mistakes, but their errors can have far more serious consequences than can those of any juggler.

In order to deal with the **Miller Limit** (a.k.a. **Hrair Limit**[2] [Adams 1972]), software engineers use the principle of **abstraction**—that is, concentrating on the most important or essential capabilities, properties, or aspects of something (relative to the observer) while temporarily suppressing or ignoring less important, immaterial, or diversionary details. By properly using abstraction, software engineers manage complexity and promote correctness, extensibility, maintainability, reusability, and understandability. *Abstraction* is also the name given to the result obtained by using the principle of abstraction. An *abstraction* is therefore a model that includes all essential capabilities, properties, or aspects of what is being modeled without any extraneous details.

Abstraction is used to both decompose (or partition) a complex system into its component parts and to compose a complex system out of its component parts. Both decomposition and composition produce architectures (of requirements, design, and code) that are hierarchical by *abstraction level*. See Figure 2-3: Levels of Abstraction.

---

[2]After the book Watership Down by R. Adams, in which the rabbits had trouble counting past three and called all larger numbers "hrair." Apparently, we software engineers are a little over twice as smart as those rabbits.

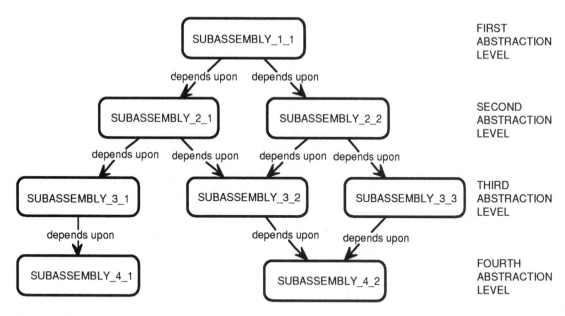

**Figure 2-3: Levels of Abstraction**

In order to promote understandability and to minimize errors, each abstraction should be understandable as a whole without regard to its lower-level abstractions. The same is true of a collection of logically related abstractions and abstraction levels. Thus, the number of items (e.g., essential objects and classes) in an abstraction level should typically be less than or equal to what can be readily attended to at one time by the human mind.

Determining what belongs (and does not belong) in a given abstraction and abstraction level is one of the most difficult jobs for most analysts and designers. Developers tend to violate the Miller Limit by including too many abstractions in a collection of abstractions (e.g., by placing too many nodes on a single diagram) and by inserting information that properly belongs at lower levels of abstraction.

There are several important types of abstraction, depending on what is being modeled. We use the following six types of abstraction in this book:

1. Object abstractions
2. Class abstractions
3. Data abstractions
4. Functional abstractions
5. Process abstractions
6. Exception abstractions

*Objects* are abstractions that model individual application-domain or solution-space entities. *Classes* are abstract templates that model similar application-domain or solution-space entities. **Data abstractions** model data and are used when dealing with the attributes of objects and classes. **Functional abstractions** model sequential operations, whereas **process abstractions** model concurrent operations. Both functional and process abstractions are used when dealing with the operations of objects and classes. **Exception abstractions** model error conditions and error handling and are used to create robust objects and classes. See Figure 2-4: Types of Abstraction.

## 2.3.2    Encapsulation

Software-development methods must ensure that the appropriate information is properly encapsulated into the right type of entity. **Encapsulation** is the combination of the software-engineering principles of modularity, localization, and information hiding. Each of these is very important for the efficient development of robust, reliable, and maintainable systems.

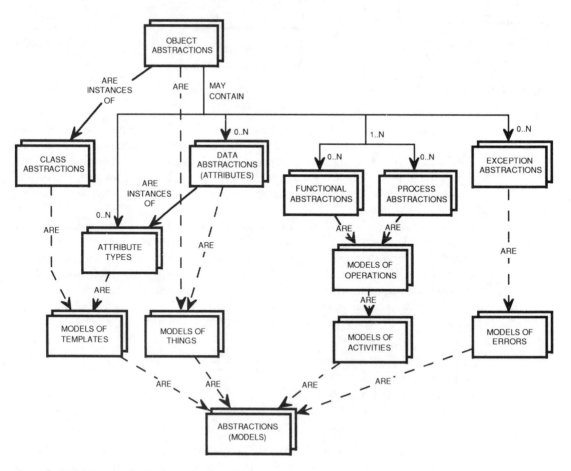

**Figure 2-4: Types of Abstractions**

**Modularity** is the purposeful partitioning of requirements, design, and software into collections of the appropriate size and complexity, consistent with software-engineering goals. Modularity is used to construct larger components (i.e., modules) and smaller operations in OOD than when using functional methods because

- Modules are created for object abstractions rather than functional abstractions
- Operations must be allocated to and encapsulated within objects and classes

**Localization** is the purposeful partitioning of requirements, design, and software into collections so that logically related resources are physically grouped together to increase cohesion and to decrease coupling. It is more important to localize a complete abstraction (using the principles of abstraction, completeness, and localization) than it is to create a small module (using modularity).

Almost all software-development methods localize capabilities and resources into entities in terms of one type of abstraction. OOD methods (e.g., ADM3) localize along object and class abstraction lines, while data-driven methods (e.g., Warnier-Orr [Orr 1981]) are based on data abstraction. Functional-decomposition methods (e.g., Structured Analysis [SA; DeMarco 1978] and Structured Design [SD; Yourdon and Constantine 1979]) localize along functional-abstraction lines, whereas process-abstraction methods (e.g., Hasan Gomaa's ADARTS [Gomaa 1984], George Cherry's original Process Abstraction Method for Embedded Large Applications [PAMELA; Cherry 1988] and Buhr's original design method [Buhr 1983]) localize software into process-abstraction modules.

Traditional development methods scatter the parts of objects and classes to different functional and process abstractions, abstraction levels, computer software configuration items (CSCIs), and developers or developer teams. This in turn:

- Increases data coupling
- Decreases extensibility, maintainability, and understandability
- Makes the creation of complete classes and objects more difficult, which considerably decreases reusability
- Makes the tracing from functional requirements considerably more difficult
- Results in configuration-management and maintenance nightmares

**Information hiding** is the deliberate hiding of information (e.g., design decisions, implementation details) in order to promote abstraction, support incremental top-down development, protect against accidental corruption, and promote the achievement of software-engineering goals. All resources of a component should be hidden unless specifically needed by another component. Common global data are not used, but rather attributes are hidden within objects and classes. Each component should be divided into two separately developable (and compilable) parts: the specification (or interface) and the body (or implementation).

The *specification* declares the outside, user view of the entity. It specifies what the entity is and does, but not how it does it. It provides the visible interface of the entity to other entities. Objects, classes, and subassemblies are said to *export* their visible resources. When properly supported by either the specification and design language or the implementation language, the specification becomes a contract between the entity and its clients that is enforced by the compiler and possibly the run-time environment.

The *body* declares the inside, developer view of the entity. It declares how the entity does what it does. It also provides the hidden implementation of the entity.

This logical and physical separation of specification and body has many advantages. It increases understandability by limiting the scope of what a software engineer has to deal with at any one time. It increases maintainability by ensuring that other entities need not be affected by changes to a specific entity's body, so long as its specification is not affected (assuming adequate language and compiler support). It promotes a high degree of parallelism, allowing multiple developers to work simultaneously on different parts (i.e., specification, body, operation body) of the same object. It minimizes recompilation efforts if supported by the implementation language's compiler.

In order to obtain an overview of a set of interacting objects, classes, and/or subassemblies, it may only be necessary to document the name and type of entity on analysis and design diagrams. However, in order to understand an entity, it is almost always necessary to understand the entity's specification and is often useful to understand its body. Using a single icon to represent the entity is thus often inadequate to determine whether the entity is correct. Specifications are often also shown when it is important to document the resources exported by these entities in order to provide a user view of the objects, classes, and subassemblies. When the developer's view is also needed, the body may be added, to provide details of hidden resources. Specifications and bodies can be shown graphically, either by using icons for specifications and bodies or by socketing icons of specification resources and nesting icons of body resources in the icon of the parent entity.

The first approach, using icons for specifications and bodies, is shown in Figure 2-5. The *icon for a specification* for an object, class, or subassembly is a rectangle drawn with thin lines hung below the icon for the object, class, or subassembly. The *icon for a body* is a rectangle drawn with dotted lines and is either hung below the icon for the specification or to the right of the icon for the specification. These rectangles may be divided by horizontal solid and dotted lines to separate the different types of resources that may be exported from or hidden within objects, classes, and subassemblies.

The second approach, using socketing and nesting for documenting specifications and bodies, is shown in Figure 2-6. The icons for valid *exported resources* declared in the specification are drawn socketed in the border of the icon for the parent entity, whereas those for valid *hidden resources* declared in the body are shown nested inside the icon for the parent entity.

## 2.3.3    Completeness, Confirmability, Independence, and Uniformity

**Completeness** is the degree to which entities (e.g., objects and classes) contain all necessary and useful characteristics, properties, and resources. That is, they should

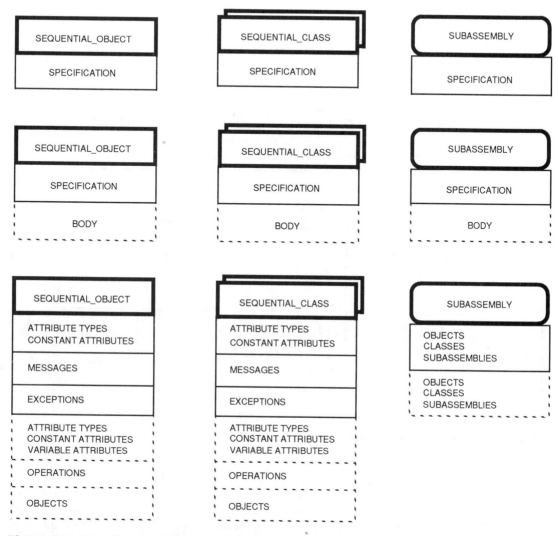

**Figure 2-5: Icons for Specifications and Bodies**

*store* all appropriate *data* (i.e., have all necessary attributes), *provide* all appropriate *services* (i.e., accept all appropriate messages and perform all appropriate operations), and *handle* and raise all appropriate *exceptions*. Generic classes should also have all appropriate generic formal parameters.

Proper use of this principle makes the objects and classes much more reusable, increases developer productivity, and decreases configuration management problems. This is especially true (although much more difficult to achieve) if a functional

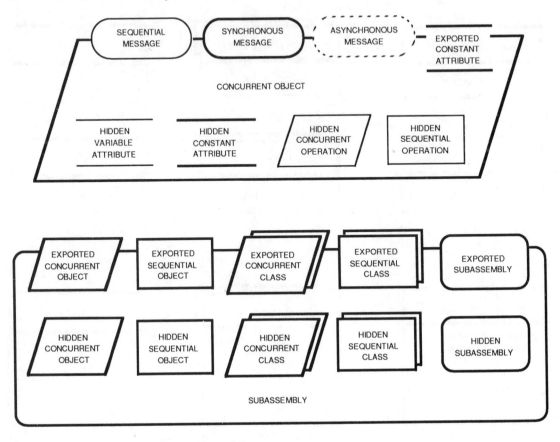

**Figure 2-6: Socketing and Nesting of Resources**

decomposition approach is used as a front end to the OOD, in which case, pieces of the objects and classes are scattered to the four winds, both vertically and horizontally throughout the functional hierarchy. Often, different aspects of the same object or class are therefore assigned to different developers, resulting in the redundant development of multiple partial versions of the same object or class. Document and code size increases, and understandability is lost. When the requirements change or bugs are found, the same changes must be simultaneously made in the same way to all of the variants, or quality suffers.

**Confirmability** is the degree to which the software engineers can readily determine whether the software is correct, reliable, and robust. The localization of attributes, operations, and exceptions into individual objects and classes makes it easier to confirm that they meet their requirements without unexpected side effects of coupling. The globally recursive nature of OOD supports confirmability through the incremental verification and validation of the software and ensures that errors are found earlier in the development process.

**Independence** is the degree to which the software does not rely on other entities. The coupling between objects and classes should be minimized. Where practical, objects and classes should be independent of the underlying hardware and operating system.

As with functional approaches, the important concepts of coupling and cohesion are still useful with OOD, but they have slightly different interpretations and effects. *Coupling* refers to the number of relationships and the amount of information flow between entities. Coupling should be minimized to support information hiding. Each component (i.e., object, class, subassembly) should thus communicate as little as possible and with as few components as possible. Because objects and classes primarily interact via message passing, the number of message paths and of messages along these paths should be minimized. Inheritance, which is discussed later herein, unfortunately increases coupling between classes in a way that is unique to OOD. *Cohesion* refers to the extent to which the resources of an abstraction are localized within that abstraction. Whereas *functional* cohesion is critical for messages and operations, it is inappropriate for objects and classes, which are based on object and class abstraction rather than functional abstraction. Unlike coupling, cohesion should be maximized, to support abstraction and localization.

**Uniformity** is the degree to which the same paradigm, models, notations, and concepts are consistently applied throughout the development process. Unnecessary differences should be avoided. Many older methods (e.g., SA/SD) used different diagrams (e.g., DFDs, structure charts) and different concepts (e.g., transforms and modules) during different development activities, and this resulted in difficult transitions among these activities. OOD, however, tends to use the same paradigm, models, diagrams, and concepts during all development activities.

## 2.3.4   Concurrency and Real-Time

Concurrency and real-time constraints are critical issues that must be properly addressed in many application domains, such as avionics, embedded software, process control, and telecommunications. Although they are less important in the data-processing world, they are still important in several areas (e.g., transaction processing) and have something to offer, even when developing batch applications. Yet concurrency and real-time are often ignored or underemphasized in the object-oriented community, which has instead tended to emphasize static architecture design and reuse over dynamic behavior design. One of the goals of this book is to present a more balanced approach to both software architecture and software behavior.

Before addressing how to model concurrency, it may help to ask, Why is concurrency critical? For several important reasons. The application domain entities that objects and classes model are for the most part naturally concurrent. The universe is not scheduled by some cosmic cyclic executive, and reality is not controlled by a heavenly operating system using round-robin scheduling. If objects and classes are properly to model all relevant characteristics and behavior of the application domain entities, then their concurrency and timing properties should be addressed because concurrent entities behave differently than sequential ones. If the software to be developed is to react to the real world (e.g., via asynchronous hardware interrupts), concurrency and real-time issues are important.

Thus, some means of addressing concurrency seems essential. For some situations, one way of doing so is to use cyclic executives and polling to sequentialize everything into a single thread of control, but this has several major drawbacks. By forcing concurrent entities into sequential objects and classes, complexity increases and understandability decreases because additional "scheduler" objects must be added. Also, cyclic executives are notoriously inefficient and brittle when requirements change (as they always do). Often, timing requirements demand that certain messages must be passed and certain operations must execute at certain absolute times or within certain time limits. In some cases, when the right answer is too late, it is definitely the wrong answer. Sometimes, messages may be safely dropped (e.g., because replacement data will arrive within some allowable time limit), and sometimes they may not. Sometimes, objects must react to external inputs within critically short time limits. For example, the navigation objects in a fighter aircraft may need to be interrupted when particular radar objects detect that an enemy missile has locked on so that electronic countermeasure objects can immediately execute, and these objects have only a very short time in which to react to this change in system mode.

Another factor to consider is that once there is any concurrency (i.e., multiple threads of control) in the objects, there often needs to be significantly more. For example, if two concurrent objects can send messages to a third object, the third object will probably have to be concurrent. Otherwise, one or more attributes of the third object may be accidentally corrupted due to interleaved access (i.e., one operation may only partially update the attribute before its time slice is complete and the second operation may then start with a partially updated attribute).

For these reasons, most objects and classes should be concurrent during requirements analysis and logical design, even if many are later sequentialized during implementation design, due to limitations of the implementation language, run-time, and operating system and for inherent efficiency reasons.

If concurrency must be addressed, there are three possibilities. One can address objects first and concurrency second [Booch 1991]; at the other extreme, one can address concurrency first and objects second [Shumate 1992]; or one can address them concurrently and iteratively, as recommended by this book. Although I agree with Shumate that concurrency is critical and must be addressed early, I disagree that it should be addressed prior to objects and classes. Relying initially on process abstraction and data/control flow diagrams has many of the same disadvantages as relying on functional abstraction and decomposition. The pieces of the objects and classes tend to be scattered horizontally and vertically throughout the software, and, like Humpty Dumpty, all the manager's designers and all the manager's programmers cannot easily put the objects back together again.

On the other hand, addressing objects first without consideration of concurrency and timing issues is also somewhat dangerous, although not as dangerous as the other way around. Additional objects (e.g., buffers) and operations (e.g., to protect the attributes) must often be added. Because the entities modeled by objects and classes are often naturally concurrent, proper object and class identification usually produces objects and classes that can easily be made concurrent (although the important issues of priority, priority inversion, deadlock, livelock, starvation, mutual exclusion, race conditions, etc. still have to be correctly handled). The best approach seems to be to consider both issues simultaneously, with concurrency and timing issues addressed in terms of both *objects*, which may be concurrent or sequential, and *messages*, which may be sequential, synchronous, and asynchronous. Concurrency and timing are addressed later in this book in terms of icons, diagrams (e.g., timing diagrams), and such things as timed event lists.

## 2.4  ENTITIES

### 2.4.1    Objects

As the name implies, OOD (including OODA, OORA, and OOLD) is founded on the concept of an object. An **object** is defined as a software abstraction that models all relevant aspects of a single tangible or conceptual entity or thing from the application domain or solution space. An object is one of the primary software entities in an object-oriented application, typically corresponds to a software module, and consists of a set of related attribute types, attributes, messages, exceptions, operations, and optional component objects. An object may be documented in terms of requirements, design, code, etc. On projects using the U.S. military standard [DOD-STD-2167A], an object often corresponds to a computer software unit (CSU).[3]

In order to model properly all relevant aspects of such entities, an object must store attributes (including data such as state information) of specific types, accept messages, hide operations that may or may not affect the encapsulated attributes, and raise exceptions that are usually associated with operations. As an abstraction, an object encapsulates these resources and only exports information and resources (e.g., messages and exceptions) at a high, user-oriented level of abstraction while hiding the implementation details of all encapsulated resources. Data, function, process, and exception abstractions are therefore required to implement object abstraction. Each object has both a specification and a body that declare these localized resources.

For example, the following is the specification and body of THE_ DESIRED_TEMPERATURE object written in the object-oriented specification and design language (OOSDL) described in Chapter 6:

```
object THE_DESIRED_TEMPERATURE is concurrent
 parent subassembly DIGITAL_THERMOSTAT;
specification
-- no exported attribute types or constants.
```

---

[3]This mapping from objects to CSUs depends on how the object is implemented in the programming language. An object is a CSU if it is implemented as a module (e.g., an Ada package or task), but not if it is implemented as a part of a module (e.g., as a variable).

```
message DECREMENT            raise FAILURE_OCCURRED_IN is synchronous;
message INCREMENT            raise FAILURE_OCCURRED_IN is synchronous;
message START                raise FAILURE_OCCURRED_IN is synchronous;
message STOP                 raise FAILURE_OCCURRED_IN is synchronous;
message USE_CELSIUS          raise FAILURE_OCCURRED_IN is synchronous;
message USE_FAHRENHEIT       raise FAILURE_OCCURRED_IN is synchronous;
exception FAILURE_OCCURRED_IN;
end;


object THE_DESIRED_TEMPERATURE
 needs THE_MEAN_TEMPERATURE;
 needs CLOCKS.PREDEFINED;
body
 type Modes   is (Celsius,Fahrenheit);
 type States is (On,Off);
 constant The_Delay_Amount        : Seconds.THE_CLOCK       ::=   10;
 constant The_Maximum_Difference  :
        Degrees_Celsius.THE_SET_OF_TEMPERATURE_SENSORS  ::=    2;
 variable The_Current_Value       :
        Degrees_Celsius.THE_SET_OF_TEMPERATURE_SENSORS;
 variable The_Mean_Temperature    :
        Degrees_Celsius.THE_SET_OF_TEMPERATURE_SENSORS;
 variable  The_Mode               : Modes                  ::=  Celsius;
 variable  The_State              : States                 ::=  Off;
 modifier  operation   DECREMENT            raise FAILURE_OCCURRED_IN;
 modifier  operation   DISPLAY              raise FAILURE_OCCURRED_IN;
 modifier  operation   INCREMENT            raise FAILURE_OCCURRED_IN;
 modifier  operation   MAINTAIN             raise FAILURE_OCCURRED_IN,
                                                  INCOMPATIBLE_STATE_IN
                                            is concurrent;

 preserver operation   ROUTE_MESSAGES_FOR   raise FAILURE_OCCURRED_IN
                                            is concurrent;

 modifier  operation   START                raise FAILURE_OCCURRED_IN;
 modifier  operation   STOP                 raise FAILURE_OCCURRED_IN;
 modifier  operation   USE_CELSIUS          raise FAILURE_OCCURRED_IN;
 modifier  operation   USE_FAHRENHEIT       raise FAILURE_OCCURRED_IN;
 object THE_CLOCK            : CLOCKS.PREDEFINED;
start
 CONSTRUCT(THE_CLOCK).CLOCKS;
 ROUTE_MESSAGES_FOR;
end;
```

Because an object is an abstraction, it captures only the relevant characteristics of the physical or conceptual entity being modeled and ignores the entity's immaterial properties. For example, if a missile is being modeled as part of a software launch application, one attribute might be The_Current_Status_Of.THE_MISSILE, while a valid operation might be LAUNCH.THE_MISSILE. There is probably no need for the attribute The_Color_Of.THE_MISSILE or the questionable operation SELL_TO_HIGHEST_BIDDER.THE_MISSILE. Similarly, the abstraction should always be modeled with respect to a specific user or development viewpoint. For example, a built-in test (BIT) might have a very different view of what is important to model in a radar application than an operator who is only interested in range, altitude, velocity, acceleration, etc.

We use the icons in Figure 2-7 for objects on the object-oriented diagrams in this book. The icon for concurrent objects is a parallelogram drawn with thick lines, and the icon for a sequential object is a rectangle drawn with thick lines. The parallelogram reminds the software engineer of the parallel processing of concurrency, the rectangle and the thick borders reminds the software engineer that objects are the software black boxes that protect their contents.

Objects also have specifications and bodies. An object specification is repre-

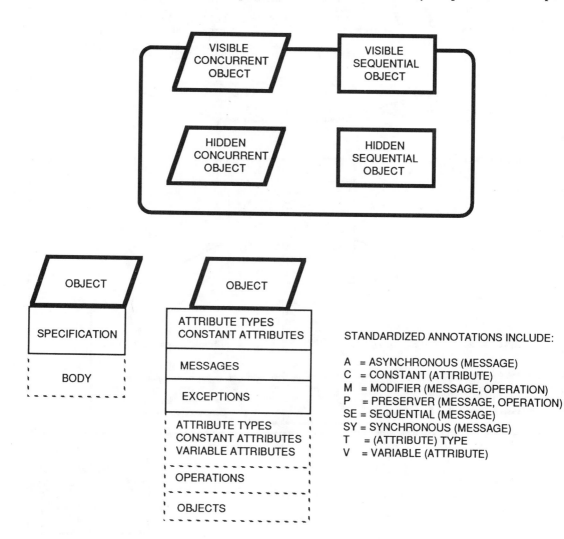

**Figure 2-7: Icons for Objects**

sented graphically by a rectangle drawn with thin lines hung below the object icon and divided into three areas by two solid horizontal lines. Visible attribute types and constant attributes are listed in the top area, messages are listed in the middle area, and visible exceptions are listed in the bottom area. Bodies are represented graphically by a thin dotted rectangle hung below or to the right of the specification icon. The object body icon is divided into three areas by two horizontal dotted lines. Hidden attributes types and attributes are listed in the top area, hidden operations are

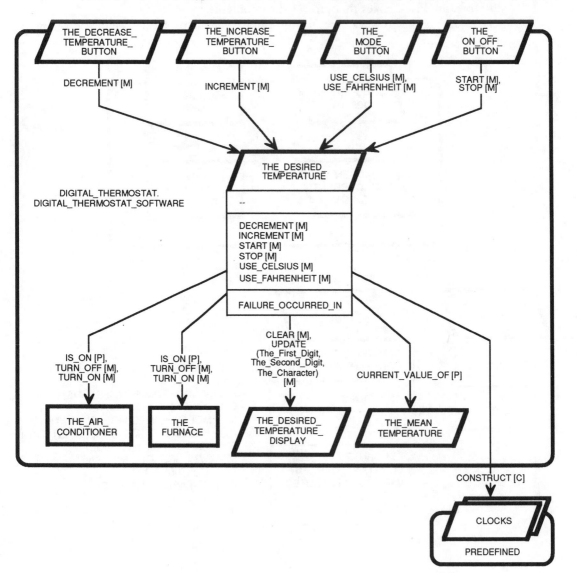

**Figure 2-8: Example Object with Specification**

listed in the middle area, and component objects are listed in the bottom area. Figure 2-8 shows an object-level interaction diagram that shows the specification of the object THE_DESIRED_TEMPERATURE.

Objects can and should be categorized in many ways. Most of the same categories can also be applied to classes and subassemblies with identical or analogous definitions (e.g., an atomic class is a class for which the instances are atomic objects).

Objects may model many different things. Some of the more common types are as follows:

- *Device objects* model individual devices, such as sensors, actuators, motors, valves, keyboards, and lights.
- *Property objects* model important properties or characteristics from the application domain, such as altitude, velocity, temperature, and pressure.
- *Role objects* model persons and the roles they play in the system, such as customer, teller, and operator.
- *Organization objects* model organizations (e.g., accounting, division headquarters).
- *Location objects* model locations (e.g., a street intersection, a drilling site).
- *Event objects* model events (e.g., accidents, flights, launches).
- *Interaction objects* model interactions among other objects (e.g., a license or purchase) and are often used when ternary relationships exist.

Interaction objects are rare and should be handled with great care because functional abstractions can often be misidentified as interaction objects. Many words in English can be both nouns and verbs (i.e., objects and operations, respectively). For example, the word *purchase* either can refer to a purchase object or can describe the purchase operation of some other object(s). Software engineers should also be on their guard against verbs turned into nouns by the addition of —*er* or —*or* to the end of a verb (e.g., contro*ler*, manag*er*, creat*or*), for these are almost always operations masquerading as objects.

Objects may also be either tangible or intangible, and this distinction is important because intangible objects are harder to identify and model than tangible objects. Intangible objects are therefore often overlooked.

- *Intangible objects* model intangible entities (e.g., account, position, temperature) that can not be touched.
- *Tangible objects* model tangible intangible entities (e.g., actuators, keyboards, sensors).

Objects may be either essential or nonessential, depending on the system requirements.

- *Essential objects* are those for which their existence and capabilities are required. They typically model aspects of the real-world application (or problem) domain. Essential objects are typically known and understood by the customer or the application-domain specialist. Essential objects (and their essential resources) should be identified and analyzed during OODA and OORA. They should be specified in the appropriate project software requirements specification (SRS), either as a required capability or as a design constraint.

- *Nonessential objects* are those for which their existence and capabilities are design decisions. They typically model aspects of the solution space. Nonessential objects are identified during object-oriented logical and implementation design. Both essential and nonessential objects are designed and documented in the appropriate project software design document (SDD). See Figure 2-9: Essential and Nonessential Objects.

Objects can relate to the entities that they model in many ways. For each entity that it models, an object might do the following:

- Control the entity (e.g., THE_ACTUATOR)
- Emulate, simulate, or stimulate the entity (e.g., THE_SIMULATED_PLANE)
- Interface with the entity (e.g., THE_SENSOR)
- Store information about or keep track of the entity

In addition, intangible objects often enforce the abstraction of the concepts that they model. Ultimately, objects implement in software the models of their associated entities.

Objects may either be atomic or aggregate:

- *Atomic objects* do not contain subobjects or classes.
- *Aggregate objects* contain at least one nested object. Aggregate objects are used to model aggregate entities, and they restrict visibility to their component objects.

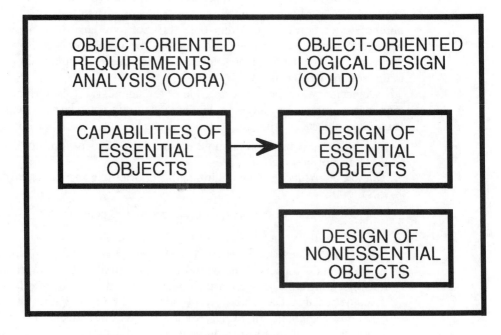

**Figure 2-9: Essential and Nonessential Objects**

Objects can either be sequential or concurrent [HTG 1991], and the difference has a significant impact on their behavior and robustness:

- **Concurrent objects** have their own thread of control or contain resources (i.e., operations, subobjects) that have their own thread of control. Most objects should be concurrent (at least during requirements analysis and logical design) because most of the entities that they model in the real world are inherently concurrent, and this concurrency is an important characteristic to be modeled.
- *Sequential objects* do not have their own thread of control at any level. They are thus simpler than concurrent objects to implement.

Collections of concurrent objects are often easier to understand because they more naturally model the application domain entities and their interactions. With the proper scheduling algorithms, they can run faster than sequential objects, even on single-processor systems. They can also more readily protect their attributes from corruption due to interleaved access than can sequential objects. On the other hand, errors due to improper interactions (e.g., starvation, deadlock, livelock, priority inversion, excessive polling) among concurrent objects can be difficult to identify and avoid.

A critical issue related to concurrency is how objects handle mutual exclusion in order to ensure robustness. When multiple threads of control exist (especially on a single processor), merely hiding attributes in the bodies of sequential objects is inadequate to protect them from accidental corruption. If one operation that updates an attribute is only partially completed during a time slice, a second operation accessing the same, partially updated attribute may execute during a later time slice, producing erroneous results. This problem can be avoided by ensuring mutual exclusion to critical regions (i.e., contiguous segments of code guaranteed to execute to completion without interruption). Objects may therefore be categorized as only one of the following:

- *Corruptible objects* do not address mutual exclusion and are typically sequential.
- *Guardable objects* permit mutually exclusive use (e.g., via binary semaphores) but do not enforce or guarantee mutual exclusion.
- *Guarded objects* enforce and guarantee mutually exclusive access to their resources. They are preferable because they ensure robustness in a concurrent environment.

Persistence is another important characteristic of objects that should be addressed, especially when databases are used:

- *Transient objects* may be created and destroyed while the program runs and are therefore not guaranteed to exist for the duration of the program run.
- *Temporary objects* persist while the program runs but cease to exist when the program stops.
- *Permanent objects* are stored in permanent storage, such as an object-oriented database. They may exist before the program begins and after the program stops.

Objects primarily interact by sending messages to one another, and the direction of message passing introduces a client–server relationship among objects. See Figure 2-10: Master, Agent, and Servant Objects and Classes.

- *Master objects* depend on (i.e., send messages to) other objects or classes but are not depended on (i.e., do not receive messages from) any objects or classes. However, master objects may be depended on by external entities, such as hardware, people, systems, or external software.
- *Agent objects* both depend on, and are depended on by, other objects and classes.
- *Servant objects* do not themselves depend on, but are depended on by, other objects or classes. Servant objects also may depend on external entities, such as hardware, people, systems, or external software.

An object should be uniquely identified within a project, if necessary, using identifiers extended with the dot notation. Object identifiers should be singular proper nouns, noun phrases, or direct references that are meaningful from the user viewpoint, rather than only from the developer viewpoint. Object identifiers are shown in all capital letters in this book, in order to emphasize them and to differentiate them from attributes. Object identifiers should not be plural nouns (which should be reserved for classes and attribute types), lowercase singular nouns (which should be reserved for attribute data), verbs (which should be reserved for operations), or nouns made from verbs (which often imply operations masquerading as objects). For example, the following are examples of both good and bad object identifiers:

| *Good Identifiers* | *Bad Identifiers* | |
|---|---|---|
| ACCELEROMETER_5 | ACCELEROMETERS | --Plural implies class |
| BACKUP_CONVEYOR_BELT | States | --Lowercase implies type |
| BAROMETRIC_ALTIMETER | CONTROL | --Verb implies operation |
| BUS_1553 | LAUNCH | --May be noun or verb |
| FLIGHT_NUMBER_36 | CONTROLLER | --May be masquerading operation |
| HEADS_UP_DISPLAY_SCREEN | | |
| INTERSECTION | | |
| MISSILE_GYROSCOPE | | |
| PRESENT_POSITION | | |
| PRIMARY_INTAKE_VALVE | | |
| RADAR_TRANSMITTER | | |
| SECONDARY_REHEAT_FURNACE | | |
| SIGNAL_BEACON | | |
| THE_CUSTOMER[4] | | |
| THE_DESIRED_FLOW | | |
| THE_DESIRED_FLOW.COLD_WATER | | |
| THE_DESIRED_FLOW.CONTROL_PANEL | | |
| THE_PURCHASE_ORDER | | |
| WATER_STORAGE_TANK | | |

---

[4]The prefix "THE_" is often used to make messages read better in English (e.g., LAUNCH.THE_MISSILE).

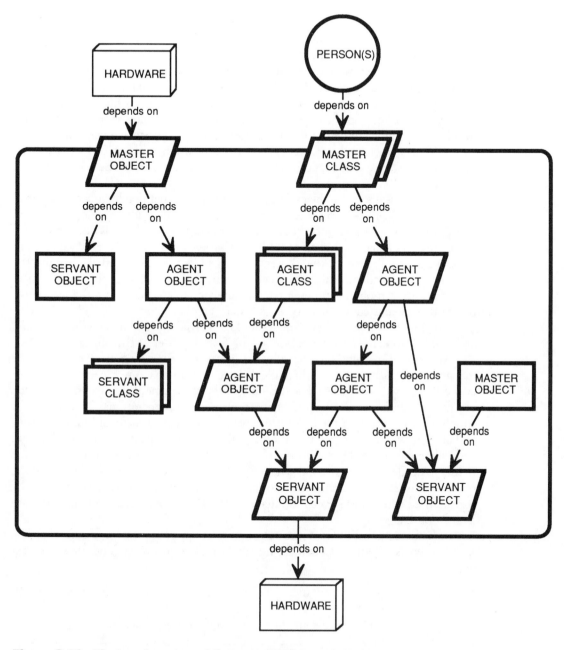

**Figure 2-10:  Master, Agent, and Servant Objects and Classes**

A *class* is a template for generating objects, and an *object* may (or may not)[5] be an **instance** of one or more classes, the members of which share the same or similar characteristics and rules of behavior. *Single classification* exists if an object is an instance of only one class, whereas **multiple classification** exists if an object is an instance of two or more classes in different classification hierarchies. For example, a person may be an instance of both the employees class and the athletes class, and the employees class may not be in the same classification hierarchy as the athletes class, which may include animals (e.g., race horses). *Static classification* exists if an object's class is fixed, whereas *dynamic classification* exists when the class(es) of which an object is an instance vary over time (e.g., a person is an instance of the classes children and adults at different times).

An object is a software **black box**, having a sharply defined boundary and interface. It has an outside, user-oriented viewpoint and an inside, developer-oriented viewpoint. The separation of specification from body is used for this distinction. An object uses information hiding to hide and protect the structure and value of its attributes, including state, the existence of its hidden auxiliary attributes, and the existence of its hidden operations. Access is provided to attributes only via messages to operations. An object is therefore completely characterized (from the user viewpoint) by its exported attribute types, constant attributes, messages, and exceptions. The structure of the encapsulated data should be considered an implementation detail and is thus protected by information hiding from the user of the object.

An object is usually influenced by its history as well as by outside influences. It may thus have *state* in the mathematical sense. A state machine's behavior is influenced by its own state, as well as the state of its environment. For example, a stack object with a maximum size would export push and pop operations, the behavior of which would depend on the current size of the stack (i.e., they could raise overflow and underflow operations if the stack was full or empty, respectively, rather than add and delete entries to the stack). An object usually stores its state but may calculate it only as needed. Objects may also have aggregate states consisting of substates. If the object can be characterized as a finite state machine (FSM), then its state is usually documented with a **state transition diagram (STD)**. See Figure 2-11: Example State Transition Diagram.

It is the responsibility of the relevant software engineers to ensure that the specified goals of software engineering are met by each object (and class, for that matter):

- *Compatibility*—Each object must be compatible with the other objects with which it must be integrated.
- *Correctness*—Each object must meet its specified requirements.

---

[5]Although most OOP languages require the existence of a class before an object may be instantiated, this restriction is not appropriate for OORA, which should be language independent. Sometimes, only one object with specific properties is needed, so a class is superfluous. In this case, one might say that the object is of an anonymous class. At other times, a class may not make sense. For example, a monotheist would argue that only one god exists, and the class gods does not make sense.

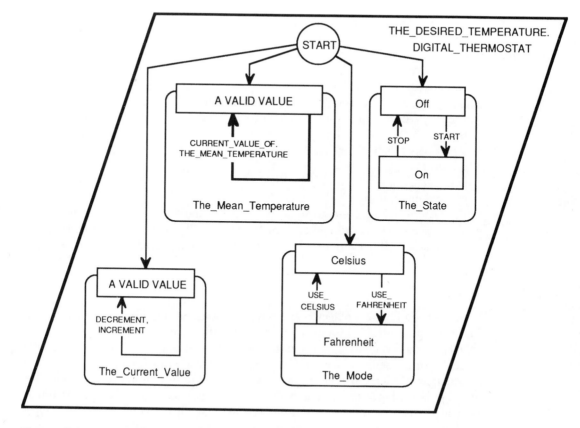

**Figure 2-11: Example State Transition Diagram**

- *Correctable*—It should be easy to find and correct any latent errors in each object.
- *Efficiency*—Each object should localize efficient resources (e.g., operations).
- *Extensibility*—Each object should be easy to modify to meet new requirements.
- *Maintainability*—Each object should be easy to maintain (i.e., be both correctable and extensible).
- *Modifiability*—Each object should be easy to change.
- *Portability*—Each object should be independent, to the extent practical, of its hardware and software environment (e.g., operating system).
- *Reliability*—Each object should enforce its own abstraction, and users should not be allowed to directly or indirectly violate its abstraction. All preconditions, postconditions, and invariants should be evaluated and enforced. Concurrency issues should be properly addressed (e.g., an object may protect its state in a concurrent environment by using monitors and critical regions).
- *Reusability*—Each object should be complete and should export all attribute types, constant attributes, messages, and exceptions needed by the intended user. This

also simplifies configuration management and significantly reduces total source and object code size.

- *Robustness*—Each object should continue to function correcty under abnormal circumstances. It should raise relevant exceptions and not allow its abstraction to be violated. It should use preconditions, postconditions, and invariants.
- *Safety*—Each object should not accidentally harm life or property.
- *Security*—Each object should protect itself from unauthorized access or modification.
- *Testability*—Each object should be easy to test for correctness, reliability, and robustness.
- *Understandability*—Each object should be easily comprehended by those who must use and maintain it.
- *Validatability*—The correctness of each object should be easy to demonstrate.
- *Verifiability*—The conformance of each object to all relevant previously developed products and all relevant development standards and procedures should be easy to demonstrate.

## 2.4.2    Classes

Wherever you find one object, you often find additional similar or identical objects. The concept of class is introduced in order to efficiently construct multiple related objects. A **class** is defined as a template for the construction of identical or similar objects. It must define object attribute types and attributes (including data such as object state information), object messages and operations that may or may not affect the object attributes encapsulated in its instances, and object exceptions usually associated with the object operations. A class may also have class attribute types, attributes, and operations that belong to the class as a whole rather than to its instances.

A *generic class* is parameterized with formal generic parameters. Its instances may vary, depending on the actual parameters that are supplied.

This abstraction may be documented in terms of requirements, design, code, etc. On projects using the U.S. military standard DOD-STD-2167A, a class almost always corresponds to a computer software unit (CSU). The objects constructed using a class are called "instances" of that class, and all instances of the same class have the same or similar architecture (i.e., attribute types, attributes, messages, operations, exceptions, and nested objects) and rules of behavior (e.g., states and state transitions).

As an abstraction, a class encapsulates its resources and only exports information and resources (e.g., messages and exceptions) at a high, user-oriented level of abstraction while hiding the implementation details of all encapsulated resources. Data, function, process, and exception abstraction are therefore required within the context of class abstraction. Each class has a specification and a body that declare these encapsulated resources. Thus, a generic class for constructing stacks may have the following specification and body, written in the OOSDL specification and design language:

```
class GENERIC_STACKS
 needs THE_SET_OF_INTEGERS.PREDEFINED;
 parent subassembly  CLASS_REPOSITORY;
 superclass ARRAYS;
 parameter type       Entries is visible;
 parameter constant   The_Maximum_Stack_Size :
                       Values.THE_SET_OF_INTEGERS;
 specification
  introduces
   message     CONSTRUCT    (A_STACK)
                     raise    CONSTRUCT_FAILED   is sequential;
   message     DESTRUCT     (A_STACK)
                     raise    DESTRUCT_FAILED    is sequential;
   message     INITIALIZE
                     raise  ABSTRACTION_VIOLATED      is sequential;
   message     MAXIMUM_SIZE_OF return Values.THE_SET_OF_INTEGERS
                     raise  ABSTRACTION_VIOLATED      is sequential;
   message     POP (An_Entry :   out Entries)
                   raise ENTRY_NOT_REMOVED,INCORRECT_SIZE,IS_EMPTY
                                             is sequential;
   message     PUSH (An_Entry : in    Entries)
                   raise ENTRY_NOT_ADDED,INCORRECT_SIZE,IS_FULL
                                             is sequential;
 message   SIZE_OF       return Values.THE_SET_OF_INTEGERS
              raise INCORRECT_SIZE           is sequential;
 exception   ABSTRACTION_VIOLATED;
 exception   ENTRY_NOT_ADDED;
 exception   ENTRY_NOT_REMOVED;
 exception   INCORRECT_SIZE;
 exception   IS_EMPTY;
 exception   IS_FULL;
end;

class GENERIC_STACKS
body
 introduces
  type The_Stacks is new The_Arrays range 1 .. The_Maximum_Stack_Size;
  variable The_Current_Size  : Values.THE_SET_OF_INTEGERS := 0;
  variable The_Top           : Entries;
  constructor operation  CONSTRUCT   (A_STACK)  raise  CONSTRUCT_FAILED;
  destructor operation   DESTRUCT    (A_STACK)  raise  DESTRUCT_FAILED;
  modifier operation     INITIALIZE             raise  ABSTRACTION_VIOLATED;
  preserver operation    MAXIMUM_SIZE_OF return Values.THE_SET_OF_INTEGERS;
  modifier operation     POP (An_Entry :   out Entries)
              raise ENTRY_NOT_REMOVED,INCORRECT_SIZE,IS_EMPTY;
  modifier operation     PUSH (An_Entry : in    Entries)
              raise ENTRY_NOT_ADDED,INCORRECT_SIZE,IS_FULL;
  preserver operation    SIZE_OF        return   Values.THE_SET_OF_INTEGERS
                                      raise INCORRECT_SIZE;
 invariants
 require
  The_Current_Size <= The_Maximum_Stack_Size
```

```
  else
    raise INCORRECT_SIZE;
  end require;
end;
```

We use the following icons for classes on the object-oriented diagrams in this book: The icon for a *concurrent class* is two thick overlapping parallelograms, and the icon for a *sequential class* is two thick overlapping rectangles. The parallelograms remind the software engineer of the parallel processing of concurrency. The rectangles with the thick borders remind the software engineer that, like objects, classes are software black boxes that protect their resources. See Figure 2-12: Primary Icons for Classes.

Classes also have specifications and bodies and may have generic parameters. Generic parameters are listed in a thin rounded rectangle, hung below the class icon (see Figure 2-13: Example Class with Generic Parameters, Specifications, and Bodies). A class specification is represented graphically by a thin solid rectangle hung below the generic parameters icon (if it is used) and below the class icon otherwise. The specification is divided into three areas by two solid horizontal lines (see Figure 2-14). Visible attribute types are listed in the top area, messages are listed in the middle area, and visible exceptions are listed in the bottom area. Bodies are represented graphically by a thin dotted rectangle hung in one of three places: (1) below the specification icon if it is used, (2) below the generic parameters icon if it is used and the specification icon if not, or (3) below the class icon if the generic parameters and the specification icons are not used. The class body icon is divided into three areas by two horizontal dotted lines (see Figure 2-14). Hidden attribute types and

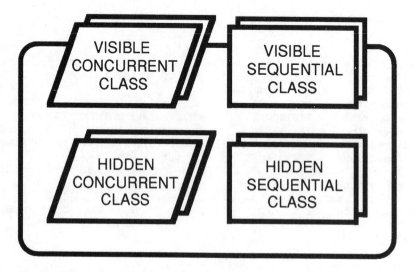

**Figure 2-12: Primary Icons for Classes**

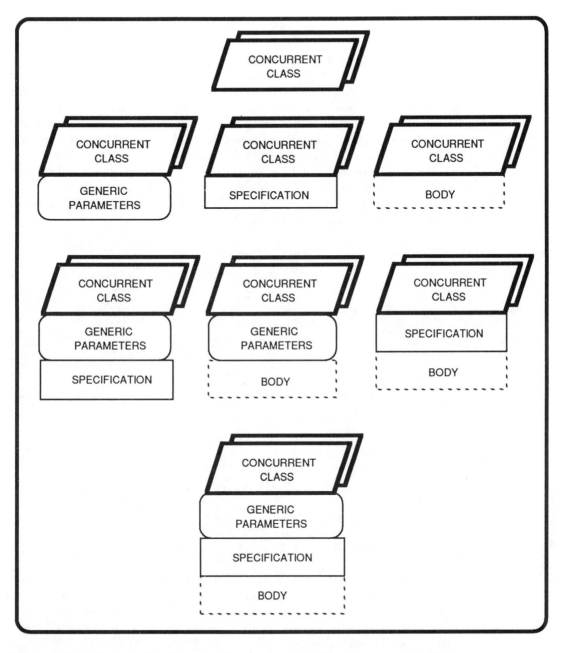

**Figure 2-13: Classes with Generic Parameters, Specifications, and Bodies**

attributes are listed in the top area, operations are listed in the middle area, and component objects are listed in the bottom area.

Each class should be uniquely identifiable within a project—if necessary, by using identifiers extended with the dot notation. Class identifiers should be plural proper nouns, noun phrases, or direct references that are meaningful from the user viewpoint, rather than only the developer viewpoint. Software engineers should be able to easily differentiate between objects and classes because object identifiers are singular and class identifiers are plural. Class identifiers are shown in all-capital letters in this book, in order to emphasize them and to differentiate them from attribute types. Class identifiers should not be singular nouns (which are reserved for objects and attribute data), verbs (which are reserved for operations), or nouns made from verbs (which often imply operations masquerading as objects). For example, the following are examples of good and bad class identifiers:

*Good Identifiers*                    *Bad Identifiers*

ACCELEROMETERS              ACCELEROMETER        --Singular implies object
ALTIMETERS                  Altimeters           --Lowercase implies attribute type
BONDS
CONVEYOR_BELTS
CROSSWALK_SIGNALS
CUSTOMERS
FLIGHTS
FLOWS
FLOWS.CONTROL_PANEL_CLASSES
HEADS_UP_DISPLAY_SCREENS
INTAKE_VALVES
TRAFFIC_LIGHTS
PURCHASE_ORDERS
RADAR_TRANSMITTERS
REHEAT_FURNACES
SENSORS
STOCKS
TURN_SIGNALS
TARGETS
UNITS
WATER_STORAGE_TANKS
WEAPONS

Figure 2-14 shows a nongeneric example class developed as part of a robotics arm application. Figure 2-15 shows a generic class developed as part of an avionics navigation application. The annotations "[T]" and "[T_D]" mean type and deferred type, respectively. On the generic parameters, the annotation "[C]" means constant attribute. On the operations, the annotations "[CN]," "[MN]," and "[PN]" mean noniterator constructor, modifier, and preserver, respectively. On the hidden attributes, the annotations "[C]" and "[V]" mean constant and variable, respectively.

*Single classification* occurs when each object is an instance of only a single class. While this is the typical situation (and the only situation allowed by most current

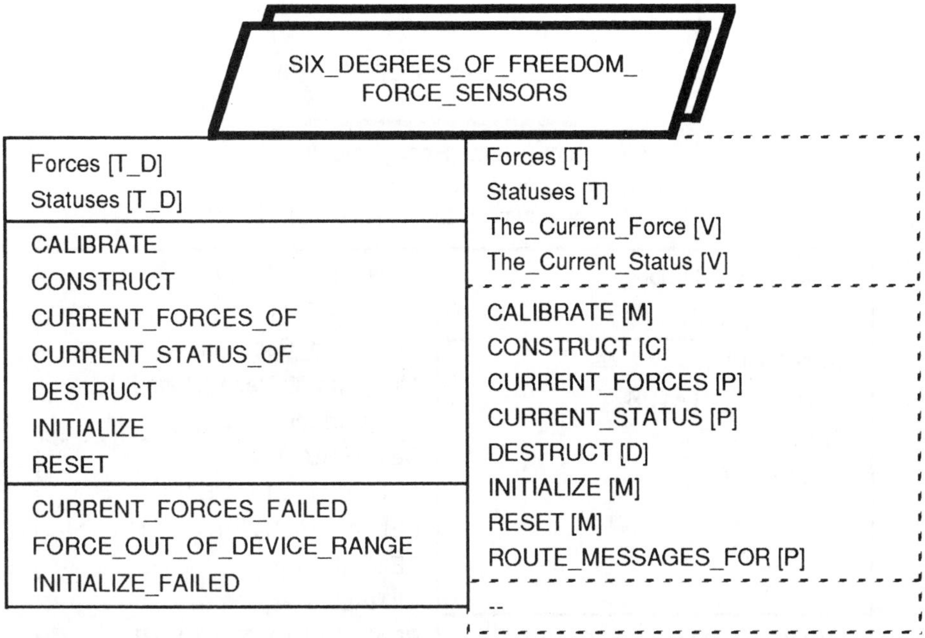

**Figure 2-14: Example Class:** SIX_DEGREES_OF_FREEDOM_FORCE_SENSORS

OOPLs), it is important to remember that the same object can be an instance of multiple classes (i.e., **multiple classification**). As an example of multiple classification, a specific person, Jane Doe, can be both an executive and an athlete. Thus, the object JANE_DOE is an instance of the classes EXECUTIVES and ATHLETES. See Figure 2-16: Single vs. Multiple Classification.

*Static classification* occurs when the objects that are instances of some class remain instances of that class from the moment they are constructed to the moment they are destroyed. On the other hand, *dynamic classification* occurs when a single object can have different classes at different times. *Conditional classification* occurs when a single object is an instance of a class only under certain conditions and is another way of looking at dynamic classification. As an example of dynamic and conditional classification, consider a specific person, John Doe, who can be a legal driver (e.g., when he has a valid driver's license) during part of his life and not a legal driver during other times (e.g., when he is under age or has lost his license). Thus, the object JOHN_DOE is a conditional instance of the class LEGAL_DRIVERS. See Figure 2-17: Dynamic and Conditional Classification.

## 2.4.3    Subassemblies

Nontrivial applications often consist of more than 50 objects and classes, and it is not unusual for large complex applications to have hundreds or even thousands. Clearly,

GYROSCOPES

Delta_Theta_Read_Rate [C]
Maximum_Rotation_Rate [C]
Minimum_Rotation_Rate [C]

| Delta_Thetas [T_D] | Delta_Thetas [T_D] |
|---|---|
| Statuses [T_D] | Statuses [T_D] |
| | Calibration_Constants [C] |
| | The_Current_Delta_Theta [V] |
| | The_Current_Status [V] |
| CONSTRUCT | CONSTRUCT [C] |
| CURRENT_STATUS | CURRENT_STATUS [P] |
| DELTA_THETA | DELTA_THETA [P] |
| DESTRUCT | DESTRUCT [D] |
| INITIALIZE | INITIALIZE [M] |
| TURN_OFF | READ_DELTA_THETA [M] |
| TURN_ON | ROUTE_MESSAGES_FOR [P] |
| | TURN_OFF [M] |
| MAXIMUM_RATE_EXCEEDED | TURN_ON [M] |
| OBSOLETE_DELTA_THETA_DATA | -- |

**Figure 2-15: Example Generic Class** GYROSCOPES

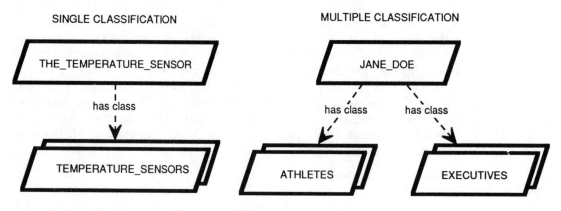

SINGLE CLASSIFICATION

THE_TEMPERATURE_SENSOR

has class

TEMPERATURE_SENSORS

MULTIPLE CLASSIFICATION

JANE_DOE

has class          has class

ATHLETES          EXECUTIVES

**Figure 2-16: Single vs. Multiple Classification**

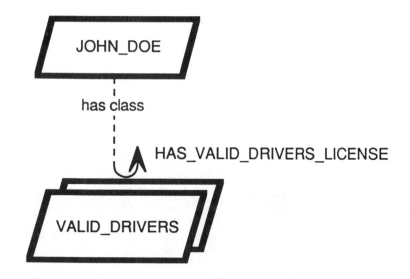

**Figure 2-17: Dynamic and Conditional Classification**

if software engineers are not to be overwhelmed by the sheer number of objects and classes, they must have some means of dividing the problem into small, manageable pieces that can be handled individually. Only by using an incremental identification and development process tied to the Miller Limit can errors be minimized and productivity enhanced. This leads to the concept of a subassembly.

A **subassembly** is defined as a small, manageable set of logically related objects, classes, other subassemblies, and possibly other software entities (if a hybrid development approach is used) that are typically identified, analyzed, designed, coded, and tested together. A subassembly should be logically cohesive and should have minimal coupling to other subassemblies. Subassemblies typically contain from 5 to 15 (and no more than 20) components, in order to remain small, manageable, and easy to document (e.g., via various diagrams). Subassemblies tend to grow with age, so that older subassemblies being maintained and reused tend to be larger than newly created ones. Subassemblies usually contain no more objects and classes than can be analyzed, designed, programmed, and tested by a team of two to five developers in a few weeks or months. On projects using the U.S. military standard DOD-STD-2167A, a subassembly should almost always correspond to a computer software component (CSC). The *subassembly specification* consists of the visible components of the subassembly— that is, those components to which messages can be sent from outside of the subassembly. The *subassembly body* consists of the hidden components that can only receive messages from other components of the same subassembly, including those in the corresponding specification. For example, the following is a subassembly specification and body written in OOSDL:

```
subassembly DIGITAL_THERMOSTAT is concurrent
  parent assembly DIGITAL_THERMOSTAT_SOFTWARE;
specification
  object  THE_DECREMENT_TEMPERATURE_BUTTON   is concurrent;
  object  THE_INCREMENT_TEMPERATURE_BUTTON   is concurrent;
  object  THE_MODE_BUTTON                    is concurrent;
  object  THE_ON_OFF_BUTTON                  is concurrent;
end;

subassembly DIGITAL_THERMOSTAT
  needs PREDEFINED;
body
  object  THE_AIR_CONDITIONER;
  object  THE_DESIRED_TEMPERATURE           is concurrent;
  object  THE_DESIRED_TEMPERATURE_DISPLAY   is concurrent;
  object  THE_FURNACE;
  object  THE_MEAN_TEMPERATURE              is concurrent;
  object  THE_MEAN_TEMPERATURE_DISPLAY      is concurrent;
  object  THE_SET_OF_TEMPERATURE_SENSORS    is concurrent;
end;
```

We use a thick rounded rectangle as the subassembly icon in this book (see Figure 2-18: Icons for Subassemblies). Icons of visible components are socketed to the border of the subassembly, and icons for hidden components are nested within the subassembly icon. Subassembly specifications are represented graphically by thin solid rectangles hung below the subassembly icon. The exported objects and classes are listed in the subassembly specification icon. Subassembly bodies are represented graphically by thin dotted rectangles hung below the subassembly specification icon. The hidden objects and classes are listed in the subassembly body icon (not shown in Figure 2-18). These icons are used on subassembly general semantic nets (GSNs) (see Figure 2-19), on subassembly interaction diagrams (IDs) (see Figure 2-20), subassembly control flow diagrams (CFDs) (see Figure 2-21), and assembly diagrams (ADs) (see Figure 2-22). Figures 2-19 through 2-21 show three successive views of the same subassembly.

The term *subassembly* is not yet a standard in the OOD community. The most popular synonym is **subsystem** [Booch 1987, Rumbaugh et al. 1991, Wirfs-Brock et al. 1990], which has two major problems. First, OOD subsystems contain only software, while systems engineers have long recognized that true subsystems also typically contain hardware and people. The term is also confusing on projects using the U.S. military standard, DOD-STD-2167A, because a subassembly maps to a CSC, and a military subsystem contains CSCIs, which in turn contain CSCs. Another synonym is **subject** [Coad and Yourdon 1989], which is not very intuitive, does not imply that it is a subcomponent of a larger collection, and is more arbitrary. A relatively new synonym is **domain** [Shlaer and Mellor 1992], which has the disadvantage that it may be confused with the word *domain* in domain analysis, which is a much larger concept. A final synonym is *cluster* [Meyer 1988], which also does not imply that it is a subcomponent of a larger collection.

There are several ways to categorize subassemblies. As noted in Figure 2-23, subassemblies, like objects and classes, may be either essential or nonessential, depending on system requirements:

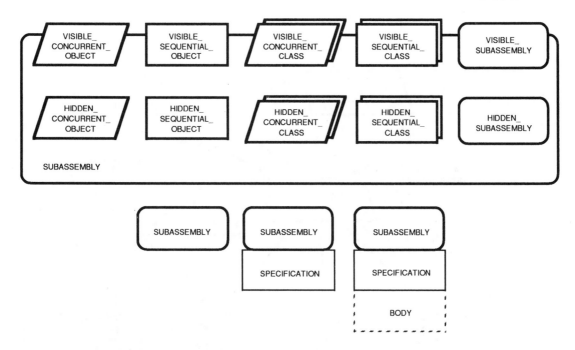

**Figure 2-18: Icons for Subassemblies**

- *Essential subassemblies* contain essential objects or classes. Essential subassemblies (and their essential objects and classes) should be identified and analyzed during OODA and OORA. They should be specified in the appropriate project SRS, either as a required capability or as a design constraint.
- *Nonessential subassemblies* do not contain any essential resources. During object-oriented logical and implementation design, nonessential subassemblies are identified, and both essential and nonessential subassemblies are designed. They should be documented in the appropriate project SDD.

Subassemblies can be masters, agents, or servants, depending on their dependency relationships to other subassemblies:

- *Master subassemblies* depend on (i.e., have components that send messages to components in) other subassemblies, but other subassemblies do not depend on them (i.e., master subassemblies do not have components that receive messages from components in any subassemblies). However, external entities such as hardware, people, systems, or external software may depend on master subassemblies.
- *Agent subassemblies* depend on other subassemblies, and other subassemblies depend on the agent subassemblies.
- *Servant subassemblies* do not themselves depend on other subassemblies, but other subassemblies depend on these servant subassemblies. Servant subassemblies also may depend on external entities, such as hardware, persons, systems, or external software.

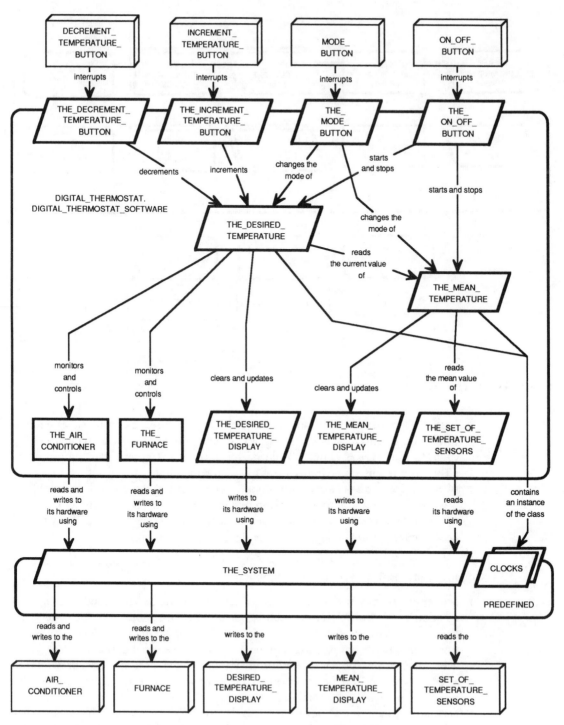

**Figure 2-19: Example Subassembly General Semantic Net (GSN)**

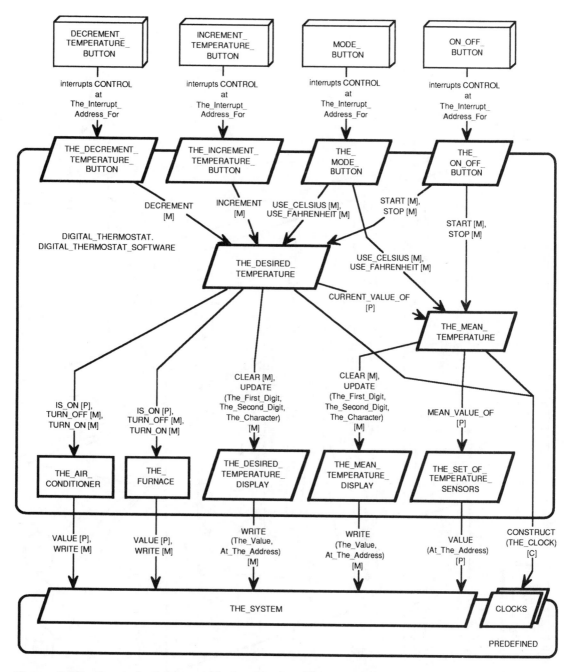

**Figure 2-20: Example Subassembly Interaction Diagram (ID)**

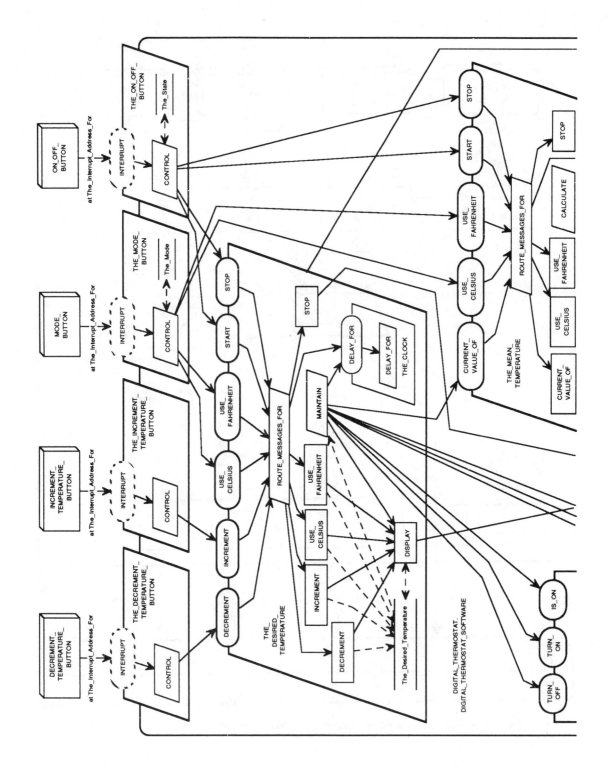

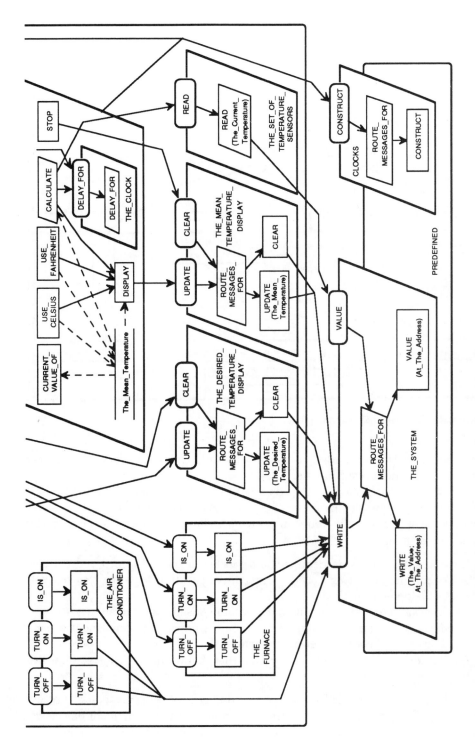

**Figure 2-21: Example Subassembly Control Flow Diagram (CFD)**

53

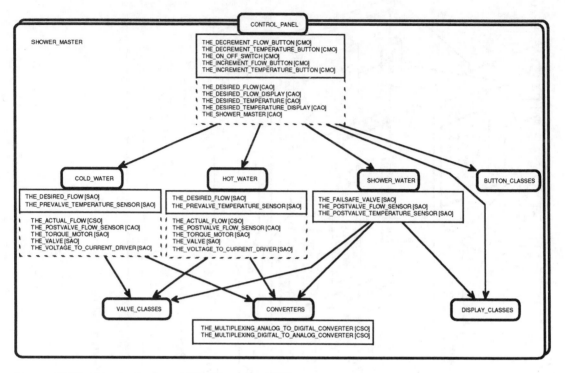

**Figure 2-22: Example Assembly Diagram (AD)**

Figure 2-24 shows an example assembly that illustrates the relationships among master, agent, and servant subassemblies.

Most subassemblies are developed as part of a recursive, incremental, top-down development process. Some subassemblies are used to contain classification hierarchies, while others are built around major requirements. Still others are developed in an ad hoc manner:

- *Recursive subassemblies* are identified (and possibly analyzed, designed, coded, tested, and/or integrated) during a single nonrecursive pass through some recursive software-development method.
- *Classification subassemblies* are used to contain classification hierarchies.
- *Requirements subassemblies* contain all resources required to implement a major capability (i.e., a cohesive set of requirements).
- *Ad hoc subassemblies* are all subassemblies that do not meet the foregoing definitions.

All subassemblies are object-oriented, in the sense of being composed of objects and classes. They also may be considered functional if their component objects and classes implement a major function (e.g., requirements subassemblies or recursive

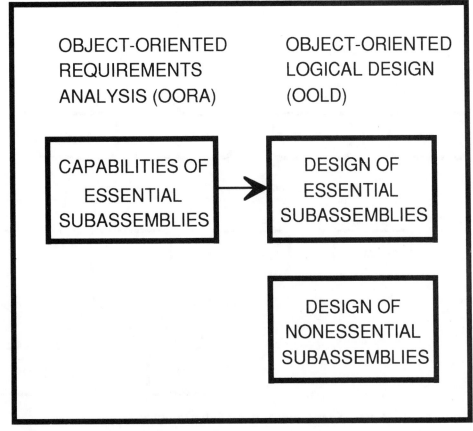

**Figure 2-23: Essential and Nonessential Subassemblies**

subassemblies providing the resources needed by a stubbed operation of an object or class in the parent subassembly).

Subassemblies may be either atomic or aggregate, depending on their aggregation relationships:

- An *atomic subassembly* does not contain any other subassemblies and thus only consists of objects, classes, and possibly other software entities (if a hybrid approach is used).
- An *aggregate subassembly* contains one or more subassemblies, as well as possibly objects, classes, etc. On many projects, only atomic subassemblies are used, although aggregate subassemblies are sometimes used to enforce information hiding and to limit access to the nested subassemblies. Whether atomic or aggregate, the number of subassembly components should not significantly exceed the Miller Limit of seven, plus or minus two.

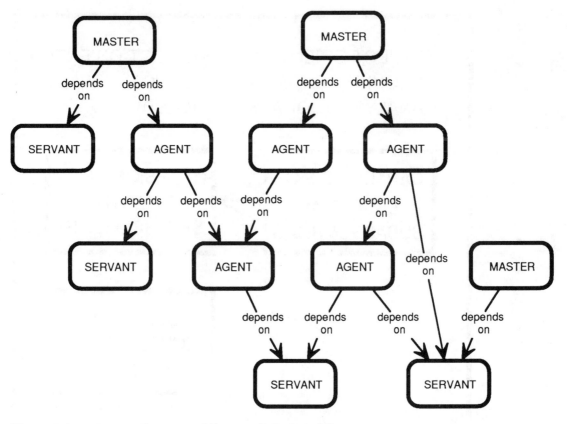

**Figure 2-24: Master, Agent, and Servant Subassemblies**

Figure 2-25 illustrates the difference between atomic and aggregate subassemblies.

Every object and class should be localized into at least one subassembly. An object may belong to more than one subassembly due to its reuse, but one subassembly should be chosen as the main one for purposes of configuration management, documentation, and maintenance.

The following guidelines have proven useful when identifying, analyzing, and designing subassemblies: Subassemblies should have stable interfaces that minimize coupling, with volatile objects and classes hidden within the bodies of the subassemblies where practical. The amount and type of documentation per subassembly should not excessively drive the choice and size of subassemblies.

## 2.4.4 Assemblies

An **assembly** is defined as a complete set of logically related subassemblies. It typically corresponds to either a single program or a major, reusable, contiguous part of a single

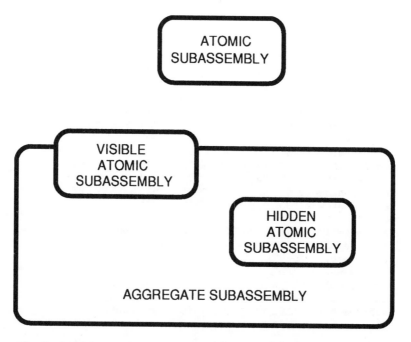

**Figure 2-25: Atomic and Aggregate Subassemblies**

program. It is often the largest software item placed under configuration management. It typically has staffing and work-breakdown implications. Assemblies should be logically cohesive and should have minimal coupling to other assemblies. Every subassembly should be allocated to at least one assembly. Unlike the number of objects and classes that compose subassemblies, which are subject to the Miller Limit, there is no clear limit to the number of subassemblies that may make up an assembly. On projects using the U.S. military standard DOD-STD-2167A, an assembly typically corresponds to a CSCI.

Assemblies have specifications and bodies. The *assembly specification* consists of the visible subassemblies of the assembly—that is, those subassemblies with components to which messages can be sent from outside of the assembly. The *assembly body* consists of the hidden subassemblies, the components of which can only receive messages from other components of the same assembly. For example, the specification and body of the SHOWER_MASTER subassembly, written in OOSDL, are as follows:

```
assembly SHOWER_MASTER is concurrent
specification
   subassembly     CONTROL_PANEL is concurrent;
end;

assembly SHOWER_MASTER
   needs hardware ACTUAL_FLOW_DISPLAY;
   needs hardware ACTUAL_TEMPERATURE_DISPLAY;
```

```
    needs hardware COLD_WATER_PREVALVE_TEMPERATURE_SENSOR;
    needs hardware COLD_WATER_POSTVALVE_FLOW_SENSOR;
    needs hardware COLD_WATER_TORQUE_MOTOR;
    needs hardware COLD_WATER_TORQUE_MOTOR_VALVE;
    needs hardware COLD_WATER_VOLTAGE_TO_CURRENT_DRIVER;
    needs hardware DESIRED_FLOW_DISPLAY;
    needs hardware DESIRED_TEMPERATURE_DISPLAY;
    needs hardware HOT_WATER_PREVALVE_TEMPERATURE_SENSOR;
    needs hardware HOT_WATER_POSTVALVE_FLOW_SENSOR;
    needs hardware HOT_WATER_TORQUE_MOTOR;
    needs hardware HOT_WATER_TORQUE_MOTOR_VALVE;
    needs hardware HOT_WATER_VOLTAGE_TO_CURRENT_DRIVER;
    needs hardware SHOWER_WATER_POSTVALVE_FLOW_SENSOR;
    needs hardware SHOWER_WATER_POSTVALVE_TEMPERATURE_SENSOR;
    needs hardware SOLENOID_FAILSAFE_VALVE;
body
    subassembly    BUTTON_CLASSES     is concurrent;
    subassembly    COLD_WATER         is concurrent;
    subassembly    CONVERTERS         is concurrent;
    subassembly    DISPLAY_CLASSES    is concurrent;
    subassembly    HOT_WATER          is concurrent;
    subassembly    SHOWER_WATER       is concurrent;
    subassembly    VALVE_CLASSES      is concurrent;
end;
```

We use two thick, rounded rectangles as the assembly icon in this book (see Figure 2-26). Icons of visible subassemblies are socketed to the border of the assembly icon, and icons for hidden subassemblies are nested within the assembly icon (see Figure 2-28). Assembly specifications are represented graphically by thin solid rectangles hung below the assembly icon (see Figure 2-26). The exported subassemblies should be listed in the assembly specification icon. Assembly bodies are represented graphically by thin dotted rectangles hung below the assembly specification icon (see Figure 6-26), and the hidden subassemblies should be listed in the assembly body icon. Figure 2-26 uses a generic context diagram to show the icons for an assembly and its specification and body. These icons are primarily used on SNs used as context diagrams (see Figure 2-27) and as assembly diagrams (see Figure 2-28).

## 2.4.5    Frameworks

A **framework** is defined as a reusable, application-domain-specific template that can be used as a skeleton from which to build a complete application. Frameworks consist of reusable specifications, designs [Johnson and Foote 1988], and one or more objects, classes, and/or subassemblies that implement some important common capabilities. Many frameworks are limited to application-specific class libraries [Winblad et al. 1990]. Frameworks are abstractions developed from a set of related applications, and the development of specifications for one or more frameworks should be a major goal of OODA. Frameworks are not complete applications but are intended to be fleshed out by their users, with application-specific objects and classes. Often, some of the

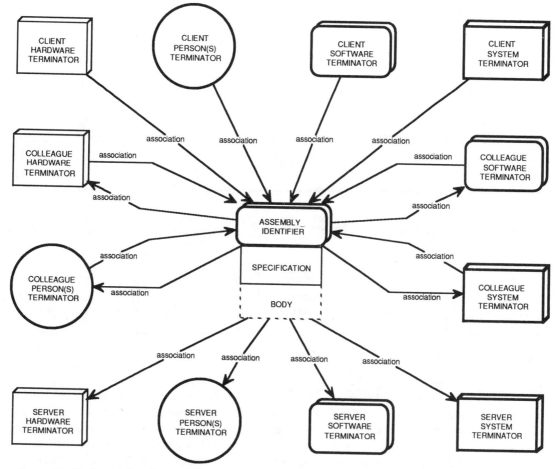

**Figure 2-26: Icons for Assemblies**

classes within frameworks are generic, requiring application-specific parameters for instantiation. Frameworks can and should be developed for any application domain with common architectures (e.g., windowing, simulation, accounting, avionics, human–machine interface software).

A standard example of a framework is the MacApp™ system [Schmucker 1986], developed by Apple Computer for developing Macintosh applications. A generic MacApp application consists of an application object, one or more windows, and one or more documents. Each window displays one or more views, and each view displays part of the state of a document. MacApp also consists of commands and printer handlers. Most applications inherit menu options and a command interpreter. By providing all of the basic classes, MacApp makes it significantly easier to write interactive programs that meet the Macintosh user-interface standard. Other similar

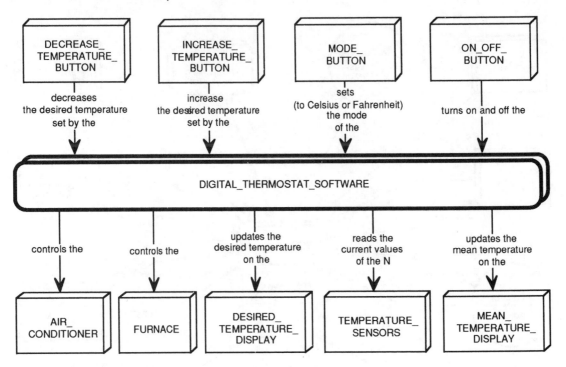

**Figure 2-27:** *Semantic Net used as a Context Diagram*

frameworks include the Lisa Toolkit [Apple 1984] and the Smalltalk-80 Model/View/ Controller (MVC) framework for constructing user interfaces [Goldberg 1984]. While most frameworks are oriented for language- or computer-specific user interfaces (because of the corresponding large pool of users), other frameworks show the potential of frameworks in other application domains. For example, Battery Simulation [Foote 1988] is a framework for constructing real-time psychophysiological experiments.

Frameworks potentially represent a major step forward for OOD. Frameworks promote massive reuse and standardization at a significantly higher level than objects and classes. This makes application development significantly faster, easier, and more cost-effective. There are, however, several problems limiting the current use of frameworks: Frameworks require a significant investment of time and effort to de-velop. Although the potential return on investment is great, many organizations are not yet willing to make that investment, especially when the effort should often be done during domain development, using organizational overhead money, rather than the development of a specific application. Because of the newness of the topic, frameworks do not yet exist for most application domains. It will be several years before an organization can purchase production-quality frameworks in avionics, banking, command and control, communications, process control, etc. All of the problems concerning massive reuse, such as certification, data rights, and the not-

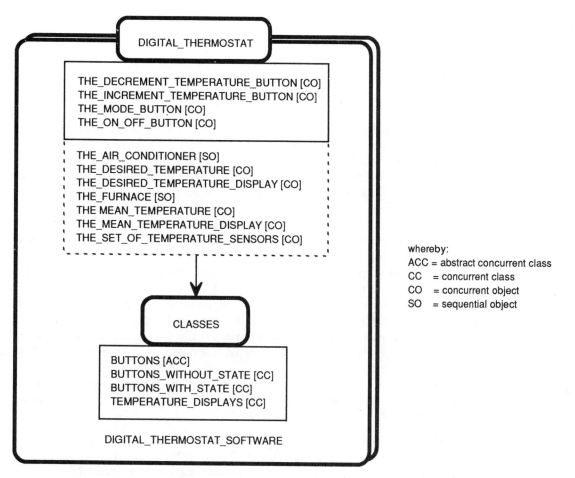

**Figure 2-28: Example Assembly Diagram**

invented-here (NIH) syndrome, must be dealt with. Frameworks must be adequately tuned to the specific application domain, yet flexible and generic enough for widespread reuse. Frameworks require a significant learning curve prior to effective use, although once mastered, productivity of development increases rapidly.

## 2.5 RESOURCES

Objects and classes have resources that must be understood if the objects and classes themselves are to be understood. Objects and classes are primarily localizations of attribute types, attributes, messages, operations, and exceptions, but they can also encapsulate nested objects, as well. The following sections define and address these resources.

## 2.5.1   Attributes and Attribute Types

An **attribute** is a discrete, inherent characteristic, property, trait, quantity, or quality of an object or class. Attributes are used to identify, describe, provide the state of, or act as a pointer to objects or classes. Attributes are data that may either be constants or variables. Data abstraction is therefore used to model attributes and to hide their implementations.

Constant attributes may be declared in object or class specifications because they may be safely exported from their objects and classes. In order to ensure proper information hiding and to avoid the classic problems associated with common global data, variable attributes should always be hidden in the body of the corresponding object or class. Variable attributes should only be accessible indirectly, via messages to operations of the object or class.

Although in some object-oriented languages, attributes are also considered to be objects, and types are considered to be classes, this book maintains the distinction, in order to handle implementation with hybrid languages such as Ada and C++.

An **attribute type** is a template for the construction of attributes that share the same structure and operations. Attribute types declare the common structure, allowed values, and behavior of an arbitrary set of related attributes, in terms of applicable operations. An attribute type may need to be named in the specification of the object or class because attributes of that type may need to be used as parameters of messages and operations. The definition of attribute types should be hidden in the body of the corresponding objects and classes.

Attributes and attribute types can and should be categorized in several ways. For example, they can be either essential or nonessential, depending on the system requirements:

- *Essential attributes* and *essential attribute types* are required, are resources of essential objects or classes, and are identified, analyzed, and specified during OORA.
- On the other hand, *nonessential attributes* and *nonessential attribute types* represent the results of design decisions and may be encapsulated in either essential or nonessential objects or classes. Nonessential attributes and nonessential attribute types are identified and designed during either logical or implementation design.

Attributes and attribute types can belong to either objects or classes, depending on their scope:

- *Object attributes* and *object attribute types* belong to individual objects and may be defined either separately for each object of an anonymous class or as part of the definition of a template class.
- *Class attributes* and *class attribute types* belong to individual classes and refer to the class as a whole, as opposed to its instances.

Attributes and attribute types should be named using nouns or noun phrases with initial capitalization that are meaningful from the user perspective. We use plural nouns for attribute types and singular nouns for attributes. For example, the TEMPERATURE_SENSOR_1 object may export the attribute type, Valid_

Temperatures_In_Degrees_Celsius, and hide the variable attribute, The_Current_Temperature, which may have the value 45.

The specification of a type attribute should define the identifier, range, units of measure, precision, and accuracy of its instances, and all allowable operations on the type. The design of a type attribute should define the structure of its allowable instances. The specification of a data attribute should define its type and initial value (if any). For example, using OOSDL,

```
type  Lists_Of_Sensor_Values   is array   (1 .. Number_Of_Sensors)
                                of          Sensor_Values;
type  Kilometers                is new Values.THE_SET_OF_REAL_NUMBERS
                                delta 0.001;
type  Voltage                   is new Values.THE_SET_OF_REAL_NUMBERS
                                digits 5   range 0.0 .. 120.0;
type  Kilometers_Per_Hour       is new Values.THE_SET_OF_INTEGERS
                                                   range   0 ..  500;
type  Valid_Temperatures        is new Degrees_Celsius    range   0 ..  120;
type  Safe_Temperatures         is sub Valid_Temperatures range  10 ..  100;
type  States                    is     (Off,Enabled,Disabled,Failed);

constant The_Delay_Aamount       : Seconds.THE_CLOCK            ::=       10;
constant The_Maximum_Difference  :
         Degrees_Celsius.THE_SET_OF_TEMPERATURE_SENSORS         ::=        2;
variable The_Mode                : Modes                        ::= Celsius;
variable The_State               : States                       ::=      Off;
variable The_Mean_Temperature    :
         Degrees_Celsius.THE_SET_OF_TEMPERATURE_SENSORS;
variable The_Desired_Temperature :
         Degrees_Celsius.THE_SET_OF_TEMPERATURE_SENSORS;
```

### 2.5.2   Messages

A **message** is a call, possibly bound at run-time, to an object or class that requests a specific service, provides needed data, or provides the notification of a specific event. Messages thus address the specific responsibilities of objects and classes. Messages to sequential objects and classes map exactly to a corresponding operation that provides the service requested by the message. However, messages to concurrent objects and classes must be routed to the appropriate operation in such a manner that one operation completes before the next message to that operation is received. The mapping between messages and operations in a concurrent environment must consider both synchronization and critical regions  and therefore may not be one-to-one. The object or class is responsible for ensuring that the messages are received by theappropriate operations. (Later in this section, this kind of situation is shown for the ROUTE_MESSAGES_FOR.THE_DESIRED_TEMPERATURE operation in Figure 2-30.)

Messages come in three main types, with regard to concurrency and threads of control: sequential, synchronous, and asynchronous. The servant object or class determines which of these three types of messages to export in the message declaration.

- A *sequential message* involves only a single thread of control and can only be sent to a sequential object or class; the thread of control is passed from the client to the server until the corresponding operation is completed.
- A *synchronous message* involves two threads of control that must synchronize during the execution of the corresponding operation; it can only be exported by a concurrent object or class.
- An *asynchronous message*, on the other hand, does not involve synchronization and is essentially a fire-and-forget message; such a message can only be exported by a concurrent object or class.

Messages can be documented as arcs on IDs, CFDs, and timing diagrams (TDs). On IDs, the identifiers of one or more messages are written on the message arcs. On CFDs, the arcs point to the corresponding message sockets and operations. On event TDs, the horizontal message arcs are drawn between the vertical bars that represent the objects and classes.

Figure 2-29 is an example ID, showing the arcs relating to messages. Messages are documented as arrows that point from the sender to the receiver of the message. These arcs are then labeled with the identifiers of the messages.

Figure 2-30 is an example object-oriented CFD, showing the icons relating to messages. Message sockets are documented using ovals that straddle the borders of objects and classes. Sequential message sockets are drawn with a thin line, synchronous message sockets are drawn with a thick line, and asynchronous message sockets are drawn with a dashed line. Messages are drawn with an arrow. Sequential messages can only be routed to sequential operations, whereas synchronous and asynchronous messages may only be routed to a concurrent operation in a concurrent object or class. Figure 2-30 shows the same message arcs between the same objects and class as shown on Figure 2-29.

Figure 2-31 illustrates message arcs on an event TD for the TURN_ON Scenario of the DIGITAL_THERMOSTAT_SOFTWARE assembly.

Each message should be documented (e.g., using the OOSDL). This documentation should include the specification of the message, the identifiers of the source and destination of the message, and the specification of the associated operation, as well as a description of the functional or process abstraction it implements. For example:

Message: **message** TURN_OFF **raise** FAILURE_OCCURRED_IN **is sequential;**
   Sent by: **object** THE_DESIRED_TEMPERATURE **is concurrent;**
   Sent to: **object** THE_AIR_CONDITIONER;
   Operation:
      **modifier operation** TURN_OFF.THE_AIR_CONDITIONER **raise**
        FAILURE_OCCURRED_IN;
Abstraction:
      This message asks THE_AIR_CONDITIONER software object to turn off
      the hardware AIR_CONDITIONER.

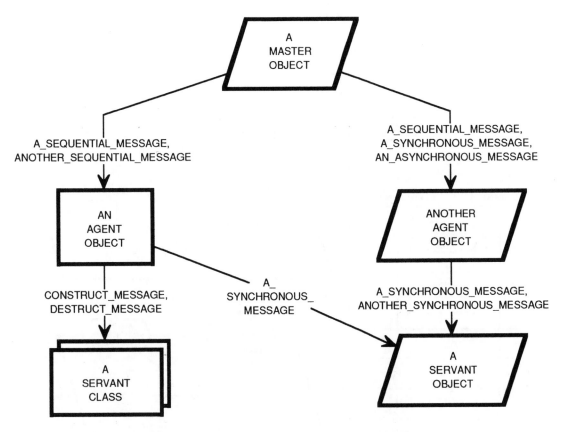

**Figure 2-29: Example Message Arcs on an Interaction Diagram (ID)**

Message:     **message** START
                    **raise** INCOMPATIBLE_STATE_IN
                    **is synchronous**;
Sent by: **object** THE_ON_OFF_BUTTON **is concurrent**;
Sent to: **object** THE_DESIRED_TEMPERATURE **is concurrent**;
Operation:
     **preserver operation** ROUTE_MESSAGES_FOR
                         **raise** INCOMPATIBLE_STATE_IN **is concurrent**;
Abstraction:
     This message is used to turn on THE_DESIRED_TEMPERATURE object.

Message:     **message INTERRUPT**(The_Interrupt_Address_For)**is asynchronous**;
Sent by: **hardware** ON_OFF_BUTTON;
Sent to: **object** THE_ON_OFF_BUTTON **is concurrent**;

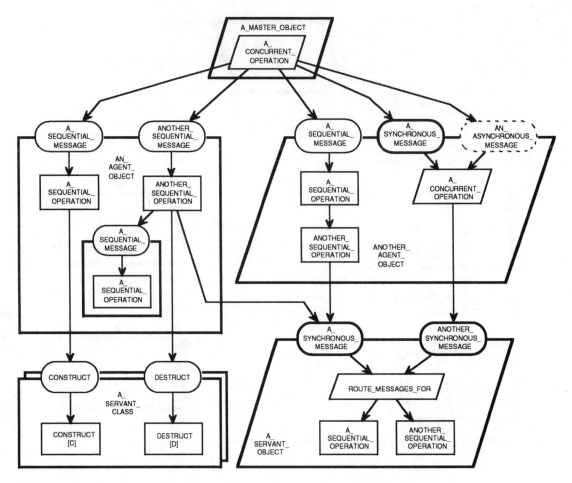

**Figure 2-30: Example Message Arcs on a Control Flow Diagram (CFD)**

Operation:

    **modifier operation** CONTROL.THE_ON_OFF_BUTTON

                **is concurrent;**

Abstraction:

This message causes THE_ON_OFF_BUTTON object to send the START and the STOP messages to THE_DESIRED_TEMPERATURE object when interrupted by the hardware ON_OFF_BUTTON when it is in the Off and On states, respectively.

Messages are declared analogously to operations and are declared in the specifications of the objects, classes, and operations that can receive them. The following specifications, written in OOSDL for an object, class, and operation, illustrate message declarations:

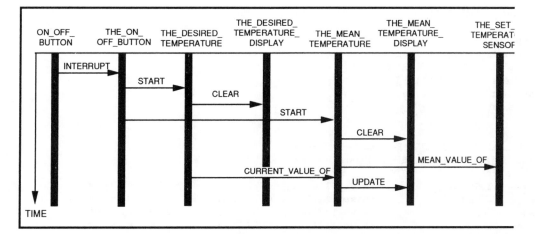

**Figure 2-31: Example Message Arcs on an Event Timing Diagram**

```
object THE_AIR_CONDITIONER is concurrent
  parent subassembly DIGITAL_THERMOSTAT;
specification
  type          Booleans        is (True,False);
  message       IS_ON           return Booleans
                                raise FAILURE_OCCURRED_IN is sequential;
  message       TURN_OFF        raise FAILURE_OCCURRED_IN is sequential;
  message       TURN_ON         raise FAILURE_OCCURRED_IN is sequential;
  exception     FAILURE_OCCURRED_IN;
end;

class GENERIC_STACKS
  needs THE_SET_OF_INTEGERS.PREDEFINED;
  parent subassembly   CLASS_REPOSITORY;
  superclass ARRAYS;
  parameter type       Entries is visible;
  parameter constant   The_Maximum_Stack_Size :  Values.THE_SET_OF_INTEGERS;
specification
  introduces
   message       CONSTRUCT      (A_STACK)
                      raise CONSTRUCT_FAILED           is sequential;
   message       DESTRUCT       (A_STACK)
                      raise DESTRUCT_FAILED            is sequential;
   message       INITIALIZE
                      raise ABSTRACTION_VIOLATED       is sequential;
   message       MAXIMUM_SIZE_OF return Values.THE_SET_OF_INTEGERS
                      raise ABSTRACTION_VIOLATED       is sequential;
   message       POP (An_Entry :   out Entries)
                      raise ENTRY_NOT_REMOVED,INCORRECT_SIZE,IS_EMPTY
                                                       is sequential;
   message       PUSH (An_Entry : in      Entries)
                      raise ENTRY_NOT_ADDED,INCORRECT_SIZE,IS_FULL
                                                       is sequential;
```

```
    message      SIZE_OF            return Values.THE_SET_OF_INTEGERS
                        raise INCORRECT_SIZE              is sequential;
    exception    ABSTRACTION_VIOLATED;
    exception    ENTRY_NOT_ADDED;
    exception    ENTRY_NOT_REMOVED;
    exception    INCORRECT_SIZE;
    exception    IS_EMPTY;
    exception    IS_FULL;
end;


operation ROUTE_MESSAGES_FOR is concurrent
  parent object THE_DESIRED_TEMPERATURE.DIGITAL_THERMOSTAT;
specification
  message DECREMENT        raise FAILURE_OCCURRED_IN    is synchronous;
  message INCREMENT        raise FAILURE_OCCURRED_IN    is synchronous;
  message START            raise FAILURE_OCCURRED_IN    is synchronous;
  message STOP             raise FAILURE_OCCURRED_IN    is synchronous;
  message USE_CELSIUS      raise FAILURE_OCCURRED_IN    is synchronous;
  message USE_FAHRENHEIT   raise FAILURE_OCCURRED_IN    is synchronous;
end;
```

### 2.5.3    Operations

An **operation** (a.k.a. method, service) is a discrete activity, action, or behavior performed by an object or class. Operations provide both the behavior of and the access to the attributes of objects and classes. Functional or process abstraction is used to model operations and to hide their implementation. The following paragraphs discuss several important varieties of operations.

Like objects, classes, and subassemblies, operations can be either essential or nonessential, depending on the system requirements:

- *Essential operations* are the required operations of essential objects or classes and are identified, analyzed, and specified during OORA.
- *Nonessential operations* represent the results of design decisions and may be encapsulated in either essential or nonessential objects and classes. Nonessential operations are identified and designed during either logical or implementation design.

Operations may be either object or class operations, depending on their scope:

- *Object operations* operate on individual objects.
- *Class operations* operate on the entire class or on more than one instance of the class. For example, **CONSTRUCT** and **DESTRUCT** are class operations of the SETS class, whereas NUMBER_OF_ELEMENTS, INTERSECTION, and UNION are object operations exported by each instance of the SETS class.

Operations may be categorized as constructors, destructors, modifiers, or preservers, depending on how they behave:

- **Constructor operations** are class operations that *construct* instances of the associated class.
- **Destructor operations** *destroy* instances of the associated class.
- **Modifier operations** *modify* the state of the associated object or class.
- **Preserver operations** *preserve* the state of the associated object or class. They are like functions without side effects and are used only to return values of attributes.

Operations may be either iterators or noniterators.

- An *iterator* accesses either multiple resources within an object or multiple instances of a class. An example of an iterator operation is the operation that averages the current temperatures measured by all instances of a TEMPERATURE_SENSORS class in THE_SET_OF_TEMPERATURE_SENSORS object.
- A *noniterator* accesses only a single object or class. An example of a noniterator operation is the operation that calibrates an individual sensor in the aforementioned aggregate object.

Operations may be either atomic or aggregate.

- *Atomic operations* require knowledge of the underlying implementation of the object or class. Atomic operations must exist, and all essential operations that are not the result of design constraints are atomic.
- *Aggregate operations* are based on simple operations and are typically nonessential. Aggregate operations are often used to improve user-friendliness and reusability by simplifying the specification of objects and classes.

Another categorization of operations has to do with concurrency issues. Operations may be sequential or concurrent.

- *Sequential operations* do not have their own thread of control and exist in sequential objects and classes. For example, they would be implemented in Ada as a subprogram (i.e., a procedure or function) not nested inside a task.
- **Concurrent operations** have their own thread of control and, for example, could be implemented in Ada as a task without entries.

Preserver operations should be named by using nouns or noun phrases because, like functions, they are often used in place of the attribute for which they return a value. Modifier operations should be named using verbs and verb phrases because they are activities or actions, and they implement behavior. These identifiers should be meaningful from the users' perspective. We use all-capital-letter identifiers for operations. For example, the TEMPERATURE_SENSORS class will have the **CONSTRUCT** constructor operation and the **DESTRUCT** destructor operation, and each instance may have the CALIBRATE modifier operation and the CURRENT_VALUE_OF preserver operation.

Operations may (or may not) have parameters, and these parameters may be of mode **in** (i.e., read only), **out** (i.e., write only), or **inout** (i.e., both read and write). For example:

```
constructor operation CONSTRUCT (TEMPERATURE_SENSOR_1)
                                    raise  CONSTRUCT_FAILED;


destructor operation DESTRUCT (TEMPERATURE_SENSOR_1);
                                    raise  DESTRUCT_FAILED;


modifier operation CALIBRATE.TEMPERATURE_SENSOR_1
        (The_Actual_Temperature : in Valid_Temperatures_In_Degrees_Celsius)
                                    raise FAILURE_OCCURRED_IN;


preserver operation CURRENT_VALUE_OF.TEMPERATURE_SENSOR_1
        return Valid_Temperatures_In_Degrees_Celsius
                                    raise FAILURE_OCCURRED_IN;
```

Sequential operations execute only upon receipt of the corresponding message. Concurrent operations begin execution upon *elaboration* (i.e., the process by which declarations take effect) of their corresponding object or class and in the order in which they are listed in the initialization list. Concurrent operations may or may not receive messages.

The following is the specification and body for a sequential operation. Notice that the declaration of the operation and of the corresponding message are identical.

```
preserver operation CURRENT_PERCENT_OF              return Percents
                                                    raise  FAILURE_OCCURRED_IN
 parent object THE_FUEL_SENSOR.GAUGES.AUTOMOTIVE_DASHBOARD_APPLICATION;
specification
 message CURRENT_PERCENT_OF                          return Percents
                                                    raise  FAILURE_OCCURRED_IN
                                                    is sequential;

end;


operation CURRENT_PERCENT_OF
body
statements
 receive CURRENT_PERCENT_OF;
 The_Current_Percent := The_Conversion_Factor *
  CONVERT(VALUE_OF(The_Fuel_Sensor_Address).SYSTEM).SET_OF_INTEGERS;
 return The_Current_Percent;
end;
```

The following is the specification and body, written in OOSDL, for a concurrent operation that receives (and routes) two messages. Notice that the declaration of the operation and the corresponding message are not identical. The purpose of this operation is to ensure that THE_SHOWER_MASTER object only receives and handles one message at a time in a concurrent environment.

```
operation ROUTE_MESSAGES_FOR  is  concurrent
 parent object THE_SHOWER_MASTER.CONTROL_PANEL.SHOWER_MASTER;
```

```
        specification
         message TURN_OFF    raise       FAILURE_OCCURRED_IN is sequential;
         message TURN_ON     raise       FAILURE_OCCURRED_IN is sequential;
        end;

        operation ROUTE_MESSAGES_FOR
        body
        statements
         FOREVER : loop
          select
           receive TURN_OFF;     -- message
           TURN_OFF;   -- execute TURN_OFF operation
          or
           receive TURN_ON; -- message
           TURN_ON;    -- execute TURN_ON  operation
          end select;
         end loop FOREVER;
        end;
```

The following is the specification and body for a concurrent operation that does not receive any messages:

```
preserver operation MAINTAIN raise FAILURE_OCCURRED_IN is concurrent
 parent object
   THE_DESIRED_TEMPERATURE.DIGITAL_THERMOSTAT.DIGITAL_THERMOSTAT_SOFTWARE;
specification
 -- This master operation does not receive any messages.
end;

operation MAINTAIN
 needs THE_AIR_CONDITIONER;
 needs THE_FURNACE;
 needs THE_MEAN_TEMPERATURE;
body
preconditions
 require
   The_Current_Value = 21 and The_Mode = Celsius and The_State = Off
 else
   raise INCOMPATIBLE_STATE_IN.THE_DESIRED_TEMPERATURE;
 end require;
statements
 FOREVER : loop
  INNER : while The_State = On loop
   The_Mean_Temperature ::= CURRENT_VALUE_OF.THE_MEAN_TEMPERATURE;
   if -- The_Mean_Temperature is too low.
    The_Mean_Temperature < The_Current_Value - The_Maximum_Difference
   then
    if not    IS_ON.THE_FURNACE          then TURN_ON.THE_FURNACE;
    if        IS_ON.THE_AIR_CONDITIONER  then TURN_OFF.THE_AIR_CONDITIONER;
   end if;
   if -- The_Mean_Temperature is too high.
```

```
        The_Mean_Temperature > The_Current_Value + The_Maximum_Difference
     then
       if not      IS_ON.THE_AIR_CONDITIONER              then TURN_ON.THE_AIR_CONDITIONER;
       if          IS_ON.THE_FURNACE                      then TURN_OFF.THE_FURNACE;
       end if;
     DELAY(The_Delay_Amount).THE_CLOCK;
    end loop INNER;
    DELAY(The_Delay_Amount).THE_CLOCK;
  end loop FOREVER;
exception_handler
 when FAILURE_OCCURRED_IN.THE_AIR_CONDITIONER        then
   if IS_ON.THE_FURNACE                              then TURN_OFF.THE_FURNACE;
 end when;
 when FAILURE_OCCURRED_IN.THE_FURNACE                then
   if IS_ON.THE_AIR_CONDITIONER                      then TURN_OFF.THE_AIR_CONDITIONER;
 end when;
 when FAILURE_OCCURRED_IN.THE_MEAN_TEMPERATURE       then
   if IS_ON.THE_AIR_CONDITIONER                      then TURN_OFF.THE_AIR_CONDITIONER;
   if IS_ON.THE_FURNACE                              then TURN_OFF.THE_FURNACE;
 end when;
 when others                                         then
   if IS_ON.THE_AIR_CONDITIONER                      then TURN_OFF.THE_AIR_CONDITIONER;
   if IS_ON.THE_FURNACE                              then TURN_OFF.THE_FURNACE;
 end when;
 raise FAILURE_OCCURRED_IN.THE_DESIRED_TEMPERATURE;
end;
```

Note the nontraditional use of the dot notation in the preceding example. The resource is listed before its source (i.e., TURN_OFF.THE_AIR _CONDITIONER) so that non-Boolean messages (the most common kind) can be read as standard imperative English sentences of the form "VERB.DIRECT_OBJECT."

The specifications and bodies of the three preceding operations were specified algorithmically and therefore include design decisions, as well as requirements. Operation specifications and bodies can also be specified using preconditions, postconditions, and invariants.

The following specification and body of the operation PUSH    (An_ Entry).THE_STACK illustrates the use of preconditions and postconditions.

```
modifier operation PUSH (An_Entry :     in Entries)
                                        raise ENTRY_NOT_ADDED,INCORRECT_SIZE,IS_FULL
 parent object GENERIC_STACKS;
specification
  message PUSH (An_Entry : in Entries)
                                        raise ENTRY_NOT_ADDED,INCORRECT_SIZE,IS_FULL
                                        is sequential;
end;


operation PUSH (An_Entry : in Entries)
                                        raise ENTRY_NOT_ADDED,INCORRECT_SIZE,IS_FULL
```

```
body
preconditions
  require
    The_Size < The_Maximum_Size          else raise IS_FULL;
  end require;
postconditions
  require
    post(The_Size) <= The_Maximum_Size   else raise IS_FULL;
  end require;
  require
    post(The_Size) =  The_Size + 1       else raise INCORRECT_SIZE;
  end require;
  require
    post(The_Top) =  An_Entry            else raise ENTRY_NOT_ADDED;
  end require;
end;
```

The following specification and body of the operation MAINTAIN. THE_DESIRED_TEMPERATURE illustrates the use of invariants.

```
preserver operation MAINTAIN  raise _OCCURRED_IN, INCOMPATIBLE_STATE_IN
                                is concurrent
 parent object
  THE_DESIRED_TEMPERATURE.DIGITAL_THERMOSTAT.DIGITAL_THERMOSTAT_SOFTWARE;
specification
-- This master operation does not receive any messages.
end;


operation MAINTAIN
 needs THE_AIR_CONDITIONER;
 needs THE_FURNACE;
body
invariants
    not (IS_ON.THE_AIR_CONDITIONER and IS_ON.THE_FURNACE);
end;
```

## 2.5.4 Exceptions

Most specifications and designs naturally emphasize the normal capabilities and behavior of the software but unfortunately also underemphasize how the software is to behave under abnormal circumstances. *Exceptions* are error conditions that are identified and raised by the operations of objects and classes so that they can be properly handled by calling operations, possibly in other objects or classes. The following are example exception statements and handlers:

```
if    The_Pressure > The_Maximum_Safe_Pressure  then
  raise PRESSURE_ABOVE_MAXIMUM_SAFE_VALUE;
or_if The_Pressure < The_Minimum_Safe_Pressure  then
  raise PRESSURE_BELOW_MINIMUM_SAFE_VALUE;
else
```

```
    CONTROL;
end if;

exception_handler
  when PRESSURE_ABOVE_MAXIMUM_SAFE_VALUE
  or TEMPERATURE_ABOVE_MAXIMUM_SAFE_VALUE            then
    OPEN.THE_FAILSAFE_VALVE;
    SHUT_DOWN.THE_SYSTEM;
  end when;
  when PRESSURE_BELOW_MINIMUM_SAFE_VALUE             then
    INCREASE_RATE;
  end when;
  when TEMPERATURE_BELOW_MINIMUM_SAFE_VALUE          then
    TURN_ON.THE_FURNACE;
  end when;
  when others                                        then
    SHUT_DOWN.THE_SYSTEM;
  end when;
  SOUND_ALARM_OF.THE_OPERATOR;
  UPDATE.THE_ERROR_LOG;
```

## 2.6 RELATIONSHIPS

No object or class is an island, independent of all others. They are related to one another in several important ways. At the highest level of abstraction, objects and classes interact and depend on one another. One or more groups of collaborating objects is usually required to implement any significant capability. Objects typically depend on other objects for services (via message passing) or possibly for declarations of visible attribute types, constant attributes, and exceptions. Objects are typically instances of classes, and classes may inherit resources from other classes. Some objects are components or parts of larger aggregate objects.

A *relationship* exists between any two entities (e.g., objects, classes, hardware devices) that are somehow associated or connected.

Relationships may be binary (i.e., between two entities), ternary (i.e., among three entities), or of higher order. *Binary relationships* are the most common and the easiest to understand and represent. Although *ternary relationships* are sometimes important, higher-order relationships are much more complex and should be avoided where practical. See Figure 2-32: Binary and Higher-Order Relationships.

For the sake of understandability, all relationships should be labeled, either with an identifier or with a graphic arc type. For example, associations and message arcs have labels, whereas inheritance relationships in this book have visible arc styles (e.g., dotted or dashed).

Directional relationships introduce client and server roles. An entity that depends on or uses (e.g., sends a message to) another entity has the **client** role, while the subservient entity has the role of **server**. If two related entities both play the role of client with regard to one relationship and the role of server with regard to another relationship, then each has the **colleague** role. However, two entities usually should

BINARY RELATIONSHIP                    TERNARY RELATIONSHIP

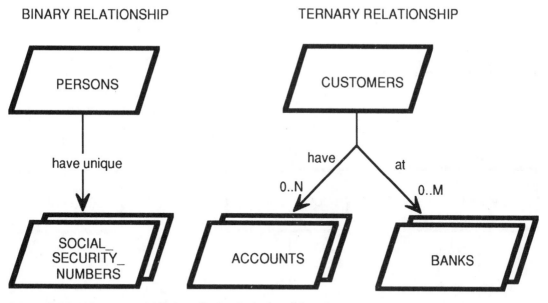

**Figure 2-32: Binary and Higher-Order Relationships**

not be both clients and servers of each other, in order to promote understandability and reliability. The client/server roles can, in turn, be used to differentiate entities into three roles by the dependency (i.e., using) relationships between them. A **master** is the client of all other entities with which it is related but is the server of none. A **servant** is the server of all other entities with which it is related but is the client of none. An **agent** is the client of some entities and the server of others. See Figure 2-33: Roles in Relationships

In order to promote the understandability of the diagrams showing relationships, we use the following conventions: Relationships are drawn using arrows from the client entity to the server entity (i.e., in the direction of dependency), so that they are consistent with the direction of dependency and message passing. The client entities are drawn above the associated server entities, so that the arrows all run from top to bottom, making the distinctions among masters, agents, and servants clearer.

The **cardinality** (a.k.a. *multiplicity* [Rumbaugh et al. 1991]) of relationships can be important when dealing with relationships involving classes (which may have multiple instances) or aggregate objects (which contain multiple objects). Relationships may be one-to-one, one-to-zero-or-one, one-to-many, many-to-many, etc. Sometimes, the cardinality varies over time, but when the cardinality is fixed and known, simple classifications such as one-to-many may be insufficient. The recommended notation for cardinality is shown on Figure 2-34: Cardinality of Relationships. If the relationship is one-to-one, no cardinality need be shown, as in the relationship between employees and social security numbers. If the cardinality of the client is one, then only the cardinality of the server needs to be documented. The

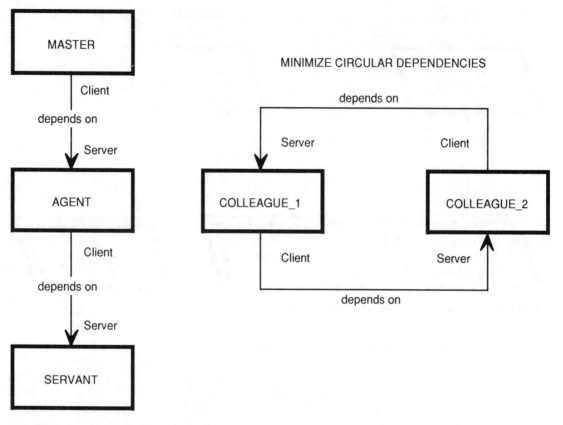

**Figure 2-33: Roles in Relationships**

cardinality of the server can be given by a number (e.g., "5"), a range (e.g., "0..1," "1..100"), a set of values (e.g., "2,4"), a set of ranges ("1..10,21..30"), or an arbitrary number (e.g., "N"). If the cardinality of the client is not one, then the two cardinalities can be separated by a colon (e.g., "0..1:1..10," "M:N").

A **conditional** relationship is, by definition, a relationship that only exists when a specific condition is met. If it is adequate merely to note that the relationship is conditional, a curved arc is used, as shown on the bottom left of Figure 2-35. When it is important to document the specific condition that must be met on the diagram, it is written near the arrowhead; this recommended notation for conditional relationships is shown on Figure 2-35: Conditional Relationships.

## 2.6.1 Associations

An **association** [Rumbaugh et al. 1991] (a.k.a. *connection* [Coad and Yourdon 1989]) is a general relationship that exists at the highest level of abstraction. It can be used

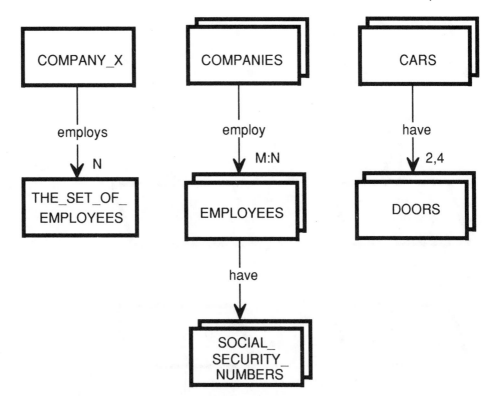

**Figure 2-34: Cardinality of Relationships**

for literally any relevant relationship among any entities and is used to address the high-level, abstract responsibilities of the objects and classes. Because it is usually described in everyday English, it can be used to communicate with non–software developers and is often developed very early during requirements analysis, to provide a top-level overview of the relationships between entities. Associations are documented on general semantic nets (a.k.a. *information models* [Shlaer and Mellor 1988]).

Associations between two entities can usually be read as standard English sentences of the form "`SUBJECT verb_phrase DIRECT_OBJECT`" by first reading the identifier of the client, then reading the identifier of the association, and finally reading the identifier of the server. Binary associations are inherently bidirectional, but relationship identifiers are not. The choice of words (e.g., "`THE_SENSOR provides a value to THE_GAUGE`" vs. "`THE_GAUGE obtains a value from THE_SENSOR`") or the word order (e.g., "The manager controls the project" vs. "The project controls the manager") makes a difference. For example, if the sensor is the master and the gauge is the server, then the association can be read "`THE_SENSOR provides a value to THE_GAUGE`." On the other hand, if the gauge is the master and the sensor is the server, then the association can be read "`THE_GAUGE obtains a value from THE_SENSOR`." See Figure 2-36: Association Directions.

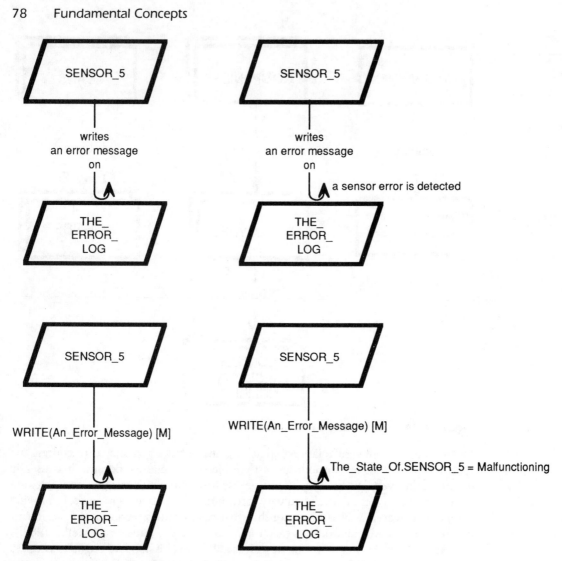

**Figure 2-35: Conditional Relationships**

## 2.6.2 Message Passing

Objects primarily interact via *messages*[6] (i.e., a call, possibly bound at run-time, to an operation of an object or class). Classes can also send and accept messages, including **CONSTRUCT** and **DESTRUCT** messages, requesting the construction and destruction of instances. The client object or class will send a message to the server requesting the

---

[6]Objects can also interact in terms of exception passing and of having visibility to exported attribute types and constants (if one allows the strong typing of attributes).

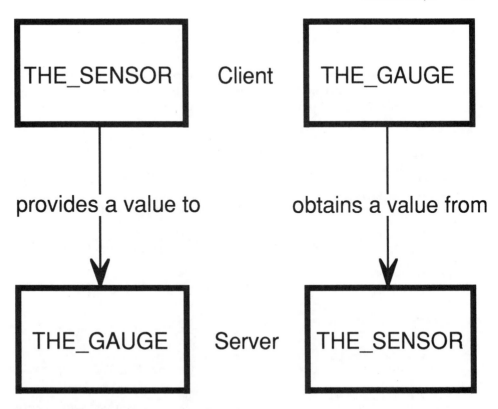

**Figure 2-36: Association Directions**

server to perform a service, provide needed data, or provide notification of a specific event. The destination object or class must be part of the message if the client and the server are different. If objects can send messages to themselves, then the destination is assumed and does not have to be provided. If the client and server are different, then the message must be exported from the server and so must be declared in the server's specification. If the message requires any formal parameters, then the corresponding actual parameters must be supplied in the message by the client.

The specification of the server object thus acts as a contract between the client and the server, which declares the responsibilities of each. It is the *client's responsibility* (a) to send the message to the right server, (b) to only send messages that are declared in the server's specification, and (c) to supply compatible actual parameters in the message for all formal parameters required by the corresponding message exported by the server. It is the *server's responsibility* (a) to check the compatibility of all actual parameters with the corresponding formal parameters; (b) to ensure that the correct operation receives the message; (c) to correctly perform the operation if possible; (d) to ensure that the object's abstraction is not violated by the performance of the operation, by ensuring that all preconditions, postconditions, and invariants of the corresponding operation have been met; (e) to return to the client all required actual parameters of mode **inout** or **out**; and (f) in the case that the operation could not be correctly and safely performed, to raise an appropriate visible exception to the client and to return to the state it had prior to receiving the message.

Messages are received by the appropriate operation body. The following operation body, written in OOSDL, illustrates the receipt of a message:

```
operation ROUTE_MESSAGES_FOR
body
statements
 FOREVER : loop
   select
     receive DECREMENT;               -- message
     DECREMENT;                       -- execute the DECREMENT operation
   or
     receive INCREMENT;               -- message
     INCREMENT;                       -- execute the INCREMENT operation
   or
     receive START;                   -- message
     START;                           -- execute the START operation
   or
     receive STOP;                    -- message
     STOP;                            -- execute the STOP operation
   or
     receive USE_CELSIUS;             -- message
     USE_CELSIUS;                     -- execute the USE_CELSIUS operation
   or
     receive USE_FAHRENHEIT;          -- message
     USE_FAHRENHEIT;                  -- execute the USE_FAHRENHEIT operation
   end select;
 end loop FOREVER;
end;
```

## 2.6.3    Inheritance

If there were no way to directly reuse and extend the resources of previously developed classes, each new object and class would have to declare and implement all of the resources it exports and hides (except for those exported resources it obtains from its servers). **Inheritance** is the relationship between classes that allows **subclasses** to be built as extensions or specializations of **superclasses**. As Bertrand Meyer [1988, p. 229] so aptly put it,

> This favors a style of software development completely different from traditional approaches. Instead of trying to solve every new problem from scratch, the idea is to build on previous accomplishments and extend their results. The spirit is one of economy—why redo what has already been done?—and humility, in the line of Newton's famous remark that he could reach so high only because he stood on the shoulders of giants.

Objects that are instances of different classes are often related to one another because part of their architecture and behavior is identical or similar. Thus, they must export or encapsulate analogous or related resources. For example, different device objects (e.g., THE_FAN,  THE_HEATER) of different device classes (e.g., FANS, HEATERS) may nevertheless have a common behavior (e.g., TURN_OFF and TURN_ON). As objects, they all may export the following type, messages, and exception and may hide the following attribute type and attribute:

```
type       Booleans       is (True,False);
message    IS_ON          return Booleans
                          raise FAILURE_OCCURRED_IN is sequential;
message    TURN_OFF       raise FAILURE_OCCURRED_IN is sequential;
message    TURN_ON        raise FAILURE_OCCURRED_IN is sequential;
exception  FAILURE_OCCURRED_IN;


type       States is (On,Off,Malfunctioning);
variable   The_State : States ::= Off;
```

The classes of these similar, yet different, objects must be related in an analogous way. As templates for their respective objects, these classes must declare the resources of their objects. If their objects encapsulate analogous resources, the different classes must declare them. Rather than repeating and maintaining the identical declarations in the two classes, the software engineer should factor out these common declarations and place them in a new superclass (i.e., DEVICES). The two original subclasses may now inherit the common declarations from their parent superclass, the root class of the hierarchy. Inheritance is the mechanism used to model these relationships among analogous classes. A *subclass* can be an extension, modification, or specialization of its parent superclass(es), depending on whether resources are added to, modified, or deleted from those inherited from its parents. See Figure 2-37: Example Inheritance Hierarchy.

For example, the following are specifications and bodies for the root superclass DEVICES and its two subclasses FANS and HEATERS:

```
class DEVICES
 parent subassembly TBD;
specification
 introduces
   message   CONSTRUCT  (A_DEVICE)  raise CONSTRUCT_FAILED    is sequential;
   message   DESTRUCT   (A_DEVICE)  raise DESTRUCT_FAILED     is sequential;
   message   IS_ON                  raise FAILURE_OCCURRED_IN is sequential;
   message   TURN_OFF               raise FAILURE_OCCURRED_IN is sequential;
   message   TURN_ON                raise FAILURE_OCCURRED_IN is sequential;
   exception     FAILURE_OCCURRED_IN;
end;

class DEVICES
body
 introduces
   type         States is (On,Off,Malfunctioning);
   variable     The_State : States ::= Off;
   constructor  operation  CONSTRUCT  (A_DEVICE)  raise  CONSTRUCT_FAILED;
```

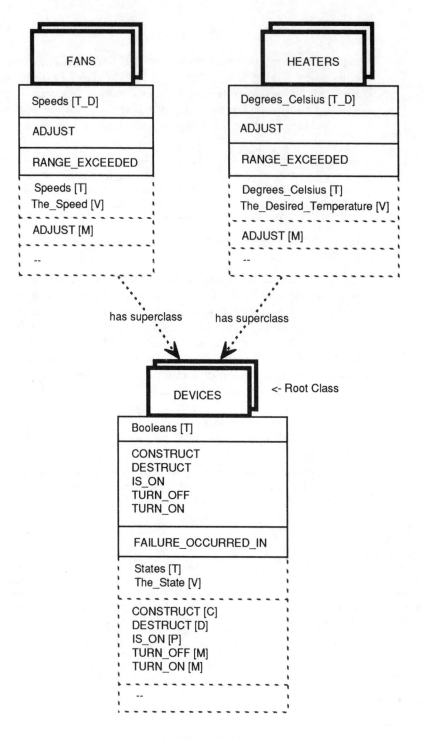

**Figure 2-37: Example Inheritance Hierarchy**

```
   destructor     operation  DESTRUCT    (A_DEVICE)  raise  DESTRUCT_FAILED;
   preserver      operation  IS_ON                   raise  FAILURE_OCCURRED_IN;
   modifier       operation  TURN_OFF                raise  FAILURE_OCCURRED_IN;
   modifier       operation  TURN_ON                 raise  FAILURE_OCCURRED_IN;
end;

class FANS
 parent subassembly TBD;
 superclass DEVICES;
specification
 introduces
   type Speeds is (Low,Medium,High);
   message       ADJUST(The_Speed : in Speeds)          raise RANGE_EXCEEDED;
                                                        is sequential;
   exception     RANGE_EXCEEDED;
end;

class FANS
body
 introduces
   variable The_Speed : Speeds ::= Low;
   modifier operation ADJUST(The_Speed : in Speeds) raise RANGE_EXCEEDED;
end;

class HEATERS
 parent subassembly TBD;
 superclass DEVICES;
specification
 introduces
   type Degrees_Celsius is new Values.THE_SET_OF_INTEGERS range 0 .. 100;
   message       ADJUST(The_Desired_Temperature : in Degrees_Celsius)
                              raise RANGE_EXCEEDED is sequential;
   exception     RANGE_EXCEEDED;
end;

class HEATERS
body
 introduces
   variable The_Desired_Temperature : Degrees_Celsius ::= 0;
   modifier  operation       ADJUST(The_Desired_Temperature : in Degrees_Celsius)
                              raise RANGE_EXCEEDED;
end;
```

As another example of a classification hierarchy in the application domain that is properly modeled using inheritance during requirements analysis and logical design, consider the different types of bank accounts that exist. Some accounts have an associated interest rate (e.g., savings accounts), whereas others do not (e.g., most checking accounts). With some accounts, the interest is positive (e.g., savings accounts), whereas with others it is negative (e.g., loan accounts). Some accounts have minimum balances and terms (e.g., certificates of deposit [CDs]), whereas others do not (e.g., passbook accounts). Figure 2-38 shows a classification diagram for a bank accounts classification hierarchy.

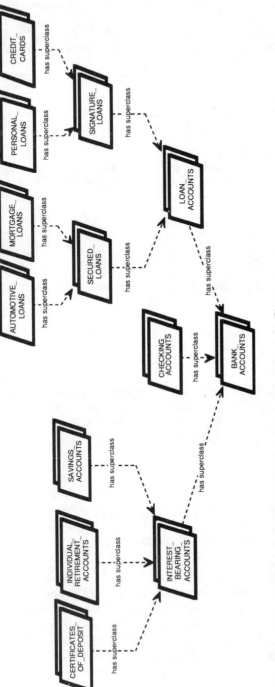

**Figure 2-38: Classification Hierarchy for the** BANK_ACCOUNTS **Class**

*Concrete* classes are complete and may be instantiated. *Abstract* classes, on the other hand, are incomplete superclasses. They are missing necessary declarations for additional resources, which must be defined in subclasses before meaningful objects can be instantiated. *Deferred* classes are abstract classes, which include stubs for the missing declarations that must be supplied by subclasses. By listing the deferred (i.e., stubbed) resources, deferred classes make it clear what missing resources must be supplied by the subclasses prior to instantiation. For example, the FANS and HEATERS subclasses both export an ADJUST operation, although ADJUST.FANS and ADJUST.HEATERS are different operations. Thus, one could define an intermediate deferred class ADJUSTABLE_DEVICES that export a deferred ADJUST operation that would be supplied by the FANS and HEATERS subclasses.

Figure 2-39 shows a body-level CLD of the TRAFFIC_SIGNALS class hierarchy. The subclasses STANDARD_SIGNALS and TURN_SIGNALS introduce exported messages and a hidden attribute, some operations, and a component object that were nonexistent or deferred in the superclass TRAFFIC_SIGNALS.

Because inheritance is often primarily used as a way of avoiding duplicate effort and documentation, some methodologists have argued that inheritance is purely a design issue and should not be addressed during requirements analysis. After all, what contractual difference does it make whether the same requirement is duplicated in the SRS under different objects and classes or is only listed once under the superclass? There are, however, good counterarguments for using inheritance during requirements analysis. If inheritance is truly used to model classification relationships in the application domain rather than for random reuse of unrelated common requirements, an important aspect of the problem space is captured. By avoiding redundancy, configuration management, quality assurance, testing, and requirements tracing are less costly. All of the advantages of inheritance during coding have their analogs during requirements analysis. The SRSs are smaller and easier to read. Unfortunately, the limitations and risks of inheritance that are discussed in a later paragraph also apply.

Inheritance clearly involves both generalization and specialization. A class can be considered a generalization of its instances, which factors out all common properties of the related instances. Similarly, a superclass can be considered a generalization of its subclasses (e.g., DEVICES can be considered more general than FANS and HEATERS). Conversely, instances of a class and subclasses of a superclass can be considered different specializations (e.g., FANS are more specialized than DEVICES). While both views are appropriate, different views tend to be more appropriate during different development activities. Thus, ADM3, the development method recommended in this book, emphasizes generalization during analysis and design by stating that objects should be identified before their corresponding classes and that these classes can be generalized to create superclasses. Because of language and compiler constraints, many OOPLs emphasize specialization during coding by mandating that objects must be instantiated from preexisting classes.

The relationships between objects and classes and between subclasses and superclasses can be considered from the viewpoint of either generalization or specialization.

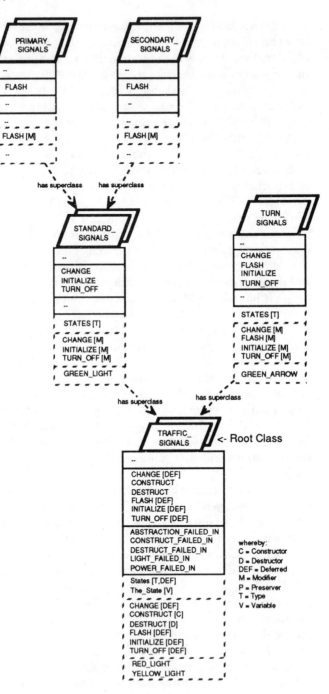

**Figure 2-39: Subclasses Introducing Additional Resources**

Each object is an instance of its class, and each class is a subclass of its superclasses. For example, FAN_1 is an instance of FANS, and FANS is a subclass of DEVICES. These two different relationships are often considered a single generic "is-a" relationship. With the right name changes (e.g., FAN instead of FANS), one can then say that FAN_1 is a FAN and that each FAN is a DEVICE. Because these first two approaches are popular in the OOP community, classification diagrams are often drawn with the arrows pointing from the instance to the class and from the subclass to the instance. On the other hand, each class has objects as instances and each superclass has classes as subclasses. For example, DEVICES has subclass FANS, and FANS has instance FAN_1. See Figure 2-40: The Three Approaches. The use of "is-a" arcs is not recommended because classes would have to be labeled with singular nouns for the relationship to be correct English, which is counterintuitive. Otherwise, the three viewpoints are equivalent, and the direction and labeling of the arcs is ultimately a matter of taste.

Inheritance can be either single or multiple. With single inheritance, each child subclass inherits resources from only one parent superclass. Species exhibit single inheritance. For example, apes can be chimpanzees, gorillas, or orangutans. See Figure 2-41, which shows the recent branches of humanity's family tree. With multiple inheritance, however, a single subclass has multiple parent superclasses. Thus, children inherit genes from both their biological fathers and their biological mothers. See Figure 2-42: Examples of Single and Multiple Inheritance From Biology.

Inheritance has a significant impact on concurrency issues. A subclass is concurrent if and only if it inherits a concurrent resource or it introduces a concurrent resource. A subclass is thus sequential if and only if it does not inherit any concurrent resources and does not introduce any concurrent resouces. Therefore, concurrent superclasses typically have concurrent subclasses, and sequential superclasses typically have sequential subclasses.

Inheritance is considered a critical part of any object-oriented method by many software engineers because it offers many significant benefits. Inheritance models the important analogous relationship in the application domain. By factoring out the common declarations, classes are simplified, and their differences are clearly emphasized. Their common declarations can be reused, not only by current subclasses but also by any future ones that need the same declarations. Inheritance thus greatly increases the reuse of related capabilities and minimizes specification and design documentation. Classification, the ability to see common characteristics and behavior in different situations, is a basic human tool for understanding and dealing with complexity. Inheritance can also increase understandability and maintainability by emphasizing the important, shared capabilities and differences and by physically separating different sets of declarations. Reliability is increased by allowing subclasses to be used safely in any context where one of its ancestor superclasses can be used.

On the other hand, inheritance also has numerous significant risks and limitations that cannot safely be ignored. Inheritance greatly limits the software engineering principles of localization and encapsulation. Instead of localizing all class declarations in the class itself and encapsulating all hidden resources in the class body,

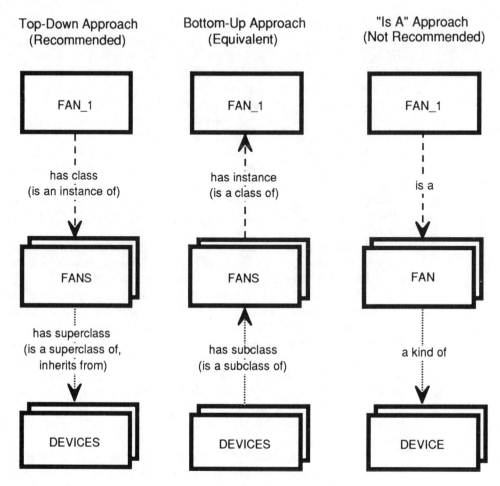

**Figure 2-40: The Three Approaches**

these declarations are scattered throughout the inheritance hierarchy in the class and all of its superclasses. Understandability can be greatly diminished because all parts of a class are not collected in a single location. If inheritance hierarchies are large, it is often difficult for a software engineer to determine which resources the subclasses are inheriting and from which superclasses they are inheriting these resources. This is especially true of multiple inheritance, in which either the same resource may be inherited via multiple superclasses or incompatible resources may be inherited from different superclasses.

Multiple inheritance also has the added problem that two different versions of the same resource may be inherited from multiple parents, leading to problems in over-loading and conflict resolution. Reliability may decrease because modifications to

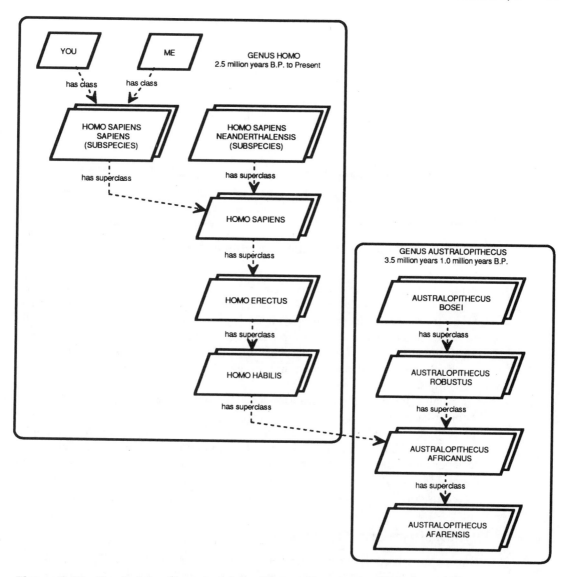

**Figure 2-41: Single Inheritance and the Recent Human Family Tree**

superclasses may have unexpected effects on their subclasses. Inheritance is also often misused. Instead of being restricted to a way of simplifying related classes in true classification hierarchies, some developers use it as a way to reuse unrelated capabilities that do not logically belong to objects of the same superclass. Because they do not implement any real abstraction, such random-reuse "superclasses" are inherently difficult to understand, costly to maintain, and difficult to extend when the require-

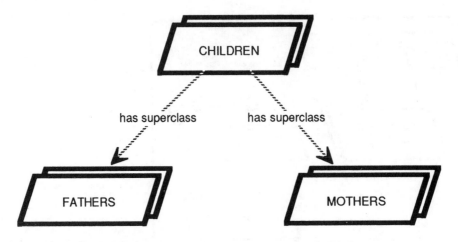

**Figure 2-42: Example of Multiple Inheritance From Biology**

ments change. Although parameterization (i.e., generics) is often more natural and reliable than inheritance in many situations, some approaches advocate using inheritance for all reuse. In fact, some methods and languages force all objects to be instances of classes and all classes to be part of a single massive classification hierarchy. This often forces totally unrelated abstractions to be related by inheritance, which requires significant effort and which results in questionable classification hierarchies.

Finally, not every implementation language supports inheritance. If the language is object-based (e.g., Ada-83) or procedural (e.g., C, COBOL, or FORTRAN) rather than object-oriented, then significant redesign and programming is required to implement an OOLD. Because of these risks and limitations, other software engineers consider inheritance to be of limited value and dangerous if misused. They advocate a limited number of small disjoint classification hierarchies, rather than one massive hierarchy containing all classes, as required by the language SMALLTALK.

## 2.6.4    Polymorphism and Overloading

*Polymorphism* literally means being able to take on many forms. The term is very important in OOP and has been considered to be one of the defining properties of object orientation by many authors. **Polymorphism** is "the ability of an entity to refer at run-time to instances of various classes" [Meyer 1988]. Polymorphism promotes the extensibility of software and requires dynamic (i.e., run-time) binding to function. Whereas polymorphism (and dynamic binding) are critical concerns during OOP, they are relatively irrelevant during requirements analysis and logical design, where implementation concerns should be deferred.

*Overloading*, on the other hand, is critical during the entire development cycle. If attribute types, attributes, messages, exceptions, and operations are to be localized within and developed specifically for individual objects and classes, it is common for different objects and classes to need analogous resources. Thus, different objects belonging to different classes may well need an attribute type (e.g., `States`), an attribute (e.g., `The_Current_State`), a preserver operation (e.g., `CURRENT_STATE_OF`), and an exception (e.g., `INVALID_STATE_IN`). Similarly, different but analogous objects and classes may need to exist in different subassemblies, or different but analogous subassemblies may need to exist in different assemblies. **Overloading** is the reuse of identifiers for different, but analogous, entities. Overloaded identifiers can and must be differentiated by entity type (e.g., subassembly or object), parameter profile (i.e., the number and types of formal parameters), and the use of identifiers extended with the dot notation. For example, the messages `CURRENT_STATE_OF` and `CURRENT_VALUE_OF` are overloaded in the following message statements:

```
CURRENT_STATE_OF.THE_DISPLAY;
CURRENT_STATE_OF.THE_SENSOR;

CURRENT_VALUE_OF.THE_TEMPERATURE_SENSOR.DINING_ROOM;
CURRENT_VALUE_OF.THE_TEMPERATURE_SENSOR.MASTER_BEDROOM;
```

### 2.6.5    Parameterization and Generics

Like inheritance, parameterization (i.e., generics) is an important mechanism for making classes more flexible and reusable. A *generic class* is parameterized with formal parameters that must be replaced with actual parameters before an instance can be created. Although less powerful than inheritance [Meyer 1988], genericity is a powerful technique for small-scale reuse and avoids some of the problems of inheritance, especially when large classification hierarchies exist. Parameterization is also primarily important when attributes are strongly typed and operations must be defined for specific attribute types.

The following is an example of a generic class with the formal generic parameters `Entries` and `The_Maximum_Stack_Size`:

```
class GENERIC_STACKS
 needs THE_SET_OF_INTEGERS.PREDEFINED;
 parent subassembly  CLASS_REPOSITORY;
 superclass ARRAYS;
 parameter type Entries is visible;
 parameter constant  The_Maximum_Stack_Size : Values.THE_SET_OF_INTEGERS;
specification
 introduces
  message  CONSTRUCT     (A_STACK)
                raise CONSTRUCT_FAILED           is sequential;
  message  DESTRUCT      (A_STACK)
                raise DESTRUCT_FAILED            is sequential;
  message  INITIALIZE
                raise ABSTRACTION_VIOLATED       is sequential;
```

```
      message    MAXIMUM_SIZE_OF return Values.THE_SET_OF_INTEGERS
                       raise ABSTRACTION_VIOLATED     is sequential;
      message    POP (An_Entry :     out Entries)
                       raise ENTRY_NOT_REMOVED, INCORRECT_SIZE, IS_EMPTY
                                          is sequential;
      message    PUSH (An_Entry : in      Entries)
                       raise ENTRY_NOT_ADDED, INCORRECT_SIZE, IS_FULL
                                          is sequential;
      message    SIZE_OF          return Values.THE_SET_OF_INTEGERS
                       raise INCORRECT_SIZE    is sequential;
      exception  ABSTRACTION_VIOLATED;
      exception  ENTRY_NOT_ADDED;
      exception  ENTRY_NOT_REMOVED;
      exception  INCORRECT_SIZE;
      exception  IS_EMPTY;
      exception  IS_FULL;
end;

class GENERIC_STACKS
 body
  introduces
    type The_Stacks is new The_Arrays range 1 .. The_Maximum_Stack_Size;
    variable The_Current_Size : Values.THE_SET_OF_INTEGERS := 0;
    variable The_Top : Entries;
    constructor operation  CONSTRUCT   (A_STACK)  raise  CONSTRUCT_FAILED;
    destructor operation   DESTRUCT    (A_STACK)  raise  DESTRUCT_FAILED;
    modifier operation     INITIALIZE            raise  ABSTRACTION_VIOLATED;
    preserver operation    MAXIMUM_SIZE_OF return      Values.THE_SET_OF_INTEGERS;
    modifier operation     POP (An_Entry :       out Entries)
              raise ENTRY_NOT_REMOVED, INCORRECT_SIZE, IS_EMPTY;
    modifier operation     PUSH (An_Entry :      in      Entries)
              raise ENTRY_NOT_ADDED, INCORRECT_SIZE, IS_FULL;
    preserver operation    SIZE_OF return Values.THE_SET_OF_INTEGERS
              raise INCORRECT_SIZE;
  invariants
   require
    The_Current_Size <= The_Maximum_Stack_Size
   else
    raise INCORRECT_SIZE;
   end require;
end;
```

## 2.6.6    Aggregation

Developers are constantly confronted with aggregate entities consisting of component entities. Systems and subsystems are composed of hardware, software (e.g., assemblies), and people. Hardware devices may have components (i.e., computer boards are composed of chips, resisters, etc.). Assemblies are almost always composed of multiple subassemblies. Aggregate subassemblies consist of objects, classes, and other subassemblies. Aggregate classes can contain nested classes and objects, and aggregate objects may contain other objects.

Aggregation has several important uses. One is to better model application-domain entities. For example, each instance of a TANKS class in a computer game may be composed of a TURRET and a BODY object because real-world tanks are composed of turrets and bodies. Another use of aggregates is to ensure the proper visibility (or hiding) of—and interaction among—the components of an aggregate entity. For example, the individual lights of a traffic signal must be turned on and turned off in a specific sequence if the abstraction of the traffic light as a whole is to be ensured. Therefore, each instance of the TRAFFIC_SIGNALS class should have three instances of the TRAFFIC_LIGHTS class as components, and these component objects should be controlled only by the instance of the TRAFFIC_SIGNALS class.

Aggregation has several interesting properties that must be correctly addressed. Aggregation is a *transitive relationship*: If object A is a component of object B and object B is a component of object C, then object A is indirectly a component of object C. Aggregation is also *antisymmetric*: If object A is a component of object B, then object B is *not* a component of object A.

Aggregation may be either static or dynamic, and a component of an aggregate may also be conditional:

- A *static aggregate* has fixed components.
- A *dynamic aggregate* has components that may vary over time.
- A *conditional component* either is or is not a component of an aggregate, depending on whether a specific condition holds.

On the other hand, aggregation and object decomposition should not be overemphasized and should only be used where *relevant* aggregation hierarchies must be modeled. Many subassemblies consist of collections of objects that collaborate and depend on one another, but that are not related to one another via any significant aggregation hierarchy. Although some object-oriented methods, such as HOOD [HTG 1991], imply that all objects exist as part of a single massive aggregation hierarchy, this approach has significant flaws and should be avoided. Constructing aggregate objects merely to contain existing objects and making subassemblies into objects leads to massive hierarchies of "call-through" message passing, with chains of overloaded messages being sent from parent to child to child ad nauseam until terminal children are reached. Such hierarchies are difficult to understand and impossible to implement efficiently.

Composition diagrams (CMDs) are specialized semantic nets that document individual aggregation hierarchies. CMDs can be at the level of the system, hardware, assembly, subassembly, class, or object. System-level and hardware-level CMDs are used during systems and hardware analysis and design. Assembly-level and subassembly-level CMDs, while legitimate, are usually not created because other diagrams are used instead to provide the same information. Typically, only object-level CMDs are used for software requirements analysis and logical design. Each CMD shows the relevant

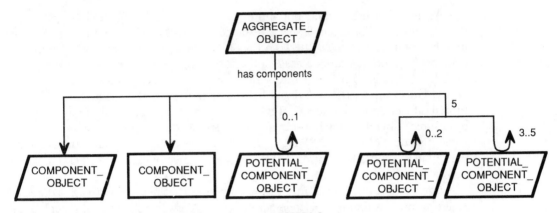

**Figure 2-43: Common Composition Diagram (CMD) Icons**

- Aggregate entity and its actual and potential component entities
- "Has components" relationships among these entities

For each composition hierarchy, the subassembly development team develops a CMD showing the aggregate object in terms of its component objects. All subassemblies and objects that have concurrent objects as components must themselves be concurrent. The "has components" relationship arcs that are drawn to connect with mandatory components are constrained to the vertical and horizontal axes, whereas

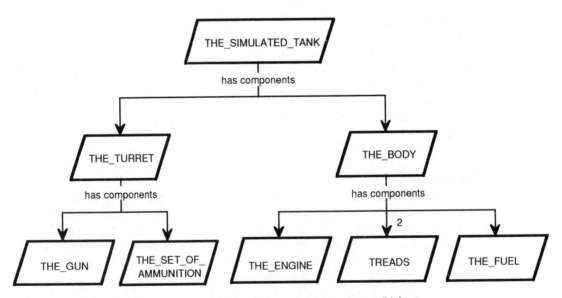

**Figure 2-44: Example Composition Diagram of an Aggregate Object**

the "has components" arcs drawn to potential components subject to choice are not so constrained. A curved arrow is used to label each potential component on the CMD. Note that a CMD documents the logical nesting of objects, and no implementation decisions concerning the physical nesting of modules is implied. See Figure 2-43: Common Composition Diagram (CMD) Icons. Figure 2-44 shows the CMD of an example aggregate object.

Variants of CMDs are also used, under different names and with slightly different notation, in several OOD methods. Colbert has object hierarchy diagrams (OHDs) [1989], and the object model of Rumbaugh et al. [1991] also documents aggregates.

## 2.7 STRUCTURE OF SOFTWARE SPECIFICATIONS AND DESIGNS

The basic structure of software requirements specifications should mirror the structure of the resulting design of the software. This use of the software-engineering principle of uniformity provides several important benefits: The design will be significantly more understandable. Requirements traceability will be simplified with the mapping being roughly one-to-one from the essential-requirements entities to the resulting design entities. This in turn supports confirmability and verifiability. Likewise, the basic structure of the logical design should mirror the structure of the resulting software and its implementation design. How does object orientation affect the structure of the software specifications and designs? How does this relate to the structure of the resulting software?

### 2.7.1    Structure of Functional Software

The basic building block of the functional-decomposition methods was the *function*, a relatively independent operation that was often specified algorithmically. Software-requirements specifications were organized in terms of the major functions that the software must perform, their subfunctions, and their subsubfunctions. Because decomposing requirements by function scattered the data throughout the software, with significant data coupling between many of the resulting functions, data dictionaries were necessary, to keep track of common data definitions. The functions and the data were thus analyzed and documented separately, with significant effort required to ensure consistency. The software designs, in turn, were decomposed into functional modules and their common global data.

This decomposition of the specifications and designs corresponded to the basic building block of the older languages, such as ALGOL, C, FORTRAN, and Pascal. The modules (i.e., subroutines) in these procedural languages did the following:

- Theoretically implemented a single functional requirement or abstraction
- Were therefore presumed to maximize functional cohesion

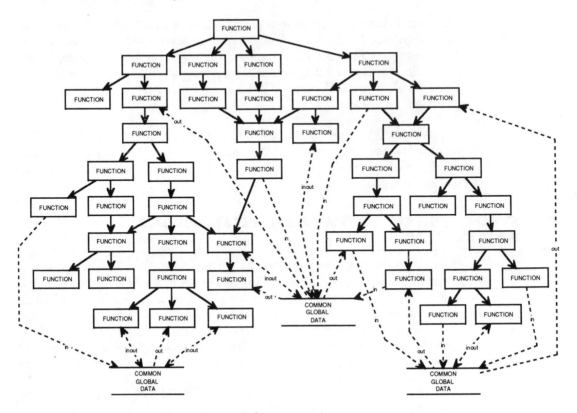

**Figure 2-45: Structure of Functional Software**

- Interfaced with other modules via
  —subroutine calls
  —common global data

The structure of such functional specifications, designs, and software was relatively simple because there were only two types of entities (i.e., functions and common global data) and two types of hierarchies (i.e., the calling "tree" and the data structures). For this reason, DFDs (which showed how the functions decomposed and how the functions and data interacted) and classic structure charts (which showed the calling trees) were both appropriate and reasonably adequate. Figure 2-45 shows an example of the structure of functional software, ignoring aggregation (i.e., nesting) and database interfaces.

## 2.7.2    Structures of Object-Oriented Software

Object-oriented software has a radically different structure from software written in more traditional languages. The basic building blocks of object-oriented methods are objects, classes of objects, and subassemblies of objects and classes. Each of these, in turn, has its own hierarchies. *Objects* interact primarily via message passing, so there are interaction hierarchies of collaborating objects. *Classes* are related primarily via inheritance, so there are classification hierarchies of subclasses and superclasses. The object and class hierarchies are connected via "has-class" relationships between instances (i.e., objects) and their classes. Objects and classes are grouped into subassemblies for methodological and management reasons, and there exist hierarchies of subassemblies related by dependency.

Because subassemblies contain objects and classes that contain as resources attribute types, attributes, messages, exceptions, and operations, their specifications and designs should be organized accordingly. The software-requirements specification and software-design documents should be formatted in a uniform manner, sorted first by subassembly, second by class (and object), third by attribute type and attribute (when using a strongly typed language), and then by the remaining resources (e.g., messages and operations).

The basic building blocks of object-oriented specifications, designs, and software are different and larger than the basic building blocks of functional software. The basic relationships and corresponding hierarchies are different, too. This is the main reason that new (and different) methods are needed. If the old analysis and design methods do not understand objects, classes, subassemblies, and their hierarchies, then they will provide little if any guidance in how to identify, analyze, and design them.

Object-oriented software (and its designs and specifications) have three relatively orthogonal structures. Figure 2-46 shows the basic structure of object-oriented

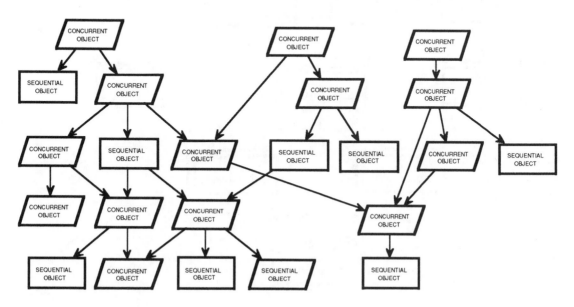

**Figure 2-46: Structure of Software in Terms of Objects**

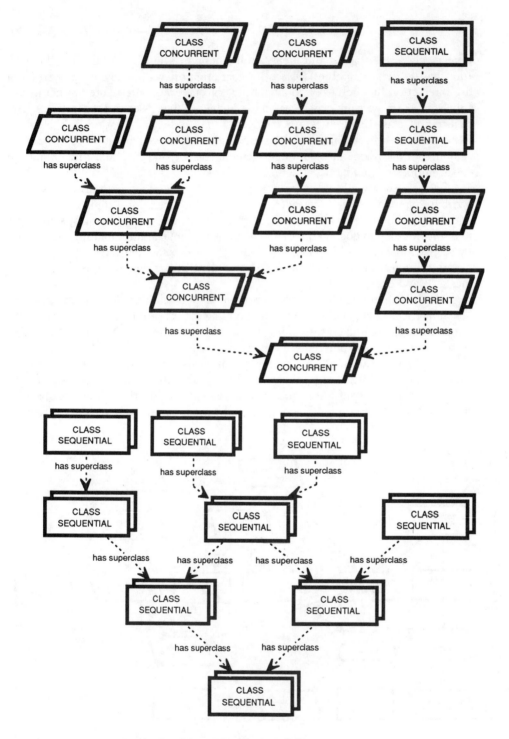

**Figure 2-47: Structure of Software in Terms of Classes**

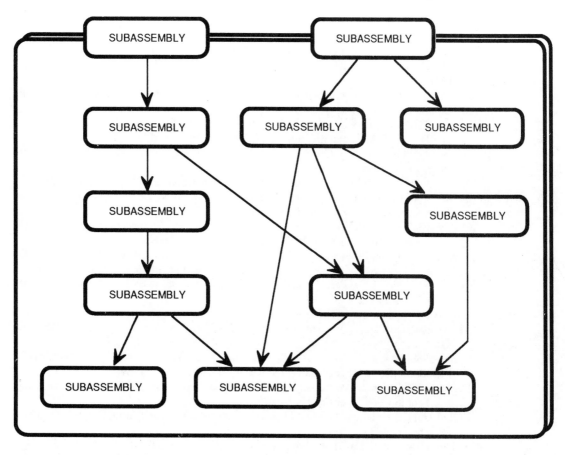

**Figure 2-48: Structure of Software in Terms of Subassemblies**

software in terms of its objects. Figure 2-47 shows the basic structure of object-oriented software in terms of its classes, and Figure 2-48 shows the basic structure of object-oriented software in terms of its subassemblies.

## 2.8 CHAPTER REFERENCES

[Adams 1972] R. Adams, *Watership Down*, McMillan, 1983, page 3.

[Apple 1984] Apple Computer, Inc., *Lisa Toolkit 3.0*, Cupertino, CA, Apple Computer Inc., 1984.

[Bailin 1989] Sidney C. Bailin, "An Object-Oriented Specification Method for Ada," *Communications of the ACM*, 32(5), May 1989, 608–632.

[Berard 1991a] Edward V. Berard, "Object-Oriented Design," 101 Lakeforest Blvd, Suite 360, Gaithersburg, MD 20877, Berard Software Engineering, Inc., 10 February 1991.

[Berard 1991b] Edward V. Berard, "Object-Oriented Domain Analysis," 101 Lakeforest Blvd, Suite 360, Gaithersburg, MD 20877, Berard Software Engineering, Inc., 10 February 1991.

[Berard 1991c] Edward V. Berard, "Object-Oriented Requirements Analysis," 101 Lakeforest Blvd, Suite 360, Gaithersburg, MD 20877, Berard Software Engineering, Inc., 10 February 1991.

[Booch 1983] Grady Booch, *Software Engineering with Ada*, Menlo Park, CA, Benjamin Cummings, 1983.

[Booch 1987] Grady Booch, *Software Components with Ada: Structures, Tools, and Subsystems*, Menlo Park, CA, Benjamin Cummings, 1987.

[Booch 1991] Grady Booch, *Object-Oriented Design: with Applications*, Menlo Park, CA, Benjamin Cummings, 1991.

[Buhr 1984] R. J. A. Buhr, *System Design with Ada*, Englewood Cliffs, NJ, Prentice Hall, 1984.

[Bulman 1987] Dave Bulman, "Model-Based Object-Oriented Design for Ada," P.O. Box 3020, Waikoloa, Hawaii 96743, Pragmatics, Inc., 14 July 1987.

[Cherry 1988] George W. Cherry, *Software Construction by Object-Oriented Pictures*, 5151 Emerson Road, Canandaigua, NY 14425, Thought**Tools, Inc., 1988.

[Coad and Yourdon 1989] Peter Coad and Edward Yourdon, *OORA—Object-Oriented Requirements Analysis*, Englewood Cliffs, NJ, Prentice Hall, 1989.

[Coad and Yourdon 1991] Peter Coad and Edward Yourdon, *Object-Oriented Design*, Englewood Cliffs, NJ, Prentice Hall, 1991.

[Colbert 1989] Ed Colbert, "The Object-Oriented Software Development Method: A Practical Approach to Object-Oriented Development," TRIAa Conference Proceedings,1989, 400–415.

[Comer 1989] Edward R. Comer, *Ada Box Structures Methodology Handbook*, P.O. Box 361697, Melbourne FL 32936, Software Productivity Solutions, Inc., 1989.

[DeMarco 1978] Tom DeMarco, *Structured Analysis and System Specification*, Englewood Cliffs, NJ, Yourdon Press/Prentice Hall, 1978.

[DOD 1986] Department of Defense, *Defense Systems Software Development*, DOD-STD-2167A, 29 February 1986.

[Embley et al. 1992] David W. Embley, Barry D. Kurtz, and Scott N. Woodfield, *Object-Oriented Systems Analysis: A Model-Driven Approach*, Englewood Cliffs, NJ, Yourdon Press, 1992.

[Firesmith 1993] Donald G. Firesmith, *Object-Oriented Requirements Analysis and Logical Design*, New York, NY, Wiley, 1993.

[Foote 1988] Brian Foote, *Designing to Facilitate Change with Object-Oriented Frameworks*, Master's Thesis, University of Illinois at Urbana-Champaign, 1988.

[Gibson 1990] E. Gibson, "Objects—Born and Bred," *BYTE Magazine*, October 1990, 245–254.

[Goldberg 1984] Adele Goldberg, *Smalltalk-80: The Interactive Programming Environment*, Reading, MA, Addison-Wesley, 1984.

[Gomaa 1984] Hasan Gomaa, "A Software Design Method for Real-Time Systems," *Communications of the ACM*, 27(9), September 1984.

[Henderson-Sellers 1992] Brian Henderson-Sellers, *A Book of Object-Oriented Knowledge*, New York, Prentice Hall, 1992.

[Henderson-Sellers and Edwards 1990] Brian Henderson-Sellers and J. M. Edwards, "The Object-Oriented Systems Life Cycle," *Communications of the ACM*, 33(9), September 1990, 142–159.

[HTG 1991] HOOD Technical Group, *HOOD Reference Manual, Issues 3.1*, HOOD User Group, Noordwijk, Netherlands, European Space Agency, July 1991.

[Jacobson and Linstrøm 1991] Ivar Jacobson and Frederik Linstrøm, "Re-engineering of Old Systems to an Object-Oriented Architecture," *OOPSLA'91 Conference Proceedings*, SIGPLAN Notices, 26(11), 340–350, November 1991.

[Johnson and Foote 1988] Ralph E. Johnson and Brian Foote, "Designing Reusable Classes," *Journal of Object-Oriented Programming*, 1(2), June/July 1988, 22–35.

[Meyer 1988] Bertrand Meyer, *Object-Oriented Software Construction*, Hertfordshire, England, Prentice Hall International, 1988.

[Miller 1956] George A. Miller, "The Magical Number Seven, Plus or Minus Two: Some Limits on Our Capacity for Processing Information," *Psychological Review*, 63 (2), March 1956.

[Nielsen and Shumate 1988] Kjell Nielsen and Ken Shumate, *Designing Large Real-Time Systems with Ada*, New York, NY, McGraw-Hill, 1988.

[Orr 1981] Kenneth T. Orr, *Structured Requirements Definition*, 1725 Gage Boulevard, Topeka, Kansas 66604, Ken Orr and Associates, 1981.

[Ross et al. 1975] Douglas T. Ross, John B. Goodenough, and C. A. Irvine, "Software Engineering: Process, Principles, and Goals," *IEEE Computer Magazine*, 8(5), May 1975, 17–27.

[Rumbaugh et al. 1991] James Rumbaugh, Michael Blaha, William Premerlani, Frederick Eddy, and William Lorensen, *Object-Oriented Modeling and Design*, Englewood Cliffs, NJ, Prentice Hall, 1991.

[Schmucker 1986] K. J. Schmucker, *Object-Oriented Programming for the Macintosh*, Hasbrouck Heights, NJ, Hayden Books, 1986.

[Seidewitz 1989] Ed Seidewitz, *Object-Oriented Systems Analysis*, Greenbelt, MD, NASA Goddard Space Flight Center, 1989.

[Seidewitz and Stark 1986] Ed Seidewitz and Mike Stark, *General Object-Oriented Software Development*, Greenbelt, MD, NASA Goddard Space Flight Center, August 1986.

[Shlaer and Mellor 1988] Sally Shlaer and Stephen J. Mellor, *Object-Oriented Systems Analysis, Modeling the World in Data*, Englewood Cliffs, NJ, Yourdon Press, 1988.

[Shlaer and Mellor 1992] Sally Shlaer and Stephen J. Mellor, *Object Lifecycles, Modeling the World in State*, Englewood Cliffs, NJ, Yourdon Press, 1992.

[Shumate 1992] Ken Shumate, *Software Specification and Design: A Disciplined Approach for Real-Time Systems*, New York, NY, Wiley, 1992.

[SofTech 1978] SofTech, *An Introduction to SADT Structured Analysis and Design Technique*, 9022-78R, 460 Totten Pond Road, Waltham, MA, SofTech, 1978.

[Vidale and Hayden 1986] Richard F. Vidale and Charlene Roberts Hayden, "A Student Project to Extend Object-Oriented Design," *Proceedings of the Second ASEET Symposium*, Washington, DC, Ada Joint Program Office, 1987.

[Ward and Mellor 1985] Paul Ward and Stephen J. Mellor, *Structured Development for Real-Time Systems, Volume 1: Introduction and Tools; Volume 2: Essential Modelling Techniques; Volume 3: Implementation Modelling Techniques*, New York, NY, Yourdon Press, 1985.

[Winblad et al. 1990] Ann L. Winblad, Samuel D. Edwards, and David R. King, *Object-Oriented Software*, Reading, MA, Addison Wesley, 1990, p. 34.

[Wirfs-Brock et al. 1990] Rebecca Wirfs-Brock, Brian Wilkerson, and Lauren Wiener, *Designing Object-Oriented Software*, Englewood Cliffs, NJ, Prentice-Hall, 1990.

[Yourdon and Constantine 1979] Edward Yourdon and Larry Constantine, *Structured Design*, Englewood Cliffs, NJ, Prentice Hall, 1979.

# Chapter 3

# Object-Oriented Models

Models are critical tools in all engineering disciplines. Because the application domains and their relevant entities are typically too complex to understand holistically, abstractions must be used to model their essential characteristics and behavior. A *model* is a useful abstraction of the entity being modeled. Software objects, as abstractions of application-domain entities, are by definition models that encapsulate the essential attributes (i.e., characteristics), operations (i.e., behavior), and exceptions of the entities.

Good software models are built using the following principles of software engineering to achieve the appropriate levels of the goals of software engineering:

*Abstraction*, to represent essential characteristics and behaviors of the entities being modeled

*Completeness*, to ensure that all essential characteristics and behaviors are modeled (although different modeling techniques are typically used to model different aspects of the entities being modeled)

*Confirmability*, to ensure that the correct models are being built correctly

*Independence*, to ensure that unnecessary coupling among the objects and classes is minimized

*Information hiding*, to suppress extraneous details from the view of the model's users, which might otherwise limit understanding of the entities being modeled

*Localization*, to ensure that all essential characteristics and behaviors of each entity are used to model that entity

*Modularity*, to ensure that the model is not too large and complex

*Uniformity*, to ensure that the models are consistent and do not exhibit unnecessary differences

Different models must be used in order to model all relevant architectural and behavioral aspects of the software at all relevant levels of abstraction. No single modeling approach is sufficient to describe all relevant views of the software. This

chapter documents the six recommended object-oriented models of software requirements analysis and logical design:[1]

- Assembly model
- Object model
- Class model
- State model
- Control model
- Timing model

The *assembly model* is developed for each assembly and documents the interfaces
and static architecture of the assembly as a whole. The remaining five aforementioned
models are developed for each subassembly, on a subassembly-by-subassembly basis.
The *object model* documents the objects of the subassembly, their general and aggregation relationships, and the messages passed among them. The *class model* documents
the classes of the subassembly and their inheritance (i.e., "has class" and "has superclass")
relationships. The *state model* documents the behavior of the objects as abstract state
machines (ASMs). The *control model* documents the behavior of the objects in terms
of control flows and possibly data flows. The *timing model* documents the temporal
behavior of the objects.

The object, class, and assembly models are primarily concerned with static
architecture, whereas the state, control, and timing models are primarily concerned
with dynamic behavior. The different models also have different scopes. The scope
of the assembly model is an entire assembly. The scope of each object, control, and
timing model is either a subassembly, a thread of control, or an individual object or
class. The scope of each class model is either a subassembly or a class hierarchy. The
scope of the state model is an individual object or class. The applicability of the
models in terms of their scope and area of concern is documented in Figure 3-1:
Applicability of the Models.

Each model has associated diagrams. The applicability of these diagrams in terms
of their scope and area of concern is documented in Figure 3-2: Applicability of the
Associated Diagrams.

This book provides many models and diagram types for the sake of completeness
and to support the engineer under all probable circumstances. It recognizes that no
single model or diagram can do everything. It is based on the philosophy that it is
easier to tailor out unneeded diagrams than to tailor in missing ones. However, models
and diagrams should support analysis, design, and understanding. They should also be
both practical and cost-effective. Managers and software engineers must remember
that not all models and diagrams will be useful, practical, cost-effective, or even
semantically meaningful under all circumstances. For example, state transition diagrams (STDs) only make sense if the objects and classes can be modeled as finite state
machines. The timing model and timing diagrams (TDs) only make sense if temporal

---

[1] The implementation model can be used during implementation design to document
the implementation language-specific design decisions if a hybrid language is used, as
well as to document the mapping of the software modules to the hardware processors
and the operating system processes.

| MODEL APPLICABILITY | | AREA OF CONCERN | |
|---|---|---|---|
| | | STATIC ARCHITECTURE | DYNAMIC BEHAVIOR |
| SCOPE | ASSEMBLY | ASSEMBLY MODEL | CONTROL MODEL TIMING MODEL |
| | SUBASSEMBLY | OBJECT MODEL CLASS MODEL | CONTROL MODEL TIMING MODEL |
| | AGGREGATION HIERARCHY | OBJECT MODEL | |
| | INHERITANCE HIERARCHY | CLASS MODEL | |
| | THREAD OR SCENARIO | OBJECT MODEL | CONTROL MODEL TIMING MODEL |
| | CLASS | OBJECT MODEL CLASS MODEL | STATE MODEL CONTROL MODEL TIMING MODEL |
| | OBJECT | OBJECT MODEL CLASS MODEL | STATE MODEL CONTROL MODEL TIMING MODEL |

**Figure 3-1: Applicability of the Models**

requirements or design are important. Similarly, many diagrams can be used with different scope. For example, general semantic nets (GSNs) can be used at the subassembly, major scenario/thread of control, and object/class levels. Whereas GSNs should probably always be developed at the subassembly level, they should only be developed at the scenario/thread-of-control level if major scenarios or threads of control exist and must be documented. They should only be drawn at the object/class level if doing so provides "value added" to the documentation and can be done easily (e.g., reverse engineering the diagram using a computer-aided software-engineering [CASE] tool). Only a limited number of diagrams of this book should be mandated on a project basis, and developers should have the flexibility to determine whether the other diagrams should be developed on a case-by-case basis.

## 3.1  THE CHAPTER EXAMPLE

In order to better explain the models documented in this chapter, a single example is used, where practical. Consider DOOR_MASTER, an assembly, the primary ob-

| DIAGRAM APPLICABILITY | | AREA OF CONCERN | |
|---|---|---|---|
| | | STATIC ARCHITECTURE | DYNAMIC BEHAVIOR |
| SCOPE | ASSEMBLY | CONTEXT DIAGRAM<br>ASSEMBLY DIAGRAM | OO CONTROL FLOW DIAGRAM<br>TIMING DIAGRAM |
| | SUBASSEMBLY | GENERAL SEMANTIC NET<br>INTERACTION DIAGRAM<br>COMPOSITION DIAGRAM<br>CLASSIFICATION DIAGRAM | OO CONTROL FLOW DIAGRAM<br>TIMING DIAGRAM |
| | AGGREGATION HIERARCHY | COMPOSITION DIAGRAM | |
| | INHERITANCE HIERARCHY | CLASSIFICATION DIAGRAM | |
| | THREAD OR SCENARIO | INTERACTION DIAGRAM | OO CONTROL FLOW DIAGRAM<br>TIMING DIAGRAM |
| | CLASS | GENERAL SEMANTIC NET<br>INTERACTION DIAGRAM<br>CLASSIFICATION DIAGRAM | STATE TRANSITION DIAGRAM<br>STATE OPERATION TABLE<br>OO CONTROL FLOW DIAGRAM<br>TIMING DIAGRAM |
| | OBJECT | GENERAL SEMANTIC NET<br>INTERACTION DIAGRAM<br>CLASSIFICATION DIAGRAM | STATE TRANSITION DIAGRAM<br>STATE OPERATION TABLE<br>OO CONTROL FLOW DIAGRAM<br>TIMING DIAGRAM |

**Figure 3-2: Applicability of the Associated Diagrams**

jective of which is to control access of personnel through a secured door. It does this by providing the following capabilities, which are written in a relatively functional manner:

- *Allow free access when disabled.* When DOOR_MASTER is in the DISABLED state, the door shall be unlocked.
- *Allow restricted access when enabled.* When DOOR_MASTER is in the enabled state, the door shall be unlocked only when the correct entry code is entered on the numeric keypad and shall be relocked after 30 seconds if the door is closed.
- *Change the entry code.* Security personnel shall be able to change the five-digit entry code by pressing the change-entry-code button, entering the current security code on the numeric keypad, and then entering the new entry code on the numeric keypad. If the two codes are not correctly entered within 2 minutes, the current entry code shall remain in effect. The initial entry code shall be "12345."

- *Change the security code.* Security personnel shall be able to change the 10-digit security code by pressing the change-security-code button, entering the current security code on the numeric keypad, and then entering the new security code on the numeric keypad. If the two security codes are not correctly entered within 2 minutes, the current security code shall remain in effect. The initial security code shall be "1234567890."
- *Control alarms.* When DOOR_MASTER is in the disabled state, the alarm bell and alarm light shall be turned off. When DOOR_MASTER is in the enabled state, the alarm bell and alarm light shall be turned on if the door remains open longer than 40 seconds. The alarm bell shall then be turned off when the correct security code is entered on the numeric keypad.
- *Disable* DOOR_MASTER. Security personnel shall be able to disable DOOR_MASTER by pressing the disable button and then entering the current security code on the numeric keypad within 1 minute. The initial state of DOOR_MASTER is DIS-ABLED.
- *Enable* DOOR_MASTER. Security personnel shall be able to enable DOOR_MASTER by pressing the enable button and then entering the current security code on the numeric keypad within 1 minute. The door shall be locked as soon as the door is closed when DOOR_MASTER is in the ENABLED state.
- *Enter the entry code.* Employees shall be able to enter the five-digit entry code on the numeric keypad by pressing five digits, followed by pressing the enter key. If the correct entry code is not entered within 1 minute, the numeric keypad shall be reinitialized.
- *Enter the security code.* Security personnel shall be able to enter the 10-digit security code on the numeric keypad by pressing the correct 10 digits, followed by pressing the enter key. If the correct security code is not entered within 1 minute, the numeric keypad shall be reinitialized.

## 3.2  THE ASSEMBLY MODEL

The *assembly model* is the first of the six major object-oriented models to be started and the last to be completed during subassembly requirements analysis and logical design. The purpose of the assembly model is to provide a top-level view of the assembly consisting of its abstraction, its terminators, its static architecture in terms of subassemblies, and its specification and body. The assembly model of a single assembly consists of the following information:

- Purpose and description of the assembly
- Context diagrams (CDs)
- Assembly diagram (AD)
- Specification and body
- Purpose and description of each subassembly

The assembly model is incrementally developed. The purpose, description, and CDs for the assembly is developed prior to starting on any of the other models. However, the AD and the assembly specification and body are incrementally developed, one subassembly (and its information) at a time.

The system-level requirements and the individual subassembly object and class models are the primary source of information used for developing the assembly model. The assembly model is developed by the assembly development team and is documented in the assembly part of the project repository.

## 3.2.1    Purpose and Description of the Assembly

The assembly development team should collectively document the purpose and description of the assembly as a whole. For example:

- The purpose of the DOOR_MASTER assembly is to control access of personnel through a secured door.
- The purpose of the SHOWER_MASTER assembly is to implement all shower-master software capabilities. The SHOWER_MASTER assembly (1) is controlled by decrement flow, decrement temperature, increment flow, increment temperature, and on/off buttons; (2) reads the cold water, hot water, and shower water flow and temperature sensors; (3) controls the cold water and hot water voltage to current drivers, torque motors, and valves; (4) controls the solenoid fail-safe valve; and (5) displays the actual and desired flows and temperatures on the actual and desired flow and temperature displays.

## 3.2.2    Context Diagrams (CDs)

A CD is a top-level GSN that is restricted in scope to the entire assembly and its terminators. CDs are used to provide a high-level, analysis view of the assembly, treated as a software black box. They are useful for communication with the customer and those requiring an introduction to the application. Specifically, a CD documents

- The assembly
- Its system, hardware, software, and people terminators
- All associations among them

The assembly development team should incrementally draw the CD by first drawing the assembly and terminator nodes and then connecting appropriate nodes with the appropriate association arcs. The icons for CDs form a small subset of the icons used for GSNs and are documented in Figure 3-3. Assemblies are drawn with two thick rounded rectangles, hardware is drawn with thin boxes, systems are drawn with thick boxes, and people are drawn with thick circles. Assemblies, systems, hardware, and people may not be drawn socketed or nested in each other. Notice that when using an object-oriented requirements analysis (OORA) method, CDs should be based on SNs rather than on data flow diagrams (DFDs), as in Structured Analysis (SA) [DeMarco 1978].

For example, Figure 3-4 shows the CD for the DOOR_MASTER assembly, which shows the hardware terminators mandated by systems engineering.

As another example, Figure 3-5 shows the CD for the SHOWER_MASTER assembly. This software controls the temperature and flow rate of shower water, based on user commands entered via hardware buttons. It measures the temperature and flow of

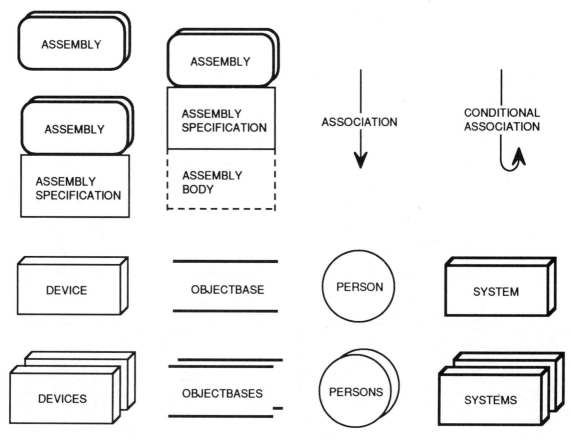

**Figure 3-3: Icons for CDs**

water through the cold water, hot water, and shower water pipes and controls the flow by means of two torque motor valves. A solenoid valve is used as a fail-safe valve to prevent accidental scalding in case of failure of the system. The desired and actual temperatures and flow rates are displayed on four light-emitting diode (LED) displays. These hardware terminators have been mandated by a systems engineering group, and the software must respond accordingly.

### 3.2.3 Assembly Diagrams (ADs)

An AD is incrementally developed, a subassembly at a time. ADs are used to provide a high-level, static view of the as-built physical architecture of the assembly. They are useful for communication with the customer and those requiring an introduction to the application, as well as for configuration-management purposes. Specifically, an AD documents

- The assembly
- Its component subassemblies, optionally including their specifications and bodies
- The dependency relationships among them

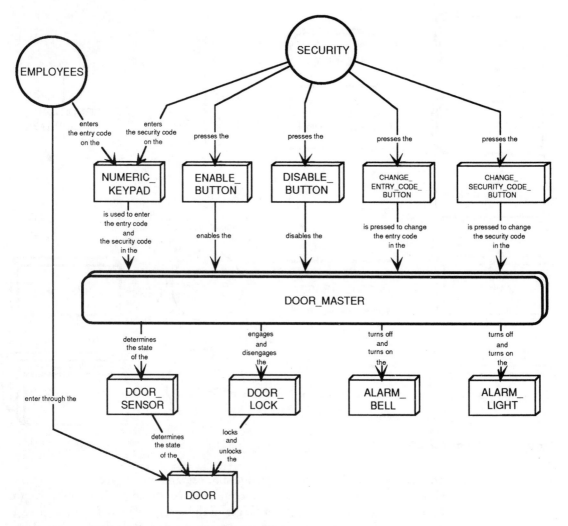

**Figure 3-4: CD for the** DOOR_MASTER **Assembly**

The assembly development team should incrementally draw the AD by first drawing the initial subassemblies and then adding additional child subassemblies as they are completed by their subassembly development teams. The icons for ADs are a small subset of the icons used for GSNs and are documented in Figure 3-6. The icon for the assembly is two rounded rectangles drawn with thick lines. The icons for the subassemblies are single rounded rectangles drawn with thick lines. The optional icons for subassembly specifications are single rectangles drawn with thin lines, hung below the subassembly icon, whereas the optional icons for subassembly bodies are single rectangles drawn with dotted lines hung below the corresponding subassembly specification icon. The subassembly icons are nested inside the assembly icon. Figure 3-7 shows the overview AD for the SHOWER_MASTER assembly, whereas Figure 3-8 shows the corresponding detailed AD.

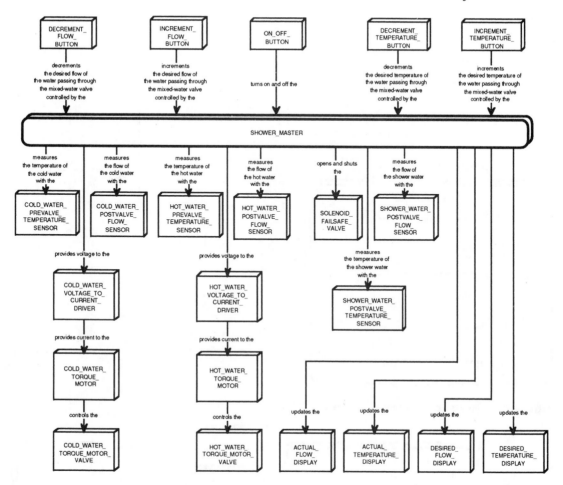

**Figure 3-5: CD for the** SHOWER_MASTER **Assembly**

## 3.2.4    Specification and Body of the Assembly

The purpose of the assembly specification and body is to provide the static architectural specification and design of the assembly in a compact, machine-readable form. The assembly development team should incrementally specify and logically design the specification and body of the assembly, using OOSDL. In fact, most of the subassembly specification and body should be automatically generated from the information in the AD, provided adequate CASE tool support.

When completed, an assembly specification documents the visible subassemblies (i.e., those with master terminators). When completed, an assembly body documents the hidden subassemblies (i.e., those with servant terminators).

For example, the DOOR_MASTER assembly only has two subassemblies: ACCESS_CONTROL_FOR and CLASSES_FOR. Its specification and body are trivial. On the other hand, the SHOWER_MASTER assembly has one exported subassembly

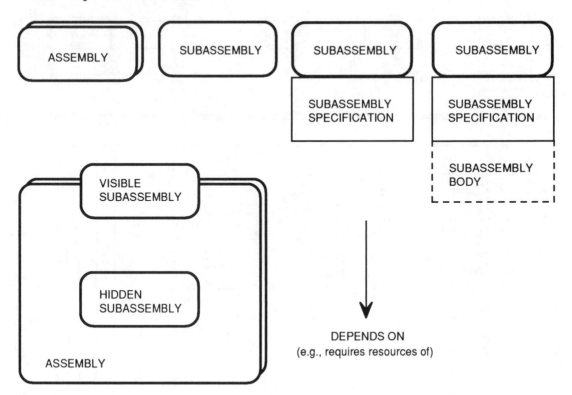

**Figure 3-6: Icons for Assembly Diagrams (ADs)**

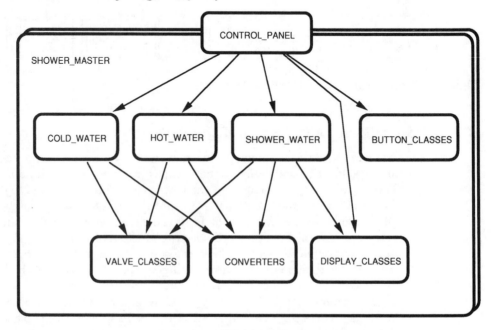

**Figure 3-7: Overview AD for the SHOWER_MASTER Assembly**

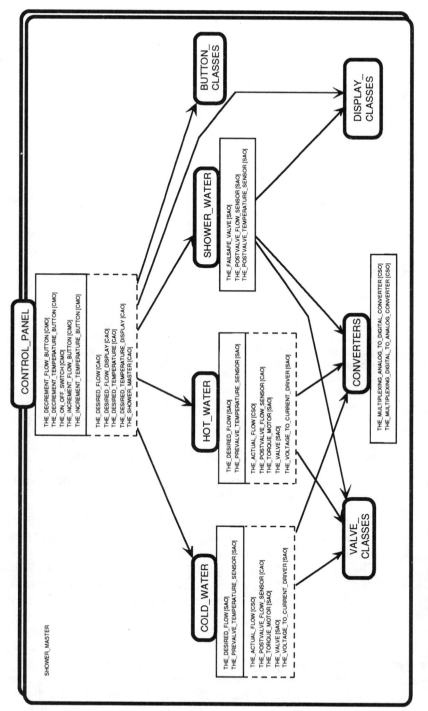

**Figure 3-8: Detailed AD for the** SHOWER_MASTER **Assembly**

SHOWER_MASTER

CONTROL_PANEL

THE_DECREMENT_FLOW_BUTTON [CMO]
THE_DECREMENT_TEMPERATURE_BUTTON [CMO]
THE_ON_OFF_SWITCH [CMO]
THE_INCREMENT_FLOW_BUTTON [CMO]
THE_INCREMENT_TEMPERATURE_BUTTON [CMO]

THE_DESIRED_FLOW [CAO]
THE_DESIRED_FLOW_DISPLAY [CAO]
THE_DESIRED_TEMPERATURE [CAO]
THE_DESIRED_TEMPERATURE_DISPLAY [CAO]
THE_SHOWER_MASTER [CAO]

BUTTON_CLASSES

DISPLAY_CLASSES

SHOWER_WATER

THE_FAILSAFE_VALVE [SAO]
THE_POSTVALVE_FLOW_SENSOR [SAO]
THE_POSTVALVE_TEMPERATURE_SENSOR [SAO]

HOT_WATER

THE_DESIRED_FLOW [SAO]
THE_PREVALVE_TEMPERATURE_SENSOR [SAO]

THE_ACTUAL_FLOW [CSO]
THE_POSTVALVE_FLOW_SENSOR [CAO]
THE_TORQUE_MOTOR [SAO]
THE_VALVE [SAO]
THE_VOLTAGE_TO_CURRENT_DRIVER [SAO]

COLD_WATER

THE_DESIRED_FLOW [SAO]
THE_PREVALVE_TEMPERATURE_SENSOR [SAO]

THE_ACTUAL_FLOW [CSO]
THE_POSTVALVE_FLOW_SENSOR [CAO]
THE_TORQUE_MOTOR [SAO]
THE_VALVE [SAO]
THE_VOLTAGE_TO_CURRENT_DRIVER [SAO]

CONVERTERS

THE_MULTIPLEXING_ANALOG_TO_DIGITAL_CONVERTER [CSO]
THE_MULTIPLEXING_DIGITAL_TO_ANALOG_CONVERTER [CSO]

VALVE_CLASSES

and seven hidden subassemblies. Their assembly specifications and bodies are as follows, written in OOSDL, which is described in Chapter 6 of this book:

```
assembly DOOR_MASTER is concurrent
specification
  subassembly  ACCESS_CONTROL_FOR  is concurrent;
end;


assembly DOOR_MASTER
body
  subassembly  CLASSES_FOR        is concurrent;
end;



assembly SHOWER_MASTER is concurrent
specification
  subassembly  CONTROL_PANEL      is concurrent;
end;


assembly SHOWER_MASTER is concurrent
body
  subassembly  BUTTON_CLASSES     is concurrent;
  subassembly  COLD_WATER         is concurrent;
  subassembly  CONVERTERS         is concurrent;
  subassembly  DISPLAY_CLASSES    is concurrent;
  subassembly  HOT_WATER          is concurrent;
  subassembly  SHOWER_WATER       is concurrent;
  subassembly  VALVE_CLASSES      is concurrent;
end;
```

### 3.2.5    Purpose and Description of Each Subassembly

The subassembly development team should collectively document the purpose and description of each subassembly as a whole. For example:

- The purpose of the ACCESS_CONTROL_FOR.DOOR_MASTER subassembly is to provide software capabilities of DOOR_MASTER. It is an initial subassembly and in this case is the only subassembly of DOOR_MASTER.
- The objective of the CRUISE_CONTROL.AUTOMOTIVE_DASHBOARD_APPLI-CATION subassembly is to implement the cruise-control abstraction by grouping and controlling the visibility of all software objects that provide the cruise-control capability.

## 3.3  THE OBJECT MODEL

The *object model* is the first of the five subassembly-level object-oriented models created during subassembly requirements analysis and logical design. The purpose of the object model is to provide a static view of the architecture of the subassembly in terms of the existence, abstraction, and visibility of the subassembly's component objects, the terminators with which the individual objects must interface, and the important relationships (e.g., aggregation and association) and the messages passed among them. It identifies the basic essential and logical structure of the subassembly software to be developed. The object model of a single subassembly consists of the following information:

For the subassembly—

- List of all objects
- GSN
- Initial specification and body
- Interaction diagram (ID)

For each major thread of control in the subassembly—ID
For each message passed in the subassembly—purpose and description
For each aggregation hierarchy in the subassembly—composition diagram (CMD)
For each object in the subassembly—

- Purpose and description
- Specification and initial body
- Description of each attribute type and attribute
- Description of each message
- Description of each operation
- Description of each exception

The object model is typically developed prior to the class model if the subassembly is to contain specific objects that model specific known entities (e.g., as typically occurs when developing embedded applications). On the other hand, the object model is typically developed after the class model if the subassembly is to contain classes that model arbitrary collections of entities (e.g., as typically occurs when developing general solutions for management information systems [MIS] and automatic data processing [ADP] applications or when promoting reuse during domain analysis). The object and class models may also be developed simultaneously and iteratively, and the subassembly development team should have the freedom to choose the appropriate order in which to develop the models.

The object model is developed prior to the class model when modeling specific entities because the objects should be identified and analyzed prior to considering their classes. The higher-level requirements allocated to the subassembly primarily concern the essential objects of the subassembly, their characteristics and behavior, and how they relate to one another. Until a software engineer knows what objects must exist and understands their properties and behavior, it is very difficult to properly generalize them into the classes that will define them and will act as templates for their construction. Notice that this is the reverse order in which many object-oriented programmers have been forced to think by their object-oriented programming languages (OOPLs), which only allow them to construct an object from a preexisting class, and so the class must be developed first. During requirements analysis and logical design, this OOP order is best reversed so that optimum classes for the application may be created. For totally new software, generalization from objects to classes is recommended, while specialization from classes to objects is recommended if complete class libraries already exist and reuse of existing software is the norm.

The higher-level, as yet unanalyzed requirements allocated to the subassembly are the primary source of information used to develop the object model. In turn, the object model will be used to develop the class model. The object model is developed by the subassembly development team and is documented in the subassembly part of the project database.

## 3.3.1    List of Subassembly Objects

The subassembly development team should collectively identify, name, and agree on the initial objects of the subassembly, using an appropriate[2] subset of the following approaches:

- Recommended approaches
  - using object abstraction
    - using the types of the modeled entities
    - using the definition of an object
    - using object decomposition
  - using inheritance
    - using generalization
    - using subclasses
  - using object-oriented domain analysis (OODA)
  - using repositories of previously developed software
    - reusing application frameworks
    - reusing class hierarchies
    - reusing individual objects and classes
  - using specification and design languages
  - using personal experience
- Traditional approaches
  - using nouns
  - using traditional DFDs
    - using terminators on CDs
    - using data stores on DFDs
    - using complex data flows on DFDs
- Miscellaneous approaches
  - using abstract data types and abstract state machines
  - using states
  - using resources
    - using attributes
    - using operations
    - using exceptions
  - using requirements
  - using class responsibility collaboration (CRC) cards
    - using traditional CRC cards

---

[2] Guidance on the following approaches is provided in Chapter 4: identification guidelines for objects, classes, and subassemblies.

   – using Post-it® Notes
—using entities on entity relationship attribute (ERA) diagrams
—using object-oriented diagrams
   – using nodes on semantic nets (SNs)
   – using nodes on interaction diagrams (IDs)

Once the objects are identified, the subassembly development team should list and characterize them in the subassembly part of the project database. Objects are either essential or nonessential, are sequential or concurrent, and are masters, agents, or servants.

For example, the ACCESS_CONTROL_FOR.DOOR_MASTER subassembly contains objects that were identified using an informal combination of the following identification approaches:

- Using the types of the modeled entities
- Using the definitions
- Using object decomposition
- Using personal experience
- Using nouns

For example, the ACCESS_CONTROL_FOR.DOOR_MASTER subassembly contains the following 14 objects:

| *Object* | *Characteristics* |
|---|---|
| • THE_ALARM_BELL | Essential Sequential Agent |
| • THE_ALARM_LIGHT | Essential Sequential Agent |
| • THE_CHANGE_ENTRY_CODE_BUTTON | Essential Concurrent Master |
| • THE_CHANGE_SECURITY_CODE_BUTTON | Essential Concurrent Master |
| • THE_CLOCK | Nonessential Concurrent Servant |
| • THE_DISABLE_BUTTON | Essential Concurrent Master |
| • THE_DOOR | Essential Sequential Agent Aggregate |
| • THE_DOOR_LOCK | Essential Sequential Agent |
| • THE_DOOR_SENSOR | Essential Sequential Agent |
| • THE_ENTRY_CODE | Essential Sequential Servant |
| • THE_ENABLE_BUTTON | Essential Concurrent Master |
| • THE_GUARD | Essential Concurrent Agent |
| • THE_NUMERIC_KEYPAD | Essential Concurrent Master |
| • THE_SECURITY_CODE | Essential Sequential Servant |

## 3.3.2    General Semantic Nets (GSNs)

A GSN usually shows the entire subassembly and its terminators. Sometimes, a GSN is also drawn for each individual object, especially if the subassembly is so large and complex that it makes a subassembly GSN impractical. The GSN is used to provide a high-level, user-oriented overview of the subassembly and its component black-box objects. It is useful for communication with the customer and those requiring an introduction to the application. Specifically, a subassembly GSN shows

- The existence and visibility of its component objects, classes, and any component subassemblies

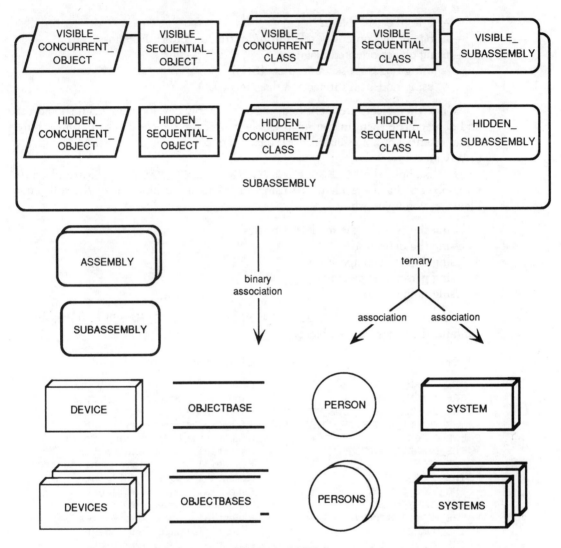

**Figure 3-9: Icons for General Semantic Nets (GSNs)**

- The system, hardware, software, and people terminators
- All important associations[3] among them

The subassembly development team should incrementally draw a GSN by first drawing some or all of its nodes and then connecting appropriate nodes with the appropriate arcs representing their relationships. The icons for GSNs are documented in Figure 3-9. Assemblies are drawn with two thick rounded rectangles, subassemblies

---

[3] Any relationship with significant meaning.

are drawn with thick rounded rectangles, concurrent objects are drawn with thick parallelograms, sequential objects are drawn with thick rectangles, concurrent classes are drawn with thick double parallelograms, sequential classes are drawn with thick double rectangles, hardware is drawn with thin boxes, systems are drawn with thick boxes, and the roles that persons play are drawn with thick circles. Visible objects and subassemblies are drawn on the boundary of the subassembly, whereas hidden objects and subassemblies are drawn fully nested within the parent subassembly. Assemblies, systems, hardware, and persons may not be drawn socketed or nested in subassemblies. Objects are used on GSNs when individual entities in the real world are being modeled (the typical case when working with embedded applications), and classes are used when relationships may exist among any objects of the same classes (the typical case when working with MIS).

SNs come from the field of artificial intelligence and represent a significant advance over entity-relationship (ER) or Chen diagrams [Chen 1976]. Variants of GSNs are used, under different names and with slightly different notation, in several object-oriented development (OOD) methods. Both Shlaer and Mellor's information model [1988] and the object model of Rumbaugh et al. [1991] are variants of GSNs.

Arcs on GSNs are associations (i.e., general semantic relationships) and are used to represent any general relationship considered significant by the subassembly development team. Associations are drawn using a solid arrow labeled with the relationship and can be drawn to connect any two or more nodes on a GSN.

Associations on GSNs should be drawn from the client node to the servant node so that IDs can reuse the topology of the GSNs. The client nodes should be drawn above the servant nodes to facilitate understanding the client-servant relationship between the nodes. Associations can be read as standard English sentences, with the identifier of the client node as the subject, the identifier of the association as the verb phrase, and the identifier of the servant node as the direct object of the sentence. Note that the same object may be a colleague (i.e., both a client and server) of another object.

The recommended notation for cardinality is shown on Figure 3-10: Associations on General Semantic Nets. If the relationship is one-to-one, no cardinality need be shown, as in the relationship between employees and social security numbers. If the cardinality of the client is one, then only the cardinality of the server must be documented. The cardinality of the server can be given by a number (e.g., "5"), a range (e.g., "0..1," "1 .. 100"), a set of values (e.g., "2,4"), a set of ranges ("1.. 10,21..30"), or an arbitrary number (e.g., "N"). If the cardinality of the client is not one, then the two cardinalities can be separated by a colon (e.g., "0..1:1..10," "M:N"). The arrowheads of conditional associations are bent back, possibly labeled by a specific condition.

Figure 3-11 shows a GSN for the ACCESS_CONTROL_FOR.DOOR_MASTER subassembly, which contains five exported concurrent master objects and nine hidden objects. Five objects in the ACCESS_CONTROL_FOR.DOOR_MASTER subassembly depend on the concurrent object THE_SYSTEM exported by the child subassembly PREDEFINED.

Consider software that is intended to control the crosswalk signals and traffic signals of a street intersection, based on input from a set of six traffic sensors and a

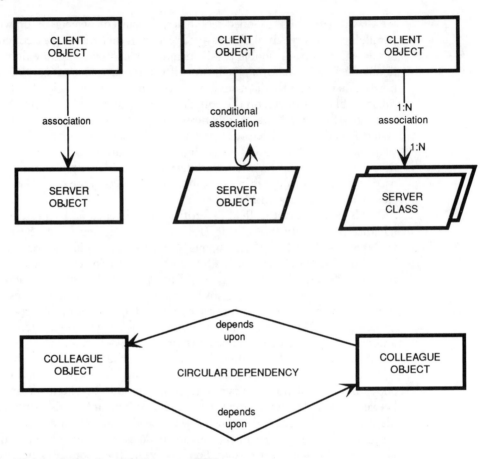

**Figure 3-10: Associations on GSNs**

switch. Figure 3-12 shows the GSN for the INTERSECTION.TRAFFIC_SYSTEM subassembly. Notice the mirror image effect at the bottom, where the four software objects mirror the external hardware with which they interface. Notice also the conceptual objects THE_CLOCK and THE_INTERSECTION, which correspond to concepts rather than to tangible hardware terminators.

The subassembly development team should therefore especially consider the important ramifications (e.g., polling, interrupts) of concurrency decisions on the relationships among different objects and between objects and the external entities with which they interface.

### 3.3.3    Initial Specification and Body of the Subassembly

The purpose of the subassembly specification and body is to provide the static architectural specification and design of the subassembly in a compact, machine-readable form. The subassembly development team should specify and logically design the initial specification and body of the subassembly, using the object-oriented

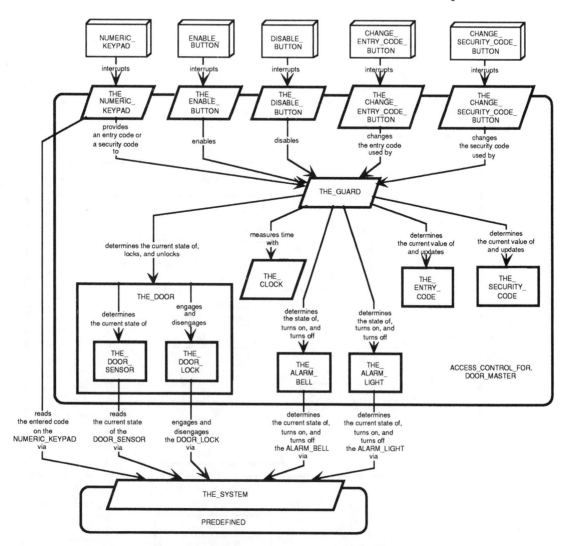

**Figure 3-11: GSN for the** ACCESS_CONTROL_FOR.DOOR_MASTER **Subassembly**

specification and design language (OOSDL). In fact, adequate CASE tool support should generate most of the subassembly specification and body automatically from the information in the subassembly GSN.

When completed, a subassembly specification documents the subassembly's parent assembly or subassembly; any child subassemblies needed by something listed in the specification; whether or not it is concurrent; and the subassembly's visible objects, classes, and subassemblies. Only the subassembly's immediate parent is listed. If more than one immediate parent exists, then only the parent in which it is defined is listed. A parent subassembly needs a child subassembly if the parent subassembly contains an object or class that needs to send a message to a visible object or class in

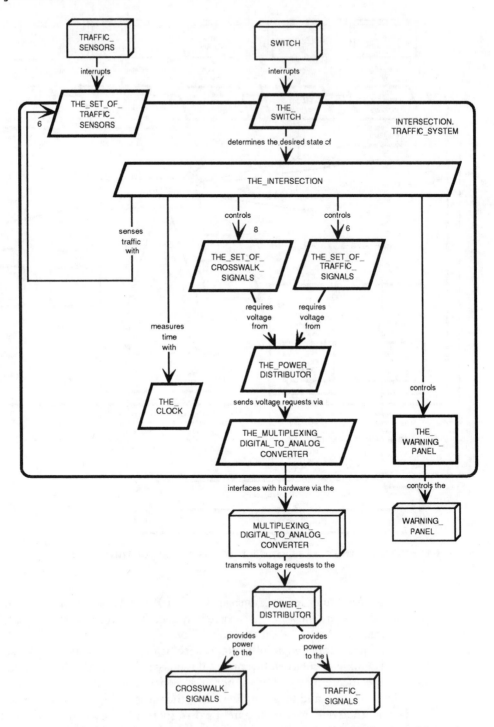

**Figure 3-12: GSN for the** INTERSECTION.TRAFFIC_SYSTEM **Subassembly**

the child subassembly. A subassembly is concurrent if it contains a concurrent object or class. A component subassembly is visible if it contains at least one object or class that may receive messages from outside its subassembly. When completed, a subassembly body documents any child subassemblies needed by something listed in the body and documents the subassembly's hidden component objects, classes, and subassemblies.

For example, the following is the specification and body of the ACCESS_ CONTROL_FOR.DOOR_MASTER subassembly written in OOSDL which is described in Chapter 6 of this book:

```
subassembly ACCESS_CONTROL_FOR is concurrent
 parent assembly DOOR_MASTER;
specification
  object      THE_CHANGE_ENTRY_CODE_BUTTON           is concurrent;
  object      THE_CHANGE_SECURITY_CODE_BUTTON        is concurrent;
  object      THE_DISABLE_BUTTON                     is concurrent;
  object      THE_ENABLE_BUTTON                      is concurrent;
  object      THE_NUMERIC_KEYPAD                     is concurrent;
end;

subassembly ACCESS_CONTROL_FOR
body
  object      THE_ALARM_BELL;
  object      THE_ALARM_LIGHT;
  object      THE_CLOCK               is concurrent;
  object      THE_DOOR;
  object      THE_DOOR_LOCK;
  object      THE_DOOR_SENSOR;
  object      THE_ENTRY_CODE;
  object      THE_GUARD               is concurrent;
  object      THE_SECURITY_CODE;
  end;
```

### 3.3.4    Interaction Diagrams (IDs)

The purpose of the IDs is to specify the existence, type, and objective of all interactions between any two objects (and possibly classes and terminators). An ID may show the entire subassembly and its terminators, a major thread of control through the subassembly, or an individual object and its terminators. Specifically, an initial subassembly ID shows:

- The existence and visibility of its component objects, classes, and subassemblies
- (Optionally) their generic parameters, specifications, and bodies
- The hardware, person, software, and system terminators
- All interactions among them, including
    —the visibility of exported attribute types and constant attributes
    —the messages passed (optionally including message type and parameters)
    —the exceptions raised

The subassembly development team should develop an initial subassembly ID for the subassembly, an initial scenario-level ID for each major scenario involving the subassembly, and optionally an object-level ID for each object and class. IDs are the primary overview diagram of subassembly requirements analysis and logical design. They may have three different scopes (i.e., subassembly, scenario, and object levels) and three levels of detail (i.e., black box, specification, and body).

Figure 3-13 shows the icons used in IDs. Note that the only difference between the icons for IDs and those for GSNs is that IDs have arcs for listing interactions, whereas GSNs have arcs for association relationships.

Black-box IDs treat objects and classes as software black boxes, while specification IDs also show the specifications of the objects and classes. Body IDs show both the specifications and the bodies. Figure 3-14 shows representative nodes on black box, specification, and body IDs, respectively.

Variants of IDs are used, under different names and with slightly different notation, in several OOD methods. Booch has object diagrams [1991], Colbert has

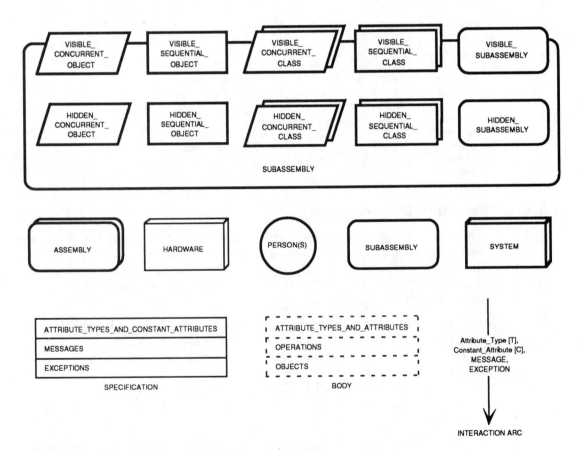

**Figure 3-13: Icons for Interaction Diagrams (IDs)**

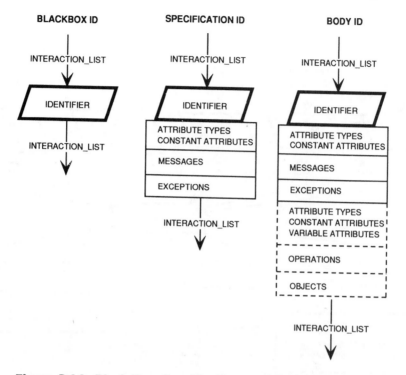

**Figure 3-14: Black Box, Specification, and Body IDs**

object-interaction diagrams (OIDs) [1989], and the object model of Rumbaugh et al. [1991] documents the passing of messages between objects.

The messages may be annotated with the type of the corresponding operation (e.g., "[M]" for modifier and "[P]" for preserver) and parameters (if useful). The IDs expand on the information in the subassembly GSNs, and with proper CASE tool support, a skeleton ID can be automatically generated from the corresponding GSN.

Subassembly IDs are the main IDs and should be mandatory. A subassembly ID shows the entire subassembly and has the same nodes and topology as the corresponding subassembly GSN from which it was derived. The arcs on the ID have a different meaning and thus have different labels than the corresponding arcs on the subassembly GSN. While the GSN remains useful for providing an introduction to the subassembly, the ID documents the messages that implement the corresponding associations.

Figure 3-15 shows an example subassembly ID for the ACCESS_CONTROL_ FOR.DOOR_MASTER subassembly, which contains five exported concurrent objects and nine hidden objects. Note that this diagram is identical to Figure 3-11 except for the labels of the arcs.

Scenario-level or thread-level IDs show all nodes involved with a single scenario or thread of control, respectively. They are useful for generating subassembly integration tests and are highly recommended for all significant scenarios and threads of

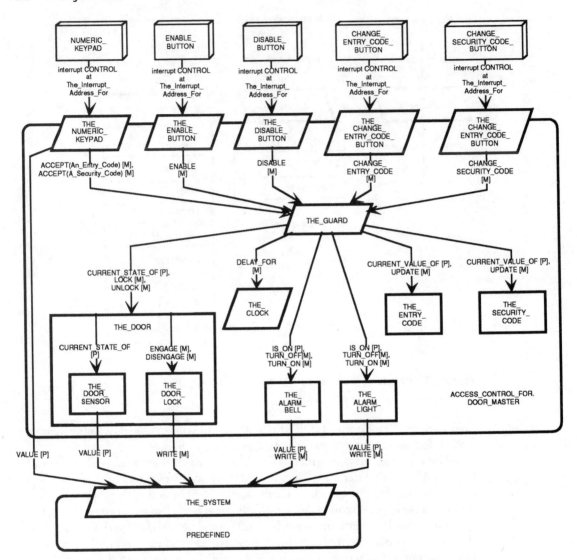

**Figure 3-15: ID for the** ACCESS_CONTROL_FOR.DOOR_MASTER **Subassembly**

control. Because scenarios and threads of control often cross subassembly boundaries, these diagrams may not be restricted to a single subassembly. For example, Figure 3-16 shows the ID for the scenario DISABLE.ACCESS_CONTROL_FOR. DOOR_MASTER

Object- and class-level IDs show only a single object or class; possibly its resources, including generic parameters (if it is a class), specification, and body; and its terminators. Although providing no new information other than the optional specification and body, they are often a useful part of the deliverable documentation of individual objects. They should be largely generated automatically from the information in the associated subassembly ID by a good CASE tool. Figure 3-17 shows an example

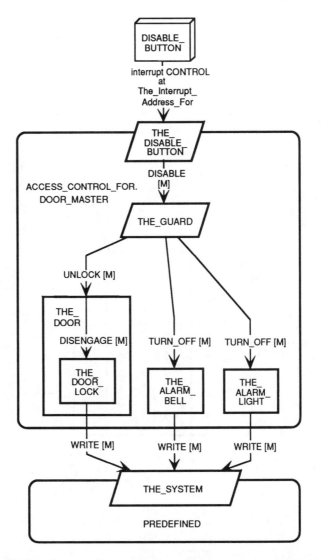

**Figure 3-16: ID for the** DISABLE.ACCESS_CONTROL_FOR.DOOR_MASTER **Scenario**

object-level ID for THE_GUARD.ACCESS_CONTROL_FOR.DOOR_MASTER object, which is the servant of five client objects and the client of six objects. The box below THE_GUARD object represents its specification with its exported attribute types and constant attributes (in this case, none), its messages, and its exceptions. Note that the interaction arcs do not necessarily list all messages of the object or class that they point to, but rather only those exported operations that are used in order to implement the relationship on the corresponding arc on the corresponding GSN. Note also that two interaction arcs that point to the same entity do not necessarily list the same set of messages.

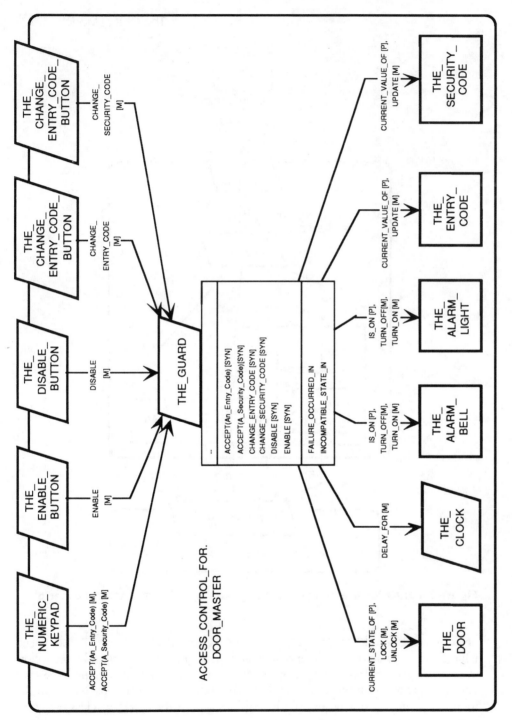

**Figure 3-17: ID for THE_GUARD Object**

### 3.3.5 Composition Diagrams (CMDs)

CMDs are specialized GSNs that are restricted to documenting individua_
hierarchies and the associated "has-components" relationships. CMDs can ι
level of the system, hardware, assembly, subassembly, hierarchy, or object. Systε
level and hardware-level CMDs are used during systems and hardware analysis and
design. Assembly-level and subassembly-level CMDs, while legitimate, are usually
not created because hierarchy-level and object-level diagrams are used instead to
provide the same information. Typically, only object-level CMDs are used for software requirements analysis and logical design. Each CMD shows the relevant aggregate entity and its actual and potential component entities:

- System
  —assemblies
  —hardware
  —people
- Hardware—hardware
- Assembly—subassemblies
- Subassembly
  —subassemblies
  —objects
  —classes
- Composition hierarchy—objects
- Object—objects.

Each CMD also shows the relevant "has-components" relationships among these
entities.

For each composition hierarchy, the subassembly development team develops a
CMD showing the aggregate object or class in terms of its component objects. All
classes and objects that have concurrent objects as components must themselves be
concurrent. A bent back arrowhead is used to label each potential component on the
CMD. See Figure 3-18: Icons for CMDs. Figure 3-19 shows the CMD of an example
aggregate object. Note that the has-components relationships on a CMD document
the logical nesting of objects, and no implementation decisions concerning the
physical nesting of modules is implied.

A set is defined as an aggregate object that is composed of a number of instances
from the same class. It is used to model such a collection. Figure 3-20 shows the CMD
of an example set.

Variants of CMDs are also used, under different names and with slightly different
notation, in several OOD methods. Object-hierarchy diagrams (OHDs) [Colbert
1989] and the object model [Rumbaugh et al. 1991] also document aggregation
hierarchies.

### 3.3.6 Description of the Objects

Every object should exist for a specific purpose (i.e., to model a specific conceptual
or physical entity in the application domain). The subassembly development team

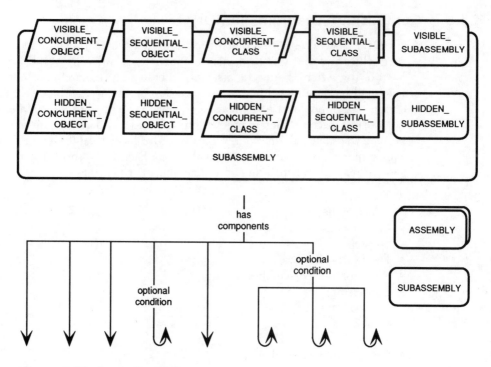

**Figure 3-18: Icons for CMDs**

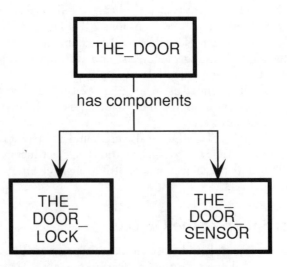

**Figure 3-19: CMD for** THE_DOOR **Aggregate Object**

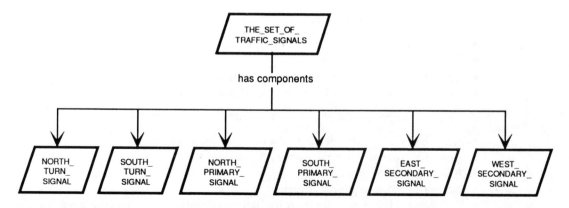

**Figure 3-20: CMD for** `THE_SET_OF_TRAFFIC_SIGNALS` **Object**

should provide a description of the abstraction implemented by each object in the subassembly and should categorize the objects as described in Chapter 2. For example, the following are descriptions of two objects in the `ACCESS_CONTROL_FOR.DOOR_MASTER` assembly.

- `THE_ALARM_BELL.ACCESS_CONTROL_FOR.DOOR_MASTER` object models, controls, and determines the state of the hardware alarm bell. This object has the following categorization:
  - essential
  - tangible
  - device
  - atomic
  - sequential
  - corruptible
  - agent (i.e., server of `THE_GUARD` and client of `THE_SYSTEM`)
- `THE_GUARD.ACCESS_CONTROL_FOR.DOOR_MASTER` object controls the door and alarm objects, based on input from the keypad and button objects. This object has the following categorization:
  - essential
  - intangible
  - role
  - atomic
  - concurrent
  - guarded
  - agent (i.e., server and client of several objects)

### 3.3.7   Specifications and Initial Bodies of the Objects

The subassembly development team should specify and logically design the specification and initial body of each object in the subassembly, using OOSDL. In fact, some of the object specifications should be automatically generated from the information in the subassembly IDs, provided adequate CASE tool support.

A complete object specification documents

- Whether or not the object is concurrent
- The object's immediate parent.[4]
- Any objects or classes needed[5] by a resource listed in the specification
- The object's visible attribute types, constant attributes, messages, and exceptions

When completed, an object body documents

- Any objects or classes needed by a resource listed in the body
- Any hidden attribute types, attributes, operations
- Any component objects
- An optional list of object invariants
- An optional list of messages to initialization operations that execute as soon as the object body is elaborated

For example, the following are object specifications and bodies written in OOSDL:

```
object THE_GUARD is concurrent
 parent subassembly ACCESS_CONTROL_FOR.DOOR_MASTER;
 needs THE_ENTRY_CODE;
 needs THE_SECURITY_CODE;
specification
 message ACCEPT(An_Entry_Code    : in Codes.THE_ENTRY_CODE)
                                   raise INCOMPATIBLE_STATE_IN  is synchronous;
 message ACCEPT(A_Security_Code : in Codes.THE_SECURITY_CODE)
                                   raise INCOMPATIBLE_STATE_IN  is synchronous;
 message CHANGE_ENTRY_CODE        raise INCOMPATIBLE_STATE_IN  is synchronous;
 message CHANGE_SECURITY_CODE     raise INCOMPATIBLE_STATE_IN  is synchronous;
 message DISABLE                  raise INCOMPATIBLE_STATE_IN  is synchronous;
 message ENABLE                   raise INCOMPATIBLE_STATE_IN  is synchronous;
 exception FAILURE_OCCURRED_IN;
 exception INCOMPATIBLE_STATE_IN;
end;


object THE_GUARD
body
 type States      is (Disabled,Enabled);
 type Substates is (Disabled,Raising_The_Alarms,Standby,
                    Waiting_For_The_Door_To_Close,Waiting_For_New_Entry_Code,
                    Waiting_For_New_Security_Code);
 variable The_State    : States    ::= Disabled;
 variable The_Substate : Substates ::= Disabled;
 modifier    operation ALLOW_ACCESS_IF_AUTHORIZED;
```

---

[4] The object's immediate parent is the lowest-level (with regard to aggregation) object, class, or subassembly in which the object is nested.
[5] An object needs a lower-level object or class if it needs:
  - Visibility of its exported attribute types and constant attributes
  - To send messages to the lower-level object or class
  - To handle exceptions that the lower-level object or class may raise.

```
modifier     operation CHANGE_THE_ENTRY_CODE;
modifier     operation CHANGE_THE_SECURITY_CODE;
preserver    operation CONTROL raise FAILURE_OCCURRED_IN  is concurrent;
modifier     operation DISABLE_IF_AUTHORIZED;
modifier     operation ENABLE_IF_AUTHORIZED;
modifier     operation WAIT_FOR_THE_DOOR_TO_CLOSE;
start
 CONTROL;
end;

object SET_OF_TRAFFIC_SIGNALS
 parent subassembly INTERSECTION;
specification
 message   CHANGE_PRIMARY      raise LIGHT_FAILED,POWER_FAILED is synchronous;
 message   CHANGE_SECONDARY    raise LIGHT_FAILED,POWER_FAILED is synchronous;
 message   CHANGE_TURN         raise LIGHT_FAILED,POWER_FAILED is synchronous;
 message   FLASH_PRIMARY       raise LIGHT_FAILED,POWER_FAILED is synchronous;
 message   FLASH_SECONDARY     raise LIGHT_FAILED,POWER_FAILED is synchronous;
 message   FLASH_TURN          raise LIGHT_FAILED,POWER_FAILED is synchronous;
 message   INITIALIZE          raise LIGHT_FAILED,POWER_FAILED is synchronous;
 message   TURN_OFF            raise ABSTRACTION_VIOLATED       is synchronous;
 exception  ABSTRACTION_VIOLATED;
 exception  LIGHT_FAILED;
 exception  POWER_FAILED;
end;

object SET_OF_TRAFFIC_SIGNALS
 needs   PRIMARY_SIGNALS;
 needs   SECONDARY_SIGNALS;
 needs   TURN_SIGNALS;
body
 type               States              is (Primary,Secondary,Turn);
 variable           The_State : States ::= PRIMARY;
 modifier operation CHANGE_PRIMARY      raise LIGHT_FAILED,POWER_FAILED;
 modifier operation CHANGE_SECONDARY    raise LIGHT_FAILED,POWER_FAILED;
 modifier operation CHANGE_TURN         raise LIGHT_FAILED,POWER_FAILED;
 modifier operation FLASH_PRIMARY       raise LIGHT_FAILED,POWER_FAILED;
 modifier operation FLASH_SECONDARY     raise LIGHT_FAILED,POWER_FAILED;
 modifier operation FLASH_TURN          raise LIGHT_FAILED,POWER_FAILED;
 modifier operation INITIALIZE          raise LIGHT_FAILED,POWER_FAILED;
 modifier operation TURN_OFF            raise ABSTRACTION_VIOLATED;
 object   EAST_SECONDARY : SECONDARY_SIGNALS;
 object   NORTH_PRIMARY  : PRIMARY_SIGNALS;
 object   NORTH_TURN     : TURN_SIGNALS;
 object   SOUTH_PRIMARY  : PRIMARY_SIGNALS;
 object   SOUTH_TURN     : TURN_SIGNALS;
 object   WEST_SECONDARY : SECONDARY_SIGNALS;
end;
```

## 3.3.8    Description of the Attribute Types and Attributes of the Objects

The subassembly development team should also document a description of the abstraction of each attribute type and each attribute of each object. This description should provide all necessary information about the attribute not already provided in the specification or body of the object. For example:

Type States.THE_GUARD is an enumeration type with the possible values Disabled and Enabled and represents the current state of THE_GUARD object.

The constant The_Interrupt_Address_For.THE_ACCELERATION_BUTTON of type ADDRESSES.SYSTEM is a specific memory location in the system, which is interrupted by the hardware CRUISE_CONTROL_ACCELERATION_BUTTON, with a value of 0 when the CRUISE_CONTROL_ACCELERATION_BUTTON is released and a value of 1 when the CRUISE_CONTROL_ACCELERATION_BUTTON is pressed.

The variable The_Substate.THE_GUARD of type SUBSTATES represents the substate of the ENABLED state and may take on the values Disabled, Raising_The_Alarms, Standby, Waiting_For_The_Door_To_Close, Waiting_For_New_Entry_Code, and Waiting_For_New_Security_Code.

## 3.3.9    Description of the Messages

In order to fully understand and document each message, the subassembly development team should document each message passed in the subassembly (e.g., using OOSDL). This documentation should include the specification of the message, the identifiers of the source and destination of the message, the specification of the associated operation that receives the operation, the specification of the operation that implements it (if different), and a description of the functional or process abstraction that the message implements. For example:

```
Message:      message TURN_OFF raise FAILURE_OCCURRED_IN is sequential;
  Sent by:    object THE_GUARD is concurrent;
  Sent to:    object THE_ALARM_BELL;
  Received by:
    modifier operation TURN_OFF.THE_ALARM_BELL raise FAILURE_OCCURRED_IN;
  Abstraction:
    This message turns off the alarm bell.


Message:      message ACCEPT (An_Entry_Code : in CODES.THE_ENTRY_CODE)
              raise INCOMPATIBLE_STATE_IN is synchronous;
  Sent by: object THE_NUMERIC_KEYPAD is concurrent;
  Sent to: object THE_GUARD          is concurrent;
  Received by:
    preserver operation CONTROL
  Implemented by:
    modifier operation CHANGE_THE_ENTRY_CODE
              (An_Entry_Code : in CODES.THE_ENTRY_CODE)
              raise INCOMPATIBLE_STATE_IN;
  Abstraction:
    This message passes a potential entry code to the guard.


Message:      message CURRENT_STATE_OF return STATES.THE_DOOR is sequential;
  Sent by: object THE_GUARD is concurrent;
  Sent to: object THE_DOOR;
```

Received by:
    **preserver operation** CURRENT_STATE_OF.THE_DOOR
        **return** States.THE_DOOR
        **is concurrent;**
Abstraction:
This message causes THE_DOOR object to return the value of its The_Current_State attribute, which may be Open, Closed, or Locked.

Message:    **message** INTERRUPT(THE_INTERRUPT_ADDRESS_FOR) **is asynchronous;**
Sent by:  **hardware** ENABLE_BUTTON;
Sent to:  **object** THE_ENABLE_BUTTON **is concurrent;**
Received by:
    **preserver operation** CONTROL.THE_ENABLE_BUTTON **is concurrent;**
Abstraction:
    This message causes THE_ENABLE_BUTTON object to send the ENABLE message to THE_GUARD object when interrupted by the hardware ENABLE_BUTTON.

### 3.3.10   Description of the Operations

The subassembly development team should also document a description of the abstraction of each operation of each object. This description should provide all necessary information about the operation not already provided in the body of the object. For example:

The concurrent CONTROL.THE_GUARD operation provides the thread of control of the concurrent THE_GUARD object and routes messages to the appropriate operations.

The sequential ALLOW_ACCESS_IF_AUTHORIZED.THE_GUARD operation unlocks the door and calls the WAIT_FOR_THE_DOOR_TO_CLOSE operation if the state is ENABLED, the substate is STANDBY, and the correct entry code is entered.

### 3.3.11   Description of the Exceptions

The subassembly development team should also document a description of the abstraction of each exception of each object. This description should provide all necessary information about the exception not already provided in the specification of the object. For example, the exception FAILURE_OCCURRED_IN.THE_GUARD signifies that the execution of THE_GUARD object has failed and that any operation returning this exception did not successfully complete and is not to be trusted.

## 3.4  THE CLASS MODEL

The class model is the second of the five subassembly-level object-oriented models created during subassembly requirements analysis and logical design, and it is derived largely from the object model. It provides a static view of the inheritance architecture of the subassembly in terms of the existence and abstraction of its component classes and the "has-class" and "has-superclass" relationships among them and between them and their instances. Whereas the object model dealt with the specific objects that make up the subassembly, the class model generalizes this information into classes in order to better support abstraction and reuse. The class model of a subassembly consists of the following information:

For the subassembly

- List of all classes
- Updated GSN
- Updated IDs

For each inheritance hierarchy in the subassembly—classification diagram (CLD)
For each class in the subassembly

- Purpose and description
- Specification and initial body

The class model is developed by the subassembly development team and is documented in the subassembly section of the project object.

## 3.4.1    List of Subassembly Classes

The subassembly development team should collectively identify, name, and agree on the initial classes of the subassembly, using an appropriate subset of the following approaches:

- Recommended approaches
  —using object abstraction
    - using the types of the modeled entities
    - using the definition of a class
    - using object decomposition
  —using inheritance
    - using generalization
    - using subclasses
  —using OODA
  —using repositories of previously developed software
    - reusing application frameworks
    - reusing class hierarchies
    - reusing individual objects and classes
  —using specification and design languages
  —using personal experience
- Traditional approaches
  —using nouns
  —using traditional DFDs
    - using terminators on CDs
    - using data stores on DFDs
    - using complex data flows on DFDs
- Miscellaneous approaches
  —using abstract data types and abstract state machines
  —using states

—using resources
  – using attributes
  – using operations
  – using exceptions
—using requirements
—using CRC cards
  –using traditional CRC cards
  –using Post-it® Notes
—using entities on ERA diagrams
—using object-oriented diagrams
  – using nodes on SNs
  – using nodes on IDs

Once the classes are identified, the subassembly development team should list and characterize them in the subassembly section of the project database. They are either essential or nonessential, sequential or concurrent, and abstract or concrete. For example, the CLASSES_FOR.DOOR_MASTER subassembly and the TRAFFIC_SYSTEM.INTERSECTION_CLASSES subassembly contain the following classes:

- CLASSES_FOR.DOOR_MASTER:
  - ALARMS                  Essential Sequential Concrete Generic
  - BUTTONS                 Essential Concurrent Concrete
  - CODES                   Essential Sequential Concrete
- TRAFFIC_SYSTEM.INTERSECTION_CLASSES:
  - PRIMARY_SIGNALS         Essential Concurrent Concrete
  - SECONDARY_SIGNALS       Essential Concurrent Concrete
  - STANDARD_SIGNALS        Essential Concurrent Abstract
  - TRAFFIC_LIGHTS          Essential Concurrent Concrete
  - TRAFFIC_SIGNALS         Essential Concurrent Abstract
  - TURN_SIGNALS            Essential Concurrent Concrete

## 3.4.2    Classification Diagrams (CLDs)

CLDs are specialized GSNs that are restricted to documenting individual inheritance hierarchies and the associated "has class" and "has superclass" relationships. Each CLD shows (see Figure 3-21) the relevant:

- Objects (where appropriate)
- Classes
- Generic parameters of generic classes (where appropriate)
- Specification of objects and classes (where appropriate)
- Bodies of objects and classes (where appropriate)
- "Has superclass" relationships between subclasses and superclasses
- "Has class" relationships between instances and classes

For each inheritance hierarchy, the subassembly development team develops or updates an overview CLD showing the classification hierarchy in terms of its superclasses, subclasses, and optionally instances. See Figure 3-22: Example Overview

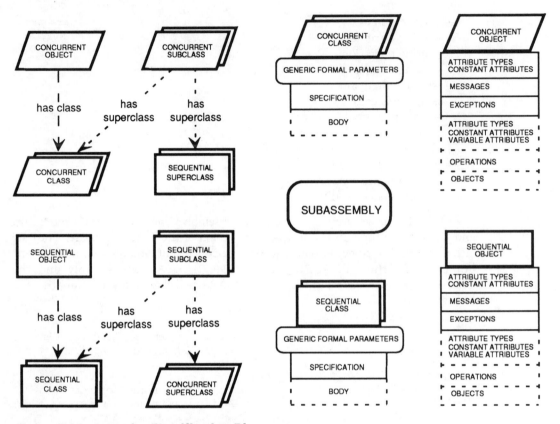

**Figure 3-21: Icons for Classification Diagrams**

Classification Diagrams. Later, as the resources of the classes are identified, the subassembly development team should use either specification-level or body-level CLDs showing specifications and bodies and what capabilities are added, modified, or deleted from subclasses. Capabilities of a superclass are inherited by each subclass unless the capability is overwritten (i.e., relisted in the subclass) or deleted (i.e., relisted with a minus sign in the subclass). Considerable iteration should be expected until the classification hierarchy stabilizes.

Specification-level CLDs provide additional information not available from overview CLDs. CLDs at the specification level show the required generic formal parameters (if any) and the exported attribute types and constant attributes, messages, and exceptions. However, specification-level CLDs take up somewhat more space than overview CLDs and do not show any of the resources hidden in the bodies of the classes. Figure 3-23 shows a specification-level CLD of the BUTTONS class hierarchy.

Body-level CLDs provide additional information not available from overview or specification-level CLDs. These body-level CLDs show the hidden attributes types and attributes, operations, and component objects; they also permit inferences regarding the mapping of the messages to the operations. However, body-level CLDs take

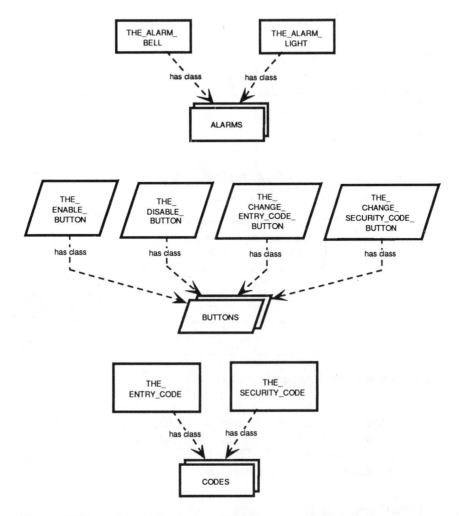

**Figure 3-22: Example Overview CLDs**

up considerably more space and are impractical for large class hierarchies. If the classification hierarchy is too large to show on a single diagram, it can be decomposed into subdiagrams or replaced with an indented list of subclasses and resources. Figure 3-24 shows a body-level CLD of the BUTTONS class hierarchy.

It is important to note that the same object can be an instance of multiple classes (i.e., multiple classification) and that the same class can be a subclass of multiple superclasses (i.e., multiple inheritance). As an example of multiple classification, a specific person—Jane Doe—can be both an executive and an athlete. Thus, the object JANE_DOE is an instance of the classes EXECUTIVES and ATHLETES. Similarly, property owners can be businesses, governments, and persons. Thus, the class PROPERTY_OWNERS is a (restricted) subclass of the classes BUSINESSES, GOVERNMENTS, and PERSONS. See Figure 3-25: Examples of Multiple Classification and Inheritance.

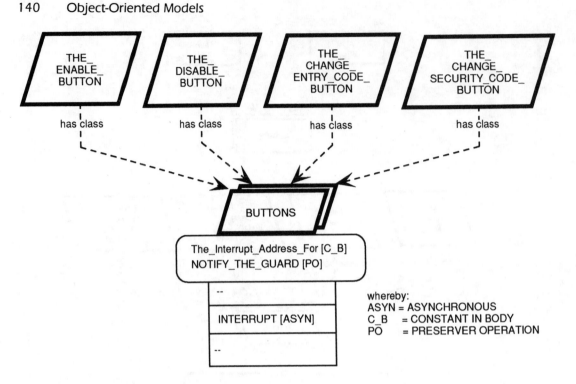

**Figure 3-23: Example Specification-Level CLD**

Variants of CLDs are also used, under different names and with slightly different notation, in several OOD methods. Booch has class diagrams [1991], Colbert has object-class diagrams (OCDs) [1989], and the object model of Rumbaugh et al. [1991] also documents inheritance hierarchies.

## 3.4.3    Description of the Classes

Every class should exist as a template for a specific group of related conceptual or tangible entities in the application domain. The subassembly development team should provide a description of the abstraction implemented by each class in the subassembly. For example, the following are descriptions of the abstraction implemented by several classes.

- The BUTTONS.CLASSES.DOOR_MASTER concrete class models the common properties of all hardware buttons controlling the DOOR_MASTER assembly. This class has the following categorization:
  — essential
  — tangible
  — device
  — atomic
  — concurrent
  — guarded

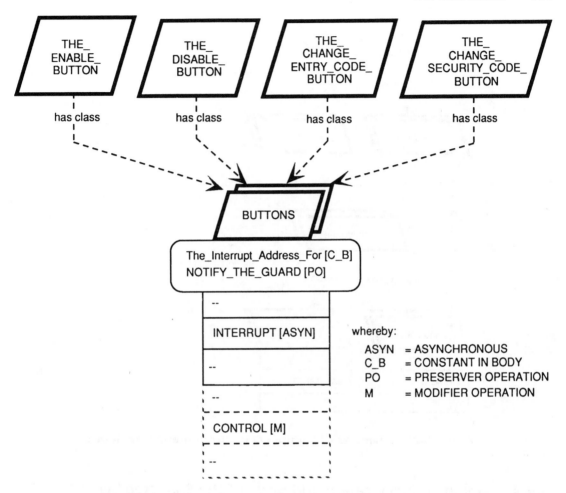

**Figure 3-24: Example Body-Level CLD**

- The TRAFFIC_SIGNALS.INTERSECTION_CLASSES.TRAFFIC_SYSTEM abstract superclass models the common properties of all traffic signals in the street intersection.
- The TURN_SIGNALS.INTERSECTION_CLASSES.TRAFFIC_SYSTEM subclass models the unique properties of all turn signals in the street intersection.
- The STANDARD_SIGNALS.INTERSECTION_CLASSES.TRAFFIC_SYSTEM abstract subclass models the common properties of all signals other than turn signals in the street intersection.
- The PRIMARY_SIGNALS.INTERSECTION_CLASSES.TRAFFIC_SYSTEM subclass models the unique properties of the standard signals in the street intersection that control the primary road and the flashing yellow signals late at night.
- The SECONDARY_SIGNALS.INTERSECTION_CLASSES.TRAFFIC_SYSTEM subclass models the unique properties of the standard signals in the street intersection that control the secondary road and the flashing red signals late at night.

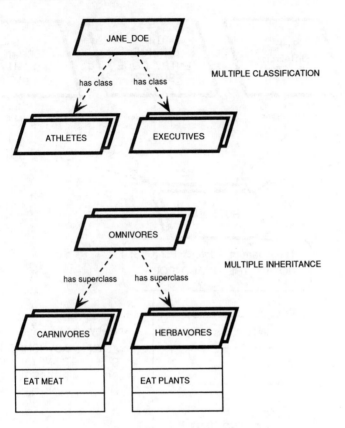

**Figure 3-25: Examples of Multiple Classification and Inheritance**

### 3.4.4 Updated Specification and Body of the Subassembly

The subassembly development team should either update the initial specification and body of the subassembly with its component classes (e.g., if the subassembly is small, compared with the Miller limit of seven—plus or minus two) or else create a new subassembly to contain them. In fact, the update or the new subassembly specification and body should be automatically generated from the information in the subassembly CLDs provided adequate CASE tool support.

The following is an example subassembly specification and body, written in OOSDL:

```
subassembly INTERSECTION_CLASSES is concurrent
  parent assembly TRAFFIC_SYSTEM;
specification
  class      PRIMARY_SIGNALS        is concurrent;
  class      SECONDARY_SIGNALS      is concurrent;
  class      TURN_SIGNALS           is concurrent;
end;
```

```
subassembly INTERSECTION_CLASSES
body
  class      STANDARD_SIGNALS    is concurrent;
  class      TRAFFIC_LIGHTS      is concurrent;
  class      TRAFFIC_SIGNALS     is concurrent;
end;
```

### 3.4.5    Specifications and Bodies of the Classes

The subassembly development team should specify and logically design the specification and body of each class in the subassembly (e.g., using OOSDL). In fact, skeleton specifications and bodies should be automatically generated from the information in the subassembly CLDs if adequate CASE tool support exists.

A class specification documents

- Whether or not the instances are concurrent
- The class's immediate parent
- Any objects or classes needed by a resource listed in the specification
- A list of its superclasses
- Any generic parameters
- Whether or not the class is abstract[6]
- The visible attribute types, constant attributes, messages, and exceptions of its instances, which the class introduces, completes, redefines, and removes

A class body documents

- Any objects or classes needed by a resource listed in the body
- Any hidden attribute types, attributes, and operations that it introduces, completes, redefines, and removes
- An optional list of object or class invariants
- An optional list of messages to initialization operations that execute as soon as the instance is instantiated

A resource must be introduced the first time (i.e., at the highest place) that it is listed in an inheritance hierarchy. Then, it can be completed, redefined, or removed in a subclass (i.e., lower in the hierarchy). A resource must be completed in a subclass if it was incomplete when it was introduced in an abstract superclass. A resource is incomplete if it was not defined when it was introduced (i.e., it was left as a stub).

A class must contain at least one attribute and one operation. For example, the following are class specifications and bodies written in OOSDL:

```
class TRAFFIC_SIGNALS is concurrent
 parent subassembly INTERSECTION_CLASSES;
specification is abstract
 introduces
  message   CHANGE      is deferred;
  message   CONSTRUCT   (A_TRAFFIC_SIGNAL) raise CONSTRUCT_FAILED is synchronous;
```

---

[6] A class is *abstract* if one or more subclasses must supply resources in order for an instance to be constructed.

```
  message    DESTRUCT    (A_TRAFFIC_SIGNAL) raise DESTRUCT_FAILED   is synchronous;
  message    FLASH       is deferred;
  message    INITIALIZE  is deferred;
  message    TURN_OFF    is deferred;
  exception  ABSTRACTION_FAILED_IN;
  exception  CONSTRUCT_FAILED_IN;
  exception  DESTRUCT_FAILED_IN;
  exception  LIGHT_FAILED_IN;
  exception  POWER_FAILED_IN;
end;

class TRAFFIC_SIGNALS
 needs  TRAFFIC_LIGHTS;
body
 introduces
  type                      States              is deferred;
  variable                  The_State           : States := Red;
  operation                 CHANGE              is deferred;
  constructor operation     CONSTRUCT   (A_TRAFFIC_SIGNAL)
                            raise CONSTRUCT_FAILED;
  destructor operation      DESTRUCT    (A_TRAFFIC_SIGNAL)
                            raise DESTRUCT_FAILED;
  operation                 FLASH               is deferred;
  operation                 INITIALIZE          is deferred;
  operation                 TURN_OFF            is deferred;
  object                    THE_RED_LIGHT    : TRAFFIC_LIGHTS;
  object                    THE_YELLOW_LIGHT : TRAFFIC_LIGHTS;
start
  CONSTRUCT(THE_RED_LIGHT).TRAFFIC_LIGHTS;
  CONSTRUCT(THE_YELLOW_LIGHT).TRAFFIC_LIGHTS;
  INITIALIZE;
end;

class TURN_SIGNALS is concurrent
 parent subassembly INTERSECTION_CLASSES;
 superclass TRAFFIC_SIGNALS is visible;
specification
 completes
  message    CHANGE      raise LIGHT_FAILED_IN, POWER_FAILED_IN is synchronous;
  message    FLASH       raise LIGHT_FAILED_IN, POWER_FAILED_IN is synchronous;
  message    INITIALIZE  raise LIGHT_FAILED_IN, POWER_FAILED_IN is synchronous;
  message    TURN_OFF    raise ABSTRACTION_FAILED_IN            is synchronous;
end;

class TURN_SIGNALS
 needs  TRAFFIC_LIGHTS;
body
 completes
  type    States is (Green_Arrow, Yellow, Red);
  modifier operation  CHANGE      raise LIGHT_FAILED_IN, POWER_FAILED_IN;
  modifier operation  FLASH       raise LIGHT_FAILED_IN, POWER_FAILED_IN;
  modifier operation  INITIALIZE  raise LIGHT_FAILED_IN, POWER_FAILED_IN;
  modifier operation  TURN_OFF    raise ABSTRACTION_FAILED_IN;
  introduces
  object THE_GREEN_ARROW : TRAFFIC_LIGHTS;
```

```
  start
    CONSTRUCT(THE_GREEN_ARROW).TRAFFIC_LIGHTS;
  end;


  class STANDARD_SIGNALS is concurrent
   parent subassembly INTERSECTION_CLASSES;
   superclass TRAFFIC_SIGNALS is visible;
  specification is abstract
   introduces
     message   CHANGE      raise LIGHT_FAILED_IN,POWER_FAILED_IN is synchronous;
     message   INITIALIZE  raise LIGHT_FAILED_IN,POWER_FAILED_IN is synchronous;
     message   TURN_OFF    raise ABSTRACTION_FAILED_IN            is synchronous;
  end;

  class STANDARD_SIGNALS
   needs  TRAFFIC_LIGHTS;
  body
     type      States is (Green_Light,Yellow,Red);
     modifier operation  CHANGE     raise LIGHT_FAILED_IN,POWER_FAILED_IN;
     modifier operation  INITIALIZE raise LIGHT_FAILED_IN,POWER_FAILED_IN;
     modifier operation TURN_OFF    raise ABSTRACTION_FAILED_IN;
     object  THE_GREEN_LIGHT : TRAFFIC_LIGHTS;
  start
   CONSTRUCT(THE_GREEN_LIGHT).TRAFFIC_LIGHTS;
  end;

  class PRIMARY_SIGNALS is concurrent
   parent subassembly INTERSECTION_CLASSES;
   superclass STANDARD_SIGNALS is visible;
  specification
   completes
     message FLASH raise LIGHT_FAILED_IN,POWER_FAILED_IN is synchronous;
  end;

  class PRIMARY_SIGNALS
  body
   completes
     modifier operation  FLASH raise LIGHT_FAILED_IN,POWER_FAILED_IN;
  end;


  class SECONDARY_SIGNALS is concurrent
   parent subassembly INTERSECTION_CLASSES;
   superclass STANDARD_SIGNALS is visible;
  specification
   completes
     message FLASH raise LIGHT_FAILED_IN,POWER_FAILED_IN is synchronous;
  end;

  class SECONDARY_SIGNALS
  body
   completes
     modifier operation  FLASH raise LIGHT_FAILED_IN raise POWER_FAILED_IN;
  end;
```

```
class TRAFFIC_LIGHTS is concurrent
 parent subassembly INTERSECTION_CLASSES;
specification is abstract
 introduces
  message CONSTRUCT   (A_TRAFFIC_LIGHT)   raise CONSTRUCT_FAILED
                                          is synchronous;
  message DESTRUCT    (A_TRAFFIC_LIGHT)   raise DESTRUCT_FAILED
                                          is synchronous;
  message CHANGE                          raise LIGHT_FAILED_IN, POWER_FAILED_IN
                                          is synchronous;
  exception       CONSTRUCT_FAILED_IN;
  exception       DESTRUCT_FAILED_IN;
  exception       LIGHT_FAILED_IN;
  exception       POWER_FAILED_IN;
end;

class TRAFFIC_LIGHTS
body
 introduces
  type     States is (Failed,Off,On);
  variable The_State   : States := Off;
  constructor operation  CONSTRUCT  (A_TRAFFIC_LIGHT) raise CONSTRUCT_FAILED;
  destructor operation   DESTRUCT   (A_TRAFFIC_LIGHT) raise DESTRUCT_FAILED;
  modifier operation     CHANGE raise LIGHT_FAILED_IN POWER_FAILED_IN;
end;
```

## 3.5 THE STATE MODEL

The state model is the third of the five subassembly-level object-oriented models created during subassembly requirements analysis and logical design. It is typically developed simultaneously and iteratively with the control model and the timing model. The objective of the state model is to specify the behavior of the subassembly objects and classes in terms of their states and the nonpreserver operations and exceptions that transition between them. It provides a dynamic view of the behavior of the objects in terms of their states, and the modifier operations and exceptions that transition the objects from state to state. The state model for an object or class consists of the following information:

- For each object and class in the subassembly that can be modeled as an individual or a set of finite-state machines:
  - Object-oriented state transition diagram (STD)
  - State operation table (SOT)
- For each state of the object or class—its purpose and description

### 3.5.1 State Transition Diagrams (STDs)

The subassembly development team should develop an object-oriented state transition diagram (STD) for each object and class of objects that can be modeled as a finite state machine. The object-oriented STD documents the individual and compound states of a single object or class and documents the modifier operations and exceptions that cause or may conditionally cause state transitions.

Modifier operations documented on STDs come in the following two varieties: (1) encapsulated within the current class or object, and (2) encapsulated within some other class, object, or external hardware or software. If a modifier operation of the current class or object also causes another class or object to change its state, this should also be documented on the current STD. When an event (such as the passing of time) triggers a transition, it should be considered a modifier operation on some other object, such as DELAY_FOR(A_Specific_Time).THE_CLOCK or DELAY_UNTIL(A_Specific_Time).THE_CLOCK.

Variants of STDs are used, with slightly different notation, in most OOD methods. Booch [1991], Colbert [1989], Rumbaugh et al. [1991], and Shlaer and Mellor [1988] all use STDs.

Figure 3-26 documents the nodes and arcs recommended for object-oriented STDs. The STD is surrounded by the icon of the object or class being modeled. The initial state or states, if any, are indicated with an arrow from a circle labeled START. Aggregate states [Harrell 1988] are represented by rounded rectangles; terminal states ("END STATE" on Figure 3-26) are represented by solid ovals drawn with a thick line; and simple, nonterminal states (e.g., "PRIOR STATE") are represented by rectangles. Modifier operations are represented by a solid line, and exceptions are represented by a dotted line. Operations and exceptions belonging to the current object or class are represented by thin lines, whereas operations and exceptions belonging to other entities (e.g., hardware devices) are represented by a thick line. Conditional transitions are annotated with a bent arrowhead, optionally labeled with the condition (not shown on Figure 3-26).

Figure 3-27 shows an example object STD with a aggregate state. The DISABLED state is the initial state and the ENABLED state is an aggregate state that decomposes into the five substates STANDBY, RAISING_THE_ALARMS, WAITING_FOR_THE_DOOR_TO_CLOSE, WAITING_FOR_THE_NEW_ENTRY_CODE, and WAITING_FOR_THE_NEW_SECURITY_CODE.

Figure 3-28 shows an example object STD with transitions other than modifier operations on the current object.

Figure 3-29 shows an example class STD that shows the states and transitions for all instances of the class.

## 3.5.2    Description of the States

The subassembly development team should describe each state of each object and class. For example:

The Disabled state of the THE_GUARD.ACCESS_CONTROL_FOR. DOOR_MASTER object signifies that the DOOR_MASTER assembly is disabled. It is automatically entered as the starting state, may be exited by means of the ENABLE.THE_GUARD operation, and may be entered by means of the DISABLE.THE_GUARD operation.

The aggregate Enabled state of THE_GUARD.ACCESS_CONTROL_

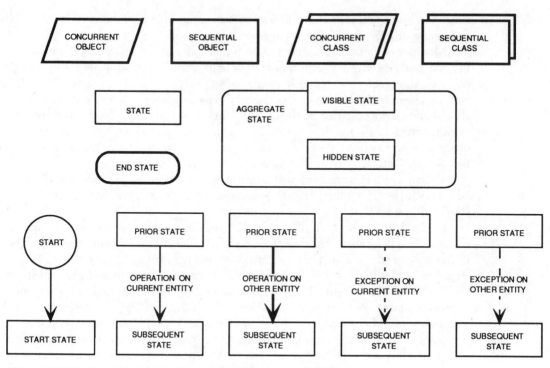

**Figure 3-26: Icons for State Transition Diagrams (STDs)**

FOR.DOOR_MASTER object signifies that the DOOR_MASTER assembly is enabled. It consists of the following four substates: Standby, Raising_The_Alarms, Waiting_For_New_Entry_Code, Waiting_For_New_Security_Code, and Waiting_For_The_Door_To_Close. It may be exited by means of the DISABLE.THE_GUARD operation and may be entered by means of the ENABLE.THE_GUARD operation.

### 3.5.3    State Operation Tables (SOTs)

While the object-oriented STD documents the relationship between states and nonpreserver operations, it does not document which preserver operations may execute in which states. The subassembly development team may develop a *state operation table* (SOT) for each object or class that can be modeled as a finite-state machine. An SOT documents the valid prior, temporary, and post states of each modifier operation and exception. The following is an example SOT that corresponds to the STD provided in Figure 3-27.

Operation: ALLOW_ACCESS_IF_AUTHORIZED.THE_GUARD
    Valid Prior States:        Standby.Enabled
    Valid Post States:        Standby.Enabled
                                    Waiting_For_The_Door_To_Close.Enabled

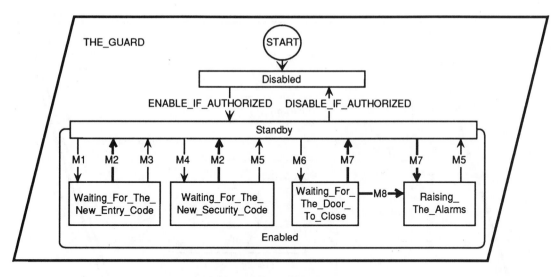

M1 = CHANGE_THE_ENTRY_CODE
M2 = DELAY_FOR(60_SECONDS).THE_CLOCK
M3 = ACCEPT(AN_ENTRY_CODE)
M4 = CHANGE_THE_SECURITY_CODE
M5 = ACCEPT(A_SECURITY_CODE)
M6 = ALLOW_ACCESS_IF_AUTHORIZED
M7 = CURRENT_STATE_OF.THE_DOOR
M8 = DELAY_FOR(40_SECONDS).THE_CLOCK

**Figure 3-27: STD of** THE_GUARD.ACCESS_CONTROL_FOR.DOOR_MASTER **Object**

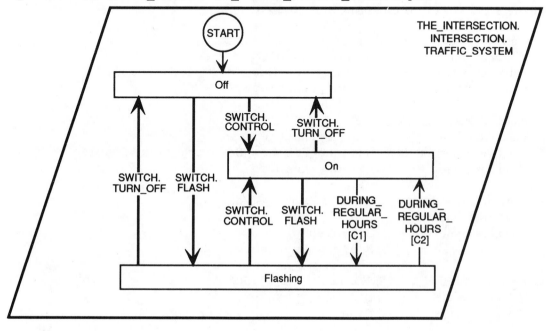

**Figure 3-28: STD of** THE_INTERSECTION **Object**

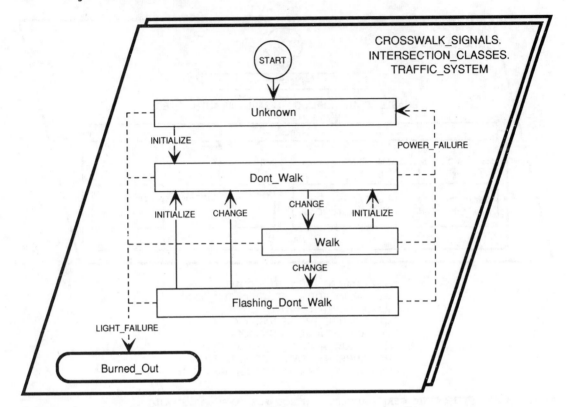

**Figure 3-29: STD of the** CROSSWALK_SIGNALS **Class**

Operation: CHANGE_THE_ENTRY_CODE.THE_GUARD
    Valid Prior States:          Standby.Enabled
    Valid Temporary States:      Waiting_For_New_Entry_Code.Enabled
    Valid Post States:           Standby.Enabled

Operation: CHANGE_THE_SECURITY_CODE.THE_GUARD
    Valid Prior States:          Standby.Enabled
    Valid Temporary States:      Waiting_For_New_Security_Code.Enabled
    Valid Post States:           Standby.Enabled

Operation: DISABLE_IF_AUTHORIZED.THE_GUARD
    Valid Prior States:          Standby.Enabled
    Valid Post States:           Disabled
                                 Standby.Enabled

Operation: ENABLE_IF_AUTHORIZED.THE_GUARD
    Valid Prior States:          Disabled
    Valid Post States:           Disabled
                                 Standby.Enabled

Operation: WAIT_FOR_THE_DOOR_TO_CLOSE.THE_GUARD
    Valid Prior States:           Waiting_For_The_Door_To_Close.Enabled
    Valid Post States:           Standby.Enabled

        The information documented in the SOT can be used to ensure that each operation may only be performed in a consistent state. This supports the principle that all objects and classes should be responsible for preserving their own abstraction from violation. The following is the body of the DISABLE_IF_AUTHORIZED operation. It ensures consistency with the state of its object, THE_GUARD, by using a precondition:

```
modifier operation DISABLE_IF_AUTHORIZED
 parent object
   THE_GUARD.ACCESS_CONTROL_FOR.DOOR_MASTER;
specification
 message ACCEPT(A_Security_Code : in Codes.THE_SECURITY_CODE) is synchronous;
end;


operation DISABLE_IF_AUTHORIZED
 needs THE_SECURITY_CODE;
body
preconditions
 require
   The_State = Enabled and The_Substate = Standby
 else
    raise INCOMPATIBLE_STATE_IN;
 end require;
statements
 select
   receive ACCEPT(A_Security_Code);
   if
   A_Security_Code = CURRENT_VALUE_OF.THE_SECURITY_CODE
 then
   The_State    := Disabled;
   The_Substate := Disabled;
 end if;
or
   DELAY_FOR(One_Minute).THE_CLOCK;
 end select;
end;
```

## 3.6 THE CONTROL MODEL

        The control model is the fourth of the five subassembly-level object-oriented models created during subassembly requirements analysis and logical design. The control model is typically developed simultaneously and iteratively with the state model and the timing model. It is derived from and must be consistent with the three previous models and any higher-level requirements allocated to the subassembly. It provides a dynamic view of (a) the subassembly, (b) its major behaviors (including scenarios and threads of control), and (c) the objects in the subassembly in terms of (i) the objects' operations, (ii) the control flows among the objects, (iii) the objects' attributes, and (iv) the data flows between the operations and the attribute stores. The control model of a single subassembly consists of the following information:

- For the subassembly—subassembly control flow diagram (CFD)
- For each major scenario or thread of control in the subassembly—behavior-level CFD
- Optionally, for each object and class in the subassembly—object-level or class-level CFD
- For each operation in the subassembly—specification and body

In order to develop the control model, the subassembly development team should first develop detailed *scenarios*[7] of both expected and error-handling threads of control among and within the objects and classes of the subassembly. They should then use these scenarios to analyze the associated messages and exceptions (i.e., control flows) among and within the objects, classes, and terminators. For each object in the subassembly, they should identify all hidden

- Messages:
  — sequential
  — synchronous (i.e., rendezvous)
    – standard
    – balking
    – timed
    – guarded
  — asynchronous
- Operations (i.e., methods)

Note that the analysis and logical design of synchronous message passing to avoid concurrency problems (e.g., starvation, deadlock, priority inversion, unnecessary polling) may involve a reversal of the direction of message passing. It may therefore require iterating back to correct the associated object and class interactions on SNs, IDs, and STDs.

## 3.6.1    Control Flow Diagrams (CFDs)

The subassembly development team should use the scenarios to develop one or more *object-oriented* CFDs. See Figure 3-30: Icons for Control Flow Diagrams (CFDs). The scope of each CFD may be as follows:

1. A *single object or class*—See Figure 3-31, which shows an example object-level CFD
2. A *scenario or thread of control involving multiple objects and classes within the subassembly*—see Figure 3-32, which shows an example CFD with primary and secondary threads of control that cause the signals of a street intersection to flash

---

[7] A scenario is a theoretically possible sequence of operation calls and/or exception flows among or within objects and classes.

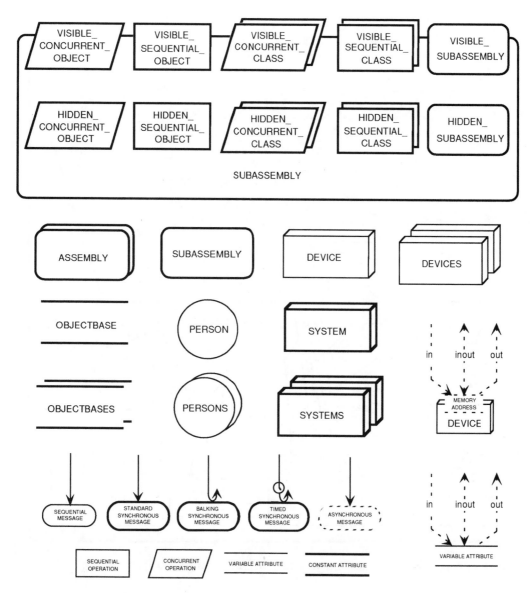

**Figure 3-30: Icons for Control Flow Diagrams (CFDs)**

3. *An entire subassembly*—see Figures 3-33, which shows an example subassembly CFD for an automatic carwash application.

Figure 3-31 shows an object-level CFD for THE_GUARD object in the ACCESS_CONTROL_FOR subassembly of the DOOR_MASTER assembly. It shows THE_GUARD object, the six synchronous messages it can receive from its five client and six server terminators, its one concurrent and six sequential operations, its two

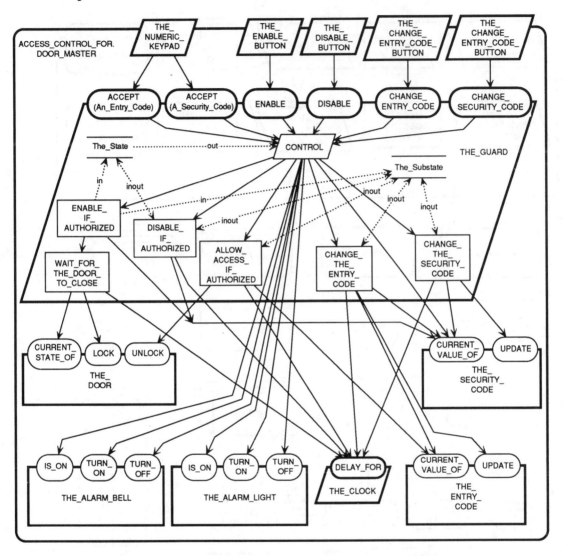

**Figure 3-31: CFD for** `THE_GUARD.ACCESS_CONTROL_FOR.DOOR_MASTER` **Object**

attributes, and the control flows and data flows associated with THE_GUARD object. Compare this figure with Figure 3-15, which shows the ID for the same subassembly. While IDs treated the objects as software black boxes, CFDs open up these black boxes and show the encapsulated operations and attributes and how they interact. Note that CASE tools should be able to generate skeleton CFDs automatically from the corresponding IDs.

Figure 3-33 shows a subassembly-level CFD for the WASHER subassembly of the CARWASH assembly.

Object-oriented CFDs are extensions of traditional DFDs [DeMarco 1978] and

CFDs [Ward and Mellor 1985]. Variants of CFDs are used, with slightly different notation, in several OOD methods. Booch's object model [1991], Shlaer and Mellor's process model [1988], and the functional model of Rumbaugh et al. [1991] use variants of CFDs.

Where cost-effective, the subassembly development team may choose to add data stores and data flows to the CFDs to make them into object-oriented control/data flow diagrams (OO C/DFDs). Note that an object or class may have more than one data store if it has more than one attribute. Identifying an object or class for each individual data store is often misleading. The OO C/DFD is used to identify hidden operations (via transforms) and attributes (via data flow arrows and stores). The OO DFD differs from traditional functional DFDs because

1. It is object-oriented rather than functionally decomposed.
2. Its scope is restricted to a *single* class, object, scenario involving or thread of control among objects and classes, or subassembly. Functional DFDs document only pieces of objects or classes, and pieces of the same class or object appear on more than one DFD.
3. All data stores and transforms are allocatable to the class or object as attributes and as operations, respectively.

CFDs are to object-oriented requirements analysis and logical design step what structure charts are to Structured Design [Yourdon and Constantine 1979].

### 3.6.2    Updated Bodies of the Objects and Classes

The bodies of the objects and classes should be updated with any attribute types, attributes, and operations identified as part of the control model.

### 3.6.3    Specification and Body of Each Operation

For each class and object of anonymous class in the subassembly, the development team should specify and logically design the specification and body of each operation. The operations can be specified formally or algorithmically in OOSDL. For example:

```
modifier operation  PUSH (An_Entry : in Entries)
                                        raise
                                        ENTRY_NOT_ADDED, INCORRECT_SIZE, IS_FULL
  parent object GENERIC_STACKS;
specification
  message PUSH (An_Entry : in Entries)

                                        raise
                                        ENTRY_NOT_ADDED, INCORRECT_SIZE, IS_FULL
                                        is sequential;
end;


operation  PUSH (An_Entry : in Entries)

                                        raise
                                        ENTRY_NOT_ADDED, INCORRECT_SIZE, IS_FULL
body
```

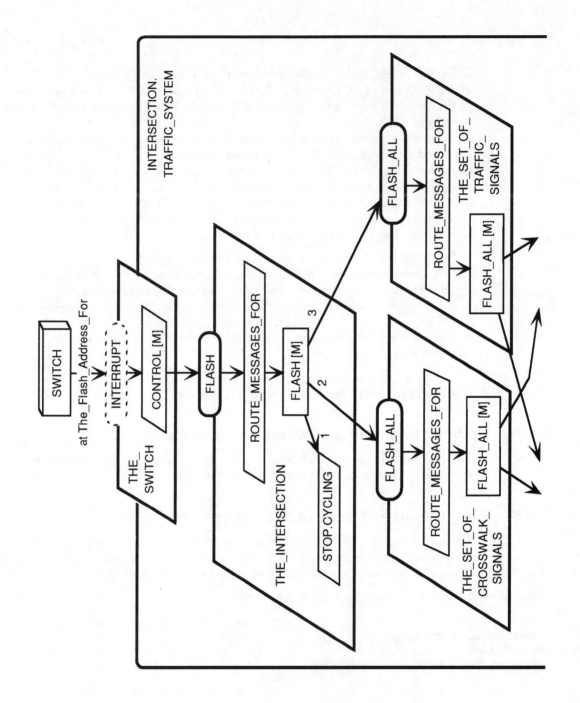

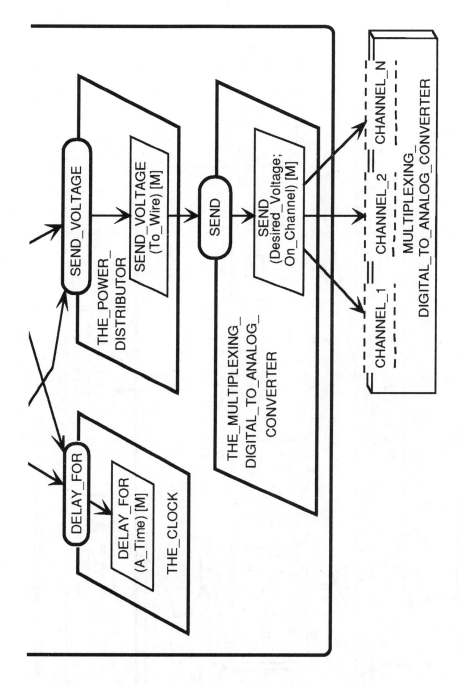

**Figure 3-32: Behavior-Level CFD for the FLASH Thread**

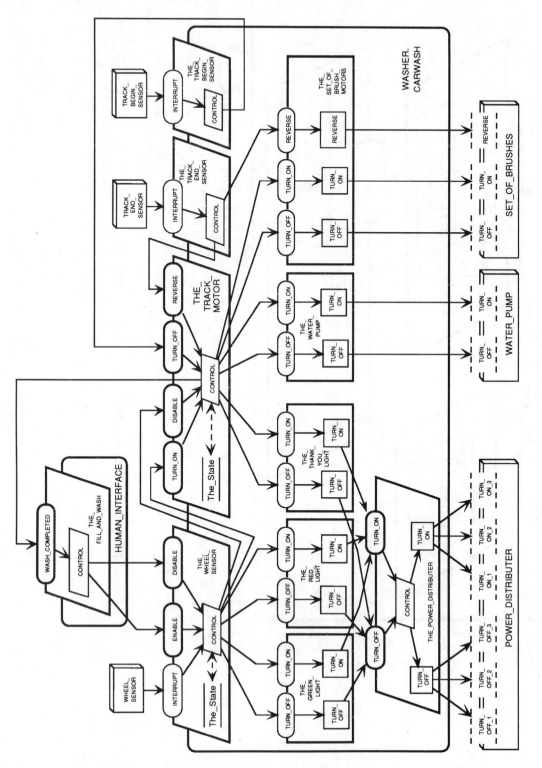

**Figure 3-33: Example CFD for the WASHER Subassembly**

```
preconditions
  require
    The_Size < The_Maximum_Size           else raise IS_FULL;
  end require;
postconditions
  require
    post(The_Size) <= The_Maximum_Size    else raise IS_FULL;
  end require;
  require
    post(The_Size) =  The_Size + 1        else raise INCORRECT_SIZE;
  end require;
require
post(The_Top)   =  The_Item              else raise ENTRY_NOT_ADDED;
end require;
end;
```

Operations may be specified algorithmically if preconditions and postconditions prove impractical. The logical design of operations should be done algorithmically. The CONTROL.THE_GUARD.ACCESS_CONTROL_FOR.DOOR_MASTER operation, when algorithmically specified and designed, has the following specification and body:

```
preserver operation  CONTROL is concurrent
  parent object THE_GUARD.ACCESS_CONTROL_FOR.DOOR_MASTER;
specification
  message ACCEPT(An_Entry_Code    : in Codes.THE_ENTRY_CODE)     is synchronous;
  message ACCEPT(A_Security_Code  : in Codes.THE_SECURITY_CODE)  is synchronous;
  message CHANGE_THE_ENTRY_CODE                                  is synchronous;
  message CHANGE_THE_SECURITY_CODE                               is synchronous;
  message DISABLE                                                is synchronous;
message ENABLE                                                   is synchronous;
end;

operation  CONTROL
  needs   THE_ALARM_BELL;
  needs   THE_ALARM_LIGHT;
  needs   THE_ENTRY_CODE;
  needs   THE_SECURITY_CODE;
body
statements
  FOREVER : loop
    FIRST : while The_State = Disabled loop
      receive ENABLE;
      ENABLE_IF_AUTHORIZED;
    end loop FIRST;
    SECOND : while The_State = Enabled loop
      select
        receive ACCEPT(An_Entry_Code);
        ALLOW_ACCESS_IF_AUTHORIZED
      or
        receive CHANGE_THE_ENTRY_CODE;
        CHANGE_THE_ENTRY_CODE;
      or
        receive CHANGE_THE_SECURITY_CODE;
        CHANGE_THE_SECURITY_CODE;
```

```
    or
      receive DISABLE;
      DISABLE_IF_AUTHORIZED;
    end select
  end loop SECOND;
 end loop FOREVER;
exception_handler
  when FAILURE_OCCURRED_IN.THE_DOOR then
  TURN_ON.THE_ALARM_BELL;
  TURN_ON.THE_ALARM_LIGHT;
  FAILURE : while IS_RINGING.THE_ALARM_BELL = True loop
   receive ACCEPT(A_Security_Code);
   if
    A_Security_Code = CURRENT_VALUE_OF.THE_SECURITY_CODE
   then
    TURN_OFF.THE_ALARM_BELL;
    TURN_OFF.THE_ALARM_LIGHT;
   end if;
  end loop FAILURE;
 end when;
end;
```

The ALLOW_ACCESS_IF_AUTHORIZED.THE_GUARD.ACCESS_CONTROL _FOR.DOOR_MASTER operation has the following specification and body, written in OOSDL:

```
modifier operation ALLOW_ACCESS_IF_AUTHORIZED
 parent object
  THE_GUARD.ACCESS_CONTROL_FOR.DOOR_MASTER;
specification
end;


operation ALLOW_ACCESS_IF_AUTHORIZED
 needs THE_ENTRY_CODE;
body
preconditions
 require
  The_State = Enabled and The_Substate = Standby
 else
  raise INCOMPATIBLE_STATE_IN;
 end require;
statements
 if
  An_Entry_Code = CURRENT_VALUE_OF.THE_ENTRY_CODE
 then
  UNLOCK.THE_DOOR;
  The_Substate := Waiting_For_The_Door_To_Close;
  WAIT_FOR_THE_DOOR_TO_CLOSE;
 end if;
end;
```

The CHANGE_THE_ENTRY_CODE.THE_GUARD.ACCESS_CONTROL_ FOR.DOOR_MASTER operation has the following specification and body, written in OOSDL:

```
modifier operation CHANGE_THE_ENTRY_CODE
 parent object THE_GUARD.ACCESS_CONTROL_FOR.DOOR_MASTER;
specification
 message ACCEPT(An_Entry_Code    : in Codes.THE_ENTRY_CODE)    is synchronous;
 message ACCEPT(A_Security_Code : in Codes.THE_SECURITY_CODE)    is synchronous;
end;


operation CHANGE_THE_ENTRY_CODE
 needs THE_ENTRY_CODE;
 needs THE_SECURITY_CODE;
body
preconditions
 require
  The_State = Enabled and The_Substate = Standby
 else
  raise INCOMPATIBLE_STATE_IN;
 end require;
statements
 The_Substate := Waiting_For_New_Entry_Code;
 select
  receive ACCEPT(A_Security_Code);
  if
   A_Security_Code = CURRENT_VALUE_OF.THE_SECURITY_CODE
  then
   select
    receive ACCEPT(An_Entry_Code);
    UPDATE(An_Entry_Code).THE_ENTRY_CODE
    The_Substate := Standby;
   or
    DELAY_FOR(One_Minute).THE_CLOCK;
    The_Substate := Standby;
   end select;
  end if;
 or
  DELAY_FOR(One_Minute).THE_CLOCK;
  The_Substate := Standby;
 end select;
end;
```

The specification and body of the CHANGE_THE_SECURITY_
CODE.THE_GUARD.ACCESS_CONTROL_FOR.DOOR_MASTER operation is
analogous to the CHANGE_THE_ENTRY_CODE operation.

The DISABLE_IF_AUTHORIZED.THE_GUARD.ACCESS_CONTROL_
FOR.DOOR_MASTER operation has the following specification and body, written in
OOSDL:

```
modifier operation DISABLE_IF_AUTHORIZED
 parent object THE_GUARD.ACCESS_CONTROL_FOR.DOOR_MASTER;
specification
 message ACCEPT(A_Security_Code : in Codes.THE_SECURITY_CODE) is synchronous;
end;
```

```
operation DISABLE_IF_AUTHORIZED
 needs THE_SECURITY_CODE;
body
preconditions
 require
  The_State = Enabled and The_Substate = Standby
 else
  raise INCOMPATIBLE_STATE_IN;
 end require;
statements
 select
  receive ACCEPT(A_Security_Code);
  if
   A_Security_Code = CURRENT_VALUE_OF.THE_SECURITY_CODE
  then
   The_State    := Disabled;
   The_Substate := Disabled;
  end if;
 or
  DELAY_FOR(One_Minute).THE_CLOCK;
 end select;
end;
```

The specification and body of the ENABLE_IF_AUTHORIZED.THE_
GUARD.ACCESS_CONTROL_FOR.DOOR_MASTER operation is analogous to that
of the DISABLE_IF_AUTHORIZED operation.

## 3.7  THE TIMING MODEL

The timing model is typically the last of the five subassembly-level object-oriented
models created during subassembly requirements analysis and logical design. It is
typically developed simultaneously and iteratively with the preceding state model and
control model. It provides a temporal view of the subassembly in terms of the timing
of the messages passed within and among objects. The timing model of a single
subassembly consists of the following information:

For the subassembly (where appropriate)

- Event or duration timing diagram (TD)
- Annotated ID
- Annotated STD
- Annotated CFD
- Timed message list

For each major scenario or thread of control in the subassembly (where appropriate)

- TD
- Annotated ID
- Annotated STD
- Annotated CFD
- Timed message list

For each object and class in the subassembly (where appropriate)

- TD
- Annotated ID
- Annotated STD
- Annotated CFD
- Timed message list

The timing model is the least understood and advanced of the object-oriented models and suffers from several serious limitations. Nontrivial software applications often have very complex temporal behavior, especially if both concurrency and asynchronous message passing occurs. Often, there is virtually an unlimited number of ways in which the system can behave in terms of the temporal sequencing of message passing. Software engineers must often limit their analysis to the most obvious or important scenarios and hope that their analysis generalizes to all scenarios. Thus, often, only a small percentage of the possible TDs are actually developed. Even so, the timing model is critical to many applications (e.g., embedded real-time systems) and is of great value during analysis, design, and testing.

### 3.7.1     Timing Diagrams (TDs)

A timing diagram (TD) is used to assess performance issues and to allocate timing goals and requirements to the interactions of the object and classes. It usually shows the entire subassembly if the subassembly is small enough to make a subassembly TD practical. Sometimes, a TD is also drawn for each major scenario or thread of control and each individual object and class with significant temporal behavior. The TD is used to provide a temporal overview of the subassembly and its component objects and classes. Specifically, event TDs show the existence and timing of messages among and within:

- Objects and classes
- The system, hardware, software, and people terminators

Figure 3-34 shows the event TD icons, and Figure 3-35 shows an example event TD. These TDs are read in temporal order from top to bottom.

The subassembly event TD is an enhanced Booch TD [1991], is object-oriented, and documents the subassembly behavior in terms of the timing of operation calls among the stubbed operations or the stubbed objects and the remaining classes and objects.

Duration TDs show the durations of the operations and the timing of the control flows (i.e., message passing and raising of exceptions). Duration TDs use different notation and are used to do timing budgets.

### 3.7.2     Annotated IDs, STDs, and CFDs

The subassembly development teams may choose to annotate the IDs, STDs, or CFDs with temporal information instead of creating TDs in order to document the temporal aspects of a scenario or thread of control. They may either annotate existing diagrams or annotate simplified diagrams that show only the relevant nodes and arcs. The

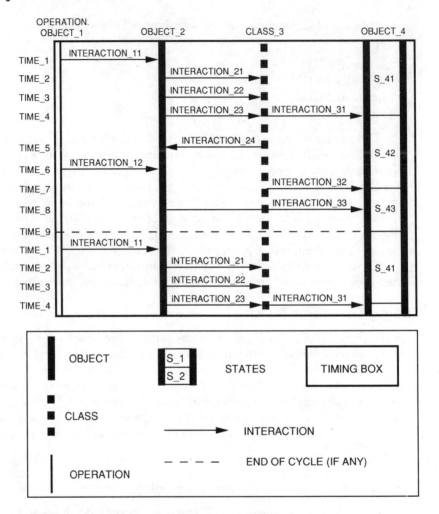

**Figure 3-34: Icons for Timing Diagrams (TDs)**

advantage of using annotated diagrams is the elimination of two additional diagram types (i.e., TDs). The disadvantage is that the linear aspect of time is lost in the topology of the other diagrams, and it is difficult to tell at a glance the order in which events should occur.

For example, Figure 3-36 shows an annotated ID, Figure 3-37 shows an annotated STD, and Figure 3-38 shows an annotated CFD.

Figure 3-37 shows an annotated STD for THE_SET_OF_TRAFFIC_SIGNALS object, which has the transitions among states annotated with the times when they should occur.

Figure 3-38 shows a partial, annotated object-level CFD for the CYCLING operation of THE_INTERSECTION object, which has the messages annotated with the times when they should be passed.

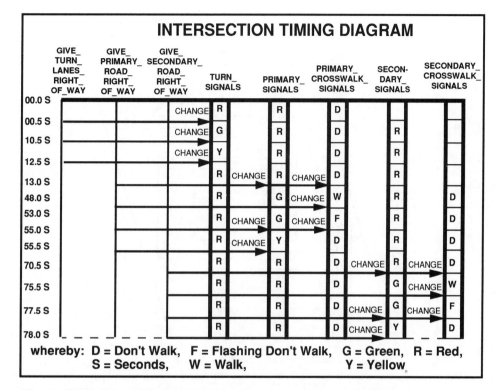

**Figure 3-35: Event Timing Diagram for THE_INTERSECTION Object**

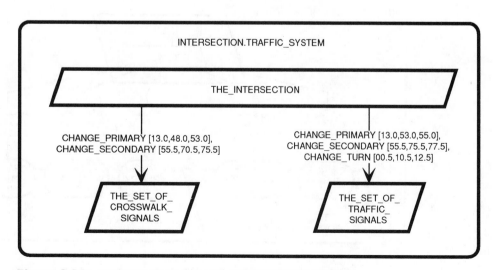

**Figure 3-36: Annotated ID for THE_INTERSECTION Object**

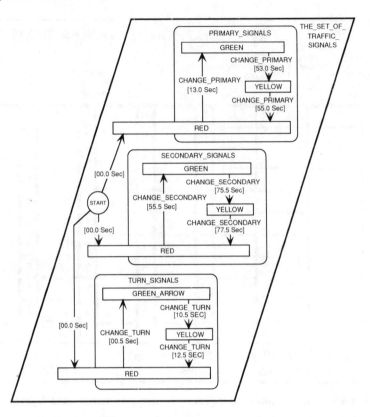

**Figure 3-37: Annotated STD for for THE_SET_OF_TRAFFIC_SIGNALS Object**

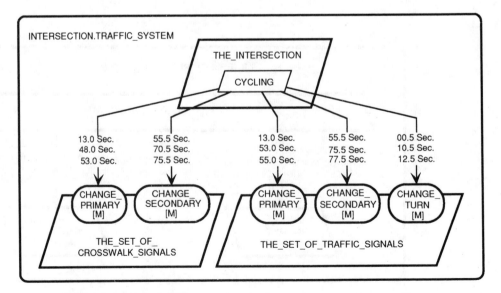

**Figure 3-38: Annotated CFD**

| Sec | Sender | Message | Receiver | Resulting State |
|-----|--------|---------|----------|-----------------|
| 00.5 | THE_INTERSECTION | CHANGE_TURN | THE_SET_OF_TRAFFIC_SIGNALS | GREEN_ARROW |
| 10.5 | THE_INTERSECTION | CHANGE_TURN | THE_SET_OF_TRAFFIC_SIGNALS | YELLOW |
| 12.5 | THE_INTERSECTION | CHANGE_TURN | THE_SET_OF_TRAFFIC_SIGNALS | RED |
| 13.0 | THE_INTERSECTION | CHANGE_PRIMARY | THE_SET_OF_TRAFFIC_SIGNALS | GREEN |
| 13.0 | THE_INTERSECTION | CHANGE_PRIMARY | THE_SET_OF_CROSSWALK_SIGNALS | WALK |
| 48.0 | THE_INTERSECTION | CHANGE_PRIMARY | THE_SET_OF_CROSSWALK_SIGNALS | FLASHING_DONT_WALK |
| 53.0 | THE_INTERSECTION | CHANGE_PRIMARY | THE_SET_OF_TRAFFIC_SIGNALS | YELLOW |
| 53.0 | THE_INTERSECTION | CHANGE_PRIMARY | THE_SET_OF_CROSSWALK_SIGNALS | DONT_WALK |
| 55.0 | THE_INTERSECTION | CHANGE_PRIMARY | THE_SET_OF_TRAFFIC_SIGNALS | RED |
| 55.5 | THE_INTERSECTION | CHANGE_SECONDARY | THE_SET_OF_TRAFFIC_SIGNALS | GREEN |
| 55.5 | THE_INTERSECTION | CHANGE_SECONDARY | THE_SET_OF_CROSSWALK_SIGNALS | WALK |
| 70.5 | THE_INTERSECTION | CHANGE_SECONDARY | THE_SET_OF_CROSSWALK_SIGNALS | FLASHING_DONT_WALK |
| 75.5 | THE_INTERSECTION | CHANGE_SECONDARY | THE_SET_OF_TRAFFIC_SIGNALS | YELLOW |
| 75.5 | THE_INTERSECTION | CHANGE_SECONDARY | THE_SET_OF_CROSSWALK_SIGNALS | DONT_WALK |
| 77.5 | THE_INTERSECTION | CHANGE_SECONDARY | THE_SET_OF_TRAFFIC_SIGNALS | RED |

**Figure 3-39: Timed Message List for the BUSY_STREETS Scenario**

### 3.7.3    Timed Message Lists

The subassembly development teams generate a timed message list for each scenario, which lists each relevant message and its associated timing requirements. Each event occurs in a specific order or at a specific time and consists of a message sent from a sender to a receiver (which may be the same). The resulting state of the receiver may also be listed.

For example, Figure 3-39 shows a timed message list for the BUSY_STREETS scenario of the INTERSECTION.TRAFFIC_SYSTEM subassembly.

## 3.8  CHAPTER REFERENCES

[Booch 1991] Grady Booch, *Object-Oriented Design with Applications*, Menlo Park, CA, Benjamin Cummings, 1991.

[Chen 1976] Peter Pin-Shan Chen, "The Entity-Relationship Model—Toward a Unified View of Data," ACM *Transactions on Database Systems*, 1(1), 9-36, March 1976.

[Coad and Yourdon 1989] Peter Coad and Edward Yourdon, *OORA—Object-Oriented Requirements Analysis*, Englewood Cliffs, NJ, Prentice Hall,1989.

[Colbert 1989] Ed Colbert, "The Object-Oriented Software Development Method: A Practical Approach to Object-Oriented Development," *Proceedings of TRI-Ada'89 — Ada Technology in Context: Application, Development, and Deployment, 23-26 October 1989*, 400-415, 1989.

[DeMarco 1978] Tom DeMarco, *Structured Analysis and System Specification*, New York, NY, Yourdon Press/Prentice Hall, 1978.

[Harrell 1988] David Harell, "On Visual Formalisms", *Communications of the ACM*, 31 (5), pages 514-530, May 1976.

[Rumbaugh et al. 1991] James Rumbaugh, Michael Blaha, William Premerlani, Frederick Eddy, and William Lorensen, *Object-Oriented Modeling and Design*, Englewood Cliffs, NJ, Prentice Hall, 1991.

[Shlaer and Mellor 1988] Sally Shlaer and Stephen J. Mellor, *Object-Oriented Systems Analysis, Modeling the World in Data*, Englewood Cliffs, NJ, Yourdon Press, 1988.

[Ward and Mellor 1985] Paul Ward and Stephen J. Mellor, *Structured Development for Real-Time Systems, Volume 1: Introduction and Tools, Volume 2: Essential Modelling Techniques, Volume 3: Implementation Modelling Techniques*, New York, NY, Yourdon Press,1985.

[Yourdon and Constantine 1979] Edward Yourdon and Larry Constantine, *Structured Design*, New York, NY, Prentice Hall, 1979.

# Chapter 4

# Identification of Objects, Classes, and Subassemblies

## 4.1 IDENTIFICATION OF OBJECTS AND CLASSES

One of the most important and difficult steps in any object-oriented software development method is that of identifying objects and classes of objects. It is vitally important because the requirements specification, design, and code will consist of interacting objects and classes, and any mistakes in proper identification will have a significant impact on the quality of the resulting software. It is difficult (at least for most beginners) because it requires both knowledge and skill, and it typically requires at least 3 to 6 months of practice for the necessary skills to mature, depending on the developer's aptitude, attitude (toward object orientation), and amount of on-the-job training and experience.

Identification of objects and classes should not be difficult. After all, we deal with thousands of real-world objects and classes each day of our lives, and software objects and classes are merely models of application-domain objects and classes. Making mental models and using abstraction are standard human approaches for dealing with the complexity of everyday life. Even very young children understand and effectively deal with models of real-world entities. For example, a child's doll is merely a model of a real baby. It has attributes that are either constant (e.g., size, hair and skin color) or variable (e.g., battery level and relative state of newness or disrepair), operations (e.g., move arms, move legs, say "mama"), and exceptions (e.g., broken joint, battery drained). Therefore, if software engineers understand their application domain and the identification of objects and classes requires merely the identification of relevant models of application-domain entities, then why is identification so difficult?

The biggest problem is that most software engineers have spent years practicing a much less natural and less powerful approach to software development: functional decomposition. Because of the extreme limitations of early computers and languages and the need to deal with them in terms of their procedural step-by-step modes of operation, early methods forced developers essentially to think as if they were computers. Because of human inertia, this is often a hard habit to break. Although thinking in terms of objects is easy in everyday life, thinking in terms of their software analogs often seems unnatural until the skill redevelops. Although "the objects are just there for the picking" [Meyer 1988], developers are often blind to them when they first learn OOD because they are too accustomed to functional designs and building blocks. Developers are often unsure of just what software objects and classes are, and they are not always sure that something meets the definition of an object or class, even when they know the definition.

Luckily, over the past 10 years, software engineers have developed numerous, often indirect approaches to combat this temporary blindness. If one is unsure of just what an object or class is, there nevertheless often exists a one-to-one mapping between objects and classes and something else that we *can* identify. If developers find the one, they have indirectly found the other. This allows the object-oriented neophyte to do useful work as he or she is developing the necessary skills and experience prior to achieving the paradigm shift. Unfortunately, many of these approaches also have significant risks, and software engineers must be aware of these risks in order to manage them. Because the mapping is not always one-to-one, using indirect approaches can be unreliable and can produce numerous false-positive identifications. This is especially important early on, when a little knowledge is a dangerous thing, and functional entities are likely to masquerade as objects and classes. Because of advances in identification techniques, some approaches are now relatively obsolete, whereas others are currently state-of-the-art. Different methodologists have their own favorite approaches, and so particular methods are tightly coupled to only a few approaches. Most books and articles teach only a small number of identification techniques, and some approaches are rarely taught. Some approaches are well suited for object-oriented design but only of minimal use during object-oriented domain analysis (OODA) or requirements analysis (OORA). Some approaches are easy and safe to use but only identify a small number of the most obvious objects and classes.

Multiple sources of information can be used to identify objects and classes. Objects and classes can be found in system and software requirements specifications (SRSs), system and software design documents (SDDs), and data dictionaries, although the information concerning any one object or class may be scattered throughout the source document if functional decomposition was used to create it. Information can be obtained from users, customers, and application-domain experts and from the software engineer's own experience. Software engineers can often use *browsers* (i.e., CASE tools used to search reuse repositories and class libraries).

Once some objects and classes are identified, they can be documented in many ways. Software engineers can use graphics (such as SNs and IDs), CRC cards, Post-it® Notes as object and class stickers, and tabular forms such as description tables. By using these documentation means, software engineers can then identify additional objects and classes by looking for missing interactions and players in the current set of collaborating objects and classes.

Objects and classes can also be identified during one or more steps of different overall development processes. They can be identified informally as part of a brain-storming session or more formally during one or more steps of an OOD method. They can be identified in either a big bang or a locally recursive manner during the requirements analysis and design phases of the traditional waterfall development cycle. They can also be identified in a globally recursive manner during the requirements analysis and design activities of a recursive, incremental development process.

This chapter provides numerous ways to identify objects and classes for several reasons. It is not hard to find some objects and classes, but it is hard to find *all* relevant objects and classes. Finding only tangible objects and classes is relatively easy, but finding the intangible objects and classes is harder. As Ken Auer [1991] notes, "Finding objects is not hard; finding *good* objects is." No single cookbook approach can be used to find all objects and classes, nor is any approach a substitute for adequate training, experience, and practice.

This chapter discusses all major, and several minor, approaches currently used to identify objects and classes. These approaches may be divided into three main categories: recommended, traditional, and miscellaneous. *Recommended approaches* are the most powerful and state-of-the-art, although they often require significant training and experience to use effectively. *Traditional approaches* (circa 1980–1986) are relatively obsolete, highly indirect, and are easy to use and misuse, especially by beginners. *Miscellaneous approaches* are often of limited scope and value, though they are sometimes useful.

1. Recommended approaches
   - Using object abstraction
     — Using the types of the modeled entities
     — Using the definitions of objects and classes
     — Using object decomposition
   - Using inheritance
     — Using generalization
     — Using subclasses
   - Using OODA
   - Using repositories of previously developed software
     — Reusing application frameworks
     — Reusing class hierarchies
     — Reusing individual objects and classes
       - Using specification and design languages
       - Using personal experience
2. Traditional approaches
   - Using nouns
   - Using traditional DFDs

—Using terminators on context diagrams (CDs)
—Using data stores on DFDs
—Using complex data flows on DFDs

3. Miscellaneous approaches
- Using abstract data types and abstract state machines
- Using states
- Using resources
  —Using attributes
  —Using operations
  —Using exceptions
- Using requirements
- Using CRC cards
- Using entities on ERA diagrams
- Using object-oriented diagrams
  —Using nodes on SNs
  —Using nodes on IDs

Some readers may question the inclusion of all of the foregoing approaches in this chapter. After all, many are of limited value, some have numerous associated risks, and others are clearly poor. Why not just provide the one or two best approaches and leave it at that?

There are several important reasons to include this breadth of approaches: For one thing, all of these approaches are in current use in industry, to varying degrees, and software engineers should therefore be aware of them, and especially aware of their limitations and risks. Also, when learning a new paradigm and method, it often helps to learn several ways of doing the same thing. Not only does this provide flexibility and reality cross-checks, but also different developers often have different preferences and learn and understand some approaches more easily than others. By learning the limitations of weaker approaches, one may better appreciate the power of the more advanced ones. Every approach can be misused and often is. As some anonymous sages have observed, "When you only have a hammer, everything starts to look like a nail," and "a craftsman is known by his tools." Thus, just as master craftpersons have many tools in their toolboxes, so software engineers should know many ways of identifying objects and classes, even if they usually rely on only a small percentage of them. Therefore, software engineers should first learn many different approaches, including their strengths and weaknesses and then choose and practice those approaches they think best.

## 4.1.1    Recommended Approaches

These approaches are the main ones in the arsenal of the experienced software engineer. They are powerful and can be used in most situations to identify all, or almost all, of the relevant objects and classes. Unlike most of the other approaches, they produce few misidentifications because they are direct or are based on previous work. Although often difficult for the novice, these approaches should be studied carefully and practiced until mastered.

### 4.1.1.1  Using Object Abstraction

#### 4.1.1.1.1  Using the Entities to be Modeled

This approach is the preferred choice of the experienced software engineer and recognizes that software engineers should identify the application-domain entities to be modeled before they identify the associated objects and classes:

1. Identify individual (or sets of) important systems devices, persons, roles, organizations, locations, events, and interactions that must be modeled by the software.
2. Identify the corresponding objects and classes.

This approach has powerful advantages. It is natural, quite direct, and highly reliable. It also intuitively reinforces the concept of an object and is consistent with the next approach, "Using the Definitions." This approach is advocated by ADM3, as well as by such major methods as Coad and Yourdon's Object-Oriented Analysis [1990] and Shlaer and Mellor's Object-Oriented Systems Analysis [1988].

Unfortunately, this approach requires a significant paradigm shift to the object-oriented mindset, although this paradigm shift should be the main goal of on-the-job training. It also tends to underemphasize all objects and classes other than terminators and tangible objects and classes which are the easiest entities to identify.

For example, consider an assembly of software that is to implement the following capabilities:

The digital thermostat (DT) shall start in the off state. The DT shall toggle between the off and on states each time the user presses the on/off button. The DT shall start in the Celsius mode. When the DT is in the on state, the DT shall toggle between the Celsius and Fahrenheit modes each time the user presses the mode button. When the DT transitions from the off to the on state, the desired temperature of the DT shall start with the value of 21 Celsius. When the DT is in the on state, the desired temperature of the DT shall increase by 1 degree each time the user presses the increment temperature button, until a maximum of 32 degrees Celsius (when in Celsius mode) or 90 degrees Fahrenheit (when in Fahrenheit mode). When the DT is in the on state, the desired temperature of the DT shall decrease by 1 degree each time the user presses the decrement temperature button until a minimum of 4 degrees Celsius (when in Celsius mode) or 40 degrees Fahrenheit (when in Fahrenheit mode). When the DT is in the on state, the DT shall sample members of a set of temperature sensors, at least once, every 10 seconds. The range of each temperature sensor shall be from 0 through 37 degrees Celsius, with an accuracy of 0.1 degrees Celsius. When in the on state, the DT shall control an air conditioner and furnace in order to keep the mean temperature of a room within 2 degrees of the desired temperature, as set by a user. When in the on state and functioning properly, the DT shall display the two-digit desired and mean temperatures, followed by a "C" for Celsius or an "F" for Fahrenheit on the desired temperature display and the mean temperature display, respectively. When in the off state or when malfunctioning, the DT shall turn off the air conditioner, furnace, desired temperature display, and mean temperature display.

Using this approach, one obtains the following initial mapping between entities to be modeled and their corresponding objects:

| *Application-Domain Entity* | *Corresponding Object* |
|---|---|
| air conditioner | THE_AIR_CONDITIONER |
| decrement temperature button | THE_DECREMENT_TEMPERATURE_BUTTON |
| desired temperature | THE_DESIRED_TEMPERATURE |
| desired temperature display | THE_DESIRED_TEMPERATURE_DISPLAY |
| digital thermostat | THE_DIGITAL_THERMOSTAT |
| furnace | THE_FURNACE |
| increment temperature button | THE_INCREMENT_TEMPERATURE_BUTTON |
| mean temperature | THE_MEAN_TEMPERATURE |
| mean temperature display | THE_MEAN_TEMPERATURE_DISPLAY |
| mode | THE_MODE |
| mode button | THE_MODE_BUTTON |
| on/off button | THE_ON_OFF_BUTTON |
| set of temperature sensors | THE_TEMPERATURE_SENSORS |

### 4.1.1.1.2  Using the Definitions of Objects and Classes

This approach assumes that the most effective approach is the direct one. It also assumes that the software engineers have adequate experience in identifying objects and classes:

> Directly use object abstraction, application domain knowledge, and the definition of "object" and "class" to intuitively identify them in the same way that an experienced developer would recognize functional and process abstractions.

The primary benefit is that this is a very natural, direct, and effective approach. This approach provides the best partitioning of the requirements into object-oriented capabilities. When used properly, this approach produces the fewest false-positive identifications.

This approach has few limitations, but it requires significant training, practice, intuition, and experience. To be effective, this approach requires a significant paradigm shift, which can take 3–6 months of on-the-job training. Finally, there is little or no tool support because the tools are designed only to document the results of this step. Using this approach, one should obtain the same initial objects (e.g., THE_AIR_CONDITIONER) as before because each object meets the definition of an object (i.e., an abstraction of an application-domain entity).

### 4.1.1.1.3  Using Object Decomposition

This approach assumes that many objects and classes are aggregates of component objects and classes, that some of these aggregate objects and classes have already been identified, and that using object decomposition is a good way to identify these component objects and classes:

1. Look for aggregate objects and classes.
2. Use object decomposition to identify their component objects and classes.

This approach has some advantages. It is the natural way to deal with aggregate objects and classes. Composition diagrams (CMDs; see Figure 4-1) can be used to document object and class decomposition.

Unfortunately, only a small percentage of objects and classes are typically aggregates, so that this approach can only be used to identify a small percentage of the objects and classes. Because real aggregates physically contain their components, beginning designers and coders often nest the component software objects and classes inside their associated software aggregates instead of using dependency relationships. This can lead to problems involving recompilation, reuse, and maintenance.

As an example of this approach, one notes that each instance of a traffic-signals class contains a yellow-light object, a red-light object, and either a green-arrow object or a green-light object, as depicted on Figure 4-1: Example Composition Diagram (CMD).

### 4.1.1.2  Using Inheritance

#### 4.1.1.2.1   Using Generalization

This approach assumes that objects are identified prior to their classes, that each object must be an instance of some class, and that commonalities among related objects can be used to generalize classes:

1. Identify all *objects*.
2. Look for collections of two or more objects that share the same attributes, operations, and exceptions.
3. Generalize these common resources to identify a *class*, the instances of which make up the collection.

The primary benefit of this approach is that it promotes reuse and supports the development of one or more classification hierarchies.

#### 4.1.1.2.2   Using Subclasses

This is a very popular approach to the identification of classes with software engineers experienced in using inheritance; it assumes that separate classes often contain resources in common and that they can be changed into subclasses that inherit the common resources from a common superclass:

1. Identify classes that share common resources (i.e., attribute types, attributes, operations, exceptions, and component objects).
2. Factor out these common resources to produce a common abstract superclass and new simpler subclasses.

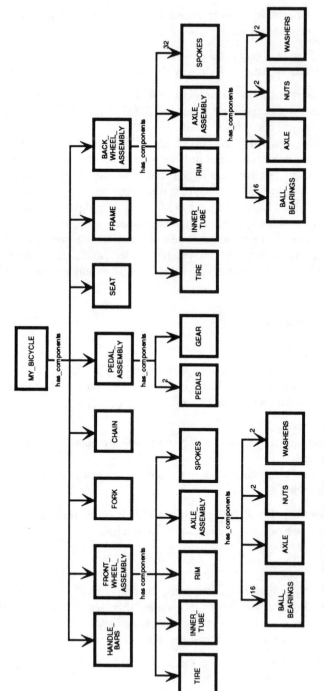

**Figure 4-1: Example Composition Diagram (CMD)**

The primary benefit of this approach is that it promotes reuse and supports the development of one or more classification hierarchies.

This approach has drawbacks: (1) When misused, it often leads to unmaintainable and opaque classes that reuse random unrelated capabilities that do not logically belong to subclasses of the same superclass. (2) It also limits encapsulation and may produce inappropriate or excessive inheritance coupling.

### 4.1.1.3  Using Object-Oriented Domain Analysis (OODA)

This enhancement of the "Using Personal Experience" approach (see 4.1.1.6) assumes that relevant OODA has been previously performed:

1. Analyze the results of previously performed OODA of the same application domain.
2. Reuse (with or without modification) objects and classes previously identified during OODA.

This approach naturally tends to produce highly reusable objects and classes that maximize cohesion while minimizing message and inheritance coupling. This approach thus tends to identify the best objects and classes. By building on previous experience, this approach provides a reasonable "reality check" on the current project and often improves the quality of the identified objects and classes because they are based on ones that have been previously built and tested. Many relevant objects and classes may be found if the OODA was complete and relevant. Considerable time and effort may be saved using this approach.

Unfortunately, even this approach has limitations. Obviously, adequate relevant OODA must be completed prior to the use of this approach. Yet OODA is often incomplete or not performed at all. The domain must also be relatively well documented and understood by the software engineers who will reuse the previously identified objects and classes. Finally, the results of OODA might not be tailored adequately for the project at hand. It must be easier to reuse than to reinvent, and the not-invented-here (NIH) syndrome must be successfully combated (e.g., with appropriate incentives).

### 4.1.1.4  Using Repositories of Previously Developed Software

Many objects and classes can be identified by browsing the entries in reuse repositories. Software engineers can look for relevant reusable application frameworks, class hierarchies, or individual objects and classes.

The three approaches based on using existing repositories have several common advantages. Like the approach using OODA, these three approaches naturally tend to produce highly reusable objects and classes that maximize cohesion while minimizing message and inheritance coupling. They thus tend to identify the best objects and classes. By building on previous experience, these approaches provide a reasonable reality check on the current project and often improve the quality of the identified objects and classes because they are based on ones that have been previously built and tested. By reusing pretested and preapproved objects and classes, these approaches produce more standardized objects and classes than do other approaches. Many relevant objects and classes may be found or derived if the repositories are complete and relevant, and significant time and effort may be saved.

Unfortunately, there are general limitations to the use of repositories. Clearly, the developers must have access to one or more existing reuse repositories. Even so, the existing repositories might not contain all of the needed entries relevant to the current application. In addition, the entries in the repository may be hard to match to the current application (e.g., because repository tools may be missing or because their names may not match those required for the current application). Also, those objects and classes that are identified may need to be tailored for the current application. This approach therefore does not help if one is developing one's first object-oriented application. As noted previously, it must be easier to reuse than to reinvent, and the "Not Invented Here (NIH)" syndrome must be successfully combated (e.g., with appropriate incentives). Existing classes may need to be parameterized, or new objects and classes may need to be derived for the current application.

### 4.1.1.4.1   Reusing Application Frameworks

This approach is an enhancement to the previous using-OODA approach for the identification of objects and classes. It assumes that OODA has been previously used to create one or more application frameworks that contain reusable objects and classes. An *application framework* is a reusable, application-domain-specific application template consisting of one or more objects, classes, and/or subassemblies that implement some common capabilities. To use this approach, the development team must:

1. Identify one or more relevant application frameworks in the same application domain.
2. Reuse (with or without modification) objects and classes from these previously developed application frameworks.

This approach has additional limitations in addition to those listed for OODA and repositories. One or more relevant application frameworks must have been developed previously, stored in the appropriate repository, and then identified by the current software engineers. Not all needed objects and classes may exist in the application framework(s) examined.

### 4.1.1.4.2   Reusing Class Hierarchies

This approach assumes that a reuse repository with relevant reusable class hierarchies has been developed and is accessible by the software engineers:

1. Examine the reuse repository for relevant class hierarchies that contain classes that can be reused, either with or without modification.

2. Group common attributes and operations to create abstract classes and supply generic formal parameters to parameterized classes as necessary.

This approach has several benefits, in addition to the general benefits listed above. First, it is a natural approach when using object-oriented programming languages (OOPLs) such as Smalltalk. Also, many relevant (sub)classes may be found or derived if the classification hierarchies are complete and relevant. Further, this approach maximizes the benefits of inheritance.

This approach also has additional limitations beyond those involving frameworks and repositories. One or more relevant classification hierarchies must be accessible to the developers, and even then existing classification hierarchies might not be relevant to the current application. In addition, existing classes may need to be parameterized, new subclasses may need to be derived for the current application, and new classes may need to be developed, beyond those in the classification hierarchies examined.

### 4.1.1.4.3   Reusing Individual Objects and Classes

This approach assumes that a reuse repository with relevant reusable objects and classes has been developed and is accessible by the software engineers:

1. Examine the reuse repository for relevant objects and classes that can be reused, either with or without modification.
2. Supply generic formal parameters to parameterized classes, as necessary.

This approach has additional limitations. One or more relevant reusable objects and classes must have been developed previously and must be identified by the current software engineers.

## 4.1.1.5  Using Specification and Design Languages

This approach assumes that the developers are incrementally developing subassemblies, using a recursive development method such as the one recommended by this book. Any nonterminal subassembly, by definition, contains one or more components that depend on (e.g., need to send messages to) one or more components in one or more child subassemblies at the next-lower level of abstraction. When the current nonterminal subassembly is being developed, these lower-level child subassemblies do not yet exist. The current components that depend on components in the child subassemblies must therefore temporarily remain incomplete because the current components refer to as-yet-unidentified objects or classes in these child subassemblies. The specification or design of these incomplete components may be used to identify lower-level objects and classes that must export the needed resources. To implement this approach, the developers:

1. Identify one or more objects or classes in the current nonterminal subassembly that must remain temporarily incomplete because they depend on one or more as-yet-unidentified objects or classes in child subassemblies.

2. Develop a skeleton specification and/or design for the stubbed-out objects and classes (or their relevant operations), using either (1) a narrative English description (i.e., the "using nouns" approach [Abbott 1983]), (2) an object-oriented specification language and design language, such as OOSDL, or (3) an appropriate program design language (PDL) such as Eiffel or Ada.[1] In this case, some objects and classes in the child subassemblies will be named in the English description, specification language, or the PDL.

This approach has several benefits: It is the primary approach used by most OOD methods, and it naturally supports the incremental identification of objects and classes. It also identifies the most important objects and classes in the child subassembly, and it can be either informal with narrative English or formal with a specification language.

There are, however, some risks that must be addressed. This approach can only be used with child subassemblies and only identifies the exported objects and classes of the child subassembly. Because it cannot be used to identify the components of the initial subassemblies, it cannot be used to identify all objects and classes.

As an example of this approach, assume that the five objects in the parent subassembly have already been identified and that the operation, MAINTAIN.THE_DESIRED_FLOW, must be stubbed and depends upon some as-yet-unidentified objects in an as-yet-unidentified child subassembly. See Figure 4-2. The two objects, THE_ACTUAL_FLOW and THE_FLOW_CONTROL_VALVE, may be identified using this approach.

The following is an example of this approach, using narrative English, combined with Abbott's "using nouns" approach. The newly identified objects are listed in bold.

As long as THE_DESIRED_FLOW object is in the ENABLED state, the MAINTAIN. THE_DESIRED_FLOW operation shall do the following: It shall get the current value of THE_DESIRED_FLOW_POTENTIOMETER and convert it to the current value of THE_DESIRED_FLOW. It shall then update THE_DESIRED_FLOW_DISPLAY with the current value of THE_DESIRED_FLOW. If the current value of THE_DESIRED_FLOW is above the maximum safe value, then it shall sound THE_DESIRED_FLOW_ALARM. It shall get the current value of **THE_ACTUAL_FLOW**. If the current value of **THE_ACTUAL_FLOW** is more than .01 meters per second less than the current value of THE_DESIRED_FLOW, then it shall open **THE_FLOW_CONTROL_VALVE** 5 degrees. If the current value of **THE_ACTUAL_FLOW** is more than .01 meters per second more than the current value of THE_DESIRED_FLOW, then it shall close **THE_FLOW_CONTROL_VALVE** 5 degrees. It shall then delay for 1 second and repeat this sequence of actions.

The following is an example of this approach applied to the same stubbed operation MAINTAIN.THE_DESIRED_FLOW, using OOSDL for this approach:

---

[1] Although Ada83 is an class-based, rather than object-oriented, programming language, it strongly supports software-engineering principles and the development of large complex applications (unlike Smalltalk and C++) and has been used numerous times to produce excellent object-based designs.

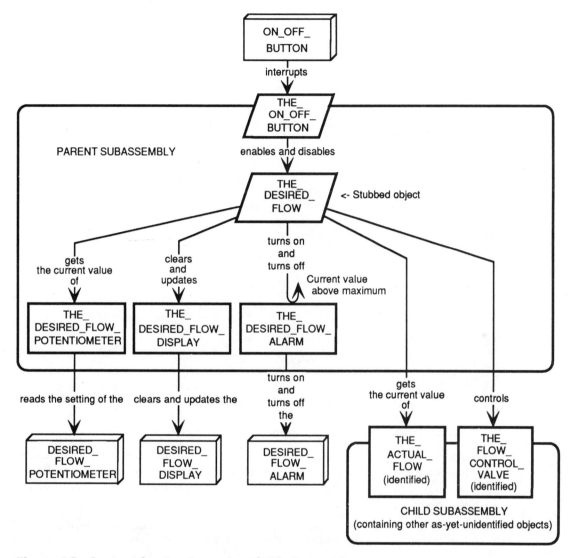

**Figure 4-2: Context for the Examples of this Approach**

```
operation MAINTAIN
 parent object THE_DESIRED_FLOW;
 needs THE_ACTUAL_FLOW.CHILD_SUBASSEMBLY;
 needs THE_DESIRED_FLOW_ALARM;
 needs THE_DESIRED_FLOW_DISPLAY;
 needs THE_DESIRED_FLOW_POTENTIOMETER;
 needs THE_FLOW_CONTROL_VALVE.CHILD_SUBASSEMBLY;
```

```
body
statements
 FOREVER : loop
  INNER : while The_State = Enabled loop
   The_Current_Value_Of :=
                    CONVERT(CURRENT_VALUE_OF.THE_DESIRED_FLOW_POTENTIOMETER);
   UPDATE(An_Amount := The_Current_Value_Of).THE_DESIRED_FLOW_DISPLAY;
   if -- The_Current_Value_Of.THE_DESIRED_FLOW is too low.
    The_Current_Value_Of > The_Maximum_Safe_Value
   then
    SOUND.THE_DESIRED_FLOW_ALARM;
   end if;
   if
    The_Current_Value_Of.THE_ACTUAL_FLOW -- is too low
    < The_Current_Value_Of - The_Maximum_Difference
   then
    OPEN(An_Angle := Five_Degrees).THE_FLOW_CONTROL_VALVE;
   end if;
   if
    The_Current_Value_Of.THE_ACTUAL_FLOW -- is too high
    > The_Current_Value_Of - The_Maximum_Difference
   then
    OPEN(An_Angle := Five_Degrees).THE_FLOW_CONTROL_VALVE;
   end if;
   DELAY(The_Delay_Amount).THE_CLOCK; -- one second.
  end loop INNER;
  DELAY(The_Minimum_Delay_Amount).THE_CLOCK ;
 end loop FOREVER;
end;
```

### 4.1.1.6 Using Personal Experience

This approach to the identification of objects and classes will eventually become more popular once more software engineers gain experience using object-oriented software. It assumes that the software engineers have previously developed one or more relevant objects and classes:

> **Identify objects and classes that correspond to the ones that have been identified previously on similar projects in the same application domain.**

The primary benefit of this approach is that it comes naturally to the software engineer and that it can be used by any software engineer with previous experience in the application domain. By building on previous experience, this approach provides a reasonable "reality check" on the current project and often improves the quality of the identified objects and classes because they are based on ones that have been previously built and tested.

This approach has many drawbacks. First of all, it assumes *relevant* previous experience and cannot be used for an initial object-oriented project. Because past experience is often with functional-decomposition projects and the first few objects and classes that an engineer identifies and develops tend to be suboptimal, past experience may be of limited value and possibly even misleading. This approach is very informal, and different software engineers may identify quite different objects and classes, given the same starting information. This approach may not minimize message and inheritance coupling. Finally, this approach is "not *objective* but subjective" [van der Loo 1992] and will not produce consistent results across developers.

## 4.1.2    Traditional Approaches

These approaches were developed between 1980 and 1986, and they were the main approaches used by the first two generations of object-oriented design methods. For the most part, they are indirect and had a large number of limitations and risks. They are primarily included as fallback approaches and as crutches for novices prior to their making the paradigm shift to object-oriented thinking.

### 4.1.2.1  Using Nouns

This is the oldest approach. Pioneered by Russell J. Abbott [1983], it was expanded and popularized by Grady Booch [1983] in the classic, *Software Engineering with Ada*. This approach became very popular between 1983 and 1986 and was included in many first-generation object-oriented software development methods:

1. Either obtain (e.g., from a software requirements specification) or use narrative English to develop an informal description of the problem to be solved in terms of application entities (i.e., real-world objects and classes) and their interactions.
2. Uses nouns, pronouns, and noun phrases to identify the objects and classes. Singular proper nouns (e.g., "sensor number 5") and nouns of direct reference (e.g., "the fifth sensor") are used to identify objects, while plural (e.g., "sensors") and common (e.g., "sensor") nouns are used to identify classes. Verbs (e.g., "activate" and "read") and predicate phrases (e.g., "are simultaneously activated") are used to identify the associated operations.

This approach has many benefits. It is straightforward and well defined. Narrative English (or German, French, or Japanese on projects in the associated countries) is well understood by everyone on the project and can be an effective communication medium for both nontechnical and technical developers. Developers naturally think and communicate in their native tongue, and software engineers should know a noun when they see one. A one-to-one mapping usually exists between nouns and objects and classes. This approach can even be used with preexisting textual requirements specifications, so an informal strategy paragraph need not necessarily be developed. Best of all, this approach does not require a complete paradigm change, and it can be used by beginners.

Unfortunately, this approach also has many risks, which were discovered during the first 5 years that it was used. Other, more modern approaches have been developed, which avoid many of these problems, and this method has become much less popular in the past few years. The rest of this section addresses the various known risks and how the software engineer can best manage them.

First of all, the noun approach is very indirect; many nouns do not refer to objects or classes. Sentences also often have the wrong form for correct identification. Imperative sentences of the form "verb direct object" (e.g., Fire the missile) are best because the subjects of such sentences are often neither objects nor classes (e.g., "*This software* shall fire the missile"). For example, the nouns (especially subjects of sentences) may refer to

- An entire assembly or computer software configuration item (CSCI)
- A subassembly or computer software component (CSC)
- An attribute
- An operation (if the operation is a function)

Another problem has to do with English, the language used to document the informal strategy. Many software engineers are weak in grammar, prefer graphics to text, consider this approach mere documentation, and hate doing documentation. English is also flexible to the point of being vague. Nouns can be used as verbs, and some objects and classes may therefore be misidentified as operations. Worse, many verbs (e.g., *purchase, record*) can be used as nouns (e.g., "the *control* of the spacecraft" as opposed to "*control* the spacecraft"), and some operations may thus be misidentified as objects or classes. This is especially likely if the software engineer's primary experience is with functional-decomposition methods. As W. M. Turski [1980] of the Institute of Informatic at Warsaw University noted in 1980, "and they told me that in English, every noun can be 'verbed.'" Because of the risk of beginners misidentifying functions as objects, software engineers should beware of nouns ending with "-er" because merely adding "-er" to the end of a verb (e.g., *controller, manager*) does not change a functional abstraction into an object abstraction.

Similar problems exist for using verbs to identify the operations on objects and classes. Verbs often have the wrong form and do not map directly into operation identifiers, especially if they are taken from textual requirements specifications (e.g., "shall fire" as opposed to "fire"). Also, functions should have noun identifiers because they are used like attributes in the code.

Remember that nouns and verbs are often overloaded to represent similar attributes and operations of different objects and classes. If functionally decomposed textual requirements are used, the same verb often represents different (though similar) operations operating on different objects.

The noun approach assumes that the starting text (e.g., a requirements specification) is coherent, complete, consistent, and correct. However, the choice and meaning of nouns may vary throughout the text. Many relevant objects and classes may not be addressed, whereas some nouns in the text may not be relevant. Thus, this approach can only be used to identify some of the objects and classes. It must be combined with other approaches to be effective.

The noun approach is often used during object-oriented design. Thus, essential objects and classes may not be identified when they should be, during object-oriented domain and requirements analysis. The use of narrative English is also a problem during design because it essentially uses a noncompilable, nonexecutable PDL when compilable specification and design (e.g., Eiffel, Ada) languages could be used more efficiently.

A final problem has to do with tool support. Most object-oriented CASE tools are based on graphics (e.g., semantic nets, interaction diagrams, object-oriented data/control flow diagrams) and programming languages (e.g., Ada, C++). Only minimal object-oriented tool support exists for identifying objects and classes using nouns embedded in narrative English.

With all of these potential problems, does that mean that software engineers should ignore nouns when identifying objects and classes? No. Because the mapping from nouns to objects and classes is natural, and relevant nouns are easy to identify, this is still a useful (if supplemental) technique, as long as its limitations are known and its risks are managed.

For example, consider the initial problem description taken from a system requirements specification:

> The Heads-Up Display (HUD) CSCI shall cyclically get updates of the target, armament status, flight parameters, and target box, and then use this information to update the display. The pilot shall be able to terminate HUD upon command.

The subject of the first sentence is an assembly rather than an object or class, and the verbs (e.g., shall get, shall be able to terminate) have the wrong form if they are to be used as operation identifiers. The description should be changed to imperative sentences to avoid these problems. The compound sentences should be broken into multiple simple sentences, because the verbs and some of the attributes are overloaded and refer to multiple objects. Note that *update* is used both as a noun (i.e., attribute) and a verb (i.e., operation). An improved problem description reads:

> Cyclically get updates of the target.
> Cyclically get updates of the armament status.
> Cyclically get updates of the flight parameters.
> Cyclically get updates of the target box.
> Cyclically update the Heads-Up Display.
> Simultaneously, upon pilot command, terminate the Heads-Up Display.

Using nouns to identify the objects and attributes and using verbs to identify the operations in the improved problem description yields:

```
object: ARMAMENT_STATUS
   attribute:     Updates
   operation:     GET
object: FLIGHT_PARAMETERS
   attribute:     Updates
   operation:     GET
object: HEADS_UP_DISPLAY
   operation:     TERMINATE
   operation:     UPDATE
```

```
object: TARGET
    attribute:      Updates
    operation:      GET
object: TARGET_BOX
    attribute:      Updates
    operation:      GET
```

### 4.1.2.2  Using Traditional Data Flow Diagrams (DFDs)

This is the second oldest approach and was discovered independently by several developers around 1985 when the limitations of the noun approach were first encountered. This approach was first published by Ed Seidewitz and Mike Stark of NASA Goddard Space Flight Center [1986]. In some sense, this approach was the result of the "search for the Holy Grail" of many software developers and managers who desperately needed a way to make the transition from functional-decomposition requirements analysis methods (e.g., Structured Analysis) to object-oriented design, who were familiar with and often had large numbers of DFDs, and who had invested large sums of money in expensive CASE tools that only supported DFDs. This approach comes in the following three flavors:

- Using terminators on CDs
- Using data stores on DFDs
- Using complex data flows on DFDs

#### 4.1.2.2.1  Using Terminators on Context Diagrams (CDs)

To use this approach, the development team must:

1. Create a CD, a DFD showing the external entities (i.e., terminators) with which the software must interface.
2. Identify one object to encapsulate the interface to each individual terminator.
3. Identify one class to encapsulate the interface to each set of similar or identical terminators.

For example, consider Figure 4-3, which shows a traditional (i.e., data flow) CD of an example automotive dashboard application. An object can be identified for each of the 11 terminators on the DFD. Figure 4-4 shows the corresponding objects on an OO CFD.

This approach also has numerous benefits. It is trivial to use and does not require any paradigm shift to use. Because terminators almost always correspond by definition to objects and classes, it is highly reliable, and false-positive identifications are very rare. CDs are commonly used, and significant CASE tool support is often available.

Unfortunately, this approach also has some important risks. First and foremost is that on nontrivial projects, it only identifies a small percentage of the most obvious

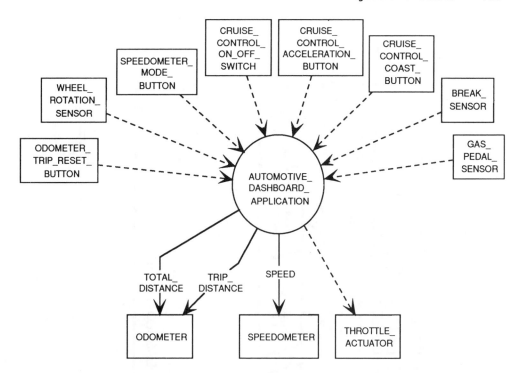

**Figure 4-3: Example of Terminators on a CD**

objects and classes. There are typically many more objects and classes than termina-tors. It tends to identify only the tangible (rather than the intangible) objects and classes because most terminators tend to be physical. Because CDs are one of the first intermediate products produced by a project, the corresponding objects and classes also tend to be identified early. These objects and classes are often identified as part of one or more initial subassemblies, even though they may properly belong to lower-level subassemblies. This may cause subassemblies to grow beyond manageable sizes. This may also result in poor, top-heavy architectures, when the caller objects actually belong lower down in the architecture.

As an example of these risks, consider Figure 4-5, which shows an improved architecture over Figure 4-4, which is consistent with this terminator–CD approach. Figure 4-4 has all 11 objects corresponding to terminators as part of the same subassembly, whereas Figure 4-5 has the objects corresponding to terminators allo-cated to two subassemblies at two different levels of abstraction, improving both subassembly modularity and cohesion. Note that Figure 4-5 also shows 2 intangible objects, THE_CRUISE_CONTROL and THE_MODE, which do not correspond to terminators, and which the terminator–CD approach would miss. The terminator–CD approach would produce one subassembly with 11 tangible and 2 conceptual

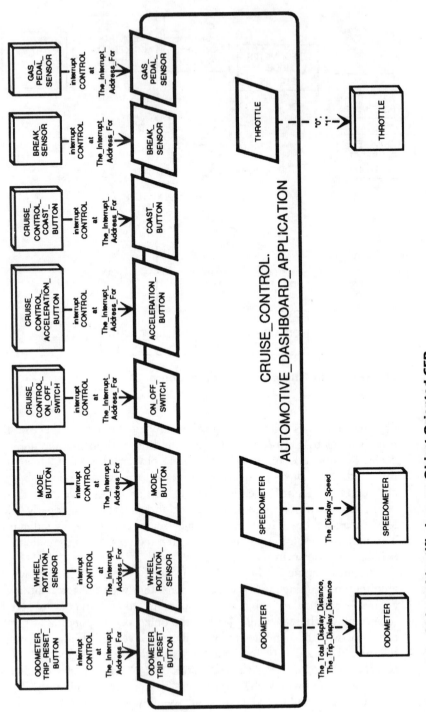

**Figure 4-4: Objects Identified on an Object-Oriented CFD**

objects (rather than two subassemblies with 7 or 6 objects each). Thus, this approach leads to subassemblies that exceed the Miller limit [Miller 1956] of seven plus or minus two and therefore would probably lead to increased errors and decreased productivity.

Sometimes, this approach is only useful for identifying objects or classes corresponding to terminators that are called by the software to be developed. Such *callee* objects (i.e., objects that are called) and classes provide a logical interface to these callee terminators, thereby allowing the rest of the software to be independent of changes to these terminators. On the other hand, objects and classes corresponding to terminators that call the software to be developed may not be required because these caller terminators may be able to call operations of other objects and classes. If always used for both callee and caller terminators, this approach may occasionally produce unnecessary and partially redundant objects and classes for some caller terminators. For example in Figure 4-6, `THE_SPEEDOMETER` and `THE_THROTTLE_ACTUATOR` are caller objects that map to callee terminators. On the other hand, all three caller terminators (at the top of the figure) are mapped into the single callee object, `THE_CRUISE_CONTROL`.

Another drawback to this approach is that the wrong CD may be used. CDs based on DFDs are often the result of the functional decomposition of the system into functional CSCIs or assemblies. By showing only data flows (which are much less important in OOD) and unlabeled control flows, they ignore the important associations behind the flows and the messages that are shown on SNs and IDs, respectively. These object-oriented diagrams should be used as CDs because they provide a better view of the terminators (i.e., in terms of relationships and operations required instead of data flows). For example, compare Figure 4-7 with Figure 4-3. Figure 4-7 shows a general semantic net (GSN) used as a CD for the same automotive-dashboard application shown on the traditional data-flow CD in Figure 4-3. GSNs can be used earlier than DFDs and can provide information at a higher level of abstraction. IDs can then be used later to provide detailed information in a more complete manner than can DFDs.

Although this approach is certainly worth using, software engineers should be well aware of its associated risks and limitations. They should concentrate on other, more modern and effective approaches (e.g., SNs, IDs, object-oriented STDs).

Finally, developers must be careful if the software to be developed interfaces to one terminator via another terminator. An important mirror-image reflection in the order of the objects must occur at the boundary if the proper client–servant relationships between them is to hold. For example, Figure 4-8 shows such a mirror-image effect involving the following four objects and their associated hardware:

1. `THE_SET_OF_CROSSWALK_SIGNALS`
2. `THE_SET_OF_TRAFFIC_SIGNALS`
3. `THE_POWER_DISTRIBUTOR`
4. `THE_MULTIPLEXING_DIGITAL_TO_ANALOG_CONVERTER`

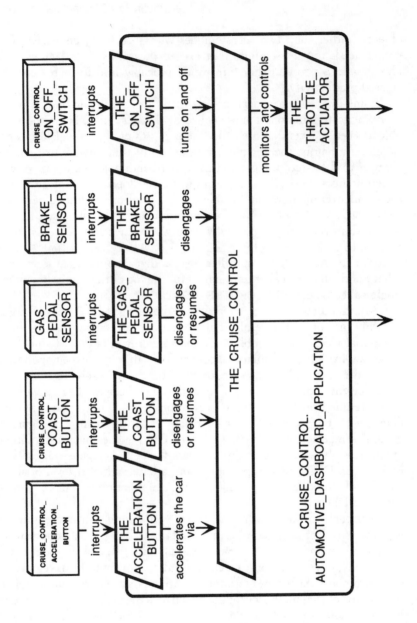

190

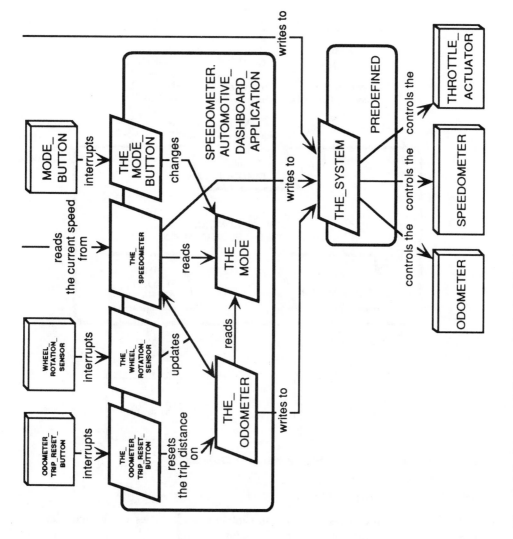

**Figure 4-5: Improved Subassembly Architecture**

191

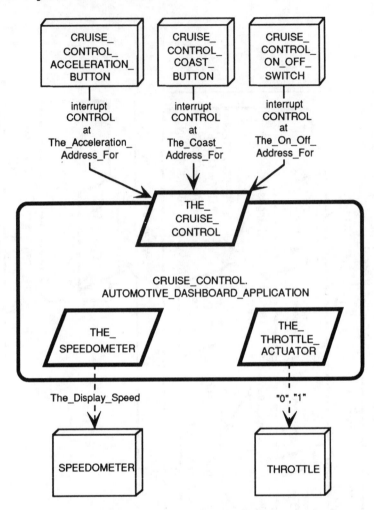

**Figure 4-6: Caller and Callee Terminator Objects**

### 4.1.2.2.2  Using Data Stores on DFDs

This approach assumes that because objects and classes encapsulate both attributes (i.e., data) and operations on those data, it is reasonable to map (a) data stores to attributes, (b) transforms to operations, and (c) the combination of data stores and associated transforms to objects and classes:

1. Identify one object for each data store on each DFD.
2. Identify an aggregate object or class if the data store contains more than one data value.
3. Map (all or part of) the data transforms associated with the data store to the operations of the object or class. Where possible, control transforms are also

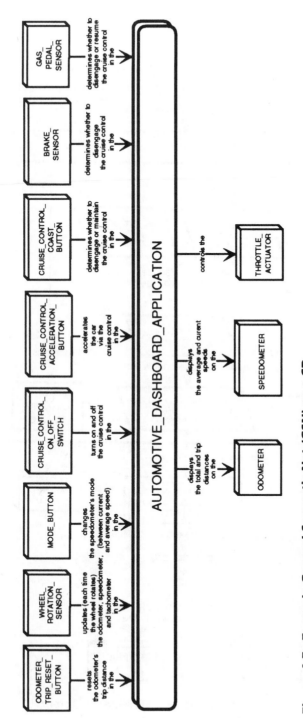

**Figure 4-7: Example General Semantic Net (GSN) as a CD**

193

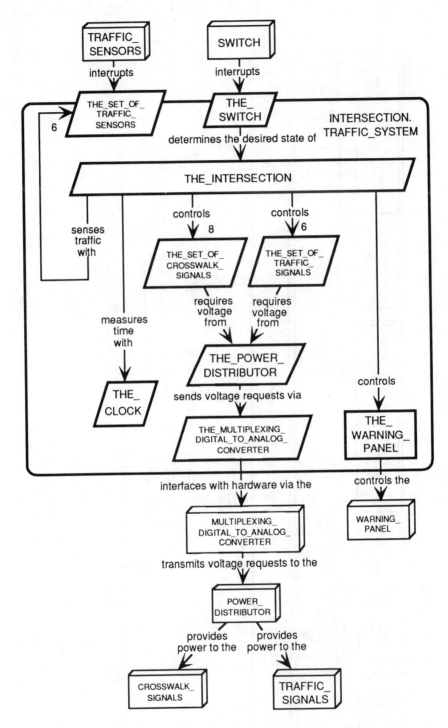

**Figure 4-8: Reflection of Terminators and Terminator Objects**

mapped to operations on objects or classes, although the allocation of these operations is less obvious because they typically do not directly involve data stores. Each object or class therefore encapsulates a single data store and all (or part ) of each associated transform.

This approach has several benefits, including some advantages over the previous approaches. For contractual and historical reasons, many projects must use traditional requirements analysis methods (e.g., Structured Analysis) that are based on DFDs. This approach can act as a bridge between functionally decomposed requirements specifications and object-oriented design. Many analysts and software engineers have been trained to use DFDs, and significant, production-quality tool support exists for these DFDs. This approach is more rigorous and less prone to misinterpretation than when using nouns and narrative English. It also helps to identify many of the objects and classes missed by only using terminators. Also, like the other traditional methods, it does not require a paradigm shift and can be used by software engineers new to object-oriented methods.

On the other hand, this approach probably has the most risks and is most likely to yield questionable identifications. It is very indirect and is based more on data abstraction than on object abstraction. Because many objects and classes contain more than one data store, their attributes may be misidentified as objects and classes, while the associated objects and classes may go unidentified.

The objects and classes identified may be incomplete. Because DFDs are often functionally decomposed, pieces of an object or class may be scattered, both horizontally and vertically, across several DFDs assigned to different analysts. Thus, different variants of the same object or class may be redundantly and independently identified and these partial objects and classes may be developed and maintained, leading to a configuration-management nightmare if they must be modified. For example, Figure 4-9 shows a functional DFD in which two data stores (i.e., The_Total_Distance and The_Trip_Distance) would be allocated to two different misidentified "objects" (i.e., TOTAL_DISTANCE and TRIP_DISTANCE) by this approach. Figure 4-10 shows an object-oriented CFD in which the same two data stores are correctly allocated as attributes of the single object THE_ODOMETER. Because most DFDs are functionally decomposed, transforms were not required to be operations on objects or classes. Transforms are therefore often compound and cannot be allocated to objects or classes. Thus, different parts of a single compound operation may have to be allocated to multiple misidentified classes. For example, Figure 4-9 shows a functional DFD in which the compound transform UPDATE would have to be divided among the three misidentified objects THE_TRIP_DISTANCE, THE_TOTAL_DISTANCE, and THE_CURRENT_SPEED.

Traditional DFDs have the wrong scope. These DFDs usually contain more than one data store and thus map to more than one object or class using this approach. Functional DFDs usually do not document an entire subassembly because they would then violate the Miller limit [Miller 1956] by containing too many nodes (especially transforms) to be easily understandable. Therefore, pieces (i.e., operations and at-

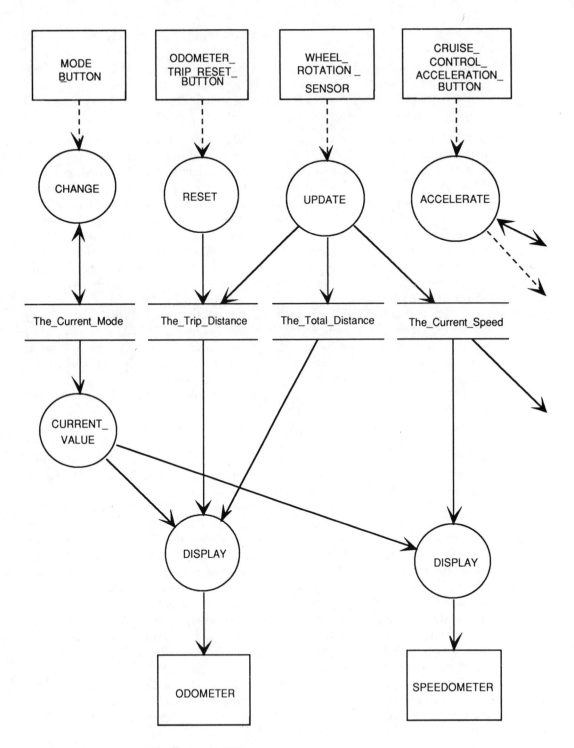

**Figure 4-9: Example Functional DFD**

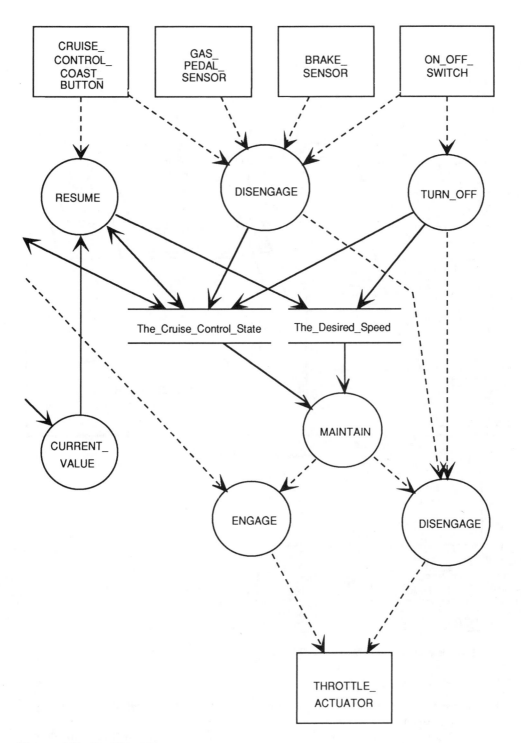

**Figure 4-9: Continued**

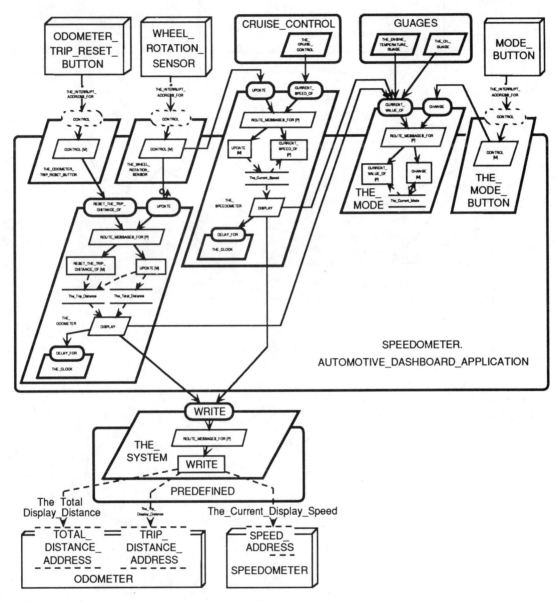

**Figure 4-10: Example Object-Oriented CFD**

tributes) of the same object or class are often allocated to several DFDs by functional decomposition.

Another problem is the emphasis on data flow as opposed to control flow on functional DFDs. Data should be encapsulated and protected inside objects and classes, which interact via message passing (i.e., control flow). Because control flow is more important and natural in an object-oriented specification and design than is data flow, object-oriented CFDs (annotated with data flow where appropriate) are much more useful than functional DFDs.

Finally, on projects using Structured Analysis and the classic waterfall development cycle, functional DFDs are often documented in software requirements specifications that are placed under formal software-configuration management, upon approval. The software engineers typically discover the inappropriateness of the initial functional partitioning of the DFDs only later, during object-oriented design, and they are then faced with significant bureaucratic overhead and schedule pressure if they try to repartition the approved functional DFDs along object and class lines.

It is clearly not cost-effective to develop the DFDs twice: first incorrectly as functional DFDs and then correctly in an object-oriented manner. A better approach is to do the job right the first time. The aforementioned risks can be largely avoided by drawing object-oriented CFDs, which typically have the following properties: All operation (i.e., transform) and attribute (i.e., data store) nodes can be allocated to objects, classes, or objects or classes. All parts of an object or class are on the same CFD. The scope of most object-oriented CFDs is (1) a single object or class (and possibly its terminators); (2) a single thread of control through several objects, classes, and possibly terminators; or (3) a subassembly of objects and classes (and possibly its terminators). Object-oriented CFDs can also help one identify multiple data stores and hidden operations.

Unfortunately, many objects and classes contain so many (often interacting) operations that even object-oriented CFDs are not always useful. Many analysts and software engineers are also so accustomed to developing functional DFDs that it is difficult for them to produce object-oriented CFDs. This is one reason why the traditional icons of Structured Analysis were not used for the CFDs of this book; the new icons help software engineers break out of the functional-DFD habit. Because of the many aforementioned risks, some methodologists (e.g., Ed Berard) advise not using DFDs or CFDs at all. However, if software engineers are aware of the many risks of non-object-oriented DFDs and develop object-oriented CFDs only when cost-effective, such CFDs often are of value and should not be banned outright. Certainly, functional DFDs should only be used either if they already exist and can provide useful information or if contractual or corporate political considerations require their use. The software engineer should definitely concentrate on other, more modern and effective approaches.

### 4.1.2.2.3  Using Complex Data Flows on DFDs

This approach is based on the premise that a complex data flow (e.g., a record with numerous fields or with multiple parameters of different types) may require subtransforms to manipulate the different parts of the data flow. Objects and classes could perhaps be identified to encapsulate the data and its associated operations. To implement this approach, the developers:

1. Identify one object for each complex data flow on each DFD.
2. Identify subtransforms associated with the parts of the data flow and then map these subtransforms to the operations of the object. Each object therefore encapsulates a single complex data flow and all (or part of all) of each associated (sub)transform.

This approach has most of the same benefits and disadvantages of the previous data-store approach. It also has some additional risks that must be recognized and properly handled. It is rarely used or useful because data flows with the necessary structural complexity are rare, so only a very small percentage of the objects and classes will be identified this way, and such data flows often imply that the original DFD is incomplete and should be further decomposed to the point where the simpler data-store approach can be used instead.

## 4.1.3     Miscellaneous Approaches

These approaches, while interesting and occasionally useful, should not be relied on as primary approaches. They are very limited in scope and should only be used as backup approaches.

### 4.1.3.1  Using Abstract Data Types (ADTs) and Abstract State Machines (ASMs)

This approach is based on the following observations concerning how objects and classes are implemented. Because objects encapsulate state attributes and operations that modify the object's state, objects can be modeled (and are often implemented) as **abstract state machines** (ASMs). For examples of ASMs, see Figure 4-11, which is an interaction diagram (ID) showing eight ASM objects in two subassemblies, from an automotive dashboard example. Because classes model a set of objects that share the same or similar structure and behavior (i.e., the same attributes and operations), classes can be modeled (and are usually implemented) as **abstract data types** (ADTs). For examples of ADTs, see Figure 4-12, which shows an ID containing several ADT classes from a simulation example.

To implement this approach, the developers:

1. Identify places in the requirements specification or design where ASMs and ADTs may be appropriately used.
2. Identify an object for each ASM.
3. Identify a class for each ADT or set of ASMs.[2]

---

[2] Some OOPLs (e.g., Smalltalk) require that all objects are instances of preexisting classes, implying to many object-oriented programmers that classes must be identified first. Other approaches identify objects first and then identify classes, as a way to reuse common resources across objects.

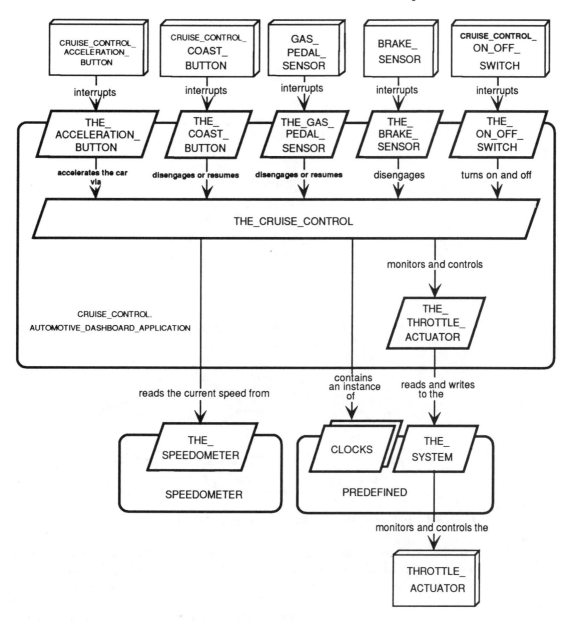

**Figure 4-11: Example Abstract State Machine (ASM)**

This approach has many benefits. It is straightforward and well defined. It is relatively easy for beginners to use and does not require a complete shift to the object-oriented paradigm. If the software engineer is experienced in ASMs and ADTs and

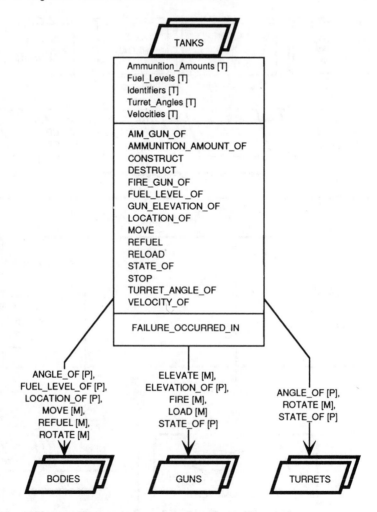

**Figure 4-12: Example Abstract Data Types (ADTs)**

can effectively spot places where they can be used, this approach can usually identify a large percentage of the objects and classes. This approach can also be used in almost all application domains, although ASMs prove more useful with embedded and process-control applications, whereas ADTs prove more useful with any data-intensive application domain, such as typical management information system (MIS) and command, control, and communications (C3) applications.

Nonetheless, some risks must be addressed. To avoid these risks, the software engineer must understand and be experienced in the identification and use of ASMs and ADTs. This approach is indirect and may promote premature design decisions (e.g., the use of generic ASMs instead of ADTs) when used during requirements analysis. It is therefore best used during object-oriented design. Software engineers must use both ASMs and ADTs to be effective because using only ASMs will miss most classes except generic ASMs or classes of generic ASM instances, whereas using only ADTs will miss objects of **anonymous classes** (i.e., unspecified classes for solitary objects, for which the class need not be discussed). This approach is also less effective if the objects and classes contain more than one primary data type (e.g., an ASM with a complex state).

The software engineer should therefore concentrate on other, more modern and effective approaches and should use this only as a supplemental approach.

### 4.1.3.2  Using States

This approach is based on the observation that objects tend to encapsulate state attributes and can be considered to be ASMs (see the previous approach):

1. Identify important states of the system and its entities.
2. Identify an object (or class) for each entity (or set of entities) that has a state.

This approach has only limited benefits: It is relatively straightforward and is reasonably well defined; also, this approach certainly can be used any time that an object or class has a finite number of obvious states.

For example, Figure 4-13 shows an object-oriented STD of THE_ CRUISE_CONTROL, a concurrent object that could have been identified using this approach.

Unfortunately, this approach as several significant limitations. The object or class may have (a) an infinite number of states, (b) one or more states that are not at all obvious, or (c) only a small number of trivial states. The states may even belong to the entire assembly, a subassembly, or an operation. Thus, this approach tends not to be useful, in that it is typically used only to identify a small percentage of the objects and classes, and it may misidentify some other entities as objects and classes. Finally, the objects and classes identified using this approach are often obvious or can more easily be identified using other approaches. It certainly cannot be relied on as the main identification approach.

### 4.1.3.3  Using Resources

These approaches are based on the observation that all attributes, operations, and exceptions are resources that should be encapsulated in objects and classes in an object-oriented application. If software engineers start with (a) known data to be stored or manipulated; (b) functional requirements; or (c) error conditions to be identified and handled, they may identify corresponding attributes, operations, and exceptions before identifying the objects or classes to which they belong. Attributes, operations, and exceptions of an anonymous object or class can therefore be used as the starting points from which to identify the corresponding objects and classes. These approaches, however, work in the reverse order of the much better paradigm of identifying the objects and classes first, and then identifying all of their encapsu-

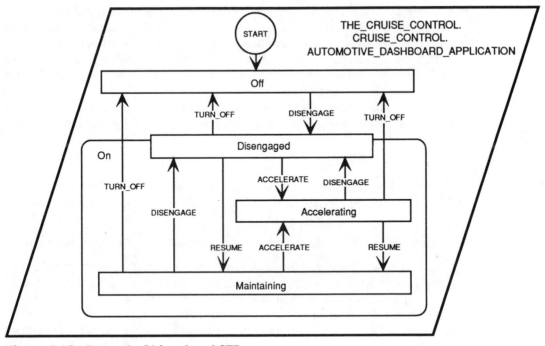

**Figure 4-13: Example Object-Level STD**

lated resources. These approaches can nevertheless be useful on occasion and should not be rejected totally a priori.

### 4.1.3.3.1 Using Attributes

To implement this approach, the developers:

1. Identify relevant attributes by looking for important data abstractions.
2. Identify the object or class associated with each attribute.

This approach has several benefits. It is relatively straightforward and reasonably well defined. Typically, data are relatively easy to identify, and all data (i.e., attributes) should be encapsulated inside objects and classes. Also, the project's data dictionary (if it exists) can be used to identify many objects and classes. This approach directly combats the common global-data mindset and guarantees that each identified attribute is allocated to some object or class.

Unfortunately, this approach has several significant limitations. It is relatively indirect and depends on an obvious many-to-one mapping from attributes to objects or classes. Overloading of attributes may lead to underidentification of objects and classes. With object-based languages, one still has to determine whether a data abstraction should merely be implemented as an attribute or should be mapped to an entire object or class. If a single object or class has more than one attribute (especially if the attributes are of different types), it promotes the tendency to identify an individual object for each attribute and class for each attribute type (which is inappropriate if the objects have multiple attributes and attribute types), and it may be difficult to identify the higher-level object or class that contains these objects. If a functional-decomposition approach to requirements analysis (or preliminary design) has been used, operations are decomposed regardless of the data they access or modify. This separation of data and operations tends to produce common global data and makes it difficult to identify all of the operations that correspond to an attribute. This in turn makes it difficult to create complete objects and classes. This common global-data mindset may be difficult to overcome. The data-dictionary mindset may also inhibit the development of a more powerful and useful object/class dictionary.

### 4.1.3.3.2   Using Operations

To implement this approach, the developers:

1. Identify relevant operations by looking for important functional and process abstractions.
2. Identify the object or class associated with each operation.

This approach has several benefits. It is comparatively straightforward and reasonably well defined. Operations are typically relatively easy to identify. All operations should be encapsulated inside objects and classes. Operations are easy to identify for software engineers with a strong functional-decomposition background.

Unfortunately, this approach has even more significant limitations. The software engineer must understand and be experienced in the identification and use of functional and process abstractions. It is relatively indirect and depends on a mapping from operations to objects or classes that is probably not one-to-one. If a functional-decomposition approach to requirements analysis (or preliminary design) has been used, then the operation may be compound and may operate on more than one object or class. Operations belonging to the same object or class may be scattered across the project and may lead to the multiple, redundant identification of the same object or class. The overloading of operations may lead to underidentification of objects and classes. This approach also reinforces a functional-decomposition mindset, which is then all the more difficult to overcome.

### 4.1.3.3.3   Using Exceptions

To implement this approach, the developers:

1. Identify relevant exceptions by looking for important error conditions.
2. Identify the object or class that must raise the exception and the objects or classes that must handle the exception.

This approach has very few benefits and should be used sparingly. It is relatively straightforward and reasonably well defined. All exceptions and exception handlers should be encapsulated inside objects and classes.

Unfortunately, this approach has very significant limitations. The software engineer must understand and be experienced in the identification and use of exceptions, which many developers tend to overlook. It is very indirect and depends on an obvious many-to-one mapping from exceptions to objects or classes. Overloading of exceptions may lead to underidentification of objects and classes. Finally, most software engineers tend to ignore exceptions, so relatively few objects and classes will be identified using this approach. This approach may be safely ignored as a practical way of identifying objects and classes.

### 4.1.3.4  Using Requirements

This approach is based on the observation that each requirement is the responsibility of and should be allocated to one or more objects and classes:

1. Identify all relevant requirements.
2. Identify the object or class corresponding to each requirement by answering the question, "What object or class should be allocated the responsibility of implementing this requirement?"

This approach has some benefits. Every requirement corresponds to one or more objects and classes. This approach naturally emphasizes requirements traceability.

Unfortunately, this approach tends to emphasize the functional-decomposition mindset if traditional requirements specifications are used. Objects and classes are not (and should not be) functionally cohesive. This approach therefore tends to identify poor objects and classes, and it suffers from a significant number of false-positive identifications. The mapping between requirements and objects and classes is not one-to-one. A single requirement may be implemented via the collaboration of several objects and classes, whereas a single object or class often implements multiple requirements. This approach therefore tends to redundantly identify different variants of the same object and class.

### 4.1.3.5  Using Class-Responsibility-Collaboration (CRC) Cards

This approach is based on the observation that the identification of objects and classes is a human activity and that the identification process can be stimulated by using small pieces of paper (i.e., CRC cards and Post-it® Notes) that correspond to objects and classes, which can be handed from software engineer to engineer. Software engineers with experience, creativity, and intuition can often identify new objects and classes by noticing holes in the current set of cards and notes, which correspond to missing objects and classes. Thus, these pieces of paper are not merely used to document previously identified objects and classes; they also trigger insight and can be used to iteratively and incrementally identify new objects and classes not currently documented.

A CRC card [Beck and Cunningham 1989] is typically a 4-by-6-inch index card that documents the name of a class and lists both its responsibilities (i.e., requirements) and collaborators (i.e., the objects and classes to which it sends messages). See Figure 4-14: Example CRC Card. The developers:

1. Document known classes on CRC cards.
2. Identify missing objects and classes that should be added to existing set of CRC cards. They do this by looking for responsibilities that cannot be allocated to existing cards and collaborators that do not yet have cards.

The recommended alternative version of this approach uses Post-it® Notes in lieu of CRC cards. The developers:

1. Document known objects and classes on large Post-it® Notes.
2. Position them on a whiteboard, and draw association arcs among them.
3. Identify new objects and classes that should be added to the existing set of Post-it® Notes. Do this by looking both for attributes and operations that cannot be allocated to existing notes and for additional objects and classes that do not yet have cards.

This approach has several benefits. CRC cards and Post-it® Notes are very cheap, easy to use, and quite object-oriented. Little effort is invested in them, so they promote iteration and can be discarded if they do not prove useful. They stimulate communication and are not intimidating to the beginner.

Unfortunately, CRC cards and Post-it® Notes are better for thinking about and designing objects and classes than for identifying them. A significant number of objects and classes must already exist for this approach to prove useful for identification, and only a small number of objects and classes are typically identified using these approaches. CRC cards are typically restricted to classes and do not directly help identify objects. Finally, significant experience, creativity, and intuition is required for this approach to be consistently successful.

Post-it® Notes are more flexible than CRC cards in terms of what they document and better elicit the relationships among the objects and the classes. This, in turn,

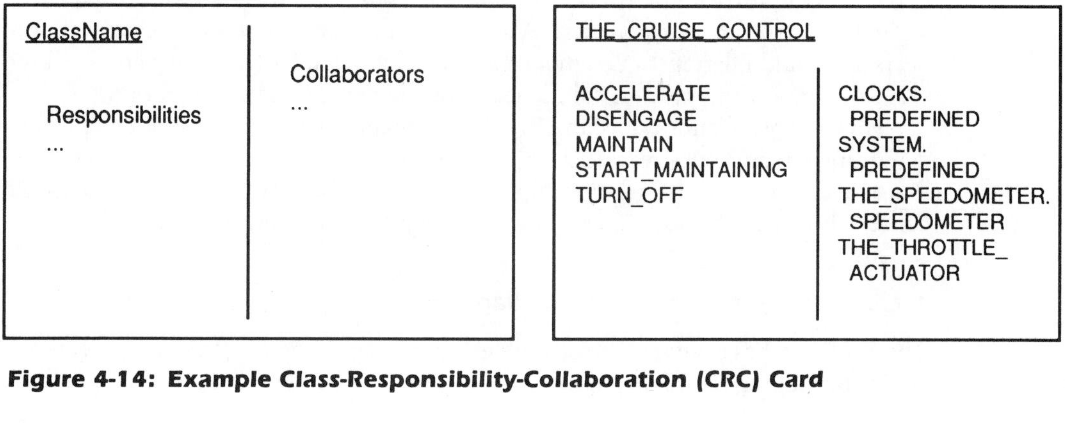

**Figure 4-14: Example Class-Responsibility-Collaboration (CRC) Card**

provides a better feel for the architecture and thus helps identify holes in that architecture.

### 4.1.3.6  Using Entity Relationship Attribute (ERA) Diagrams

This was the initial object-oriented approach that replaced the use of functional DFDs. It assumes that the nodes on entity relationship attribute (ERA) diagrams are often objects and classes. An ERA diagram (a.k.a. Chen diagram [Chen 1976], ER diagram) is a diagram for which (a) its nodes are important entities and (b) its arcs are the important relationships among the nodes. To implement this approach, the developers

**Identify an object or class for each entity node on an ERA diagram.**

This approach has several advantages. ERA diagrams are relatively object-oriented, in that most nodes do correspond to objects and classes. ERA diagrams are a significant improvement over, and more object-oriented than, Abbott's approach and the use of DFDs. They are understood and preferred by many software engineers and are appropriate for requirements analysis. Also, significant CASE tool support for ERA diagrams exists.

There are several risks and limitations associated with ERA diagrams. This approach is still somewhat indirect. Because entities do not necessarily map one-to-one to objects and classes, developers must still understand object abstraction to use this approach effectively.

There are also general problems with ERA diagrams that are unrelated to the identification of objects. ERA diagrams are less powerful and user-friendly than semantic nets. For example, compare the ERA ("Chen") diagram provided by Figure 4-15 with the more informative semantic net provided by Figure 4-8. On standard ERA diagrams, there is no way to differentiate among application domain entities, attributes, objects, classes of objects, and classes of classes. There is no way to document anything (e.g., operations) other than entities and attributes, conditional relationships, and the cardinality of relationships. There is no graphic way to differentiate important varieties of relationships such as "depends on," "has class," "has superclass," and "has components." Also, relationships may not always map well into operations, and relationship diamonds are not user-friendly (e.g., they are often too small to contain the meaningful identifier of the corresponding operation).

For example, Figure 4-15 shows an ERA diagram in which one cannot graphically determine which nodes represent objects and which nodes represents classes. Note that the direction of the relationship is often ambiguous and must be guessed from context because it is not always graphically depicted with arrowheads.

### 4.1.3.7  Using Object-Oriented Diagrams

These approaches assume that software engineers can often identify new objects and classes by looking for missing nodes on existing object-oriented diagrams, such as on

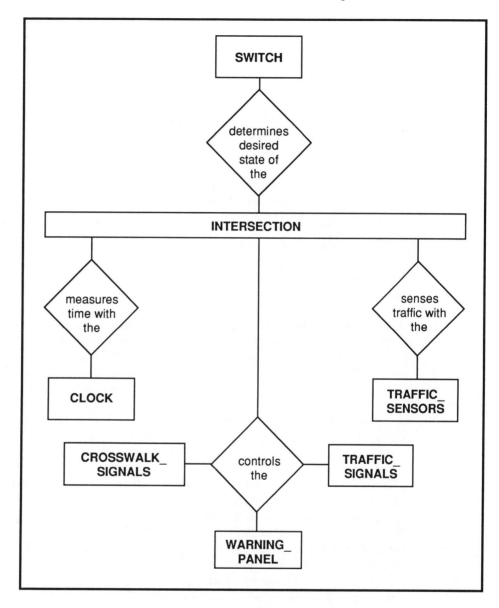

**Figure 4-15: Example of an Entity on a Chen Diagram**

various SNs, and on IDs. Thus, these diagrams are not merely used to document previously identified objects and classes; they also trigger insight and can be used to iteratively and incrementally identify new objects and classes not currently nodes on existing diagrams.

### 4.1.3.7.1   Using Nodes on Semantic Nets (SNs)

This approach assumes that software engineers will use SNs to document the relationships between objects and classes. A SN (a.k.a. *information model*) is a diagram for which (a) its nodes are objects, classes, and possibly other important entities; and (b) its arcs are the important, primarily semantic relationships among these entities. To implement this approach, the developers

**Look for missing objects and classes that should be added to existing SNs**

This approach has several advantages: SNs are very object-oriented and are the best (i.e., most powerful, user-friendly, object-oriented, understandable) current graphic approach. Several specialized SNs document important relationships (e.g., "depends on," "has class," "has superclass," or "has components").

SNs are the basis of several of the best OORA methods. In addition to the ADM3 described in this book, Berard's OORA [1991] uses semantic networks. Colbert's Object-Oriented Software Development [1989] uses only CLDs and CMDs. Shlaer and Mellor's Object-Oriented Systems Analysis [1988] refers to SNs as information models. Because the relationships on the SNs often refer to some of the exported operations of the objects and classes, SNs support the object-oriented paradigm and trace easily to IDs.

This approach also has numerous limitations and risks. This is a "chicken-and-egg" problem because object-oriented SNs are hard to draw if at least some objects and classes have not already been identified. SNs are best used to document, rather than to identify, objects and classes. Few analysts or software engineers are familiar with SNs. In addition, some OORA methods (e.g., Berard's OORA [1991]) restrict the SNs to too few semantic relationships.

The graphic notation for SNs is not standardized and is rapidly changing. Some SNs (e.g., Shlaer and Mellor's Information Model) use arrowheads to represent cardinality and thus unnecessarily require the software engineer to list the relationships twice (i.e., from both directions). Some SNs do not differentiate among objects, classes of objects, classes of classes, and attributes. Some semantic nets do not (adequately) document conditional relationships, the cardinality of relationships, the different varieties of relationships (e.g., "depends on," "has class," "has superclass," or "has components").

CASE tool support for SNs is very limited. *ObjectMaker* by Mark V Systems currently supports the largest number of SNs, while ProtoSoft's *Paradigm Plus* supports some SNs. Cadre's *Teamwork/IM* originally used Chen diagrams instead of Shlaer and Mellor's Information Model.

Figure 4-16 shows an example GSN with 10 objects as nodes in three subassemblies.

Figures 4-17 and 4-18 show two specialized SNs with classes and objects as nodes. Figure 4-17 shows a CLD, and Figure 4-18 shows a CMD.

### 4.1.3.7.2   Using Nodes on Interaction Diagrams (IDs)

This approach assumes that software engineers will use interaction diagrams to document the message passing between objects and classes. An *interaction diagram* (ID) is a diagram for which (a) its nodes are objects, classes, and possibly other important entities; and (b) its arcs list the constant attributes, attribute types, messages, and exceptions passed among these entities. IDs are also called "object diagrams" [Booch 1991] and "object-interaction diagrams" [Colbert 1989]. To implement this approach, the developers

**Look for missing objects and classes that should be added to existing IDs**

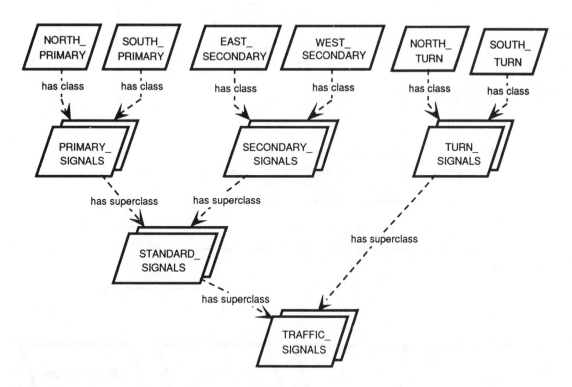

**Figure 4-16: Example General Semantic Net (GSN)**

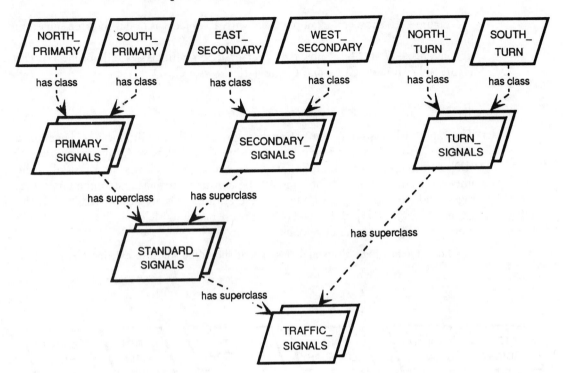

**Figure 4-17: Example CLD**

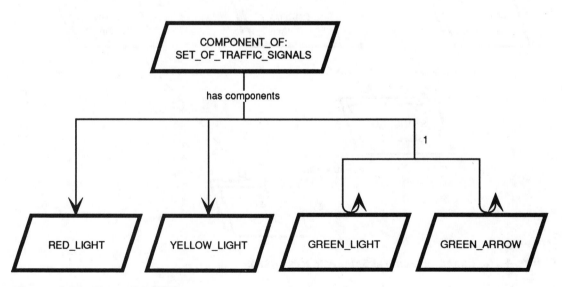

**Figure 4-18: Example CMD**

This approach has some advantages: IDs are very object-oriented and IDs are the basis of several of the best object-oriented requirements analysis methods (e.g., ADM3, Colbert's OOSD).

On the other hand, few analysts or software engineers are familiar with IDs. Object-oriented IDs are impossible to draw if at least some objects and classes have not already identified. Not every node on an ID is an object or class; some may be terminators or subassemblies. CASE tool support is very limited with *ObjectMaker* currently supporting the largest number of IDs. The graphic notation is not standardized and is rapidly changing. IDs, like SNs, are best used to document, rather than to identify, objects and classes.

For example, Figure 4-19 shows an ID with three exported objects and seven hidden objects.

## 4.1.4    Recommendations

The best approach to identifying objects and classes is to look for tested objects and classes in tested architectures by using relevant application frameworks to identify them. If they do not already exist, then a separate project using OODA should be commenced to create the relevant application frameworks. If adequate OODA has not been performed, then a separate project should be commenced to perform it. If a relevant reuse repository does not exist, it should be created either as part of the project if the current project is large enough to justify it or else as part of a separate project.

If the previous approaches are inappropriate or inadequate, then the "using-object-abstraction" approaches should be used to identify new objects and classes. If the software engineers are not experienced with object orientation for these approaches (a common occurrence with beginners), then a combination of the "using-nouns," "using-ADTs-and-ASMs," "using-states," and "using-resources" approaches should be used to identify the primary objects and classes. The "using-object-oriented-diagrams" approach is recommended as a secondary approach.

The "using-traditional-DFDs" approach is not recommended because of its many risks and limitations, although existing DFDs may be examined for useful information if done very carefully to avoid functional design influences. The "using-requirements" approach is likewise not recommended if the requirements are functionally decomposed and is superfluous if they are object-oriented. The "using-ERA-diagram" approach is not recommended because object-oriented diagrams are better.

Thus, those approaches emphasizing the reuse of previously developed and tested objects and classes receive the highest recommendations but are often impractical for an organization's first few object-oriented projects. Object abstraction should be the guide to identifying new objects and classes, and most of the other approaches can be combined. Only the approaches emphasizing functional decomposition should be avoided altogether.

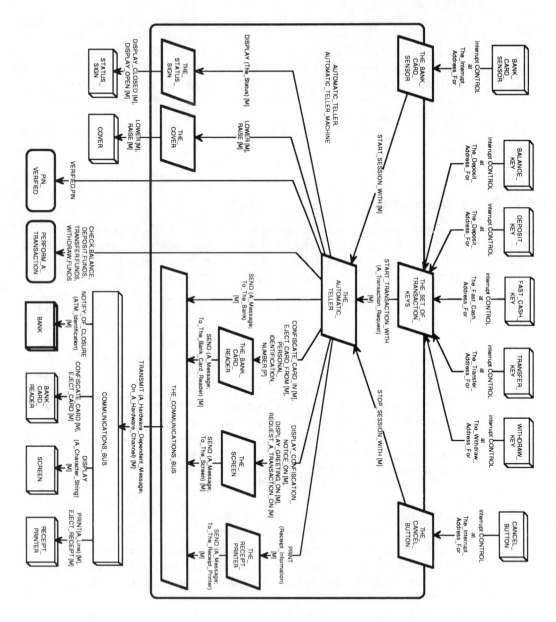

**Figure 4-19: Example ID**

## 4.2 IDENTIFICATION OF SUBASSEMBLIES

Most significant applications and many assemblies contain hundreds, if not thousands, of objects and classes. It is not cost-effective, is certainly impractical, and is sometimes impossible to identify all objects and classes at once. Even if the objects could somehow be identified as part of some "identify the objects" activity of an OOD method, identifying that many objects and classes are beyond human understanding [Miller 1956]. *Subassemblies* (a.k.a. *subsystems, subjects, computer software components, clusters*) are the small, manageable collections of logically related objects and classes that software engineers use to partition significant *assemblies* (a.k.a., *systems, computer software configuration items*) into useful groupings for understandability, documentation, and development.

The identification of subassemblies is therefore almost as important as the identification of objects and classes of objects. It is important because the project will be managed in terms of subassemblies, and the requirements specifications and design documents will be organized by subassemblies. Any mistakes in proper identification will have a significant impact on the quality of the resulting software. It is difficult to identify subassemblies (at least for most beginners) because identification requires both knowledge and skill. It typically requires 3–6 months of practice for the necessary skills to mature.

Fortunately, there are numerous approaches that can be used to identify subassemblies, and these approaches vary widely. Several approaches (e.g., cohesion and coupling, master terminators) are better for getting started, while other approaches (e.g., recursion) are better for incremental development once the initial subassemblies have been identified. Some approaches (e.g., application frameworks) require previous work, whereas other approaches (e.g., requirements) may be used on an initial application. Some approaches (e.g., recursion) tend to produce subassemblies of manageable size, whereas other approaches (e.g., requirements) tend to produce subassemblies that are too large. Some approaches (e.g., classification hierarchies) tend to maximize reuse, whereas other approaches (e.g., recursion) may lead to reinventing the wheel on multiple subassemblies. Finally, some approaches (e.g., recursion) emphasize application development, whereas other approaches (e.g., classification hierarchies, domain analysis) emphasize the development of class libraries and reuse repositories. This chapter addresses the following approaches to the identification of subassemblies.

- Using recursion
- Using cohesion and coupling
- Using masters
  —Using master terminators
  —Using master objects and classes
- Using object decomposition
- Using classification hierarchies
- Using requirements

- Using personal experience
- Using OODA
- Using repositories of previously developed software
  —Reusing application frameworks
  —Reusing individual subassemblies

## 4.2.1    Using Recursion

This is the oldest approach and dates back to the original object-oriented design method expanded and documented by Grady Booch [1983] in his classic book, *Software Engineering with Ada*. It is based on the premise that with nontrivial applications, the total number of objects and classes significantly exceeds the Miller Limit [Miller 1956] and is therefore too large to allow identification of all of them at once. By using a globally recursive OOD method, subassemblies can be incrementally identified in a top-down (with respect to dependency) manner, based on the resources required by objects and classes of currently identified subassemblies. To implement this approach, developers:

1. On any project using a globally recursive OOD method, identify (on a subassembly-by-subassembly basis) all classes, objects, or operations in the parent (i.e., current) subassembly that must be stubbed out because they depend on (e.g., must send messages to) lower-level objects and classes that have not yet been identified as part of the current subassembly.
2. Identify one or more child subassemblies to export the resources required by these stubbed classes, objects, or operations.

This approach has significant benefits: It is straightforward and well defined, and if the assembly contains numerous subassemblies, this approach can be used to identify the majority of subassemblies. This approach helps achieve the numerous benefits of top-down, globally recursive, incremental development, and it offers a clear way of incrementally identifying subassemblies, so that not all subassemblies need to be identified at once. Also, unlike some other approaches, recursion can be used on the first project.

There are, however, certain limitations and risks to this approach: It assumes the existence of parent subassemblies, and only identifies child subassemblies. Because it offers no support for getting started (i.e., for identifying the initial subassemblies), it cannot be used as the only approach to identifying the subassemblies. This approach also may lead to the reinvention of the same object or class in multiple subassemblies and thus may not maximize reuse. This approach may not minimize message and inheritance coupling. This approach requires the use of a globally recursive development cycle, with associated major changes in the traditional management of software development.

An example illustrating the results of this approach is shown in Figure 4-20: Using Recursion. Note that three child subassemblies were spawned from the same

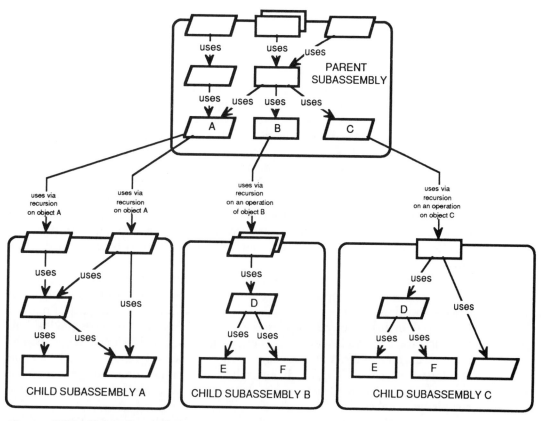

**Figure 4-20: Using Recursion**

parent subassembly, a common occurrence that promotes parallel development. Note that child subassembly A is due to recursion on a stubbed object, whereas child subassemblies B and C are due to recursion on stubbed operations. Note that a risk associated with this approach is the redundant identification of the same objects by different subassembly development teams (e.g., the redundant development of objects D, E, and F).

## 4.2.2    Using Cohesion and Coupling

This is the second oldest approach and is often the approach used when software engineers new to OOD first realize that the recursive approach will not identify all subassemblies. It is based on the premise that if you can identify all objects and classes, you should be able to group them into subassemblies that maximize some type of cohesion while minimizing cross-subassembly coupling. To implement this approach, developers:

1. Identify as many objects and classes as is practical.
2. Group the resulting set of objects and classes into subassemblies in such a manner as to maximize [object] cohesion while minimizing message and inheritance coupling.

This approach has some benefits: This brute force approach is straightforward, well defined, and works well with very small applications having fewer than 25 objects and classes and can even be used up to approximately 100 objects and classes (though much less efficiently than with other approaches). Even if the number of objects and classes is quite large, it can provide some guidance in identifying initial subassemblies if restricted to the most obvious and important objects and classes. This approach can be used if no prior object-oriented domain experience exists so that the use of classification hierarchies, application frameworks, and domain analysis is impractical. Certainly, the more objects and classes that have been identified, the more knowledge exists that can be used to maximize subassembly cohesion and minimize subassembly coupling. Unlike some other approaches, decomposition can be used on the first project.

On the other hand, assemblies often contain hundreds of objects and classes, making this approach impractical because it is impossible to identify all important objects and classes up front. This approach is cost-effective only if a trivial number (i.e., less than 40) of objects and classes exist to be grouped into subassemblies. This approach also does not achieve the benefits of incremental development obtained by using recursion and often restricts developers to the classic (and obsolete) waterfall development cycle. This approach must rely heavily on iteration and is therefore not very efficient. This approach breaks down when it is needed most—with large complex assemblies.

An example illustrating the results of this approach is shown in Figure 4-21: Using Coupling and Cohesion. Note that each subassembly is relatively cohesive and that coupling between subassemblies has been minimized. This approach also avoids the potential redundancy that might occur when using recursion as the primary approach (compare objects D, E, and F on Figures 4-20 and 4-21).

## 4.2.3    Using Masters

### 4.2.3.1  Using Master Terminators

This approach was developed as a precursor to the "using-recursion" approach. It is based on the observation that the master objects and classes that model master terminators are often at the top of the software architecture and therefore are often the main objects and classes in the initial subassemblies. If this approach can be used to identify all initial subassemblies, then recursion can be used to identify all child subassemblies, and the combination of the two approaches can be used to identify all subassemblies. To implement this approach, developers:

1. Identify an object or class for each master terminator or set of related terminators.

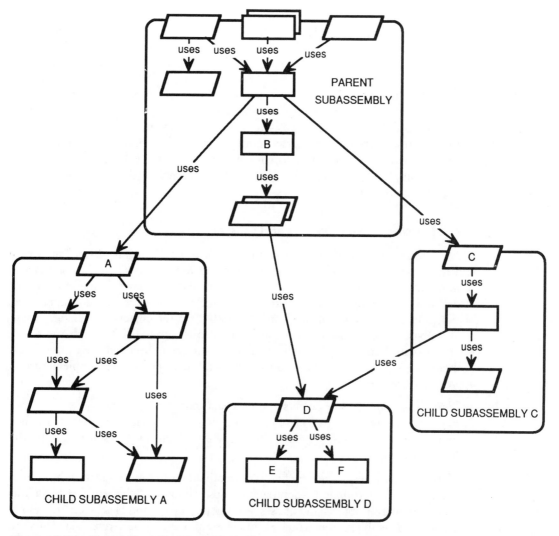

**Figure 4-21: Using Coupling and Cohesion**

2. Partition the resulting set of objects and classes into subassemblies in such a manner as to maximize [object] cohesion while minimizing message and inheritance coupling.

This approach has some benefits. It is straight forward, well defined, and easy for beginners to use. This is a reasonable first approach to use because the terminators are often identified early during the development of the assembly's CD. This approach allows the software engineers to get started by identifying initial master subassemblies and thus serves as a precursor to the "using-recursion" approach.

There are, however, significant limitations to this approach. First of all, master terminators can only be used to identify a small percentage of subassemblies if the assembly is nontrivial. Also, while the identification of terminators is relatively easy, differentiating between master and server terminators is often difficult for software engineers, especially if application domain and hardware experience is limited. Further, this approach tends to allocate the objects and classes that model master terminators to initial top-level subassemblies even though they may properly belong to lower-level subassemblies; this is especially true if there are large numbers of master objects and classes that do not model master terminators. Finally, this approach might only identify a small percentage of subassemblies if the assembly is large.

An example illustrating the results of this approach is shown in Figure 4-22: Using Master Terminators.

### 4.2.3.2 Using Master Objects and Classes

This approach was also developed as a precursor to the "using-recursion" approach and was designed to avoid some of the risks and limitations of the "using-master-terminators" approach. It is based on the observation that the initial subassemblies are by definition at the top of the software architecture and therefore must contain master objects and classes. Thus, if one can identify all master objects and classes, these master objects and classes in turn can be used to identify all initial subassemblies. Recursion can then be used to identify all child subassemblies, and the combination of these two approaches can be used to identify all subassemblies. To implement this approach, developers:

1. Identify as many master objects and classes as possible.
2. Partition the resulting set of objects and classes into subassemblies, in such a manner as to maximize [object] cohesion while minimizing message and inheritance coupling.

This approach has some benefits. It correctly identifies more subassemblies than the "using-master-terminators" approach because all master subassemblies by definition contain master objects and classes. All master objects and classes should belong to master subassemblies, from which child subassemblies may be derived via recursion. This approach allows the software engineers to get started by identifying initial master subassemblies and thus serves as a precursor to the "using-recursion" approach.

On the other hand, this approach has more risks associated with it than the "using-master-terminators" approach. Not all master objects and classes may be easy to identify, especially if they are not abstractions of terminators. Only essential master objects and classes tend to be identified early. Grouping the master objects and classes into subassemblies is not trivial. The subassemblies identified with this approach tend to contain a large number of master objects and classes. When nonessential objects and classes are later added, the subassembly tends to grow beyond the Miller limit and may become difficult to develop efficiently and correctly. Finally, this approach might only identify a small percentage of subassemblies if the assembly is large.

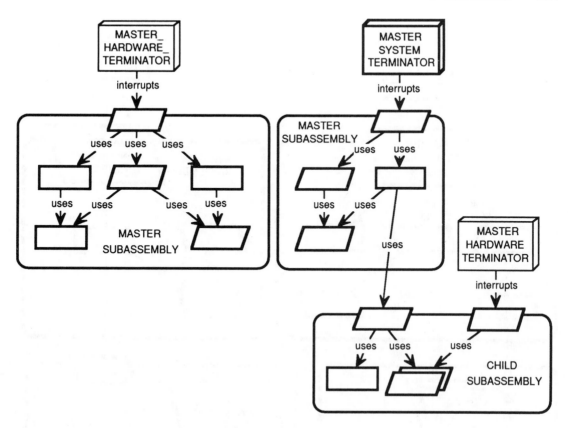

**Figure 4-22: Using Master Terminators**

An example of this approach is shown in Figure 4-23: Using Master Objects and Classes.

## 4.2.4    Using Object Decomposition

This is the appropriate approach to use for the identification of subassemblies if also using the Hierarchical Object-Oriented Design (HOOD) method [HTG 1991]. It is based on the premise that most objects can be decomposed into subobjects and that subassemblies provide a natural way to group these related subobjects (and possibly their clients) together. To implement this approach, developers:

1. Decompose each object or class into its component objects and classes.
2. Group the component objects and classes into a subassembly.

A natural extension of HOOD, which is quite popular in Europe, this approach has several benefits. It is straightforward and easy to understand, and it is consistent

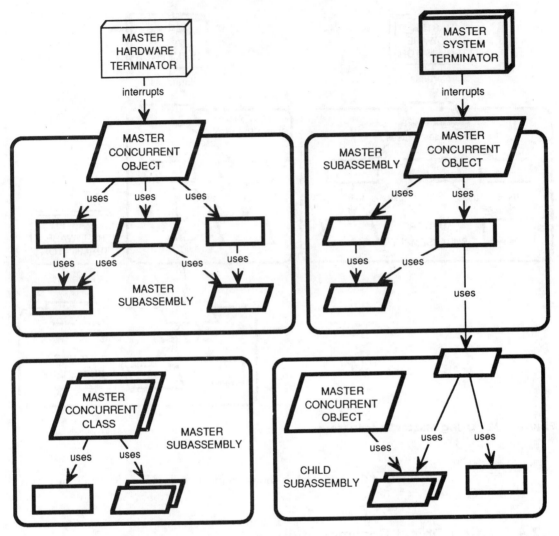

**Figure 4-23: Using Master Objects and Classes**

with the "using-recursion" approach if recursion is based on object decomposition rather than on stubs and required resources.

It does, however, have numerous limitations and risks. First of all, this approach is somewhat inconsistent with HOOD because HOOD does not recognize subassemblies and nests objects inside nonterminal objects. Also, this approach cannot easily be used to identify most subassemblies because most objects cannot reasonably be decomposed into component objects and classes. This approach tends to overemphasize object and class decomposition at the expense of "depends-on" relationships. Like the "using-recursion" approach, it may lead to the reinvention of the same object or class in multiple subassemblies and thus may not maximize reuse. Because it offers no support for getting started (i.e., in identifying the initial subassemblies), it cannot be used as the only approach to identifying subassemblies. Finally, this approach may not minimize message and inheritance coupling.

An example of this approach is shown in Figure 4-24: Using Object Decomposition.

## 4.2.5    Using Classification Hierarchies

This is a fundamentally different approach to the identification of subassemblies. It is based on the premise that classification (i.e., inheritance) hierarchies are fundamental and that the decomposition of assemblies into subassemblies should mirror the grouping of classes into classification hierarchies. To implement this approach, developers:

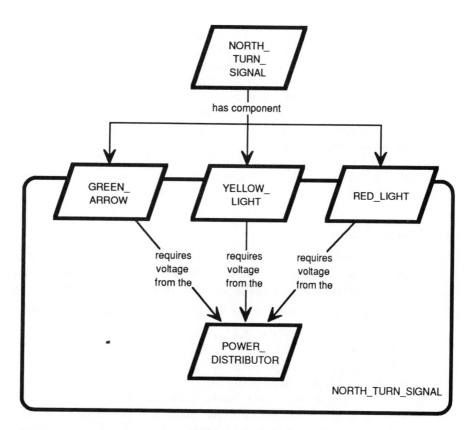

**Figure 4-24: Using Object Decomposition**

1. Identify one or more classification hierarchies.
2. Identify one subassembly for each previously identified classification hierarchy. If there is only one massive classification hierarchy, then the software engineers may identify one subassembly for each major branch in the classification hierarchy. Software engineers may either add all instances to the subassembly of the corresponding classification hierarchy or identify for each classification subassembly a separate subassembly to contain its instances.

This approach has several benefits: It maximizes the benefits of inheritance, improves the reusability of classification hierarchies, and is useful during domain analysis and the development of reusable classes. This approach produces object-oriented subassemblies and usually works well for the allocation of software engineers to subassemblies because application-domain experience often corresponds to individual classification hierarchies.

Conversely, this approach has certain significant risks. It tends to produce subassemblies that contain far too many classes if the classification hierarchies are large and not broken into subassemblies for each major branch. For example, this approach tends to produce only one massive subassembly if the implementation language is taken into account and it is a language such as Smalltalk, in which all classes must be part of the same classification hierarchy. This approach tends to be less useful when developing an initial object-oriented application and has not yet identified the classification hierarchies. It is important to note that this approach may overemphasize inheritance, especially if one is intending to use an object-based or hybrid implementation language. Finally, this approach ignores all important relationships (e.g., general, aggregation, message passing) other than the "has class" and "has superclass" relationships.

An example of the results of the "using-classification-hierarchies" approach is shown in Figure 4-25, which shows two subassemblies, each containing a classification hierarchy.

## 4.2.6    Using Requirements

This is another fundamentally different approach, based on the premise that the decomposition architecture of assemblies into subassemblies should naturally mirror the architecture of the requirements specification:

**Identify a subassembly for each major software requirement or capability.**

The primary benefit of this approach is that it naturally supports requirements traceability, testing, and validation. Subassemblies are easy to identify and have well-defined scope. This approach is also consistent with the functional-decomposition mindset and is therefore easy for beginners to use.

This approach has many drawbacks and is generally not recommended. First of all, this approach minimizes object cohesion and maximizes functional cohesion (which is often inappropriate for projects using OOD) if the requirements are not

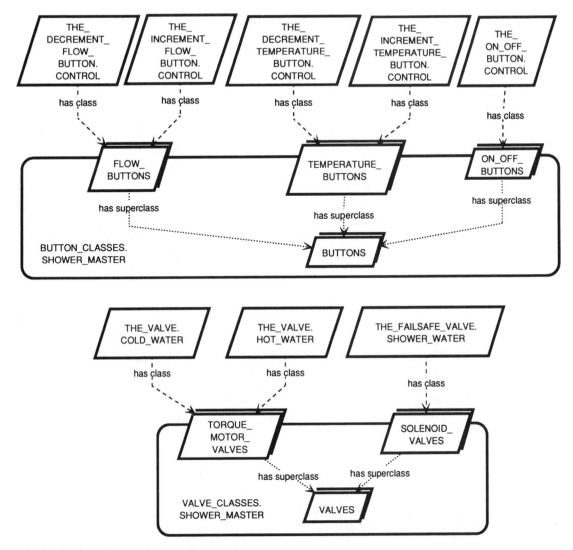

**Figure 4-25: Using Classification Hierarchies**

organized along object lines. It also tends not to minimize message and inheritance coupling. This approach may lead to the identification of incomplete objects and classes if functional-decomposition requirements analysis methods were used. Such subassemblies also may be too large, containing too many objects and classes; different subassemblies may contain the same or similar objects and classes, leading to the redundant development of the same object or class by different teams. This, in turn, may significantly limit reuse. Finally, it is not clear how far down one should go in the requirements hierarchy with this approach. Different software engineers may consider different requirements to be major and thus may develop significantly different subassembly architectures from the same requirements specifications.

### 4.2.7    Using Personal Experience

This is another fundamentally different approach to the identification of subassemblies, based on the premise that the software engineers have previously developed one or more closely related subassemblies:

> **Identify subassemblies that correspond to the subassemblies that you have previously identified on similar projects in the same application domain.**

The primary benefit of this approach is that it comes naturally to the software engineer and that it can be used by any software engineer with previous experience in the application domain. By building on previous experience, this approach provides a reasonable reality check on the current project and often improves the quality of the identified subassemblies because they are based on subassemblies that have been previously built and tested.

This approach has many drawbacks. First of all, it assumes *relevant* previous experience and cannot be used on an initial object-oriented project. Because past experience is often with functional decomposition projects and the first few object-oriented subassemblies that are identified and developed tend to be suboptimal, past experience may be of limited value and even misleading. This approach is very informal, and different software engineers may identify quite different subassemblies, given the same starting information. This approach also may lead to the reinvention of the same object or class in multiple subassemblies and thus may not maximize reuse. This approach might not minimize message and inheritance coupling.

### 4.2.8    Using Object-Oriented Domain Analysis

This is a more formal and effective version of the previous "using-experience" approach to the identification of subassemblies and is based on the premise that someone has previously performed relevant OODA:

> **Identify one or more subassemblies for reuse (with or without modification), which were previously identified and analyzed during OODA of the same application domain.**

This approach has essentially the same advantages and limitations as the analogous approach for the identification of objects and classes.

### 4.2.9    Using Repositories of Previously Developed Software

This approach is based on the premise that someone has previously developed software that contains many of the necessary subassemblies, and that many subassemblies can be identified by browsing the entities in reuse repositories. Software engineers can look for relevant reusable application frameworks, class hierarchies, or individual subassemblies. To implement this approach, developers:

1. Locate repositories of previously developed software in the same application domain.
2. Browse the repositories to identify one or more subassemblies for reuse (with or without modification).

Like the "using-OODA" approach, this approach also has essentially the same advantages and limitations as the analogous approach for the identification of objects and classes.

### 4.2.9.1  Reusing Application Frameworks

This is an enhancement to the previous "using domain analysis" approach to the identification of subassemblies. It is based on the premise that domain analysis has been previously used to create one or more application frameworks (described in Section 4.1.1.4.1) that have been divided into reusable subassemblies. To implement this approach, the developers:

1. Identify one or more relevant application frameworks in the same application domain.
2. Reuse (with or without modification) subassemblies from these previously developed application frameworks.

This approach has an additional limitation. One or more relevant application frameworks must have previously been developed and must be identified by the current software engineers.

### 4.2.9.2  Reusing Individual Subassemblies

This approach is based on the premise that a reuse repository with relevant reusable subassemblies (as well as objects, classes, and classification hierarchies) has been developed and is accessible by the software engineers:

**Examine the reuse repository for relevant subassemblies that can be reused, either with or without modification.**

This approach has the same advantages and limitations listed for reusing application frameworks.

## 4.2.10  Recommendations

The best approach for identifying subassemblies is to reuse tested subassemblies in tested subassembly architectures by using relevant application frameworks to identify the subassemblies. If these frameworks do not exist, then a separate project should be commenced to create the relevant application frameworks, and OODA and repositories should be used. Recommendations for creating such frameworks were given in Section 4.1.4.

If the previous approaches are inappropriate or inadequate, and the current project is small, then the "using-cohesion-and-coupling" approach should be used. If the project is too large for that approach (the usual case), then the "using-master-terminators" and "using-master-objects-and-classes" approaches should be used to identify the initial subassemblies, and the "using-recursion" approach should be used to identify child subassemblies. If the software engineers have significant object-oriented experience, then the "using-personal-experience" approach may also be useful as a secondary approach. If there is a significant amount of inheritance in the system, then the "using-classification-hierarchies" approach may prove useful if the implementation language does not require all objects and classes to belong to a single massive classification hierarchy. The "using-requirements" approach is only recommended as a secondary approach and only if the requirements have been organized along object and class lines by an object-oriented software requirements analysis approach.

Thus, those approaches emphasizing the reuse of previously developed and tested subassemblies receive the highest recommendations but are often impractical for an organization's first few object-oriented projects. In such cases, brute force can be applied to trivially small projects, and a top-down approach using masters followed by recursion is recommended for significant initial projects.

## 4.3 CHAPTER REFERENCES

[Abbott 1983] Russell J. Abbott, "Program Design by Informal English Description," *Communications of the* ACM, 26(11), 882–895, November 1983.

[Auer 1991] Ken Auer, "Position Paper" delivered at the Identifying Objects Workshop at OOPSLA'91, November 1991.

[Beck and Cunningham 1989] Kent Beck and Ward Cunningham, "A Laboratory for Teaching Object-Oriented Thinking, " *OOPSLA'89 Conference Proceedings*, Special Issue of SIGPLAN Notices, 24(10), 1–6, October 1989.

[Berard 1991] Ed V. Berard, "Object-Oriented Requirements Analysis," Gaithersburg, MD, Berard Software Engineering, 10 February 1991.

[Booch 1983] Grady Booch, *Software Engineering with Ada*, Menlo Park, CA, Benjamin Cummings, 1983.

[Booch 1991] Grady Booch, *Object-Oriented Design with Applications*, Menlo Park, CA, Benjamin Cummings, 1991.

[Chen 1976] Peter Pin-Shan Chen, "The Entity-Relationship Model—Toward a Unified View of Data," ACM *Transactions on Database Systems*, 1(1), 9–36, March 1976.

[Coad and Yourdon 1990] Peter Coad and Edward Yourdon, *Object-Oriented Analysis*, Englewood Cliffs, NJ, Yourdon Press, 1990.

[Colbert 1989] Ed Colbert, "The Object-Oriented Software Development Method: A Practical Approach to Object-Oriented Development," *Proceedings of TRI-Ada'89 — Ada Technology in Context: Application, Development, and Deployment*, 400–415, 23–26 October 1989.

[HTG 1991] HOOD Technical Group, *HOOD Reference Manual*, Issues 3.1, HOOD User Group, July 1991.

[Meyer 1988] Bertrand Meyer, *Object-Oriented Software Construction*, Englewood Cliffs, NJ, Prentice Hall, 1988.

[Miller 1956] George A. Miller, "The Magical Number Seven, Plus or Minus Two," *Psychological Review*, 63(2), March 1956.

[Seidewitz and Stark 1986] Ed Seidewitz and Mike Stark, *General Object-Oriented Software Development*, Greenbelt, MD, NASA Goddard Space Flight Center Software Engineering Laboratory, SEL-86-002, August 1986.

[Shlaer and Mellor 1988] Sally Shlaer and Stephen J. Mellor, *Object-Oriented Systems Analysis: Modeling the World in Data*, Englewood Cliffs, NJ, Yourdon Press, 1988.

[Turski 1980] W. M. Turski, personal communication, July 1980; with Dale Gaumer at the Summer Computer Science Institute at the University of California at Santa Cruz.

[van der Loo 1992] Ken van der Loo, personal communication, March 1992.

[Wirfs-Brock et al. 1990] Rebecca Wirfs-Brock, Brian Wilkerson, and Lauren Wiener, *Designing Object-Oriented Software*, Englewood Cliffs, NJ, Prentice-Hall, 1990.

# Chapter 5

# The ASTS Development Method 3

This chapter documents the software requirements analysis and logical design steps of the Advanced Software Technology Specialists (ASTS) Development Method 3 (ADM3), as well as the activities that precede and follow them. ADM3 is a third-generation, object-oriented software development method for use on large, complex, real-time projects. Software developed with this method should be implemented in object-oriented languages (e.g., C++, Eiffel, Smalltalk), or at least in class-based languages (e.g., Ada and Modula 2) that support the implementation of objects and classes. Nonetheless, it may even be used with traditional procedural languages (e.g., C, FORTRAN, Pascal), although the physical design and implementation aspects will require significant tailoring, due to the limitations of the languages.

ADM3 improves on most other object-oriented methods in several important ways. It has a very rich, consistent set of models and diagram classes, which can be used to model all major aspects of almost all applications. Specifically, ADM3 can be used for the following:

- *Embedded and real-time applications*, because of its strong support for concurrency and timing issues
- *Large systems*, due to its support for subassemblies and both local and global recursion
- *Projects requiring robustness*, due to its support for preconditions, postconditions, invariants, and exceptions
- *Consistency throughout the entire software development cycle*, due to its ability to handle more than merely requirements analysis or design

- *Military projects*, due to its tailoring and interpretation guidelines
- *Projects requiring reliability and responsivity to technological improvements* because it has been constantly maintained and upgraded as the technology has advanced.

ADM3 has been derived from ADM1 [Firesmith 1989], which was developed from 1985 to 1989, and ADM2 [Firesmith and Gaumer 1991], which was developed from 1989 to 1991. ADM3 is currently supported by the following CASE tools [Firesmith 1991], and negotiations with several other CASE vendors are being held:

- *ObjectMaker*
  Mark V Systems Limited
  16400 Ventura Blvd., Suite 303
  Encino, CA 91436 USA
  voice: (818) 995-7671
  fax: (818) 995-4267
- *Paradigm Plus*
  ProtoSoft
  17629 El Camino Real, Suite 202
  Houston, TX 77058 USA
  voice: (713) 480-3233
  fax: (713) 480-6606

While ADM3 covers all software development activities, the scope of this book is only software requirements analysis and logical design. Therefore, only the analysis and logical design steps of ADM3 are presented in complete detail herein. The remaining steps, either prior to analysis or after logical design, are presented in an abbreviated form.

As noted in the beginning of Chapter 2, "Fundamental Concepts," there are a great number of object-oriented analysis and design methods to choose from. What are the technical and managerial reasons for choosing the ASTS Development Method 3 (ADM3)?

First of all, ADM3 is highly comprehensive. It supports and addresses all of the following:

- The major concepts of objects, classes, subassemblies, assemblies, scenarios, and frameworks
- The visibility aspects of these entities in terms of specifications and bodies
- The resources localized and encapsulated in objects and classes, including attribute types, attributes, messages, exceptions, and operations
- Single and multiple classification, as well as static and dynamic classification
- All major relationships among objects and classes, including association, aggregation, interactions (especially message passing, but also type and constant visibility and the raising of exceptions), instantiation, inheritance (both single and multiple), and control flows

- The object, class, state, control, and timing models of requirements analysis and logical design, as well as the system model for systems analysis and the implementation model of physical, implementation design
- Static architecture specification and design at the object/class, subassembly, assembly, and framework levels
- Dynamic behavior specification and design in terms of object-oriented state transition diagrams (STDs) with substates, object-oriented control flow diagrams (CFDs), timing diagrams (TDs), and timed event and message lists
- Concurrency at both the object/class and operation levels
- Formal specification of object-oriented requirements and designs in terms of the OOSDL object-oriented specification and design language (see Chapter 6) and the ADL diagramming language (see Appendix D)
- Iteration and both global and local recursion
- All aspects of software development, from software requirements analysis through assembly integration
- Detailed format and content guidelines on documenting object-oriented specifications and designs, including tailoring and interpretation for dealing with military standards.

ADM3 currently has second-generation CASE-tool support, and negotiations are currently underway to add more vendors. Finally, training and consulting are available from ASTS to support the adoption and tailoring of ADM3 for both specific projects and organizational usage.

As a third-generation object-oriented method, ADM3 has been able to profit from considerable real-world experience and to learn from the strengths and weaknesses of predecessor methods, both earlier versions of ADM and methods developed by other methodologists. In true object-oriented fashion, ADM3 has been based on considerable reuse from all relevant sources. Whenever another method or methodologist has introduced a useful concept or technique missing in ADM, these advances have been evaluated, adapted, improved on, and added to ADM3 as rapidly as practical. While this has resulted in a comprehensive (and therefore large) method, it is our firm belief that it is easier to tailor out what is not needed than to discover or invent a needed part of the method in the midst of an ongoing project. The reader is advised to use what is useful when and where practical, and to either modify or ignore the rest of the method, on a case by case basis.

The ADM3 software development method can be divided into the following five major steps performed by the project software development organization (see Figure 5-1):

1. Perform the initial planning
2. Perform project-specific domain analysis
3. Prepare for globally recursive development
4. Perform globally recursive development
5. Complete the build

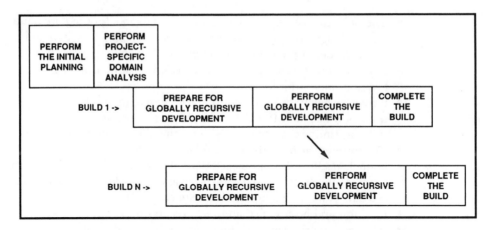

**Figure 5-1: Overview of the ADM3 Development Cycle**

ADM3 assumes that large projects contain multiple assemblies of software that are incrementally developed using multiple builds (and releases). The first two steps are performed once at the beginning of each project, whereas the last three steps are performed once for each build (and release) of each project. Most object-oriented requirements analysis (OORA) and logical design (OOLD) methods are limited to Step 4 of ADM3.

## 5.1  PERFORM THE INITIAL PLANNING

Those who fail to plan plan to fail. The project software development organization therefore performs the following six substeps of the first major step of ADM3 (see Figure 5-2) in order to properly plan for object-oriented development (OOD):

1.1.  Determine the overall development process
1.2.  Tailor ADM3
1.3.  Tailor the software standards and procedures
1.4.  Develop the training plan
1.5.  Develop the risk management plan
1.6.  Develop the software development plan (SDP)

In order for the customer to evaluate the project proposal properly, these substeps should be completed before the proposal is completed so that the project SDP is delivered with the proposal.

### 5.1.1  Determine the Overall Development Process

Project management should determine the overall development approach and associated development cycle, based on management experience with global recursion, contractual requirements (especially with regard to schedule and formal reviews), and

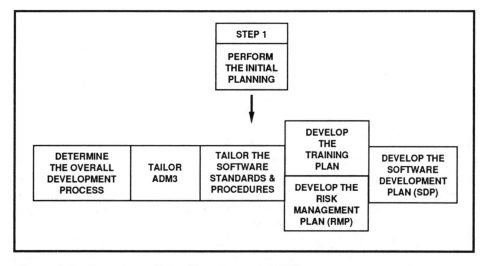

**Figure 5-2: Overview of the First Step of ADM3**

the application domain, as well as management's relative understanding of the system requirements and the degree to which the application breaks new ground. A very conservative (and inefficient) approach would be to use no global recursion and thus to force-fit OOD into the classic (and obsolete) waterfall development cycle. A very avant-garde approach would be to perform all development in a globally recursive manner, using a pure globally recursive development cycle. Other approaches lie between these two ends of this spectrum.

The waterfall development cycle should only be used when the application domain is well known, the system requirements are stable and well documented, and the project personnel have significant experience developing similar applications using similar (i.e., object-oriented) methods.

Project (technical) management should determine the following:

- The amount, if any, of project-specific object-oriented domain analysis (OODA) to be performed, based on the size of the project and whether or not adequate organizational OODA has been previously completed
- The amount, if any, of initial, *locally recursive* OORA to be performed, as well as the amount of any initial incremental development, including rapid prototyping, that shall precede the *globally recursive* OOD
- The project approach to formal reviews; for example, they could choose traditional reviews [DOD-STD-2167A] such as software specification reviews (SSRs), preliminary design reviews (PDRs), and critical design reviews (CDRs), or they might instead use object-oriented in-process reviews (IPRs)
- The project approach to concurrency (e.g., none at all, language-specific tasking, operating-system processes) and scheduling (e.g., rate monotonic scheduling algorithm or hard-deadline scheduling)

Finally, the project technical management should tailor the object-oriented method to fit the process, the global development decisions, the application domain, and the organizational culture. The tailored method should be backed by project-level standards and procedures and by training classes (at the appropriate level) for the software engineers, quality-assurance and configuration-management personnel, and project administrative and technical management.

## 5.1.2    Tailor ADM3

The software-development organization should tailor ADM3 for the development process and cycle chosen. ADM3 should also be tailored for the amount of project-specific OODA to be performed, based on the amount, if any, of initial, locally recursive OORA and of rapid prototyping. Other factors to consider are the project approach to formal reviews, concurrency, and task scheduling. The application domain, the size and complexity of the project, the implementation language, and the culture of the development organization also affect the amount and type of tailoring needed.

## 5.1.3    Tailor the Software Standards and Procedures

Although generic software-development standards and procedures that implement ADM3 should exist prior to the start of the project, they will require tailoring, based on the results of the previous two substeps:

1. Determine the overall development process
2. Tailor ADM3

## 5.1.4    Develop the Training Plan

In order to ensure that the software-development organization is properly prepared to efficiently develop high-quality object-oriented software, a detailed training plan should be developed. This plan should cover the type, scope, amount, and schedule of the training, so that (a) adequate funding and facilities can be obtained, and (b) the training schedule can be coordinated with the development schedule. The training plan should recognize that although initial classroom training provides the necessary knowledge, legitimate on-the-job-training (OJT) is also required to develop the necessary skills.

Technical managers usually require more training than their respective staffs. This is because of their responsibility to be leaders, guiding their staffs through the transition to the improved technology. Managers typically have more to unlearn because of their greater prior experience with functional-decomposition development methods. Finally, technical managers must usually perform the mentor role in the mentor–apprentice relationship required for OJT.

A "toy" (i.e., small, non-critical) training project should be considered to transition the software development organization over the learning curve "hump" as rapidly as practical so that productivity and quality improve as rapidly as practical. The scope of the training should include the application domain, OODA, the tailored ADM3, the project's software standards and procedures, the CASE tools, and the implementation language and associated tools.

Different personnel require different levels of training in different areas. Personnel to be trained include administrative and technical managers, developers, quality assurance and configuration management personnel, appropriate personnel from the customer's organization, and any independent verification and validation (IV&V) personnel. The schedule of training should include initial and advanced classroom training, ongoing OJT, and public seminars and conferences. Facilities for training should include textbooks, CASE tool(s), compilers, browsers, debuggers, etc. Training should probably be validated and improved via testing.

### 5.1.5　Develop the Risk-Management Plan (RMP)

At the same time that the training plan is developed, project management should also develop a complete, object-oriented, project-specific risk management plan (RMP), which identifies, analyzes, and prioritizes risks concerning, but not limited to, the

- Overall development process and development cycle
- Personnel requirements and training plan
- Tailored version of ADM3
- Tailored associated standards and procedures
- Object-oriented CASE tools, implementation language, compilers, and databases
- Personnel training, experience, and learning-curve issues
- Customer standards and expectations
- Contractual restrictions

The RMP should also document, schedule, and allocate risk-management activities to address these risks.

### 5.1.6　Develop the Software Development Plan (SDP)

Project management should develop a complete, object-oriented, project-specific software development plan (SDP) that addresses the project-specific

- Overall development process
- Development cycle
- Risk management
- Personnel requirements and training plan
- Tailored version of ADM3
- Tailored associated standards and procedures
- Plans concerning object-oriented CASE tools, compilers, and databases

Developers on military projects using DOD-STD-2167A should read Appendix E for more details.

## 5.2 PERFORM PROJECT-SPECIFIC DOMAIN ANALYSIS

The second step of ADM3 consists of seven substeps (see Figure 5-3). The software director staffs the domain-analysis team, consisting of personnel with expertise in the application domain, object-oriented domain analysis (OODA), and the project CASE tool(s) to be used during OODA. The domain-analysis team attends the initial classroom training, performs any project-specific OODA, and identifies the assemblies. The software director also attends the initial classroom training, develops the build plan, determines and schedules the formal reviews, and updates the Software Development Plan (SDP).

### 5.2.1    Staff the Domain-Analysis Team

The project software director staffs the domain-analysis team with lead software engineers having expertise in the application domain, OODA, and the project CASE tool(s) to be used during OODA. The purpose of the team is to perform project-specific OODA, identify the assemblies, allocate assemblies to the various **builds**, and update the SDP.

### 5.2.2    Attend the Initial Classroom Training

The software-development organization provides adequate and appropriate initial classroom training to both the software-management personnel and the domain-

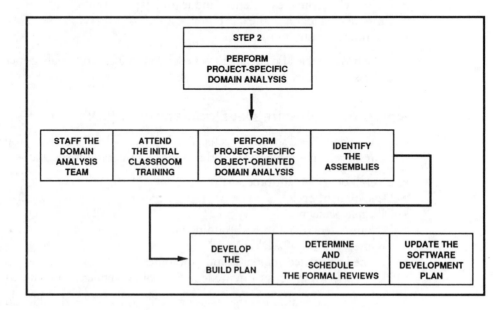

**Figure 5-3: Overview of the Second Step of ADM3**

analysis team. This training should cover the application domain, OODA, the tailored ADM3 and its corresponding project software standards and procedures, the project CASE tools, and the implementation language and its associated tools.

### 5.2.3 Perform Project-Specific Object-Oriented Domain Analysis (OODA)

Although OODA is best performed for the objective of supporting multiple projects and is performed prior to the start of any specific project, some project-specific OODA is recommended if (1) adequate organizational OODA has not been completed, and (2) the project is large enough to justify project-specific OODA to identify objects, classes, subassemblies, and assemblies with significant potential for project reuse.

The project domain-analysis teams should use the results of object-oriented systems analysis (OOSA) and OODA to identify all of the assemblies and builds, the most reusable objects and classes, and the classification and composition hierarchies.

OOSA and OODA use the same techniques as object-oriented requirements analysis and logical design (OORALD) in a less top-down manner to identify, analyze, and possibly logically design the most important objects and classes from the application domain of the project.

### 5.2.4 Identify the Assemblies

The project domain-analysis team should identify all assemblies to be developed, using the results of OOSA and OODA, software-engineering principles, and configuration-management principles. Configuration management is important because assemblies should map to computer software configuration items (CSCIs). The project domain-analysis team should also allocate the system requirements to the assemblies.

Functional assemblies should be avoided in order to ensure that multiple, partial variants of the same objects and classes are not redundantly allocated to different assemblies.

### 5.2.5 Develop the Build Plan

The software director and the project domain-analysis team should identify all builds and releases in terms of the assemblies. For these builds and releases, they should then (a) allocate the system requirements to each, and (b) schedule each one. Finally, they should develop the project build plan for inclusion into the project SDP.

### 5.2.6 Determine and Schedule the Formal Reviews

The software director and the project domain-analysis team should determine the number and type of formal reviews and determine the type of products to be reviewed. They should also determine the acceptance criteria for passing the reviews and schedule the formal reviews of the builds and releases. Finally, they should determine the amount of products to be completed at each formal review.

### 5.2.7    Update the SDP

The software director and the project domain-analysis team should update the SDP to address the build plan, the formal reviews (including type of review, the products to be reviewed, and the acceptance criteria for passing), and the schedule of the builds, the releases, and the formal reviews.

## 5.3  PREPARE FOR GLOBALLY RECURSIVE DEVELOPMENT

The third step of ADM3 consists of six substeps (see Figure 5-4) and is repeated for each build or release. The software director staffs the assembly development teams, which consist of personnel with expertise in the application domain, in OOD, and in the project CASE tool(s) to be used during this step. For each build, the assembly-development teams attend the initial classroom training. For each assembly to be developed during the current build, the relevant assembly-development team develops the assembly context diagram (CD) and the assembly event list, identifies the initial subassemblies, performs any initial locally recursive assembly-specific OORA, and performs any initial rapid prototyping.

### 5.3.1    Staff the Assembly-Development Teams

The project software director staffs the assembly-development teams with software engineers, based on in-house productivity estimates, assembly size and effort estimates, projected staffing curves, and training requirements. Each team should have training, experience, and expertise in the application domain, OOD and ADM3, the project software standards and procedures, the CASE tools, and the implementation language and associated tools.

### 5.3.2    Attend the Initial Classroom Training

The software development organization provides adequate and appropriate initial classroom training to the assembly-development teams, quality assurance personnel, and customer and independent verification and validation (IV&V) personnel. This classroom training should cover the tailored ADM3 method, the project software standards and procedures, the project CASE tools, and the implementation language and tools.

### 5.3.3    Develop the Assembly Context Diagram and Timed Event List

In order to place the software to be developed in context and to document the terminators with which it must interface, the assembly-development teams should develop a CD for each assembly. Each CD shows

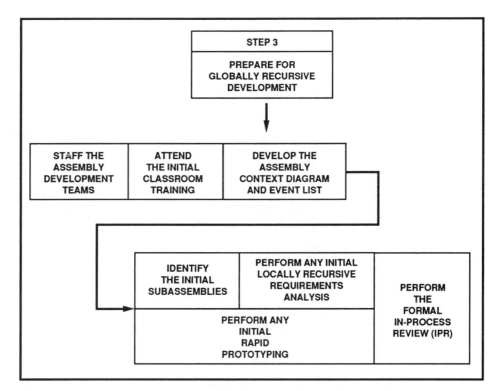

**Figure 5-4: Overview of the Third Step of ADM3**

- The assembly
- Its terminators
  - hardware
  - people
  - software
  - systems
- All important interface relationships among them

General semantic nets (GSNs) should be used as CDs rather than using the less object-oriented, traditional data flow diagrams (DFDs) of Structured Analysis. GSNs have several benefits when used as CDs. They differentiate different classes of terminators (i.e., hardware, people, software, and system, master vs. servant). GSN CDs are also very understandable. Each relationship on the GSN can be read as a standard English sentence, such as "The DECREMENT_FLOW_BUTTON decreases the desired flow of the water passing through the hardware SOLENOID_ FAILSAFE_VALVE." and "THE_SHOWER_MASTER object reads the actual temperature of the THE_PREVALVE_TEMPERATURE_SENSOR.COLD_WATER." Note that the subject of the sentence is the starting node, the verb phrase is the relationship, and the direct object of the sentence is the ending node. GSNs are at a higher level of abstraction than DFDs and can be developed earlier. GSNs used as CDs are also more general than DFDs used as CDs. Because the directions of the relationship arcs on GSNs imply *control* flow rather than *data* flow, the software engineers should ensure that the relationships are drawn from the client (i.e., caller) entity to the server (i.e., callee) entity so that dependency relationships are correctly implied and the GSNs will have the same topology as the interaction diagrams to be developed later. By providing an overview of the assembly and its relationships to its terminators, GSNs are useful for communication with the customer and those requiring an introduction to the application.

To describe and explain the steps of ADM3, a single, relatively simple example is highlighted throughout this chapter. Shower Master is a hypothetical commercial product that provides shower water at a flow rate and temperature specified by the bather, by means of a set of buttons on a control panel. See Figure 5-5: Control Panel for Shower Master. The bather can turn Shower Master on and off with the on/off button on the control panel. The bather can increment and decrement the desired flow and temperature of the shower water with the associated buttons on the control panel. When turned on, the control panel also displays the actual and desired flow and temperature of the shower water.

The cold water, the hot water, and the shower water are controlled by a valve,

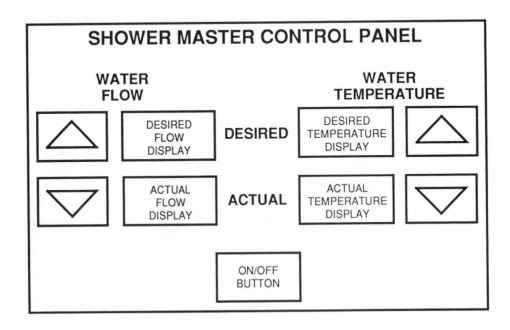

**Figure 5-5: Control Panel for Shower Master**

a flow sensor, and a temperature sensor on each of the three water pipes. See Figure 5-6: Valves, Motors, Drivers, and Sensors for Shower Master. The valves on the cold and hot water pipes are controlled by a torque motor, which is driven by a voltage to current driver. These valves can be partially opened and are used to control the actual flow and temperature of the shower water. The solenoid fail-safe valve on the shower-water pipe is used to prevent accidental injury due to scalding. The Shower Master software is to read the sensors and control the three valves in order to achieve the desired flow and temperature, as specified by the buttons on the control panel.

Figure 5–7 is the corresponding CD for the hardware described in Figure 5–6.

The assembly-development team should also document (a) a description of the abstraction implemented by the assembly, (b) the objective of the assembly, (c) a description of each terminator, and (d) an elaboration (if necessary) of each relationship. For example:

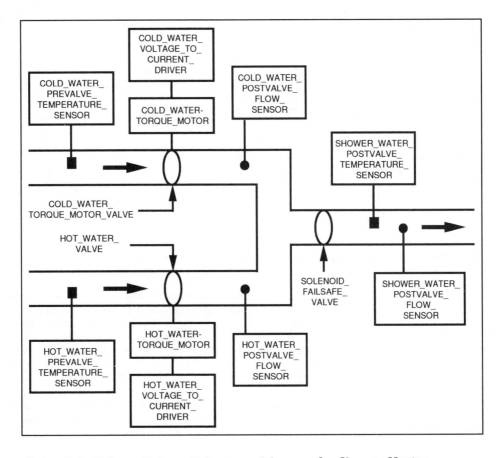

**Figure 5-6: Valves, Motors, Drivers, and Sensors for Shower Master**

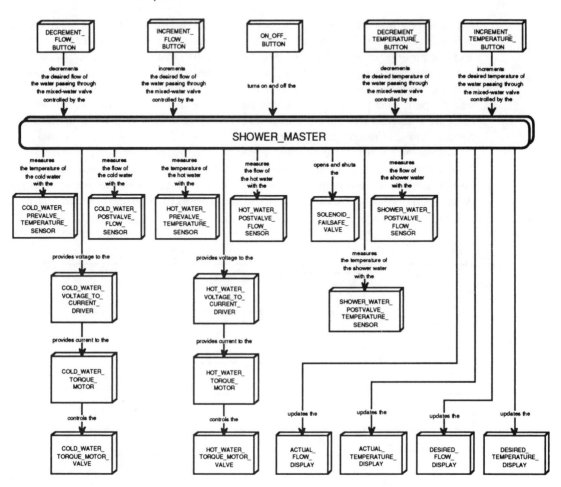

**Figure 5-7: Context Diagram (CD) for the** SHOWER_MASTER **Assembly**

The SHOWER_MASTER assembly contains all of the objects and classes required to implement the Shower Master capabilities and (1) is controlled by decrement flow, decrement temperature, increment flow, increment temperature, and on/off buttons; (2) reads the cold water, hot water, and shower water flow and temperature sensors; (3) controls the cold water and hot water voltage to the current drivers, torque motors, and valves; (4) controls the solenoid failsafe valve; and (5) displays the actual and desired flows and temperatures on the actual and desired flow and temperature displays.

The DECREMENT_TEMPERATURE_BUTTON is the hardware terminator that decrements the desired temperature of the SHOWER_MASTER assembly by 1 degree when pressed, given that the desired temperature is above its minimum value.

The assembly development teams should also generate a timed event list for each scenario, which lists each relevant event and its associated timing requirements. Each event consists of a message sent across the assembly boundary. For an example event list associated with a street intersection, see Figure 5-8: Event List for the TURN_OFF Thread of the SHOWER_MASTER Assembly.

### 5.3.4    Identify the Initial Subassemblies

Most nontrivial assemblies contain far more objects and classes than can efficiently and reliably be identified, analyzed, and designed at once. The assembly must therefore be partitioned into small, manageable subassemblies (a.k.a. *subsystems, subjects*) that can be individually analyzed and designed by subassembly-development teams comprising two to five software engineers. Developers with years of experience with traditional software-development methods restricted to the classic waterfall development cycle tend to want to identify all subassemblies prior to identifying and developing any of their component objects and classes. Most OOD methods, however, use a more modern and efficient recursive development approach to incrementally develop assemblies, one subassembly at a time. Unfortunately, recursion is not adequate by itself for this objective. While recursion is useful for identifying child subassemblies, it requires the existence of stubbed objects or classes in initial subassemblies to provide the motivation for the child subassemblies at the next-lower level of abstraction.

The assembly development team identifies one or more initial subassemblies, using some of the following approaches:

- Using cohesion and coupling
- Using masters
  —Using master terminators
  —Using master object and classes
- Using object decomposition
- Using classification hierarchies
- Using requirements
- Using personal experience

| Sec | Sender | Message | Receiver |
|-----|--------|---------|----------|
| 0.00 | ON_OFF_BUTTON.CONTROL | interrupt | SHOWER_MASTER |
| 0.04 | SHOWER_MASTER | clear | DESIRED_FLOW_DISPLAY |
| 0.04 | SHOWER_MASTER | clear | DESIRED_TEMPERATURE_DISPLAY |
| 0.05 | SHOWER_MASTER | zero voltage | COLD_WATER_VOLTAGE_TO_CURRENT_DRIVER |
| 0.05 | SHOWER_MASTER | zero voltage | HOT_WATER_VOLTAGE_TO_CURRENT_DRIVER |
| 0.06 | COLD_WATER_VOLTAGE_TO_CURRENT_DRIVER | zero current | COLD_WATER_TORQUE_MOTOR |
| 0.06 | HOT_WATER_VOLTAGE_TO_CURRENT_DRIVER | zero current | HOT_WATER_TORQUE_MOTOR |
| 0.07 | COLD_WATER_TORQUE_MOTOR | close | COLD_WATER_VALVE |
| 0.07 | HOT_WATER_TORQUE_MOTOR | close | HOT_WATER_VALVE |
| 0.08 | SHOWER_MASTER | clear | ACTUAL_FLOW_DISPLAY |
| 0.08 | SHOWER_MASTER | clear | ACTUAL_TEMPERATURE_DISPLAY |

**Figure 5-8: Event List for the TURN_OFF Thread of the SHOWER_MASTER Assembly**

- Using OODA
- Using repositories of previously developed software
  —Reusing application frameworks
  —Reusing individual subassemblies

The software engineers should maximize object cohesion while minimizing message and inheritance coupling among these initial subassemblies. Due to the difficulty of this step, some errors in identification should be expected. The software engineers should iterate until a reasonable set of top-level subassemblies exists from which all other child subassemblies can be developed, using recursion.

The assembly-development team should allocate to each initial subassembly the appropriate subset of the systems requirements that were allocated to the assembly. For each initial subassembly, the associated requirements will include both those requirements implemented directly by the objects and classes that make up the subassembly and those that will be passed down to any child subassemblies. Thus, if only one initial subassembly is identified, all assembly requirements will be allocated to the initial subassembly, some of which are to be implemented by the subassembly and the others of which are to be passed through to the initial subassembly's children.

The software engineers should also document the mapping of assembly requirements to the initial subassemblies with a requirements trace. Both this mapping of assembly requirements to initial subassemblies and this requirements trace will require significantly less effort if an object-oriented approach is used to analyze the system requirements, to identify the assemblies, and to allocate the system software requirements to assemblies.

## 5.3.5    Perform Any Initial Locally Recursive Requirements Analysis

The assembly development teams may use the steps of the method in a locally recursive manner to optionally perform some initial OORA. The method should be restricted to essential objects and classes, and to their essential attributes, operations, and exceptions. The objective of this step is to

- Meet contractual schedule requirements
- Improve software size and schedule estimates
- Determine the initial subassemblies of the assembly
- Lower the risk associated with the global recursion of high-risk capabilities

In order to maximize productivity and quality, this should be limited to a preliminary analysis of the top two or three levels of abstraction and their high-risk capabilities.

## 5.3.6    Perform Any Initial Rapid Prototyping

The assembly development teams may optionally perform some initial, incremental OOD and traditionlal rapid prototyping. The primary objective of this step is to develop common reusable software identified with the OODA. This step can also be used to develop any high-risk objects and classes and the main reusable classes of the classification hierarchies.

# 5.4  PERFORM GLOBALLY RECURSIVE DEVELOPMENT

The fourth step of ADM3 consists of eight substeps (see Figure 5-9) and is repeated for each build or release. On a subassembly-by-subassembly basis, the assembly de-

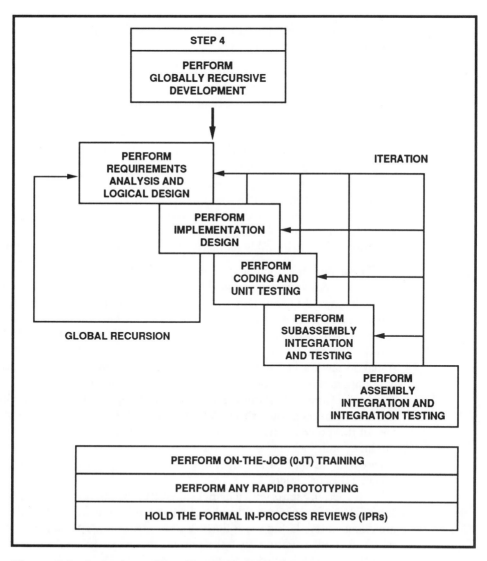

**Figure 5-9: Overview of the Fourth Step of ADM3**

velopment teams perform requirements analysis and logical design, implementation design, programming and unit testing, subassembly integration and testing, and assembly integration, and integration testing. On an assembly-by-assembly basis, the assembly development teams implement on-the-job training (OJT), any additional rapid prototyping, and formal IPRs.

## 5.4.1    Object-Oriented Requirements Analysis and Logical Design (OORALD)

The objectives of the software OORALD activity are to identify, analyze, specify the requirements for, and logically design all subassembly objects and classes. The individual steps of this activity are

- Staff and schedule subassembly development
- State the subassembly objective
- Obtain and review the subassembly requirements
- Develop the object model
- Develop the class model
- Organize the subassembly requirements
- Check the reuse repository
- Develop the state model
- Develop the control model
- Develop the timing model
- Update the deliverable documentation
- Perform the subassembly requirements and logical design inspection

These steps are documented in Figure 5-10: Overview of Object-Oriented Requirements Analysis and Logical Design (OORALD). The steps that are listed vertically adjacent to one another are interrelated and can be effectively implemented simultaneously. For example, because objects and classes are the primary nodes on the semantic nets, one must first identify some of the initial objects and classes before one can develop the semantic model. However, one often identifies the need for additional objects and classes by recognizing the incompleteness of existing semantic nets. The important models developed during this activity are depicted by rounded rectangles on Figure 5-10. Although the individual steps are listed in chronological order without iteration arrows, this is definitely not intended to imply that iteration is not part of this process. The individual steps often include planned iteration of previous products, and the members of the subassembly-development team are encouraged to iterate back, as appropriate, whenever they discover mistakes or ways to improve the specification or design.

This activity starts with a management step, which is followed by two preparatory steps. The next seven steps develop the five fundamental models of this activity with are documented during the following step. The final step is a peer-level inspection, which is used to ensure that the activity has been successfully completed before starting the next activity, implementation design.

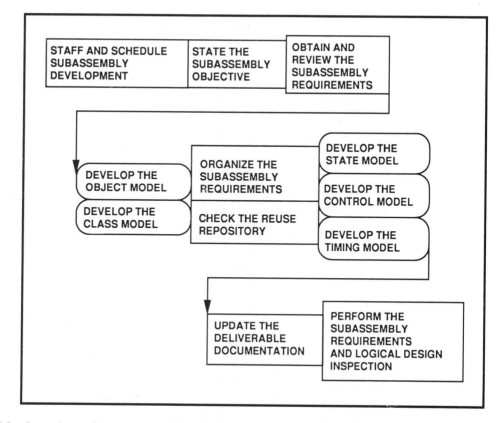

**Figure 5-10: Overview of Object-Oriented Requirements Analysis and Logical Design (OORALD)**

The steps of the method are applied on a subassembly-by-subassembly basis. The subassembly requirements are the inputs to the method, and the outputs of the method are the object, class, state, control, and timing models; the subassembly part of the project repository; and the software requirements specification (SRS) and the software design document (SDD), which are updated with the subassembly requirements and logical design, respectively. The first step of the method is a management activity, the last step is a verification activity, and the other steps are development activities. See Figure 5-11: A Second Overview of OORALD.

### 5.4.1.1  Staff and Schedule Subassembly Development

The first step of the OORALD activity of an individual subassembly is the technical management step of staffing and scheduling the subassembly development. The technical manager responsible for the development of the current subassembly should assign the members of the subassembly-development team and should schedule all

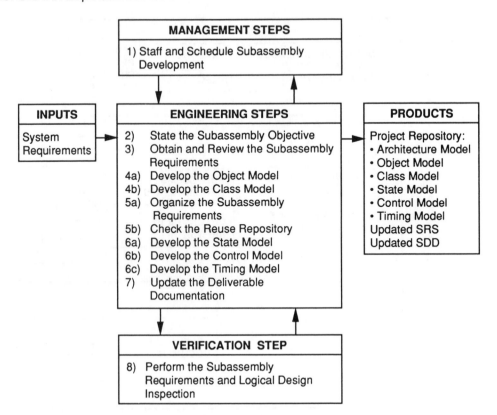

**MANAGEMENT STEPS**

1) Staff and Schedule Subassembly Development

**INPUTS**

System Requirements

**ENGINEERING STEPS**

2)  State the Subassembly Objective
3)  Obtain and Review the Subassembly Requirements
4a) Develop the Object Model
4b) Develop the Class Model
5a) Organize the Subassembly Requirements
5b) Check the Reuse Repository
6a) Develop the State Model
6b) Develop the Control Model
6c) Develop the Timing Model
7)  Update the Deliverable Documentation

**PRODUCTS**

Project Repository:
• Architecture Model
• Object Model
• Class Model
• State Model
• Control Model
• Timing Model
Updated SRS
Updated SDD

**VERIFICATION STEP**

8)  Perform the Subassembly Requirements and Logical Design Inspection

**Figure 5-11: A Second Overview of OORALD**

subassembly milestones, including a date for the start and the completion of each activity (i.e., not just the OORALD). He or she should then document the assignments and milestone dates in the subassembly part of the project repository.

The members of the subassembly-development team are drawn from the relevant assembly-development team and typically comprise two to five software engineers. The members of the team should have adequate training and experience in the application domain and in OOD, including analysis, design, coding, and testing. A minimum of at least two software engineers should be assigned to each subassembly, in order to ensure an adequate amount of peer-level interaction and review because no individual is truly aware of his or her own limitations. Assigning only one developer per subassembly tends to significantly lower both quality and productivity, due to the large number of mistakes that are typically made and not caught until much later, when they require significantly more effort to correct and are thus less likely to be corrected properly. Because of the small size of subassemblies (i.e., typically three to ten objects and classes, usually requiring less than 1000–2000 lines of source code), it is often inappropriate to assign more than four or five software engineers, as that would result in too much interaction and designs by committee. The specific number of software engineers assigned naturally depends on availability and experience, with new hires and the less experienced being assigned to the project experts for OJT.

Subassembly scheduling is typically done on an individual subassembly-by-subassembly basis as the subassemblies are identified. The duration of subassembly development typically runs 3 to 10 weeks. The schedule depends on the subassembly-development team size, training, and experience, with larger (within limits), highly trained, and experienced teams being naturally faster. Large and complex subassemblies with significant concurrency are often harder and take more time. Even the application domain has an impact with hard real-time embedded applications often taking longer than management information systems (MIS) applications of equal size. Because the size and complexity of subassemblies can only be roughly estimated at this stage, the schedule is typically inexact at the subassembly level and should be updated often. This step is also made more difficult for many projects because OOD is relatively new, and few—if any—metrics have been collected that can be used to calibrate project estimates.

The technical manager should informally evaluate the subassembly staffing and schedule prior to having the subassembly-development team start the next step: Does the software development team contain too few or too many members? Do the members of the software development team have adequate training and experience in both the application domain and OOD? If the subassembly interfaces with one or more other subassemblies, has a member from each subassembly-development team been temporarily assigned to the current subassembly-development team, as liaison, to ensure consistent interfaces? Is the schedule adequate? Have all subassembly milestones been scheduled? Is the subassembly schedule consistent with the assembly schedule?

### 5.4.1.2  State the Subassembly Objective

During this step, the subassembly-development team states the primary objective of the subassembly in a single complete sentence (or a very small paragraph) that clearly conveys the objective of the subassembly to be developed. The objective should be written using the terms of the application domain and should be understandable to all members of the subassembly-development team, their management, quality assurance, maintenance personnel, and any customer or user representatives. If an essential subassembly is being developed, this objective should be written in terms of "what" rather than "how" and specifically in terms of required entities and their interactions and capabilities rather than in terms of the design of their corresponding objects and classes.

By having a single objective, the members of the subassembly-development team derive two primary benefits. (1) They can better cooperate to solve the *same* problem rather than working at cross objectives due to miscommunication; without this, subassembly-development teams often create subassemblies that are too large and that contain objects and classes that should not belong to the same subassembly. (2) The subassembly-development team can better identify the *relevant* objects and classes (i.e., those that belong to this subassembly and at this level of abstraction).

If this is the sole initial subassembly, the subassembly objective is the objective of the entire assembly. For example, "The objective of the INTERSECTION subassembly of the TRAFFIC_SYSTEM assembly is to control the crosswalk signals, traffic signals, and traffic sensors of the street intersection."

If this is one of several initial subassemblies, the subassembly objective is the associated major subobjective of the entire assembly. For example, "The objective of the CONTROL_PANEL.SHOWER_MASTER subassembly is to implement the control panel abstraction by grouping and controlling the visibility of all software objects associated with the control panel terminators." As another example, "The objective of the VALVE_CLASSES.SHOWER_MASTER subassembly is to contain all classes for the torque-motor and solenoid valves."

If this is a child subassembly due to recursion on a stubbed entity, the subassembly objective is the objective of the stubbed entity. For example, "The objective of the COLD_WATER.SHOWER_MASTER child subassembly is to provide all objects directly related to the cold water."

The subassembly-development team should informally evaluate the subassembly objective prior to starting the next step: Does the sentence or paragraph state only the primary objective? Does the objective emphasize "what" over "how"? Is the objective understandable to all interested parties (e.g., software engineers, managers, customers, maintenance personnel, quality assurance)? Is the objective appropriate in terms of the type of the subassembly (i.e., initial vs. child)?

### 5.4.1.3  Obtain and Review the Subassembly Requirements

The subassembly-development team must next obtain the subset of the assembly requirements that were allocated to the current subassembly and store them in the subassembly part of the project repository. If this is an initial subassembly of the assembly, this subset of requirements were allocated during the "identify-the-initial-subassemblies" activity, prior to the start of globally recursive development. If this is a child subassembly produced by recursion, this subset of requirements were allocated as part of the development of the parent subassembly, during the "make-any-additional-design-decisions" step of the "implementation-design" activity.

After the members of the subassembly-development team agree on a subassembly objective, they prepare to identify the relevant objects and classes by reviewing the subassembly requirements. This review need not be lengthy or deep because the requirements will be analyzed in more detail during the subsequent steps. This review should emphasize the most important, top-level remaining entities because the objective of the current step is only to prepare for the next step, when the corresponding objects and classes will be identified. The subassembly-development team should informally list the relevant entities (perhaps by highlighting them in the requirements) and the places where they are addressed in the requirements.

Not all of the requirements allocated to the current subassembly may be relevant. Some may well need to be passed down to child subassemblies to be implemented by objects and classes at lower levels of abstraction. However, *all* of the requirements allocated to the current subassembly should probably be reviewed, if time allows, because the requirements for individual objects and classes are often scattered through the set of subassembly requirements, especially if they were sorted by functional abstraction.

The subassembly-development team should informally evaluate the subassembly requirements prior to starting the next step: Have all subassembly requirements been found? Are they properly stored? Have all relevant requirements been reviewed by each member of the subassembly-development team? Has the review been performed at the right level—neither too shallow nor too deep? Have potential objects and classes been noted?

### 5.4.1.4 Develop the Object Model

The subassembly-development team should develop the subassembly object model and should document it in the subassembly part of the project repository. When making concurrency decisions, they should especially consider these decisions' important ramifications (e.g., polling, interrupts) for the relationships among the objects and between the objects and the external entities with which they interface.

The object model provides a static view of the essential and logical architecture of the subassembly. The model documents the existence, abstraction, and visibility of its component objects (and possibly classes), the terminators with which the individual objects must interface, and the important relationships and messages passed among them.

Development of the object model typically precedes the development of the class model if the subassembly is to contain specific objects that model specific known entities (e.g., as typically occurs when developing embedded applications). On the other hand, the object model is typically developed after the class model if the subassembly is to contain classes that model arbitrary collections of entities (e.g., as typically occurs when developing general solutions for MIS/ADP (automatic data processing) applications or when promoting reuse during domain analysis). The object and class models may also be developed simultaneously and iteratively, and the subassembly-development team should have the freedom to choose the appropriate order in which to develop the models.

The object model of a subassembly consists of the following (where practical and useful):

- A list of all objects in the subassembly
- A GSN for the subassembly
- The specification and body of the subassembly (e.g., written in OOSDL), listing all subassembly objects
- An interaction diagram (ID) for the subassembly, each major thread of control through the subassembly, and each object within the subassembly

- A description of each message passed to and from each object in the subassembly
- A composition diagram (CMD) for each subassembly aggregation hierarchy
- The objective of each object of the subassembly and a description of the abstraction implemented by each
- The specification and initial body of each object in the subassembly
- A description of each attribute type and attribute of each object in the subassembly
- A description of each operation of each object in the subassembly
- A description of each exception of each object in the subassembly

### 5.4.1.4.1    Identify the Subassembly Objects

The subassembly-development team should then collectively identify, name, and agree on the initial objects of the subassembly, using an appropriate subset of the following approaches:

- Recommended approaches
  —Using object abstraction
    - Using the types of the modeled entities
    - Using the definition of an object
    - Using object decomposition
  —Using inheritance
    - Using generalization
    - Using subclasses
  —Using OODA
  —Using repositories of previously developed software
    - Reusing application frameworks
    - Reusing class hierarchies
    - Reusing individual objects and classes
  —Using specification and design languages
  —Using personal experience
- Traditional approaches
  —Using nouns
  —Using traditional DFDs
    - Using terminators on CDs
    - Using data stores on DFDs
    - Using complex data flows on DFDs
- Miscellaneous approaches
  —Using abstract data types (ADTs) and abstract state machines (ASMs)
  —Using states
  —Using resources
    - Using attributes
    - Using operations
    - Using exceptions
  —Using requirements

—Using class responsibility collaboration (CRC) cards
—Using entities on entity relationship attribute (ERA) diagrams
—Using object-oriented diagrams
  - Using nodes on semantic nets (SNs)
  - Using nodes on IDs

This substep is one of the most difficult of OOD; it involves some creativity and requires practice and experience. Additional objects can often be identified during the next step, when the GSNs are developed.

Once the objects are identified, the subassembly-development team should list and characterize them in the subassembly part of the project repository. They are (a) essential or nonessential, (b) sequential or concurrent, and (c) masters, agents, or servants. For example, the CONTROL_PANEL.SHOWER_MASTER and the COLD_WATER.SHOWER_MASTER subassemblies contain the following objects, respectively:

CONTROL_PANEL:
| | | | |
|---|---|---|---|
| • THE_DECREMENT_FLOW_BUTTON | Essential | Concurrent | Master |
| • THE_DECREMENT_TEMPERATURE_BUTTON | Essential | Concurrent | Master |
| • THE_DESIRED_FLOW | Essential | Concurrent | Agent |
| • THE_DESIRED_FLOW_DISPLAY | Essential | Concurrent | Agent |
| • THE_DESIRED_TEMPERATURE | Essential | Concurrent | Agent |
| • THE_DESIRED_TEMPERATURE_DISPLAY | Essential | Concurrent | Agent |
| • THE_INCREMENT_FLOW_BUTTON | Essential | Concurrent | Master |
| • THE_INCREMENT_TEMPERATURE_BUTTON | Essential | Concurrent | Master |
| • THE_ON_OFF_BUTTON | Essential | Concurrent | Master |
| • THE_SHOWER_MASTER | Essential | Concurrent | Agent |

COLD_WATER:
| | | | |
|---|---|---|---|
| • THE_ACTUAL_FLOW | Essential | Concurrent | Servant |
| • THE_DESIRED_FLOW | Essential | Sequential | Agent |
| • THE_PREVALVE_TEMPERATURE_SENSOR | Essential | Sequential | Agent |
| • THE_POSTVALVE_FLOW_SENSOR | Essential | Concurrent | Agent |
| • THE_TORQUE_MOTOR | Essential | Sequential | Agent |
| • THE_VALVE | Essential | Sequential | Agent |
| • THE_VOLTAGE_TO_CURRENT_DRIVER | Essential | Sequential | Agent |

Prior to completing this step, the subassembly-development team should informally ensure that the initial objects have been properly identified: Do all candidate objects meet the definition of an object? Is the total number of objects not significantly more than the Miller (a.k.a., Hrair) limit of seven plus or minus two? Are all objects relevant, and do they all belong at the current level of abstraction? Have all objects been given understandable, project-unique identifiers that are singular nouns?

If a specification or design language was used as part of the identification process, several questions should be answered: Is it compilable, executable, and testable? Was it successfully compiled, executed, and tested? Does it fulfill the objective of the subassembly? Does it address all relevant objects? Does it address all or most of their major attributes and operations?

### 5.4.1.4.2    Develop the General Semantic Nets (GSNs)

The subassembly-development team should check the reuse repository for a reusable subassembly GSN previously developed for a similar subassembly or as part of a relevant application framework. If no such GSN exists, the subassembly-development team should incrementally draw a subassembly GSN by first drawing some or all of its nodes and then connecting appropriate nodes with the appropriate arcs, representing relationships. The nodes on GSNs are assemblies, subassemblies, objects, systems, hardware, and people. Assemblies are drawn with two thick rounded rectangles; subassemblies are drawn with thick rounded rectangles; concurrent objects are drawn with thick parallelograms; sequential objects are drawn with thick rectangles; hardware is drawn with thin boxes; systems are drawn with thick boxes; and people are drawn with thick circles. Visible objects and subassemblies are drawn on the boundary of the subassembly, whereas hidden objects and subassemblies are drawn fully nested within the parent subassembly. Assemblies, systems, hardware, and people may not be drawn socketed or nested in subassemblies. See Figure 5-12: Icons for General Semantic Nets (GSNs).

The subassembly-development team should also label the cardinality and conditionality of the associations on the subassembly GSN. The recommended notation for cardinality is shown on Figure 5-13: Associations on GSNs. If the relationship is one-to-one, no cardinality need be shown, as in the relationship between employees and social security numbers. If the cardinality of the client is one, then only the cardinality of the server needs to be documented. The cardinality of the server can be given by a number (e.g., "5"), a range (e.g., "0..1", "1..100"), a set of values (e.g., "2,4"), a set of ranges ("1..10, 21..30"), or an arbitrary number (e.g., "N"). If the cardinality of the client is not one, then the two cardinalities can be separated by a colon (e.g., "0..1:1..10","M:N").

Figure 5-14 shows a GSN for the initial CONTROL_PANEL.SHOWER_MASTER subassembly, which contains five exported concurrent master objects and five hidden concurrent agent objects. THE_SHOWER_MASTER object depends on seven objects in three child subassemblies.

Figure 5-15 shows the GSN for the child COLD_WATER.SHOWER_MASTER subassembly, which controls the flow of cold water through the torque-motor cold water valve. The GSN for the HOT_WATER.SHOWER_MASTER subassembly is analogous.

### 5.4.1.4.3    Develop the Initial Specification and Body of the Subassembly

The subassembly-development team should specify and logically design the initial specification and body of the subassembly (e.g., using OOSDL). In fact, most of the subassembly specification and body should be automatically generated from the information in the subassembly GSN.

When completed, a subassembly specification documents the subassembly's parent assembly or subassembly, any child subassemblies needed by something listed in

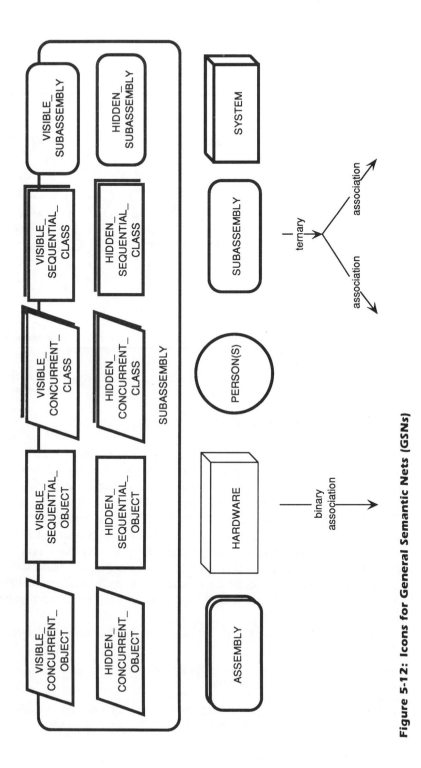

**Figure 5-12: Icons for General Semantic Nets (GSNs)**

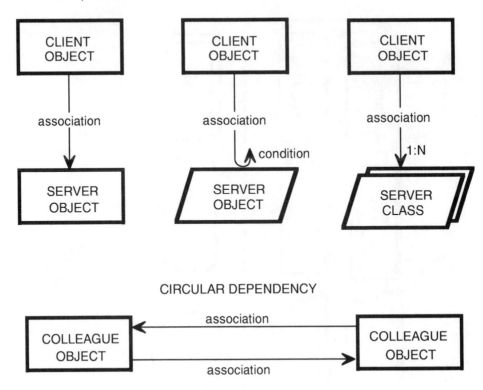

**Figure 5-13: Associations on GSNs**

the specification, whether or not the subassembly is concurrent, and the subassembly's visible objects, classes, and subassemblies. Only the subassembly's immediate parent is listed. If more than one immediate parent exists, then only the parent in which it is defined is listed. A parent subassembly needs a child subassembly if the parent subassembly contains an object or class that needs to send a message to a visible object or class in the child subassembly. A subassembly is concurrent if it contains a concurrent object or class. A component subassembly is visible if is contains at least one object or class that may receive messages from outside its subassembly. When completed, a subassembly body documents (a) any child subassemblies needed by something listed in the body, and (b) the subassembly's hidden component objects, classes, and subassemblies.

The following is an example subassembly specification and body written in OOSDL:

```
subassembly CONTROL_PANEL is concurrent
 parent assembly SHOWER_MASTER;
specification
 object   THE_DECREMENT_FLOW_BUTTON          is concurrent;
 object   THE_DECREMENT_TEMPERATURE_BUTTON   is concurrent;
 object   THE_INCREMENT_FLOW_BUTTON          is concurrent;
```

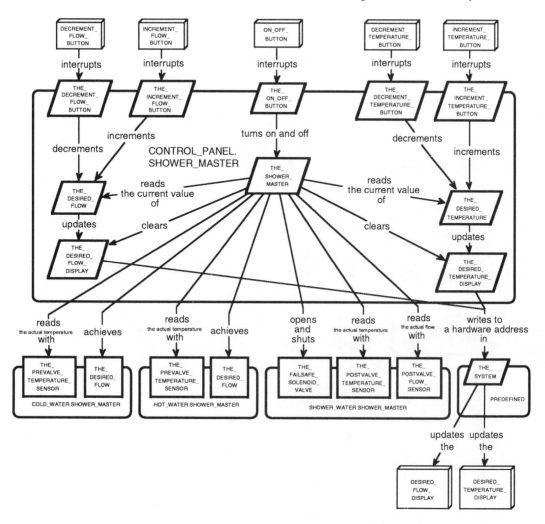

**Figure 5-14: GSN for the** CONTROL_PANEL.SHOWER_MASTER **Subassembly**

```
    object    THE_INCREMENT_TEMPERATURE_BUTTON    is concurrent;
    object    THE_ON_OFF_BUTTON                   is concurrent;
end;

subassembly CONTROL_PANEL
body
    object    THE_DESIRED_FLOW                    is concurrent;
    object    THE_DESIRED_FLOW_DISPLAY            is concurrent;
    object    THE_DESIRED_TEMPERATURE             is concurrent;
    object    THE_DESIRED_TEMPERATURE_DISPLAY     is concurrent;
    object    THE_SHOWER_MASTER                   is concurrent;
end;
```

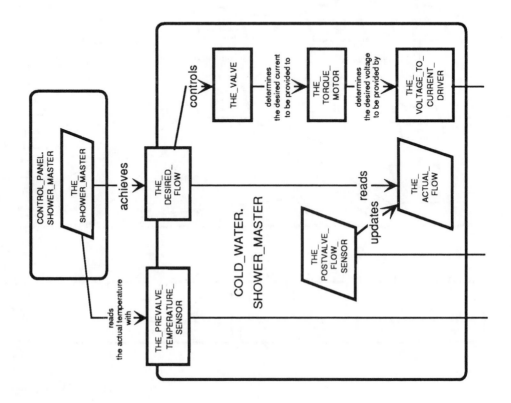

260

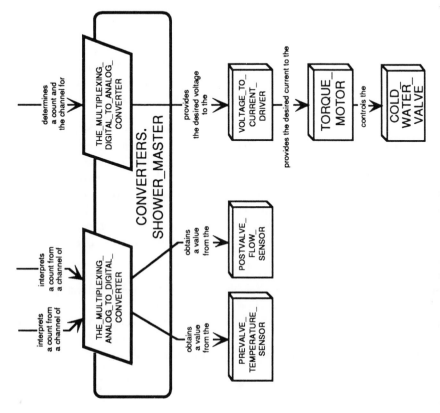

**Figure 5-15: GSN for the** COLD_WATER.SHOWER_MASTER **Subassembly**

261

### 5.4.1.4.4    Develop the Interaction Diagrams (IDs)

The subassembly-development team should check the reuse repository for appropriate reusable IDs previously developed for a similar subassembly or as part of a relevant application framework. If no such IDs exists, the subassembly-development team should incrementally draw an initial subassembly ID for the subassembly, an initial scenario-level ID for each major scenario involving the subassembly, and an object-level ID for each object and class. IDs are primary overview diagrams of subassembly OORALD. They may have three different scopes (i.e., subassembly, scenario, and object level) and three levels of detail (i.e., black box, specification, and body).

Subassembly IDs are the main IDs and should be mandatory. They show an entire subassembly and have the same scope and topology as subassembly GSNs, but the arcs are now labeled with the interactions, typically a list of the messages that can be passed. Scenario-level IDs show all nodes involved with a single scenario, are useful for generating subassembly integration tests, and are highly recommended. Object-level IDs show only a single object or class and its terminators. They are useful in the deliverable documentation if they can be generated quickly and easily. The IDs expand on the information in the subassembly GSNs, and with proper CASE tool support, a skeleton ID can be automatically generated from them.  The IDs show:

- The existence and visibility of objects and classes
- Their generic parameters (classes), specifications, and bodies (optionally)
- The system, hardware, software, and people terminators
- The attribute types, constant attributes, messages, and exceptions that may be passed among the objects and classes
- The type and parameters of the messages (optionally)

Figure 5-16 shows the icons used in IDs. The messages may be annotated with the type of operation (i.e., [C] for constructor, [D] for destructor, [M] for modifier, and [P] for preserver) and the parameters (if useful).

Figure 5-17 shows an example subassembly ID for the CONTROL_PANEL. SHOWER_MASTER. Note that this diagram is identical to Figure 5-14 except for the arcs, which are now labeled with the messages that implement the relationships on Figure 5-14.

Scenario IDs show all nodes involved with a single scenario. They are useful for generating subassembly integration tests and are highly recommended for all significant scenarios. Figure 5-18 shows an example scenario-level ID for the TURN_OFF. SHOWER_MASTER scenario. The hardware ON_OFF_BUTTON interrupts the CONTROL operation of THE_ON_OFF_BUTTON object at THE_INTERRUPT_ ADDRESS_FOR.THE_ON_OFF_BUTTON object sends the TURN_OFF message to THE_SHOWER_MASTER object. THE_SHOWER_MASTER object then sends the CLEAR message to THE_DESIRED_FLOW_DISPLAY and to THE_DESIRED_TEMPERATURE_DISPLAY objects, which then clear the corresponding hardware devices by writing the the appropriate hardware addresses, using

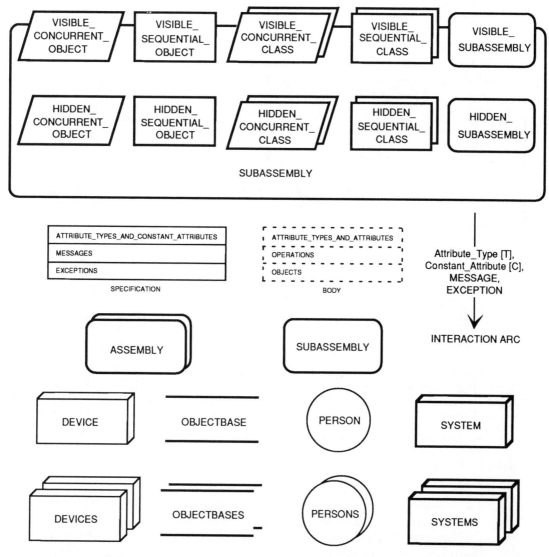

**Figure 5-16: Icons for IDs**

**THE_SYSTEM.PREDEFINED** object. THE_SHOWER_MASTER object also shuts the hardware COLD_WATER_VALVE and HOT_WATER_VALVE by sending the ACHIEVE an amount of zero message to THE_DESIRED_FLOW.COLD_WATER and THE_DESIRED_FLOW.HOT_WATER objects. If either of the ACHIEVE.THE_ DESIRED_FLOW messages fails and returns an exception, then THE_SHOWER_ MASTER sends the SHUT message to THE_FAILSAFE_SOLENOID_VALVE to ensure that the shower water stops flowing.

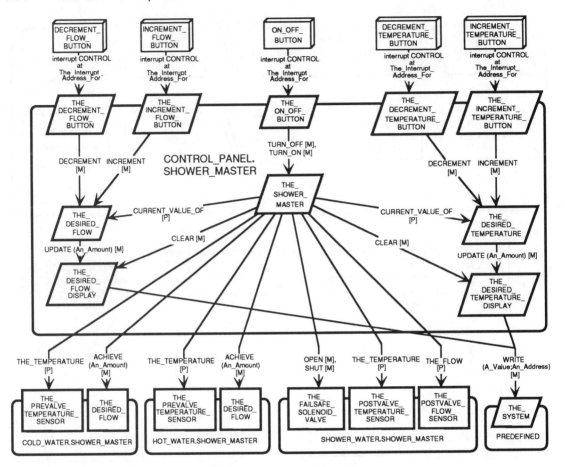

**Figure 5-17: ID for the** CONTROL_PANEL.SHOWER_MASTER **Subassembly**

Figure 5-19 shows an example object-level ID for THE_DESIRED_FLOW object, which is the server of three client objects and the client of one agent object. The box below THE_DESIRED_FLOW object represents its specification, with its exported attribute types, messages, and exceptions. Note that the interaction arcs do not necessarily list all exported resources of the object or class that they point to, but rather only those that are used in order to implement the relationship on the corresponding arc on the corresponding GSN. Note also that if two or more inter-action arcs point to the same entity, they do not necessarily have to list the same set of interactions.

Black-box IDs treat objects and classes as software black boxes, while specifica-tion IDs also show the specifications of the objects and classes. Body IDs show both the specifications and the bodies. See Figure 5-20: Example Black Box, Specification, and Body IDs.

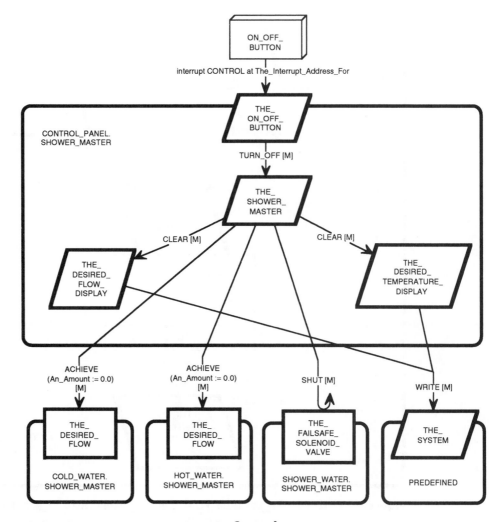

**Figure 5-18: ID for the** TURN_OFF.SHOWER_MASTER **Scenario**

### 5.4.1.4.5   Develop the Composition Diagrams (CMDs)

The subassembly-development team should check the reuse repository for appropriate reusable CMDs previously developed for a similar subassembly or as part of a relevant application framework. If no such CMDs exists, the subassembly-development team should develop a CMD for each composition hierarchy in the subassembly. Each CMD shows the aggregate object in terms of its component objects. Concurrent subassemblies and objects may have concurrent objects as components, but sequential ones may not. The choice oval is used to document the number of potential components to be chosen. See Figure 5-21: Icons for Composition Diagrams (CMDs). Figure

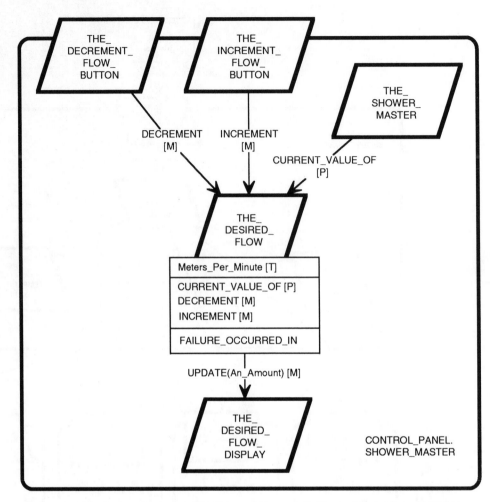

**Figure 5-19: ID for** `THE_DESIRED_FLOW.CONTROL_PANEL.SHOWER_MASTER` **Object**

5-22 shows the CMD of an example aggregate object. Note that a CMD documents the logical nesting of objects, and no implementation decisions concerning the physical nesting of modules is implied.

### 5.4.1.4.6   Describe and Categorize the Objects

The subassembly-development team should describe the abstraction implemented by each object in the subassembly. For example, the following are descriptions of the abstraction implemented by several objects.

• `THE_DESIRED_TEMPERATURE.CONTROL_PANEL.SHOWER_MASTER` object models the

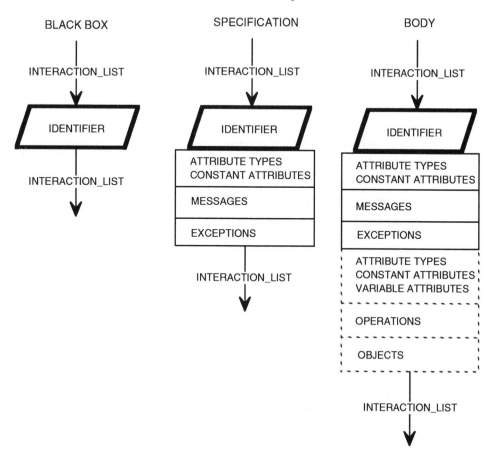

**Figure 5-20: Example Black Box, Specification, and Body IDs**

desired temperature of the Shower Master. This object has the following categorization:
- Essential
- Intangible
- Property
- Atomic
- Concurrent
- Guarded
- Agent (i.e., server of three objects and client of one).

- THE_INCREMENT_TEMPERATURE_BUTTON.CONTROL_PANEL.SHOWER_MASTER object models the hardware increment-temperature button and increments THE_DESIRED_TEMPERATURE object each time that the hardware button is pushed.

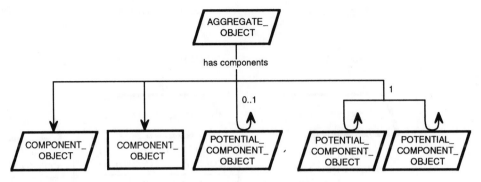

**Figure 5-21: Icons for Composition Diagrams (CMDs)**

This object has the following categorization:

- Essential
- Tangible
- Device
- Atomic
- Concurrent
- Guarded
- Master (i.e., server of no objects and client of one).

5.4.1.4.7   Develop the Specifications and Initial Bodies of the Objects

The subassembly-development team should specify and logically design the specification and initial body of each object in the subassembly, using OOSDL. In fact, some

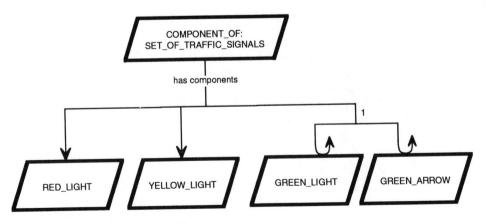

**Figure 5-22: CMD for a Traffic Signal**

of the object specifications should be automatically generated from the information in the subassembly IDs.

In order to develop the specifications and bodies of the objects, the subassembly-development team should identify each resource of each object in the subassembly. This can be done incrementally, using informal *object description tables* (ODTs). Description tables are updated versions of Class-Responsibility-Collaboration (CRC) cards [Beck 1989] that are used as a memory aid to ensure that all relevant information concerning objects and classes is considered and documented. See Figure 5-23, which shows an example ODT. For each object, the subassembly-development team may document

- The identifier and type of the object
- Its location in terms of assembly and subassembly
- All exported and hidden attribute types and attributes, using data abstraction
- All exported and hidden operations, using functional and process abstraction
- All exported exceptions, using exception abstraction
- All hidden component objects
- All objects and classes on which it depends

The subassembly-development team should also add additional nonessential operations to the objects, as appropriate to (a) complete the abstraction; (b) promote reuse; (c) simplify use; (d) decrease client source-code size. They should also update the IDs and CMDs, where appropriate.

The following is an example object specification and body written in OOSDL:

```
object THE_DESIRED_FLOW is concurrent
 parent subassembly CONTROL_PANEL;
 needs THE_SET_OF_INTEGERS.PREDEFINED;
specification
 type Meters_Per_Minute is new Values.SET_OF_INTEGERS range 0 .. 200;
 message   CURRENT_VALUE_OF   return METERS_PER_MINUTE
                              raise  FAILURE_OCCURRED_IN is synchronous;
 message   DECREMENT          raise  FAILURE_OCCURRED_IN is synchronous;
 message   INCREMENT          raise  FAILURE_OCCURRED_IN is synchronous;
 exception FAILURE_OCCURRED_IN;
end;


object THE_DESIRED_FLOW
body
 variable The_Current_Value : Meters_Per_Minute := 0;
 preserver operation   CURRENT_VALUE_OF   return METERS_PER_MINUTE
                                          raise  FAILURE_OCCURRED_IN;
 modifier  operation   DECREMENT          raise  FAILURE_OCCURRED_IN;
 modifier  operation   INCREMENT          raise  FAILURE_OCCURRED_IN;
 preserver operation   ROUTE_MESSAGES_FOR raise  FAILURE_OCCURRED_IN;
start
ROUTE_MESSAGES_FOR;
end;
```

| OBJECT DESCRIPTION TABLE | |
|---|---|
| **OBJECT:** <br> *THE_DESIRED_FLOW.CONTROL_PANEL.SHOWER_MASTER* | |
| **CLASS:** <br> *none* | |
| **SPECIFICATION** | **BODY** |
| **ATTRIBUTE TYPES AND CONSTANTS:** <br><br> *type Meters_Per_Minute* | **ATTRIBUTE TYPES AND ATTRIBUTES:** <br><br> *variable The_Current_Value* |
| **MESSAGES:** <br><br> *CURRENT_VALUE_OF* <br> *DECREMENT* <br> *INCREMENT* | **OPERATIONS:** <br><br> *preserver CURRENT_VALUE_OF* <br> *modifier DECREMENT* <br> *modifier INCREMENT* <br> *preserver ROUTE_MESSAGES_FOR* |
| **EXCEPTIONS:** <br><br> *FAILURE_OCCURRED_IN* | **OBJECTS:** <br><br> *none* |
| **DEPENDS UPON:** <br> *THE_SET_OF_INTEGERS.PREDEFINED* | |

**Figure 5-23: Object Description Table (ODT) for** THE_DESIRED_FLOW **Object**

5.4.1.4.8    Describe the Attribute Types and Attributes of the Objects

The subassembly-development team should also document a description of the abstraction of each attribute type and attribute of each object. This description should provide all necessary information about the attribute not already provided in the body of the object. For example,

- Type `Meters_Per_Minute.THE_DESIRED_FLOW` is derived from the type `Values.`**`SET_OF_INTEGERS.PREDEFINED`** and represents the desired flow of the shower water measured in meters per minute.
- The variable `The_Current_Value_of.THE_DESIRED_FLOW` of type `Meters_Per_Minute` represents the desired flow of the shower water measured in meters per minute.

### 5.4.1.4.9 Describe the Messages of the Objects

The subassembly-development team should document each message passed in the subassembly (e.g., using OOSDL). This documentation should include the specification of the message, the identifiers of the source and destination of the message, the specification of the associated operation that receives the operation, the specification of the operation that implements it (if different), and a description of the functional or process abstraction the message implements. For example,

```
Message: ACHIEVE (An_Amount : in Meters_Per_Minute) is synchronous;
    Sent by:  object THE_SHOWER_MASTER.CONTROL_PANEL is concurrent;
    Sent to:  object THE_DESIRED_FLOW.COLD_WATER;
              object THE_DESIRED_FLOW.HOT_WATER;
    Received by:
     preserver operation ROUTE_MESSAGES_FOR
    Implemented by:
     modifier operation ACHIEVE
        (An_Amount : in Meters_Per_Minute)
        raise FAILURE_OCCURRED_IN
         is concurrent;
    Functional abstraction:
      This message causes THE_DESIRED_FLOW objects to achieve An_Amount.
```

### 5.4.1.4.10 Describe the Exceptions of the Objects

The subassembly-development team should also document a description of the abstraction of each exception of each object. For example, "The exception `FAILURE_OCCURRED_IN.THE_DESIRED_FLOW` signifies that the execution of `THE_DESIRED_FLOW` object has failed and that any operation returning this exception did not successfully complete and is not to be trusted."

### 5.4.1.4.11 Describe the Operations of the Objects

The subassembly-development team should also document a description of the abstraction of each operation of each object. For example, "The `CURRENT_VALUE_OF.THE_DESIRED_FLOW` preserver message returns the value of

The_Current_Value attribute." As another example, "The DECREMENT.
THE_DESIRED_FLOW modifier message decrements the value of The_Current_Value
attribute if it is greater than zero."

### 5.4.1.4.12 Evaluate the Object Model

Prior to starting the next step of the method, the subassembly-development team
should evaluate and approve the quality of the following intermediate products
making up the object model:

- The objective of the subassembly and each object in it
- A description of the abstraction implemented by the subassembly and by each
  object in it
- A list of all objects in the subassembly
- A GSN for the subassembly
- The specification and body of the subassembly (e.g., written in OOSDL) listing all
  subassembly objects, as well as the specification and initial body of each of its
  objects
- An *ID* for the subassembly, each scenario involving the subassembly, and each
  object within the subassembly
- A description of each message passed to and from each object in the subassembly
- A CMD for each subassembly aggregation hierarchy
- A description of each attribute type and attribute of each object in the subassembly

This peer-level evaluation of the object model should provide satisfactory answers
to the following questions:

- Has a clear, correct, and understandable objective of the subassembly been developed
  and documented in the subassembly part of the project repository?
- Have all objects in the subassembly been identified in the subassembly part of the
  project repository and been given proper singular-noun identifiers?
- Does the number of objects in the subassembly not significantly exceed the Miller
  limit of seven plus or minus two?
- Have all objects in the subassembly been properly characterized?
- Is each object concurrent unless there is a requirement or logical design reason[1] to
  have it be sequential?
- Has a proper subassembly GSN been developed and documented in the subassembly
  part of the project repository?
- Does the subassembly GSN contain each object in the subassembly?
- Are all important relationships among objects documented on the subassembly
  GSN?

---

[1] A concurrent object or class may later be made sequential for implementation reasons,
such as language or compiler limitations, efficiency considerations, etc.

- Are all nodes, arcs, and annotations on the GSNs defined in the associated set of GSN icons?
- Has an initial specification and body been developed for the subassembly and documented in the subassembly part of the project repository?
- Are the subassembly specification and body syntactically and semantically correct OOSDL?
- Is each object hidden in the subassembly body unless there is a good reason to export it in the subassembly specification?
- Are the subassembly specification and body consistent with the subassembly GSN?
- Has a proper ID been developed for the subassembly, for each scenario, and for each object in the subassembly?
- Are all IDs properly documented in the subassembly part of the project repository?
- Does the subassembly ID include all subassembly objects and messages?
- Is the subassembly ID consistent with the subassembly GSN in terms of nodes and arc topology?
- Are all nodes, arcs, and annotations on the IDs defined in the associated set of ID icons?
- Has a complete and correct description of each message been documented in the subassembly part of the project repository?
- Has a proper CMD been developed for each composition hierarchy in the subassembly?
- Are all CMDs properly documented in the subassembly part of the project repository?
- Is each node on each CMD also a node on the corresponding GSN?
- Is each aggregate or component node on the GSN also such a node on some CMD for the subassembly?
- Do sequential aggregate objects contain no concurrent objects?
- Has a clear, correct, and understandable objective for each object in the subassembly been developed and documented in the subassembly part of the project repository?
- Has a complete specification and an initial body been developed for each object in the subassembly and documented in the subassembly part of the project repository?
- Are the specification and body of each object syntactically correct OOSDL?
- Has a proper description of each attribute type and attribute been developed and documented in the subassembly part of the project repository?
- Has a proper description of each operation and each exception been developed and documented in the subassembly part of the project repository?

### 5.4.1.5 Develop the Class Model

The subassembly-development team should develop and document the subassembly class model in the subassembly part of the project repository. They should carefully consider the important positive and negative effects of inheritance (e.g., improved reuse, decreased encapsulation, increased coupling) on the resulting subassembly requirements and logical design.

The class model provides a static view of the classification and inheritance architecture of the subassembly, in terms of the existence and abstraction of its component classes and the "has class" and "has superclass" relationships among them and between them and their instances. Refer to Section 5.4.1.4 regarding which model to develop first—the class model or the object model.

The class model of a subassembly consists of

- A list of all classes in the subassembly
- A *classification diagram* (CLD) for each inheritance hierarchy of the subassembly
- The objective of each class of the subassembly, as well as a description of the abstraction implemented by each class therein
- The specification and body of each class, written in OOSDL

### 5.4.1.5.1   Identify the Subassembly Classes

The subassembly-development team should then collectively and iteratively identify, name, and agree on the initial classes of the subassembly, using an appropriate subset of the approaches listed in Section 5.4.1.4.1, with the one change being that among the recommended approaches using object abstraction, the definition of a class would be used in place of the definition of an object.

Once the classes are identified, the subassembly-development team should list and characterize them in the subassembly part of the project repository. They are (a) essential or nonessential, (b) sequential or concurrent, and (c) abstract or concrete. For example, the BUTTONS_CLASSES.SHOWER_MASTER subassembly contains following classes:

- BUTTONS                                    Essential  Concurrent  Abstract
- DECREMENT_FLOW_BUTTONS                      Essential  Concurrent  Concrete
- DECREMENT_TEMPERATURE_BUTTONS               Essential  Concurrent  Concrete
- FLOW_BUTTONS                                Essential  Concurrent  Abstract
- INCREMENT_FLOW_BUTTONS                      Essential  Concurrent  Concrete
- INCREMENT_TEMPERATURE_BUTTONS               Essential  Concurrent  Concrete
- TEMPERATURE_BUTTONS                         Essential  Concurrent  Abstract

### 5.4.1.5.2   Develop the Classification Diagrams (CLDs)

CLDs are specialized SNs restricted to documenting individual inheritance hierarchies and the associated "has class" and "has superclass" relationships. Each CLD (see Figure 5-24) shows the relevant

- Objects (where appropriate)
- Classes
- Generic parameters of generic classes (where appropriate)
- Specification of objects and classes (where appropriate)
- Bodies of objects and classes (where appropriate)

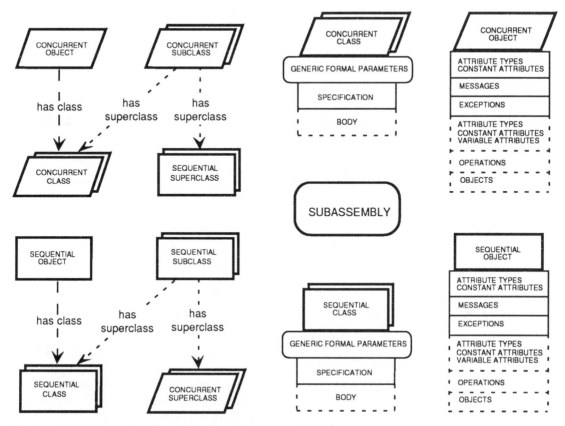

**Figure 5-24: Icons for Classification Diagrams (CLDs)**

- "Has superclass" relationships between subclasses and superclasses
- "Has class" relationships between instances and classes

For each inheritance hierarchy, the subassembly-development team develops an initial overview CLD showing the classification hierarchy in terms of its superclasses, subclasses, and optionally instances. (See Figure 5-25: example of an overview CLD.) Later, as the resources of the classes are identified, the subassembly-development team should use detailed CLDs showing the specifications and bodies and the capabilities that are added, modified, or deleted from subclasses. Capabilities of a superclass are inherited by each subclass unless the capability is *overwritten* (i.e., relisted in the subclass) or *deleted* (i.e., relisted with a minus sign in the subclass). (See Figure 5-26: example of a detailed Classification Diagram.) If the classification hierarchy is too large to show on a single diagram, the classification hierarchy can be decomposed into subdiagrams. If the classification hierarchy is too large to show on a single diagram and if only single inheritance is used, the classification hierarchy can be replaced with an indented list of subclasses and resources. (See Figure 5-27: example of an indented list.)

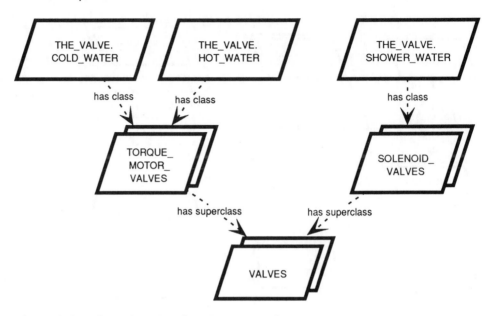

**Figure 5-25: Overview CLD for the** VALVES **Class**

The subassembly-development team should evaluate the inheritance relationships carefully. Although inheritance has many advantages, it is inconsistent with encapsulation and can also decrease quality, understandability, and maintainability. The software engineers should use inheritance to simplify related classes but *not* merely to reuse random unrelated capabilities that do not logically belong to objects of the same superclass. Engineers should also avoid unnecessary inheritance coupling.

In order to develop the detailed CLDs, the subassembly-development team should identify each resource of each class in the subassembly. This can be done incrementally, using informal *class description tables* (CDTs). CDTs are updated versions of CRC cards [Beck 1989], which are used as a memory aid to ensure that all relevant information concerning classes is considered and documented. (See Figure 5-28: example class description table.) For each class, the subassembly-development team may document

- The identifier and type of the class
- Any parameters
- Its superclasses, subclasses, and instances
- All exported and hidden attribute types and attributes using data abstraction
- All exported and hidden operations using functional and process abstraction
- All exported exceptions using exception abstraction
- All hidden component objects
- All objects and classes on which the subassembly depends

The subassembly-development team should also add additional nonessential

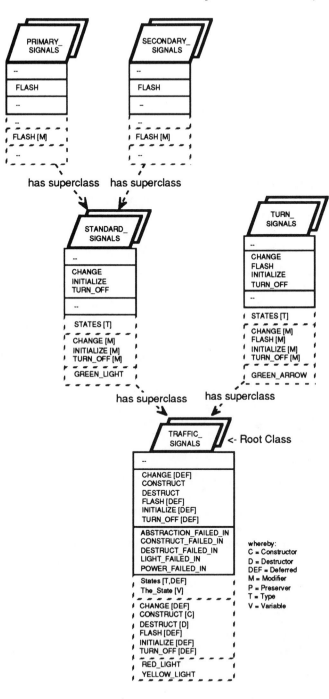

**Figure 5-26: Detailed CLD for the TRAFFIC_SIGNALS Class**

```
class BUTTONS is concurrent
   class FLOW_BUTTONS is concurrent
      class DECREMENT_FLOW_BUTTONS is concurrent
      class INCREMENT_FLOW_BUTTONS is concurrent
   class TEMPERATURE_BUTTONS is concurrent
      class DECREMENT_TEMPERATURE_BUTTONS is concurrent
      class INCREMENT_TEMPERATURE_BUTTONS is concurrent
```

**Figure 5-27: Indented List for the BUTTONS Class**

operations to the classes, as appropriate, (a) to complete the abstraction, (b) promote reuse, (c) simplify use, and (d) decrease the user's source-code size. They should also update the CLDs and the IDs with specifications and bodies, where appropriate.

### 5.4.1.5.3   Describe and Categorize the Classes

The subassembly-development team should provide a description of the abstraction implemented by each class in the subassembly. For example, the following are descriptions of the abstraction implemented by several classes:

* The BUTTONS.BUTTONS_CLASSES.SHOWER_MASTER abstract superclass models the common properties of all buttons in the SHOWER_MASTER assembly.
* For all buttons in the SHOWER_MASTER assembly, the FLOW_BUTTONS. BUTTONS_CLASSES.SHOWER_MASTER abstract subclass models the common properties associated with the desired flow of the shower water.
* The DECREMENT_FLOW_BUTTONS.BUTTONS_CLASSES.SHOWER_MASTER concrete subclass is used to instantiate THE_DECREMENT_FLOW_BUTTON object.

### 5.4.1.5.4   Update or Create a Subassembly Specification and Body

The subassembly-development team should either update the initial specification and body of the subassembly (with its component classes) or create a new subassembly to contain them. In fact, the update or the new subassembly specification and body should be automatically generated from the information in the subassembly CLDs.

The following is an example subassembly specification and body, written in OOSDL:

```
subassembly BUTTON_CLASSES is concurrent
  parent assembly SHOWER_MASTER;
specification
  class   DECREMENT_FLOW_BUTTONS          is concurrent;
  class   DECREMENT_TEMPERATURE_BUTTONS   is concurrent;
  class   INCREMENT_FLOW_BUTTONS          is concurrent;
  class   INCREMENT_TEMPERATURE_BUTTONS   is concurrent;
end;

subassembly BUTTON_CLASSES
body
```

| CLASS DESCRIPTION TABLE | |
|---|---|
| **CLASS:** <br> *STANDARD_SIGNALS.INTERSECTION_CLASSES.TRAFFIC_SYSTEM is abstract* | |
| **PARAMETERS:** <br> *none* | |
| **SUPERCLASSES:** <br> *TRAFFIC_SIGNALS.INTERSECTION_CLASSES.TRAFFIC_SYSTEM is visible* | |
| **SUBCLASSES:**   *PRIMARY_SIGNALS.INTERSECTION_CLASSES.TRAFFIC_SYSTEM* <br> *SECONDARY_SIGNALS.INTERSECTION_CLASSES.TRAFFIC_SYSTEM* | |
| **INSTANCES:** <br> *none* | |

| SPECIFICATION | BODY |
|---|---|
| **ATTRIBUTE TYPES AND CONSTANTS:** <br> *none* | **ATTRIBUTE TYPES AND ATTRIBUTES:** <br> *introduces:* <br> *type STATES* |
| **MESSAGES:** <br> *introduces :* <br> *CHANGE* <br> *INITIALIZE* <br> *TURN_OFF* | **OPERATIONS:** <br> *introduces :* <br> *modifier CHANGE* <br> *modifier INITIALIZE* <br> *modifier TURN_OFF* |
| **EXCEPTIONS:** <br> *none* | **OBJECTS:** <br> *introduces:* <br> *object GREEN_LIGHT* |

| DEPENDS UPON: |
|---|
| *TRAFFIC_LIGHTS (Body).INTERSECTION_CLASSES.TRAFFIC_SYSTEM* |

**Figure 5-28: Class Description Table (CDT) for the** TRAFFIC_SIGNALS **Class**

```
class   BUTTONS                 is concurrent;
class   FLOW_BUTTONS            is concurrent;
class   TEMPERATURE_BUTTONS     is concurrent;
end;
```

### 5.4.1.5.5    Develop the Specifications and Bodies of the Classes

The subassembly-development team should specify and logically design the specification and body of each class in the subassembly, using OOSDL. In fact, skeleton specifications and bodies should be automatically generated from the information in the subassembly CLD.

The following is an example class specification and body:

```
class TRAFFIC_SIGNALS is concurrent
  parent subassembly INTERSECTION_CLASSES;
specification is abstract
  introduces
    message      CHANGE        is deferred;
    message      CONSTRUCT   (A_TRAFFIC_SIGNAL)  raise CONSTRUCT_FAILED
                                                 is synchronous;
    message      DESTRUCT    (A_TRAFFIC_SIGNAL)  raise DESTRUCT_FAILED
                                                 is synchronous;
    message      FLASH         is deferred;
    message      INITIALIZE    is deferred;
    message      TURN_OFF      is deferred;
    exception    ABSTRACTION_FAILED_IN;
    exception    CONSTRUCT_FAILED_IN;
    exception    DESTRUCT_FAILED_IN;
    exception    LIGHT_FAILED_IN;
    exception    POWER_FAILED_IN;
end;

class TRAFFIC_SIGNALS
  needs TRAFFIC_LIGHTS;
body
  introduces
    type         States        is deferred;
    variable     The_State     : States := Red_Light;
    operation    CHANGE        is deferred;
    constructor operation      CONSTRUCT   (A_TRAFFIC_SIGNAL)
                               raise CONSTRUCT_FAILED;
    destructor operation       DESTRUCT    (A_TRAFFIC_SIGNAL)
                               raise DESTRUCT_FAILED;
    operation    FLASH         is deferred;
    operation    INITIALIZE    is deferred;
    operation    TURN_OFF      is deferred;
    object       RED_LIGHT     : TRAFFIC_LIGHTS;
    object       YELLOW_LIGHT  : TRAFFIC_LIGHTS;
start
    CONSTRUCT(RED_LIGHT).TRAFFIC_LIGHTS;
    CONSTRUCT(YELLOW_LIGHT).TRAFFIC_LIGHTS;
    INITIALIZE;
end;
```

### 5.4.1.5.6    Evaluate the Class Model

Prior to starting the next step of the method, the subassembly-development team should evaluate and approve the quality of the intermediate products making up the class model:

- A list of all classes in the subassembly
- A CLD for each inheritance hierarchy of the subassembly
- The objective of each class of the subassembly, and a description of the abstraction implemented by each one
- The specification and body of each class, written in OOSDL

This peer-level evaluation of the class model should provide satisfactory answers to the following questions:

- Have all classes in the subassembly been identified in the subassembly part of the project repository and been given proper plural noun identifiers?
- Does the number of classes in the subassembly not significantly exceed the Miller limit of seven plus or minus two?
- Have all classes in the subassembly been properly characterized?
- Is each class concurrent unless there is a requirement or logical design reason to have it be sequential?
- Has a proper CLD been (a) developed for each subassembly classification hierarchy and (b) documented in the subassembly part of the project repository?
- Do the CLDs contain each class in the subassembly?
- Are classification hierarchies used only to show true inheritance relationships and not merely to maximize random reuse at the expense of maintainability?
- Is each instance on a CLD also on the subassembly GSN?
- Is each object on the subassembly GSN also an instance on some CLD?
- Are all nodes, arcs, and annotations on the CLDs defined in the associated set of CLD icons?
- Has a proper description of each class been developed and documented in the subassembly part of the project repository?
- Has the subassembly specification and body been updated with the classes, or has a new subassembly specification and body been developed for the classes?
- Has a specification and body been developed for each class in the subassembly and documented in the subassembly part of the project repository?
- Are the class specifications and bodies syntactically and semantically correct OOSDL?

### 5.4.1.6 Organize the Subassembly Requirements

This step can be done concurrently and iteratively with the previous step. The subassembly-development team should allocate the relevant subassembly requirements to the objects and classes, in order to promote the analysis and development of complete and correct objects and classes. They should then document this allocation with a requirements trace. Finally, they should organize the relevant requirements by sorting them by:

1. Class and object of anonymous class
2. Attributes (first types, then data)
3. Operations

4. Exceptions
5. Instances

By organizing the requirements along class and object lines, the requirements will be easier to understand and use as inputs to the following steps.

### 5.4.1.7  Check the Reuse Repository

This step can be done concurrently and iteratively with the previous step. The subassembly-development team should check the project reuse repository (if it exists) to determine whether appropriate, object-oriented requirements and logical designs already exist for any of the subassembly objects and classes. If requirements or a logical design for an object or class already exists, then it should be reused. If requirements or a logical design for a variant of the object or class already exists, then it should be used as a starting point to develop or generalize a new one.

### 5.4.1.8  Develop the State Model

This step should be performed concurrently and iteratively with the next two steps. The subassembly-development team should develop and document the subassembly state model in the subassembly part of the project repository. Specifically, the state model of the subassembly consists of

- An object-oriented state transition diagram for each object and class, which can be modeled as an individual or a set of finite state machines (FSMs)
- A description of each state
- A state operation table (SOT) for each object and class that can be modeled as an individual or a set of FSMs
- A description of any event (other than an operation call or an exception raise) that initiates the transition

The objective of the state model is to specify the behavior of the subassembly objects and classes in terms of their states and the nonpreserver operations and exceptions that transition among them.

The subassembly-development team should develop an object-oriented **state transition diagram (STD)** for each object and class that can be modeled as an individual or a set of FSMs. The object-oriented STD documents (a) the atomic and aggregate states of a single object or class, and (b) the modifier operations and exceptions that cause or may conditionally cause state transitions.

Modifier operations documented on STDs come in the following three varieties: (1) exported by the current class or object; (2) hidden within the current class or object; (3) and exported by some other class, object, or external hardware or software. If a modifier operation of the current class or object also causes another class or object to change its state, this should also be documented on the current STD. When an event (such as the passing of time) triggers a transition, it should be considered a modifier operation on some other object, such as DELAY_FOR(A_Specific_Time).THE_CLOCK or DELAY_UNTIL(A_Specific_Time).THE_CLOCK.

Operations are depicted using a solid line, and exceptions are depicted using a dotted line. Operations and exceptions belonging to the current object or class are depicted using thin lines, whereas operations and exceptions belonging to other entities (e.g., hardware devices) are depicted using thick lines. Conditional transitions are annotated with a bent arrow. See Figure 5-29: STDs for Icons. Figures 5-30, 5-31, and 5-32 provide examples of object-oriented STDs.

The subassembly-development team should also describe each state of each object and class. If the transition is not initiated by the operation call or the raising of the exception, the team should then describe the event that initiated the transition. For example, "The Off state of THE_CRUISE_CONTROL object signifies that the automobile's cruise control is not functioning and should not be confused with the Disabled state. It is automatically entered as the starting state and may be transitioned to by means of the TURN_OFF.THE_CRUISE_CONTROL operation."

Note on the STD in Figure 5-30 that the Off state is the initial state and the On state is an aggregate state that decomposes into the three substates: Accelerating, Disengaged, and Maintaining.

While the object-oriented STD documents the relationship between states and nonpreserver operations, it does not document which preserver operations may be run in which states. The subassembly-development team develops an SOT for each object

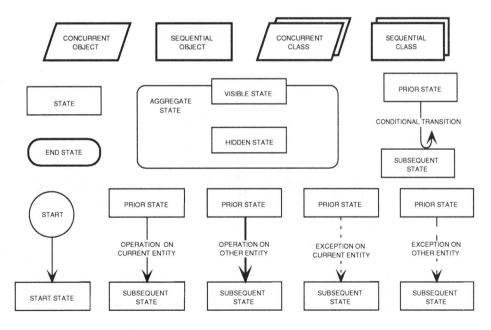

**Figure 5-29: Icons for State Transition Diagrams (STDs)**

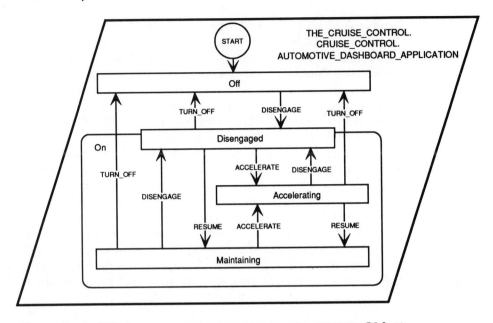

**Figure 5-30: STD for** `THE_CRUISE_CONTROL.CRUISE_CONTROL` **Object**

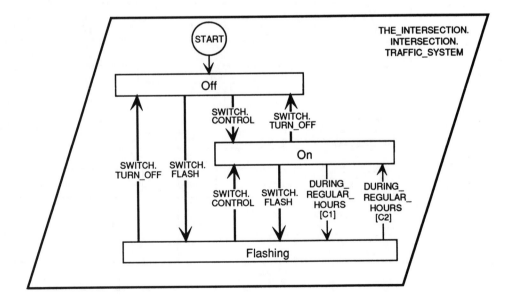

**Figure 5-31: STD for** `THE_INTERSECTION.INTERSECTION` **Object**

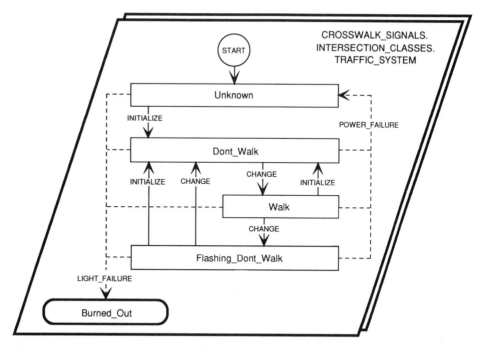

**Figure 5-32: STD for the** CROSSWALK_SIGNALS.INTERSECTION_CLASSES **Class**

or class that can be modeled as an individual or set of finite state machines. An SOT documents the operations and their types (i.e., C for constructor, D for destructor, M for modifier, and P for preserver) that can execute in each state. The SOT also documents the exception that is to be raised if an object or class attempts to execute an operation that is not valid for its current state. Figure 5-33 provides an example SOT for THE_SHOWER_MASTER object:

The information documented in the SOT can be used to ensure that each operation may only be performed in a consistent state, and thus to support the principle that all objects and classes should be responsible for preserving their own abstraction from violation. The following is the body of the ACCELERATE operation shown in Figure 5-30, which ensures consistency with the state of its object, THE_CRUISE_CONTROL, by using preconditions and postconditions:

```
Operation:  TURN_OFF.THE_SHOWER_MASTER
   Valid Prior States:    On
   Valid Post States:     Off
Operation:  TURN_ON.THE_SHOWER_MASTER
   Valid Prior States:    Off
   Valid Post States:     On
```

**Figure 5-33: State Operation Table (SOT) for** THE_SHOWER_MASTER **Object**

```
operation ACCELERATE raise FAILURE_OCCURRED_IN,INCOMPATIBLE_PRIOR_STATE_IN
 parent object THE_CRUISE_CONTROL.CRUISE_CONTROL.AUTOMOTIVE_DASHBOARD_APPLICATION;
specification
 message ACCELERATE raise FAILURE_OCCURRED_IN,INCOMPATIBLE_PRIOR_STATE_IN
  is sequential;
end;


operation ACCELERATE
 needs THE_THROTTLE_ACTUATOR;
body
 variable The_Temporary_State : STATES;
preconditions
 require
  The_State = DISENGAGED or The_State = MAINTAINING
 else
  raise INCOMPATIBLE_PRIOR_STATE_IN;
 end require;
statements
 receive ACCELERATE; -- message
 ENGAGE.THE_THROTTLE_ACTUATOR;
 The_Temporary_State := The_State;
 The_State := ACCELERATING;
postconditions
 require
  post(The_State) = ACCELERATING and
  post(IS_ENGAGED.THE_THROTTLE_ACTUATOR) = TRUE
 else
  The_State := The_Temporary_State;
  raise FAILURE_OCCURRED_IN;
 end require;
exception_handler
 when others then
  TURN_OFF;
  raise FAILURE_OCCURRED_IN;
end;
```

The subassembly-development team should update the IDs and object and class specifications and bodies, as necessary.

Prior to starting the "update-the-subassembly-documentation" step, the subassembly-development team should evaluate and approve the quality of the following aspects of the state model:

- Each STD
- The description of each nonpreserver operation and exception
- A description of any event (other than operation call or exception raise) that initiates the transition
- Each SOT
- Any updated ID
- Any updated object and class specification and body

This peer-level evaluation of the state model should provide satisfactory answers to the following questions:

- Does each STD show all states and state transitions of a single object or class?
- Are the STDs consistent with the description tables and with the object and class specifications and bodies?
- Is there a state transition for each constructor, modifier, and destructor operation, and for each exception?
- Are all state transitions caused by external operations of other objects and classes shown on the STD?
- Is there only one start state labeled with a single start icon and an associated unlabeled arc, for each STD?
- Are all compound states and associated substates depicted?
- Are all stop states labeled as such on the STDs?
- Are all nodes, arcs, and annotations on the STDs defined in the associated set of STD icons?
- Has an SOT been developed for each object and class with a finite number of states?
- Have all necessary modifications been made to the IDs and the object and class specifications and bodies?

### 5.4.1.9  Develop the Control Model

This step should be performed concurrently and iteratively with the preceding and following steps. The subassembly-development team should develop and document the subassembly control model in the subassembly part of the project repository. Specifically, the control model consists of

- An object-oriented CFD for
  — The subassembly
  — Each important scenario through the subassembly
  — Each object and class
- The body of each operation

The objective of the control model is to specify the behavior of the subassembly and its objects and classes in terms of

- Their operations
- The control flows between them
- Their attributes
- The data flows between the operations and attribute stores

In order to develop the control model, the subassembly-development team should first develop detailed scenarios of both expected and error-handling *threads of control*[2] among and within the objects and classes of the subassembly. They should then use

---

[2] A theoretically possible sequence of operation calls and/or exception flows between or within objects and classes.

these scenarios to analyze the associated messages and exceptions (i.e., control flows) among and within the objects, classes, and terminators. For each object and class in the subassembly, they should identify all hidden

- Operations (a.k.a., methods)
- Messages
  —Sequential
  —Synchronous (i.e., rendezvous)
  - Simple
  - Conditional
  - Timed
  - Guarded
  —Asynchronous

Note that analysis of synchronous message passing to avoid concurrency problems (e.g., deadlock, starvation, priority inversion, unnecessary polling)[3] may involve reversing the direction of message passing and may therefore require iterating back to correct the associated object and class interactions on SNs, IDs, and STDs.

Where appropriate, the subassembly-development team should use the Software Engineering Institute's rate monotonic scheduling algorithm and hard deadline scheduling [Sha and Goodenough 1990] as the default method for the scheduling and prioritization of concurrent operations.

The subassembly-development team should use the scenarios to develop one or more *object-oriented control flow diagrams (CFDs)*. See Figure 5-34: Icons for Control Flow Diagrams (CFDs). The scope of each CFD may be

1. A single essential or logical object or class (Figure 5-35 shows an example object-level CFD).
2. A scenario involving multiple objects and classes within the subassembly (Figure 5-36 shows an example scenario-level CFD).
3. An entire subassembly (Figure 5-37 shows an example subassembly CFD).

Where cost-effective, the subassembly-development team may choose to add data stores and data-visibility arrows to the CFDs to make them also object-oriented (OO) DFDs. Note that an object or class may have more than one data store if it has more than one attribute. Using an individual data store to identify an object or class may therefore be misleading. The OO CFD/DFD is used to identify hidden operations (via transforms) and attributes (via data-visibility arrows and stores). The OO DFD differs from traditional functional DFDs because

---

[3] *Deadlock* occurs when two or more concurrent operations are waiting on each other so that none are ever executed. *Starvation* occurs when a concurrent operation must wait indefinitely for execution. *Priority inversion* occurs when a high priority concurrent operation is blocked from execution because it is waiting on a low priority concurrent operation that is waiting on a medium priority concurrent operation. *Polling* or *busy waiting* occurs when a client concurrent operations must continually send synchronous messages to a server concurrent operation in order to determine whether an event has occured instead of being sent a message once upon occurance of the event.

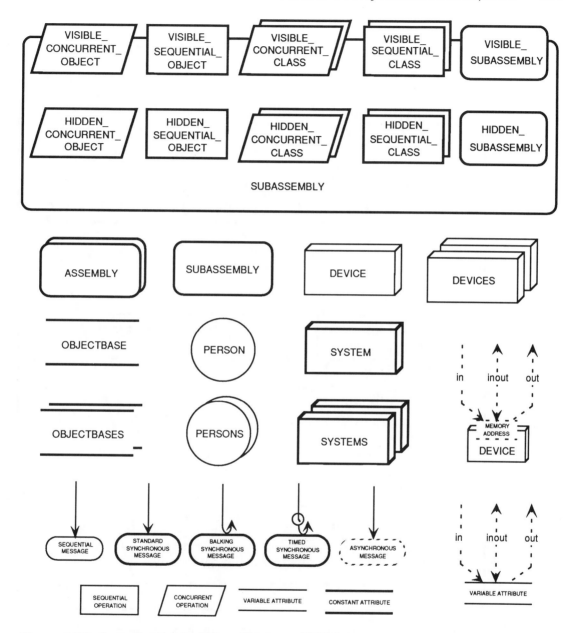

**Figure 5-34: Icons for Control Flow Diagrams (CFDs)**

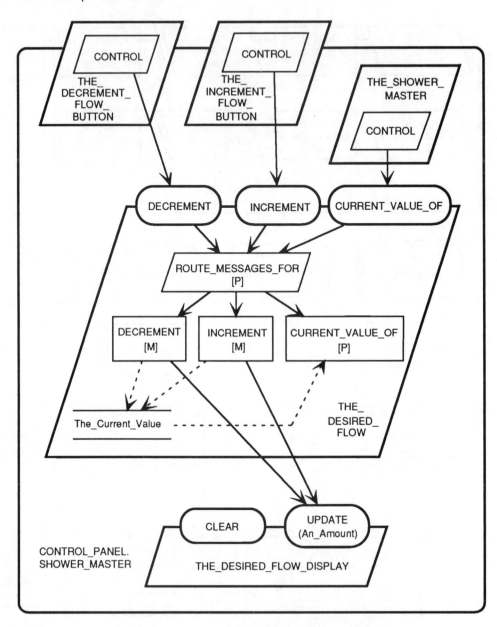

**Figure 5-35: CFD for** THE_DESIRED_FLOW.CONTROL_PANEL **Object**

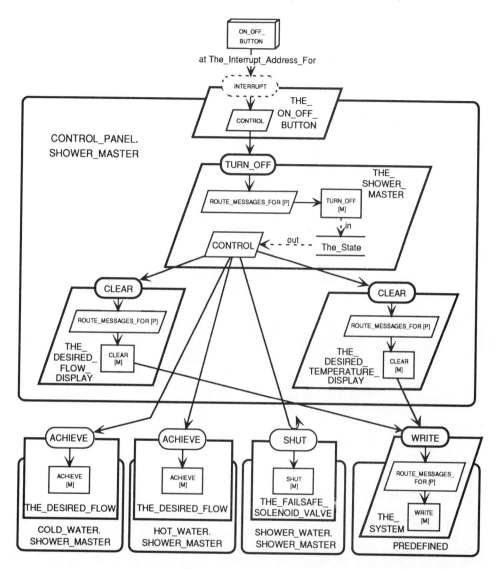

**Figure 5-36: CFD for the** TURN_OFF **Scenario**

1. Its scope is restricted to a *single* class, object, scenario involving objects and classes, or a subassembly of objects and classes; functional DFDs document only pieces of an object or class, and pieces of the same class or object appear on more than one DFD

2. All data stores and transforms are allocatable to the class or object, as attributes and operations, respectively

CFDs are to OORALD what structure charts are to Structured Design.

The subassembly-development team should associate attributes with the parameters of each operation and determine the mode of the parameters.

Figure 5-35 shows the object-level CFD for THE_DESIRED_FLOW object in the CONTROL_PANEL subassembly of the SHOWER_MASTER assembly. It shows THE_DESIRED_FLOW concurrent object, the three synchronous messages it can receive, its one concurrent operation and three sequential operations, its one variable attribute (i.e., The_Current_Value), and its four terminators (i.e., three client objects and one servant object), as well as the control flows (i.e., synchronous messages) among them and the data flows within THE_DESIRED_FLOW object.

Figure 5-36 shows a scenario-level CFD for the TURN_OFF scenario involving the CONTROL_PANEL subassembly of the SHOWER_MASTER assembly. The conditional message to the SHUT.THE_FAILSAFE_SOLENOID_VALVE occurs if an exception is raised.

Figure 5-37 shows a subassembly-level CFD for the CONTROL_PANEL subassembly of the SHOWER_MASTER assembly. Compare this figure with Figure 5-17, which shows the ID for the same subassembly. While IDs treat the objects as software black boxes, CFDs open up these black boxes and show the encapsulated operations and attributes and how they interact. Note that CASE tools should automatically generate skeleton CFDs for the corresponding IDs.

For each class and object of anonymous class in the subassembly, specify and logically design the body of each operation (e.g., using OOSDL). The operations can be specified formally or algorithmically. For example, the following is the design of the CONTROL.THE_SHOWER_MASTER and the CHOOSE.THE_SHOWER_MASTER operations:

```
operation CONTROL
 parent object THE_SHOWER_MASTER;
specification
end;

operation CONTROL
 needs THE_DESIRED_FLOW;
 needs THE_DESIRED_FLOW_DISPLAY;
 needs THE_DESIRED_FLOW.COLD_WATER;
 needs THE_DESIRED_FLOW.HOT_WATER;
 needs THE_DESIRED_TEMPERATURE;
 needs THE_DESIRED_TEMPERATURE_DISPLAY;
 needs THE_FAILSAFE_SOLENOID_VALVE.SHOWER_WATER;
 needs THE_POSTVALVE_FLOW_SENSOR.SHOWER_WATER;
 needs THE_POSTVALVE_TEMPERATURE_SENSOR.SHOWER_WATER;
 needs THE_PREVALVE_TEMPERATURE_SENSOR.COLD_WATER;
 needs THE_PREVALVE_TEMPERATURE_SENSOR.HOT_WATER;
body
statements
 FOREVER : loop
  case The_State is
   when OFF then
```

```
      ACHIEVE(An_Amount  := 0.0).THE_DESIRED_FLOW.COLD_WATER;
      ACHIEVE(An_Amount  := 0.0).THE_DESIRED_FLOW.HOT_WATER;
      CLEAR.THE_DESIRED_FLOW_DISPLAY;
      CLEAR.THE_DESIRED_TEMPERATURE_DISPLAY;
    when ON then
      Actual_Cold_Temperature         :=  THE_TEMPERATURE.
                                          THE_PREVALVE_TEMPERATURE_SENSOR.COLD_WATER;
      Actual_Hot_Temperature          :=  THE_TEMPERATURE.
                                          THE_PREVALVE_TEMPERATURE_SENSOR.HOT_WATER;
      Current_Desired_Flow            :=  CURRENT_VALUE_OF.THE_DESIRED_FLOW;
      Current_Desired_Temperature     :=  CURRENT_VALUE_OF.THE_DESIRED_TEMPERATURE;
      Cold_Desired_Flow               :=  Current_Desired_Flow *
                      (Actual_Hot_Temperature - Current_Desired_Temperature) /
                      (Actual_Hot_Temperature - Actual_Cold_Temperature);
      Hot_Desired_Flow                    :=  Current_Desired_Flow *
                      (Current_Desired_Temperature - Actual_Cold_Temperature) /
                      (Actual_Hot_Temperature - Actual_Cold_Temperature);
      ACHIEVE(An_Amount := Cold_Desired_Flow).THE_DESIRED_FLOW.COLD_WATER;
      ACHIEVE(An_Amount := Hot_Desired_Flow ).THE_DESIRED_FLOW.HOT_WATER;
    end case;
    DELAY(THE_DELAY_AMOUNT).THE_CLOCK;
  end loop FOREVER;
end;

operation ROUTE_MESSAGES_FOR is concurrent
  parent object THE_SHOWER_MASTER;
specification
  message TURN_OFF;
  message TURN_ON;
end;

operation ROUTE_MESSAGES_FOR
body
statements
  FOREVER : loop
    select
      receive TURN_OFF;
      TURN_OFF;
    or
      receive TURN_ON;
      TURN_ON;
    end select;
  end loop FOREVER;
end;
```

Prior to starting the "update-the-subassembly-documentation" step, the subassembly-development team should evaluate and approve the quality of the following components of the control model:

- The object-oriented CFD for
  — The subassembly (where practical)
  — Each important scenario involving the subassembly
  — Each object and class (where cost-effective)
- The body of each operation

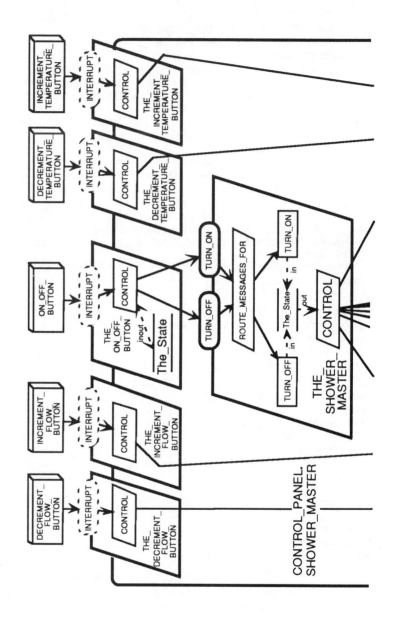

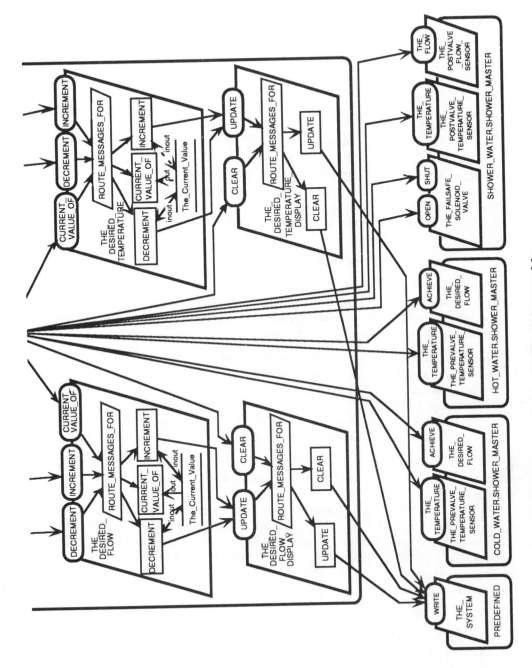

**Figure 5-37: CFD for the** CONTROL_PANEL.SHOWER_MASTER **Subassembly**

This peer-level evaluation of the control model should provide satisfactory answers to the following questions:

- Is the scope of each CFD a single object, class, or scenario, or is it the entire subassembly?
- Is each CFD complete and correct?
- Is each CFD consistent with the object, class, and state models and the corresponding description tables?
- Are all nodes, arcs, and annotations on the CFDs defined in the associated set of CFD icons?
- Is there a complete and agreed-on body for each operation?
- Is each body consistent with the object, class, and state models, the corresponding description table, and the associated CFDs?
- Is each operation body syntactically correct OOSDL?

### 5.4.1.10   Develop the Timing Model

This step should be performed concurrently and iteratively with the previous two steps. The subassembly-development team should develop and document the subassembly timing model in the subassembly part of the project repository. Specifically, the timing model of the subassembly consists of

- The **timing diagram** (TD), where appropriate and cost-effective, for
  — The subassembly (where appropriate)
  — Each scenario involving the subassembly
  — Each object and class
- Any IDs, STDs, or CFDs annotated with timing information
- Any timed event lists internal to the subassembly

The objective of the timing model is to specify the temporal behavior of the subassembly in terms of the messages passed among and within objects and classes in the subassembly.

A TD usually shows the entire subassembly if the subassembly is small enough to make a subassembly TD practical. Sometimes, a TD is also drawn for each major scenario and each individual object and class with significant temporal behavior. The TD is used to provide a temporal overview of the subassembly and its component objects and classes. Specifically, TDs show the existence and timing of messages among and within

- Objects and classes
- The system, hardware, software, and people terminators

Figure 5-38 shows the TD icons, and Figure 5-39 shows an example TD.

The subassembly TD is a modified Booch TD, is object-oriented, and documents the subassembly behavior in terms of the timing of messages between (a) the stubbed operation, object or class, and (b) the remaining classes and objects.

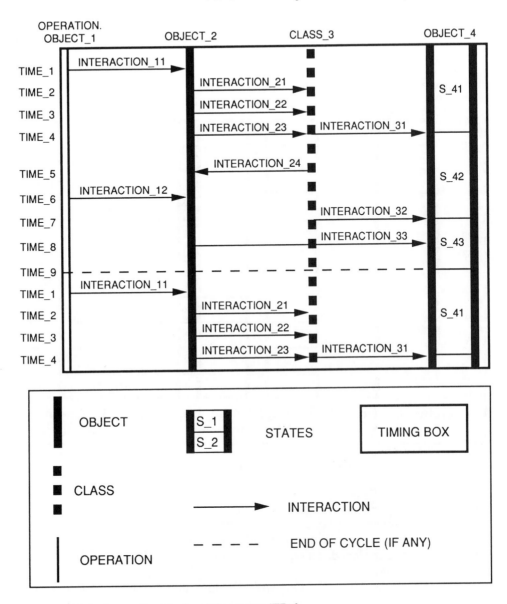

**Figure 5-38: Icons for Timing Diagrams (TDs)**

Prior to starting the "update-the-subassembly-documentation" step, the subassembly-development team should evaluate and approve the quality of the intermediate products produced during this step of the method, including all of the aforementioned elements of the timing model. This peer-level evaluation of the timing model should provide satisfactory answers to the following questions:

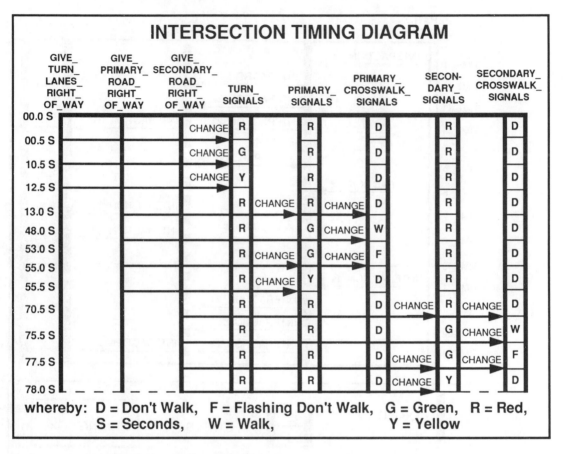

**Figure 5-39: TD for** THE_INTERSECTION **Object**

- Is the scope of each TD a single object, class, scenario, or the entire subassembly?
- Is each TD complete and correct?
- Is each TD consistent with the object, class, state, and control models?
- Are all nodes, arcs, and annotations on the TDs defined in the associated set of TD icons?
- Are the IDs, STDs, and CFDs annotated with timing information (if any) correct and complete?
- Are the timed message lists (if any) internal to the subassembly correct and complete?

### 5.4.1.11   Update the Subassembly Documentation

The subassembly-development team uses the diagrams, description tables, and program design language (PDL) to update the software requirements specification (SRS) and initial software design document (SDD) for the current subassembly, including each object and class. The team should sort both requirements and design by the following categories:

| | |
|---|---|
| A. | Assembly |
| A.B. | Subassembly |
| A.B.C. | Class and object of anonymous class |
| A.B.C.1. | Visible resources |
| A.B.C.1.1. | Attribute types and constant attributes |
| A.B.C.1.2. | Messages |
| A.B.C.1.3. | Exceptions |
| A.B.C.2. | Hidden resources |
| A.B.C.2.1. | Attributes types and attributes |
| A.B.C.2.2. | Operations |
| A.B.C.2.3. | Exceptions |
| A.B.C.2.4. | Component objects |
| A.B.C.3. | Instances |
| B. | Aggregation hierarchies |
| C. | Classification hierarchies |
| D. | Scenarios |

The subassembly-development team should document the following information:

- The assembly-unique identifier of the subassembly, written as an understandable, singular noun phrase from the application domain
- The classification of the subassembly
- The location of the subassembly in terms of assembly and subassembly
- The abstraction implemented by the subassembly
- The cardinality of the subassembly in terms of the number of actual component objects, classes, and nested subassemblies
- The specification and body of the subassembly
- The subassembly-level capabilities allocated to, and implemented by, the subassembly
- The object model of the subassembly
- The class model of the subassembly
- The state model of the subassembly
- The control model of the subassembly
- The timing model of the subassembly
- Any analysis or design trade-offs made concerning the subassembly

### 5.4.1.12  Perform the Subassembly Requirements and Logical Design Inspection

After completing all previous steps for the subassembly, the subassembly-development team should perform the peer-level *subassembly requirements and design inspection* of all intermediate products produced during subassembly OORALD. The team should use tool(s) and the scenarios to test—as well as peer-level inspection to evaluate—the completeness, consistency, and correctness of all models and graphics. The team should ensure that all product evaluation criteria have been considered and properly enforced during the previous steps. For example, the team might use the following for product evaluation:

- Peer-level review
- Tool support (e.g., *ObjectMaker* by Mark V Systems or *Paradigm Plus* by ProtoSoft)
- Software quality assurance (SQA)

## 5.4.2    Implementation Design

The objective of this activity is to produce a compiled implementation design of the specification and body of each object, class, and auxiliary unit in the subassembly. It consists of the following steps:

1. Determine the language-specific implementations.
2. Develop language-specific diagrams.
3. Analyze the concurrency design.
4. Identify any auxiliary modules.
5. Examine the project reuse repository.
6. Code and compile the module specifications.
7. Code and compile the initial module bodies.
8. Make any additional design decisions.
9. Update the Software Design Document (SDD).

Several steps of implementation design can safely be ignored if the logical and physical designs are identical. When using *object-oriented* languages such as Smalltalk and Eiffel, classes are both logical-design entities and modules. No further language-specific design may be necessary. The situation, however, is very different with many *object-based* languages that are hybrids of the procedural and the object-oriented paradigms. These languages allow many different ways to implement objects and classes. They even allow the implementation of objects without corresponding classes.

The subassembly-development team should perform those steps shown in rounded rectangles in Figure 5-40 only if the implementation language (e.g., Ada, Modula-2) is a hybrid language that

- Provides multiple ways to implement objects and classes
- Allows for the separate design and compilation of object bodies and methods

### 5.4.2.1  Determine the Language-Specific Implementations

The subassembly-development team should skip this step if the implementation language (e.g., Smalltalk) only provides one way to implement objects and classes. If

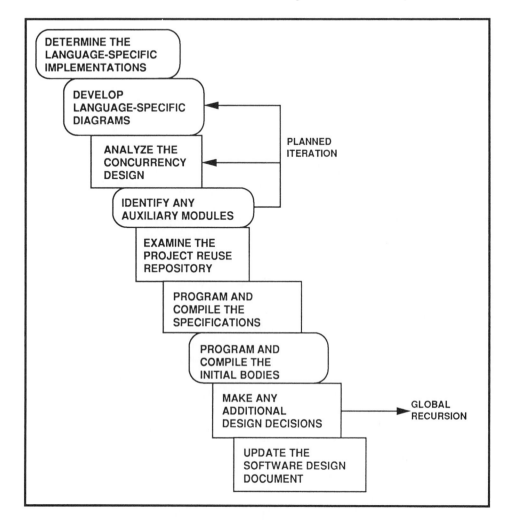

**Figure 5-40: Overview of Implementation Design**

the language (e.g., Ada, Modula-2) provides more than one way to implement objects, classes, and subassemblies, then, the team must determine the language-specific implementations for each entity.

While the choice of programming languages is beyond the scope of this book, several points should probably be addressed. There are only two primary languages for *engineering* significant software projects today: the class-based language Ada and the hybrid object-oriented language C++. While Eiffel shows great promise from an engineering standpoint (and can be argued to be technically superior to C++), its lack of popularity and infrastructure probably remove it from consideration by many organizations. Smalltalk is often eliminated because it was not designed for large, complex applications and does not strongly support software engineering.

With Ada and C++ as the primary competitors, one might readily choose C++ over Ada because C++ is object-oriented (i.e., it supports inheritance, polymorphism, and dynamic binding), whereas Ada is merely class-based (i.e., supporting object and class abstraction and encapsulation). However, a recent business-case analysis of Ada vs. C++ [Mosemann 1991] found Ada the clear winner from a business and software-engineering standpoint. Ada typically saves 35% during development and 70% during maintenance over C++. Whereas C++ is a major improvement over C, which can clearly be characterized as antagonistic to software engineering, the extent to which the engineering features of C++ are used is totally left up to the programmer. According to the director of the study [Mosemann 1992], "no cases were found in 7 firms and 23 C++ projects where any significant use was being made of the C++ engineering features." On the other hand, Ada was designed to support software engineering, and its software engineering features are an integral part of the language. While it is possible to hack an Ada program that fails to significantly achieve the goals of software engineering, it seldom occurs to the extent that it does with C++ because engineering with Ada is the most natural way to use the language. Therefore, Ada83[4] is currently recommended over C++ for all large, complex applications. Once the newest version of Ada—Ada9X—is available (probably in 1994), Ada will also strongly support inheritance and polymorphism.

The remainder of this section is specific to Ada83. Determine how each object and class will be implemented in terms of Ada. (An extended library unit consists of the library unit (i.e., the specification), the associated body, and all associated subunits.) Remember that there are various ways to implement objects, classes of objects, and classes of classes in hybrid languages.

The following three lists document the typical ways in which (1) objects, (2) classes of objects, and (3) subassemblies are implemented in Ada. The most popular methods are italicized in the following three lists.

1. Object
   - Implemented as a *library package*:
     - A sequential or concurrent abstract state machine (ASM) package
     - An instance of a sequential or concurrent generic ASM package
     - A package of sequential or concurrent ASM packages
     - A package of instances of a sequential or concurrent generic ASM package
     - A package of ASM tasks
     - A package of instances of a sequential or concurrent abstract data type (ADT) package

---

[4]The original Ada standard was approved in 1983, and the current version of Ada is often called Ada83 in order to differentiate it from Ada9X, the next version of Ada planned for 1994.

- Implemented as a *subunit*:
  - an encapsulated ASM task body
- Implemented as a *variable*:
  - an *instance of a sequential or concurrent ADT*
2. Class of objects
   - Implemented as a *library package*:
     - A sequential or concurrent ADT package
     - An instance of a sequential or concurrent generic ADT package
     - A sequential or concurrent generic ASM package
     - A sequential or concurrent generic ADT package
   - Implemented as a *type*:
     - An ASM task type
3. Subassembly
   - A package (in order to enforce visibility constraints)
   - A library (if the library management system enforces visibility constraints)

If a package or a generic package only contains a single object or object class task, it is usually the package or generic package and not the task that is considered the object or class. In consideration of modularity considerations,

- Typically, only one ASM object is encapsulated per package
- Typically, only one object class is encapsulated per package or ASM generic package

### 5.4.2.2 Develop the Language-Specific Diagrams

The subassembly-development team should skip this step if the implementation language (e.g., Eiffel, Smalltalk) has only a single way of implementing objects and classes. If the implementation language is hybrid (e.g., Ada, C++) and there are multiple ways of implementing objects and classes, then the ID and the CFD are inadequate to show these design decisions, and language-specific module and submodule diagrams are useful to document the choices of modules (e.g., package, generic package) and of submodules (e.g., subprogram, task).

**Module diagrams** (MDs) deal with the physical architecture of the subassembly. They treat the objects and classes as software black boxes and show the dependency relationships (e.g., **with** clauses in Ada) among them. Submodule diagrams treat objects and classes as software *white boxes*. They open up the modules to show the nested submodules, and they deal with the interactions of the objects in terms of the physical implementation of the message passing (e.g., subprogram calls and task rendezvous in Ada) among and within the modules.

The initial-draft MD documents the static architecture of the subassembly objects and classes in terms of the subassembly's component modules (e.g., object and class packages and generic packages in Ada), their exported resources, and their dependencies (e.g., in terms of **with** clauses in Ada).

Figure 5-41 shows MD icons for the Ada programming language. Figure 5-42 shows an MD for an intersection subassembly.

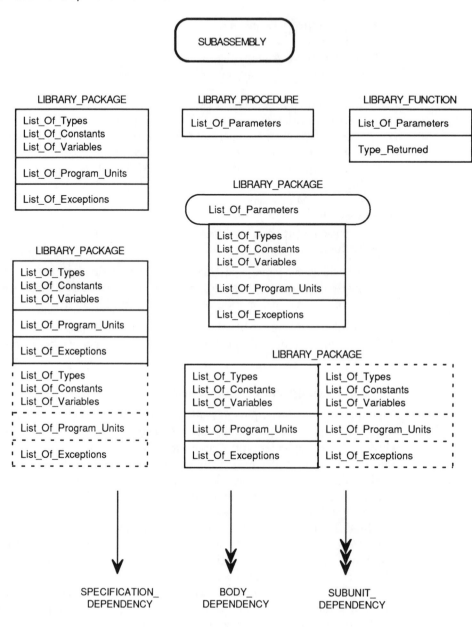

**Figure 5-41: Icons for Module Diagrams (MDs) for Ada**

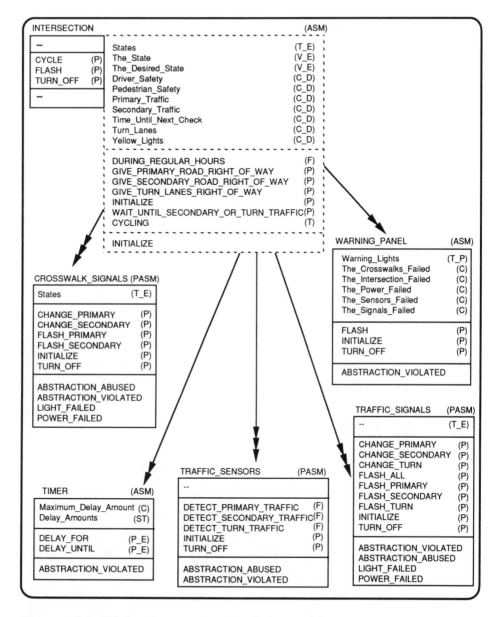

**Figure 5-42: MD for the INTERSECTION Subassembly**

MDs come in the following four versions, depending on the scope of the information they present; these MDs may show the following:

1. Without module resources
2. Only specifications

3. Both specifications and bodies, but not subunits

4. Specifications, bodies, and [selected] subunits

Figures 5-43 through 5-46 show MDs with these four levels of detail.

The current-draft MD does not contain auxiliary or process-abstraction modules. This is the traditional diagram of OOD and provides the same type of information as (however with more detail than) the Booch module diagram [Booch 1983] and the Cherry library graph [Cherry 1988].

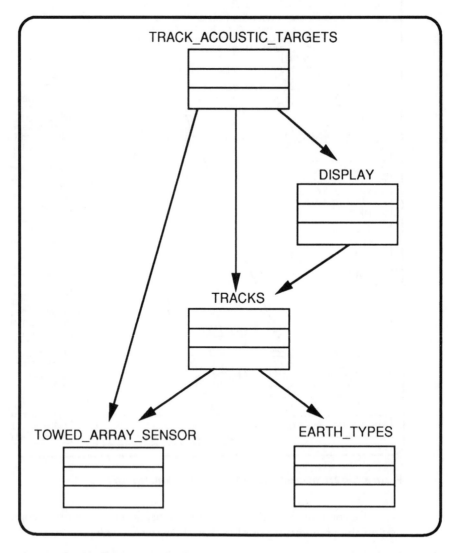

**Figure 5-43: Overview MD for the** TRACK_ACOUSTIC_TARGETS **Subassembly (No Module Resources Shown)**

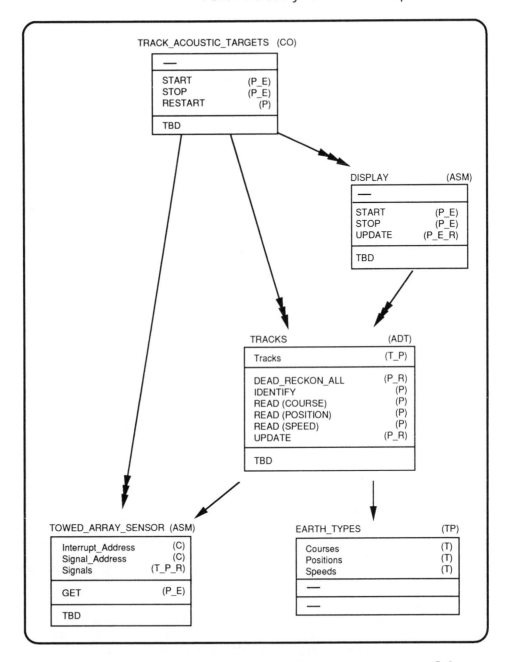

**Figure 5-44: Specification-Level MD for the** TRACK_ACOUSTIC_TARGETS **Subassembly**

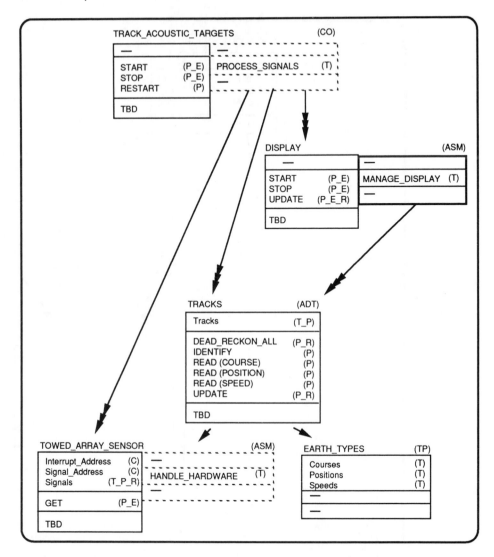

**Figure 5-45: Body-Level MD for the** `TRACK_ACOUSTIC_TARGETS` **Subassembly**

If the language is Ada, the subassembly-development team should also develop draft *submodule diagrams* (SMDs) to document the module's internal design. While the MD emphasizes static architecture, the SMD emphasizes the design of the dynamic behavior. More than one is usually needed to document an entire subassembly, due to the increased detail shown. SMDs are slightly modified Buhr structure graphs [Buhr 1984] and document the dynamic behavior in terms of subprograms, subprogram calls, tasks, task entries, and task rendezvous (calls). Notice that the icons

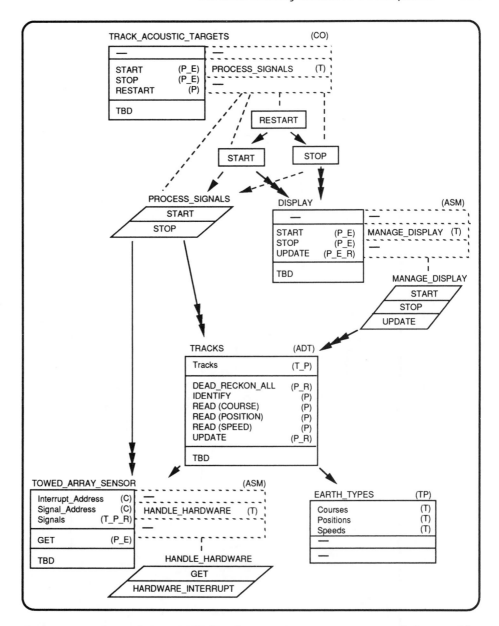

**Figure 5-46: Subunit-Level MD for the** TRACK_ACOUSTIC_TARGETS **Subassembly**

for exported resources do not straddle the parent icon's boundary, so that these diagrams may be better differentiated from CFDs. See Figure 5-47: Icons for Submodule Diagrams (SMDs).

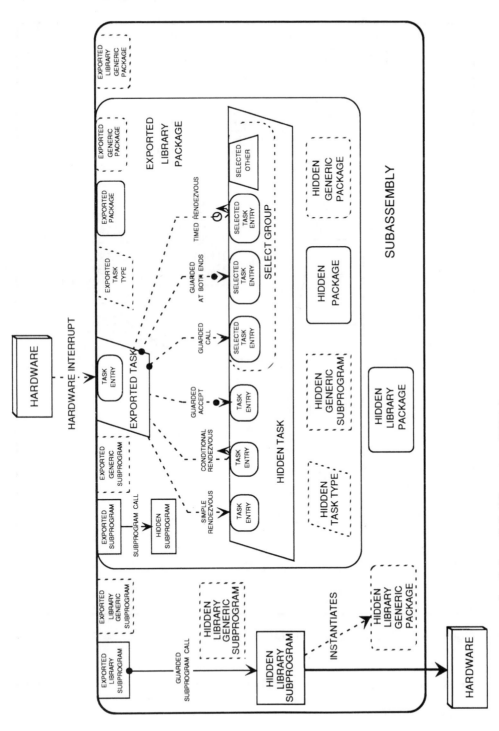

**Figure 5-47: Icons for Submodule Diagrams (SMDs)**

Where cost-effective and useful, either update or develop additional (e.g., Buhr) TDs, as necessary to document the expected timing of task rendezvous (and possibly of subprogram calls).

Figure 5-48 provides an example SMD for the CRUISE_CONTROL subassembly of the AUTOMOTIVE_DASHBOARD_APPLICATION assembly.

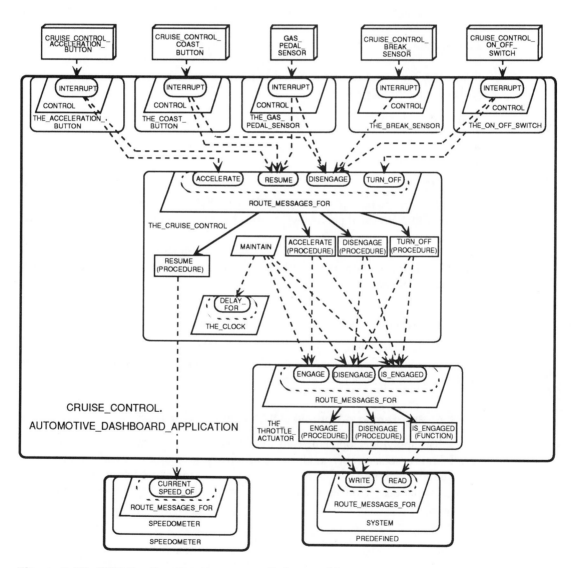

**Figure 5-48: SMD for the** CRUISE_CONTROL **Subassembly**

### 5.4.2.3  Analyze the Concurrency Design

If necessary, the subassembly-development team should analyze the operating system- and language-specific concurrency design. Several tools, including some based on Petri net analysis,[5] can be used.

### 5.4.2.4  Identify Any Other Auxiliary Modules

The subassembly-development team should skip this step if the implementation language (e.g., Smalltalk) does not allow non-object-oriented modules. Identify any auxiliary units (e.g., object relationship packages, types and constants packages), as necessary. The subassembly-development team should identify any intermediate or third-party tasks and their associated process-abstraction library units (e.g., library packages or generic packages):

- Buffers
- Pumps
- Queues
- Relays
- Transporters

Remember that projects using OOD with hybrid languages such as Ada will typically contain a small percentage of units that do not implement objects or object classes.

As necessary, the subassembly-development team should update both the sub-assembly MD with these auxiliary units and the subassembly SMD with the intermediate tasks and process-abstraction library units.

### 5.4.2.5  Examine the Project-Reuse Repository

The subassembly-development team should examine the project-reuse repository, in order to determine opportunities for reuse, now that the subassembly's main units have been identified but not yet coded.

### 5.4.2.6  Program and Compile All Module Specifications

The subassembly-development team should program and compile the specifications of all known subassembly modules (e.g., library packages in Ada), using object-oriented programming (OOP) techniques. This substep may be omitted if the implementation language, rather than OOSDL, was used as a specification and design language.

---

[5]*Petri nets are a popular European diagramming technique with a solid foundaiton of matehmatical theory used to analyze dynamic behavior.*

### 5.4.2.7  Program and Compile the Initial Bodies

The subassembly-development team should program and compile the initial bodies of the subassembly modules, but not the module subunits. In Ada, they should use

- Subprogram specification stubs and the **separate** clause
- Task specifications
- Task body stubs and the separate clause

### 5.4.2.8  Make Any Additional Design Decisions

The subassembly-development team should make additional design decisions based on software-engineering considerations, such as the following:

- Determine the classes, objects, and operations requiring recursive development as part of one or more child subassemblies (i.e., at the next lower level of abstraction). These contain (or are) the subprograms, active tasks, and task entries that must remain temporarily stubbed because they would either (a) be too large or complex to exhibit good modularity, or (b) depend on as-yet-unidentified resources exported by one or more classes or objects in the child subassemblies.
- Allocate any unmet requirements to the resulting child subassemblies, as necessary

If any nested subassemblies, classes, objects, and their operations depend on as-yet-unidentified resources (i.e., of classes and objects) at the next lower level of abstraction and therefore must remain stubbed out until these resources are identified, the current software-development team notifies their technical manager that global recursion is required on these incomplete entities.

The technical manager will form a new software-development team to develop each child subassembly spawned by this recursion process. Meanwhile, the current subassembly-development team will continue on with the remaining steps of the ADM3 process to code, integrate, and test the current subassembly while the new teams start developing the child subassemblies in parallel.

### 5.4.2.9  Update the Software Design Document (SDD)

The subassembly-development team updates the initial SDD for the current subassembly, with implementation-design information and any changes that were made to the logical design.

## 5.4.3  Programming and Unit Testing

The objective of this activity is to produce a complete, compiled, and unit-tested physical implementation of each object, class, and auxiliary unit (if any) in the subassembly. It consists of the following steps (see Figure 5-49):

1. Program and compile all operations not requiring recursion.
2. Informally debug all operations not requiring recursion.

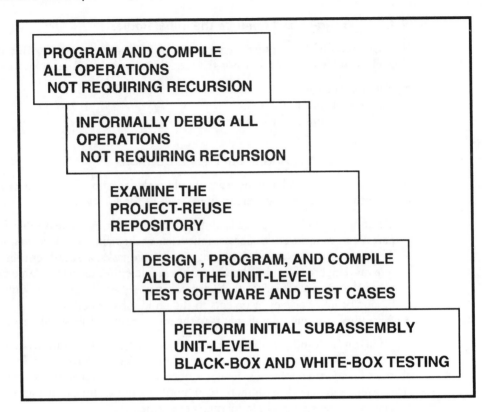

**Figure 5-49: Overview of Programming and Unit Test**

3. Examine the project-reuse repository for unit-level test software and test cases.
4. Design, program, and compile all of the unit-level test software and test cases not found in the project-reuse repository.
5. Perform initial unit-level black box testing (e.g., using equivalence class and boundary value testing) and perform white-box testing (e.g., basis path testing).

## 5.4.4    Subassembly Integration and Testing

The objective of this activity is to integrate the objects, classes, and any auxiliary modules into a functioning subassembly and to perform integration testing on the subassembly. It consists of the following steps (see Figure 5-50):

1. Place the subassembly software into the subassembly library.
2. Plan subassembly integration and testing.
3. Examine the project-reuse repository for subassembly-level test software and test cases.

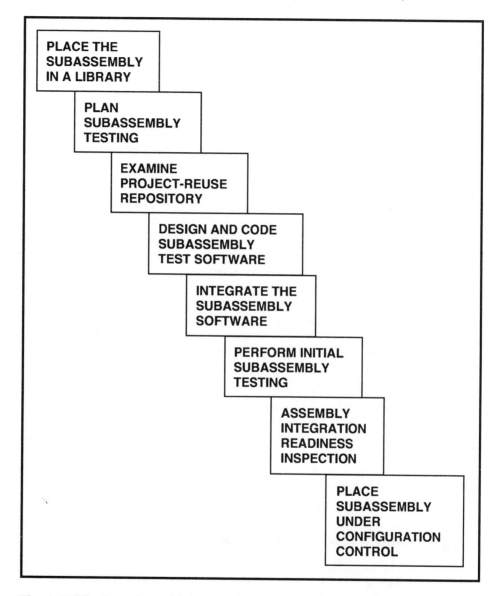

**Figure 5-50: Overview of Subassembly Integration and Testing**

4. Design, code, and compile all of the subassembly-level test software and test cases not found in the project-reuse repository.
5. Integrate the objects, classes, and auxiliary units (if any) into a functioning subassembly.
6. Perform the initial subassembly-integration testing.

7. Perform the peer-level assembly-integration readiness inspection, to determine whether the subassembly is ready to turn over for integration with the growing assembly.
8. Place the subassembly software and documentation under developer configuration control.

### 5.4.5 Assembly Integration and Integration Testing

The objective of this activity is to further integrate the integrated subassembly into the growing assembly and to perform integration testing at the assembly level. It consists of the following steps (see Figure 5-51):

1. Place the integrated subassembly into the assembly library.
2. Plan assembly integration and testing for the current subassembly.
3. Examine the project-reuse repository for assembly-level test software and test cases.
4. Design, code, and compile all of the assembly-level test software and test cases not found in the project-reuse repository.
5. Integrate the integrated subassembly into the growing assembly.
6. Perform the initial assembly integration testing.
7. Update the assembly diagram (AD).
8. Update the deliverable documentation, including the Software Requirements Specification (SRS) and Software Design Document (SDD).
9. Add the subassembly software, test software and test cases, and documentation to the project-reuse repository.

The AD documents the static architecture of the assembly in terms of its subassemblies and the recursion relationships between them. The AD is also an important management tool for scheduling, staffing, and work breakdown, as well as for configuration management. The AD contains more than the information in the software organization chart of DOD-STD-2167A [DOD 1986]. Figure 5-52 shows the icons for assembly diagrams. Figure 5-53 shows an example overview AD, and Figure 5-54 shows an example detailed AD.

### 5.4.6 Perform on-the-Job Training (OJT)

The members of the subassembly-development teams receive continual OJT from their lead software engineers in the areas of the application domain, object-oriented development, ADM3, the CASE tool(s), and the implementation language.

### 5.4.7 Perform Any Additional Rapid Prototyping

The assembly-development teams may optionally perform additional rapid prototyping to develop any high-risk objects and classes sooner than they would be reached via normal globally recursive development.

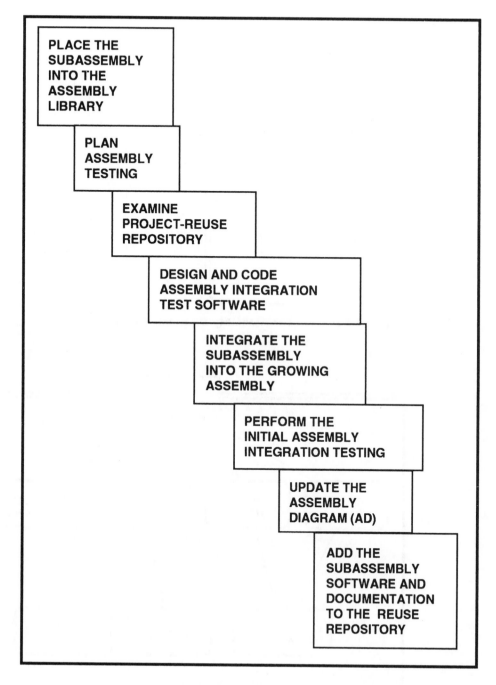

**Figure 5-51: Overview of Assembly Integration and Integration Testing**

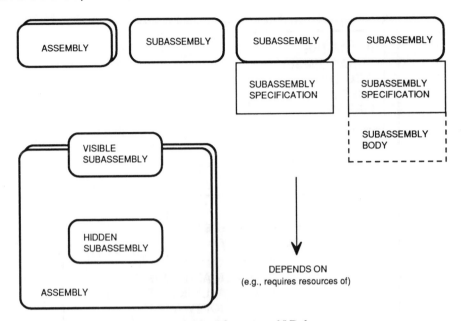

**Figure 5-52: Icons for Assembly Diagrams (ADs)**

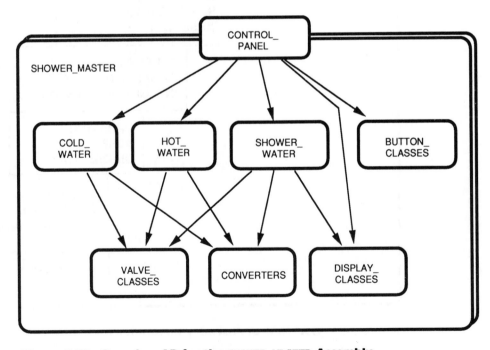

**Figure 5-53: Overview AD for the** SHOWER_MASTER **Assembly**

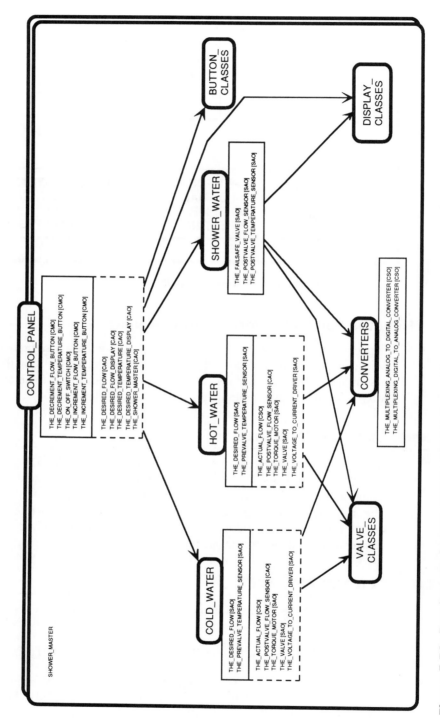

**Figure 5-54: Detailed AD for the SHOWER_MASTER Assembly**

319

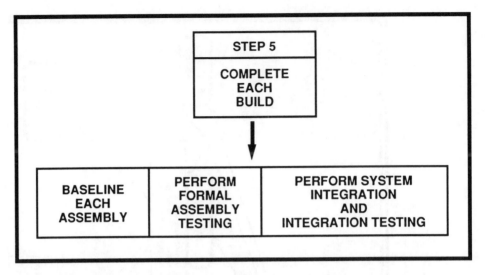

**Figure 5-55: Overview of Step 5 of ADM3**

### 5.4.8     Hold the Formal In-Process Reviews (IPRs)

Independently of the globally recursive development of the subassemblies, the assembly-development teams hold formal (i.e., customer witnessed) IPRs of the completed subassemblies. IPRs are scheduled so as to provide adequate customer oversight and feedback without unduly prolonging the development effort.

## 5.5 COMPLETE EACH BUILD

The final step of ADM3 contains three substeps (see Figure 5-55) and is performed on a build-by-build basis. Project software configuration management baselines each assembly as it is completed (for the current build) so that it can safely be turned over to the independent test organization for formal (i.e., customer witnessed) assembly testing. On successful completion of assembly testing, the assembly is integrated into the system, and system integration testing is performed.

## 5.6 CHAPTER REFERENCES

[Beck 1989] Kent Beck and Ward Cunningham, "A Laboratory for Teaching Object-Oriented Thinking," *OOPSLA '89 Conference Proceedings*, Special Issue of *SIGPLAN Notices*, 24(10), 1-6, October 1989.

[Booch 1983] Grady Booch, *Software Engineering with Ada*, Menlo Park, CA, Benjamin Cummings, 1983.

[Buhr 1984] R. J. A. Buhr, *System Design with Ada*, Englewood Cliffs, NJ, Prentice Hall, 1984.

[Cherry 1988] George W. Cherry, *Software Construction by Object-Oriented Pictures*, Thought**Tools, 1988.

[DOD 1986] Department of Defense, *Defense Systems Software Development*, DOD-STD-2167A, 29 February 1986.

[Firesmith 1989] Donald G. Firesmith, "The Ada Development Method (ADM): An Object-Oriented Development Method for the Entire Development Cycle," *Summer 1989 SIGAda Conference Program and Abstracts*, 8–11 August 1989, xvii–xxvi.

[Firesmith 1991] Donald G. Firesmith, "ObjectMaker 2.0: The power of choice, customization, and extensibility," *Object Magazine*, *1*(4), November/December 1991.

[Firesmith and Gaumer 1991] Donald G. Firesmith and Dale Gaumer, *Ada Development Method 2 User's Manual*, Version 1.2, Advanced Software Technology Specialists, 17124 Lutz Road, Ossian Indiana 46777, 10 February 1991.

[Mosemann 1991] Lloyd K Mosemann II, *Ada and C++: A Business Case Analysis*, Deputy Assistant Secretary of the Air Force (Communications, Computers, and Logistics), US Department of Defense, July 1991.

[Mosemann 1992] Lloyd K Mosemann II, "Ada: Vital to the Industrial Base," a speech presented at George Mason University and quoted in full in *CrossTalk, the Monthly Technical Report of the US Air Force Software Technology Support Center*, 14 January 1992.

[Sha and Goodenough 1990] Lui Sha and John B. Goodenough, "Real-Time Scheduling Theory and Ada," *Computer*, *23*(4), 53–62, April 1990.

# Chapter 6

# Object-Oriented Specification and Design Language

The object-oriented specification and design language, OOSDL, was primarily developed to improve the specification, design, and documentation of object-oriented software applications. OOSDL is a strongly typed, quasi-formal, textual, object-oriented specification and design language roughly based on the Ada programming language [AJPO 1983]; it is both simplified and extended with concepts from Eiffel [Meyer 1988], DRAGOON [Atkinson 1991], and ASTS Development Method 3 (ADM3). Although OOSDL could reasonably be used as an implementation language if production-quality compilers were available, it is intended to be used earlier, during specification and language-independent design. OOSDL specifications and designs are intended to evolve incrementally as analysis and design progresses. Eventual CASE-tool support in terms of both language-sensitive editors (LSEs) and documentation generators is envisioned to support the automatic generation of OOSDL specifications and designs from CASE databases, the automatic generation of implementation-language software from OOSDL information, the automatic reverse engineering of database information from updated OOSDL specifications and designs, and the automatic reverse engineering of OOSDL from implementation-language software.

The syntax of OOSDL is defined using a simple modification of Backus-Naur-Form (BNF), and the semantics of OOSDL is defined using standard narrative English. OOSDL terms may contain embedded underlines to promote readability (e.g., "Assembly_Body"). OOSDL terms are syntactically defined in modified BNF declarations of the form "Construct ::= Syntax." OOSDL terms in boldface

323

(e.g., "**abstract**") denote reserved words. Square brackets enclose an optional item (e.g., "[**is concurrent**]"), whereas curly braces enclose a potentially repeated item (e.g., "{ , Range_Integer }") that may appear zero or more times, with the repetitions occurring from left to right. Alternative items are separated by vertical bars (e.g., "First Alternate|Second Alternative"), whereby the vertical bars do not occur in OOSDL. Semicolons are used as terminators in OOSDL, and the number of spaces used as separators is not significant. Comments in OOSDL are preceded by two hyphens (i.e., "--") and continue to the end of the line. The format (e.g., indentation, line breaks, capitalization) in the definitions and examples represent the optional recommended style.

The following nonterminal constructs of OOSDL are defined in a top-down manner in this chapter, using the aforementioned notation and conventions:

- **Assemblies**
  - Assembly_Specification
  - Assembly_Body
  - ASSEMBLY_IDENTIFIER
- **Subassemblies**
  - Subassemblies_List
  - Subassembly_Specification
  - Subassembly_Body
  - EXTENDED_SUBASSEMBLY_IDENTIFIER
  - SUBASSEMBLY_PATH
  - SUBASSEMBLY_IDENTIFIER
- **Objects and Classes**
  - COMPONENT_PATH
  - COMPONENT_IDENTIFIER
  - Objects
    - Objects_List
    - Object_Declaration
    - Object_Specification
    - Object_Body
    - EXTENDED_OBJECT_IDENTIFIER
    - OBJECT_IDENTIFIER
  - Classes
    - Classes_List
    - Class_Specification
    - Class_Body
    - Introduces_List
    - Completes_List
    - Redefines_List
    - Removes_List
    - EXTENDED_CLASS_IDENTIFIER
    - CLASS_IDENTIFIER

- **Relationships**
  - Generics
    - Generic_Parameters_List
    - Generic_Parameter_Declaration
    - Generic_Parameter
  - Needs
    - Needs_List_Subassembly
    - Needs_List_Component
  - Parents
    - Parent_Clause_Subassembly
    - Parent_Clause_Object
    - Parent_Clause_Operation
  - Superclasses
    - Superclasses_List
- Resources
  - Attribute Types
    - Attribute_Types_List_Specification
    - Attribute_Types_List_Body
    - Attribute_Type_Declaration_Specification
    - Attribute_Type_Declaration_Body
    - Attribute_Type_Definition
    - Attribute_Type_Definition_Array
    - Attribute_Type_Definition_Derived
    - Attribute_Type_Definition_Enumeration
    - Attribute_Type_Definition_Integer
    - Attribute_Type_Definition_Real
    - Attribute_Type_Definition_Record
    - Attribute_Type_Definition_Subtype
    - ATTRIBUTE_TYPE_IDENTIFIER
    - A_Range
    - Range_Enumeration
    - Range_Integer
    - Range_Real
  - Attributes
    - Attributes_List
    - Attribute_Declaration
    - Attribute_Declaration_Constant
    - Attribute_Declaration_Variable
    - Attribute_Identifier
    - ATTRIBUTE_IDENTIFIER_CONSTANT
    - Attribute_Identifier_Variable
  - Messages
    - Message_List
    - Message_Declaration

- – Operations
    - – Operations_List_Modifier
    - – Operations_List_Preserver
    - – Operation_Declaration_Class
    - – Operation_Declaration_Constructor_Class
    - – Operation_Declaration_Destructor_Class
    - – Operation_Declaration_Modifier
    - – Operation_Declaration_Preserver
    - – OPERATION_IDENTIFIER_CONSTRUCTOR
    - – OPERATION_IDENTIFIER_DESTRUCTOR
    - – OPERATION_IDENTIFIER_MODIFIER
    - – OPERATION_IDENTIFIER_PRESERVER
    - – Operation_Specification
    - – Operation_Body
    - – Actual_Parameters_List
    - – Parameter_Association
    - – Actual_Parameter
    - – Formal_Parameters_List
    - – Parameter_Declaration
    - – Formal_Parameter
    - – Mode
- – Exceptions
    - – Exceptions_List
    - – Exception_Declaration
    - – Exception_Handler
    - – Exception_Choice
    - – EXCEPTION_IDENTIFIER
- • Low-Level Constructs
    - – Statements
    - – Statements_List
    - – Statement
    - – Sequence_Of_Statements
    - – Assignment_Statement
    - – If_Statement
    - – Interrupt_Statement
    - – Case_Statement
    - – Set_Of_Choices
    - – More_Choices
    - – Choice
    - – Construct_Statement
    - – Destruct_Statement
    - – Loop_Statement
    - – Null_Statement
    - – Raise_Statement
    - – Renames_Statement

- — Return_Statement
- — Select_Statement
- — TBD_Statement
- Assertions
  - — Invariants_List
  - — Invariant
  - — Condition
  - — Preconditions_List
  - — Precondition
  - — Postconditions_List
  - — Postcondition
- Expressions
  - — Expression
  - — Expression_Boolean
  - — Expression_Integer
  - — Expression_Real
- Values
  - — Value
  - — Value_Boolean
  - — Value_Enumeration
  - — Value_Integer
  - — Natural_Number
  - — Comma
  - — Minus_Sign
  - — Value_Real
- Identifiers
  - — UPPER_CASE_IDENTIFIER
  - — NOUN_IDENTIFIER
  - — SINGULAR_NOUN_IDENTIFIER
  - — PLURAL_NOUN_IDENTIFIER
  - — VERB_IDENTIFIER
  - — Identifier
  - — Letter_Or_Digit
  - — Letter
  - — Upper_Case_Letter
  - — Lower_Case_Letter
  - — Digit
  - — Underline

## 6.1  RESERVED WORDS

The following list of reserved words of OOSDL are printed in boldface for readability because they have special significance. They may not be used as names for assemblies, subassemblies, objects, classes, attribute types, attributes, operations, and exceptions.

- abstract
- array
- at
- case
- completes
- CONSTRUCT
- deferred
- DESTRUCT_FAILED
- else
- exception_handler
- hardware
- INTEGERS
- invariants
- message
- new
- of
- or_if
- out
- post
- PREDEFINED
- raise
- record
- renames
- select
- THE_SET_OF_REAL_NUMBERS
- statements
- superclass
- TBD
- then
- when

- ALL
- assembly
- body
- class
- concurrent
- CONSTRUCT_FAILED
- delta
- destructor
- end
- False
- if
- interrupt
- is
- modifier
- null
- operation
- others
- parameter
- postconditions
- preserver
- range
- redefines
- require
- sequential
- specification
- sub
- synchronous
- terminate
- type
- while

- and
- asynchronous
- BOOLEANS
- CLOCK
- constant
- constructor
- DESTRUCT
- digits
- exception
- for
- in
- introduces
- loop
- needs
- object
- or
- otherwise
- parent
- preconditions
- priority
- receive
- removes
- return
- THE_SET_OF_INTEGERS
- start
- subassembly
- SYSTEM
- True
- visible

## 6.2 ASSEMBLIES

An assembly is the highest-level software entity, typically corresponds to a major software configuration item, and consists of a set of related subassemblies that are to be developed from a single cohesive set of requirements. Each assembly has its own thread of control and is therefore concurrent. Each assembly consists of an assembly specification and an assembly body. Each *assembly identifier* is unique for each project. An *assembly specification* documents the assembly's visible subassemblies (i.e., those that contain objects or classes that may receive messages from outside the assembly). An *assembly body* documents the assembly's hidden component subassemblies.

```
Assembly_Specification ::=

  assembly ASSEMBLY_IDENTIFIER
  specification
    Subassemblies_List
  end;

Assembly_Body ::=
```

```
assembly ASSEMBLY_IDENTIFIER
body
  Subassemblies_List
end;
```

```
ASSEMBLY_IDENTIFIER ::= UPPER_CASE_IDENTIFIER
```

An assembly must contain at least one subassembly. An assembly specification need not contain any subassemblies as long as the corresponding body contains at least one subassembly. Likewise, an assembly body need not contain any subassemblies as long as the corresponding specification contains at least one subassembly. The following are example assembly specifications and bodies:

```
assembly AUTOMATIC_DASHBOARD_APPLICATION
specification
  subassembly CRUISE_CONTROL   is concurrent;
  subassembly GAUGES           is concurrent;
  subassembly SPEEDOMETER      is concurrent;
end;
```

```
assembly AUTOMATIC_DASHBOARD_APPLICATION
body
end;
```

```
assembly AUTOMATIC_TELLER_MACHINE
specification
  subassembly AUTOMATIC_TELLER is concurrent;
end;
```

```
assembly AUTOMATIC_TELLER_MACHINE
body
  subassembly PERFORM_A_TRANSACTION is concurrent;
  subassembly PIN_VERIFIED          is concurrent;
end;
```

```
assembly DIGITAL_THERMOSTAT_SYSTEM
specification
  subassembly MAIN is concurrent;
end;
```

```
assembly DIGITAL_THERMOSTAT_SYSTEM
body
end;
```

```
assembly SHOWER_MASTER
specification
  subassembly CONTROL_PANEL is concurrent;
end;
```

```
assembly SHOWER_MASTER
body
```

```
    subassembly COLD_WATER      is concurrent;
    subassembly CONVERTERS      is concurrent;
    subassembly FAIL_SAFE       is concurrent;
    subassembly HOT_WATER       is concurrent;
    subassembly SHOWER_WATER    is concurrent;
end;
```

## 6.3  SUBASSEMBLIES

A subassembly is the second-highest-level software entity, typically corresponds to a major software component, and consists of a set of related objects, classes, and subassemblies. A subassembly has its own thread of control only if it contains, either directly or indirectly, one or more concurrent objects or classes. A *subassemblies list* documents the existence of zero or more subassemblies. Each subassembly consists of a subassembly specification and a subassembly body. An *extended subassembly identifier* includes the full subassembly path, using the dot notation. Each subassembly identifier is unique within its assembly. The identifier is often the same as the main object or class in the subassembly or else the name of the stubbed operation, object or class in the parent subassembly that caused the current subassembly to be formed via recursion.

A *subassembly specification* documents the subassembly's parent assembly or subassembly; any child subassemblies needed by something listed in the specification, whether or not it is concurrent; and the subassembly's visible objects, classes, and subassemblies. Only the subassembly's immediate parent is listed. If more than one immediate parent exists, then only the one in which it is defined is listed. A parent subassembly needs a child subassembly if the parent subassembly contains an object or class that needs to send a message to a visible object or class in the child subassembly. A subassembly is *concurrent* if it contains a concurrent object or class. A component subassembly is *visible* if it contains at least one object or class that may receive messages from outside its subassembly. A *subassembly body* documents both any child subassemblies needed by something listed in the body and the subassembly's hidden component objects, classes, and subassemblies.

```
Subassemblies_List ::= {subassembly SUBASSEMBLY_IDENTIFIER [ is concurrent];}


Subassembly_Specification  ::=

 subassembly SUBASSEMBLY_IDENTIFIER[ is concurrent]
  Parent_Clause_Subassembly
  Needs_List_Subassembly
 specification
  Objects_List
  Classes_List
  Subassemblies_List
 end;

Subassembly_Body  ::=
```

```
subassembly SUBASSEMBLY_IDENTIFIER
  Needs_List_Subassembly
body
  Objects_List
  Classes_List
  Subassemblies_List
end;
```

EXTENDED_SUBASSEMBLY_IDENTIFIER   ::= SUBASSEMBLY_IDENTIFIER.[SUBASSEMBLY_PATH]

SUBASSEMBLY_PATH                  ::= {[SUBASSEMBLY_IDENTIFIER.]}ASSEMBLY_IDENTIFIER

SUBASSEMBLY_IDENTIFIER            ::= UPPER_CASE_IDENTIFIER

Lists of zero or more subassemblies occur in the specifications and bodies of assemblies and subassemblies. The following are examples of subassembly lists:

```
subassembly COLD_WATER      is concurrent;
subassembly CONVERTERS      is concurrent;
subassembly FAIL_SAFE       is concurrent;
subassembly HOT_WATER       is concurrent;
subassembly SHOWER_WATER    is concurrent;
```

```
subassembly MAIN is concurrent;
```

A subassembly must contain at least one object, class, or subassembly. The following are example subassembly specifications and bodies:

```
subassembly CRUISE_CONTROL is concurrent
  parent assembly AUTOMOTIVE_DASHBOARD_APPLICATION;
specification
  object   THE_ACCELERATION_BUTTON   is concurrent;
  object   THE_BREAK_SENSOR          is concurrent;
  object   THE_COAST_BUTTON          is concurrent;
  object   THE_GAS_PEDAL_SENSOR      is concurrent;
  object   THE_ON_OFF_SWITCH         is concurrent;
end;
```

```
subassembly CRUISE_CONTROL
body
  object   THE_CRUISE_CONTROL     is concurrent;
  object   THE_THROTTLE_ACTUATOR  is concurrent;
end;
```

```
subassembly GAUGES is concurrent
  parent assembly AUTOMOTIVE_DASHBOARD_APPLICATION;
specification
  object   THE_ENGINE_ROTATION_SENSOR    is concurrent;
end;
```

```
subassembly GAUGES
body
  object   THE_ENGINE_TEMPERATURE_GAUGE   is concurrent;
```

```
object   THE_ENGINE_TEMPERATURE_SENSOR;
object   THE_FUEL_GAUGE                      is concurrent;
object   THE_FUEL_SENSOR;
object   THE_OIL_GAUGE                       is concurrent;
object   THE_OIL_PRESSURE_SENSOR;
object   THE_TACHOMETER                      is concurrent;
end;

subassembly CONTROL_PANEL                        is concurrent
 parent assembly SHOWER_MASTER;
specification
object   THE_DECREASE_FLOW_BUTTON              is concurrent;
object   THE_DECREASE_TEMPERATURE_BUTTON       is concurrent;
object   THE_ON_OFF_SWITCH                     is concurrent;
object   THE_INCREASE_FLOW_BUTTON              is concurrent;
object   THE_INCREASE_TEMPERATURE_BUTTON       is concurrent;
end CONTROL_PANEL;

subassembly CONTROL_PANEL
 needs COLD_WATER;
 needs FAIL_SAFE;
 needs HOT_WATER;
 needs SHOWER_WATER;
body
 object   THE_DESIRED_FLOW          is concurrent;
 object   THE_DESIRED_TEMPERATURE   is concurrent;
 object   THE_DISPLAY               is concurrent;
 object   THE_SHOWER_MASTER         is concurrent;
end CONTROL_PANEL;

subassembly INTERSECTION is concurrent
 parent assembly TRAFFIC_SYSTEM;
specification
 object   THE_SET_OF_TRAFFIC_SENSORS  is concurrent;
 object   THE_SWITCH                  is concurrent;
end;

subassembly INTERSECTION
body
 object   THE_CLOCK                                          is concurrent;
 object   THE_INTERSECTION                                   is concurrent;
 object   THE_MULTIPLEXING_DIGITAL_TO_ANALOG_CONVERTER       is concurrent;
 object   THE_POWER_DISTRIBUTOR                              is concurrent;
 object   THE_SET_OF_CROSSWALK_SIGNALS                       is concurrent;
 object   THE_SET_OF_TRAFFIC_SIGNALS                         is concurrent;
 object   WARNING_PANEL;
end;
```

The following are examples of extended subassembly identifiers:

```
COLD_WATER.SHOWER_MASTER
CRUISE_CONTROL.AUTOMOTIVE_DASHBOARD_APPLICATION
FAIL_SAFE.SHOWER_MASTER
```

```
GAUGES.AUTOMOTIVE_DASHBOARD_APPLICATION
HOT_WATER.SHOWER_MASTER
SHOWER_MASTER.SHOWER_WATER
SPEEDOMETER.AUTOMOTIVE_DASHBOARD_APPLICATION
```

## 6.4  OBJECTS AND CLASSES

Objects and classes are the main components of object-oriented applications.

```
COMPONENT_PATH        ::=
{COMPONENT_IDENTIFIER.}{SUBASSEMBLY_IDENTIFIER.}SUBASSEMBLY_IDENTIFIER.
ASSEMBLY_IDENTIFIER
COMPONENT_IDENTIFIER ::= OBJECT_IDENTIFIER | CLASS_IDENTIFIER
```

The following are examples of valid component identifiers for objects and classes:

```
THE_DECREASE_FLOW_BUTTON.CONTROL_PANEL
THE_DECREASE_TEMPERATURE_BUTTON.CONTROL_PANEL
THE_DESIRED_FLOW
THE_DESIRED_TEMPERATURE
THE_DISPLAY
THE_INCREASE_FLOW_BUTTON.CONTROL_PANEL
THE_INCREASE_TEMPERATURE_BUTTON.CONTROL_PANEL
THE_ON_OFF_SWITCH.CONTROL_PANEL
THE_SHOWER_MASTER
THE_SET_OF_TRAFFIC_SIGNALS
```

### 6.4.1    Objects

An object is one of the primary software entities in an object-oriented application, typically corresponds to a software unit, and consists of a set of related attribute types, attributes, operations, exceptions, optional component objects, and optional main operation. An *objects list* documents zero or more object declarations. An object declaration declares the existence of a single object and documents whether the declared object is concurrent. An object is concurrent and has one or more threads of control only if it contains, either directly or indirectly, one or more concurrent operations. Each object consists of an object specification and an object body. An *extended object identifier* includes the full component path, using the dot notation. Each object identifier is a singular noun phrase, unique within its subassembly.

An *object specification* documents whether the object is concurrent, its immediate parent, any objects or classes needed by something listed in the specification, and the object's visible attribute types, operations, and exceptions. Only the object's immediate parent object, class, or subassembly is listed. If more than one immediate parent exists, then only the one in which it is defined is listed. An object needs a lower-level object if it needs to send a message to the lower-level object. An object needs a lower-level class if it needs to instantiate the lower-level class. An attribute type or exception listed in an object's specification may be referenced by the operations of objects and classes needed by the current object. Objects may send messages to the current object (if it is visible to these objects) if the messages correspond to operations listed in the specification of the current object. An *object body* documents any objects or classes needed by something listed in the body; any hidden attribute types, attributes, or operations; any component objects; an optional list of object invariants; and an optional list of messages to initialization operations that execute as soon as the object body is elaborated.

```
Objects_List            ::= {Object_Declaration}

Object_Declaration      ::= object OBJECT_IDENTIFIER [is concurrent];

Object_Specification  ::=

  object OBJECT_IDENTIFIER [is concurrent]
   Parent_Clause_Object
   Needs_List_Component
  specification
   Attribute_Types_List_Specification
   Message_List
   Exceptions_List
  end;

Object_Body        ::=

  object OBJECT_IDENTIFIER
   Needs_List_Component
  body
   Attribute_Types_List_Body
   Attributes_List
   Operations_List_Modifier
   Operations_List_Preserver
   Objects_List
   Invariants_List
   Initialization_Messages_List
  end;

EXTENDED_OBJECT_IDENTIFIER   ::= OBJECT_IDENTIFIER.COMPONENT_PATH

OBJECT_IDENTIFIER            ::= SINGULAR_NOUN_IDENTIFIER;
```

Lists of zero or more objects occur in the specifications and bodies of subassemblies and in the bodies of objects and classes. The following are examples of object lists:

```
object   THE_ENGINE_TEMPERATURE_GAUGE    is concurrent;
object   THE_ENGINE_TEMPERATURE_SENSOR;
object   THE_FUEL_GAUGE                  is concurrent;
object   THE_FUEL_LEVEL_SENSOR;
object   THE_OIL_GAUGE                   is concurrent;
object   THE_OIL_PRESSURE_SENSOR;
object   THE_TACHOMETER                  is concurrent;
```

```
object    THE_DESIRED_FLOW                is concurrent;
object    THE_DESIRED_TEMPERATURE         is concurrent;
object    THE_DISPLAY                     is concurrent;
object    THE_SHOWER_MASTER               is concurrent;
```

An object usually contains at least one attribute and must contain one operation. The following is an example specification and body for the concurrent object THE_DESIRED_TEMPERATURE.DIGITAL_THERMOSTAT:

```
object THE_DESIRED_TEMPERATURE is concurrent
 parent subassembly DIGITAL_THERMOSTAT;
specification
 - no exported attribute types or constants.
 message DECREMENT          raise FAILURE_OCCURRED_IN is synchronous;
 message INCREMENT          raise FAILURE_OCCURRED_IN is synchronous;
 message START              raise FAILURE_OCCURRED_IN is synchronous;
 message STOP               raise FAILURE_OCCURRED_IN is synchronous;
 message USE_CELSIUS        raise FAILURE_OCCURRED_IN is synchronous;
 message USE_FAHRENHEIT    raise FAILURE_OCCURRED_IN is synchronous;
 exception FAILURE_OCCURRED_IN;
end;


object THE_DESIRED_TEMPERATURE
 needs THE_MEAN_TEMPERATURE;
 needs CLOCKS.PREDEFINED;
body
 type Modes  is (Celsius,Fahrenheit);
 type States is (Off,On);
 constant The_Delay_Amount          : Seconds.THE_CLOCK      ::=      10;
 constant THE_MAXIMUM_DIFFERENCE  :
         Degrees_Celsius.THE_SET_OF_TEMPERATURE_SENSORS  ::=      2;
 variable The_Current_Value         :
         Degrees_Celsius.THE_SET_OF_TEMPERATURE_SENSORS;
 variable The_Mean_Temperature    :
         Degrees_Celsius.THE_SET_OF_TEMPERATURE_SENSORS;
 variable The_Mode              : Modes               ::= Celsius;
 variable The_State             : States              ::=     Off;
 modifier operation   DECREMENT         raise FAILURE_OCCURRED_IN;
 modifier operation   DISPLAY           raise FAILURE_OCCURRED_IN;
 modifier operation   INCREMENT         raise FAILURE_OCCURRED_IN;
 modifier operation   MAINTAIN          raise FAILURE_OCCURRED_IN,
                                              INCOMPATIBLE_STATE_IN
                                   is concurrent;
 preserver operation  ROUTE_MESSAGES_FOR  raise FAILURE_OCCURRED_IN
                                   is concurrent;
 modifier operation   START             raise FAILURE_OCCURRED_IN;
 modifier operation   STOP              raise FAILURE_OCCURRED_IN;
 modifier operation   USE_CELSIUS       raise FAILURE_OCCURRED_IN;
 modifier operation   USE_FAHRENHEIT    raise FAILURE_OCCURRED_IN;
 object THE_CLOCK              : CLOCKS.PREDEFINED;
start
 CONSTRUCT(THE_CLOCK).THE_CLOCKS;
 ROUTE_MESSAGES_FOR;
end;
```

The following is an example specification and body for the concurrent object THE_SET_OF_TRAFFIC_SIGNALS.INTERSECTION:

```
object THE_SET_OF_TRAFFIC_SIGNALS
 parent subassembly INTERSECTION;
specification
 message    CHANGE_PRIMARY      raise LIGHT_FAILED,POWER_FAILED  is synchronous;
 message    CHANGE_SECONDARY    raise LIGHT_FAILED,POWER_FAILED  is synchronous;
 message    CHANGE_TURN         raise LIGHT_FAILED,POWER_FAILED  is synchronous;
 message    FLASH_PRIMARY       raise LIGHT_FAILED,POWER_FAILED  is synchronous;
 message    FLASH_SECONDARY     raise LIGHT_FAILED,POWER_FAILED  is synchronous;
 message    FLASH_TURN          raise LIGHT_FAILED,POWER_FAILED  is synchronous;
 message    INITIALIZE          raise LIGHT_FAILED,POWER_FAILED  is synchronous;
 message    TURN_OFF            raise LIGHT_FAILED,POWER_FAILED  is synchronous;
 exception  FAILURE_OCCURRED_IN;
 exception  LIGHT_FAILED;
 exception  POWER_FAILED;
end;


object THE_SET_OF_TRAFFIC_SIGNALS
 needs PRIMARY_SIGNALS.INTERSECTION_CLASSES;
 needs SECONDARY_SIGNALS.INTERSECTION_CLASSES;
 needs TURN_SIGNALS.INTERSECTION_CLASSES;
body
 type       States is (Primary,Secondary,Turn);
 variable   The_State      : States ::= Primary;
 modifier   operation CHANGE_PRIMARY;
 modifier   operation CHANGE_SECONDARY;
 modifier   operation CHANGE_TURN;
 modifier   operation FLASH_PRIMARY;
 modifier   operation FLASH_SECONDARY;
 modifier   operation FLASH_TURN;
 modifier   operation INITIALIZE;
 preserver  operation ROUTE_MESSAGES_FOR  raise FAILURE_OCCURRED_IN  is concurrent;
 modifier   operation TURN_OFF;
 object    EAST_SECONDARY  : SECONDARY_SIGNALS.INTERSECTION_CLASSES;
 object    NORTH_PRIMARY   : PRIMARY_SIGNALS.INTERSECTION_CLASSES;
 object    NORTH_TURN      : TURN_SIGNALS.INTERSECTION_CLASSES;
 object    SOUTH_PRIMARY   : PRIMARY_SIGNALS.INTERSECTION_CLASSES;
 object    SOUTH_TURN      : TURN_SIGNALS.INTERSECTION_CLASSES;
 object    WEST_SECONDARY  : SECONDARY_SIGNALS.INTERSECTION_CLASSES;
end;
```

The following are example extended object identifiers of the objects in the three subassemblies of the automotive dashboard application assembly:

```
THE_ACCELERATION_BUTTON.CRUISE_CONTROL.AUTOMOTIVE_DASHBOARD_APPLICATION
THE_BREAK_SENSOR.CRUISE_CONTROL.AUTOMOTIVE_DASHBOARD_APPLICATION
THE_COAST_BUTTON.CRUISE_CONTROL.AUTOMOTIVE_DASHBOARD_APPLICATION
THE_CRUISE_CONTROL.CRUISE_CONTROL.AUTOMOTIVE_DASHBOARD_APPLICATION
THE_GAS_PEDAL_SENSOR.CRUISE_CONTROL.AUTOMOTIVE_DASHBOARD_APPLICATION
THE_ON_OFF_SWITCH.CRUISE_CONTROL.AUTOMOTIVE_DASHBOARD_APPLICATION
THE_THROTTLE_ACTUATOR.CRUISE_CONTROL.AUTOMOTIVE_DASHBOARD_APPLICATION
```

```
THE_ENGINE_ROTATION_SENSOR.GAUGES.AUTOMOTIVE_DASHBOARD_APPLICATION
THE_ENGINE_TEMPERATURE_GAUGE.GAUGES.AUTOMOTIVE_DASHBOARD_APPLICATION
THE_ENGINE_TEMPERATURE_SENSOR.GAUGES.AUTOMOTIVE_DASHBOARD_APPLICATION
THE_FUEL_GAUGE.GAUGES.AUTOMOTIVE_DASHBOARD_APPLICATION
THE_FUEL_LEVEL_SENSOR.GAUGES.AUTOMOTIVE_DASHBOARD_APPLICATION
THE_OIL_GAUGE.GAUGES.AUTOMOTIVE_DASHBOARD_APPLICATION
THE_OIL_PRESSURE_SENSOR.GAUGES.AUTOMOTIVE_DASHBOARD_APPLICATION
THE_TACHOMETER.GAUGES.AUTOMOTIVE_DASHBOARD_APPLICATION


THE_MODE.SPEEDOMETER.AUTOMOTIVE_DASHBOARD_APPLICATION
THE_MODE_BUTTON.SPEEDOMETER.AUTOMOTIVE_DASHBOARD_APPLICATION
THE_ODOMETER.SPEEDOMETER.AUTOMOTIVE_DASHBOARD_APPLICATION
THE_ODOMETER_TRIP_RESET_BUTTON.SPEEDOMETER.AUTOMOTIVE_DASHBOARD_APPLICATION
THE_SPEEDOMETER.SPEEDOMETER.AUTOMOTIVE_DASHBOARD_APPLICATION
THE_WHEEL_ROTATION_SENSOR.SPEEDOMETER.AUTOMOTIVE_DASHBOARD_APPLICATION
```

## 6.4.2   Classes

A **class** is the primary software entity for inheritance in an object-oriented application, is a template for constructing objects, typically corresponds to a software unit, and consists of a set of instance resources, including attribute types, attributes, operations, optional exceptions, optional component objects, and optional main operation. A *classes list* documents zero or more classes and whether the classes are concurrent. A class is concurrent only if its instances are concurrent. Each class consists of a class specification and a class body. An *extended class identifier* includes the full component path, using the dot notation. Each class identifier is a plural noun phrase unique within its subassembly.

A *class specification* documents whether the class is concurrent, its immediate parent, any objects or classes needed by something listed in the specification, a list of its superclasses, any generic parameters, whether it is abstract, and the visible attribute types, operations, and exceptions of its instances that it introduces, completes, redefines, and removes. Only the class's immediate parent subassembly is listed. If more than one immediate parent exists, then only the one in which it is defined is listed. A class needs a lower-level object or class if it needs to send a message to the lower-level object or class. A class is abstract if one or more subclasses must supply resources for an instance to be constructed. An attribute type or exception listed in a class's specification may be referenced by the operations of objects and classes that send messages to instances of the current class. Objects and classes may send messages to instances of the current class (if it is visible to them) if the messages correspond to operations listed in the specification of the current class. A *class body* documents any objects or classes needed by something listed in the body; any hidden attribute types, attributes, or operations that it introduces, completes, redefines, and removes; any component objects; and an optional list of messages to initialization operations that execute as soon as the instance is instantiated.

A resource must be introduced the first time it is listed in an inheritance hierarchy. It then can be completed, redefined, or removed in a subclass. A resource must be completed in a subclass if it is incomplete when it is introduced. A resource is incomplete if it is not defined when it is introduced.

```
Classes_List                      ::= {class CLASS_IDENTIFIER [ is concurrent];}

Class_Specification               ::= class CLASS_IDENTIFIER [ is concurrent]
                                      Parent_Clause_Class
                                      Needs_List_Component
                                      Superclasses_List
                                      Generic_Parameters_List
                                      specification [is abstract]
                                      Introduces_List_Specification
                                      Completes_List_Specification
                                      Redefines_List_Specification
                                      Removes_List_Specification
                                      end;

Class_Body                        ::= class CLASS_IDENTIFIER
                                      Needs_List_Component
                                      body
                                      Introduces_List_Body
                                      Completes_List_Body
                                      Redefines_List_Body
                                      Removes_List_Body
                                      end;

EXTENDED_CLASS_IDENTIFIER         ::= CLASS_IDENTIFIER.COMPONENT_PATH

CLASS_IDENTIFIER                  ::= PLURAL_NOUN_IDENTIFIER;

Introduces_List_Specification     ::= [introduces
                                      {Class_Resources_Specification}]

Completes_List_Specification      ::= [completes
                                      {Class_Resources_Specification}]

Redefines_List_Specification      ::= [redefines
                                      {Class_Resources_Specification}]

Removes_List_Specification        ::= [removes
                                      {Class_Resources_Specification}]

Class_Resources_Specification     ::= Attribute_Types_List_Specification
                                      Message_Declaration_List
                                      Exceptions_List

Introduces_List_Body              ::= [introduces
                                       {Class_Resources_Body}]
```

```
Completes_List_Body             ::=   [completes
                                        {Class_Resources_Body}]

Redefines_List_Body             ::=   [redefines
                                        {Class_Resources_Body}]

Removes_List_Body               ::=   [removes
                                        {Class_Resources_Body}]

Class_Resources_Body            ::=   Attribute_Types_List_Body
                                      Attributes_List
                                      Operations_List_Modifier
                                      Operations_List_Preserver
                                      Objects_List
                                      Invariants_List
                                      Initialization_Messages_List
```

Lists of zero or more classes occur in the specifications and bodies of subassemblies. The following is an example class list:

```
class PRIMARY_SIGNALS    is concurrent;
class SECONDARY_SIGNALS  is concurrent;
class STANDARD_SIGNALS   is concurrent;
class TRAFFIC_SIGNALS    is concurrent;
class TURN_SIGNALS       is concurrent;
```

A class must contain at least one attribute and one operation. The following are example class specifications and bodies:

```
class TRAFFIC_SIGNALS is concurrent
  parent subassembly INTERSECTION_CLASSES;
specification is abstract
  introduces
  message   CHANGE                                                is deferred;
  message   CONSTRUCT   (A_TRAFFIC_SIGNAL)  raise CONSTRUCT_FAILED is synchronous;
  message   DESTRUCT    (A_TRAFFIC_SIGNAL)  raise DESTRUCT_FAILED  is synchronous;
  message   FLASH                                                 is deferred;
  message   INITIALIZE                                            is deferred;
  message   TURN_OFF                                              is deferred;
  exception   ABSTRACTION_FAILED_IN;
  exception   CONSTRUCT_FAILED_IN;
  exception   DESTRUCT_FAILED_IN;
  exception   LIGHT_FAILED_IN;
  exception   POWER_FAILED_IN;
end;
```

```
class TRAFFIC_SIGNALS
 needs TRAFFIC_LIGHTS;
body
 introduces
   type                  States        is deferred;
   variable              The_State     : States := Red_Light;
   operation             CHANGE        is deferred;
   constructor operation CONSTRUCT     (A_TRAFFIC_SIGNAL)
                         raise CONSTRUCT_FAILED;
   destructor operation  DESTRUCT      (A_TRAFFIC_SIGNAL)
                         raise DESTRUCT_FAILED;
   operation             FLASH         is deferred;
   operation             INITIALIZE    is deferred;
   operation             TURN_OFF      is deferred;
   object                RED_LIGHT     : TRAFFIC_LIGHTS;
   object                YELLOW_LIGHT  : TRAFFIC_LIGHTS;
start
 CONSTRUCT(RED_LIGHT).TRAFFIC_LIGHTS;
 CONSTRUCT(YELLOW_LIGHT).TRAFFIC_LIGHTS;
 INITIALIZE;
end;

class TURN_SIGNALS is concurrent
 parent subassembly INTERSECTION_CLASSES;
 superclass TRAFFIC_SIGNALS is visible;
specification
 introduces
   message  CHANGE     raise LIGHT_FAILED_IN,POWER_FAILED_IN  is synchronous;
   message  FLASH      raise LIGHT_FAILED_IN,POWER_FAILED_IN  is synchronous;
   message  INITIALIZE raise LIGHT_FAILED_IN,POWER_FAILED_IN  is synchronous;
   message  TURN_OFF   raise ABSTRACTION_FAILED_IN            is synchronous;
end;

class TURN_SIGNALS
 needs TRAFFIC_LIGHTS;
body
 introduces
   type States is (Green_ARROW,YELLOW_LIGHT,RED_LIGHT);
   modifier operation CHANGE      raise  LIGHT_FAILED_IN,POWER_FAILED_IN;
   modifier operation FLASH       raise  LIGHT_FAILED_IN,POWER_FAILED_IN;
   modifier operation INITIALIZE  raise  LIGHT_FAILED_IN,POWER_FAILED_IN;
   modifier operation TURN_OFF    raise  ABSTRACTION_FAILED_IN;
   object             GREEN_ARROW :  TRAFFIC_LIGHTS;
start
 CONSTRUCT(GREEN_ARROW).TRAFFIC_LIGHTS;
end;
```

```
class STANDARD_SIGNALS is concurrent
 parent subassembly INTERSECTION_CLASSES;
 superclass TRAFFIC_SIGNALS is visible;
specification is abstract
 introduces
   message   CHANGE      raise LIGHT_FAILED_IN, POWER_FAILED_IN  is synchronous;
   message   INITIALIZE  raise LIGHT_FAILED_IN, POWER_FAILED_IN  is synchronous;
   message   TURN_OFF    raise ABSTRACTION_FAILED_IN             is synchronous;
end;

class STANDARD_SIGNALS
 needs TRAFFIC_LIGHTS;
body
 introduces
   type States is (Green_Light, Yellow_Light, Red_Light);
   modifier operation  CHANGE      raise  LIGHT_FAILED_IN, POWER_FAILED_IN;
   modifier operation  INITIALIZE  raise  LIGHT_FAILED_IN, POWER_FAILED_IN;
   modifier operation  TURN_OFF    raise  ABSTRACTION_FAILED_IN;
   object GREEN_LIGHT  : TRAFFIC_LIGHTS;
start
 CONSTRUCT(GREEN_LIGHT).TRAFFIC_LIGHTS;
end;

class GENERIC_STACKS
 parent subassembly  CLASS_REPOSITORY;
 needs THE_SET_OF_INTEGERS.PREDEFINED;
 superclass ARRAYS;
 parameter type       Entries is visible;
 parameter constant   The_Maximum_Stack_Size : Values.THE_SET_OF_INTEGERS;
specification
 introduces
  message CONSTRUCT  (A_STACK)        raise CONSTRUCT_FAILED       is sequential;
  message DESTRUCT   (A_STACK)        raise DESTRUCT_FAILED        is sequential;
  message INITIALIZE is sequential;
  message POP        (An_Entry :  out Entries)  raise IS_EMPTY  is sequential;
  message PUSH       (An_Entry :  in  Entries)  raise IS_FULL   is sequential;
  message MAXIMUM_SIZE_OF return Values.THE_SET_OF_INTEGERS      is sequential;
  message SIZE_OF          return Values.THE_SET_OF_INTEGERS
                           raise ABSTRACTION_VIOLATED            is sequential;
  exception          ABSTRACTION_VIOLATED;
  exception          EMPTY;
  exception          FULL;
end;

class GENERIC_STACKS
body
 introduces
  type THE_STACKS is new THE_ARRAYS range 1 .. The_Maximum_Stack_Size;
  variable The_Current_Size : Values.THE_SET_OF_INTEGERS := 0;
  constructor operation  CONSTRUCT  (A_STACK)  raise  CONSTRUCT_FAILED;
  destructor operation   DESTRUCT   (A_STACK)  raise  DESTRUCT_FAILED;
  modifier operation     INITIALIZE;
  modifier operation     POP (An_Entry :  out  Entries)  raise IS_EMPTY;
```

```
modifier operation       PUSH (An_Entry : in  Entries) raise IS_FULL;
preserver operation      MAXIMUM_SIZE_OF return Values.THE_SET_OF_INTEGERS;
preserver operation      SIZE_OF  return Values.THE_SET_OF_INTEGERS
                         raise ABSTRACTION_VIOLATED;
invariants
  The_Current_Size <= The_Maximum_Stack_Size else raise ABSTRACTION_VIOLATED;
end;
```

The following are example extended class identifiers:

```
PRIMARY_SIGNALS.INTERSECTION_CLASSES.TRAFFIC_SYSTEM
SECONDARY_SIGNALS.INTERSECTION_CLASSES.TRAFFIC_SYSTEM
STANDARD_SIGNALS.INTERSECTION_CLASSES.TRAFFIC_SYSTEM
TRAFFIC_SIGNALS.INTERSECTION_CLASSES.TRAFFIC_SYSTEM
TURN_SIGNALS.INTERSECTION_CLASSES.TRAFFIC_SYSTEM
```

## 6.5  RELATIONSHIPS

### 6.5.1    Generics

A *generic parameter list* documents the zero or more generic parameter declarations of parameters needed by the current generic class. A *generic parameter* of a class is used to parameterize the instances of the class. Attribute parameters are added to the body of each instance of the class. Visible attribute type parameters are named in the specification and listed in the body of each instance of the class, while hidden attribute-type parameters are listed in the body of each instance of the class. Visible operation parameters are listed in the specification of each instance of the class, while hidden operation parameters are listed in the body of each instance of the class. Exception parameters are listed in the specification of each instance of the class. Object parameters are listed in the body of each instance of the class.

```
Generic_Parameters_List        ::= {Generic_Parameter_Declaration}

Generic_Parameter_Declaration  ::= parameter Generic_Parameter

Generic_Parameter ::=
  Attribute_Declaration                                      |
  Attribute_Type_Declaration_Specification  [is visible]     |
  Operation_Declaration_Modifier            [is visible]     |
  Operation_Declaration_Preserver           [is visible]     |
  Exception_Declaration                                      |
  Object_Declaration
```

The following are examples of generic parameters declarations:

```
parameter  constant      Maximum_Safe_Temperature;
parameter  constant      Maximum_Safe_Temperature  := 100;
parameter  variable      The_Current_Temperature;
parameter  variable      The_Current_Temperature   :=  58;
parameter  type          Safe_Temperatures;
parameter  type          Safe_Temperatures is visible;
```

```
parameter   modifier operation   MAINTAIN;
parameter   modifier operation   IS_PRESSED              is visible;
parameter   exception            MAXIMUM_SAFE_TEMPERATURE_EXCEEDED;
parameter   object               THE_SET_OF_TEMPERATURE_SENSORS is concurrent;
```

### 6.5.2   Needs

A needs list documents the resources visible to the construct that has the needs list
on which the construct depends. A *subassembly needs list* documents the one or more
immediate lower-level subassemblies that export resources needed by the current
subassembly. A *component needs list* documents the one or more immediate lower-level
objects and classes that export resources needed by the current object, class, or
operation.

```
Needs_List_Subassembly ::= {needs SUBASSEMBLY_IDENTIFIER;}

Needs_List_Component   ::= {needs COMPONENT_IDENTIFIER;}
```

The following are examples of a subassembly and component needs lists:

```
-- Subassembly needs list:
needs COLD_WATER.SHOWER_MASTER;
needs FAIL_SAFE.SHOWER_MASTER;
needs HOT_WATER;
needs SHOWER_WATER;

-- Components needs list:
needs DESIRED_TEMPERATURE.CONTROL_PANEL.SHOWER_MASTER;
needs MEAN_TEMPERATURE;
```

### 6.5.3   Parents

A *parent clause for subassemblies* documents the subassembly's immediate parent, which
is the assembly or subassembly in which it is nested. A *parent clause for objects*
documents the immediate parent of the current object, which is the object or
subassembly in which it is nested. A *parent clause for classes* documents the immediate
parent of the current class, which is the subassembly in which it is nested. A *parent
clause for operations* documents the immediate parent of the current operation, which
is the object or class in which it is nested.

```
Parent_Clause_Subassembly  ::=

    parent assembly          ASSEMBLY_IDENTIFIER;      |
    parent subassembly       SUBASSEMBLY_IDENTIFIER;

Parent_Clause_Object         ::=

    parent object            OBJECT_IDENTIFIER;        |
    parent subassembly       SUBASSEMBLY_IDENTIFIER;
```

```
Parent_Clause_Class          ::=

    parent subassembly       SUBASSEMBLY_IDENTIFIER;

Parent_Clause_Operation      ::=

    parent object            OBJECT_IDENTIFIER;   |
    parent class             CLASS_IDENTIFIER;
```

The following are examples of parent clauses:

```
parent assembly      AUTOMOTIVE_DASHBOARD_SYSTEM;
parent subassembly   CONTROL_PANEL.SHOWER_MASTER;
parent object        SHOWER_MASTER;
parent class         TEMPERATURE_SENSORS;
```

## 6.5.4    Superclasses

A *superclasses list* documents the one or more immediate superclasses from which the current class inherits resources. In order to promote information hiding, all inherited resources are hidden in the body of the subclass unless the superclass is labeled as visible, in which case the subclass inherits the visibility characteristics of the super-class.

```
Superclasses_List ::= {superclass CLASS_IDENTIFIER    [is visible];}
```

The following are examples of superclass lists for classes:

```
superclass ARRAYS;
superclass TRAFFIC_SIGNALS is visible;
```

The following are examples of superclass clauses:

```
superclass TRAFFIC_SIGNALS is visible;
superclass STANDARD_SIGNALS.INTERSECTION_CLASSES is visible;
```

## 6.6  RESOURCES

### 6.6.1    Attribute Types

An *attribute types list* may occur in the specification or body of an object or class and may document zero or more attribute-type declarations. An *attribute-type declaration for the specification* only identifies the type, whereas an *attribute-type declaration for the body* also specifies the definition of the type. An *attribute-type declaration deferred* is used in abstract classes and means that the definition must be supplied by one or more subclasses prior to instantiation.

```
Attribute_Types_List_Specification        ::=

  {Attribute_Type_Declaration_Specification}
```

```
Attribute_Types_List_Body                  ::=

  {Attribute_Type_Declaration_Body}

Attribute_Type_Declaration_Specification   ::=

  type ATTRIBUTE_TYPE_IDENTIFIER;

Attribute_Type_Declaration_Body            ::=

  type ATTRIBUTE_TYPE_IDENTIFIER is Attribute_Type_Definition;

Attribute_Type_Declaration_Deferred        ::=

  type ATTRIBUTE_TYPE_IDENTIFIER is deferred;

ATTRIBUTE_TYPE_IDENTIFIER                   ::=

  PLURAL_NOUN_IDENTIFIER[.COMPONENT_IDENTIFIER]
```

In order to promote information hiding, the definition of types is not exported from specifications. The following are example attribute-type declarations for specifications of objects and classes:

```
type States;
type Kilometers_Per_Hour;
```

The following are example attribute-type declarations for the bodies of objects and classes:

```
type Lists_Of_Sensor_Values is array  (1 .. Number_Of_Sensors) of Sensor_Values;
type Kilometers             is new Values.THE_SET_OF_REAL_NUMBERS delta 0.001;
type Voltages               is new Values.THE_SET_OF_REAL_NUMBERS digits 5
                                                                  range 0.0 .. 120.0;
type Kilometers_Per_Hour    is new Values.THE_SET_OF_INTEGERS   range    0 .. 500;
type Valid_Temperatures     is new Degrees_Celsius             range    0 .. 120;
type Safe_Temperatures      is sub Valid_Temperatures          range   10 .. 100;
type States                 is (Off,Disabled,Enabled,Failed);
type States                 is deferred;
```

An *attribute-type definition* documents the structure and the allowed values for all attributes of attribute types, which may be array, derived, enumeration, integer, real, record, or subtype.

```
Attribute_Type_Definition ::=   Attribute_Type_Definition_Array       |
                                Attribute_Type_Definition_Derived     |
                                Attribute_Type_Definition_Enumeration |
                                Attribute_Type_Definition_Integer     |
                                Attribute_Type_Definition_Real        |
                                Attribute_Type_Definition_Record      |
                                Attribute_Type_Definition_Subtype
```

```
Attribute_Type_Definition_Array          ::=

 array (Range_Integer{,Range_Integer}) of ATTRIBUTE_TYPE_IDENTIFIER

Attribute_Type_Definition_Derived        ::=

 new ATTRIBUTE_TYPE_IDENTIFIER[ range A_Range]

Attribute_Type_Definition_Enumeration    ::=

 (Value_Enumeration{,Value_Enumeration})

Attribute_Type_Definition_Integer        ::=

 Values.THE_SET_OF_INTEGERS [range Range_Integer]

Attribute_Type_Definition_Real           ::=
 Values.THE_SET_OF_REAL_NUMBERS [delta Expression_Real]     [ range Range_Real]  |
 Values.THE_SET_OF_REAL_NUMBERS [digits Expression_Integer] [ range Range_Real]

Attribute_Type_Definition_Record         ::=

 record
   Attribute_Identifier  : ATTRIBUTE_TYPE_IDENTIFIER [:= Expression];
   {Attribute_Identifier : ATTRIBUTE_TYPE_IDENTIFIER [:= Expression];}
 end record

Attribute_Type_Definition_Subtype        ::=
 sub ATTRIBUTE_TYPE_IDENTIFIER range A_Range
```

Attributes of *array types* contain multiple components of the same type. The following are examples of attribute array-type definitions:

```
array (1 .. Number_Of_Sensors)  of Sensor_Values
array (1 .. 8,1 .. 8)           of Chess_Pieces
```

*Derived types* are distinct types that inherit the properties of their parent types. The following are examples of attribute derived-type definitions:

```
new Temperature_In_Degrees
new Temperature_In_Degrees    range 10       ..     120
new States                    range Disabled .. Enabled
new Values.THE_SET_OF_INTEGERS range 1       ..      31
```

Attributes of *enumeration types* may have values from the specified ordered list of values. The following are examples of attribute enumeration-type definitions:

```
(Red, Green, Yellow)
(Monday,Tuesday,Wednesday,Thursday,Friday,Saturday,Sunday)
```

Attributes of *integer types* have integer values. The following are examples of attribute integer-type definitions:

```
Values.THE_SET_OF_INTEGERS
Values.THE_SET_OF_INTEGERS range 1 .. 31
```

Attributes of *real types* have values that approximate real numbers. The following are examples of attribute real-type definitions:

```
Values.THE_SET_OF_REAL_NUMBERS
Values.THE_SET_OF_REAL_NUMBERS              range  0.0  .. 100,000.0
Values.THE_SET_OF_REAL_NUMBERS  delta  0.01
Values.THE_SET_OF_REAL_NUMBERS  delta  0.01 range  0.01 .. 50.75
Values.THE_SET_OF_REAL_NUMBERS  digits 5
Values.THE_SET_OF_REAL_NUMBERS  digits 5    range  7.5  .. 50.0
```

Attributes of *record types* contain multiple components of different types. The following are examples of attribute record-type definitions:

```
record
  The_Current_Pressure : Valid_Pressures;
  The_State            : States      := Unread;
end record

record
  An_Employee          : Employees;
  The_Hours_Worked     : Hours_Worked := 0.0;
  The_Pay_Rate         : Pay_Rates;
  The_Salary           : Salaries    := 0.0;
end record
```

*Subtypes* are not different types from their parent types, but attributes of subtypes have their values constrained. The following are examples of attribute subtype definitions:

```
sub Temperature_In_Degrees      range  10        .. 120
sub States                      range  Disabled .. Enabled
sub Values.THE_SET_OF_INTEGERS  range  1         .. 31
```

*Range constraints* may exist for enumeration, integer, and real types, and they run from a lower to an upper bound, inclusive. Enumeration values run from left to right.

```
A_Range            ::= Range_Enumeration | Range_Integer | Range_Real

Range_Enumeration  ::= Value_Enumeration  .. Value_Enumeration

Range_Integer      ::= Expression_Integer .. Expression_Integer

Range_Real         ::= Expression_Real    .. Expression_Real
```

## 6.6.2  Attributes

An *attribute list* documents zero or more attribute declarations and may occur in the body of objects and classes. *Attribute declarations* document whether the attribute is a constant or a variable, its type, and its optional initial value. The italicized part of a construct implies semantic meaning and has no syntactic meaning.

```
Attributes_List                  ::= {Attribute_Declaration}

Attribute_Declaration            ::=

 Attribute_Declaration_Constant | Attribute_Declaration_Variable

Attribute_Declaration_Constant ::=
  constant ATTRIBUTE_IDENTIFIER_CONSTANT : ATTRIBUTE_TYPE_IDENTIFIER
   [ :=  Expression_Of_Attribute_Type];

Attribute_Declaration_Variable ::=

  variable Attribute_Identifier_Variable : ATTRIBUTE_TYPE_IDENTIFIER
   [ :=  Expression_Of_Attribute_Type];

Attribute_Identifier             ::=

 ATTRIBUTE_IDENTIFIER_CONSTANT | Attribute_Identifier_Variable

ATTRIBUTE_IDENTIFIER_CONSTANT   ::=

 SINGULAR_NOUN_IDENTIFER[.COMPONENT_IDENTIFIER]

Attribute_Identifier_Variable   ::=
 Initial_Upper_Case_Singular_Noun_Identifier
```

The following are examples of attribute declarations for the body of an object or class:

```
constant The_Delay_Amount        : Seconds.THE_CLOCK                 :=  10;
constant The_Maximum_Difference   : Pounds_Per_Square_Inch.THE_PRESSURE  :=   2;
variable The_State                : States                           := OFF;
variable The_Desired_Temperature  : Valid_Degrees.TEMPERATURES;
variable The_Mean_Temperature     : Valid_Degrees.TEMPERATURES       := 0.0;
```

## 6.6.3   Messages

A **message** is a signal that is sent to an object or class and that is received by an operation in that object or class. There are three forms of messages: sequential, synchronous, and asynchronous. A sequential message may only be received by a sequential operation. Both synchronous messages and asynchronous messages may only be received by a concurrent operation.

The specifications of objects and classes must contain a list of one or more message declarations.

```
Message_List  ::= Message_Declaration{Message_Declaration}
```

*Messages declarations* declare the identifier of the message, the destination of the message (if to another object or class), its formal parameters (possibly starting with the identifier of the object or class constructed), the type of attribute returned, a list of all exceptions that the message can raise, and the type of message. Message type is mandatory unless the message is deferred.

```
Message_Declaration ::=

  message Message_IDENTIFIER[.COMPONENT_IDENTIFIER]
    [([OBJECT_IDENTIFIER][,Formal_Parameters_List])]
    [return ATTRIBUTE_TYPE_IDENTIFIER][Raises_Clause] [Message_Type]
    [is deferred];

Message_Type  ::=  is sequential|is synchronous|is asynchronous
```

The following are example message declarations for the specification of an object or class:

```
message   TURN_OFF                      raise FAILURE_OCCURRED_IN is sequential;
message   CURRENT_PERCENT_OF   return Percents
                                        raise FAILURE_OCCURRED_IN is sequential;
message ACCELERATE                                                is synchronous;
message CURRENT_TEMPERATURE_OF return Degrees_Celsius  is sequential;
message CONTROL                                        is asynchronous;
message CHANGE                                         is deferred;
```

## 6.6.4   Operations

An operation is a functional abstraction, the execution of which is invoked by a message pass. An operation is declared in the body of an object or class. There are four forms of operations: constructors, destructors, modifiers, and preservers. A **constructor operation** creates an instance of a class and may only occur in a class. A **destructor operation** destroys an instance of a class and may only occur in a class. A **modifier operation** may modify the value of an attribute and may occur in an object or a class. A **preserver operation** may not modify the value of an attribute and may occur in an object or a class.

The bodies of objects and classes may contain a list of zero or more modifier-operation declarations and a list of zero or more preserver-operation declarations.

```
Operations_List_Modifier   ::= {Operation_Declaration_Modifier}
Operations_List_Preserver  ::= {Operation_Declaration_Preserver}
```

*Operation declarations* declare the type of the operation, its identifier, its formal parameters (possibly starting with the identifier of the object or class constructed if it is a constructor operation), the type of attribute returned if it is a preserver operation, a list of all exceptions that the operation can raise, and whether the operation is concurrent.

```
Operation_Declaration_Constructor_Class  ::=

  constructor operation CONSTRUCT
```

```
                     (OBJECT_IDENTIFIER [, Formal_Parameters_List]) [Raises_Clause];

    Operation_Declaration_Destructor_Class    ::=

       destructor operation DESTRUCT (OBJECT_IDENTIFIER)
        [Raises_Clause];

    Operation_Declaration_Modifier              ::=

       modifier operation OPERATION_IDENTIFIER_MODIFIER
        [(Formal_Parameters_List)][ Raises_Clause][ is concurrent]
        [is deferred];

    Operation_Declaration_Preserver             ::=

       preserver operation OPERATION_IDENTIFIER_PRESERVER
        [Formal_Parameters_List][ return ATTRIBUTE_TYPE_IDENTIFIER]
        [Raises_Clause][ is concurrent][is deferred];
```

The following are examples of creator, destroyer, modifier, and preserver operation declarations:

```
constructor operation  CONSTRUCT    (A_TARGET;
                                     With_Initial_Position : in Positions;
                                     With_Initial_Velocity : in Velocities)
                                     raise CONSTRUCT_FAILED;

destructor operation    DESTRUCT    (A_TARGET) raise DESTRUCT_FAILED;
modifier operation      MAINTAIN raise ABSTRACTION_CHALLENGED,INCOMPATIBLE_STATE
                                  is concurrent;
modifier operation      MAINTAIN raise ABSTRACTION_CHALLENGED,INCOMPATIBLE_STATE
                                  is deferred;

modifier operation      ADD (The_Coin : in Coins)
  raise MAXIMUM_AMOUNT_DEPOSITED_EXCEEDED,NOT_A_VALID_COIN
preserver operation     CURRENT_SPEED_OF return Kilometers_Per_Hour  is concurrent;
```

An operation's identifier must be unique among operation identifiers in its parent object or class if the operations cannot be differentiated via their parameter lists.

```
    OPERATION_IDENTIFIER_CONSTRUCTOR   ::= CONSTRUCT

    OPERATION_IDENTIFIER_DESTRUCTOR    ::= DESTRUCT

    OPERATION_IDENTIFIER_MODIFIER      ::= VERB_IDENTIFER

    OPERATION_IDENTIFIER_PRESERVER     ::= SINGULAR_NOUN_IDENTIFER
```

The following are examples of constructor, destructor, modifier, and preserver operation identifiers:

```
-- Constructor:
CONSTRUCT
-- Destructor:
DESTRUCT
-- Modifiers:
DECREMENT.THE_MONEY_DEPOSITED
INCREMENT
UPDATE
-- Preservers:
AMOUNT_OF.THE_MONEY_DEPOSITED
AVERAGE_VALUE_OF
CURRENT_INFORMATION
CURRENT_STATE_OF.THE_SENSOR
CURRENT_VALUE
```

An *operation body* documents the parent object or class of the operation, any objects or classes it needs, any parameters, a list of its local attribute types, a list of its local attributes, a list of any preconditions, a sequence of statements, a list of any postconditions, and an optional exception handler.

```
Operation_Body ::=

  operation OPERATION_IDENTIFIER[Parameters]
    Parent_Clause_Operation
    Needs_List_Component
  body
    Attributes_List_Operation
    Preconditions_List
    Sequence_Of_Statements
    Postconditions_List
    [Exception_Handler]
  end;
```

Where possible, operations should be specified with preconditions and postconditions rather than algorithmically because algorithmic specifications almost always contain design information, as well as requirements. The following are example operation bodies specified using preconditions and postconditions:

```
operation RESUME.THE_CRUISE_CONTROL
body
  preconditions
    require
      The_State = Accelerating or The_State = Disengeged
    else
      raise INCOMPATIBLE_STATE_IN;
    end require;
  postconditions
    require
      post(The_State) = Maintaining
    else
      raise INCOMPATIBLE_STATE_IN;
    end require;
end;
```

```
      operation PUSH (An_Entry : in Entries)
                          raise ENTRY_NOT_ADDED, INCORRECT_SIZE, IS_FULL
      body
      preconditions
       require
         The_Size < The_Maximum_Size          else raise IS_FULL;
       end require;
      postconditions
       require
        post(The_Size) <= The_Maximum_Size   else raise IS_FULL;
       end require;
       require
        post(The_Size) = The_Size + 1        else raise INCORRECT_SIZE;
       end require;
       require
        post(The_Top)  = The_Item            else raise ENTRY_NOT_ADDED;
       end require;
      end;
```

Operations may be specified algorithmically if preconditions and postconditions prove impractical. The logical design of operations should be done algorithmically. The following is an example operation body specified algorithmically:

```
operation MAINTAIN
 needs THE_AIR_CONDITIONER;
 needs THE_FURNACE;
 needs THE_MEAN_TEMPERATURE;
body
preconditions
 when
   not (The_Current_Value = 21 and The_Mode = Celsius and The_State = Off)
 then
     raise INCOMPATIBLE_STATE_IN.THE_DESIRED_TEMPERATURE;
 end when;
statements
 FOREVER : loop
   INNER : while The_State = On loop
    The_Mean_Temperature ::= CURRENT_VALUE_OF.THE_MEAN_TEMPERATURE;
    if -- The_Mean_Temperature is too low.
     The_Mean_Temperature < The_Current_Value - The_Maximum_Difference
    then
     if not  IS_ON.THE_FURNACE           then TURN_ON.THE_FURNACE;
     if      IS_ON.THE_AIR_CONDITIONER   then TURN_OFF.THE_AIR_CONDITIONER;
    end if;
    if -- The_Mean_Temperature is too high.
     The_Mean_Temperature > The_Current_Value + The_Maximum_Difference
    then
     if not  IS_ON.THE_AIR_CONDITIONER   then TURN_ON.THE_AIR_CONDITIONER;
     if      IS_ON.THE_FURNACE           then TURN_OFF.THE_FURNACE;
    end if;
    DELAY(The_Delay_Amount).THE_CLOCK;
   end loop INNER;
   DELAY(The_Delay_Amount).THE_CLOCK;
 end loop FOREVER;
```

```
exception_handler
  when FAILURE_OCCURRED_IN.THE_AIR_CONDITIONER      then
    if IS_ON.THE_FURNACE                 then TURN_OFF.THE_FURNACE;
  end when;
  when FAILURE_OCCURRED_IN.THE_FURNACE                 then
    if IS_ON.THE_AIR_CONDITIONER  then TURN_OFF.THE_AIR_CONDITIONER;
  end when;
  when FAILURE_OCCURRED_IN.THE_MEAN_TEMPERATURE   then
    if IS_ON.THE_AIR_CONDITIONER  then TURN_OFF.THE_AIR_CONDITIONER;
    if IS_ON.THE_FURNACE                 then TURN_OFF.THE_FURNACE;
  end when;
  when others                          then
    if IS_ON.THE_AIR_CONDITIONER  then TURN_OFF.THE_AIR_CONDITIONER;
    if IS_ON.THE_FURNACE                 then TURN_OFF.THE_FURNACE;
  end when;
  raise FAILURE_OCCURRED_IN.THE_DESIRED_TEMPERATURE;
end;
```

Operations may have parameters. Operation declarations may include a *list of formal parameters*, whereas a message statement will include a *list of actual parameters* corresponding to the formal parameters. Each *parameter association* assigns an actual parameter to the corresponding formal parameter. The *mode* refers to whether the formal parameter is read only, write only, or read/write.

```
Actual_Parameters_List   ::= (Parameter_Association {;Parameter_Association})

Parameter_Association    ::= [Formal_Parameter :=] Actual_Parameter

Actual_Parameter         ::= Attribute_Identifier | Expression

Formal_Parameters_List   ::= Parameter_Declaration {; Parameter_Declaration}

Parameter_Declaration    ::= Formal_Parameter : Mode ATTRIBUTE_TYPE_IDENTIFER
                             [:= Expression_Of_Attribute_Type]

Formal_Parameter         ::= Attribute_Identifier_Variable

Mode                     ::= in | in out | out
```

The following are examples of formal parameter lists and the corresponding actual parameter lists:

```
(The_Current_Value)

(State := Off)

(Current_Month   := The_Current_Month;
 Current_Day     := The_Current_Day)

(Current_Value   : in Values)

(Current_Month   : in Months := January;
 Current_Day     : in Days   := 1)
```

## 6.6.5    Exceptions

An exception is an error condition that can be raised by an operation and handled by the operation's parent. Lists of zero or more exceptions occur in the specifications of objects and classes. An *exception handler* documents the handling of one or more exceptions in the body of an operation.

```
Exceptions_List          ::= {Exception_Declaration}

Exception_Declaration    ::= exception EXCEPTION_IDENTIFIER;

Exception_Handler        ::=

  exception_handler
    {when Exception_Choice {or Exception_Choice} then
     Sequence_Of_Statements
    end when;}
    [Sequence_Of_Statements]

Exception_Choice         ::= EXCEPTION_IDENTIFIER | others

EXCEPTION_IDENTIFIER     ::= VERB_IDENTIFIER;
```

The following is an example exception list :

```
exception   ABSTRACTION_VIOLATED;
exception   FAILED;
exception   FAILURE_OCCURRED_IN;
exception   POSTCONDITION_FAILED;
exception   PRECONDITION_FAILED;
```

The following are example exception handlers:

```
exception_handler
 when PRESSURE_ABOVE_MAXIMUM_SAFE_VALUE
 or TEMPERATURE_ABOVE_MAXIMUM_SAFE_VALUE        then   OPEN.THE_FAILSAFE_VALVE;
  SHUT_DOWN.THE_SYSTEM;
 end when;
 when PRESSURE_BELOW_MINIMUM_SAFE_VALUE         then   INCREASE_RATE;
 end when;
 when TEMPERATURE_BELOW_MINIMUM_SAFE_VALUE      then   TURN_ON.FURNACE;
 end when;
 when others                                    then   SHUT_DOWN.THE_SYSTEM;
 end when;
SOUND_ALARM_OF.THE_OPERATOR;
UPDATE.THE_ERROR_LOG;


exception_handler
 when FAILED.AIR_CONDITIONER                    then   TURN_OFF.FURNACE;
 end when;
 when FAILED.FURNACE                            then   TURN_OFF.AIR_CONDITIONER;
 end when;
 when FAILED.MEAN_TEMPERATURE                   then   TURN_OFF.AIR_CONDITIONER;
  TURN_OFF.FURNACE;
```

```
 end when;
 when others                                         then   TURN_OFF.AIR_CONDITIONER;
   TURN_OFF.FURNACE;
 end when;
 raise FAILED;
```

# 6.7 STATEMENTS

## 6.7.1    Sequences of Statements

A sequence of one or more statements occurs in the body of operations. A statement can be one of the following: assignment, case, construct, destruct, if, loop, message, null, raise, receive, return, select, to-be-determined (TBD), or terminate.

```
Statements_List          ::= statement
                                 Sequence_Of_Statements

Sequence_Of_Statements   ::= Statement{Statement}

Statement                ::= Assignment_Statement    |
                             Case_Statement          |
                             Construct_Statement     |
                             Destruct_Statement      |
                             If_Statement            |
                             Interrupt_Statement     |
                             Loop_Statement          |
                             Message_Statement       |
                             Null_Statement          |
                             Raise_Statement         |
                             Receive_Statement       |
                             Renames_Statement       |
                             Return_Statement        |
                             Select_Statement        |
                             TBD_Statement           |
                             Terminate_Statement
```

The following are examples of statements:

```
The_State := Off;

  case The_Day is
   when Monday then
     COMPUTE_INITIAL.INVENTORY;
     GENERATE.DAILY_REPORT;
   when Tuesday .. Thursday then
     UPDATE.INVENTORY;
     GENERATE.DAILY_REPORT;
   when Friday then
     UPDATE.INVENTORY;
     GENERATE.WEEKLY_REPORT;
```

```
  when Saturday or Sunday then
  null;
 end case;

CONSTRUCT A_TARGET (With_Position := The_Position; With_Velocity := The_Velocity);

DESTRUCT A_TARGET;

if    The_Pressure > The_Maximum_Safe_Pressure   then
 raise PRESSURE_ABOVE_MAXIMUM_SAFE_VALUE;
or_if The_Pressure < the_Minimum_Safe_Pressure   then
 raise PRESSURE_BELOW_MINIMUM_SAFE_VALUE;
else
 CONTROL;
end if;

for A_Sensor in 1 .. Number_Of_Sensors loop
 READ(A_Sensor).THE_SET_OF_SENSORS;
end loop;

DELAY(Until_Next_Update).THE_CLOCK;

null;

raise PRESSURE_BELOW_MINIMUM_SAFE_VALUE;

receive CONTROL when interrupt THE_INTERRUPT_ADDRESS_FOR;

OPEN(AN_ACCOUNT).BANK_ACCOUNTS renames CONSTRUCT(AN_ACCOUNT).BANK_ACCOUNTS;

return The_State;

select
 ACCELERATE  when The_State = Disengaged    or The_State = Maintaining;
or
 DISENGAGE   when The_State = Maintaining   or The_State = Off;
or
 RESUME      when The_State = Accelerating  or The_State = Disengaged;
or
 TURN_OFF    when not The_State = Off;
end select;

TBD;

terminate;
```

## 6.7.2    Assignment Statements

An *assignment statement* assigns the value of an expression to a variable.

```
Assignment_Statement ::= Attribute_Identifier_Variable := Expression;
```

The following are examples of assignment statements:

```
The_State := Off;
The_Temperature := TEMPERATURE_SENSOR.CURRENT_VALUE;
```

## 6.7.3    Case Statements

A *case statement* selects one of the enclosed sequences of statements, depending on the value of an expression.

```
Case_Statement    ::=  case Expression is
                         when Set_Of_Choices then
                         Sequence_Of_Statements
                         {when Set_Of_Choices then
                         Sequence_Of_Statements}
                         end case;

Set_Of_Choices   ::= Choice {More_Choices}

More_Choices     ::= or Choice | .. Choice

Choice           ::= Attribute_Value | others
```

The following are examples of case statements:

```
case The_Day is
 when Monday then
  COMPUTE_INITIAL.INVENTORY;
  GENERATE.DAILY_REPORT;
 when Tuesday .. Thursday  then
  UPDATE.INVENTORY;
  GENERATE.DAILY_REPORT;
 when Friday then
  UPDATE.INVENTORY;
  GENERATE.WEEKLY_REPORT;
 when Saturday or Sunday    then
  null;
end case;

case The_Type_Of_Sensor is
 when Azimuth              then
  UPDATE(The_Sensor_Value).AZIMUTH;
 when Distance             then
  UPDATE(The_Sensor_Value).DISTANCE;
 when Elevation            then
  UPDATE(The_Sensor_Value).ELEVATION;
 when others               then
  raise FAILED;
end case;
```

### 6.7.4    Construct Statements

A *construct statement* constructs an instance of a class and may raise the predefined exception CONSTRUCT_FAILED.

```
Construct_Statement  ::=
 CONSTRUCT (OBJECT_IDENTIFIER
[;Actual_Parameters_List]).CLASS_IDENTIFIER;
```

The following are examples of construct statements used to add objects:

```
CONSTRUCT  (AN_EMPLOYEE;With_Information := The_Information).EMPLOYEES;
CONSTRUCT  (A_TARGET;   With_Position := The_Position;
                        With_Velocity := The_Velocity).TARGETS;
```

### 6.7.5    Destruct Statements

A *destruct statement* destroys an instance of a class and may raise the predefined exception DESTRUCT_FAILED.

```
Destruct_Statement  ::=
 DESTRUCT (OBJECT_IDENTIFIER).CLASS_IDENTIFIER;
```

The following are examples of destruct statements used to delete objects:

```
DESTRUCT (AN_EMPLOYEE).EMPLOYEES;
DESTRUCT (PRIMARY_TARGET).TARGETS.;
```

### 6.7.6    If Statements

An *if statement* selects one or none of the enclosed sequences of statements, depending on the truth of one or more conditions.

```
If_Statement ::=

 if Condition      then
   Sequence_Of_Statements
 [or_if Condition then
   Sequence_Of_Statements]
 [else
   Sequence_Of_Statements]
 end if;
```

The following are examples of if statements:

```
if
 The_Mean_Temperature < The_Desired_Temperature - THE_MAXIMUM_DIFFERENCE
then
 TURN_OFF.AIR_CONDITIONER;
 TURN_ON.FURNACE;
end if;
```

```
if ENOUGH_MONEY then
 PAY_BILLS;
else
 CALL_CREDITORS;
end if;

if The_Pressure > The_Maximum_Safe_Pressure        then
 raise PRESSURE_ABOVE_MAXIMUM_SAFE_VALUE;
or_if   The_Pressure < the_Minimum_Safe_Pressure   then
 raise PRESSURE_BELOW_MINIMUM_SAFE_VALUE;
else
 CONTROL;
end if;
```

## 6.7.7    Interrupt Statements

An *interrupt statement* selects one or none of the enclosed sequences of statements, depending on the truth of one or more conditions.

```
Interrupt_Statement ::= interrupt INTERRUPT_ADDRESS;
INTERRUPT_ADDRESS   ::= ADDRESS;
```

The following are examples of interrupt statements:

```
interrupt The_Interrupt_Address_For.THE_DECREMENT_FLOW_BUTTON;
```

## 6.7.8    Loop Statements

A *loop statement* may be named, has an optional iteration scheme, and includes a sequence of statements that is repeated zero or more times.

```
Loop_Statement   ::= Simple_Loop | For_Loop | While_Loop

Simple_Loop      ::=

 [LOOP_IDENTIFER:] loop
   Sequence_Of_Statements
 end loop [LOOP_IDENTIFIER];

For_Loop         ::=

 [LOOP_IDENTIFER:] for IDENTIFIER in Discrete_Range loop
   Sequence_Of_Statements
 end loop [LOOP_IDENTIFIER];

While_Loop       ::=

 [LOOP_IDENTIFER:] while condition loop
   Sequence_Of_Statements
 end loop [LOOP_IDENTIFIER];
```

The following are example simple loop, for loop, and while loop statements:

```
FOREVER: loop
  UPDATE(With_Current_Data).DISPLAY;
  WAIT_UNTIL(The_Next_Time).CLOCK;
end loop;

for A_Sensor in 1 .. Number_Of_Sensors loop
  READ(A_Sensor).THE_SET_OF_SENSORS;
end loop;

while The_State = On loop
  UPDATE_DISPLAY;
  DELAY(The_Delay_Amount).TIME;
end loop;
```

## 6.7.9    Message Statements

A *message statement* passes a message to an individual object or broadcasts a message to all visible objects. The message is passed to the current object if no object identifier is listed. The message identifies a modifier or preserver operation to be performed.

```
Initialization_Messages_List       ::= start Sequence_Of_Message_Statements

Sequence_Of_Message_Statements     ::= {Message_Statement}

Message_Statement                  ::= Individual_Message | Broadcast_Message

Individual_Message                 ::= MESSAGE_IDENTIFIER [(Actual_Parameters_List)]
                                       [.OBJECT_IDENTIFIER]
                                       [priority Expression_Integer];

Broadcast_Message                  ::= MESSAGE_IDENTIFIER [(Actual_Parameters_List)]
                                       [.ALL][priority Expression_Integer];
```

The following are examples of messages statements:

```
PRINT.ALL;
DELAY(Until_Next_Update).THE_CLOCK;
ACCELERATE.THE_CRUISE_CONTROL;
UPDATE(The_Temperature := TEMPERATURE_SENSOR.CURRENT_VALUE;
       The_Pressure    := PRESSURE_SENSOR.CURRENT_VALUE).DISPLAY;
MAINTAIN;
```

## 6.7.10   Null Statements

A *null statement* has no effect other than to sequence to the next statement and, unlike the TBD statement, may exist in the completed specification or design.

```
Null_Statement ::= null;
```

## 6.7.11   Raise Statements

A *raise statement* may only occur within a sequence of statements and raises an exception to the calling operation.

```
Raise_Statement ::= raise EXCEPTION_IDENTIFIER
```

The following are examples of raise statements:

```
raise FAILURE_OCCURRED_IN.THE_SPEEDOMETER;
raise TEMPERATURE_ABOVE_MAXIMUM_SAFE_VALUE;
```

## 6.7.12   Receive Statements

A *receive statement* may only occur within a sequence of statements and is used to receive a message.

```
Receive_Statement ::=

        receive MESSAGE_DECLARATION [at interrupt ADDRESS_IDENTIFIER];
```

The following are examples of raise statements:

```
receive ACCELERATE;
receive CURRENT_PERCENT_OF return PERCENTS;
receive CONTROL at interrupt THE_INTERRUPT_ADDRESS_FOR;
```

## 6.7.13   Renames Statements

A *renames statement* may only occur within a sequence of statements and is used to rename an identifier within the scope of the statement.

```
Renames_Statement ::= Identifier_1 renames Identifier_2;
```

The following are examples of rename statements:

```
OPEN(AN_ACCOUNT).BANK_ACCOUNTS   renames CONSTRUCT(AN_ACCOUNT).BANK_ACCOUNTS;
CLOSE(AN_ACCOUNT).BANK_ACCOUNTS renames DESTRUCT(AN_ACCOUNT).BANK_ACCOUNTS;
```

## 6.7.14   Return Statements

A *return statement* may only occur within the body of a preserver operation and returns the value of the associated attribute or expression.

```
Return_Statement ::= return ATTRIBUTE_IDENTIFIER | return Expression
```

The following are examples of return statements:

```
return The_Current_Value;  -- attribute
return The_State = On;      -- expression
```

## 6.7.15  Select Statements

A *select statement* selects the highest priority pending message.

```
Select_Statement ::= select
                     [when Condition then] [priority Expression_Integer]
                     Receive_Statement {Sequence_Of_Statements}
                     or
                     [when Condition then] [priority Expression_Integer]
                     Receive_Statement {Sequence_Of_Statements}
                     or
                     [when Condition then] [priority Expression_Integer]
                     Receive_Statement {Sequence_Of_Statements}
                     [else
                     Sequence_Of_Statements]
                     end select;
```

The following are examples of select statements:

```
select -- statement used to handle messages and ensure mutual exclusion
 when The_State = Disabled                                      then
  receive ACCEPT(An_Authorization_Code);
  INITIALIZE;
  The_Stae := Uncalibrated
 when The_State = Calibrated or The_State = Uncalibrated    then priority 3
  receive ACCEPT(An_Authorization_Code);
  The_State := Disabled;
 when The_State = Uncalibrated                              then priority 2
  receive CALIBRATE_USING(A_Value);
  CALIBRATE;
  The_State := Calibrated
 when The_State = Calibrated                                then priority 1
  receive VALUE_IS;
  return The_Current_Value;
 else
  DELAY_FOR(The_Delay_Time).THE_CLOCK;
end select;
```

## 6.7.16  Terminate Statements

A *terminate statement* terminates the thread of control of a concurrent operation.

```
Terminate_Statement ::= terminate;
```

## 6.7.17  To_Be_Determined (TBD) Statements

A *to_be_determined (TBD) statement* has no effect and is ignored. It is temporarily used as part of incremental analysis and design and may not remain in the completed specification or design.

```
TBD_Statement ::= TBD;
```

## 6.8  ASSERTIONS

### 6.8.1    Invariants

Objects and classes may include an optional *list of invariants*. An *invariant* is a condition that must always hold for an object or class. If an invariant is not met, the associated exception is raised, and further use of the object is erroneous.

```
Invariants_List   ::=   invariants
                        Invariant
                        {Invariant}

Invariant         ::=   require
                        Condition
                        else
                        {Statement}
                        raise EXCEPTION_IDENTIFIER;
                        end require;

Condition         ::=   Expression_Boolean
```

The following are examples of invariants lists:

```
require
   The_Current_Temperature <= The_Maximum_Temperature
else
   SOUND.THE_ALARM;
   raise OVERHEATED;
end require;

require
   The_Length * The_Width <= The_Maximum_Area
else
   raise AREA_TOO_BIG;
end require;
```

### 6.8.2    Preconditions

Operation bodies may include an optional *list of preconditions*. A *precondition* is a condition that must be met prior to the execution of the statements of the operation. If it is not met, the associated exception is raised, and the operation does not execute.

```
Preconditions_List   ::=   preconditions
                           Precondition
                           {Precondition}

Precondition         ::=   require Condition else
                           {Statement}
                           raise EXCEPTION_IDENTIFIER;
                           end require;
```

The following is an example preconditions lists:

```
preconditions -- PUSH.STACK
 require
  The_Size < The_Maximum_Size
 else
  raise FULL;
 end require;

preconditions -- MAINTAIN.THE_DESIRED_TEMPERATURE
 require
  The_State = On
 else
  raise INCOMPATIBLE_STATE_IN.THE_DESIRED_TEMPERATURE;
 end require;
```

### 6.8.3    Postconditions

Operation bodies may include an optional *list of postconditions*. A *postcondition* is a condition that must be met after the execution of the statements of the operation. If it is not met, the associated exception is raised, and the operation does not execute.

```
Postconditions_List   ::=   postconditions
                            Postcondition
                            {Postcondition}


Postcondition         ::=   require Condition_Post else
                            {Statement}
                            raise EXCEPTION_IDENTIFIER;
                            end require;


Condition_Post        ::= Expression_Boolean_Post
```

The following is an example postconditions list:

```
postconditions -- PUSH.STACK
 require
  post(The_Size) <= The_Maxiumum_Size    else raise IS_FULL;
 end require;
 require
  post(The_Size) =  The_Size + 1         else raise INCORRECT_SIZE;
 end require;
 require
  post(The_Top)  =  The_Item             else raise ENTRY_NOT_ADDED;
 end require;
```

## 6.9  EXPRESSIONS

A *post expression* is a formula that defines the computation of a value after the execution of an operation and contains the reserved word *post* to signify the value of an attribute or expression after the execution of an operation.

```
Expression_Post              ::=   Expression_Boolean_Post |
                                   Expression_Integer_Post |
                                   Expression_Real_Post

Expression_Boolean_Post      ::=

                                   Relation_Post {and Relation_Post} |
                                   Relation_Post {or Relation_Post}

Relation_Post                ::=

 Expression_Numerical_Post Relation_Operator Expression_Numerical_Post |
 Expression_Numerical_Post Relation_Operator Expression_Numerical      |
 Expression_Numerical      Relation_Operator Expression_Numerical_Post |
 not(Expression_Boolean_Post)

Expression_Numerical_Post  ::= Expression_Integer_Post | Expression_Real_Post

Expression_Integer_Post      ::=

 Expression_Integer_Post Integer_Operator Expression_Integer_Post |
 Expression_Integer_Post Integer_Operator Expression_Integer      |
 Expression_Integer      Integer_Operator Expression_Integer_Post |
 post(Expression_Integer Integer_Operator Expression_Integer)     |
 Attribute_Of_Integer_Type                                        |
 post(Attribute_Of_Integer_Type)

Expression_Real_Post         ::=

 Expression_Real_Post Real_Operator Expression_Real_Post          |
 Expression_Real_Post Real_Operator Expression_Real               |
 Expression_Real      Real_Operator Expression_Real_Post          |
 post(Expression_Real Real_Operator Expression_Real)              |
 Attribute_Of_Real_Type                                           |
 post(Attribute_Of_Real_Type)
```

An *expression* is a formula that defines the computation of a value.

```
Expression            ::=   Expression_Boolean      |
                            Expression_Integer      |
                            Expression_Real

Expression_Boolean    ::=   Relation {and Relation}  |
                            Relation {or Relation}

Relation              ::=

 Expression_Numerical Relation_Operator Expression_Numerical |
 not(Expression_Boolean)

Relational_Operator   ::= < | <= | = | >= | >

Expression_Numerical  ::= Expression_Integer | Expression_Real
```

```
Expression_Integer    ::=

Expression_Integer Integer_Operator Expression_Integer    |
Attribute_Of_Integer_Type                                 |
Integer

Integer_Operator       ::=  + | -- integer plus           integer = integer
                            - | -- integer minus          integer = integer
                            * | -- integer times          integer = integer
                            / | -- integer divided by     integer = integer
                            ** -- integer to the power    integer = integer

Expression_Real        ::=  Expression_Real Real_Operator Expression_Real  |
                            Attribute_Of_Real_Type                         |
                            Real_Number

Real_Operator          ::=  + | -- real plus          real = real
                            - | -- real minus         real = real
                            * | -- real times         real = real
                            / | -- real divided by    real = real
                            ** -- real to the power   real = real
```

The following are examples of Boolean expressions that might appear in invariants, if statements, loop statements, or preconditions:

```
The_Size      < The_Maximum_Size
The_Altitude < The_Maximum_Altitude and The_Speed < The_Maximum_Speed
The_Altitude < The_Maximum_Altitude or  The_Speed < The_Maximum_Speed
```

The following are examples of Boolean expressions that might appear in the postconditions of operations:

```
post(The_Size) <= The_Maximum_Size
post(The_Size) =  The_Size + 1
post(The_Top)  =  The_Item
post(The_Altitude) < The_Maximum_Altitude and post(The_Speed) < The_Maximum_Speed
post(The_Length) * post(The_Height) * post(The_Width) < The_Maximum_Volume
```

## 6.10 VALUES

```
Value              ::=  Value_Boolean      |
                        Value_Enumeration  |
                        Integer            |
                        Real_Number

Value_Boolean      ::=  True | False

Value_Enumeration  ::=  All_Upper_Case_Identifier

Integer            ::=  Natural_Number | 0 | Minus_Sign Natural_Number

Natural_Number     ::=      Nonzero_Digit {[Comma] Digit Digit Digit} |
```

```
                         Nonzero_Digit Digit {[Comma] Digit Digit Digit} |
                   Nonzero_Digit Digit Digit {[Comma] Digit Digit Digit}
```

Comma            ::= ,

Minus_Sign       ::= -

Real_Number      ::=
```
       Integer.{Digit Digit Digit [Comma]} Nonzero_Digit           |
       Integer.{Digit Digit Digit [Comma]} Digit Nonzero_Digit      |
       Integer.{Digit Digit Digit [Comma]} Digit Digit Nonzero_Digit
```

The following are examples of valid values:

```
TRUE            -- Boolean value
FALSE           -- Boolean value
RED             -- Enumeration value
FAILED          -- Enumeration value
0               -- Integer value
55              -- Integer value
93,888          -- Integer value
-3,488,947      -- Integer value
0.0             -- Real value
3.14159         -- Real value
300,946.38      -- Real value
-45.838,484,3   -- Real value
```

## 6.11 IDENTIFIERS

*Identifiers* are used as reserved words and as names for assemblies, subassemblies, objects, classes, attribute types, attributes, modifier and preserver operations, and exceptions. All characters of an identifier are significant, including any underline characters occurring between letters, digits, or a letter and digit. Spaces are used as separators and are not allowed as part of an identifier. The italicized part of a construct implies semantic meaning and has no syntactic meaning.

Attribute_Identifier      ::=  *Initial_Uppercase_Singular_Noun*_Identifier

UPPERCASE_IDENTIFIER      ::=  NOUN_IDENTIFIER | VERB_IDENTIFIER

NOUN_IDENTIFIER          ::=  SINGULAR_NOUN_IDENTIFIER | PLURAL_NOUN_IDENTIFIER

SINGULAR_NOUN_IDENTIFIER ::=  *All_Uppercase_Singular_Noun*_Identifier

PLURAL_NOUN_IDENTIFIER   ::=  *All_Uppercase_Plural_Noun*_Identifier

VERB_IDENTIFIER          ::=  *All_Uppercase_Verb*_Identifier

Identifier               ::=  Letter{[Underline] Letter_Or_Digit}

Letter_Or_Digit          ::=  Letter | Digit

```
Letter                    ::= Uppercase_Letter | Lowercase_Letter

Uppercase_Letter          ::= A | B | C | D | E | F | G | H | I | J | K | L | M |
                              N | O | P | Q | R | S | T | U | V | W | X | Y | Z

Lowercase_Letter          ::= a | b | c | d | e | f | g | h | i | j | k | l | m |
                              n | o | p | q | r | s | t | u | v | w | x | y | z

Digit                     ::= 0 | 1 | 2 | 3 | 4 | 5 | 6 | 7 | 8 | 9

Nonzero_Digit             ::= 1 | 2 | 3 | 4 | 5 | 6 | 7 | 8 | 9

Underline                 ::= _
```

The following are examples of valid identifiers:

```
AUTOMOTIVE_DASHBOARD_SYSTEM    -- Assembly
CRUISE_CONTROL                 -- Subassembly
DESIRED_TEMPERATURE            -- Object
SENSORS                        -- Class
States                         -- Attribute type
The_State                      -- Attribute
CONSTRUCT                      -- Constructor operation
DESTRUCT                       -- Destructor operation
UPDATE                         -- Modifier operation
CURRENT_VALUE                  -- Preserver operation
FAILED                         -- Exception
```

## 6.12 CHAPTER REFERENCES

[AJPO 1983] Ada Joint Program Office, *Reference Manual for the Ada Programming Language*, *ANSI/MIL-STD-1815A-1983*, United States Department of Defense, 17 February 1983.

[Atkinson 1991] Colin Atkinson, *Object-Oriented Reuse, Concurrency, and Distribution*, Reading, MA, Addison Wesley, 1991.

[Meyer 1988] Bertrand Meyer, *Object-Oriented Software Construction*, Englewood Cliffs, NJ, Prentice Hall, 1988.

# Chapter 7

# Documenting Object-Oriented Requirements Specifications and Logical Designs

The primary purpose of this chapter is to teach the proper way to document object-oriented software. It also includes representative examples of object-oriented documentation, to illustrate the guidelines and to provide the reader with prototypical documentation that can be compared with the traditional documentation. It also illustrates the application of ADM3 to a simple application.

## 7.1 GENERAL CONSIDERATIONS

Functional decomposition and the resultant separation of functionality and data have had a major impact on the traditional format of documentation. Software specifications and design documents have typically been divided into separate sections concerning operations and global data. The sections concerning functions (i.e., operations) have traditionally been further divided into subfunctions. While this approach was reasonable for functionally decomposed software, it is highly inappropriate for object-oriented software. If this approach is used, the documentation concerning individual objects and classes will tend to be scattered, both horizontally and vertically, throughout the documentation. Because of this emphasis on functional abstraction (and to a lesser extent data abstraction), functional abstractions and data

369

abstractions have tended to be reasonably well documented, but object, class, and exception abstractions have not. Traditional documentation standards (e.g., the data item descriptions [DIDs] of DOD-STD-2167A) have tended to have inappropriate format and incomplete content requirements [Technical Evaluation Research Inc. 1989].

Documentation standards and guidelines should be consistent with the structure and scope of the entities being documented. Documentation of object-oriented requirements specifications and logical designs should be consistent with the object-oriented software. Standards and guidelines should recognize that a consistent object-oriented paradigm, set of models, and notation is used throughout the entire development process. This implies that the same basic format should be used for both requirements specifications and design documents.

The difference between requirements specifications and design documents primarily lies in the purpose and scope of the two documents. The purpose of requirements specifications is to document the requirements of the associated software. The scope of the requirements specification is therefore the *essential* properties of the *essential* subassemblies, classes, objects, attribute types and attributes, operations, and exceptions. The design document is based on the requirements specification and is concerned with all nonessential design decisions. Its scope is greater than that of the software requirements specification and consists of all relevant properties of all relevant subassemblies, classes, objects, attribute types and attributes, operations, and exceptions, whether essential or not.

Because requirements and design documents should have the same format and should discuss the same entities using the same models and graphics, one might argue that justification for their division into two documents is primarily based on contractual and legal reasons (e.g., work on the design is authorized once the requirements document has been formally accepted). One might also argue that with a globally recursive approach (i.e., analyze a little, design a little, etc.), both requirements and design should be documented in the same document, which is incrementally developed along with the software. This would increase understandability because software engineers would not have to switch between documents to understand how the design implements the requirements. Traceability from the requirements to the design would be improved by the close physical proximity of the design decision to the corresponding requirement(s) in the same document, and the design would be less likely to become inconsistent with the requirements. Although the baselining of requirements would be more difficult, the iteration and update of the single document would be easier, and the documentation would be more likely to be consistent with the resulting code.

## 7.2 DOCUMENTATION GUIDELINES

The software-engineering principle of *completeness* implies that all relevant information (i.e., concerning assemblies, subassemblies, classes, objects, attribute types and attributes, messages and operations, exceptions, and scenarios and threads) will be captured and stored in the project development database. So that no useful information "falls through the cracks," this information should be incrementally captured as it is developed, preferably by the project computer-aided software engineering (CASE) tools. Prior to the formal reviews, this information should be documented in the associated deliverable documentation.

The software-engineering principle of *uniformity* implies that the format of the documentation mirrors the object-oriented architecture of the specifications and the designs. The information to be documented should therefore be organized by assembly (typically one per document):

- Subassembly within assembly
  - class or object of anonymous class within the subassembly
    - attribute type within the class or object
      - attribute within the attribute type
  - message
  - operation
  - exception
- Aggregation hierarchies within the assembly[1]
- Classification hierarchies within the assembly[2]
- Scenarios or major threads of control within the assembly[3]

If corporate or customer standards mandate a standard format for the documentation that is inconsistent with the object-oriented paradigm (e.g., DOD-STD-2167A), proper tailoring and interpretation should be performed to ensure adequate documentation of the object-oriented information.

## 7.3 DOCUMENTATION CONTENT AND FORMAT

The software specification and design document (SSDD) documents the complete requirements and design of an assembly. It is used for customer review, programming, and maintenance. It describes the assembly as consisting of subassemblies, classes, and objects.

The following content and format are recommended for an SSDD if ADM3 is used. Software requirements should be clearly stated as such and must be uniquely identified. If the SSDD is to be divided into a separate software requirements specification (SRS) and software design document (SDD) for contractual or other purposes, then the SRS and SDD should have analogous formats. All requirements concerning essential subassemblies, classes, objects, and their essential resources should be specified in the associated assembly SRS. All design decisions concerning

---

[1]Aggregation hierarchies may cross subassembly boundaries and therefore may not be documentable on a subassembly basis.
[2]Classification hierarchies may cross subassembly boundaries and therefore may not be documentable on a subassembly basis.
[3]Scenarios and threads of control may cross subassembly boundaries and therefore may not be documentable on a subassembly basis.

both essential and nonessential subassemblies, classes, objects, and their resources should be documented in the associated assembly SDD.

The SSDD consists of the following sections, paragraphs, and subparagraphs. Additional subparagraphs may be added for each generic formal parameter, attribute type, attribute, message, exception, and operation.

Cover Page
Table of Contents
1) Introduction
1.1) Identification
1.2) Purpose
1.3) Referenced Documents
2) Requirements and Design
2.1) Assembly Context
2.2) Assembly Architecture
2.3) Assembly Requirements
2.4) Subassembly Requirements and Design
2.4.1) [Identifier of first subassembly]
2.4.1.1) [Identifier of the first class or object of anonymous class in the first subassembly]
2.4.1.1.1) Generic Formal Parameters
2.4.1.1.2) Attribute Types
2.4.1.1.3) Attributes
2.4.1.1.4) Messages
2.4.1.1.5) Operations
2.4.1.1.6) Exceptions
...
2.4.X.Y) [Identifier of the last class or object of anonymous class in the last subassembly]
2.4.X.Y.1) Generic Formal Parameters
2.4.X.Y.2) Attribute Types
2.4.X.Y.3) Attributes
2.4.X.Y.4) Messages
2.4.X.Y.5) Operations
2.4.X.Y.6) Exceptions
2.5) Aggregation Hierarchies
2.5.1) [Identifier of the first aggregation hierarchy]
2.6) Classification Hierarchies
2.6.1) [Identifier of the first inheritance hierarchy]
2.7) Dynamic Behavior
2.7.1) Concurrency Requirements and Design
2.7.2) Timing Requirements and Design
2.7.3) Major Scenarios
3) Sizing Requirements and Design
4) Goals of Software Engineering
5) Notes
6) Appendices

**Cover Page.** The cover page identifies this document as either the SSDD, SRS, or SDD for the assembly, identifies its system, documents the date and version number of the document, and provides the name and address of the customer and development organization.

**Table of Contents.** The table of contents first lists the title and page number of each titled section, paragraph, and subparagraph. The table of contents then lists the title and page number of each figure, table, and appendix, in that order.

**1) Introduction.** This section provides an introduction to the document and is divided into the following paragraphs (1.1–1.3).

**1.1) Identification.** This paragraph documents the approved identifier, abbreviation, and identification number (if applicable) of the system and the assembly to which this document applies.

**1.2) Purpose.** This paragraph briefly summarizes the purpose of the system and the assembly to which this document applies.

**1.3) Referenced Documents.** This paragraph lists by title and document identifier all documents referenced in this document.

**2) Requirements and Design.** This section documents the requirements and design of the assembly and is divided into the following paragraphs (2.1–2.7.3).

**2.1) Assembly Context.** This paragraph documents the context of the assembly within the system, including the following information:

1. The identifier and purpose of all terminators of the assembly
2. One or more system semantic nets (SSNs), showing the associations between the system entities being modeled
3. A context diagram (CD), showing the associations between the assembly and its terminators

**2.2) Assembly Architecture.** This paragraph documents the static architecture of the assembly, including the following information:

1. The specification and body of the assembly
2. An assembly diagram (AD), showing the dependency and visibility relationships of the subassemblies within the assembly

**2.3) Assembly Requirements.** This paragraph identifies the system requirements allocated to the assembly as a whole, including the following information:

1. The SRS documenting the requirements from which this assembly was derived
2. Any system requirements allocated to the assembly as a whole and not further allocated to its components, including validation criteria and method

**2.4) Subassembly Requirements and Design.** This paragraph documents the requirements and design of each subassembly of the assembly.

**2.4.X) [Subassembly Identifier.]** This subparagraph is numbered 2.4.X (beginning with 2.4.1) and documents the requirements and design of the associated subassembly, including the following information:

1. The assembly-unique subassembly identifier
2. A description of the abstraction implemented by the subassembly
3. The classification of the subassembly in terms of
   - Essential vs. nonessential
   - Atomic vs. aggregate
   - Recursive vs. ad hoc vs. requirements etc.
   - Master vs. agent vs. servant
4. The specification and body of the subassembly
5. The subassembly general semantic net GSN
6. The subassembly interaction diagram ID
7. The subassembly control flow diagram (CFD) (if practical)
8. The subassembly timing diagram (TD) (or equivalent if relevant)
9. Any system requirements allocated to the subassembly as a whole and not further allocated to its components, including validation criteria and methods
10. Any analysis and design trade-offs made regarding the subassembly as a whole

**2.4.X.Y) [Class or Object Identifier.]** This subparagraph is numbered 2.4.X.Y (beginning with 2.4.X.1) and documents the requirements and design of the associated class or object of anonymous class, including the following information:

1. The subassembly-unique class or object identifier
2. A description of the abstraction implemented by the class or object
3. The classification of the class or object in terms of
   - Essential vs. nonessential
   - Concurrent vs. sequential
   - Atomic vs. aggregate
   - Master vs. agent vs. servant
   - Physical vs. conceptual
   - Generic vs. nongeneric (if class)
   - Abstract vs. concrete (if class)
   - Models of
     - devices
     - properties
     - roles
     - organizations
     - ocations
     - events
     - interactions
   - Relationships to entity being modeled
     - control
     - emulation

- implement
- interface
- simulation
- stimulation
- tracking

- Corruptible vs. guardable vs. guarded
- Transient vs. temporary vs. permanent

4. The inheritance aspects (if class)
   - The superclasses of the class (if any)
   - The subclasses of the class (if any)
   - The instances of the class (if fixed and known)
   - The allowed cardinality of the class (if known)
5. The specification and body
6. The GSN (if object)
7. The ID (if object)
8. The composition diagram (CMD) (if object)
9. The classification diagram (CLD) (if class)
10. The state transition diagram (STD) (or equivalent if relevant)
11. The CFD (if useful)
12. The TD (if useful)
13. Any system requirements allocated to the class or object as a whole and not further allocated to its resources, including validation criteria and methods
14. Any analysis and design trade-offs made regarding the class or object as a whole

**2.4.X.Y.1) [Generic Formal Parameters.]** This paragraph is numbered 2.4.X.Y.1 (beginning with 2.4.X.1.1) and documents the generic parameters of the associated class. This paragraph is not applicable if used for an object of anonymous class. The information in this paragraph may be here by reference if adequately documented at the class level. For each generic parameter, this paragraph documents the following information:

1. The class—unique parameter identifier
2. The type of generic parameter
   - Attribute type
   - Attribute
   - Message
   - Exception
   - Operation
3. A description of the abstraction implemented by the parameter
4. Any system requirements allocated to the attribute type, including validation criteria and methods
5. Any analysis and design trade-offs made regarding the attribute type

**2.4.X.Y.2) [Attribute Types.]** This paragraph is numbered 2.4.X.Y.2 (beginning with 2.4.X.1.2) and documents the attribute types of the associated class. The information in this paragraph may be here by reference if adequately documented at the class level. For each attribute type, this paragraph documents the following information:

1. The class- or object-unique attribute-type identifier
2. A description of the type of data abstraction implemented by the attribute type
3. The classification of the attribute type in terms of
   - Essential vs. nonessential
   - Class vs. object
   - Tangible vs. intangible
   - Visible vs. hidden
4. The instances of the attribute type (if known)
5. The unit of measure of the attribute type
6. The accuracy of the attribute type
7. The precision (i.e., resolution) of the attribute type
8. The declaration of the attribute type
9. Any system requirements allocated to the attribute type, including validation criteria and methods
10. Any analysis and design trade-offs made regarding the attribute type

**2.4.X.Y.3) [Attributes.]** This paragraph is numbered 2.4.X.Y.3 (beginning with 2.4.X.1.3) and documents the attributes of the associated class or object. The information in this paragraph may be here by reference if adequately documented at the class or object level. For each attribute, this paragraph documents the following information:

1. The class- or object-unique attribute identifier
2. A description of the data abstraction implemented by the attribute
3. The classification of the attribute in terms of
   - Essential vs. nonessential
   - Class vs. object
   - Tangible vs. intangible
   - Visible vs. hidden
   - Constant vs. variable
   - Name vs. description vs. state variable vs. relationship pointer
4. The attribute type of the attribute
5. The declaration of the attribute
6. Any system requirements allocated to the attribute, including validation criteria and methods
7. Any analysis and design trade-offs made regarding the attribute

**2.4.X.Y.4) [Messages.]** This paragraph is numbered 2.4.X.Y.4 (beginning with 2.4.X.1.4) and documents the messages of the associated class or object. The information in this paragraph may be here by reference if adequately documented at the class or object level. For each message, this paragraph documents the following information:

1. The class- or object-unique message identifier
2. A description of the functional or process abstraction requested by the message

3. The classification of the message in terms of
   - Essential vs. nonessential
   - Class vs. object
   - Sequential vs. synchronous vs. asynchronous
   - Standard vs. timed vs. balking
4. The declaration of the message, including
   - The formal parameters of the message, including modes (if any)
   - The exceptions that can be raised by the message (if any)
5. The objects and classes that receive the message
6. Any system requirements allocated to the message, including validation criteria and methods
7. Any analysis and design trade-offs made regarding the message

**2.4.X.Y.5) [Operations.]** This paragraph is numbered 2.4.X.Y.5 (beginning with 2.4.X.1.5) and documents the operations of the associated class or object. The information in this paragraph may be here by reference if adequately documented at the class or object level. For each operation, this paragraph documents the following information:

1. The class- or object-unique operation identifier
2. A description of the functional or process abstraction implemented by the operation
3. The classification of the operation in terms of
   - Essential vs. nonessential
   - Concurrent vs. sequential
   - Constructor vs. destructor vs. modifier vs. preserver
   - Iterator vs. noniterator
   - Class vs. object
4. The specification and body of the operation, including
   - Any preconditions required by the operation
   - The action performed by the operation
   - Any postconditions ensured by the operation
   - Any invariants ensured by the operation
5. Any timing criteria, including deadlines and frequency
6. Any system requirements allocated to the operation, including validation criteria and methods
7. Any analysis and design trade-offs made regarding the operation

**2.4.X.Y.6) [Exceptions.]** This paragraph is numbered 2.4.X.Y.6 (beginning with 2.4.X.1.6) and documents the exceptions of the associated class or object. The information in this paragraph may be here by reference if adequately documented at the class or object level. For each exception, this paragraph documents the following information:

1. The class- or object-unique exception identifier
2. A description of the exception abstraction implemented by the exception
3. The classification of the exception in terms of

- Essential vs. nonessential
- Class vs. object

4. The declaration of the exception
5. The behavior of the exception, including
   - Any preconditions required to raise the operation
   - The exception handling to be performed
   - Any postconditions ensured by the exception handling
   - Any invariants ensured by the exception handling
   - The propagation chain of the exception
   - The location of the exception handlers
6. Any timing criteria, including deadlines and frequency
7. Any system requirements allocated to the exception, including validation criteria and methods
8. Any analysis and design trade-offs made regarding the exception

**2.5) Aggregation Hierarchies.** This paragraph documents the requirements for and the design of each aggregation hierarchy of the assembly, comparing the subparagraphs 2.5.X.

**2.5.X) [Aggregation Hierarchy Identifier.]** These subparagraphs are numbered 2.5.X (beginning with 2.5.1) and document the requirements and design of the associated aggregation hierarchy. These subparagraphs document the following information, which may be provided by one or more CMDs:

1. The assembly-unique aggregation hierarchy identifier
2. The root object or class of the hierarchy
3. The subobjects of the hierarchy
4. The "has-components" relationships among them

**2.6) [Classification Hierarchies.]** This paragraph documents the requirements for and the design of each classification hierarchy of the assembly, comprising the subparagraphs 2.6.X.

**2.6.X) [Classification Hierarchy Identifier.]** These subparagraphs are numbered 2.6.X (beginning with 2.6.1) and document the requirements and design of the associated classification hierarchy. These subparagraphs document the following information, much of which may be supplied by one or more CLDs:

1. The assembly-unique classification hierarchy identifier
2. The root class of the hierarchy
3. The subclasses of the hierarchy
4. The "has-superclass" relationships between the subclasses and their superclasses in the hierarchy
5. Information on which resources are introduced, completed, redefined, or removed by which classes
6. The instances of the hierarchy (if practical and useful)

7. The "has-class" relationships between the instances and their classes in the hierarchy (if practical and useful)

**2.7) Dynamic Behavior.** This paragraph documents the requirements for and the high-level design of the dynamic behavior of the assembly. It consists of the following paragraphs (2.7.1–2.7.3).

**2.7.1) Concurrency Design.** This subparagraph documents the overall assembly approach to concurrency, including such information as

1. Whether concurrency will be implemented via language features (e.g., Ada tasks) or via operating system features (e.g., UNIX processes)
2. The approach to scheduling (e.g., rate monotonic scheduling)
3. The prioritization of threads of control
4. The approach to mutual exclusion (e.g., tasks, monitors, semaphores, protected records)

**2.7.2) Timing Requirements and Design.** This subparagraph documents the requirements for and the design of timing issues. It includes information on

1. Hard and soft deadlines
2. Minimum, average, and maximum time intervals
3. What should happen when deadlines are missed

**2.7.3) Major Scenarios.** This subparagraph documents the major scenarios that the assembly must support. This information is used to develop integration and performance tests.

**3) Sizing Requirements and Design.** This section documents the amount and location (if applicable) of the memory requirements and design of the assembly. This information includes

1. The sizing requirement
2. The method of evaluating compliance (e.g., analysis, test, inspection)
3. The design steps taken to ensure compliance

**4) Goals of Software Engineering.** This section documents the requirements and design decisions made regarding the goals of software engineering for the assembly. Each goal may be documented in its own paragraph, which should contain the following information:

1. The goal and its definition
2. The project priority of the goal
3. The required level of the goal (if practical)
4. The method of evaluating compliance (e.g., analysis, test, inspection)
5. The design steps taken to ensure compliance

**5) Notes.** This section provides general information that aids in understanding this document, such as an overview of ADM3 and any analysis and design trade-offs made regarding the assembly as a whole.

**6) Appendixes.** This section provides information published separately, for convenience in document maintenance (e.g., abbreviations list, glossary, classified data). As applicable, each appendix should be referenced in the main body of the document, where the information would normally have been provided. Appendixes may be bound as separate documents, for ease of handling.

## 7.4 THE DIGITAL THERMOSTAT SYSTEM REQUIREMENTS

This chapter uses a single example—a digital thermostat—to illustrate how object-oriented software should be documented. The primary objective of the digital thermostat is to control the temperature within a large room (see Figure 7-1). The system has the following requirements.

R.1.   The system is controlled by its hardware control panel, consisting of the following hardware devices (see Figure 7-2):
- `ON_OFF_BUTTON`
- `MODE_BUTTON`
- `DECREMENT_TEMPERATURE_BUTTON`
- `INCREMENT_TEMPERATURE_BUTTON`
- `DESIRED_TEMPERATURE_DISPLAY`
- `MEAN_TEMPERATURE_DISPLAY`

R.2.   The system controls the mean temperature of the room by monitoring and controlling the following hardware devices:
- `AIR_CONDITIONER`
- `FURNACE`

R.3.   The system measures the actual mean temperature of the room by monitoring a `SET_OF_TEMPERATURE_SENSORS`.

R.4.   The purpose of the hardware `ON_OFF_BUTTON` is to change the state of the system from `Off` to `On` and from `On` to `Off` when pressed. The system starts in the `Off` state.

R.5.   The purpose of the hardware `MODE_BUTTON` is to change the mode of the system from `Celsius` to `Fahrenheit` and from `Fahrenheit` to `Celsius` when pressed. The system starts in the `Celsius` mode.

R.6.   The purpose of the hardware `DECREMENT_TEMPERATURE_BUTTON` is to decrement the desired temperature of the system by 1 degree.

R.7.   The purpose of the hardware `INCREMENT_TEMPERATURE_BUTTON` is to increment the desired temperature of the system by 1 degree.

R.8.   The initial desired temperature of the system is 20 degrees `Celsius`.

R.9.   The purpose of the hardware `DESIRED_TEMPERATURE_DISPLAY` is to display the desired temperature of the system and the mode of the system (i.e., "C" for `Celsius`, "F" for `Fahrenheit`) as long as the system is in the `On` state.

R.10. The purpose of the hardware MEAN_TEMPERATURE_DISPLAY is to display the mean temperature of the system and the mode of the system (i.e., "C" for Celsius, "F" for Fahrenheit) as long as the system is in the On state.

R.11. The purpose of the hardware AIR_CONDITIONER is to decrease the temperature of the room. It shall be turned on if the system is in the On state and the desired temperature is at least 2 degrees less than the mean temperature. The initial state of the AIR_CONDITIONER is Off, and the AIR_CONDITIONER shall be turned off when the system is in the Off state.

R.12. The purpose of the hardware FURNACE is to increase the temperature of the room. It shall be turned on if the system is in the On state and the desired temperature is at least 2 degrees more than the mean temperature. The initial state of the FURNACE is Off, and the FURNACE shall be turned off when the system is in the Off state.

R.13. The hardware AIR_CONDITIONER and FURNACE should never be turned on at the same time.

R.14. The purpose of the hardware SET_OF_TEMPERATURE_SENSORS is to determine the actual temperature of the room at a number of strategic locations.

## 7.5 EXAMPLE DOCUMENTATION

### 7.5.1 Example Assembly Documentation

The following is an example of some of the documentation that software engineers should provide for each assembly:

- The DIGITAL_THERMOSTAT_SOFTWARE assembly provides the digital thermostat capability by reacting to all buttons and by controlling the air conditioner, the furnace, and both displays, using the information from the temperature sensors.
- It has the context diagram (CD) provided by Figure 7-3.
- The hardware DECREMENT_TEMPERATURE_BUTTON master terminator interrupts the DIGITAL_THERMOSTAT_SOFTWARE assembly, which then decrements the desired temperature by 1 degree.
- The DIGITAL_THERMOSTAT_SOFTWARE assembly has the following specification and body:
- The DIGITAL_THERMOSTAT_SOFTWARE assembly has the assembly diagram (AD) provided by Figure 7-4.

```
assembly DIGITAL_THERMOSTAT_SOFTWARE
specification
 subassembly DIGITAL_THERMOSTAT  is concurrent;
end;

assembly DIGITAL_THERMOSTAT_APPLICATION
body
 subassembly CLASSES           is concurrent;
end;
```

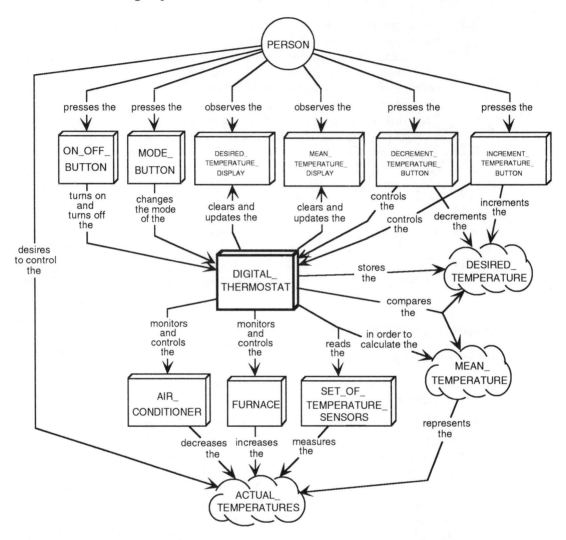

**Figure 7-1: System Semantic Net (SSN) of the** DIGITAL_THERMOSTAT **System**

## 7.5.2    Example Subassembly Documentation

The following is an example of some of the documentation that software engineers should provide for each subassembly:

- The DIGITAL_THERMOSTAT.DIGITAL_THERMOSTAT subassembly contains all objects in the DIGITAL_THERMOSTAT_SOFTWARE assembly.
- It is an essential, atomic, ad hoc, master subassembly.
- It has the following specification and body:

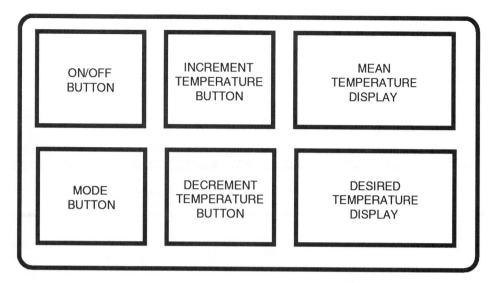

**Figure 7-2: Control Panel for the** DIGITAL_THERMOSTAT **System**

```
subassembly  DIGITAL_THERMOSTAT is concurrent
 parent assembly DIGITAL_THERMOSTAT_SOFTWARE;
specification
  object      THE_DECREMENT_TEMPERATURE_BUTTON    is concurrent;
  object      THE_INCREMENT_TEMPERATURE_BUTTON    is concurrent;
  object      THE_MODE_BUTTON                     is concurrent;
  object      THE_ON_OFF_BUTTON                   is concurrent;
end;


subassembly  DIGITAL_THERMOSTAT
body
  object      THE_AIR_CONDITIONER;
  object      THE_DESIRED_TEMPERATURE             is concurrent;
  object      THE_DESIRED_TEMPERATURE_DISPLAY     is concurrent;
  object      THE_FURNACE;
  object      THE_MEAN_TEMPERATURE                is concurrent;
  object      THE_MEAN_TEMPERATURE_DISPLAY        is concurrent;
  object      THE_SET_OF_TEMPERATURE_SENSORS;
end;
```

- The DIGITAL_THERMOSTAT.DIGITAL_THERMOSTAT subassembly has the general semantic net (GSN) provided by Figure 7-5.
- The DIGITAL_THERMOSTAT.DIGITAL_THERMOSTAT subassembly has the interaction diagram (ID) provided by Figure 7-6.
- The DIGITAL_THERMOSTAT.DIGITAL_THERMOSTAT subassembly has the control flow diagram (CFD) provided by Figure 7-7.

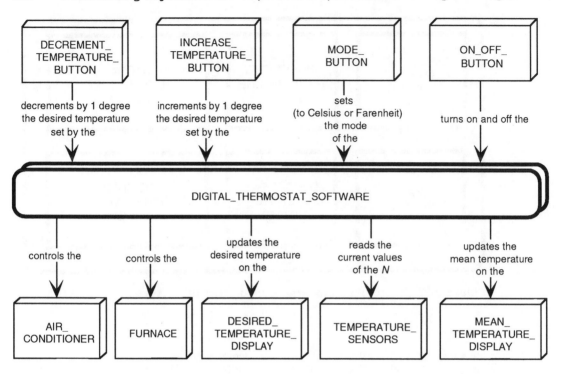

**Figure 7-3: Context Diagram (CD) for the** `DIGITAL_THERMOSTAT_SOFTWARE` **Assembly**

## 7.5.3    Example Class Documentation

The following is an example of some of the documentation that software engineers should provide for each class.

- The `CONTROLLERS.CLASSES.DIGITAL_THERMOSTAT_SOFTWARE` class is a template for `THE_AIR_CONDITIONER` and `THE_FURNACE` objects.
- It is an essential, sequential, atomic, agent, physical, device, controller, corruptable class.
- It has
  — no superclasses
  — no subclasses
  — two instances: THE_AIR_CONDITIONER and THE_FURNACE
  — cardinality 2
- It has the following specification and body:

```
class CONTROLLERS
 parent subassembly CLASSES;
 needs THE_SYSTEM.PREDEFINED;
 parameter constant Address : VALUES.THE_SYSTEM;
specification
```

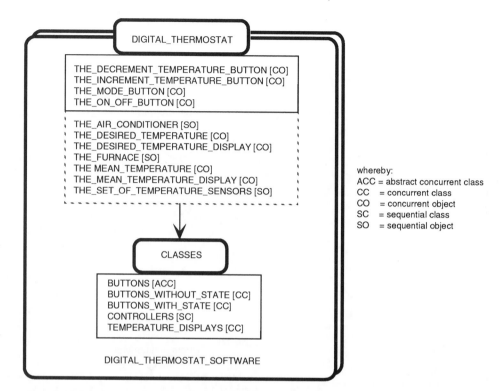

**Figure 7-4: Assembly Diagram (AD) for the** `DIGITAL_THERMOSTAT_SOFTWARE`
**Assembly**

```
introduces
  type        States is (Failed,Off,On);
  message     CONSTRUCT   (A_CONTROLLER;
                          With_Address     : in Addresses.THE_SYSTEM;
                          With_Off_Value   : in Values.THE_SYSTEM;
                          With_On_Value    : in Values.THE_SYSTEM)
                          raise CONSTRUCT_FAILED       is synchronous;
  message     DESTRUCT (A_CONTROLLER;
                          With_Address     : in Addresses.THE_SYSTEM;
                          With_Off_Value   : in Values.THE_SYSTEM;
                          With_On_Value    : in Values.THE_SYSTEM)
                          raise DESTRUCT_FAILED        is synchronous;
  message     IS_ON       return States
                          raise FAILURE_OCCURRED_IN    is synchronous;
  message     TURN_OFF    raise FAILURE_OCCURRED_IN    is synchronous;
  message     TURN_ON     raise FAILURE_OCCURRED_IN    is synchronous;
  exception   CONSTRUCT_FAILED_IN;
  exception   DESTRUCT_FAILED_IN;
  exception   FAILURE_OCCURRED_IN;
  exception   INCOMPATIBLE_STATE_IN;
end;
```

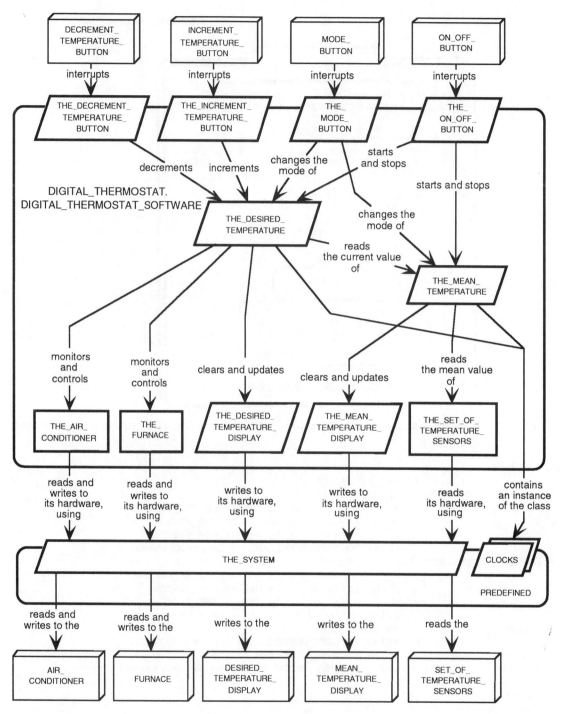

**Figure 7-5: General Semantic Net (GSN) for the** DIGITAL_THERMOSTAT **Subassembly**

386

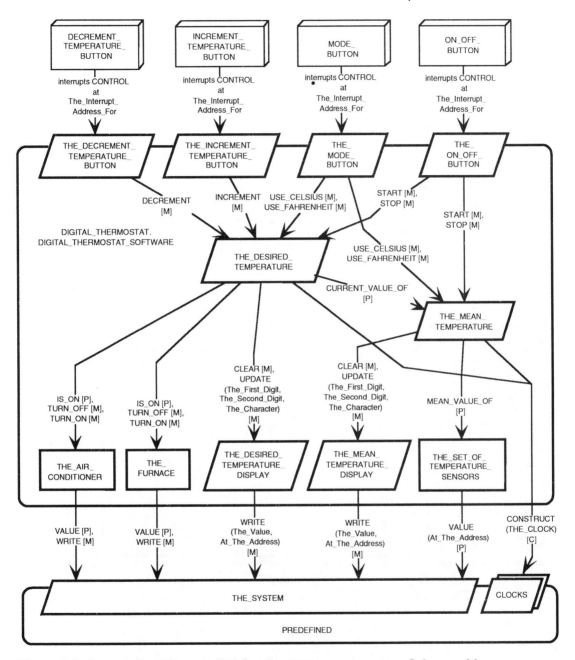

**Figure 7-6: Interaction Diagram (ID) for the** DIGITAL_THERMOSTAT **Subassembly**

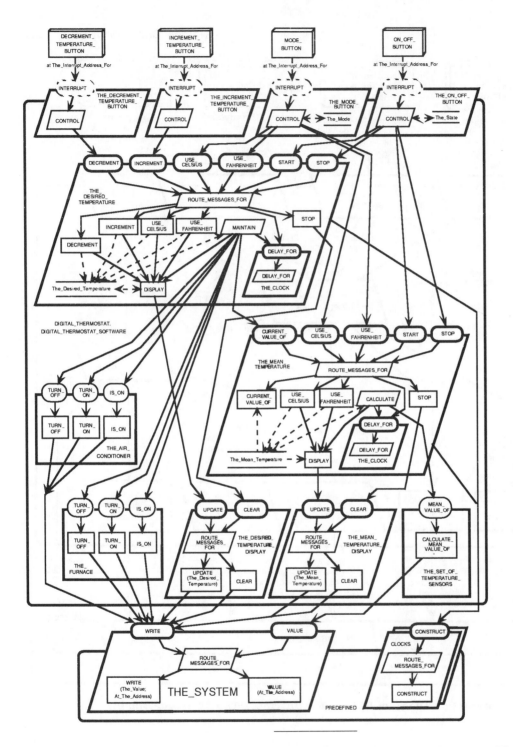

**Figure 7-7: Control Flow Diagram (CFD) for the** `DIGITAL_THERMOSTAT` **Subassembly**

```
class CONTROLLERS
body
 introduces
  variable                    The_State        : States := Off;
  constructor operation  CONSTRUCT         (A_CONTROLLER;
                              With_Address     : in ADDRESSES.THE_SYSTEM;
                              With_Off_Value   : in VALUES.THE_SYSTEM;
                              With_On_Value    : in VALUES.THE_SYSTEM)
                                      raise CONSTRUCT_FAILED    is synchronous;
  destructor operation   DESTRUCT          (A_CONTROLLER;
                              With_Address     : in ADDRESSES.THE_SYSTEM;
                              With_Off_Value   : in VALUES.THE_SYSTEM;
                              With_On_Value    : in VALUES.THE_SYSTEM)
                                      raise CONSTRUCT_FAILED    is synchronous;
  preserver operation    IS_ON                return States
                                      raise FAILURE_OCCURRED_IN is synchronous;
  modifier operation     TURN_OFF raise FAILURE_OCCURRED_IN is synchronous;
  modifier operation     TURN_ON  raise FAILURE_OCCURRED_IN is synchronous;
end;
```

- The CONTROLLERS.CLASSES.DIGITAL_THERMOSTAT_SOFTWARE class has the classification diagram (CLD) provided by Figure 7-8.
- The CONTROLLERS.CLASSES.DIGITAL_THERMOSTAT_SOFTWARE class has the state transition diagram (STD) provided by Figure 7-9.
- The CONTROLLERS.CLASSES.DIGITAL_THERMOSTAT_SOFTWARE class has the control flow diagram (CFD) provided by Figure 7-10.

## 7.5.4    Example Object Documentation

The following is an example of some of the documentation that software engineers should provide for each object of anonymous class.

- THE_DESIRED_TEMPERATURE.DIGITAL_THERMOSTAT.DIGITAL_THERMOSTAT_SOFTWARE object models and controls the desired temperature of the digital thermostat.
- It is an essential, concurrent, aggregate, agent, conceptual, property, controller, guarded, temporary object.
- It is an object of anonymous class.
- It has the following specification and body:

```
object THE_DESIRED_TEMPERATURE is concurrent
 parent subassembly DIGITAL_THERMOSTAT;
specification
 -- no exported attribute types or constants.
 message DECREMENT       raise FAILURE_OCCURRED_IN is synchronous;
 message INCREMENT       raise FAILURE_OCCURRED_IN is synchronous;
 message START           raise FAILURE_OCCURRED_IN is synchronous;
 message STOP            raise FAILURE_OCCURRED_IN is synchronous;
 message USE_CELSIUS     raise FAILURE_OCCURRED_IN is synchronous;
 message USE_FAHRENHEIT  raise FAILURE_OCCURRED_IN is synchronous;
 exception FAILURE_OCCURRED_IN;
end;
```

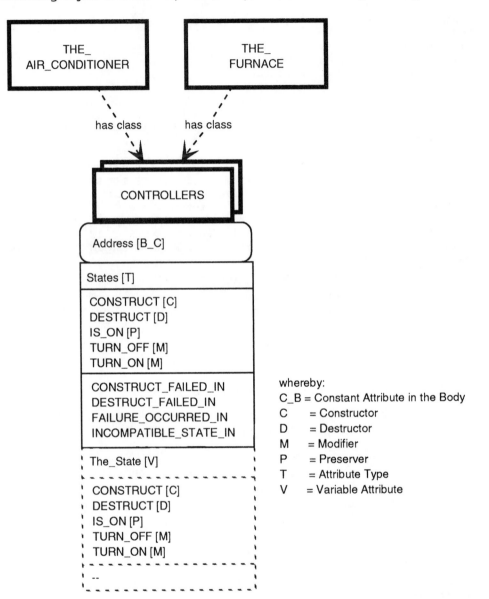

**Figure 7-8: Body-Level Classification Diagram (CLD) for the** CONTROLLERS **Class**

```
object THE_DESIRED_TEMPERATURE
 needs THE_MEAN_TEMPERATURE;
 needs CLOCKS.PREDEFINED;
body
 type Modes  is (Celsius,Fahrenheit);
```

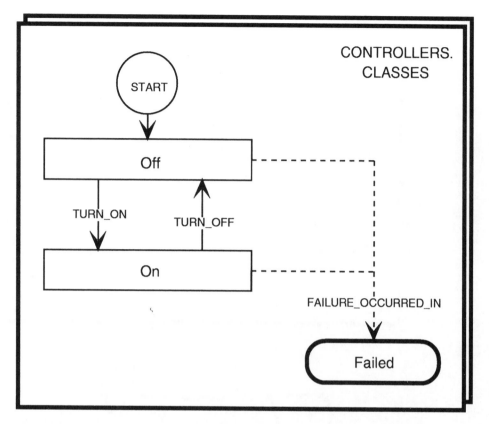

**Figure 7-9: State Transition Diagram (STD) for the** CONTROLLERS **Class**

```
type States is (On,Off);
constant The_Delay_Amount          : Seconds.THE_CLOCK                    :=      10;
constant The_Maximum_Difference   :
         Degrees_Celsius.THE_SET_OF_TEMPERATURE_SENSORS                   :=       2;
variable The_Current_Value         :
         Degrees_Celsius.THE_SET_OF_TEMPERATURE_SENSORS                   :=      20;
variable The_Mean_Temperature      :
         Degrees_Celsius.THE_SET_OF_TEMPERATURE_SENSORS;
variable The_Mode                  : Modes                               := Celsius;
variable The_State                 : States                              :=     Off;
modifier operation   DECREMENT           raise FAILURE_OCCURRED_IN;
modifier operation   DISPLAY             raise FAILURE_OCCURRED_IN;
modifier operation   INCREMENT           raise FAILURE_OCCURRED_IN;
modifier operation   MAINTAIN            raise FAILURE_OCCURRED_IN,
                                               INCOMPATIBLE_STATE_IN
                                         is concurrent;
preserver operation  ROUTE_MESSAGES_FOR  raise FAILURE_OCCURRED_IN
                                         is concurrent;
```

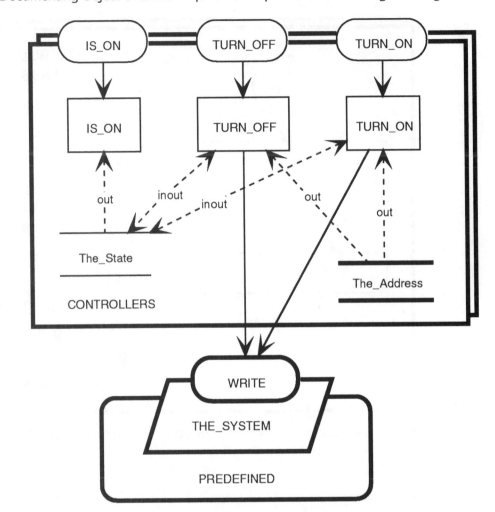

**Figure 7-10: Control Flow Diagram (CFD) for the** CONTROLLERS **Class**

```
modifier operation   START              raise FAILURE_OCCURRED_IN;
modifier operation   STOP               raise FAILURE_OCCURRED_IN;
modifier operation   USE_CELSIUS        raise FAILURE_OCCURRED_IN;
modifier operation   USE_FAHRENHEIT     raise FAILURE_OCCURRED_IN;
object THE_CLOCK                : CLOCKS.PREDEFINED;
start
CONSTRUCT(THE_CLOCK).THE_CLOCKS;
ROUTE_MESSAGES_FOR;
end;
```

- THE_DESIRED_TEMPERATURE.DIGITAL_THERMOSTAT.DIGITAL_
  THERMOSTAT_SOFTWARE object has the GSN provided by Figure 7-11: GSN for
  THE_DESIRED_TEMPERATURE Object.

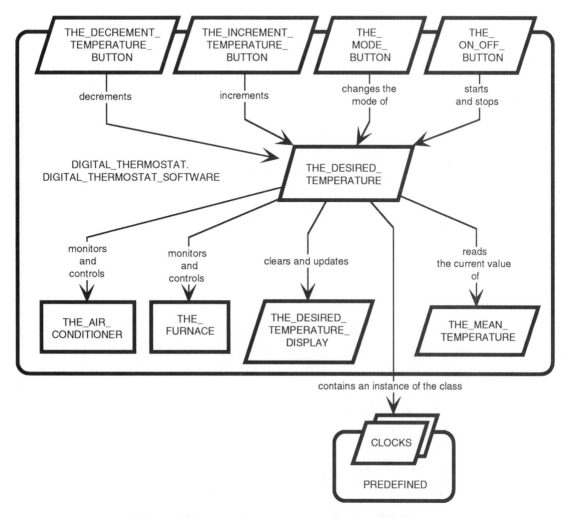

**Figure 7-11: GSN for** THE_DESIRED_TEMPERATURE **Object**

- THE_DESIRED_TEMPERATURE.DIGITAL_THERMOSTAT.DIGITAL_
  THERMOSTAT_SOFTWARE object has the ID provided by Figure 7-12: ID for
  THE_DESIRED_TEMPERATURE Object.
- THE_DESIRED_TEMPERATURE.DIGITAL_THERMOSTAT.DIGITAL_
  THERMOSTAT_SOFTWARE object has the STD provided by Figure 7-13: STD for
  THE_DESIRED_TEMPERATURE Object.
- THE_DESIRED_TEMPERATURE.DIGITAL_THERMOSTAT.DIGITAL_
  THERMOSTAT_SOFTWARE object has the CFD provided by Figure 7-14: CFD for
  THE_DESIRED_TEMPERATURE Object.

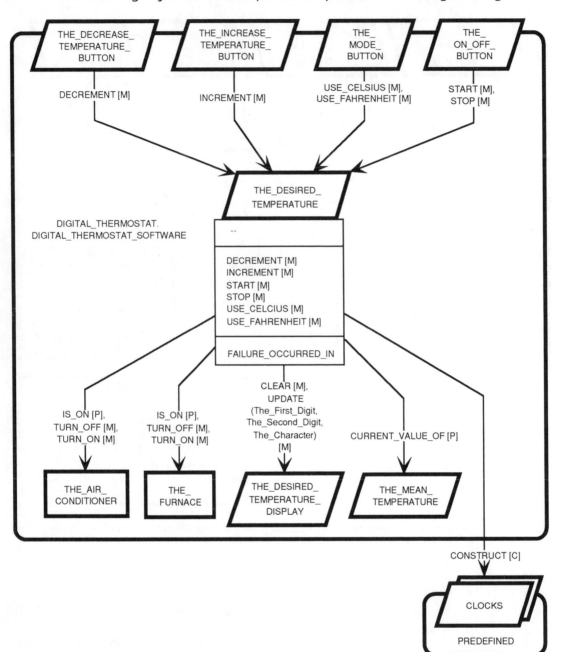

**Figure 7-12: ID for** THE_DESIRED_TEMPERATURE **Object**

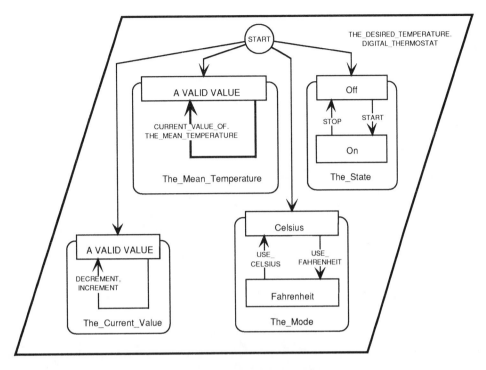

**Figure 7-13: STD for** THE_DESIRED_TEMPERATURE **Object**

## 7.5.5    Example Documentation of Resources

Objects and classes are localizations of resources—specifically attribute types, attributes, messages, operations, and exceptions. The software-engineering principle of uniformity therefore implies that the information about resources should also be localized with the information about the objects and classes as a whole. Thus, data dictionaries, like common global data, are antithetical to object orientation and should not drive the format of the documentation.

The following is an example of some of the documentation that software engineers should provide for each assembly.

### 7.5.5.1    Example Attribute Type Documentation

The following is an example of some of the documentation that software engineers should provide for each attribute type.

- The Modes.THE_DESIRED_TEMPERATURE attribute type models the modes of THE_DESIRED_TEMPERATURE object, which can be either Celsius or Fahrenheit.

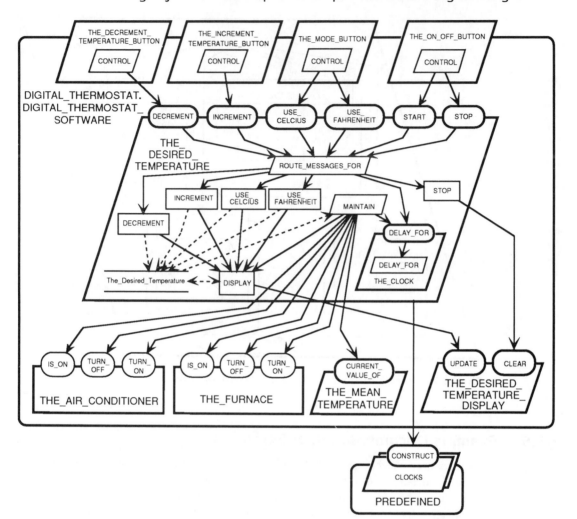

**Figure 7-14: CFD for THE_DESIRED_TEMPERATURE Object**

- It is an essential, visible, conceptual, object attribute type.
- It has the single instance The_Mode.
- Units of measure, accuracy, and precision are not applicable.
- It has the following declaration:

  **type** Modes **is** (Celsius,Fahrenheit);

- It fulfills part of system requirement R.9. See Section 7.4 (The Digital Thermostat System Requirements).

### 7.5.5.2 Example Attribute Documentation

The following is an example of some of the documentation that software engineers should provide for each attribute:

- `The_State.THE_AIR_CONDITIONER` models the state of the hardware air conditioner, which can be `Failed`, `Off`, or `On`.
- It is an essential, conceptual, hidden, object, and state variable attribute.
- It is of type `States`.
- Its initial value is `Off`.
- Its declaration is

  **variable** `The_State : States := Off;`

- It fulfills part of system requirement R.11.

### 7.5.5.3 Example Message Documentation

The following is an example of some of the documentation that software engineers should provide for each message.

- The `TURN_OFF.THE_AIR_CONDITIONER.DIGITAL_THERMOSTAT.DIGITAL_THERMOSTAT_SOFTWARE` message requests that `THE_AIR_CONDITIONER` object turn off the hardware air conditioner.
- It is an essential, sequential, object message.
- It has the following declaration:

  `TURN_OFF.THE_AIR_CONDITIONER;`

- It is sent by `THE_DESIRED_TEMPERATURE` object.
- It may raise the following exception: `FAILURE_OCCURRED_IN`.
- It fulfills part of system requirement R.11.

### 7.5.5.4 Example Operation Documentation

The following is an example of some of the documentation that software engineers should provide for each operation.

- The `MAINTAIN.THE_DESIRED_TEMPERATURE.DIGITAL_THERMOSTAT.DIGITAL_THERMOSTAT_SOFTWARE` operation maintains the desired temperature of the digital thermostat.
- It is an essential, concurrent, preserver, noniterator, object operation.
- It has the following specification and body:

```
preserver operation MAINTAIN  raise FAILURE_OCCURRED_IN, INCOMPATIBLE_STATE_IN
                            is concurrent
parent object
  THE_DESIRED_TEMPERATURE.DIGITAL_THERMOSTAT.DIGITAL_THERMOSTAT_SOFTWARE;
```

```
specification
-- This master operation does not receive any messages.
end;

operation MAINTAIN
 needs THE_AIR_CONDITIONER;
 needs THE_FURNACE;
 needs THE_MEAN_TEMPERATURE;
body
preconditions
 when
  not (The_Current_Value = 21 and The_Mode = Celsius and The_State = Off)
  then
  raise INCOMPATIBLE_STATE_IN.THE_DESIRED_TEMPERATURE;
 end when;
statements
 FOREVER : loop
  INNER : while The_State = On loop
   The_Mean_Temperature ::= CURRENT_VALUE_OF.THE_MEAN_TEMPERATURE;
   if -- The_Mean_Temperature is too low.
    The_Mean_Temperature < The_Current_Value - The_Maximum_Difference
   then
    if not  IS_ON.THE_FURNACE           then TURN_ON.THE_FURNACE;
    if      IS_ON.THE_AIR_CONDITIONER   then TURN_OFF.THE_AIR_CONDITIONER;
   end if;
   if -- The_Mean_Temperature is too high.
    The_Mean_Temperature > The_Current_Value + The_Maximum_Difference
   then
    if not  IS_ON.THE_AIR_CONDITIONER   then TURN_ON.THE_AIR_CONDITIONER;
    if      IS_ON.THE_FURNACE           then TURN_OFF.THE_FURNACE;
   end if;
   DELAY(The_Delay_Amount).THE_CLOCK;
  end loop INNER;
  DELAY(The_Delay_Amount).THE_CLOCK;
 end loop FOREVER;
exception_handler
 when FAILURE_OCCURRED_IN.THE_AIR_CONDITIONER    then
  if IS_ON.THE_FURNACE                           then TURN_OFF.THE_FURNACE;
 end when;
 when FAILURE_OCCURRED_IN.THE_FURNACE            then
  if IS_ON.THE_AIR_CONDITIONER                   then TURN_OFF.THE_AIR_CONDITIONER;
 end when;
 when FAILURE_OCCURRED_IN.THE_MEAN_TEMPERATURE   then
  if IS_ON.THE_AIR_CONDITIONER                   then TURN_OFF.THE_AIR_CONDITIONER;
  if IS_ON.THE_FURNACE                           then TURN_OFF.THE_FURNACE;
 end when;
 when others                                     then
  if IS_ON.THE_AIR_CONDITIONER                   then TURN_OFF.THE_AIR_CONDITIONER;
  if IS_ON.THE_FURNACE                           then TURN_OFF.THE_FURNACE;
 end when;
 raise FAILURE_OCCURRED_IN.THE_DESIRED_TEMPERATURE;
end;
```

- It fulfills part of system requirement R.11.

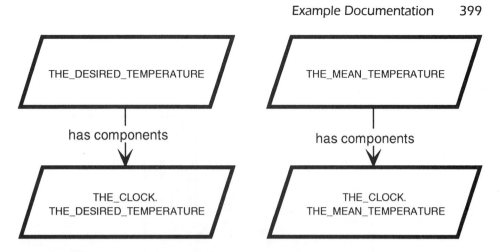

**Figure 7-15: Composition Diagram (CMD) for the** TEMPERATURE **Aggregation Hierarchies**

### 7.5.5.5  Example Exception Documentation

The following is an example of some of the documentation that software engineers should provide for each exception.

- The INCOMPATIBLE_STATE_IN.THE_AIR_CONDITIONER exception is an essential, object exception.

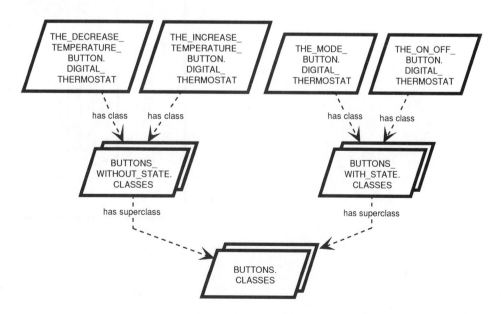

**Figure 7-16: Classification Diagram (CLD) for the** BUTTONS **Class Hierarchy**

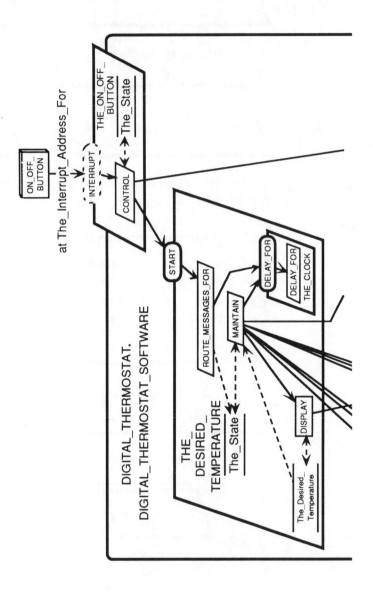

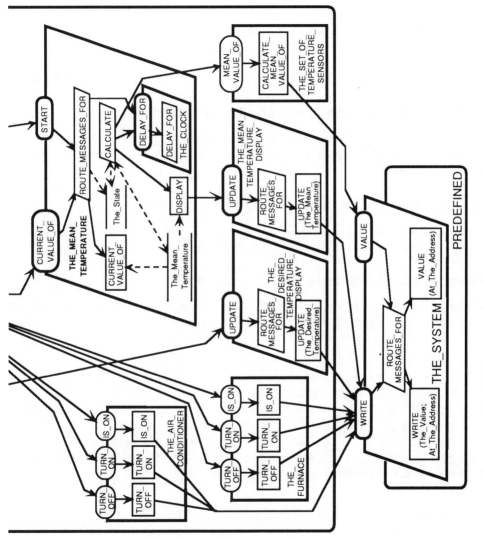

**Figure 7-17: CFD for the TURN_ON Scenario**

401

- It is raised when a message to perform an operation is received when the object is in the wrong state in which to perform the operation.
- It has the following declaration:

```
exception  INCOMPATIBLE_STATE_IN;
```

- It is raised under the following preconditions:
  - The_State = Off and the message received is TURN_OFF.
  - The_State = On  and the message received is TURN_ON.
- It is propagated back to the MAINTAIN.THE_DESIRED_TEMPERATURE operation.

### 7.5.6    Example Aggregation Hierarchy Documentation

An example of the documentation that software engineers should provide for each aggregation hierarchy is provided by Figure 7-15, which shows two trivial composition diagrams (CMDs).

### 7.5.7    Example Classification Hierarchy Documentation

An example of some of the documentation that software engineers should provide for each classification hierarchy is provided by Figure 7-16.

### 7.5.8    Example Major Scenario Documentation

The following is a partial example of some of the documentation that software engineers should provide for each major scenario.

Event 1: The user presses the hardware ON_OFF_BUTTON.

1. The ON_OFF_BUTTON interrupts THE_ON_OFF_BUTTON object.
2. THE_ON_OFF_BUTTON sends the START message to THE_DESIRED_ TEMPERATURE and THE_MEAN_TEMPERATURE objects.
3. THE_MEAN_TEMPERATURE object sends the MEAN_VALUE_OF message to THE_SET_OF_TEMPERATURE_SENSORS object.
4. THE_SET_OF_TEMPERATURE_SENSORS object repeatedly sends the VALUE_AT message to THE_SYSTEM.PREDEFINED object to read the values provided by the individual hardware temperature sensors.

etc. . . .

Figure 7-17 shows the CFD for the TURN_ON  scenario.

## 7.6 CHAPTER REFERENCES

[Technical Evaluation Research Inc. 1989] Technical Evaluation Research Inc., *Documentation Guidelines for Ada Object-Oriented Development Using DOD-STD-2167A*, Report No. TR-L801-066, US Army Communications-Electronics Command (CECOM) Advanced Systems Concepts Directorate, 5 September 1989.

# Chapter 8

# Automotive Dashboard Application

The primary purpose of this chapter is to present a relatively complete[1] example of properly documented object-oriented software. It also illustrates the application of ADM3 to a common application that is large enough to require multiple subassemblies and recursion.

## 8.1 OVERVIEW

The purpose of the AUTOMOTIVE_DASHBOARD_APPLICATION assembly is to provide the cruise control and readout capabilities by reacting to all buttons and by controlling all gauges and meters on the automotive dashboard, using the information from the appropriate sensors.

Assume that the system-level requirements state that the AUTOMOTIVE_ DASHBOARD_APPLICATION assembly has the following 8 master and 10 servant terminators:

- Master terminators
    1. **hardware** BRAKE_SENSOR
    2. **hardware** CRUISE_CONTROL_ACCELERATION_BUTTON
    3. **hardware** CRUISE_CONTROL_COAST_BUTTON

---

[1]Several objects are very similar in architecture and behavior. In order to limit the size of this book, the editors have requested that only the complete design of one of each set of related objects be given.

4. **hardware**   CRUISE_CONTROL_ON_OFF_SWITCH
5. **hardware**   GAS_PEDAL_SENSOR
6. **hardware**   MODE_BUTTON
7. **hardware**   ODOMETER_TRIP_RESET_BUTTON
8. **hardware**   WHEEL_ROTATION_SENSOR
- Servant terminators
1. **hardware**   ENGINE_TEMPERATURE_GAUGE
2. **hardware**   ENGINE_TEMPERATURE_SENSOR
3. **hardware**   FUEL_GAUGE
4. **hardware**   FUEL_LEVEL_SENSOR
5. **hardware**   ODOMETER
6. **hardware**   OIL_GAUGE
7. **hardware**   OIL_PRESSURE_SENSOR
8. **hardware**   SPEEDOMETER
9. **hardware**   TACHOMETER
10. **hardware**   THROTTLE_ACTUATOR

The AUTOMOTIVE_DASHBOARD_APPLICATION assembly has the context diagram (CD) provided by Figure 8-1: CD for the Automotive Dashboard Application.

The AUTOMOTIVE_DASHBOARD_APPLICATION assembly has the following specification and body:

```
assembly AUTOMATIC_DASHBOARD_APPLICATION
specification
 subassembly CRUISE_CONTROL   is concurrent;
 subassembly GAUGES           is concurrent;
 subassembly SPEEDOMETER      is concurrent;
end;


assembly AUTOMATIC_DASHBOARD_APPLICATION
body
end;
```

An overview of the AUTOMOTIVE_DASHBOARD_APPLICATION assembly is provided by the Assembly Diagram (AD) in Figure 8-2.

## 8.2 SUBASSEMBLY CRUISE_CONTROL

The objective of the CRUISE_CONTROL.AUTOMOTIVE_DASHBOARD_APPLICATION subassembly is to implement the cruise-control abstraction by grouping and controlling the visibility of all software objects that provide the cruise-control capability.

The CRUISE_CONTROL.AUTOMOTIVE_DASHBOARD_APPLICATION subassembly is controlled by the following five terminators:

1. **hardware**   BRAKE_SENSOR

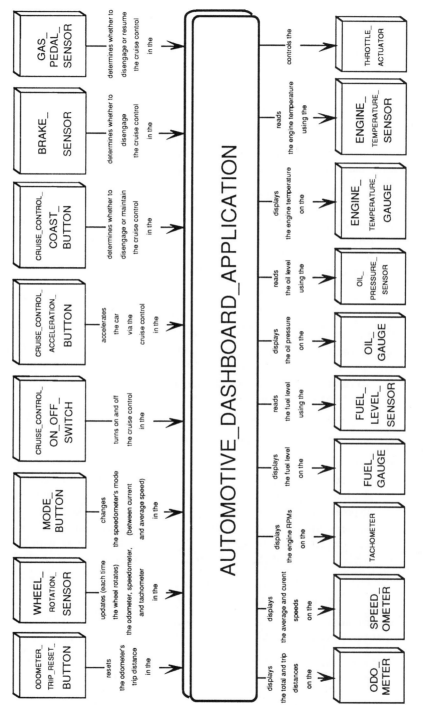

**Figure 8-1: CD for the AUTOMOTIVE_DASHBOARD_APPLICATION**

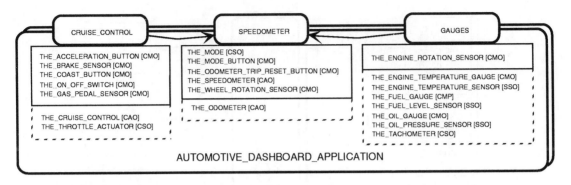

**Figure 8-2: AD for the** AUTOMOTIVE_DASHBOARD_APPLICATION

2. **hardware**    CRUISE_CONTROL_ACCELERATION_BUTTON
3. **hardware**    CRUISE_CONTROL_COAST_BUTTON
4. **hardware**    CRUISE_CONTROL_ON_OFF_SWITCH
5. **hardware**    GAS_PEDAL_SENSOR

The CRUISE_CONTROL.AUTOMOTIVE_DASHBOARD_APPLICATION sub-assembly depends on the following four terminators:

1. **class**      **CLOCKS.PREDEFINED**
2. **object**     THE_SPEEDOMETER.SPEEDOMETER.AUTOMOTIVE_
              DASHBOARD_APPLICATION
3. **object**     **THE_SYSTEM.PREDEFINED**
4. **hardware**   THROTTLE_ACTUATOR

The CRUISE_CONTROL.AUTOMOTIVE_DASHBOARD_APPLICATION sub-assembly consists of the following components:

- **object**  THE_ACCELERATION_BUTTON    Essential Concurrent Master
- **object**  THE_BRAKE_SENSOR           Essential Concurrent Master
- **object**  THE_COAST_BUTTON           Essential Concurrent Master
- **object**  THE_CRUISE_CONTROL         Essential Concurrent Agent
- **object**  THE_GAS_PEDAL_SENSOR       Essential Concurrent Master
- **object**  THE_ON_OFF_SWITCH          Essential Concurrent Master
- **object**  THE_THROTTLE_ACTUATOR      Essential Concurrent Servant

The CRUISE_CONTROL.AUTOMOTIVE_DASHBOARD_APPLICATION sub-assembly has the following specification and body:

```
subassembly CRUISE_CONTROL is concurrent
 parent assembly AUTOMOTIVE_DASHBOARD_APPLICATION;
specification
  object  THE_ACCELERATION_BUTTON    is concurrent;
  object  THE_BRAKE_SENSOR           is concurrent;
  object  THE_COAST_BUTTON           is concurrent;
  object  THE_GAS_PEDAL_SENSOR       is concurrent;
```

```
object   THE_ON_OFF_SWITCH          is concurrent;
end;

subassembly CRUISE_CONTROL
body
 object   THE_CRUISE_CONTROL         is concurrent;
 object   THE_THROTTLE_ACTUATOR      is concurrent;
end;
```

The CRUISE_CONTROL.AUTOMOTIVE_DASHBOARD_APPLICATION subassembly has the general semantic net (GSN) shown in Figure 8-3.

The CRUISE_CONTROL.AUTOMOTIVE_DASHBOARD_APPLICATION subassembly has the interaction diagram (ID) shown in Figure 8-4.

The BRAKE.CRUISE_CONTROL scenario has the interaction diagram (ID) shown in Figure 8-5.

The CRUISE_CONTROL.AUTOMOTIVE_DASHBOARD_APPLICATION subassembly has the control flow diagram (CFD) shown in Figure 8-6.

## 8.2.1   Object THE_ACCELERATION_BUTTON

The objective of the THE_ACCELERATION_BUTTON.CRUISE_CONTROL object is to model and interface with the hardware CRUISE_CONTROL_ACCELERATION_BUTTON.

THE_ACCELERATION_BUTTON.CRUISE_CONTROL object is controlled by the following terminator:

**hardware**   CRUISE_CONTROL_ACCELERATION_BUTTON

THE_ACCELERATION_BUTTON.CRUISE_CONTROL object depends on the following two terminators:

1. **object**   THE_CRUISE_CONTROL.CRUISE_CONTROL
2. **object**   **THE_SYSTEM.PREDEFINED**

THE_ACCELERATION_BUTTON.CRUISE_CONTROL object has the following specification and body:

```
object THE_ACCELERATION_BUTTON is concurrent
 parent subassembly CRUISE_CONTROL;
specification
 message CONTROL is asynchronous;
end;

object THE_ACCELERATION_BUTTON
 needs THE_SYSTEM.PREDEFINED;
body
 constant The_Interrupt_Address_For.THE_ACCELERATION_BUTTON
         : Addresses.THE_SYSTEM := TBD;
 modifier operation CONTROL is concurrent;
start
 CONTROL;
end;
```

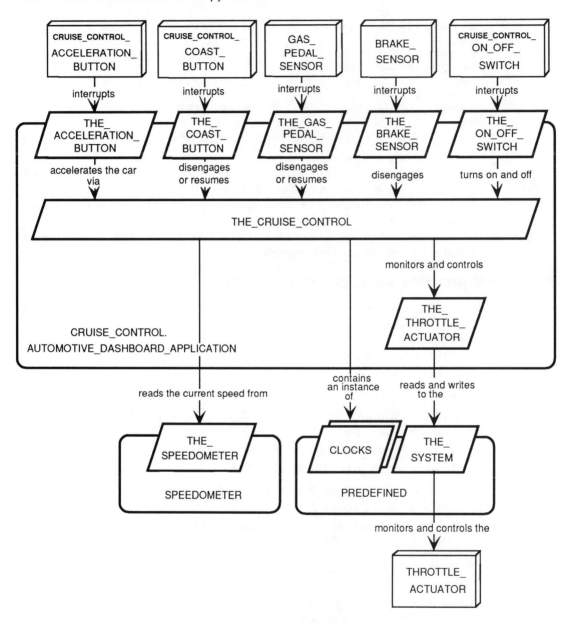

**Figure 8-3: GSN for the CRUISE_CONTROL Subassembly**

The objective of the concurrent CONTROL.THE_ACCELERATION_BUTTON operation is to control the execution of the THE_ACCELERATION_BUTTON object, based on a hardware interrupt at The_Interrupt_Address_For.THE_ACCELERATION_BUTTON.

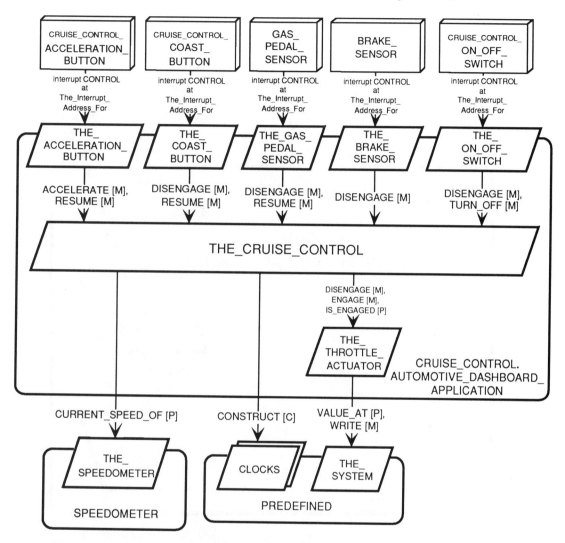

**Figure 8-4: ID for the** CRUISE_CONTROL **Subassembly**

```
modifier operation CONTROL is concurrent
 parent object THE_ACCELERATION_BUTTON;
specification
 message CONTROL is asynchronous;
end;

operation CONTROL
 needs THE_CRUISE_CONTROL;
body
statements
```

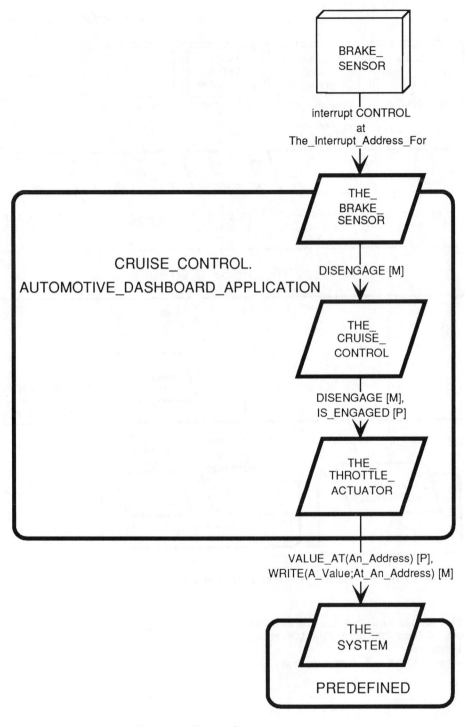

**Figure 8-5: ID for the** BRAKE **Scenario**

410

```
FOREVER : loop
 receive CONTROL when interrupt The_Interrupt_Address_For;
 case VALUE_AT(The_Interrupt_Address_For.THE_ACCELERATION_BUTTON).THE_SYSTEM is
   when 0 then -- The CRUISE_CONTROL_ACCELERATION_BUTTON is released.
    ACCELERATE.THE_CRUISE_CONTROL;
   when 1 then -- The CRUISE_CONTROL_ACCELERATION_BUTTON is pressed.
    RESUME.THE_CRUISE_CONTROL;
 end case;
 end loop FOREVER;
exception_handler
 when FAILURE_OCCURRED_IN.THE_CRUISE_CONTROL then
  TURN_OFF.THE_CRUISE_CONTROL;
end;
```

## 8.2.2  Object THE_BRAKE_SENSOR

The objective of the THE_BRAKE_SENSOR.CRUISE_CONTROL object is to model and interface with the hardware BRAKE_SENSOR.

THE_BRAKE_SENSOR.CRUISE_CONTROL object is controlled by the following terminator:

**hardware**  BRAKE_SENSOR

THE_BRAKE_SENSOR.CRUISE_CONTROL object depends on the following two terminators:

1. **object**  THE_CRUISE_CONTROL.CRUISE_CONTROL
2. **object**  **THE_SYSTEM.PREDEFINED**

THE_BRAKE_SENSOR.CRUISE_CONTROL object has the following specification and body:

```
object THE_BRAKE_SENSOR is concurrent
 parent subassembly CRUISE_CONTROL;
specification
 message CONTROL is asynchronous;
end;

object THE_BRAKE_SENSOR
 needs THE_SYSTEM.PREDEFINED;
body
 constant The_Interrupt_Address_For.THE_BRAKE_SENSOR
        : Addresses.THE_SYSTEM := TBD;
 modifier operation CONTROL is concurrent;
start
 CONTROL;
end;
```

The objective of the concurrent CONTROL.THE_BRAKE_SENSOR operation is to control the execution of the THE_BRAKE_SENSOR object, based on a hardware interrupt at The_Interrupt_Address_For.THE_BRAKE_SENSOR.

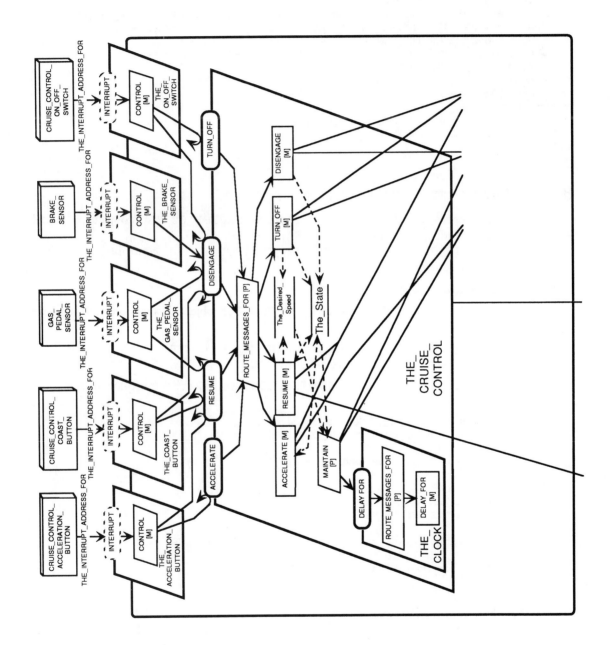

412

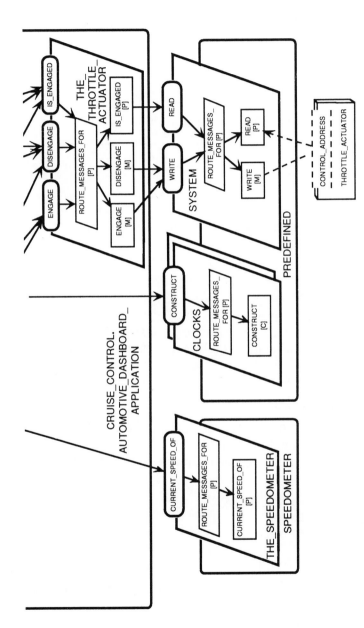

**Figure 8-6: CFD for the** CRUISE_CONTROL **Subassembly**

413

```
modifier operation CONTROL is concurrent
 parent object THE_BRAKE_SENSOR;
specification
 message CONTROL is asynchronous;
end;

operation CONTROL
 needs THE_CRUISE_CONTROL;
body
statements
 FOREVER : loop
  receive CONTROL when interrupt The_Interrupt_Address_For;
  if -- The hardware BRAKE_SENSOR detects pressure.
   VALUE_AT(The_Interrupt_Address_For.THE_BRAKE_SENSOR).THE_SYSTEM = 1
  then
   DISENGAGE.THE_CRUISE_CONTROL;
  end if;
 end loop FOREVER;
exception_handler
 when FAILURE_OCCURRED_IN.THE_CRUISE_CONTROL then
  TURN_OFF.THE_CRUISE_CONTROL;
end;
```

### 8.2.3  Object THE_COAST_BUTTON

The objective of the THE_COAST_BUTTON.CRUISE_CONTROL object is to model and interface with the hardware CRUISE_CONTROL_COAST_BUTTON.

This object has a similar architecture and behavior to THE_ACCELERATION_BUTTON. See paragraph 8.2.1.

### 8.2.4  Object THE_CRUISE_CONTROL

The objective of the THE_CRUISE_CONTROL.CRUISE_CONTROL object is to model and provide the cruise control capability.

THE_CRUISE_CONTROL.CRUISE_CONTROL object is controlled by the following five terminators:

1.  **object**  THE_ACCELERATION_BUTTON
2.  **object**  THE_BRAKE_SENSOR
3.  **object**  THE_COAST_BUTTON
4.  **object**  THE_GAS_PEDAL_SENSOR
5.  **object**  THE_ON_OFF_SWITCH

THE_CRUISE_CONTROL.CRUISE_CONTROL object depends on the following three terminators:

1.  **class**  **CLOCKS.PREDEFINED**
2.  **object**  THE_SPEEDOMETER.SPEEDOMETER
3.  **object**  THE_THROTTLE_ACTUATOR

THE_CRUISE_CONTROL.CRUISE_CONTROL object has the following specification and body:

```
object THE_CRUISE_CONTROL is concurrent
 parent subassembly CRUISE_CONTROL;
specification
 message ACCELERATE   is synchronous;
 message DISENGAGE    is synchronous;
 message RESUME       is synchronous;
 message TURN_OFF     is synchronous;
 exception FAILURE_OCCURRED_IN;
 exception INCOMPATIBLE_PRIOR_STATE_IN;
end;

object THE_CRUISE_CONTROL
 needs CLOCKS.PREDEFINED;
 needs THE_SPEEDOMETER.SPEEDOMETER;
body
 type Desired_Speeds is sub Kilometers_Per_Hour.THE_SPEEDOMETER
                                         range 0.0 .. 300.0;
 type States is (Accelerating,Disengaged,Maintaining,Off);
 variable The_Desired_Speed  : Desired_Speeds := 0.0;
 variable The_State          : States         := Off;
 modifier  operation  ACCELERATE;
 modifier  operation  DISENGAGE;
 preserver operation  MAINTAIN            is concurrent;
 modifier  operation  RESUME;
 preserver operation  ROUTE_MESSAGES_FOR  is concurrent;
 modifier  operation  TURN_OFF;
 object THE_CLOCK             : CLOCKS.PREDEFINED;
start
 CONSTRUCT(THE_CLOCK).CLOCKS;
 ROUTE_MESSAGES_FOR;
 MAINTAIN;
end;
```

THE_CRUISE_CONTROL.CRUISE_CONTROL object has the state transition
diagram (STD) shown in Figure 8-7.

The Off state of the THE_CRUISE_CONTROL object signifies that the
automobile's cruise control is not functioning and should not be confused with the
Disengaged state. It is automatically entered as the starting state and may be
transitioned to by means of the TURN_OFF.THE_CRUISE_CONTROL operation.

The aggregate On state of THE_CRUISE_CONTROL object signifies that the
automobile's cruise control is functioning and consists of the following substates:
Disengaged, Accelerating, and Maintaining. It is entered from the Off
state by means of the DISENGAGE.THE_CRUISE_CONTROL operation.

The Disengaged substate of THE_CRUISE_CONTROL object signifies that the
automobile's cruise control is functioning but is disabled. It is entered from the Off
state by means of the DISENGAGE.THE_CRUISE_CONTROL operation.

The Accelerating substate of THE_CRUISE_CONTROL object signifies that

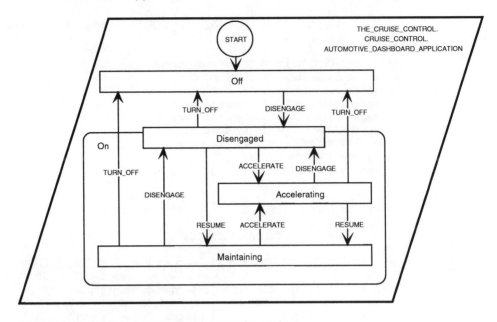

**Figure 8-7: STD for** `THE_CRUISE_CONTROL` **Object**

the automobile's cruise control is functioning and causing the automobile to accelerate by sending the `ENGAGE.THE_THROTTLE_ACTUATOR` message. It is entered from either the `Disengaged` or the `Maintaining` substate, by means of the `ACCELERATE.THE_CRUISE_CONTROL` operation.

The `Maintaining` substate of `THE_CRUISE_CONTROL` object signifies that the automobile's cruise control is functioning and causing the automobile to maintain a desired speed by sending both the `ENGAGE.THE_THROTTLE_ACTUATOR` and the `DISENGAGE.THE_THROTTLE_ACTUATOR` messages. It is entered from either the `Disengaged` or the `Accelerating` substate, by means of the `RESUME.THE_CRUISE_CONTROL` operation.

### 8.2.4.1  Operation `ACCELERATE.THE_CRUISE_CONTROL`

The objective of the sequential `ACCELERATE.THE_CRUISE_CONTROL` operation is to send the `ENGAGE` message to `THE_THROTTLE_ACTUATOR`.

```
modifier operation ACCELERATE
 parent object THE_CRUISE_CONTROL;
specification
end;

operation ACCELERATE
 needs THE_THROTTLE_ACTUATOR;
body
```

```
    variable The_Temporary_State : States;
  preconditions
   require
    The_State = Disengaged or The_State = Maintaining
   else
    raise INCOMPATIBLE_PRIOR_STATE_IN;
   end require;
  statements
   if
    not IS_ENGAGED.THE_THROTTLE_ACTUATOR
   then
    ENGAGE.THE_THROTTLE_ACTUATOR;
   end if;
   The_Temporary_State := The_State;
   The_State          := Accelerating;
  postconditions
   require
    post(The_State) = Accelerating and
    post(IS_ENGAGED.THE_THROTTLE_ACTUATOR)
   else
    The_State := The_Temporary_State;
    raise FAILURE_OCCURRED_IN;
   end require;
  exception_handler
   when others then
    TURN_OFF;
    raise FAILURE_OCCURRED_IN;
  end;
```

### 8.2.4.2  Operation `DISENGAGE.THE_CRUISE_CONTROL`

The objective of the sequential `DISENGAGE.THE_CRUISE_CONTROL` operation is to send the `DISENGAGE` message to `THE_THROTTLE_ACTUATOR`.

```
modifier operation DISENGAGE
 parent object THE_CRUISE_CONTROL;
specification
end;

operation DISENGAGE
 needs THE_THROTTLE_ACTUATOR;
body
 variable The_Temporary_State : States;
preconditions
 require
  The_State = Accelerating or The_State = Maintaining or The_State = Off
 else
  raise INCOMPATIBLE_PRIOR_STATE_IN;
 end require;
statements
 if
  IS_ENGAGED.THE_THROTTLE_ACTUATOR
```

```
 then
  DISENGAGE.THE_THROTTLE_ACTUATOR;
 end if;
  The_Temporary_State  := The_State;
  The_State            := Disengaged;
postconditions
 require
  post(The_State) = Disengaged and
  not post(IS_ENGAGED.THE_THROTTLE_ACTUATOR)
 else
  The_State := The_Temporary_State;
  raise FAILURE_OCCURRED_IN;
 end require;
exception_handler
 when others then
  TURN_OFF;
  raise FAILURE_OCCURRED_IN;
end;
```

### 8.2.4.3  Operation MAINTAIN.THE_CRUISE_CONTROL

The objective of the concurrent MAINTAIN.THE_CRUISE_CONTROL operation is
to maintain the CURRENT_VALUE_OF.THE_SPEEDOMETER when The_State
equals Maintaining.

```
preserver operation MAINTAIN is concurrent
 parent object THE_CRUISE_CONTROL;
specification
end;

operation MAINTAIN
 needs THE_SPEEDOMETER.SPEEDOMETER;
 needs THE_THROTTLE_ACTUATOR;
body
 constant The_Delay_Amount : Seconds.THE_CLOCK := 1.0; -- Second
statements
 FOREVER : loop
 while The_State = Maintaining loop
  if  -- The_Desired_Speed is too low
   CURRENT_VALUE_OF.THE_SPEEDOMETER < The_Desired_Speed - 1.0
  then
   if
    not IS_ENGAGED.THE_THROTTLE_ACTUATOR;
   then
    ENGAGE.THE_THROTTLE_ACTUATOR;
   end if;
  end if;
  if  -- The_Desired_Speed is too high
   CURRENT_VALUE_OF.THE_SPEEDOMETER > The_Desired_Speed + 1.0
  then
   if
    IS_ENGAGED.THE_THROTTLE_ACTUATOR;
```

```
    then
      DISENGAGE.THE_THROTTLE_ACTUATOR;
     end if;
    end if;
   end loop;
   DELAY_FOR(The_Delay_Amount).THE_CLOCK;
  end loop FOREVER;
exception_handler
 when others then
  DISENGAGE.THE_THROTTLE_ACTUATOR;
  TURN_OFF;
  raise FAILURE_OCCURRED_IN;
end;
```

### 8.2.4.4  Operation RESUME.THE_CRUISE_CONTROL

The objective of the sequential RESUME.THE_CRUISE_CONTROL operation is to maintain the CURRENT_VALUE_OF.THE_SPEEDOMETER.

```
modifier operation RESUME
 parent object THE_CRUISE_CONTROL;
specification
end;


operation RESUME
 needs THE_THROTTLE_ACTUATOR;
body
 variable The_Temporary_State : States;
preconditions
 require
  The_State = Accelerating or The_State = Disengaged
 else
  raise INCOMPATIBLE_PRIOR_STATE_IN;
 end require;
statements
 The_Desired_Speed     := CURRENT_VALUE_OF.THE_SPEEDOMETER;
 The_Temporary_State   := The_State;
 The_State             := Disengaged;
postconditions
 require
  post(The_State) = Maintaining
 then
  The_Desired_Speed     := 0.0;
  The_State             := The_Temporary_State;
  raise FAILURE_OCCURRED_IN;
 end require;
exception_handler
 when others then
  DISENGAGE.THE_THROTTLE_ACTUATOR;
  raise FAILURE_OCCURRED_IN;
end;
```

### 8.2.4.5  Operation `ROUTE_MESSAGES_FOR.THE_CRUISE_CONTROL`

The objective of the concurrent ROUTE_MESSAGES_FOR.THE_CRUISE_CONTROL operation is to route messages to their proper operations in a manner that ensures that only one message at a time is received and that it is completely handled before the next message is received. The ultimate objective of this operation is to ensure that the abstraction is not violated by the corruption of its attributes, due to an interleaving of messages in a concurrent environment.

```
preserver operation ROUTE_MESSAGES_FOR is concurrent
 parent object THE_CRUISE_CONTROL;
specification
 message ACCELERATE  is synchronous;
 message DISENGAGE   is synchronous;
 message RESUME       is synchronous;
 message TURN_OFF     is synchronous;
end;


operation ROUTE_MESSAGES_FOR
body
statements
 FOREVER : loop
  select
   receive ACCELERATE;
   ACCELERATE;
  or
   receive DISENGAGE;
   DISENGAGE;
  or
   receive RESUME;
   RESUME;
  or
   receive TURN_OFF;
   TURN_OFF;
  end select;
 end loop FOREVER;
end;
```

### 8.2.4.6  Operation `TURN_OFF.THE_CRUISE_CONTROL`

The objective of the sequential TURN_OFF.THE_CRUISE_CONTROL operation is to send the DISENGAGE message to THE_THROTTLE_ACTUATOR and to set The_Desired_Speed back to 0.0 Kilometers_Per_Hour.

```
modifier operation TURN_OFF
 parent object THE_CRUISE_CONTROL;
specification
end;


operation TURN_OFF
 needs THE_THROTTLE_ACTUATOR;
```

```
body
 variable The_Temporary_State : States;
preconditions
 require
  The_State = OFF
 then
  raise INCOMPATIBLE_PRIOR_STATE_IN;
 end require;
statements
 if
  IS_ENGAGED.THE_THROTTLE_ACTUATOR
 then
  DISENGAGE.THE_THROTTLE_ACTUATOR;
 end if;
 The_Desired_Speed := 0.0; -- Kilometers_Per_Hour
 The_State        := Off;
postconditions
 require
  post(The_State) = OFF and
  not post(IS_ENGAGED.THE_THROTTLE_ACTUATOR)
 else
  The_Desired_Speed := 0.0;
  The_State        := The_Temporary_State;
 raise FAILURE_OCCURRED_IN;
 end require;
exception_handler
 when others then
  DISENGAGE.THE_THROTTLE_ACTUATOR;
  raise FAILURE_OCCURRED_IN;
end;
```

## 8.2.5 Object THE_GAS_PEDAL_SENSOR

The objective of the THE_GAS_PEDAL_SENSOR.CRUISE_CONTROL object is to model and interface with the hardware GAS_PEDAL_SENSOR. The object has a similar architecture and behavior to THE_BRAKE_SENSOR. See paragraph 8.2.2.

## 8.2.6 Object THE_ON_OFF_SWITCH

The objective of the THE_ON_OFF_SWITCH.CRUISE_CONTROL object is to model and interface with the hardware CRUISE_CONTROL_ON_OFF_SWITCH.

THE_ON_OFF_SWITCH.CRUISE_CONTROL object is controlled by the following terminator:

**hardware** CRUISE_CONTROL_ON_OFF_SWITCH

THE_ON_OFF_SWITCH.THE_CRUISE_CONTROL object depends on the following two terminators:

1. **object** THE_CRUISE_CONTROL.CRUISE_CONTROL
2. **object** **THE_SYSTEM.PREDEFINED**

THE_ON_OFF_SWITCH.CRUISE_CONTROL object has the following specification and body:

```
object THE_ON_OFF_SWITCH is concurrent
 parent subassembly CRUISE_CONTROL;
specification
 message CONTROL is synchronous;
end;

object THE_ON_OFF_SWITCH
 needs THE_SYSTEM.PREDEFINED;
body
 constant The_Interrupt_Address_For.THE_ON_OFF_SWITCH
        : Addresses.THE_SYSTEM := TBD;
 modifier operation CONTROL is concurrent;
start
 CONTROL;
end;
```

The objective of the concurrent CONTROL.THE_ON_OFF_SWITCH operation is to control the execution of THE_ON_OFF_SWITCH object, based on a hardware interrupt at The_Interrupt_Address_For.THE_ON_OFF_SWITCH.

```
modifier operation CONTROL is concurrent
 parent object THE_ON_OFF_SWITCH;
specification
 message CONTROL is asynchronous;
end;

operation CONTROL
 needs THE_CRUISE_CONTROL;
body
statements
 FOREVER : loop
  receive CONTROL when interrupt The_Interrupt_Address_For;
  case VALUE_AT(The_Interrupt_Address_For.THE_ON_OFF_SWITCH).THE_SYSTEM is
   when 0 then -- The CRUISE_CONTROL_ON_OFF_SWITCH was set to OFF.
    TURN_OFF.THE_CRUISE_CONTROL;
   when 1 then -- The CRUISE_CONTROL_ON_OFF_SWITCH was set to ON.
    DISENGAGE.THE_CRUISE_CONTROL;
  end case;
 end loop FOREVER;
exception_handler
 when FAILURE_OCCURRED_IN.THE_CRUISE_CONTROL then
  TURN_OFF.THE_CRUISE_CONTROL;
end;
```

## 8.2.7    Object THE_THROTTLE_ACTUATOR

The objective of THE_THROTTLE_ACTUATOR.CRUISE_CONTROL object is to model and control with the hardware THROTTLE_ACTUATOR.

THE_THROTTLE_ACTUATOR.CRUISE_CONTROL object is controlled by the following terminator:

**object**  THE_CRUISE_CONTROL

THE_THROTTLE_ACTUATOR.CRUISE_CONTROL object controls the following terminator:

**hardware**  THROTTLE_ACTUATOR

THE_THROTTLE_ACTUATOR.CRUISE_CONTROL object has the following specification and body:

```
object THE_THROTTLE_ACTUATOR is concurrent
 parent subassembly CRUISE_CONTROL;
specification
 message   DISENGAGE     is synchronous;
 message   ENGAGE        is synchronous;
 message   IS_ENGAGED    is synchronous;
end;

object THE_THROTTLE_ACTUATOR
 needs object    THE_SYSTEM.PREDEFINED;
body
 constant Control_Address_Of : Addresses.THE_SYSTEM := TBD;
 modifier   operation   DISENGAGE;
 modifier   operation   ENGAGE;
 preserver operation   IS_ENGAGED;
 preserver operation   ROUTE_MESSAGES_FOR  is concurrent;
start
 CONTROL;
end;
```

### 8.2.7.1  Operation DISENGAGE.THE_THROTTLE_ACTUATOR

The objective of the DISENGAGE.THE_THROTTLE_ACTUATOR operation is to disengage the hardware THROTTLE_ACTUATOR on receiving the DISENGAGE message from CRUISE_CONTROL.MAINTAIN.

```
modifier operation DISENGAGE
 parent object THE_THROTTLE_ACTUATOR;
specification
end;

operation DISENGAGE
body
statements
 -- Disengage the hardware THROTTLE_ACTUATOR.
 WRITE(A_Value := 0;At_An_Address := Control_Address_Of.THE_THROTTLE_ACTUATOR).
   THE_SYSTEM;
end;
```

### 8.2.7.2  Operation `ENGAGE.THE_THROTTLE_ACTUATOR`

The objective of the `ENGAGE.THE_THROTTLE_ACTUATOR` operation is to increase the hardware `THROTTLE_ACTUATOR`, upon receiving the `INCREASE` message from `MAINTAIN.CRUISE_CONTROL`.

```
modifier operation ENGAGE
 parent object THE_THROTTLE_ACTUATOR;
specification
end;


operation ENGAGE
body
statements
 -- Engage the hardware THROTTLE_ACTUATOR.
 WRITE(A_Value := 1;At_An_Address := Control_Address_Of.THE_THROTTLE_ACTUATOR).
  THE_SYSTEM;
end;
```

### 8.2.7.3  Operation `IS_ENGAGED.THE_THROTTLE_ACTUATOR`

The objective of the `IS_ENGAGED.THE_THROTTLE_ACTUATOR` operation is to determine whether the hardware `THROTTLE_ACTUATOR` is engaged.

```
preserver operation ENGAGE return BOOLEAN;
 parent object THE_THROTTLE_ACTUATOR;
specification
end;


operation IS_ENGAGED
body
statements
 if
  VALUE_AT(An_Address := Control_Address_Of.THE_THROTTLE_ACTUATOR).THE_SYSTEM = 1
 then
  return TRUE;
 else
  return FALSE;
 end if;
end;
```

### 8.2.7.4  Operation `ROUTE_MESSAGES_FOR.THE_THROTTLE_ACTUATOR`

The objective of the concurrent `ROUTE_MESSAGES_FOR.THE_THROTTLE_ACTUATOR` operation is to route messages to their proper operations in a manner that ensures that only one message at a time is received and that it is completely handled before the next message is received. The ultimate objective of this operation is to ensure that the abstraction is not violated by the corruption of its attributes, due to an interleaving of messages in a concurrent environment.

```
preserver operation ROUTE_MESSAGES_FOR is concurrent
 parent object THE_THROTTLE_ACTUATOR;
specification
 message  DISENGAGE    is synchronous;
 message  ENGAGE       is synchronous;
 message  IS_ENGAGED   is synchronous;
end;

operation ROUTE_MESSAGES_FOR is concurrent
body
statements
 FOREVER : loop
  select
   receive ENGAGE;
   ENGAGE;
  or
   receive DISENGAGE;
   DISENGAGE;
  or
   receive IS_ENGAGED;
   IS_ENGAGED;
  end select;
 end loop FOREVER;
end;
```

## 8.3 **SUBASSEMBLY** GAUGES

The objective of the GAUGES.AUTOMOTIVE_DASHBOARD_APPLICATION initial subassembly is (a) to group and control the visibility of all software objects that model the gauges and their related sensors on the automotive dashboard, and (b) to implement the gauges capability.

The GAUGES.AUTOMOTIVE_DASHBOARD_APPLICATION subassembly is controlled by the following terminator:

**hardware**  ENGINE_ROTATION_SENSOR

The GAUGES.AUTOMOTIVE_DASHBOARD_APPLICATION subassembly is the client of the following eight servant terminators:

1. **hardware**  ENGINE_TEMPERATURE_GAUGE
2. **hardware**  ENGINE_TEMPERATURE_SENSOR
3. **hardware**  FUEL_GAUGE
4. **hardware**  FUEL_SENSOR
5. **object**    THE_SPEEDOMETER.MODE
6. **hardware**  OIL_GAUGE
7. **hardware**  OIL_PRESSURE_SENSOR
8. **hardware**  TACHOMETER

The `GAUGES.AUTOMOTIVE_DASHBOARD_APPLICATION` subassembly consists of the following eight components:

| | | | | | |
|---|---|---|---|---|---|
| 1. | **object** | THE_ENGINE_ROTATION_SENSOR | Essential | Concurrent | Servant |
| 2. | **object** | THE_ENGINE_TEMPERATURE_GAUGE | Essential | Concurrent | Master |
| 3. | **object** | THE_ENGINE_TEMPERATURE_SENSOR | Essential | Sequential | Servant |
| 4. | **object** | THE_FUEL_GAUGE | Essential | Concurrent | Master |
| 5. | **object** | THE_FUEL_SENSOR | Essential | Sequential | Servant |
| 6. | **object** | THE_OIL_GAUGE | Essential | Concurrent | Master |
| 7. | **object** | THE_OIL_PRESSURE_SENSOR | Essential | Sequential | Servant |
| 8. | **object** | THE_TACHOMETER | Essential | Concurrent | Servant |

The `GAUGES.AUTOMOTIVE_DASHBOARD_APPLICATION` subassembly has the following specification and body:

```
subassembly GAUGES is concurrent
 parent assembly AUTOMOTIVE_DASHBOARD_APPLICATION;
specification
 object  THE_ENGINE_ROTATION_SENSOR      is concurrent;
end;


subassembly GAUGES
body
 object  THE_ENGINE_TEMPERATURE_GAUGE    is concurrent;
 object  THE_ENGINE_TEMPERATURE_SENSOR;
 object  THE_FUEL_GAUGE                  is concurrent;
 object  THE_FUEL_SENSOR;
 object  THE_OIL_GAUGE                   is concurrent;
 object  THE_OIL_PRESSURE_SENSOR;
 object  THE_TACHOMETER                  is concurrent;
end;
```

The `GAUGES.AUTOMOTIVE_DASHBOARD_APPLICATION` subassembly has the general semantic net (GSN) shown in Figure 8-8.

The `GAUGES.AUTOMOTIVE_DASHBOARD_APPLICATION` subassembly has the interaction diagram (ID) shown in Figure 8-9.

The `GAUGES.AUTOMOTIVE_DASHBOARD_APPLICATION` subassembly has the control flow diagram (CFD) shown in Figure 8-10.

## 8.3.1    Object THE_ENGINE_ROTATION_SENSOR

The objective of `THE_ENGINE_ROTATION_SENSOR.GAUGES` object is to model and interface with the hardware `ENGINE_ROTATION_SENSOR` and to send the `UPDATE` message to `THE_TACHOMETER` object.

`THE_ENGINE_ROTATION_SENSOR.GAUGES` object is controlled by the following terminator:

```
hardware  ENGINE_ROTATION_SENSOR
```

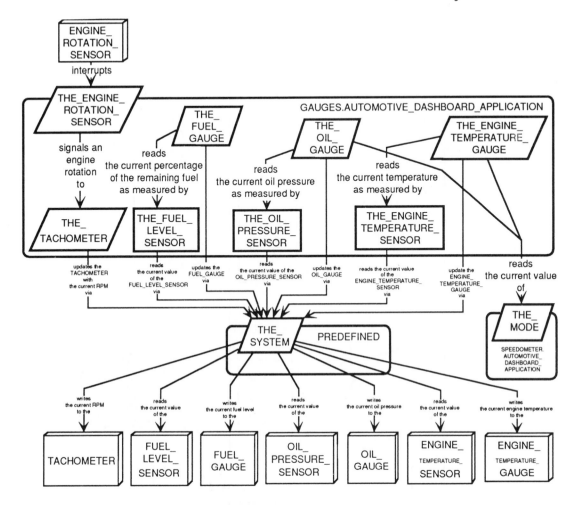

**Figure 8-8: GSN for the** GAUGES **Subassembly**

THE_ENGINE_ROTATION_SENSOR.GAUGES object is the client of the following two servant objects:

1. **object**    **THE_SYSTEM.PREDEFINED**
2. **object**    THE_TACHOMETER

THE_ENGINE_ROTATION_SENSOR.GAUGES object has the following specification and body:

```
object THE_ENGINE_ROTATION_SENSOR is concurrent
 parent subassembly GAUGES;
```

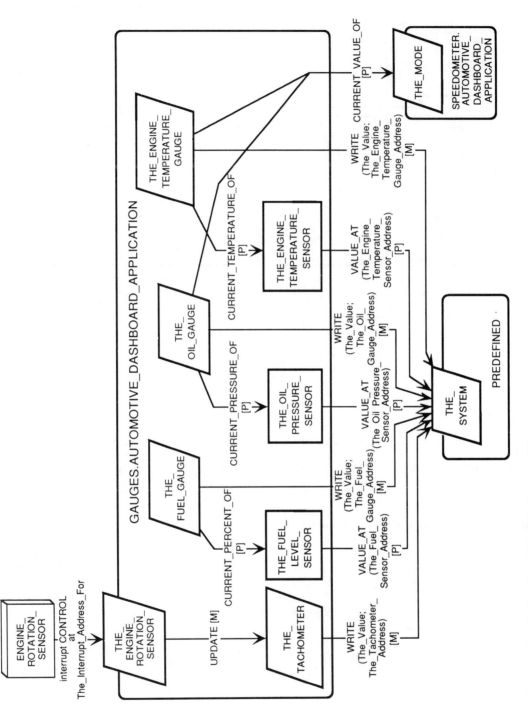

**Figure 8-9: ID for the GAUGES Subassembly**

```
specification
 message CONTROL is asynchronous;
end;

object THE_ENGINE_ROTATION_SENSOR
 needs THE_SYSTEM.PREDEFINED;
body
 constant The_Interrupt_Address_For.THE_ENGINE_ROTATION_SENSOR
                              : Addresses.THE_SYSTEM := TBD;
 modifier operation CONTROL is concurrent;
start
 CONTROL;
end;
```

The objective of the concurrent CONTROL.THE_ENGINE_ROTATION_SENSOR operation is to control the execution of THE_ENGINE_ROTATION_SENSOR object, based on a hardware interrupt at The_Interrupt_Address_For.ENGINE_ROTATION_SENSOR.

```
modifier operation CONTROL is concurrent
 parent object THE_ENGINE_ROTATION_SENSOR;
specification
 message CONTROL is asynchronous;
end;

operation CONTROL
 needs THE_TACHOMETER;
body
statements
 FOREVER : loop
  receive CONTROL when interrupt The_Interrupt_Address_For;
  if -- The ENGINE_ROTATION_SENSOR detects a complete rotation.
   VALUE_AT(The_Interrupt_Address_For.THE_ENGINE_ROTATION_SENSOR).THE_SYSTEM = 1
  then
   UPDATE.THE_TACHOMETER;
  end if;
 end loop FOREVER;
end;
```

## 8.3.2    Object THE_ENGINE_TEMPERATURE_GAUGE

The objective of THE_ENGINE_TEMPERATURE_GAUGE.GAUGES object is to model and control the hardware ENGINE_TEMPERATURE_GAUGE object.

THE_ENGINE_TEMPERATURE_GAUGE.GAUGES object is a master object that depends on the following servant objects:

- class    CLOCKS.PREDEFINED
- object   STRINGS.PREDEFINED
- object   THE_MODE.SPEEDOMETER
- object   THE_ENGINE_TEMPERATURE_SENSOR
- object   THE_SYSTEM.PREDEFINED

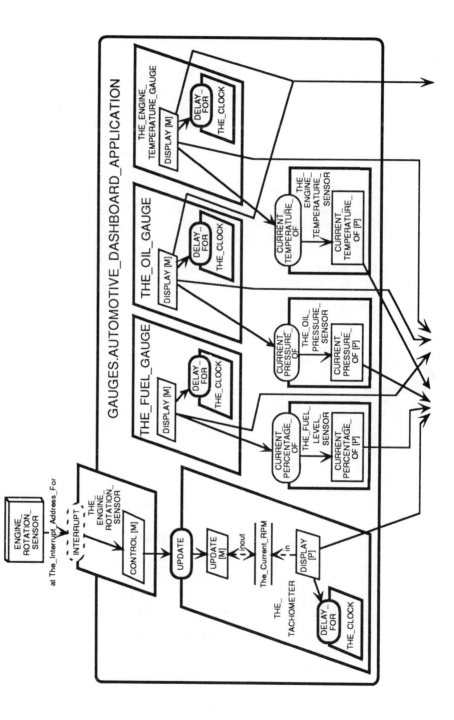

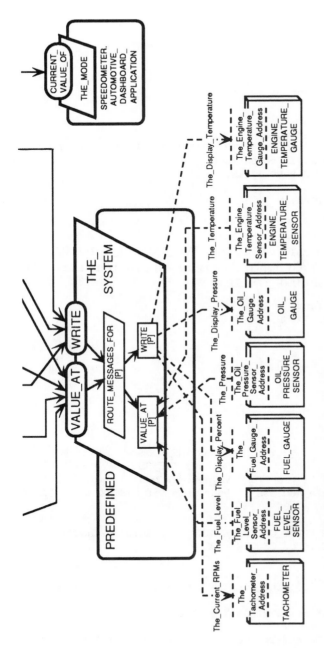

**Figure 8-10: CFD for the GAUGES Subassembly**

THE_ENGINE_TEMPERATURE_GAUGE.GAUGES object has the following specification and body:

```
object THE_ENGINE_TEMPERATURE_GAUGE is concurrent
 parent subassembly GAUGES;
specification
end;

object THE_ENGINE_TEMPERATURE_GAUGE
 needs CLOCKS.PREDEFINED;
body
 variable The_Current_Temperature
                     : Degrees_Celsius.THE_ENGINE_TEMPERATURE_SENSOR;
 modifier operation DISPLAY is concurrent;
 object THE_CLOCK  : CLOCKS.PREDEFINED;
start
 CONSTRUCT(THE_CLOCK).CLOCKS;
 DISPLAY;
end;
```

The objective of the concurrent DISPLAY.THE_ENGINE_TEMPERATURE_ GAUGE operation is to periodically display The_Current_Temperature on the hardware ENGINE_TEMPERATURE_GAUGE.

```
modifier operation DISPLAY is concurrent
 parent object THE_ENGINE_TEMPERATURE_GAUGE;
specification
end;

operation DISPLAY is concurrent
 needs STRINGS.PREDEFINED;
 needs THE_SYSTEM.PREDEFINED;
 needs THE_ENGINE_TEMPERATURE_SENSOR;
 needs THE_MODE.SPEEDOMETER;
body
 variable The_Current_Mode                 : Modes.THE_MODE       := Metric;
 constant The_Delay_Amount                 : Seconds.THE_CLOCK    :=    1.0;
 variable The_Display_Temperature          : Values.STRINGS       :=    " ";
 constant The_Engine_Temperature_Gauge_Address : Addresses.THE_SYSTEM :=    TBD;
statements
 FOREVER : loop
  The_Current_Temperature := CURRENT_VALUE_OF.THE_ENGINE_TEMPERATURE_SENSOR;
  The_Current_Mode        := CURRENT_VALUE_OF.THE_MODE;
  case The_Current_Mode is
   when English then
    The_Fahrenheit_Temperature  := (100 * The_Current_Temperature / 180) + 32;
    The_Display_Temperature     :=
      CONVERT(The_Fahrenheit_Temperature).STRINGS + " F";
   when Metric then
    The_Display_Temperature     := CONVERT(The_Current_Temperature).STRINGS + " C";
  end case;
  WRITE(
   The_Value        := The_Display_Temperature;
```

```
       To_The_Address := The_Engine_Temperature_Gauge_Address).THE_SYSTEM;
      DELAY_FOR(The_Delay_Amount).THE_CLOCK;
    end loop FOREVER;
end;
```

### 8.3.3    Object THE_ENGINE_TEMPERATURE_SENSOR

The objective of THE_ENGINE_TEMPERATURE_SENSOR.GAUGES object is to model and interface with the hardware ENGINE_TEMPERATURE_SENSOR.

THE_ENGINE_TEMPERATURE_SENSOR.GAUGES object is controlled by the following terminator:

**object**   THE_ENGINE_TEMPERATURE_GAUGE

THE_ENGINE_TEMPERATURE_SENSOR.GAUGES object depends on the following terminators:

- **hardware**  ENGINE_TEMPERATURE_SENSOR
- **object**    **THE_SYSTEM.PREDEFINED**
- **object**    **THE-SET-OF-INTEGERS.PREDEFINED**

THE_ENGINE_TEMPERATURE_SENSOR.GAUGES object has the following specification and body:

```
object THE_ENGINE_TEMPERATURE_SENSOR
 parent subassembly GAUGES;
 needs THE_SET_OF_INTEGERS.PREDEFINED;
specification
 type Degrees_Celsius is sub Values.THE_SET_OF_INTEGERS range -50 .. 250;
 message CURRENT_TEMPERATURE_OF return Degrees_Celsius is sequential;
end;
```

```
object THE_ENGINE_TEMPERATURE_SENSOR
 needs THE_SYSTEM.PREDEFINED;
body
 constant The_Engine_Temperature_Sensor_Address
                           : Addresses.THE_SYSTEM        := TBD;
 constant The_Conversion_Factor   : Values.THE_SET_OF_INTEGERS  := TBD;
 variable The_Current_Temperature : Degrees_Celsius       := 0;
 preserver operation CURRENT_TEMPERATURE_OF return Degrees_Celsius;
end;
```

The objective of the CURRENT_TEMPERATURE_OF.THE_ENGINE_TEMPERATURE_SENSOR operation is to return The_Current_Temperature, measured in Degrees_Celsius, based on the value stored in The_Engine_Temperature_Sensor_Address by the hardware ENGINE_TEMPERATURE_SENSOR.

```
preserver operation CURRENT_TEMPERATURE_OF return Degrees_Celsius
 parent object THE_ENGINE_TEMPERATURE_SENSOR;
 specification
 message CURRENT_TEMPERATURE_OF return Degrees_Celsius is sequential;
 end;
```

```
operation CURRENT_TEMPERATURE_OF return Degrees_Celsius
 needs THE_SYSTEM.PREDEFINED;
body
statements
 The_Current_Temperature := The_Conversion_Factor *
  CONVERT(VALUE_AT(The_Engine_Temperature_Sensor_Address).THE_SYSTEM).
  THE_SET_OF_INTEGERS;
 return The_Current_Temperature;
end;
```

## 8.3.4     Object THE_FUEL_GAUGE

The objective of THE_FUEL_GAUGE.GAUGES object is to model and control the hardware FUEL_GAUGE object. This object is similar to THE_ENGINE_TEMPERATURE_GAUGE. See paragraph 8.3.2.

## 8.3.5     Object THE_FUEL_SENSOR

The objective of the THE_FUEL_SENSOR.GAUGES object is to model and interface with the hardware FUEL_SENSOR. This object is similar to THE_ENGINE_TEMPERATURE_SENSOR. See paragraph 8.3.3.

## 8.3.6     Object THE_OIL_GAUGE

The objective of THE_OIL_GAUGE.GAUGES object is to model and control the hardware OIL_GAUGE object. This object is similar to THE_ENGINE_TEMPERATURE_GAUGE. See paragraph 8.3.2.

## 8.3.7     Object THE_OIL_PRESSURE_SENSOR

The objective of THE_OIL_PRESSURE_SENSOR.GAUGES object is to model and interface with the hardware OIL_PRESSURE_SENSOR. This object is similar to THE_ENGINE_TEMPERATURE_SENSOR. See paragraph 8.3.3.

## 8.3.8     Object THE_TACHOMETER

The objective of THE_TACHOMETER.GAUGES object is to model and control the hardware TACHOMETER.

THE_TACHOMETER.GAUGES object is an agent object serving the following client:

**object**   ENGINE_ROTATION_SENSOR

THE_TACHOMETER.GAUGES object is an agent object that depends on the following servant objects:

- **class**    **CLOCKS.PREDEFINED**
- **object**    **THE_SET_OF_REAL_NUMBERS.PREDEFINED**
- **object**    **STRINGS.PREDEFINED**
- **object**    **THE_SYSTEM.PREDEFINED**

The GAUGES.THE_TACHOMETER object has the following specification and body:

```
object THE_TACHOMETER is concurrent
 parent subassembly GAUGES;
specification
 message UPDATE is synchronous;
exception FAILURE_OCCURRED_IN;
end;

object THE_TACHOMETER
 needs CLOCKS.PREDEFINED;
 needs THE_SET_OF_REAL_NUMBERS.PREDEFINED;
body
 type Revolutions_Per_Minute is new Values.THE_SET_OF_REAL_NUMBERS
      delta 3 range 0.000 .. 10,000.000;
 variable The_Current_RPM  : Revolutions_Per_Minute := 0.0;
 preserver operation DISPLAY is concurrent;
 modifier  operation UPDATE  is concurrent;
 object THE_CLOCK           : CLOCKS.PREDEFINED;
start
 CONSTRUCT(THE_CLOCK).CLOCKS;
 DISPLAY;
 FOREVER : loop
  select
   UPDATE;
  end select;
 end loop FOREVER;
end;
```

### 8.3.8.1  Operation DISPLAY.THE_TACHOMETER

The objective of the concurrent DISPLAY.THE_TACHOMETER operation is to periodically display The_Current_RPM upon the hardware TACHOMETER.

```
modifier operation DISPLAY is concurrent
 parent object THE_TACHOMETER;
specification
end;

operation DISPLAY is concurrent
 parent object THE_ENGINE_TEMPERATURE_GAUGE;
 needs STRINGS.PREDEFINED;
 needs THE_SYSTEM.PREDEFINED;
body
 constant The_Delay_Amount  : Seconds.THE_CLOCK      :=    0.5;
```

```
        constant RPM_Address      : Addresses.THE_SYSTEM  :=    TBD;
      statements
       FOREVER : loop
        WRITE(
         The_Value       := CONVERT(The_Current_RPM) + " RPM").STRINGS;
         To_The_Address := RPM_Address).THE_SYSTEM;
         DELAY_FOR(The_Delay_Amount).THE_CLOCK;
        end loop FOREVER;
      end;
```

### 8.3.8.2  Operation UPDATE.THE_TACHOMETER

The objective of the concurrent UPDATE.THE_TACHOMETER operation is to update `The_Current_RPM`, upon receipt of an UPDATE message from THE_ENGINE_ROTATION_SENSOR object.

```
modifier operation UPDATE is concurrent
 parent object THE_TACHOMETER;
specification
 message UPDATE is synchronous;
end;


operation UPDATE
body
statements
 receive UPDATE;
 The_Current_Seconds          := CURRENT_TIME_IN_Seconds.THE_CLOCK;
 Seconds_Since_Last_Update    := The_Current_Seconds - The_Previous_Seconds;
 The_Current_RPM              := 60 / Seconds_Since_Last_Update;
 The_Previous_Seconds         := The_Current_Seconds;
end;
```

## 8.4  SUBASSEMBLY SPEEDOMETER

The objective of the SPEEDOMETER.AUTOMOTIVE_DASHBOARD_APPLICATION child subassembly is to provide THE_SPEEDOMETER.CURRENT_SPEED operation that is required by the stubbed CRUISE_CONTROL.MAINTAIN operation and to provide all capabilities related to THE_SPEEDOMETER.

The SPEEDOMETER.AUTOMOTIVE_DASHBOARD_APPLICATION subassembly is controlled and depended on by the following five terminators:

1. **object**    THE_CRUISE_CONTROL.CRUISE_CONTROL
2. **object**    THE_ENGINE_TEMPERATURE_GAUGE.GAUGES
3. **hardware**  ODOMETER_TRIP_RESET_BUTTON
4. **hardware**  SPEEDOMETER_THE_MODE_BUTTON
5. **hardware**  WHEEL_ROTATION_SENSOR

The SPEEDOMETER.AUTOMOTIVE_DASHBOARD_APPLICATION subassembly controls the following two terminators:

1. **hardware**    ODOMETER
2. **hardware**    SPEEDOMETER

The SPEEDOMETER.AUTOMOTIVE_DASHBOARD_APPLICATION subassembly consists of the following components:

- **object**    THE_MODE                             Essential Concurrent Servant
- **object**    THE_MODE_BUTTON                      Essential Concurrent Master
- **object**    THE_ODOMETER                         Essential Concurrent Agent
- **object**    THE_ODOMETER_TRIP_RESET_BUTTON  Essential Concurrent Master
- **object**    THE_SPEEDOMETER                      Essential Concurrent Agent
- **object**    THE_WHEEL_ROTATION_SENSOR            Essential Concurrent Master

The SPEEDOMETER.AUTOMOTIVE_DASHBOARD_APPLICATION subassembly has the following specification and body:

```
subassembly SPEEDOMETER is concurrent
 parent assembly AUTOMOTIVE_DASHBOARD_APPLICATION;
specification
 object   THE_MODE                             is concurrent;
 object   THE_MODE_BUTTON                      is concurrent;
 object   THE_ODOMETER_TRIP_RESET_BUTTON  is concurrent;
 object   THE_SPEEDOMETER                      is concurrent;
 object   THE_WHEEL_ROTATION_SENSOR            is concurrent;
end;


subassembly SPEEDOMETER
body
 object   THE_ODOMETER                         is concurrent;
end;
```

The SPEEDOMETER.AUTOMOTIVE_DASHBOARD_APPLICATION subassembly has the general semantic net (GSN) shown in Figure 8-11.

The SPEEDOMETER.AUTOMOTIVE_DASHBOARD_APPLICATION subassembly has the interaction diagram (ID) shown in Figure 8-12.

The SPEEDOMETER.AUTOMOTIVE_DASHBOARD_APPLICATION subassembly has the control flow diagram (CFD) shown in Figure 8-13.

## 8.4.1    Object THE_MODE

The objective of THE_MODE.SPEEDOMETER object is to model the mode (i.e., metric or English system) of THE_ODOMETER and THE_SPEEDOMETER objects.

THE_MODE.SPEEDOMETER object is a servant object serving the following clients:

- **object**    THE_ENGINE_TEMPERATURE_GAUGE.GAUGES
- **object**    THE_MODE_BUTTON
- **object**    THE_ODOMETER
- **object**    THE_OIL_GAUGE.GAUGES
- **object**    THE_SPEEDOMETER

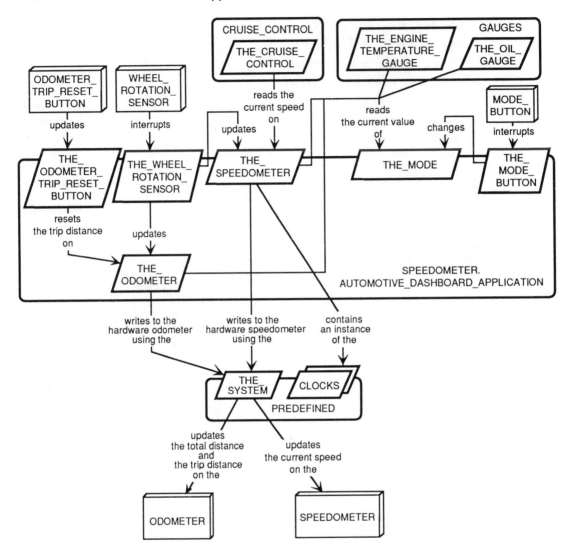

**Figure 8-11: GSN for the** SPEEDOMETER **Subassembly**

THE_MODE . SPEEDOMETER object has the following specification and body:

```
object THE_MODE is concurrent
 parent subassembly SPEEDOMETER;
specification
 type Modes is (English,Metric);
 message CHANGE                          is synchronous;
 message CURRENT_VALUE_OF return Modes   is synchronous;
 exception CONSTRAINT_ERROR;
end;
```

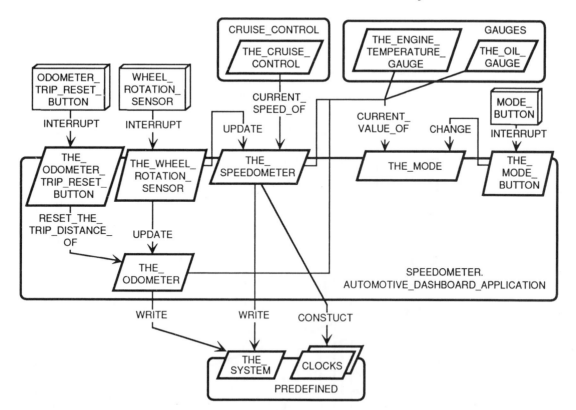

**Figure 8-12: ID for the** SPEEDOMETER **Subassembly**

```
object THE_MODE
body
 variable The_Current_Mode : Modes := Metric;
 modifier  operation   CHANGE;
 preserver operation   CURRENT_VALUE_OF    return Modes;
 preserver operation   ROUTE_MESSAGES_FOR is concurrent;
start
 ROUTE_MESSAGES_FOR;
end;
```

### 8.4.1.1 Operation CHANGE.THE_MODE

The objective of the concurrent CHANGE.THE_MODE operation is to change The_Current_Mode from English to Metric and from Metric to English, on receipt of a CHANGE message from THE_MODE_BUTTON object.

```
modifier operation CHANGE
 parent object THE_MODE;
specification
end;
```

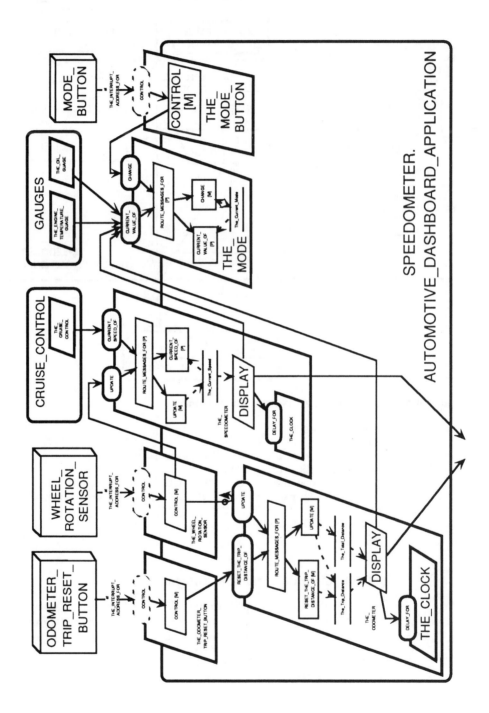

SPEEDOMETER.
AUTOMOTIVE_DASHBOARD_APPLICATION

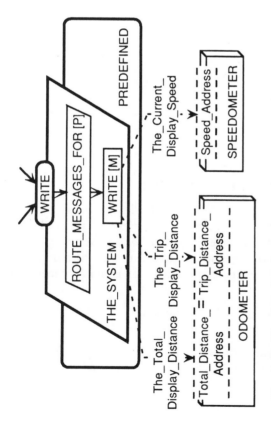

**Figure 8-13: CFD for the** SPEEDOMETER **Subassembly**

441

```
operation CHANGE
body
statements
 case The_Current_Mode is
  when English then
   The_Current_Mode := Metric;
  when Metric  then
   The_Current_Mode := English;
  when others  then
  raise CONSTRAINT_ERROR;
 end case;
end;
```

### 8.4.1.2  Operation CURRENT_VALUE_OF.THE_MODE

The objective of the concurrent CURRENT_VALUE_OF.THE_MODE operation is to return the current value of The_Current_Mode, on receipt of a CURRENT_VALUE_OF message from either THE_ODOMETER or THE_SPEEDOMETER object.

```
preserver operation CURRENT_VALUE_OF return Modes
 parent object THE_MODE;
specification
end;

operation CURRENT_VALUE_OF return Modes
 parent object THE_MODE;
body
statements
 return The_Current_Mode;
end;
```

### 8.4.1.3  Operation ROUTE_MESSAGES_FOR.THE_MODE

The objective of the concurrent ROUTE_MESSAGES_FOR.THE_MODE operation is to route messages to their proper operations in a manner that ensures that only one message at a time is received and that it is completely handled before the next message is received. The ultimate objective of this operation is to ensure that the abstraction is not violated by the corruption of its attributes, due to an interleaving of messages in a concurrent environment.

```
preserver operation ROUTE_MESSAGES_FOR is concurrent
 parent object THE_MODE;
specification
  message CHANGE           is synchronous;
 message CURRENT_VALUE_OF  is synchronous;
end;

operation ROUTE_MESSAGES_FOR
body
statements
 FOREVER : loop
```

```
select
 receive CHANGE;
 CHANGE;
or
 receive CURRENT_VALUE_OF return Modes;
 CURRENT_VALUE_OF return Modes;
 end select;
 end loop FOREVER;
end;
```

## 8.4.2  Object THE_MODE_BUTTON

The objective of THE_MODE_BUTTON.SPEEDOMETER object is to model and interface with the hardware MODE_BUTTON.

THE_MODE_BUTTON.SPEEDOMETER object is controlled by the following terminator:

**hardware**    MODE_BUTTON

THE_MODE_BUTTON.SPEEDOMETER object depends on the following two terminators:

1. **object**    THE_MODE
2. **object**    **THE_SYSTEM.PREDEFINED**

THE_MODE_BUTTON.SPEEDOMETER object has the following specification and body:

```
object THE_MODE_BUTTON is concurrent
 parent subassembly SPEEDOMETER;
specification
 message CONTROL is asynchronous;
end;
```

```
object THE_MODE_BUTTON
 needs THE_SYSTEM.PREDEFINED;
body THE_MODE_BUTTON
 constant The_Interrupt_Address_For.THE_MODE_BUTTON  :
  Addresses.THE_SYSTEM
                                                 := TBD;
 modifier operation CONTROL is concurrent;
start
 CONTROL;
end;
```

The objective of the concurrent CONTROL.THE_MODE_BUTTON operation is to control the execution of THE_MODE_BUTTON object, based on a hardware interrupt at The_Interrupt_Address_For.THE_MODE_BUTTON.

```
modifier operation CONTROL is concurrent
 parent object THE_MODE_BUTTON;
specification
```

```
  message CONTROL is asynchronous;
end;

operation CONTROL is concurrent
 needs MODE;
body
statements
 FOREVER : loop
  receive CONTROL when interrupt The_Interrupt_Address_For;
  case VALUE_AT(The_Interrupt_Address_For.THE_MODE_BUTTON).THE_SYSTEM
  is
   when 0 then -- The MODE_BUTTON is released.
    null;
   when 1 then -- The MODE_BUTTON is pressed.
    CHANGE.THE_MODE;
  end case;
 end loop FOREVER;
end;
```

## 8.4.3    Object THE_ODOMETER

The objective of THE_ODOMETER.SPEEDOMETER object is to model and control the hardware ODOMETER object.

THE_ODOMETER.SPEEDOMETER object is an agent object serving the following clients:

- **object**    THE_ODOMETER_TRIP_RESET_BUTTON
- **object**    THE_WHEEL_ROTATION_SENSOR

THE_ODOMETER.SPEEDOMETER object is an agent object that depends on the following servant objects:

- **class**    **CLOCKS.PREDEFINED**
- **object**    **THE_SET_OF_REAL_NUMBERS.PREDEFINED**
- **object**    **STRINGS.PREDEFINED**
- **object**    **THE_SYSTEM.PREDEFINED**
- **object**    THE_MODE

THE_ODOMETER.SPEEDOMETER object has the following specification and body:

```
object THE_ODOMETER is concurrent
 parent subassembly SPEEDOMETER;
specification
 message RESET_THE_TRIP_DISTANCE_ON  is synchronous;
 message UPDATE                      is synchronous;
end;

object THE_ODOMETER
 needs THE_SET_OF_REAL_NUMBERS.PREDEFINED;
body
```

```
              type Meters is new Values.THE_SET_OF_REAL_NUMBERS
                                 delta 0.001
                                 range 0.000 .. 999,999,999.999;
         variable   The_Total_Distance        : Meters := 0.0;
         variable   The_Trip_Distance         : Meters := 0.0;
         constant   The_Wheel_Circumference   : Meters := TBD;
         modifier   operation DISPLAY                is concurrent;
         modifier   operation RESET_THE_TRIP_DISTANCE_ON;
         modifier   operation ROUTE_MESSAGES_FOR   is concurrent;
         modifier   operation UPDATE;
         object THE_CLOCK                       : CLOCKS.PREDEFINED;
         start
         CONSTRUCT(THE_CLOCK).CLOCKS;
         DISPLAY;
         ROUTE_MESSAGES_FOR;
         end;
```

### 8.4.3.1  Operation DISPLAY.THE_ODOMETER

The objective of the concurrent DISPLAY.THE_ODOMETER operation is to periodically display The_Trip_Distance and The_Total_Distance on the hardware ODOMETER.

```
modifier operation DISPLAY is concurrent
 parent object THE_ODOMETER;
specification
end;

operation DISPLAY
 needs STRINGS.PREDEFINED;
 needs THE_SYSTEM.PREDEFINED;
body
 variable The_Current_Mode          : Modes.THE_MODE       :=    Metric;
 variable The_Total_Display_Distance : Values.STRINGS       :=    " ";
 variable The_Trip_Display_Distance  : Values.STRINGS       :=    " ";
 constant Meters_Per_Mile           : Values.THE_SET_OF_REAL_NUMBERS
                                                            := 1609.3472;
 constant The_Delay_Amount          : Seconds.THE_CLOCK     :=    0.5;
 constant Total_Distance_Address    : Addresses.THE_SYSTEM  :=    TBD;
 constant Trip_Distance_Address     : Addresses.THE_SYSTEM  :=    TBD;
statements
 FOREVER : loop
  The_Current_Mode := CURRENT_VALUE_OF.THE_MODE;
  case The_Current_Mode is
   when English then
    The_Total_Display_Distance :=
            (CONVERT(The_Total_Distance / Meters_Per_Mile).STRINGS /
            Meters_Per_Mile) + " MI";
    The_Trip_Display_Distance  :=
            (CONVERT(The_Trip_Distance / Meters_Per_Mile).STRINGS /
            Meters_Per_Mile) + " MI";
   when Metric then
```

```
     The_Total_Display_Distance := CONVERT(The_Total_Distance).STRINGS + " KM";
     The_Trip_Display_Distance  := CONVERT(The_Trip_Distance).STRINGS  + " KM";
   end case;
   WRITE(
    The_Value       := The_Total_Display_Distance;
    To_The_Address := Total_Distance_Address).THE_SYSTEM;
   WRITE(
    The_Value       := The_Trip_Display_Distance;
    To_The_Address := Trip_Distance_Address).THE_SYSTEM;
   DELAY_FOR(The_Delay_Amount).THE_CLOCK;
  end loop FOREVER;
end;
```

### 8.4.3.2 Operation RESET_THE_TRIP_DISTANCE_ON.THE_ODOMETER

The objective of the RESET_THE_TRIP_DISTANCE_ON.THE_ODOMETER operation is to reset The_Trip_Distance to 0.0 on receipt of a RESET_THE_TRIP_DISTANCE_ON message from THE_ODOMETER_TRIP_RESET_BUTTON object.

```
modifier operation RESET_THE_TRIP_DISTANCE_ON
 parent object THE_ODOMETER;
specification
end;


operation RESET_THE_TRIP_DISTANCE_ON
body
statements
 The_Trip_Distance := 0.0;
end;
```

### 8.4.3.3 Operation ROUTE_MESSAGES_FOR.THE_ODOMETER

The objective of the concurrent ROUTE_MESSAGES_FOR.THE_ODOMETER operation is to route messages to their proper operations in a manner that ensures that only one message at a time is received and that it is completely handled before the next message is received. The ultimate objective of this operation is to ensure that the abstraction is not violated by the corruption of its attributes, due to an interleaving of messages in a concurrent environment.

```
preserver operation ROUTE_MESSAGES_FOR is concurrent
 parent object THE_ODOMETER;
specification
 message CHANGE            is synchronous;
 message CURRENT_VALUE_OF  is synchronous;
end;


operation ROUTE_MESSAGES_FOR
body
statements
```

```
FOREVER : loop
 select
  receive RESET_THE_TRIP_DISTANCE_ON;
  RESET_THE_TRIP_DISTANCE_ON;
 or
  receive UPDATE;
  UPDATE;
 end select;
 end loop FOREVER;
end;
```

### 8.4.3.4  Operation UPDATE.THE_ODOMETER

The objective of the UPDATE.THE_ODOMETER operation is to add The_Wheel_Circumference to The_Trip_Distance and The_Total_Distance, on receipt of an UPDATE message from THE_WHEEL_ROTATION_SENSOR object.

```
modifier operation UPDATE
 parent object THE_ODOMETER;
specification
end;

operation UPDATE
body
statements
 The_Total_Distance := The_Total_Distance + The_Wheel_Circumference;
 The_Trip_Distance  := The_Trip_Distance  + The_Wheel_Circumference;
end;
```

## 8.4.4  Object THE_ODOMETER_TRIP_RESET_BUTTON

The objective of THE_ODOMETER_TRIP_RESET_BUTTON.SPEEDOMETER object is to model and interface with the hardware ODOMETER_TRIP_RESET_BUTTON. The specification and design of this object is analogous to that of THE_MODE object.

## 8.4.5  Object THE_SPEEDOMETER

The objective of THE_SPEEDOMETER.SPEEDOMETER object is to model and control the hardware SPEEDOMETER object.

THE_SPEEDOMETER.SPEEDOMETER object is an agent object serving the following clients:

- **object**   THE_CRUISE_CONTROL.CRUISE_CONTROL
- **object**   THE_WHEEL_ROTATION_SENSOR

THE_SPEEDOMETER.SPEEDOMETER object is an agent object that depends on the following servant class and objects:

- **class**   CLOCKS.PREDEFINED

- **object** **THE_SET_OF_INTEGERS.PREDEFINED**
- **object** **THE_SET_OF_REAL_NUMBERS.PREDEFINED**
- **object** **STRINGS.PREDEFINED**
- **object** **THE_SYSTEM.PREDEFINED**
- **object** THE_MODE

THE_SPEEDOMETER.SPEEDOMETER concurrent agent object has the following specification and body:

```
object THE_SPEEDOMETER is concurrent
 parent subassembly SPEEDOMETER;
 needs THE_SET_OF_INTEGERS.PREDEFINED;
 needs THE_SET_OF_REAL_NUMBERS.PREDEFINED;
specification
 type Kilometers_Per_Hour is new Values.THE_SET_OF_INTEGERS  range 0 .. 500;
 message CURRENT_SPEED_OF return Kilometers_Per_Hour  is synchronous;
 message UPDATE                                        is synchronous;
 exception FAILURE_OCCURRED_IN;
end;


object THE_SPEEDOMETER
 needs CLOCKS.PREDEFINED;
body
 type Meters is new Values.THE_SET_OF_REAL_NUMBERS
                              range 0.0 .. 999,999,999.9;
 variable The_Current_Speed         : Kilometers_Per_Hour  := 0;
 constant The_Wheel_Circumference   : Meters               := TBD;
 preserver operation CURRENT_SPEED_OF return Kilometers_Per_Hour;
 modifier  operation DISPLAY             is concurrent;
 modifier  operation ROUTE_MESSAGES_FOR is concurrent;
 modifier  operation UPDATE;
 object THE_CLOCK : CLOCKS;
start
 CONSTRUCT(THE_CLOCK).CLOCKS;
 DISPLAY;
 ROUTE_MESSAGES_FOR;
end;
```

### 8.4.5.1  Operation CURRENT_SPEED_OF.THE_SPEEDOMETER

The objective of the CURRENT_SPEED_OF.THE_SPEEDOMETER operation is to return The_Current_Speed in Kilometers_Per_Hour, on receipt of a CURRENT_SPEED_OF message from THE_CRUISE_CONTROL.CRUISE_CONTROL object.

```
preserver operation CURRENT_SPEED_OF return Kilometers_Per_Hour
 parent object THE_SPEEDOMETER;
specification
end;


operation CURRENT_SPEED_OF return Kilometers_Per_Hour
```

```
body
statements
 return The_Current_Speed;
end;
```

### 8.4.5.2  Operation `DISPLAY.THE_SPEEDOMETER`

The objective of the concurrent `DISPLAY.THE_SPEEDOMETER` operation is to periodically display `The_Current_Mode` and `The_Current_Speed` on the hardware SPEEDOMETER.

```
modifier operation DISPLAY is concurrent
 parent object THE_SPEEDOMETER;
specification
end;


operation DISPLAY is concurrent
 needs STRINGS.PREDEFINED;
 needs THE_SYSTEM.PREDEFINED;
body
 variable The_Current_Mode    : Modes.THE_MODE                   :=    Metric;
 variable The_Display_Speed    : Values.STRINGS                   :=    " ";
 constant Kilometers_Per_Mile  : Values.THE_SET_OF_REAL_NUMBERS   :=    1.609;
 constant The_Delay_Amount     : Seconds.THE_CLOCK                :=    0.5;
 constant Speed_Address        : Addresses.THE_SYSTEM             :=    TBD;
statements
 FOREVER : loop
  The_Current_Mode := CURRENT_VALUE_OF.THE_MODE;
  case The_Current_Mode is
   when English then
   The_Display_Speed :=
    CONVERT(The_Current_Speed / Kilometers_Per_Mile).STRINGS + " MPH";
   when Metric then
   The_Display_Speed := CONVERT(The_Current_Speed).STRINGS + " KPH";
  end case;
  WRITE(
   To_Address := SPEED_ADDRESS;
   The_Value  := The_Display_Speed).THE_SYSTEM;
  DELAY_FOR(The_Delay_Amount).THE_CLOCK;
 end loop FOREVER;
end;
```

### 8.4.5.3  Operation `ROUTE_MESSAGES_FOR.THE_SPEEDOMETER`

The objective of the concurrent `ROUTE_MESSAGES_FOR.THE_SPEEDOMETER` operation is to route messages to their proper operations in a manner that ensures that only one message at a time is received and that it is completely handled before the next message is received. The ultimate objective of this operation is to ensure that the abstraction is not violated by the corruption of its attributes, due to an interleaving of messages in a concurrent environment.

```
          preserver operation ROUTE_MESSAGES_FOR is concurrent
           parent object THE_SPEEDOMETER;
          specification
           message CHANGE              is synchronous;
           message CURRENT_VALUE_OF    is synchronous;
          end;


          operation ROUTE_MESSAGES_FOR
          body
          statements
           FOREVER : loop
            select
             receive CURRENT_SPEED_OF return Kilometers_Per_Hour;
             CURRENT_SPEED_OF           return Kilometers_Per_Hour;
            or
             receive UPDATE;
             UPDATE;
            end select;
           end loop FOREVER;
          end;
```

### 8.4.5.4  Operation UPDATE.THE_SPEEDOMETER

The objective of the UPDATE.THE_SPEEDOMETER operation is to add The_Wheel_Circumference to The_Trip_Distance and The_Total_Distance, on receipt of an UPDATE message from THE_WHEEL_ROTATION_SENSOR object.

```
modifier operation UPDATE
 parent object THE_SPEEDOMETER;
specification
end;

operation UPDATE
body
statements
 The_Current_Seconds         := CURRENT_TIME_IN_SECONDS.THE_CLOCK;
 Seconds_Since_Last_Update   := The_Current_Seconds -- The_Previous_Seconds;
 The_Current_Speed           := The_Wheel_Circumference /
                                (1000 * Seconds_Since_Last_Update);
 The_Previous_Seconds        := The_Current_Seconds;
end;
```

## 8.4.6     Object THE_WHEEL_ROTATION_SENSOR

The objective of THE_WHEEL_ROTATION_SENSOR.SPEEDOMETER object is to model and interface with the hardware WHEEL_ROTATION_SENSOR and to send the UPDATE message to THE_ODOMETER and THE_SPEEDOMETER objects.

THE_WHEEL_ROTATION_SENSOR.SPEEDOMETER object is controlled by the following terminator:

```
hardware  WHEEL_ROTATION_SENSOR
```

THE_WHEEL_ROTATION_SENSOR.SPEEDOMETER object is the client the following three servant objects:

- **object**    **THE_SYSTEM.PREDEFINED**
- **object**    THE_ODOMETER
- **object**    THE_SPEEDMETER

THE_WHEEL_ROTATION_SENSOR.SPEEDOMETER object has the following specification and body:

```
object THE_WHEEL_ROTATION_SENSOR is concurrent
 parent subassembly SPEEDOMETER;
specification
 message CONTROL is asynchronous;
end;

object THE_WHEEL_ROTATION_SENSOR
 needs THE_SYSTEM.PREDEFINED;
body
 constant The_Interrupt_Address_For : Addresses.THE_SYSTEM := TBD;
 modifier operation CONTROL is concurrent;
start
 CONTROL;
end;
```

The objective of the concurrent CONTROL.THE_WHEEL_ROTATION_SENSOR operation is to control the execution of THE_WHEEL_ROTATION_SENSOR object, based on a hardware interrupt at The_Interrupt_Address_For. THE_WHEEL_ROTATION_SENSOR.

```
modifier operation CONTROL is concurrent
  parent object THE_WHEEL_ROTATION_SENSOR;
specification
  message CONTROL is asynchronous;
end;

operation CONTROL
  needs THE_ODOMETER;
  needs THE_SPEEDOMETER;
body
statements
  FOREVER : loop
    receive CONTROL when interrupt The_Interrupt_Address_For;
    if -- The WHEEL_ROTATION_SENSOR detects a complete rotation.
      VALUE_AT(The_Interrupt_Address_For.THE_WHEEL_ROTATION_SENSOR).THE_SYSTEM =
      1
    then
      UPDATE.THE_ODOMETER;
      UPDATE.THE_SPEEDOMETER;
    end if;
  end loop FOREVER;
end;
```

# Chapter 9

# Development Cycles and Major Reviews

## 9.1 SOFTWARE DEVELOPMENT CYCLES

The software development cycle is primarily determined by the overall development process, which is determined by the amount of global recursion, the number and type of subassemblies, and the use of multiple **builds** and releases. The amount of global recursion used on a project could be anywhere on the spectrum from not using any global recursion at all to doing the entire software development in a globally recursive manner. The spectrum thus ranges from the extremely conservative, with few impacts on management to the avant garde with many major impacts on management. The choice of where the project lies on this spectrum is critical because this choice determines the consequent development cycle and has major effects on risk management, developer productivity, schedule, cost, the number and nature of *formal* (i.e., customer-witnessed) reviews, and the amount of required tailoring to customer standards (e.g., *Defense System Software Development* [DOD 1986]). Figure 9-1 shows how risk and productivity appear to vary inversely as a function of the amount of global recursion and object orientation on a project.

Global recursion implies parallel subassembly development, and different subassemblies take different amounts of time to develop, depending on their size and complexity. There is a method-specific average development time of approximately 3 to 8 weeks per subassembly. Different subassemblies, done by different teams, are therefore developed relatively independently and at different rates. See Figure 9-2: Globally Recursive Object-Oriented Development. Figure 9-2 is sometimes called a "species chart" because subassemblies come into existence and are completed in a manner reminiscent of the evolution and extinction of species according to the

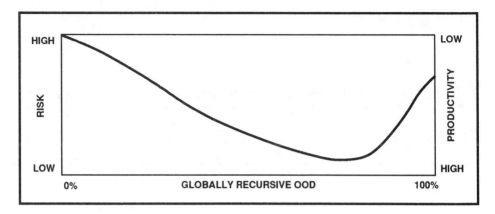

**Figure 9-1: Risk and Productivity as a Function of Global Recursion**

theory of punctuated equilibrium.[1] The small isolated boxes are not drawn to scale and represent the integration and the integration testing of the completed subassemblies into the parent subassembly and the growing assembly.

When using global recursion, software development activities exhibit massive overlap. This is because subassembly development does not stay in phase and because each subassembly passes through its own brief waterfall development cycle, often including all activities from software requirements analysis through integration. This overlap is not totally due to the globally recursive nature of OOD. Some overlap occurs on projects using languages (e.g., Eiffel, Ada) for both design and coding. For example, when Ada is used as both the design and the coding language, the development of library units (e.g., package specifications) becomes both a preliminary design and a coding activity. Developing compilable program design language (PDL) for operation subunits is both an implementation design and a programming activity. See Figure 9-3: Overlap of Development Activities.

Developers of military software often have the misconception that current military standards (e.g., DOD-STD-2167A) require the use of the waterfall development cycle and therefore prohibit the use of globally recursive OOD development cycles. For example, Figure 9-4 shows the waterfall development cycle provided as an example in *Defense System Software Development* [DOD 1986]. This was certainly true of the original, now superseded DOD-STD-2167 published in 1985. Section 4.1 ("Software Development Cycle") of that document required the classic waterfall

---

[1] Punctuated equilibrium is an evolutionary theory popularized by biologist Stephen J. Gould, which states that most species evolve into existence quite rapidly on a geologic time scale and then tend to remain little changed over their existence until they rapidly go extinct (i.e., a stable equilibrium punctuated by rapid species formation and extinction). This can be compared with the more traditional neo-Darwinism, which states that most species tend to evolve at a relatively slow and steady rate.

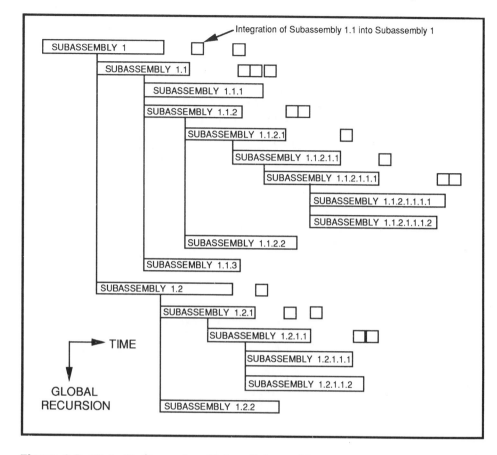

**Figure 9-2: Globally Recursive Object-Oriented Development**

development cycle when it stated that "The contractor shall implement a software development cycle that includes the following six phases: ..."

The six phases indicated were those of the classic waterfall life-cycle model. This requirement for a specific development cycle was replaced in DOD-STD-2167A with Section 4.1.1 ("Software Development Process"), which instead states that

> "The contractor shall implement a process for managing the development of the deliverable software. The contractor's software development process for each CSCI shall be compatible with the contract schedule for formal reviews and audits. The software development process shall include the following major activities, which may overlap and may be applied iteratively or recursively: ..."

"Process" replaced "Cycle," and "activities" replaced "phases," specifically to remove the requirement for the waterfall development cycle. This was specifically done to permit the globally recursive development cycle of OOD. The DOD-STD-2167A requirement is more general, in that the classic waterfall life-cycle model is

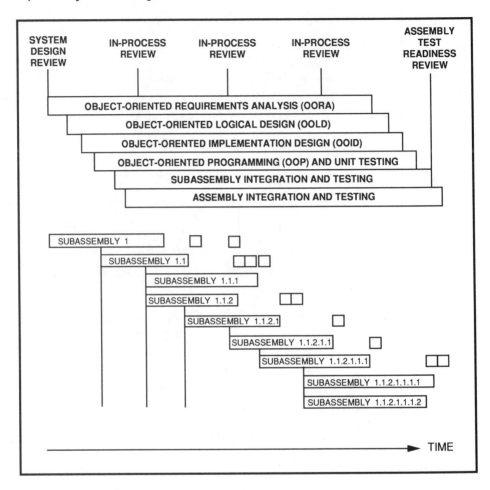

**Figure 9-3: Overlap of Development Activities**

one possible application of the requirement. The word "recursively" was added specifically to permit the use of OOD methods. Although the graphics of DOD-STD-2167A still imply a classic waterfall development cycle, these graphics are not legally binding and include the word "example." These diagrams may (and should) be removed in DOD-STD-2167B when it is issued because many people still misinterpret them as a requirement and not an example.

OOD development cycles differ radically from the traditional waterfall model, primarily due to the globally recursive nature of OOD and the aforementioned overlap. There is a wide range of options available, depending on the amount of global recursion used.

The most conservative approach to object-oriented application development would be to *not* use global recursion at all. Many initial OOD projects officially used

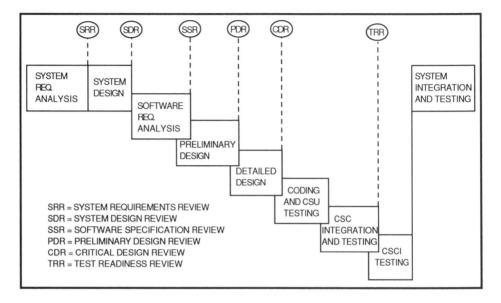

SRR = SYSTEM REQUIREMENTS REVIEW
SDR = SYSTEM DESIGN REVIEW
SSR = SOFTWARE SPECIFICATION REVIEW
PDR = PRELIMINARY DESIGN REVIEW
CDR = CRITICAL DESIGN REVIEW
TRR = TEST READINESS REVIEW

**Figure 9-4: DOD-STD-2167A's Example Waterfall Development Cycle**

this process and restricted OOD to the locally recursive design phase of the classic waterfall life cycle. This was done for numerous valid and invalid reasons, including inappropriate contractual constraints, such as adherence to obsolete military standards (e.g., DOD-STD-2167); ignorance of the negative impacts on management; the early lack of production-quality object-oriented requirements analysis (OORA) methods; and the natural desire to minimize risks by minimizing change. Unfortunately, this approach also prevented management from actualizing many OOD benefits in quality and productivity because it ignored global recursion's support for incremental design verification and validation, as well as for maximization of parallel development. By retaining the obsolete waterfall development cycle, this approach in fact decreases the quality and increases the schedule length, costs, and risks. It should not be used unless required by contract and tailoring of the relevant standards is impractical. See Figure 9-5: Object-Oriented Design Using the Traditional Waterfall Development Cycle.

A slightly less conservative and certainly more realistic approach was to recognize that any initial functional requirements analysis phase was likely to be incomplete and inappropriate as the predecessor for an object-oriented design phase. First of all, by ignoring objects and concentrating on only functional abstractions, a functional requirements analysis phase would not result in the definition and analysis of all requirements associated with essential classes, objects, attributes, operations, and exceptions. Also, because the resulting requirements would be organized along functional lines, they would not map well into an object-oriented design and made the tracing of the requirements into the design very difficult. It would thus be difficult to allocate requirements to the teams that would develop the object-oriented subas-

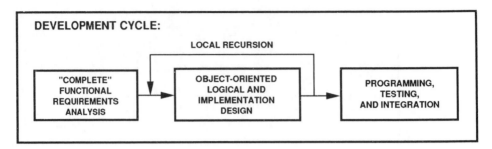

**Figure 9-5: Object-Oriented Design Using the Traditional Waterfall Development Cycle**

semblies. Therefore, those initial projects officially using the previous waterfall approach often found themselves performing a certain amount of object-oriented requirements analysis *after* requirements analysis was officially completed and the resulting software requirements baselined. Although the identification and analysis of essential classes, objects, and their resources is clearly part of requirements analysis, this further requirements analysis was often considered part of "preliminary design" because of contractual and schedule constraints. This approach also decreases software quality and increases the schedule length, costs, and risks and should not be used unless required by contract. See Figure 9-6: OOD as Often Initially Performed.

Because the Ada and Eiffel programming languages are also good design languages, it is impossible to clearly draw the line between design and coding on projects using these languages. On such projects, one naturally tends to include coding in the globally recursive OOD process. This improved approach allows the incremental verification of a compilable, executable, and even testable design and was especially popular in the Ada community prior to the advent of good OORA methods. See Figure 9-7: OOD on Some Early Projects.

With the advent of production-quality OORA methods, a new approach became possible. Although projects unfortunately still tended to use locally recursive functional-decomposition methods (e.g., Structured Analysis) during an initial software

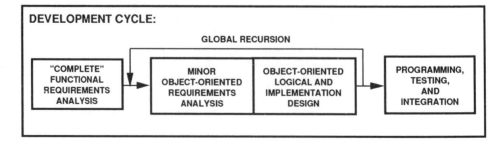

**Figure 9-6: OOD as Often Initially Performed**

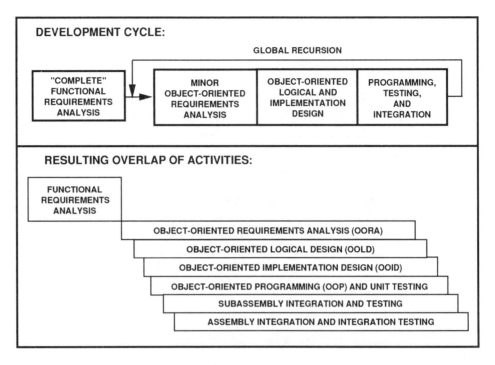

**Figure 9-7: OOD on Some Early Ada Projects**

requirements analysis phase, they then followed this with a locally recursive object-oriented analysis step, in order to (1) properly identify essential classes and objects and (2) ease the previously difficult transition to an object-oriented design. This was a significant improvement but resulted in essentially performing requirements analysis twice, once inappropriately and once correctly. Often, the initial functional requirements inhibited the following development of clean object-oriented requirements and became a significant part of the final requirements specification, especially on projects with tight schedules. Other problems were the determination of the official set of requirements to be baselined and the subsequent configuration-management headaches. See Figure 9-8: Doing Requirements Analysis Twice.

A significantly better approach would be only to perform software requirements analysis (i.e., OORA) once and to do it in a consistent object-oriented manner. Because of contractual issues and constraints, OORA is often performed in a locally recursive manner during a software requirements analysis phase prior to the initiation of globally recursive OOD. This approach minimizes risk for managers new to OOD and also comes close to maximizing quality and productivity while minimizing cost. Its only major limitation is that the requirements must be completed prior to initiating global recursion. They therefore cannot be incrementally validated as they are developed. This approach is therefore not optimal for projects (e.g., research and development) where the customers or users are not sure of their requirements/needs,

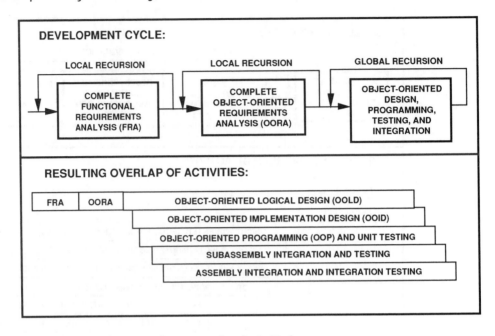

**Figure 9-8: Doing Requirements Analysis Twice**

where the system requirements are not well defined, or where the developer has limited experience with object-oriented capabilities and designs in the application domain. See Figure 9-9: Locally Recursive OORA Phase.

A somewhat better approach would be to perform only a small amount of locally recursive OORA during the software requirements analysis phase and to perform the remainder as part of a globally recursive OOD step. While allowing for the baselining of initial requirements, this approach would decrease both the costs and the schedule length while increasing quality and productivity. This approach assumes either well-specified system requirements or a cooperative contractual approach to the incremental development of software requirements. This approach is therefore not recommended for a full-scale development project with a conservative customer and project management. See Figure 9-10: Minimizing Locally Recursive OORA.

The most avant garde approach is naturally to perform all of software development in a globally recursive manner. Although it minimizes costs and schedule length while maximizing quality and productivity, this approach involves significant risks, primarily due to its major impact on project management. Because the software requirements are not completely identified and analyzed until near the end of the project, such a project is very difficult to control, particularly in terms of costs. Because errors in requirements are identified to the customer in an incremental manner, it is difficult to prevent the customer from "goldplating" the requirements after the contract is let and the price is fixed. For this reason, a fixed-price contract

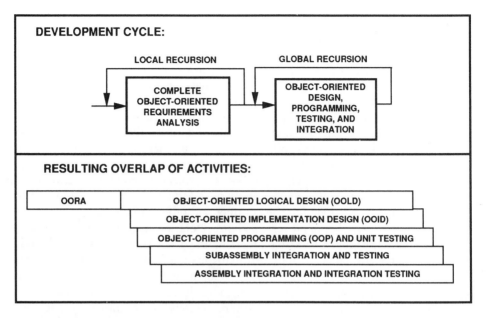

Figure 9-9: Locally Recursive OORA Phase

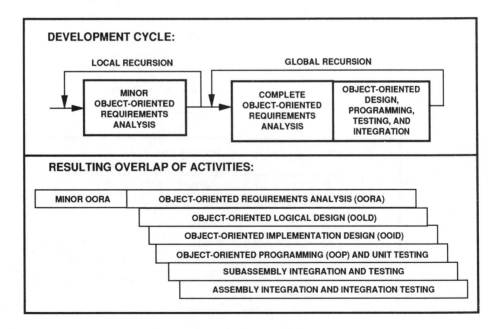

Figure 9-10: Minimizing Locally Recursive OORA

is not appropriate for this approach. Scheduling is similarly more difficult, especially considering prior management experience with projects using the waterfall development cycle. Therefore, this approach is recommended for research projects or for in-house projects where the developer and customer are the same and have adequate experience and training in the management of globally recursive projects. See Figure 9-11: Maximizing Global Recursion.

In addition to determining where on the global-recursion spectrum the project should lie, management must also determine the amount of object-oriented domain analysis (OODA) and rapid prototyping that should precede OOD and also whether global recusion will take place in the context of multiple builds and/or releases. All of these factors greatly influence project scheduling, staffing curves, training requirements, the number and type of formal reviews, the effort and cost models to be used, and therefore the contract and project planning.

Another approach maximizes iteration instead of global recursion. It is popular in the Object-Oriented Programming (OOP) community and should not be mistaken for the previous approach. This approach maximizes iteration rather than global recursion. The process and development cycle are similar, but the approach and the impacts on management are radically different. This approach starts by creating a rapid prototype of the software. This is then iterated until it meets the customer requirements (or until the project runs out of money and schedule, which is highly likely). Because no complex software is ever perfect (what human product ever is?),

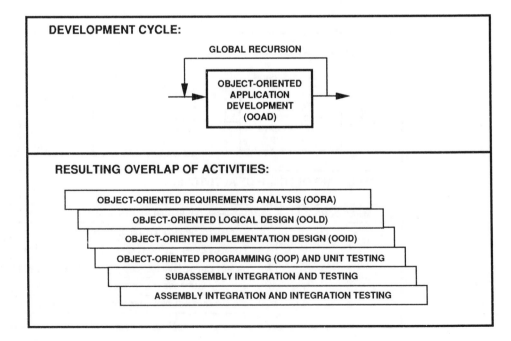

**Figure 9-11: Maximizing Global Recursion**

the developers have a tendency to want to improve it forever. As is often said, managers must sometimes "shoot the engineers" in order to "get the product out the door." Unlike the engineering approach of global recursion, this approach has the feel of flying-by-the-seat-of-the-pants hacking. While preferable to the waterfall development cycle (especially when developing something new), this approach has no completion criteria, is almost impossible to control, and can lead to contractual nightmares in which adding "bells and whistles" becomes the norm. See Figure 9-12: Maximizing Iteration.

The generic OOD development cycle shown in Figure 9-13 assumes multiple builds and assemblies and an optional locally recursive software requirements analysis phase preceding globally recursive development. It is more complex than the traditional waterfall development cycle and has multiple levels of abstraction. The generic object-oriented development cycle should also be tailored, based on such factors as

- The amount of functional software requirements analysis
- The amount of locally recursive OORA
- The existence of multiple builds or releases
- The specific OOD method used

## 9.2  CONFORMING TO THE WATERFALL DEVELOPMENT CYCLE

On a globally recursive OOD project, the increment of development is a small, manageable subassembly consisting of approximately the Miller limit of seven plus or

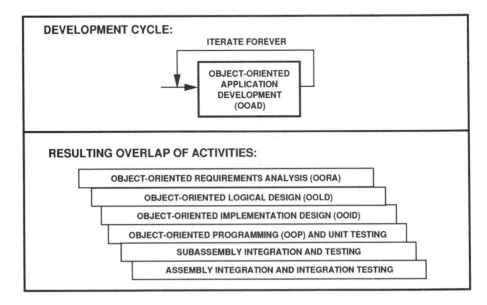

**Figure 9-12: Maximizing Iteration**

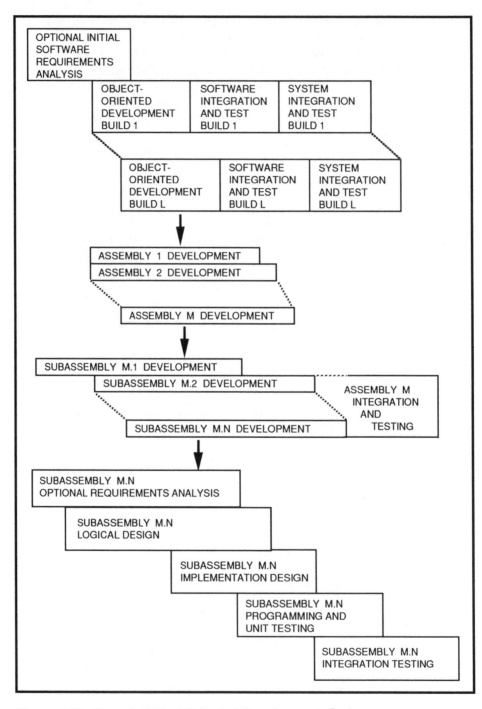

**Figure 9-13: Generic Object-Oriented Development Cycle**

minus two (or fewer) classes and objects of anonymous class. Yet on projects restricted to the classic waterfall development cycle, the increment of development is instead an entire project, build, or release, sometimes consisting of several hundred objects or classes. Conforming to the waterfall development cycle implies emphasizing local, rather than global, recursion, and the developers lose the ability incrementally to validate and verify the design throughout the process. Using the obsolete waterfall development cycle is thus significantly more expensive than using one of the modern globally recursive development cycles of OOD.

The waterfall development cycle may, however, be mandated by customer standards or chosen for various reasons (e.g., management familiarity, fear of the unknown). When this happens, there are several approaches that the developer can (or can be forced to) take. The most conservative and least cost-effective approach is to do everything in a locally recursive manner, as in Figure 9-14.

Sometimes, a better approach is to group all design activities together as in Figure 9-15. This is relatively easy grouping to accomplish contractually but suffers from the fact that logical and physical design are quite different activities, often using different models and diagrammatic techniques.

A different approach recognizes that the main argument used against globally recursive development is the perceived need to finalize requirements prior to the beginning of the design phases. Global recursion is thus allowed only after the software specification review (SSR), as in Figure 9-16.

Another approach recognizes that OORA and logical design use the same models and diagrammatic techniques and should therefore be combined, as shown in Figure 9-17. This may produce more contractual problems but will be easier for developers to implement. The primary demarcation is now between language-independent and language-dependent development. The new preliminary design review (PDR) now occurs after the logical design, but prior to physical design.

Whatever approach is used, the manager must consider and make trade-offs among the following concerns:

- Contractual requirements
- Customer and management expectations
- Cost-effectiveness and schedule limitations
- Similarity between activities
- Human psychology with regard to transitions

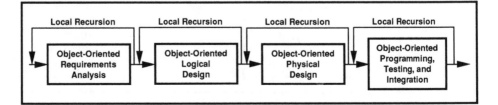

**Figure 9-14: OOD using the Traditional Waterfall Development Cycle**

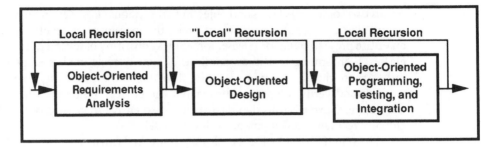

**Figure 9-15: OOD with Combined Design Activities**

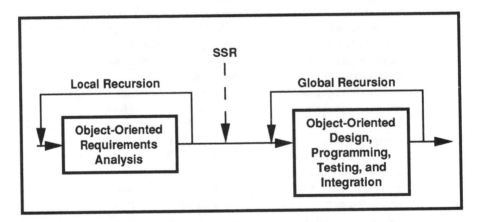

**Figure 9-16: OOD with Traditional Software Specification Review (SSR)**

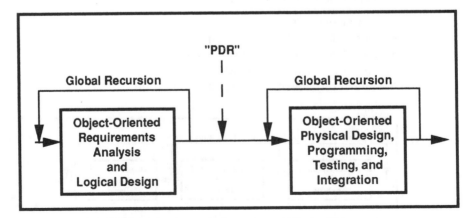

**Figure 9-17: OOD with New Preliminary Design Review (PDR)**

## 9.3 MAJOR REVIEWS

Because of OOD's globally recursive development cycle, major reviews on OOD projects tend not to be the traditional bottleneck reviews that separate the phases of the classic waterfall development cycle. With nonglobally recursive development and a strict adherence to the waterfall development cycle on software projects, many errors will not be discovered until one or more phases after they are inserted into the requirements, design, or code. This leads to significant increases in expense, a larger number of errors in the final code and documentation, and a general lack of management control.

With globally recursive development, only a small percentage of the software requirements for the entire system may be completed prior to the start of the logical (or preliminary) design of any top-level subassembly. Only a small percentage of the software logical design for the entire system will be completed prior to the start of physical (or detailed) design on any top-level subassembly. A significant amount of the coding for the entire system will be completed prior to the completion of the requirements and design for the lowest-level subassemblies.

On non-object-oriented projects, traditional reviews occur when an entire project or build completes a specific phase. For example, PDR would follow the completion of the entire preliminary design for a build. However, when a development team completes preliminary design, they are not expected to begin detailed design until approval of the PDR. There are several problems with this. On a large project, not all groups will reach the same development milestone at the same time, so some must wait, while some may have to hurry recklessly. For these reasons, reviews of this type may be referred to as "bottleneck reviews."

There are other, perhaps more expensive and damaging, effects from bottleneck reviews. They prevent global recursion (and thereby prevent incremental development), due to the exclusive concentration on one activity at a time. Therefore, for example, coding is completed for the entire system before any of it may be verified by integration or system testing. This means that the early activities are more difficult to validate than if, as with globally recursive development, the parts of the system developed early could be compiled, executed, tested, and demonstrated to the customer. When a single formal review must cover all software development performed during a single phase of a project or build, the amount of material to be reviewed is overwhelming, even if the review lasts several days. With the small-scale incremental development that occurs on globally recursive OOD projects, incremental reviews present the material in understandable and manageable amounts. Also, it is a rare project that does not have some rework to do after a review. When this is identified for all parts of the project at about the same time, there is a greater difficulty for project management to schedule the rework. With numerous, small incremental reviews, the rework is discovered for different parts of the project as they are ready.

It is still necessary to have major reviews that cover most or all of the project. With globally recursive development, a major review is primarily concerned with broader issues, such as the behavior, interaction and integration of significant subsystems. Major reviews on recursive OOD projects therefore become major in-process reviews (IPRs).

Because the requirements, design, and code are incrementally developed on recursive OOD projects, the following products should be reviewed at each IPR:

- The updated software requirements specification (SRS) for relevant assemblies— This includes the requirements specifications for each essential subassembly, class, and object of anonymous class identified and developed since the previous IPR. The SRS should include the relevant object-oriented graphics and specification language.
- The updated software design document (SDD) for relevant assemblies—This includes the design documentation for each essential, logical, and physical subassembly, class, and object of anonymous class identified and developed since the previous IPR. The SDD should include the relevant object-oriented graphics, PDL, and code.
- The evolving deliverable software of the relevant assemblies—This includes all subassemblies and component library units identified and developed since the previous IPR.

Tailoring and reinterpreting the formal reviews to be IPRs provides the most natural way of thinking about formal reviews on a recursive development project: If this is not possible for political or other reasons, some international software development standards (e.g., DOD-STD-2167A) allow for incremental reviews, which can provide the same (although less natural) result.

Figure 9-18 shows the optimal approach to scheduling IPRs for an assembly on globally recursive OOD projects. IPRs are scheduled at reasonable intervals during globally recursive development, with the final review being the test readiness review (TRR), which determines the readiness of the assembly for formal assembly testing prior to integration into the system. The optimum number of these major reviews depends on the amount of software to be developed and the overall software schedule. IPRs should not occur more often than every 3 months, or developers are so busy preparing for and conducting reviews that they will never be able to get any development done. On the other hand, IPRs should probably not occur less often than every year, or adequate customer/user oversight will be lost, and too much effort will be wasted going down inappropriate paths.

This approach is the cleanest, the most logical, and the most consistent with the globally recursive nature of OOD. Unfortunately, it also

- Requires a major paradigm shift by all involved
- Requires tailoring and or heavy reinterpretation of internationally accepted software development standards, such as
  —DOD-STD-2167A's SDD data item description (DID)
  — MIL-STD-1521B [DOD 1985], which prohibits detailed (i.e., CSU) design prior to the PDR of the computer software components (CSCs)
- Can result in significant confusion if the original terms—PDR and critical design review (CDR)—are retained for these new IPRs.

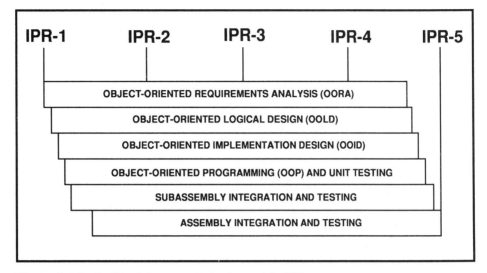

**Figure 9-18: Optimal Approach to Assembly IPRs**

Figure 9-19 shows the recommended approach to scheduling IPRs when the requirements must be officially finalized prior to the start of global recursion. The first review now becomes the traditional Software Specification Review (SSR). This approach should recognize that a minor amount of further OORA must occur after SSR, due to errors that were not discovered because using only local recursion prior to SSR prohibited the verification and validation of the requirements by implemen-

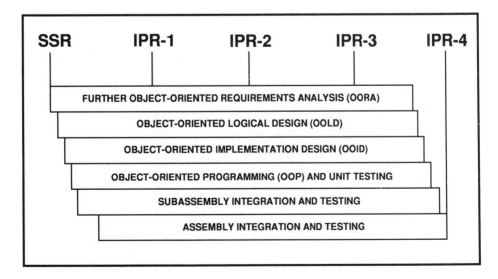

**Figure 9-19: Recommended Approach with SSR**

tation and testing prior to SSR. This approach should also recognize that a significant amount of further requirements analysis must occur if only functional-decomposition methods of requirements analysis are used. Unfortunately, this is not always politically or contractually possible. In such cases, this further requirements analysis is typically mislabeled "preliminary design."

Figure 9-20 shows the recommended approach to be used when the traditional reviews are mandated—that is, SSR, PDR, CDR, and Test Readiness Review (TRR). Incremental traditional reviews must be scheduled at the same times when the IPRs would ordinarily be scheduled.

This approach requires no tailoring or reinterpretation of U.S. military standards. It does, however, require the use of concurrently scheduled, incremental traditional formal reviews, and this is often accidentally (and inappropriately) prohibited by contracting-agency personnel when they schedule single traditional formal reviews without taking into account the contractor's software development method.

Object-oriented subassemblies are much smaller than builds (i.e., the analogous entities in waterfall projects) because each globally recursive increment (i.e., subassembly) now only involves a very small amount of software (typically less than 9–10 classes or objects of anonymous class). It is therefore not cost-effective to repeat incremental formal reviews (i.e., IPRs) for each subassembly. On very large projects, this is not even feasible, as it could require hundreds of formal reviews, with several taking place each day during much of the project. Object-oriented IPRs are orthogonal to the activities (e.g., software requirements analysis) and occur at the assembly level rather than at the subassembly level.

The major question is when to schedule the IPRs. Should each IPR be held after a specific number of abstraction levels are completed, as in Figure 9-21? Although this

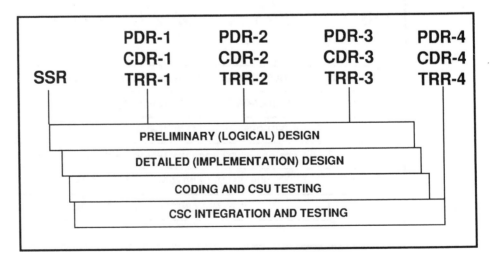

**Figure 9-20: Recommended Approach with Traditional Reviews**

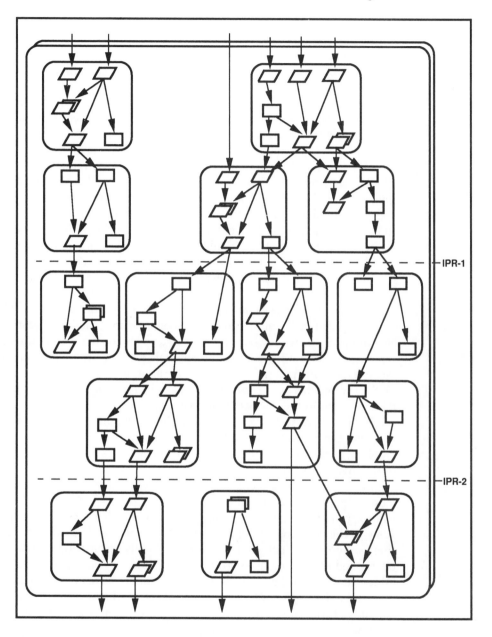

**Figure 9-21: Example IPRs, Based on Levels of Abstraction**

approach is easy to define objectively, it would require all software development teams to work in lockstep with one another and would be very inefficient.

Should each IPR be held after a specific number of subassemblies (or classes and objects) is completed, as in Figure 9-22? This would allow the manager to assign development teams, as necessary, to implement some subassemblies early while leaving others stubbed out. This could allow the early development of high-risk software or of software that is required earlier (e.g, to meet build plan schedules). Difficulties with this approach concern scheduling based on questionable estimates of total subassembly number and development-team productivity.

Should each IPR be held after a designated time interval, based on total software schedule and project build plan, as in Figure 9-23? This final and recommended approach could also allow the early development of high-risk software or of software that is required earlier (e.g, to meet build plan schedules). The manager would use an earned-value approach to determining whether the project is on schedule, as in Figures 9-24 and 9-25. IPRs should not be scheduled more often than once every 3 months or the development team productivity will suffer. IPRs should also not be scheduled more seldom than once a year or inadequate customer oversight may result.

New recursive subassemblies come into existence during the OOD process, as a result of global recursion, to provide resources at lower levels of abstraction. At the beginning, one may only have a rough concept of the number of subassemblies to be generated. When using traditional waterfall methods, the exact number of ad hoc subassemblies and their relationship to one another is generally known early on. With OOD, the number of subassemblies and their relationships cannot be known until relatively late in the development process.

With globally recursive OOD, the lower-level subassemblies cannot be scheduled in advance, but only individually as they are identified. This is not an insurmountable problem, as each subassembly is quite small and such early scheduling would amount to micromanagement.

New global scheduling approaches not tied to the waterfall development cycle must be used to determine whether the project is on schedule, and the use of earned-value approaches appear promising. The recommended approach for applying earned value to the development of an assembly is as follows: The manager first determines the total estimated size of the assembly in units of function points, subassemblies, classes and objects, modules, and/or source lines of code. The manager then determines the dates for the formal IPRs, which will be the major intermediate milestones of software development for each assembly. Next, the manager determines the target amounts of software to be completed at each IPR, based on estimated staffing and training curves and the estimated productivity of the development staff. See Figure 9-24: Initial Estimates.

Prior to each IPR, the manager reestimates the total size of the assembly. The manager then calculates the actual estimate of the percentage complete at the IPR, using the actual amount completed and the new estimate of total size. Figure 9-25 shows an example of how the initial estimates may have to be modified at the first

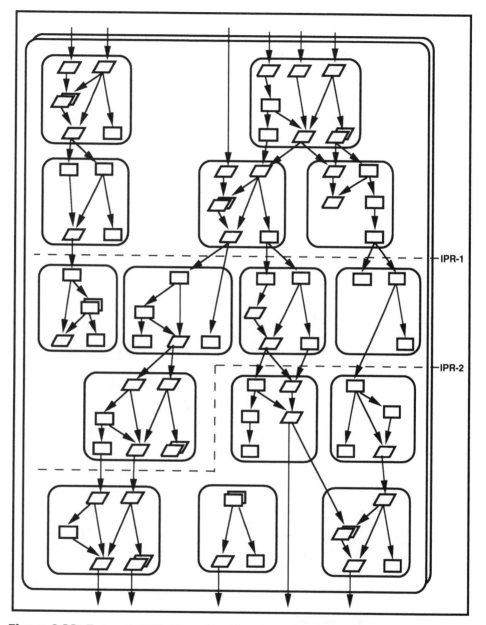

**Figure 9-22: Example IPRs Based on Number of Subassemblies**

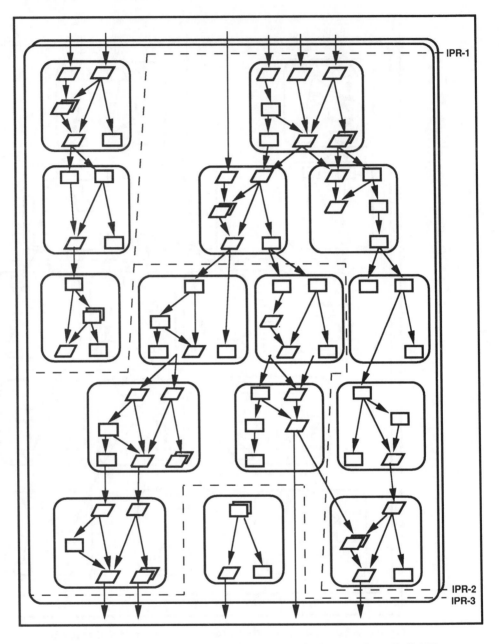

**Figure 9-23: Example IPRs, Based on Amount of Time and on Build Plan**

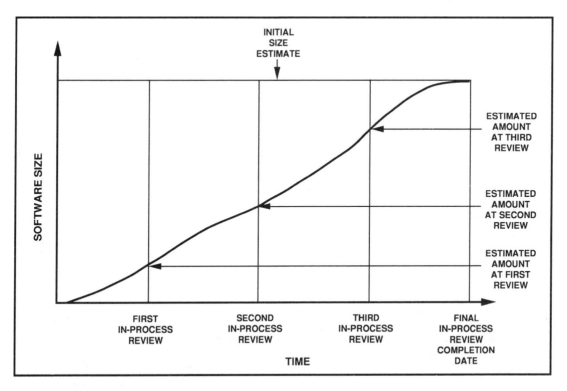

**Figure 9-24: Initial Estimates**

IPR, due to underestimating the size of the assembly. Because subassemblies are designed, coded, tested, and integrated on an individual basis, the number of completed subassemblies divided by the estimated total number of subassemblies provides a good first-order approximation of the percentage completed. Finally, the manager compares the actual percentage complete with the expected percentage complete, as estimated at the latter of the start point and the previous IPR. This comparison allows the manager to determine whether the project is on schedule.

Such an earned-value approach appears to provide a more realistic estimate than traditional waterfall-based approaches because milestones are associated with the completion of deliverable software rather than merely on paper documents. This helps mitigate the problems due to the 90–10 rule, where the first 90% of the development is on schedule and the remaining 10% takes forever.

Schedules should take into account the front-end loading of effort on projects using OOD and programming languages (e.g., Ada) that are also design languages and that have a separation of specification and body. This invalidates the traditional 40–20–40 rule of thumb, which says that requirements and design consume 40% of the

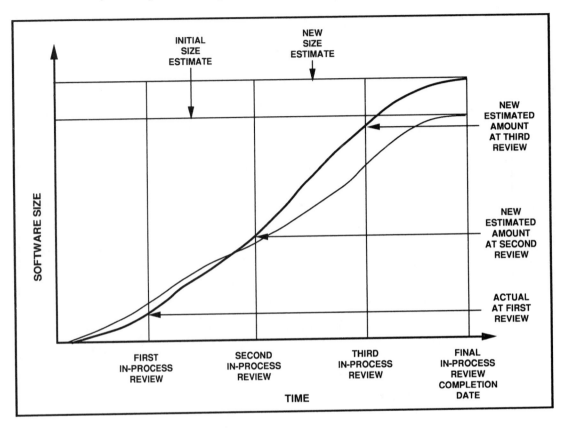

**Figure 9-25  Estimates at the First IPR**

effort, coding 20%, and integration and testing the remaining 40%. On such projects, managers can expect the following:

- Requirements analysis and design     50–60%
- Coding     10–15%
- Integration and testing     25–35%

## CHAPTER REFERENCES

[DOD 1986] Department of Defense, Defense System Software Development, DOD-STD-2167A, 29 February 1986.

[DOD 1985] Department of Defense, Technical Reviews and Audits for Systems, Equipments, and Computer Software, MIL-STD-1521B, 4 June 1985.

# Appendix A

# Abbreviations

| | | | | |
|---|---|---|---|---|
| A | attribute | | CDT | class description table |
| ACM | Association for Computing Machinery | | CFD | control flow diagram |
| | | | CLD | classification diagram |
| AD | assembly diagram | | CMD | composition diagram |
| ADARTS | Ada-Based Design Approach for Real-Time Systems | | CN | constructor, noniterative (on graphics) |
| ADL | ASTS Diagramming Language | | CRC | class responsibility collaboration |
| ADM3 | ASTS Development Method 3 | | CSC | computer software component |
| ADP | automatic data processing | | CSCI | computer software configuration item |
| ADT | abstract data type | | | |
| a.k.a. | also known as | | CSU | computer software unit |
| ASM | abstract state machine | | C3 | command, control, and communications |
| ASTS | Advanced Software Technology Specialists | | D | destructor |
| BIT | built-in test | | DFD | data flow diagram |
| BNF | Backus-Naur-Form | | DID | data item description |
| C | concurrent | | DOD | Department of Defense |
| C | constant (attribute) | | ER | entity relationship |
| C | constructor | | ERA | entity relationship attribute |
| CASE | computer-aided software engineering | | FRA | functional requirements analysis |
| | | | FSM | finite state machine |
| CD | certificate of deposit | | GOOD | Generalized Object-Oriented Design |
| CD | context diagram | | | |
| CDR | critical design review | | GSN | general semantic net |

| | | | |
|---|---|---|---|
| HOOD | Hierarchical Object-Oriented Design | OO DFD | object-oriented data flow diagram |
| I | iterator | OOD | object-oriented development |
| ID | interaction diagram | OODA | object-oriented domain analysis |
| IDD | interface design document | OODBMS | object-oriented database management system |
| IPR | in-process review | | |
| IRS | interface requirements specification | OODD | object-oriented domain development |
| IV&V | independent verification and validation | OODDes | object-oriented domain design |
| | | OODI | object-oriented domain implementation |
| LED | light-emitting diode | | |
| LSE | language sensitive editor | OODP | object-oriented domain programming |
| M | modifier | | |
| MD | module diagram | OOID | object-oriented implementation design |
| MIS | management information systems | OOIT | object-oriented integration and test |
| MN | modifier, noniterative (on graphics) | OOLD | object-oriented logical design |
| MVC | model/view/controller | OOP | object-oriented programming |
| N | noniterator (operation) | OOPL | object-oriented programming language |
| NDI | nondevelopmental item | | |
| NIH | not invented here (syndrome) | OORA | object-oriented requirements analysis |
| O | object | OORALD | object-oriented requirements analysis and logical design |
| O | operation | | |
| OBA | Object Behavior Analysis | OOSA | object-oriented systems analysis |
| OCD | object-class diagram | OOSD | Object-Oriented Software Development |
| ODT | object description table | | |
| OHD | object-hierarchy diagram | OOSDL | Object-Oriented Specification and Design Language |
| OID | object-interaction diagram | | |
| OJT | on-the-job training | OOSE | object-oriented software engineering |
| OMT | Object Modeling Technique | | |
| OOA | Object-Oriented (systems) Analysis | P | preserver |
| | | PAMELA | Process Abstraction Method for Embedded Large Applications |
| OOAD | object-oriented application development | | |
| OO C/DFD | object-oriented control/data flow diagram | PDL | program design language |
| | | PDR | preliminary design review |
| | | PN | preserver noniterator |
| OO CFD | object-oriented control flow diagram | RFP | request for proposal |
| | | RMP | risk management plan |

| | | | |
|---|---|---|---|
| SA | Structured Analysis | SQA | software quality assurance |
| SADT | Structured Analysis and Design Technique | SRR | system requirements review |
| | | SRS | software requirements specification |
| SD | Structured Design | | |
| SDD | software design document | SSDD | software specification and design document |
| SDF | software development file | | |
| SDP | software development plan | SSN | system semantic net |
| SDR | system design review | SSR | software specification review |
| SIG | special interest group | STD | state transition diagram |
| SIGPLAN | Special Interest Group for Programming Languages | T | type |
| | | TBD | to be determined |
| SMD | submodule diagram | TD | timing diagram |
| SN | semantic net | TRR | test readiness review |
| SOT | state operation table | V | variable (attribute) |

# Appendix B

# Glossary

**abstract class**  n. An incomplete superclass that requires the resources of one or more subclasses prior to the instantiation of its objects (i.e., any class that is not concrete).

**abstract data type (ADT)**  n. An encapsulation of a data type and its associated operations that hides their implementations..

**abstract state machine (ASM)**  n. An encapsulation of a set of states and operations that either change or return the states.

**abstraction**  n. A model that includes all essential capabilities, properties, or aspects of what is being modeled without any extraneous details.  v. Concentrating on the most important or essential capabilities, properties, or aspects of something while temporarily suppressing or ignoring less important, immaterial, or diversionary details in order to manage complexity and promote correctness, extensibility, maintainability, reusability, and understandability.

**aggregation hierarchy**  n. A composition hierarchy consisting of an aggregate entity, its component entities, and the "has components" relationships among them.

**agent [object, class, or subassembly]**  n. An object, class, or subassembly that (1) exports resources to one or more higher-level objects, classes, or subassemblies and (2) imports resources from one or more lower-level objects, classes, or subassemblies.

**aggregate**  n. An object, class, subassembly, or operation that has  at least one other such entity (i.e., object, class, subassembly, or operation, respectively) as a component.

**anonymous class**  n. An unspecified class for objects, the class of which is not being identified at present or in the present context.

**assembly**  n. The entire set of related subassemblies that are identified, analyzed, designed, coded, tested, and integrated from a single cohesive set of requirements.

**assembly diagram (AD)**    n.  A diagram documenting the subassemblies of an assembly, the dependency relationships among them, and possibly their specifications and bodies.

**assembly model**    n.  The major object-oriented model that provides a static view of the entire assembly in terms of its terminators, its subassemblies, and the relationships among them.

**association**    n.  A general named relationship between two or more entities.

**atomic**    adj.  Describes an object, class, or subassembly that does not have another such entity as a component.

**attribute**    n.  A discrete inherent data abstraction of a characteristic, property, trait, quantity, or quality of an object or class that identifies, describes, or provides the state of an object or class.

**attribute type**    n.  A template for creating attributes, which specifies the implementation of the attribute and the allowed operations on attributes of the designated type.

**black box**    n.  Something with a well-defined boundary separating (1) an outside, user-oriented specification providing exported resources, and (2) an inside, hidden, protected, developer-oriented body that provides the implementation of the exported resources.

**body**    n.  The hidden implementation of an entity (e.g., subassembly, class, object, programming unit), providing the inside, developer view of the entity and how it does what it does.

**bounded**    adj.  Having dynamic, yet limited, object code size.

**build**    n.  A major increment of development, usually consisting of multiple, possibly partial, assemblies.

**busy waiting**    n.  A synonym for *excessive polling*.

**capability**    n.  A major need or requirement specified by the user or customer.

**cardinality**  n.  Description of a class indicating the number of instances that (1) exist or (2) participate in a relationship.

**class**    n.  A template from which objects (i.e., instances) can be instantiated (i.e., constructed).

**class-based**    adj.  Based on the concept of classes of objects.

**classification hierarchy**  n.  An inheritance hierarchy of superclasses, subclasses, and instances and their "has-class" and "has-superclass" relationships.  Usually documented with a classification diagram (CLD).

**class model**    n.  The major object-oriented model that provides a static view of an inheritance architecture in terms of the existence and abstraction of its component classes and the "has subclass" and "has instance" relationships between them and between them and their instances.

**client [object, class, or subassembly]**    n.  The entity in a binary relationship that depends on (i.e., uses the resources of) the other (i.e., server) entity.

**colleague [object, class, or subassembly]**    n.  An entity that is both a client and a server of some other entity.

**compatibility    n.** The ease with which the software may be combined with other software.

**complete    adj.** Having all necessary and useful characteristics, properties, and resources.

**component    n.** Either an object or a class.

**computer software component (CSC)    n.** A U.S. military term for "a distinct part of a computer software configuration item (CSCI). CSCs may be further decomposed into other CSCs and Computer Software Units (CSUs)" [DOD 1986].

**computer software configuration item (CSCI)    n.** A U.S. military term for "a configuration item for computer software" [DOD 1986].

**computer software unit (CSU)    n.** A U.S. military term for "an element specified in the design of a Computer Software Component (CSC) that is separately testable" [DOD 1986].

**concrete class    n.** A class with instances (i.e., any class that is not abstract).

**concurrent class    n.** A class, the instances of which are concurrent objects.

**concurrent object    n.** An object containing one or more concurrent operations.

**concurrent operation    n.** An operation having one or more separate threads of control.

**confirmability    n.** The ability to readily determine whether software is correct, reliable, and robust.

**constructor operation    n.** An operation that constructs (i.e., creates) an instance.

**controller object    n.** An object that controls the thing(s) being modeled.

**control model    n.** The major object-oriented model that provides a dynamic view of the subassembly, its major threads of control, and its objects and classes, in terms of their operations, the control flows between them, their attributes, and the data flows between their operations and their attributes.

**correctability    n.** The ease with which latent errors can be found and corrected in the software.

**correctness    n.** The degree to which software meets its specified requirements and to which the requirements meet their associated needs.

**corruptible    adj.** Providing no support for mutual exclusion in a concurrent environment.

**data abstraction    n.** An abstraction (i.e., model) of a characteristic, property, trait, quantity, or quality of some entity (e.g., an object).

**deadlock    n.** The situation that occurs when two or more concurrent operations are waiting on each other so that none are ever executed.

**deferred class    n.** An abstract class that declares the existence of one or more resources but relies on one or more subclasses to define these resources.

**destructor    n.** An operation that destroys (i.e., deletes) an instance.

**domain    n.** (1) a synonym for subassembly; (2) a class of applications.

**efficiency    n.** The degree to which the software uses hardware resources effectively.

**emulator object    n.** An object that emulates the thing(s) being modeled.

**encapsulation**   **n.**  The combination of localization, modularity, and information hiding.

**essential**   **adj.**  Describing an object, class, or subassembly for which the following is true: (1) its existence and capabilities are required; (2) it is typically known and understood by the customer or application domain specialist; and (3) it is identified during requirements analysis and specified in the appropriate requirements specification document, either as a required capability or as a design constraint.

**exception abstraction**   **n.**  A model of an error condition and its handling.

**export**   **v.**  To make visible to clients.

**extended library unit**   **n.**  A library unit (i.e., specification), its corresponding body, and all nested subunits.

**extendibility**   **n.**  A synonym for *extensibility*.

**extensibility**   **n.**  The ease with which the software can be modified to adapt to changes in requirements.

**flexibility**   **n.**  A synonym for *extensibility*.

**framework**   **n.**  A reusable, application-domain-specific specification, design, and code template, consisting of one or more objects, classes, and/or subassemblies that implement some common capabilities.

**functional abstraction**   **n.**  A model of a sequential operation.

**globally recursive**   **adj.**  A method, the steps of which are repeated across more than one development activity (e.g., requirements analysis, design, coding, integration, and testing).

**guardable**   **adj.**  Providing, but not enforcing, support for mutual exclusion in a concurrent environment.

**guarded**   **adj.**  Providing *and* enforcing support for mutual exclusion in a concurrent environment.

**Hrair limit**   **n.**  A synonym for the Miller limit that is popular in the Ada community.

**implementer object**   **adj.**  An object that implements the thing(s) being modeled.

**independence**   **n.**  The degree to which the software does not rely on other entities. The coupling between objects and classes should be minimized. Where practical, objects and classes should be independent of the underlying hardware and operating system.

**information hiding**   **n.**  The deliberate and compiler-enforced hiding of information (e.g., design decisions, implementation details), in order to promote abstraction, support incremental top-down development, protect against accidental corruption, and promote the achievement of software-engineering goals.

**inheritance**   **n.**  The relationship among classes that allows subclasses to be built as extensions or specializations of superclasses.

**instance**   **n.**  (1) an object constructed by instantiation from a class; (2) an attribute of a type.

**instantiate**   **v.**  To create a new instance of a class or type.

**integrity**   **n.**  A synonym for *security*.

**interaction diagram (ID)**   n.  A directed graph for which (1) its primary nodes are classes and objects, and (2) its primary arcs are the interactions between them.

**interfacer object**   adj.  An object that interfaces with the thing(s) being modeled.

**iteration**   n.  The repetition of a (sub)method's steps to modify existing product(s) at the current level of abstraction, typically used to fix mistakes.

**iterator**   n.  An operation that (1) operates on all instances of a class, or (2) reads or writes to all state variables of an object.

**localization**   n.  The purposeful partitioning of things (e.g., requirements and software) into collections (e.g., capabilities and modules, respectively), so that logically related things are physically grouped together, in order to increase cohesion and to decrease coupling.

**locally recursive**   adj.  A (sub)method, the steps of which are repeated within a single development activity (i.e., requirements analysis, design, coding, integration, and testing).

**maintainability**   n.  A combination of correctability and extensibility.

**managed**   adj.  Managing its own garbage collection.

**master [object, class, or subassembly]**   n.  An object, class, or subassembly that (1) does not export resources to any higher-level objects, classes, or subassemblies, but (2) does import resources from one or more lower-level objects, classes, or subassemblies.

**message**   n.  The primary means of communication among classes and objects consisting of (1) a request for a service, (2) a notification of an event, or (3) the passing of data.

**method**   n.  (1) A popular synonym for an operation, or (2) a systematic and well-documented set of steps, with associated standards and procedures, used to perform requirements analysis, logical and physical design, coding, testing, and integration.

**Miller limit**   n.  A natural limitation on human understanding resulting from complexity, which becomes significant at approximately seven, plus or minus two. Named after the psychologist George Miller; also known as the *Hrair limit*.

**model**   n.  An abstraction that includes all essential capabilities, properties, or aspects of what is being modeled, without any extraneous details.

**modifiability**   n.  The ease with which the software can be changed.

**modifier**   n.  An operation that modifies (i.e., changes) the state of an object or class.

**modularity**   n.  The purposeful partitioning of things (e.g., requirements and software) into *small*, *simple* collections (e.g., capabilities and modules, respectively), which increase the achievement of software-engineering goals.

**module diagram (MD)**   n.  A diagram documenting one or more modules (i.e., their identification, exported resources, and possibly hidden resources) and the static relationships (e.g., dependencies) among them.

**multiple classification**   n.  The relationship that exists if a single object is an instance of more than one class.

**multiple inheritance   n.** The relationship that exists if a single class is a subclass of more than one superclass.

**nested   adj.** Hidden within the body of an object, class, subassembly, or assembly; not *socketed*.

**object   n.** An abstraction (i.e., model) in the requirements, design, and/or code of a *single* tangible or intangible object, entity, or thing from the real-world, application, or problem domain.

**object-based   adj.** Based on the concept of an object.

**object model   n.** The major object-oriented model that provides a static view of the architecture of the subassembly in terms of the existence, abstraction, and visibility of its component objects, the terminators with which the individual objects must interface, and the important relationships and messages passed among them.

**object-oriented   adj.** Based upon the concepts of encapsulation, object, class, inheritance, and aggregation.[1]

**object-oriented development (OOD)   n.** The class of *object-oriented* software development methods.

**object-oriented domain analysis (OODA)   n.** The class of object-oriented development methods used for the identification, analysis, and specification of requirements for common objects, classes, subassemblies, and frameworks from a specific application domain, typically for reuse on multiple projects within that application domain.

**object-oriented domain design (OODDes)   n.** The class of object-oriented development methods used for the design of common objects, classes, subassemblies, and frameworks from a specific application domain, typically for reuse on multiple projects within that application domain.

**object-oriented implementation design (OOID)   n.** The class of object-oriented development methods used for the *language-dependent* design of application-specific objects, classes, subassemblies, and frameworks.

**object-oriented logical design (OOLD)   n.** The class of object-oriented development methods used for the *language-independent* design of application-specific objects, classes, subassemblies, and frameworks.

**object-oriented programming (OOP)   n.** The class of object-oriented development methods used for the *programming* of application-specific objects, classes, subassemblies, and frameworks.

---

[1]This is the standard definition that probably not be changed at this late date.  More logical definitions would be as follows:

| | |
|---|---|
| object-oriented | based on the concept of objects. |
| class-oriented | based on the concept of classes of objects. |
| inheritance-oriented | based on the concept of inheritance between classes of objects. |

**object-oriented requirements analysis (OORA)**  **n.** The class of object-oriented development methods used for the analysis and specification of requirements in terms of application-specific objects, classes, subassemblies, and frameworks.

**operation**  **n.** A discrete activity, action, or behavior that (1) implements a functional (i.e., sequential) or process (i.e., concurrent) abstraction, and that (2) is typically performed by, belongs to, and is part of an object or class

**overloading**  **n.** The reuse of the same identifier for different but analogous entities (e.g., attribute types, attributes, messages, operations, exceptions, objects, classes, and subassemblies) in different contexts or with differing scopes.

**polling**  **n.** The situation that occurs when a client object must continually send messages to a server object in order to determine whether an event has occurred, instead of being sent a message once, upon occurrence of the event.

**polymorphism**  **n.** The ability of the same identifier to refer at run-time to different instances of various classes.

**portability**  **n.** The ease with which software can be transitioned to another hardware or software environment.

**preserver**  **n.** An operation that preserves (i.e., does not change) the state of an existing object or class.

**priority inversion**  **n.** The situation that occurs when a high-priority concurrent operation is blocked from execution because it is waiting on a low-priority concurrent operation that is blocked by a medium-priority concurrent operation that is currently executing.

**process abstraction**  **n.** A model of a concurrent operation.

**recursion**  **n.** The repetition of a (sub)method's steps to generate new product(s), typically at the next-lower level of abstraction.

**reliability**  **n.** The degree to which the software functions correctly over time.

**reusability**  **n.** The ease with which the software may be used for purposes other than those that were originally intended.

**robustness**  **n.** The degree to which the software continues to function correctly under abnormal circumstances.

**root class**  **n.** A class in a classification hierarchy that has no superclass.

**safety**  **n.** The degree to which the software functions without unintentional harm to life or property.

**scenario**  **n.** A coherent set of related messages and operation executions used for analysis, design, and/or testing purposes.

**security n.** The degree to which the software protects itself from unauthorized access or modification.

**semantic net**  **n.** A directed graph, the [primary] nodes of which are entities (e.g., concepts, devices, objects, classes, subassemblies) and whose arcs are the semantic relationships (i.e., associations) among them.

**sequential**  **adj.** Containing no separate thread(s) of control (i.e., tasks or calls to tasks).

**servant [object, class, or subassembly]**  **n.** An object, class, or subassembly that

1) exports resources to one or more higher-level objects, classes, or subassemblies but 2) does not import resources from any lower-level objects, classes, or subassemblies.

**server [object, class, or subassembly]**   n.   The entity in a binary relationship that provides resources to the other [client] entity and on which the other entity depends.

**simple operation**   adj.   An operation that does not rely on knowledge of the underlying implementation of the object or class.

**simulator object**   n.   An object that simulates the thing(s) being modeled.

**single inheritance**   n.   The relationship that exists if a single class is a subclass of only one superclass.

**socket**   v.   Attach to a boundary and make visible.

**specification**   n.   The visible interface of an entity (e.g., subassembly, class, object, programming unit), providing the outside, user view of the entity, its exported resources, and what it does.

**starvation**   n.   The situation that occurs when a concurrent operation must wait indefinitely for execution.

**state model**   n.   The major object-oriented model that provides a dynamic view of the behavior of the objects and classes in terms of their states, and the modifier operations and exceptions that transition them from state to state.

**state transition diagram (STD)**   n.   A diagram showing (1) the states of an object or class and (2) the operations (and exceptions) that cause the transitions between the states.

**static**   adj.   Having a constant object-code size.

**stimulator object**   n.   An object that stimulates the thing(s) being modeled.

**subassembly**   n.   A logically cohesive collection of objects, classes, subassemblies, and possibly other entities (e.g., unencapsulated data or operations). A *recursive subassembly* is a subassembly identified (and possibly analyzed, designed, coded, tested, and/or integrated) during a single, nonrecursive pass through the recursive software-development method. An *ad hoc subassembly* is any nonrecursive subassembly (e.g., one identified during domain analysis consisting of similar objects or classes).

**subclass**   n.   A class that inherits from one or more superclasses.

**subject**   n.   An arbitrary collection of objects, classes, and subjects, used for purposes of documentation and promoting understandability. Compare with *subassembly*, which requires logical cohesion, is part of the structure of the specifications and design, and is related to the recursive development process. [Coad and Yourdon 1989]

**subsystem**   n.   (1) an integrated collection of software, hardware, and roles played by people. (2) a popular, although misleading, synonym for *subassembly*.

**superclass**   n.   A class from which one or more subclasses inherit.

**testability**   n.   The degree to which and the ease with which the software can be tested for correctness, reliability, and robustness.

**thread of control**    n.  A theoretically possible sequence of operation calls and/or exception flows within objects or classes or among objects, classes, and other entities (e.g., global operations, hardware, software systems).

**timing diagram (TD)**    n.  A diagram showing the temporal aspects of (1) objects, classes, and possibly their operations, and (2) their interactions.

**timing model**    n.  The major object-oriented model that provides a temporal view of the subassembly in terms of the timing of the messages passed within and between objects.

**tracker object**    n.  An object that tracks the thing(s) being modeled.

**unbounded**    adj.  Having dynamic and unlimited object code size.

**understandability**    n.  The ease with which humans can comprehend the software (e.g., requirements, design, architecture, behavior) and its documentation.

**uniformity**    n.  The property of having the same paradigm, models, notation, and concepts consistently applied, with no unnecessary differences.

**unmanaged**    adj.  Not managing its own garbage collection.

**user-friendliness**    n.  The ease with which humans can use the software.

**validatability**    n.  The ease with which the software can be demonstrated to be correct.

**verifiability**    n.  The ease with which the software can be demonstrated to meet development standards and procedures.

## APPENDIX REFERENCES

[Coad and Yourdon 1989] Peter Coad and Edward Yourdon, *OORA - Object-Oriented Requirements Analysis*, Englewood Cliffs, NJ, Prentice Hall, 1989.

[DOD 1986] Department of Defense, *Defense Systems Software Development*, DOD-STD-2167A, 29 February 1986.

# Appendix C

# Syntax and Semantics of the Diagrams

## C.1 THE ASTS DIAGRAMMING LANGUAGE (ADL)

This appendix provides the syntax and semantics of the diagrams of the ASTS Development Method 3 (ADM3). It can be used by CASE tool vendors to provide tool support for ADM3, by developers to better understand the rules of the diagrams, and by quality assurance personnel as the requirements from which to judge conformance when evaluating the diagrams for proper syntax and semantics.

The following syntax and semantics rules are written in the ASTS Diagramming Language (ADL). Within the example, reserved words in ADL are written in boldface, whereas words written in plain text are specific to each diagram and diagram type. Comments are preceded by two hyphens and run to the end of the line. Node and arc definitions define the nodes and arcs in terms of atomic icons with associated drawing constraints. Parenting rules specify whether children nodes can or must be nested inside or socketed to the border of parent nodes. Arc rules specify the allowed start and ending nodes of the individual arcs.

The ASTS Development Method 3 requires the following 14 basic node shapes, which are documented in Figure C-1.

```
type Nodes is (Banner,Box,Building,Circle,Cloud,Data_Store,
        Diamond,Hexagon,Oval,Off_Page_Connector,Parallelogram,
        Rectangle,Rounded_Rectangle,Trapezoid);
```

The ASTS Development Method 3 requires the following 9 basic arc types, which are documented in Figure C-2.

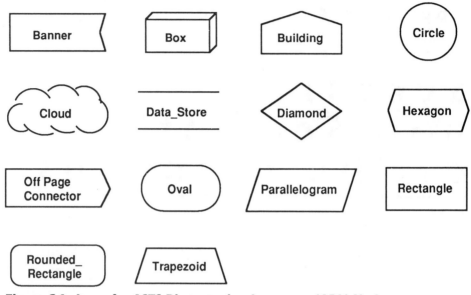

**Figure C-1: Icons for ASTS Diagramming Language (ADL) Nodes**

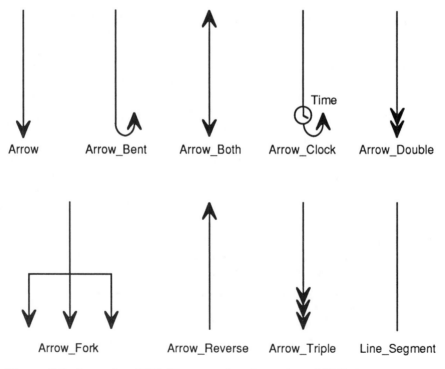

**Figure C-2: Icons for ASTS Diagramming Language (ADL) Arcs**

```
type Arcs is (Arrow,Arrow_Bent,Arrow_Both,Arrow_Clock,
              Arrow_Double,Arrow_Fork,Arrow_Reverse,
              Arrow_Triple,Line_Seqment);
```

The ASTS Diagramming Language (ADL) recognizes the following drawing parameters which are documented in Figure C-3.

```
type Label          is new Character_Strings;
type Constraints    is (X_Axis,X_Y_Axes,Y_Axis);
type Line           is (Dash,Dot,Solid);
type Multiplicity   is (1,2);
type Style          is (Thick,Thin);
type Where          is (Above,Below,Centered,Head,Inside,Outside,Right,Straddle);
```

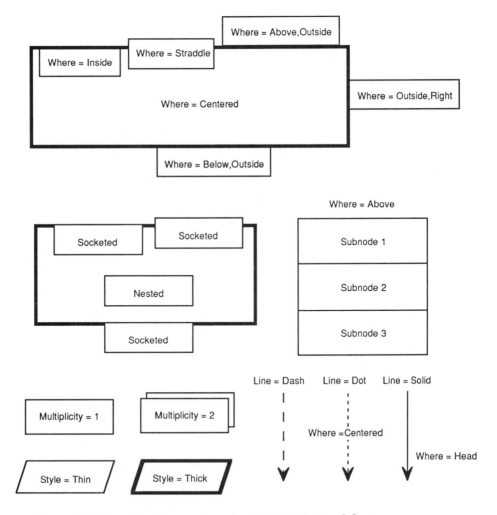

**Figure C-3: Drawing Parameters for ADL Nodes and Arcs**

Node definitions have the following syntax:

```
node NEW_NODE is A_Node (drawing parameters
              [has_label  An_Identifier (drawing parameters)]
              [has_list   Identifiers   (drawing parameters)]
              [divided_horizontally_into
                 {subnode    A_Subnode
                  [has_list  Identifiers   (drawing parameters)]}}];
```

Arc definitions have the following syntax:

```
arc ARC_TYPE is An_Arc (drawing parameters)
              [has_label  (drawing parameters)]
              [has_list   (drawing parameters)];
```

Parenting rules have the following syntax:

```
must_parent  CHILD_NODE_TYPE;
may_nest     CHILD_NODE_TYPE in PARENT_NODE_TYPE;
may_socket   CHILD_NODE_TYPE to PARENT_NODE_TYPE (drawing parameters);
```

Arc rules have the following syntax:

```
may_connect START_NODE_TYPE with ARC_TYPE to END_NODE_TYPE;
```

Comments in ADL are preceded by two hyphens (i.e., "--") and run to the end of the line.

Off page connectors are used to partition diagrams that are too large to fit on a single screen or page. Any arc can be divided and connected to two off page connectors on the two partial diagrams as indicated in Figure C-4.

## C.2  SYSTEM DIAGRAMS

ADM3 provides the following diagrams for system-level requirements analysis and design:

- System semantic nets (SSNs)
- System interaction diagrams (SIDs)
- System composition diagrams (SCMDs)
- System state transition diagrams (SSTDs)
- System event timing diagrams (SETDs)

These diagrams are similar to the analogous software level diagrams, but document system-level entities and their relationships.

## C.2.1   System Semantic Nets (SSNs)

System semantic nets (SSNs) document the application domain entities that may be modeled by the software objects and classes and also document the associations

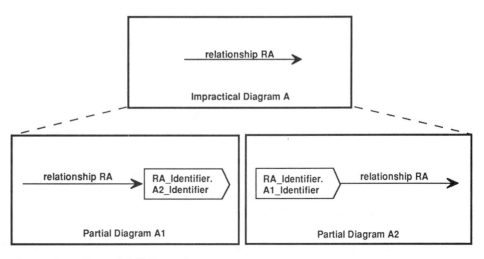

**Figure C-4: Use of Off Page Connectors**

between these entities. Figure C-5 documents the 24 valid nodes and 4 valid arcs of SSNs.

The following is the specification of the syntax and the semantics of system semantic nets (SSNs), which are part of the system model:

**diagram** SYSTEM_SEMANTIC_NET **is**

```
-- Node definitions:
-- Node icons must be labeled with the identifier of the corresponding entity.
 -- Nodes:
```

| | |
|---|---|
| **node** CONCEPT | **is Cloud**<br>(**Line** := **Solid**;    **Style** := **Thin**;    **Multiplicity** := **1**)<br>**has_label** An_Identifier (**Where** := **Centered**); |
| **node** CONCEPTS | **is Cloud**<br>(**Line** := **Solid**;    **Style** := **Thin**;    **Multiplicity** := **2**)<br>**has_label** An_Identifier (**Where** := **Centered**); |
| **node** DEVICE | **is Box**<br>(**Line** := **Solid**;    **Style** := **Thin**;    **Multiplicity** := **1**)<br>**has_label** An_Identifier (**Where** := **Centered**); |
| **node** DEVICES | **is Box**<br>(**Line** := **Solid**;    **Style** := **Thin**;    **Multiplicity** := **2**)<br>**has_label** An_Identifier (**Where** := **Centered**); |
| **node** DOCUMENT | **is Rectangle**<br>(**Line** := **Solid**;    **Style** := **Thin**;    **Multiplicity** := **1**)<br>**has_label** An_Identifier (**Where** := **Centered**); |
| **node** DOCUMENTS | **is Rectangle**<br>(**Line** := **Solid**;    **Style** := **Thin**;    **Multiplicity** := **2**)<br>**has_label** An_Identifier (**Where** := **Centered**); |

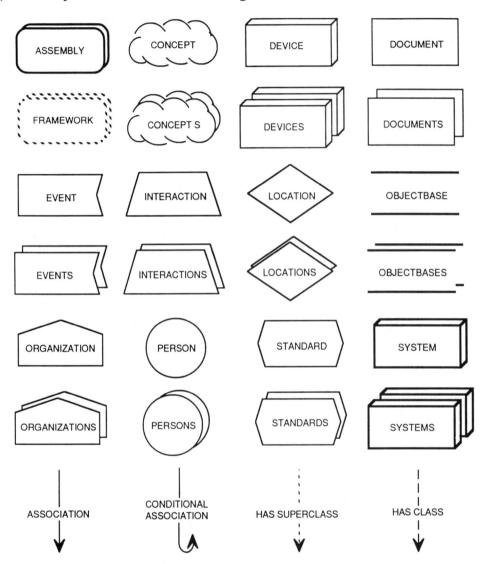

**Figure C-5: Valid Nodes and Arcs for System Semantic Nets (SSNs)**

```
node EVENT            is Banner
                      (Line := Solid;   Style := Thin;   Multiplicity := 1)
                      has_label An_Identifier (Where := Centered);
node EVENTS           is Banner
                      (Line := Solid;   Style := Thin;   Multiplicity := 2)
                      has_label An_Identifier (Where := Centered);
node INTERACTION      is Trapezoid
                      (Line := Solid;   Style := Thin;   Multiplicity := 1)
                      has_label An_Identifier (Where := Centered);
```

```
node INTERACTIONS     is Trapezoid
                          (Line := Solid;   Style := Thin;   Multiplicity := 2)
                          has_label An_Identifier (Where := Centered);
node LOCATION         is Diamond
                          (Line := Solid;   Style := Thin;   Multiplicity := 1)
                          has_label An_Identifier (Where := Centered);
node LOCATIONS        is Diamond
                          (Line := Solid;   Style := Thin;   Multiplicity := 2)
                          has_label An_Identifier (Where := Centered);
node OBJECTBASE       is Data_Store
                          (Line := Solid;   Style := Thick; Multiplicity := 1)
                          has_label An_Identifier (Where := Centered);
node OBJECTBASES      is Data_Store
                          (Line := Solid;   Style := Thick; Multiplicity := 2)
                          has_label An_Identifier (Where := Centered);
node ORGANIZATION     is Building
                          (Line := Solid;   Style := Thin;   Multiplicity := 1)
                          has_label An_Identifier (Where := Centered);
node ORGANIZATIONS    is Building
                          (Line := Solid;   Style := Thin;   Multiplicity := 2)
                          has_label An_Identifier (Where := Centered);
node PERSON           is Circle
                          (Line := Solid;   Style := Thin;   Multiplicity := 1)
                          has_label An_Identifier (Where := Centered);
node PERSONS          is Circle
                          (Line := Solid;   Style := Thin;   Multiplicity := 2)
                          has_label An_Identifier (Where := Centered);
node FRAMEWORK        is Rounded_Rectangle
                          (Line := Dash;   Style := Thick; Multiplicity := 2)
                          has_label An_Identifier (Where := Centered);
node ASSEMBLY         is Rounded_Rectangle
                          (Line := Solid;   Style := Thick; Multiplicity := 2)
                          has_label An_Identifier (Where := Centered);
node STANDARD         is Hexagon
                          (Line := Solid;   Style := Thin;   Multiplicity := 1)
                          has_label An_Identifier (Where := Centered);
node STANDARDS        is Hexagon
                          (Line := Solid;   Style := Thin;   Multiplicity := 2)
                          has_label An_Identifier (Where := Centered);
node SYSTEM           is Box
                          (Line := Solid;   Style := Thick; Multiplicity := 1)
                          has_label An_Identifier (Where := Centered);
node SYSTEMS          is Box
                          (Line := Solid;   Style := Thick; Multiplicity := 2)
                          has_label An_Identifier (Where := Centered);

-- Arc definitions:
-- Arc icons must be labeled with the identifier of the corresponding relationship.

arc ASSOCIATION                  is Arrow       (Line := Solid; Style := Thin)
         has_label An_Identifier (Where := Centered);
arc CONDITIONAL_ASSOCIATION      is Arrow_Bent  (Line := Solid; Style := Thin)
         has_label An_Identifier (Where := Centered);
```

```
-- Arc rules:

ANY_NODE := CONCEPT     or CONCEPTS     or DEVICE      or DEVICES        or
            DOCUMENT    or DOCUMENTS    or EVENT       or EVENTS         or
            INTERACTION or INTERACTIONS or LOCATION    or LOCATIONS      or
            OBJECTBASE  or OBJECTBASES  or ORGANIZATION or ORGANIZATIONS or
            PERSON      or PERSONS      or FRAMEWORK    or ASSEMBLY       or
            STANDARD    or STANDARDS    or SYSTEM       or SYSTEMS;

    may_connect ANY_NODE with ASSOCIATION             to ANY_NODE;
    may_connect ANY_NODE with CONDITIONAL_ASSOCIATION          to ANY_NODE;

end SYSTEM_SEMANTIC_NET;
```

## C.2.2    System Interaction Diagrams (SIDs)

System interaction diagrams (SIDs) document the application domain entities that
may be modeled by the software objects and classes and also document the interactions between these entities. Figure C-6 documents the 24 valid nodes and 2 valid arcs
of SIDs.

The following is the specification of the syntax and the semantics of SIDs, which
are part of the system model:

```
diagram SYSTEM_INTERACTION_DIAGRAM is

-- Node definitions:
-- Node icons must be labeled with the identifier of the corresponding entity.
  -- Nodes:
    node CONCEPT          is Cloud
                          (Line := Solid;   Style := Thin;   Multiplicity := 1)
                          has_label An_Identifier (Where := Centered);
    node CONCEPTS         is Cloud
                          (Line := Solid;   Style := Thin;   Multiplicity := 2)
                          has_label An_Identifier (Where := Centered);
    node DEVICE           is Box
                          (Line := Solid;   Style := Thin;   Multiplicity := 1)
                          has_label An_Identifier (Where := Centered);
    node DEVICES          is Box
                          (Line := Solid;   Style := Thin;   Multiplicity := 2)
                          has_label An_Identifier (Where := Centered);
    node DOCUMENT         is Rectangle
                          (Line := Solid;   Style := Thin;   Multiplicity := 1)
                          has_label An_Identifier (Where := Centered);
    node DOCUMENTS        is Rectangle
                          (Line := Solid;   Style := Thin;   Multiplicity := 2)
                          has_label An_Identifier (Where := Centered);
    node EVENT            is Banner
                          (Line := Solid;   Style := Thin;   Multiplicity := 1)
                          has_label An_Identifier (Where := Centered);
    node EVENTS           is Banner
                          (Line := Solid;   Style := Thin;   Multiplicity := 2)
                          has_label An_Identifier (Where := Centered);
```

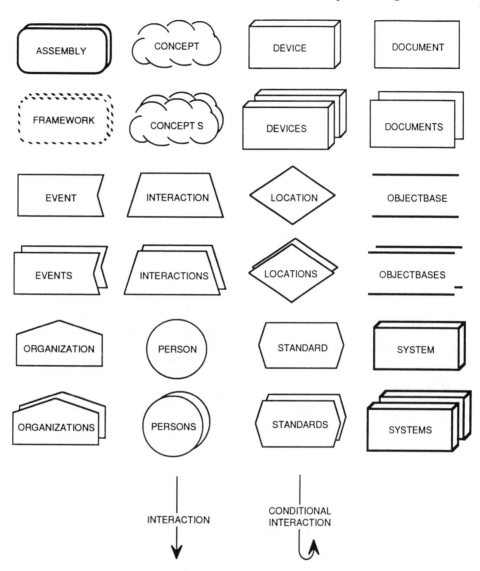

**Figure C-6: Valid Nodes and Arcs for System Interaction Diagrams (SIDs)**

```
node INTERACTION      is Trapezoid
                      (Line := Solid;   Style := Thin;   Multiplicity := 1)
                      has_label An_Identifier (Where := Centered);
node INTERACTIONS     is Trapezoid
                      (Line := Solid;   Style := Thin;   Multiplicity := 2)
                      has_label An_Identifier (Where := Centered);
node LOCATION         is Diamond
                      (Line := Solid;   Style := Thin;   Multiplicity := 1)
                      has_label An_Identifier (Where := Centered);
```

```
node LOCATIONS          is Diamond
                        (Line := Solid;   Style := Thin;  Multiplicity := 2)
                        has_label An_Identifier (Where := Centered);
node OBJECTBASE         is Data_Store
                        (Line := Solid;   Style := Thick; Multiplicity := 1)
                        has_label An_Identifier (Where := Centered);
node OBJECTBASES        is Data_Store
                        (Line := Solid;   Style := Thick; Multiplicity := 2)
                        has_label An_Identifier (Where := Centered);
node ORGANIZATION       is Building
                        (Line := Solid;   Style := Thin;  Multiplicity := 1)
                        has_label An_Identifier (Where := Centered);
node ORGANIZATIONS      is Building
                        (Line := Solid;   Style := Thin;  Multiplicity := 2)
                        has_label An_Identifier (Where := Centered);
node PERSON             is Circle
                        (Line := Solid;   Style := Thin;  Multiplicity := 1)
                        has_label An_Identifier (Where := Centered);
node PERSONS            is Circle
                        (Line := Solid;   Style := Thin;  Multiplicity := 2)
                        has_label An_Identifier (Where := Centered);
node FRAMEWORK          is Rounded_Rectangle
                        (Line := Dash;    Style := Thick; Multiplicity := 1)
                        has_label An_Identifier (Where := Centered);
node ASSEMBLY           is Rounded_Rectangle
                        (Line := Solid; Style := Thick; Multiplicity := 2)
                        has_label An_Identifier (Where := Centered);
node STANDARD           is Hexagon
                        (Line := Solid;   Style := Thin;  Multiplicity := 1)
                        has_label An_Identifier (Where := Centered);
node STANDARDS          is Hexagon
                        (Line := Solid;   Style := Thin;  Multiplicity := 2)
                        has_label An_Identifier (Where := Centered);
node SYSTEM             is Box
                        (Line := Solid;   Style := Thick; Multiplicity := 1)
                        has_label An_Identifier (Where := Centered);
node SYSTEMS            is Box
                        (Line := Solid;   Style := Thick; Multiplicity := 2)
                        has_label An_Identifier (Where := Centered);


-- Arc definitions:
-- Arc icons must be labeled with the identifier of the corresponding relationship.

   arc INTERACTION  is Arrow          (Line          := Solid; Style := Thin)
         has_label An_Identifier  (Where         := Centered);
   arc CONDITIONAL_INTERACTION  is Arrow_Bent  (Line := Solid; Style := Thin)
         has_label An_Identifier   (Where         := Centered);


-- Arc rules:

   ANY_NODE := CONCEPT     or CONCEPTS     or DEVICE       or DEVICES                or
```

```
DOCUMENT      or DOCUMENTS     or EVENT         or EVENTS         or
INTERACTION   or INTERACTIONS  or LOCATION      or LOCATIONS      or
OBJECTBASE    or OBJECTBASES   or ORGANIZATION  or ORGANIZATIONS  or
PERSON        or PERSONS       or FRAMEWORK     or ASSEMBLY       or
STANDARD      or STANDARDS     or SYSTEM        or SYSTEMS;
```

```
    may_connect ANY_NODE with INTERACTION               to ANY_NODE;
    may_connect ANY_NODE with CONDITIONAL_INTERACTION   to ANY_NODE;
```

```
end SYSTEM_INTERACTION_DIAGRAM;
```

## C.2.3   System Composition Diagrams (SCMDs)

System composition diagrams (SCMDs) document an aggregation hierarchy consisting of an aggregate entity, its component entities, and the "has components" relationships between them. Figure C-7 documents the 22 valid nodes and 2 valid arcs of SCMDs.

The following is the specification of the syntax and the semantics of system composition diagrams (SCMDs), which are part of the system model:

```
diagram SYSTEM_COMPOSITION_DIAGRAM is

-- Node definitions:
-- Node icons must be labeled with the identifier of the corresponding entity.

  -- Nodes:

  node CONCEPT        is Cloud
                      (Line := Solid;   Style := Thin;   Multiplicity := 1)
                      has_label An_Identifier (Where := Centered);
  node CONCEPTS       is Cloud
                      (Line := Solid;   Style := Thin;   Multiplicity := 2)
                      has_label An_Identifier (Where := Centered);
  node DEVICE         is Box
                      (Line := Solid;   Style := Thin;   Multiplicity := 1)
                      has_label An_Identifier (Where := Centered);
  node DEVICES        is Box
                      (Line := Solid;   Style := Thin;   Multiplicity := 2)
                      has_label An_Identifier (Where := Centered);
  node DOCUMENT       is Rectangle
                      (Line := Solid;   Style := Thin;   Multiplicity := 1)
                      has_label An_Identifier (Where := Centered);
  node DOCUMENTS      is Rectangle
                      (Line := Solid;   Style := Thin;   Multiplicity := 2)
                      has_label An_Identifier (Where := Centered);
  node EVENT          is Banner
                      (Line := Solid;   Style := Thin;   Multiplicity := 1)
                      has_label An_Identifier (Where := Centered);
  node EVENTS         is Banner
                      (Line := Solid;   Style := Thin;   Multiplicity := 2)
                      has_label An_Identifier (Where := Centered);
```

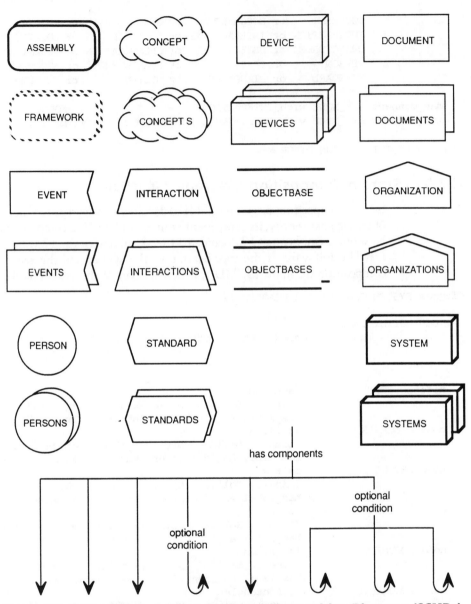

**Figure C-7: Valid Nodes and Arcs for System Composition Diagrams (SCMDs)**

```
node INTERACTION        is Trapezoid
                        (Line := Solid;   Style := Thin;   Multiplicity := 1)
                        has_label An_Identifier (Where := Centered);
```

```
  node INTERACTIONS          is Trapezoid
                             (Line := Solid;   Style := Thin;   Multiplicity := 2)
                             has_label An_Identifier (Where := Centered);
  node OBJECTBASE            is Data_Store
                             (Line := Solid;   Style := Thick; Multiplicity := 1)
                             has_label An_Identifier (Where := Centered);
  node OBJECTBASES           is Data_Store
                             (Line := Solid;   Style := Thick; Multiplicity := 2)
                             has_label An_Identifier (Where := Centered);
  node ORGANIZATION          is Building
                             (Line := Solid;   Style := Thin;   Multiplicity := 1)
                             has_label An_Identifier (Where := Centered);
  node ORGANIZATIONS         is Building
                             (Line := Solid;   Style := Thin;   Multiplicity := 2)
                             has_label An_Identifier (Where := Centered);
  node PERSON               is Circle
                             (Line := Solid;   Style := Thin;   Multiplicity := 1)
                             has_label An_Identifier (Where := Centered);
  node PERSONS              is Circle
                             (Line := Solid;   Style := Thin;   Multiplicity := 2)
                             has_label An_Identifier (Where := Centered);
  node FRAMEWORK            is Rounded_Rectangle
                             (Line := Dash;   Style := Thick; Multiplicity := 1)
                             has_label An_Identifier (Where := Centered);
  node ASSEMBLY            is Rounded_Rectangle
                             (Line := Solid;   Style := Thick; Multiplicity := 2)
                             has_label An_Identifier (Where := Centered);
  node STANDARD            is Hexagon
                             (Line := Solid;   Style := Thin;   Multiplicity := 1)
                             has_label An_Identifier (Where := Centered);
 node STANDARDS            is Hexagon
                             (Line := Solid;   Style := Thin;   Multiplicity := 2)
                             has_label An_Identifier (Where := Centered);
  node SYSTEM              is Box
                             (Line := Solid;   Style := Thick; Multiplicity := 1)
                             has_label An_Identifier (Where := Centered);
  node SYSTEMS             is Box
                             (Line := Solid;   Style := Thick; Multiplicity := 2)
                             has_label An_Identifier (Where := Centered);


-- Arc definitions:

  arc HAS_COMPONENTS          is Arrow_Fork
                       (Line := Solid; Style := Thin; Constraints := X_Y_Axes)
                      has_label "has components" (Where := Centered);
  arc MAY_HAVE_COMPONENT  is Arrow_Bent
                       (Line := Solid; Style := Thin; Constraints := X_Y_Axes);
-- Arc rules:

  may_connect CONCEPT         with HAS_COMPONENTS       to CONCEPT;
  may_connect CONCEPT         with MAY_HAVE_COMPONENT  to CONCEPT;
```

```
may_connect CONCEPTS      with HAS_COMPONENTS       to CONCEPTS;
may_connect CONCEPTS      with MAY_HAVE_COMPONENT   to CONCEPTS;
may_connect DEVICE        with HAS_COMPONENTS       to DEVICE;
may_connect DEVICE        with MAY_HAVE_COMPONENT   to DEVICE;
may_connect DEVICES       with HAS_COMPONENTS       to DEVICES;
may_connect DEVICES       with MAY_HAVE_COMPONENT   to DEVICES;
may_connect DOCUMENT      with HAS_COMPONENTS       to DOCUMENT;
may_connect DOCUMENT      with MAY_HAVE_COMPONENT   to DOCUMENT;
may_connect DOCUMENTS     with HAS_COMPONENTS       to DOCUMENTS;
may_connect DOCUMENTS     with MAY_HAVE_COMPONENT   to DOCUMENTS;
may_connect EVENT         with HAS_COMPONENTS       to EVENT;
may_connect EVENT         with MAY_HAVE_COMPONENT   to EVENT;
may_connect EVENTS        with HAS_COMPONENTS       to EVENTS;
may_connect EVENTS        with MAY_HAVE_COMPONENT   to EVENTS;
may_connect INTERACTION   with HAS_COMPONENTS       to INTERACTION;
may_connect INTERACTION   with MAY_HAVE_COMPONENT   to INTERACTION;
may_connect INTERACTIONS  with HAS_COMPONENTS       to INTERACTIONS;
may_connect INTERACTIONS  with MAY_HAVE_COMPONENT   to INTERACTIONS;
may_connect ORGANIZATION  with HAS_COMPONENTS       to ORGANIZATION;
may_connect ORGANIZATION  with MAY_HAVE_COMPONENT   to ORGANIZATION;
may_connect ORGANIZATIONS with HAS_COMPONENTS       to ORGANIZATIONS;
may_connect ORGANIZATIONS with MAY_HAVE_COMPONENT   to ORGANIZATIONS;
may_connect STANDARD      with HAS_COMPONENTS       to STANDARD;
may_connect STANDARD      with MAY_HAVE_COMPONENT   to STANDARD;
may_connect STANDARDS     with HAS_COMPONENTS       to STANDARDS;
may_connect STANDARDS     with MAY_HAVE_COMPONENT   to STANDARDS;
may_connect SYSTEM        with HAS_COMPONENTS       to DEVICE;
may_connect SYSTEM        with MAY_HAVE_COMPONENT   to DEVICE;
may_connect SYSTEM        with HAS_COMPONENTS       to DOCUMENT;
may_connect SYSTEM        with MAY_HAVE_COMPONENT   to DOCUMENT;
may_connect SYSTEM        with HAS_COMPONENTS       to OBJECTBASE;
may_connect SYSTEM        with MAY_HAVE_COMPONENT   to OBJECTBASE;
may_connect SYSTEM        with HAS_COMPONENTS       to PERSON;
may_connect SYSTEM        with MAY_HAVE_COMPONENT   to PERSON;
may_connect SYSTEM        with HAS_COMPONENTS       to ASSEMBLY;
may_connect SYSTEM        with MAY_HAVE_COMPONENT   to ASSEMBLY;
may_connect SYSTEM        with HAS_COMPONENTS       to SYSTEM;
may_connect SYSTEM        with MAY_HAVE_COMPONENT   to SYSTEM;
may_connect SYSTEMS       with HAS_COMPONENTS       to DEVICES;
may_connect SYSTEMS       with MAY_HAVE_COMPONENT   to DEVICES;
may_connect SYSTEMS       with HAS_COMPONENTS       to DOCUMENTS;
may_connect SYSTEMS       with MAY_HAVE_COMPONENT   to DOCUMENTS;
may_connect SYSTEMS       with HAS_COMPONENTS       to OBJECTBASES;
may_connect SYSTEMS       with MAY_HAVE_COMPONENT   to OBJECTBASES;
may_connect SYSTEMS       with HAS_COMPONENTS       to PERSONS;
may_connect SYSTEMS       with MAY_HAVE_COMPONENT   to PERSONS;
may_connect SYSTEMS       with HAS_COMPONENTS       to ASSEMBLY;
may_connect SYSTEMS       with MAY_HAVE_COMPONENT   to ASSEMBLY;
may_connect SYSTEMS       with HAS_COMPONENTS       to SYSTEMS;
may_connect SYSTEMS       with MAY_HAVE_COMPONENT   to SYSTEMS;

end SYSTEM_COMPOSITION_DIAGRAM;
```

## C.2.4    System State Transition Diagrams (SSTDs)

System state transition diagrams (SSTDs) document the states of system-level entities. STDs also document the transitions between the states. Figure C-8 documents the 20 valid nodes and 5 valid arcs of SSTDs.

The following is the specification of the syntax and the semantics of system state transition diagrams (SSTDs), which are part of the system model:

```
diagram SYSTEM_STATE_TRANSITION_DIAGRAM is
-- Node definitions:
-- Node icons must be labeled with the identifier of the corresponding entity.

   -- State nodes:
   node START            is Circle
                         (Line := Solid;    Style := Thin;    Multiplicity := 1)
                         has_label "START" (Where := Centered);
   node STATE            is Rectangle
                         (Line := Solid;    Style := Thin;    Multiplicity := 1)
                         has_label An_Identifier (Where := Centered);
   node AGGREGATE_STATE  is Rounded_Rectangle
                         (Line := Solid;    Style := Thin;    Multiplicity := 1)
                         has_label An_Identifier (Where := Centered);
   node END_STATE        is Rectangle
                         (Line := Solid;    Style := Thin;    Multiplicity := 1)
                         has_label An_Identifier (Where := Centered);

   -- System nodes:
   node DEVICE           is Box
                         (Line := Solid;    Style := Thin;    Multiplicity := 1)
                         has_label An_Identifier (Where := Centered);
   node DEVICES          is Box
                         (Line := Solid;    Style := Thin;    Multiplicity := 2)
                         has_label An_Identifier (Where := Centered);
   node DOCUMENT         is Rectangle
                         (Line := Solid;    Style := Thin;    Multiplicity := 1)
                         has_label An_Identifier (Where := Centered);
   node DOCUMENTS        is Rectangle
                         (Line := Solid;    Style := Thin;    Multiplicity := 2)
                         has_label An_Identifier (Where := Centered);
   node INTERACTION      is Trapezoid
                         (Line := Solid;    Style := Thin;    Multiplicity := 1)
                         has_label An_Identifier (Where := Centered);
   node INTERACTIONS     is Trapezoid
                         (Line := Solid;    Style := Thin;    Multiplicity := 2)
                         has_label An_Identifier (Where := Centered);
   node OBJECTBASE       is Data_Store
                         (Line := Solid;    Style := Thick;    Multiplicity := 1)
                         has_label An_Identifier (Where := Centered);
   node OBJECTBASES      is Data_Store
                         (Line := Solid;    Style := Thick;    Multiplicity := 2)
                         has_label An_Identifier (Where := Centered);
```

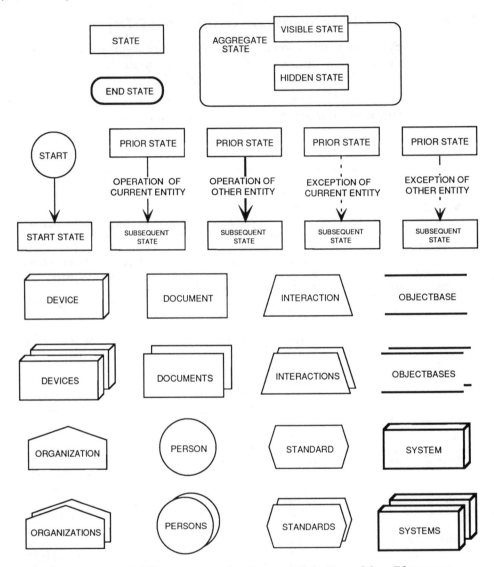

**Figure C-8: Valid Nodes and Arcs for System State Transition Diagrams (SSTDs)**

```
node ORGANIZATION      is Building
                       (Line := Solid;   Style := Thin;   Multiplicity := 1)
                       has_label An_Identifier (Where := Centered);
node ORGANIZATIONS     is Building
                       (Line := Solid;   Style := Thin;   Multiplicity := 2)
                       has_label An_Identifier (Where := Centered);
node PERSON            is Circle
                       (Line := Solid;   Style := Thin;   Multiplicity := 1)
                       has_label An_Identifier (Where := Centered);
```

```
    node PERSONS              is Circle
                              (Line := Solid;   Style := Thin;   Multiplicity := 2)
                              has_label An_Identifier (Where := Centered);
    node STANDARD             is Hexagon
                              (Line := Solid;   Style := Thin;   Multiplicity := 1)
                              has_label An_Identifier (Where := Centered);
    node STANDARDS            is Hexagon
                              (Line := Solid;   Style := Thin;   Multiplicity := 2)
                              has_label An_Identifier (Where := Centered);
    node SYSTEM               is Box
                              (Line := Solid;   Style := Thick; Multiplicity := 1)
                              has_label An_Identifier (Where := Centered);
    node SYSTEMS              is Box
                              (Line := Solid;   Style := Thick; Multiplicity := 2)
    has_label An_Identifier (Where := Centered);
```

-- Arc definitions:
    -- INTERACTIONS must be labeled with the associated messages and may be labeled
    -- with the associated attribute types, constant attributes, and exceptions.

```
    arc START_ARC                      is Arrow (Line := Solid; Style := Thin);
    arc OPERATION_OF_CURRENT_COMPONENT is Arrow (Line := Solid; Style := Thin)
                    has_label An_Identifier (Where := Centered);
    arc OPERATION_OF_OTHER_ENTITY      is Arrow (Line := Solid; Style := Thick)
                    has_label An_Identifier (Where := Centered);
    arc EXCEPTION_OF_CURRENT_COMPONENT is Arrow (Line := Dot  ; Style := Thin)
                    has_label An_Identifier (Where := Centered);
    arc EXCEPTION_OF_OTHER_ENTITY      is Arrow (Line := Dash ; Style := Thin)
                    has_label An_Identifier (Where := Centered);
```

-- Parenting rules:

```
    must_parent  START;
    must_parent  STATE;
    must_parent  COMPOUND_STATE;
    must_parent  END_STATE;

    ENTITY := DEVICE        or  DEVICES        or DOCUMENT     or DOCUMENTS    or
              INTERACTION   or  INTERACTIONS   or OBJECTBASE   or OBJECTBASES  or
              ORGANIZATION  or  ORGANIZATIONS  or PERSON       or PERSONS      or
              STANDARD      or  STANDARDS      or SYSTEM       or SYSTEMS;

    may_nest    START      in ENTITY;
    may_nest    START      in AGGREGATE_STATE;
    may_socket  START      to AGGREGATE_STATE (Where := Straddle);
    may_nest    STATE      in ENTITY;
    may_nest    STATE      in AGGREGATE_STATE;
    may_socket  STATE      to AGGREGATE_STATE (Where := Straddle);
    may_nest    END_STATE  in ENTITY;
    may_nest    END_STATE  in AGGREGATE_STATE;
    may_socket  END_STATE  to AGGREGATE_STATE (Where := Straddle);
```

```
-- Arc rules:

   may_connect START   with START_ARC                          to STATE;
   may_connect STATE   with OPERATION_OF_CURRENT_COMPONENT      to STATE;
   may_connect STATE   with OPERATION_OF_CURRENT_COMPONENT      to END_STATE;
   may_connect STATE   with OPERATION_OF_OTHER_ENTITY           to STATE;
   may_connect STATE   with OPERATION_OF_OTHER_ENTITY           to END_STATE;
   may_connect STATE   with EXCEPTION_OF_CURRENT_COMPONENT      to STATE;
   may_connect STATE   with EXCEPTION_OF_CURRENT_COMPONENT      to END_STATE;
   may_connect STATE   with EXCEPTION_OF_OTHER_ENTITY           to STATE;
   may_connect STATE   with EXCEPTION_OF_OTHER_ENTITY           to END_STATE;


end SYSTEM_STATE_TRANSITION_DIAGRAM;
```

## C.2.5    System Event Timing Diagrams (SETDs)

System event timing diagrams (SETDs) document the timing or sequence interactions between system-level entities. Figure C-9 documents the 1 valid node and 3 valid arcs of SETDs.

The following is the specification of the syntax and the semantics of SETDs, which are part of the system model:

```
diagram SYSTEM_EVENT_TIMING_DIAGRAM is

-- Node definitions:
-- Node icons must be labeled with the identifier of the corresponding entity.

   node TIMING_BOX  is Rectangle (Line := Solid; Style := Thin; Multiplicity := 1);

-- Arc definitions:
     -- INTERACTIONS must be labeled with the associated messages and may be labeled
     -- with the associated attribute types, constant attributes, and exceptions.

     -- ENTITY := CONCEPT      or CONCEPTS      or DEVICE      or DEVICES       or
                  DOCUMENT      or DOCUMENTS     or EVENT       or EVENTS        or
                  INTERACTION   or INTERACTIONS  or LOCATION    or LOCATIONS     or
                  OBJECTBASE    or OBJECTBASES   or ORGANIZATION or ORGANIZATIONS or
                  PERSON        or PERSONS       or FRAMEWORK    or ASSEMBLY      or
                  STANDARD      or STANDARDS     or SYSTEM       or SYSTEMS;

   arc ENTITY               is Line_Segment
                            (Line := Solid; Style := Thick; Constraints := Y_Axis)
                            has_label An_Identifier (Where := Above, Outside)
                            [divided_horizontally_into
                            {subnode A_State
                            has_label Identifier (Where := Centered)}];
   arc INTERACTION          is Arrow
                            (Line := Solid; Style := Thin;  Constraints := X_Axis)
                            has_label An_Identifier (Where := Above, Centered);
   arc END_OF_CYCLE         is Line_Segment
                            (Line := Dash;  Style := Thin;  Constraints := X_Axis);
```

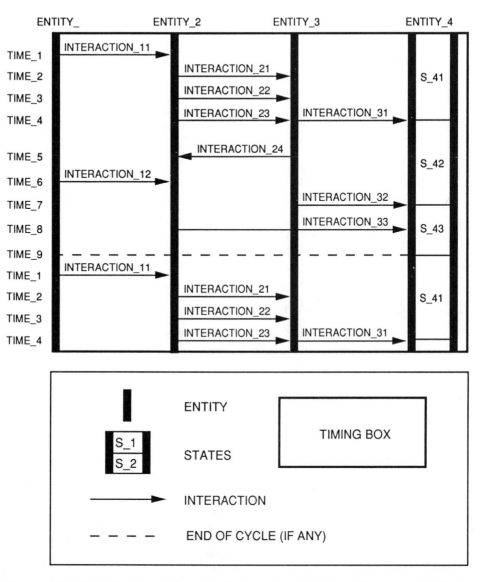

**Figure C-9: Valid Node and Arcs for System Event Timing Diagrams (SETDs)**

```
-- Arc rules:

    may_connect TIMING_BOX  with ENTITY        to TIMING_BOX;
    may_connect TIMING_BOX  with END_OF_CYCLE  to TIMING_BOX;
    may_connect ENTITY      with INTERACTION   to ENTITY;

end SYSTEM_EVENT_TIMING_DIAGRAM;
```

## C.3  SOFTWARE DIAGRAMS

ADM3 provides the following diagrams for software-level requirements analysis and design:

- Context Diagrams (CDs)
- Assembly Diagrams (ADs)
- General semantic nets (GSNs)
- Interaction diagrams (IDs)
- Composition diagrams (CMDs)
- Classification diagrams (CLDs)
- State transition diagrams (STDs)
- Control flow diagrams (CFDs)
- Event timing diagrams (ETDs)
- Module diagrams (MDs)
- Submodule diagrams (SMDs)

### C.3.1  Context Diagrams (CDs)

Context diagrams (CDs) document an assembly, its terminators, and the important associations between them. Figure C-10 documents the 11 valid nodes and 2 valid arcs of context diagrams.

The following is the specification of the syntax and the semantics of CDs, which are part of the assembly model:

```
diagram CONTEXT_DIAGRAM is

-- Node definitions:
-- Node icons must be labeled with the identifier of the corresponding entity.

-- Primary nodes:

   node ASSEMBLY          is Rounded_Rectangle
                          (Line := Solid;   Style := Thick;   Multiplicity := 2)
                          has_label An_Identifier (Where := Centered);
   node ASSEMBLY_SPECIFICATION  is Rectangle
                          (Line := Solid;   Style := Thin;   Multiplicity := 1)
                          has_list Of_Subassemblies (Where := Centered);
   node ASSEMBLY_BODY     is Rectangle
                          (Line := Dotted;  Style := Thin;   Multiplicity := 1)
                          has_list Of_Subassemblies (Where := Centered);

   -- Terminators:

   node DEVICE            is Box
                          (Line := Solid;   Style := Thin;   Multiplicity := 1)
                          has_label An_Identifier (Where := Centered);
```

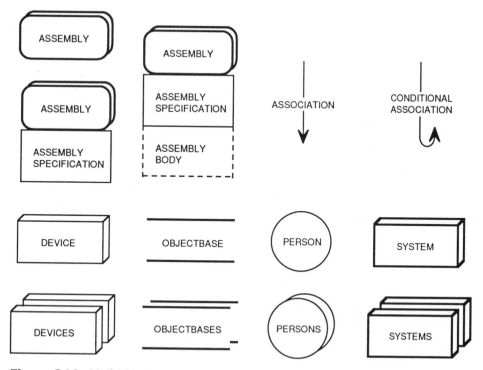

**Figure C-10: Valid Nodes and Arcs for Context Diagrams (CDs)**

```
node DEVICES              is Box
                          (Line := Solid;   Style := Thin;   Multiplicity := 2)
                          has_label An_Identifier (Where := Centered);
node OBJECTBASE           is Data_Store
                          (Line := Solid;   Style := Thick; Multiplicity := 1)
                          has_label An_Identifier (Where := Centered);
node OBJECTBASES          is Data_Store
                          (Line := Solid;   Style := Thick; Multiplicity := 2)
                          has_label An_Identifier (Where := Centered);
node PERSON               is Circle
                          (Line := Solid;   Style := Thin;   Multiplicity := 1)
                          has_label An_Identifier (Where := Centered);
node PERSONS              is Circle
                          (Line := Solid;   Style := Thin;   Multiplicity := 2)
                          has_label An_Identifier (Where := Centered);
node SYSTEM               is Box
                          (Line := Solid;   Style := Thick; Multiplicity := 1)
                          has_label An_Identifier (Where := Centered);
node SYSTEMS              is Box
                          (Line := Solid;   Style := Thick; Multiplicity := 2)
                          has_label An_Identifier (Where := Centered);
```

```
-- Arc definitions:
-- Arc icons must be labeled with the identifier of the corresponding relationship.

    arc ASSOCIATION              is arrow      (Line := Solid; Style := Thin)
                    has_label An_Identifier (Where := Centered);
    arc CONDITIONAL_ASSOCIATION is Arrow_Bent (Line := Solid; Style := Thin)
                    has_label An_Identifier (Where := Centered);


-- Parenting rules:

    must_parent ASSEMBLY SPECIFICATION:
    must_parent ASSEMBLY BODY;
    may_socket ASSEMBLY_SPECIFICATION to ASSEMBLY                (Where := Outside);
    may_socket ASSEMBLY_BODY          to ASSEMBLY                (Where := Outside);
    may_socket ASSEMBLY_BODY          to ASSEMBLY_SPECIFICATION  (Where := Outside);


-- Arc rules:

    TERMINATOR := DEVICE   or   DEVICES  or   OBJECTBASE  or OBJECTBASES  or
                  PERSON   or   PERSONS  or   SYSTEM      or SYSTEMS;

    START_NODE := ASSEMBLY or ASSEMBLY_SPECIFICATION or ASSEMBLY_BODY or TERMINATOR;
    END_NODE   := ASSEMBLY or TERMINATOR;

    if
      not START_NODE = END_NODE
    then
      may_connect START_NODE with ASSOCIATION             to END_NODE
      may_connect START_NODE with CONDITIONAL_ASSOCIATION to END_NODE
    end if;

end CONTEXT_DIAGRAM;
```

## C.3.2    Assembly Diagrams (ADs)

Assembly diagrams (ADs) document an assembly, the visibility and existence of its component subassemblies, the subassemblies' specifications and bodies, and the depends upon relationships between them. Figure C-11 documents the 4 valid nodes and 1 valid arc of ADs.

The following is the specification of the syntax and the semantics of assembly diagrams (ADs), which are part of the assembly model:

```
diagram ASSEMBLY_DIAGRAM is

-- Node definitions:
-- Node icons must be labeled with the identifier of the corresponding entity.

-- Primary nodes:
```

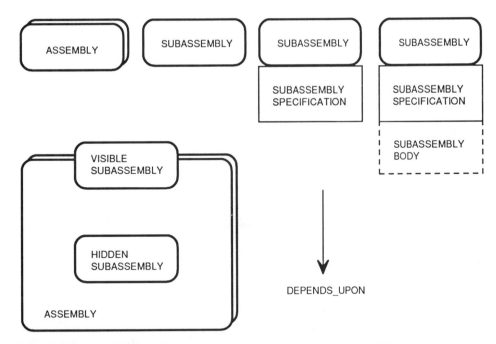

**Figure C-11: Valid Nodes and Arc for Assembly Diagrams (ADs)**

```
node ASSEMBLY            is Rounded_Rectangle
                         (Line := Solid;   Style := Thick;  Multiplicity := 2)
                         has_label An_Identifier (Where := Centered);
node SUBASSEMBLY         is Rounded_Rectangle
                         (Line := Solid;   Style := Thick;  Multiplicity := 1)
                         has_label An_Identifier (Where := Centered);
-- Resources:

 COMPONENT :=    OBJECT or CLASS or SUBASSEMBLY;

node SUBASSEMBLY_SPECIFICATION  is Rectangle
                         (Line := Solid;   Style := Thin;   Multiplicity := 1)
                         has_list Of_Components (Where := Centered);
node SUBASSEMBLY_BODY          is Rectangle
                         (Line := Dotted;  Style := Thin;   Multiplicity := 1)
                         has_list Of_Components (Where := Centered);

-- Arc definitions:
-- Arc icons must be labeled with the identifier of the corresponding relationship.

    arc DEPENDS_ON is Arrow (Line := Solid; Style := Thin);

-- Parenting rules:

    must_parent SUBASSEMBLY;
```

```
    must_parent   SPECIFICATION_SUBASSEMBLY;
    must_parent   BODY_SUBASSEMBLY;
    may_nest      SUBASSEMBLY                    in ASSEMBLY;
    may_socket    SUBASSEMBLY                    to ASSEMBLY        (Where := Straddle);
    may_socket    SUBASSEMBLY_SPECIFICATION      to SUBASSEMBLY     (Where := Outside);
    may_socket    SUBASSEMBLY_BODY               to SUBASSEMBLY     (Where := Outside);
    may_socket    SUBASSEMBLY_BODY               to SUBASSEMBLY_SPECIFICATION
                                                                   (Where := Outside);

-- Arc rules:

    START_NODE :=  SUBASSEMBLY or SUBASSEMBLY_SPECIFICATION or SUBASSEMBLY_BODY;

    if
     not START_NODE = SUBASSEMBLY
    then
     may_connect START_NODE with DEPENDS_ON to SUBASSEMBLY;
    end if;


end ASSEMBLY_DIAGRAM;
```

## C.3.3    General Semantic Nets (GSNs)

General semantic nets (GSNs) document a subassembly, the existence and visibility of its component objects and classes, its terminators, and the important associations between them. Figure C-12 documents the 14 valid nodes and 1 valid arc of GSNs.

The following is the specification of the syntax and the semantics of general semantic nets (GSNs), which are part of the object model:

```
diagram GENERAL_SEMANTIC_NET is

-- Node definitions:
-- Node icons must be labeled with the identifier of the corresponding entity.

  -- Object-Oriented nodes:

    node OBJECT(CONCURRENT)    is Parallelogram
                               (Line := Solid;  Style := Thick;   Multiplicity := 1)
                               has_label An_Identifier (Where := Centered);
    node OBJECT(SEQUENTIAL)    is Rectangle
                               (Line := Solid;  Style := Thick;   Multiplicity := 1)
                               has_label An_Identifier (Where := Centered);
    node CLASS(CONCURRENT)     is Parallelogram
                               (Line := Solid;  Style := Thick;   Multiplicity := 2)
                               has_label An_Identifier (Where := Centered);
    node CLASS(SEQUENTIAL)     is Rectangle
                               (Line := Solid;  Style := Thick;   Multiplicity := 2)
                               has_label An_Identifier (Where := Centered);
    node SUBASSEMBLY           is Rounded_Rectangle
                               (Line := Solid;  Style := Thick;   Multiplicity := 1)
                               has_label An_Identifier (Where := Centered);
```

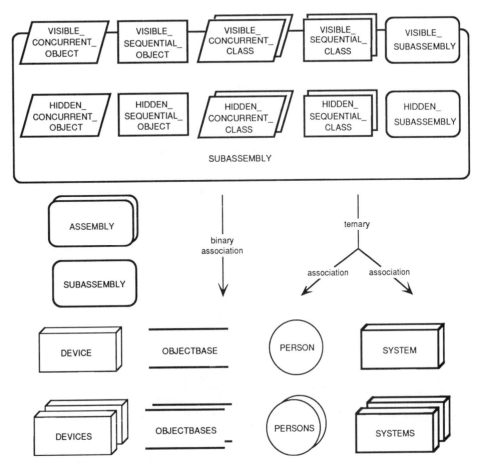

**Figure C-12: Valid Nodes and Arc for General Semantic Nets (GSNs)**

```
    node ASSEMBLY               is Rounded_Rectangle
                                (Line := Solid;    Style := Thick;    Multiplicity := 2)
                                has_label An_Identifier (Where := Centered);
-- Terminators:

    node DEVICE                 is Box
                                (Line := Solid;    Style := Thin;     Multiplicity := 1)
                                has_label An_Identifier (Where := Centered);
    node DEVICES                is Box
                                (Line := Solid;    Style := Thin;     Multiplicity := 2)
                                has_label An_Identifier (Where := Centered);
    node OBJECTBASE             is Data_Store
                                (Line := Solid;    Style := Thick;    Multiplicity := 1)
                                has_label An_Identifier (Where := Centered);
```

```
    node OBJECTBASES            is Data_Store
                                (Line := Solid;   Style := Thick;   Multiplicity := 2)
                                has_label An_Identifier (Where := Centered);
    node PERSON                 is Circle
                                (Line := Solid;   Style := Thin;    Multiplicity := 1)
                                has_label An_Identifier (Where := Centered);
    node PERSONS                is Circle
                                (Line := Solid;   Style := Thin;    Multiplicity := 2)
                                has_label An_Identifier (Where := Centered);
    node SYSTEM                 is Box
                                (Line := Solid;   Style := Thick;   Multiplicity := 1)
                                has_label An_Identifier (Where := Centered);
    node SYSTEMS                is Box
                                (Line := Solid;   Style := Thick;   Multiplicity := 2)
                                has_label An_Identifier (Where := Centered);
-- Arc definitions:
-- Arc icons must be labeled with the identifier of the corresponding relationship.

    arc ASSOCIATION is Arrow (Line := Solid; Style := Thin)
                        has_label An_Identifier (Where := Centered);


-- Parenting rules:

  -- Objects:

  OBJECT := OBJECT(CONCURRENT) or OBJECT(SEQUENTIAL);

  may_nest       OBJECT                  in OBJECT(CONCURRENT);
  may_nest       OBJECT(SEQUENTIAL)      in OBJECT(SEQUENTIAL);
  may_nest       OBJECT                  in SUBASSEMBLY;
  may_socket     OBJECT                  to SUBASSEMBLY (Where := Straddle);

  -- Classes:

  CLASS := CLASS(CONCURRENT) or CLASS(SEQUENTIAL);

  may_nest       CLASS        in SUBASSEMBLY;
  may_socket     CLASS        to SUBASSEMBLY   (Where := Straddle);

  -- Subassemblies:

  may_nest       SUBASSEMBLY  in ASSEMBLY;
  may_nest       SUBASSEMBLY  in SUBASSEMBLY;
  may_socket     SUBASSEMBLY  to ASSEMBLY      (Where := Straddle);
  may_socket     SUBASSEMBLY  to SUBASSEMBLY   (Where := Straddle);

  -- Arc rules:

  TERMINATOR :=  DEVICE  or DEVICES  or OBJECTBASE  or OBJECTBASES  or
                 PERSON  or PERSONS  or SYSTEM      or SYSTEMS;

  START_NODE :=  OBJECT or CLASS or SUBASSEMBLY or ASSEMBLY or TERMINATOR;
```

```
    END_NODE    :=   START_NODE;

if
  not START_NODE = END_NODE
then
  may_connect START_NODE with ASSOCIATION to END_NODE;
end if;
```

**end GENERAL_SEMANTIC_NET;**

## C.3.4    Interaction Diagrams (IDs)

Interaction diagrams (IDs) document a subassembly, the existence and visibility of its component objects and classes, its terminators, and the important interactions between them. Figure C-13 documents the 16 valid nodes and 1 valid arc of IDs.

The following is the specification of the syntax and the semantics of interaction diagrams (IDs), which are part of the object model:

**diagram** INTERACTION_DIAGRAM **is**

```
-- Node definitions:
-- Node icons must be labeled with the identifier of the corresponding entity.

  -- Object-Oriented nodes:

  node OBJECT(CONCURRENT)    is Parallelogram
                             (Line := Solid;   Style := Thick;   Multiplicity := 1)
                             has_label An_Identifier (Where := Centered);
  node OBJECT(SEQUENTIAL)    is Rectangle
                             (Line := Solid;   Style := Thick;   Multiplicity := 1)
                             has_label An_Identifier (Where := Centered);
  node CLASS(CONCURRENT)     is Parallelogram
                             (Line := Solid;   Style := Thick;   Multiplicity := 2)
                             has_label An_Identifier (Where := Centered);
  node CLASS(SEQUENTIAL)     is Rectangle
                             (Line := Solid;   Style := Thick;   Multiplicity := 2)
                             has_label An_Identifier (Where := Centered);
  node SUBASSEMBLY           is Rounded_Rectangle
                             (Line := Solid;   Style := Thick;   Multiplicity := 1)
                             has_label An_Identifier (Where := Centered);
  node ASSEMBLY              is Rounded_Rectangle
                             (Line := Solid;   Style := Thick;   Multiplicity := 2)
                             has_label An_Identifier (Where := Centered);
  -- Terminators:
  node DEVICE                is Box
                             (Line := Solid;   Style := Thin;   Multiplicity := 1)
                             has_label An_Identifier (Where := Centered);
  node DEVICES               is Box
                             (Line := Solid;   Style := Thin;   Multiplicity := 2)
                             has_label An_Identifier (Where := Centered);
```

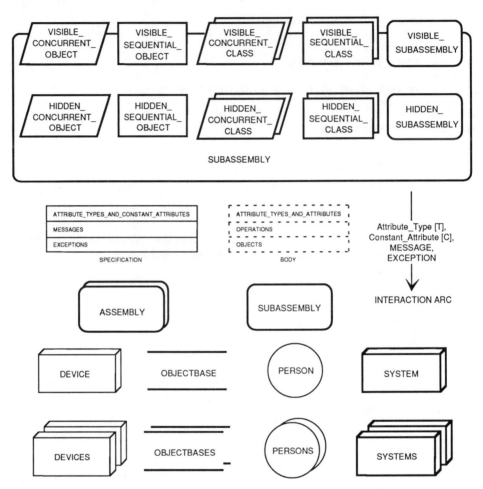

**Figure C-13: Valid Nodes and Arc for Interaction Diagrams (IDs)**

```
node OBJECTBASE          is Data_Store
                         (Line := Solid;   Style := Thick;    Multiplicity := 1)
                         has_label An_Identifier (Where := Centered);
node OBJECTBASES         is Data_Store
                         (Line := Solid;   Style := Thick;    Multiplicity := 2)
                         has_label An_Identifier (Where := Centered);
node PERSON              is Circle
                         (Line := Solid;   Style := Thin;     Multiplicity := 1)
                         has_label An_Identifier (Where := Centered);
node PERSONS             is Circle
                         (Line := Solid;   Style := Thin;     Multiplicity := 2)
                         has_label An_Identifier (Where := Centered);
node SYSTEM              is Box
                         (Line := Solid;   Style := Thick;    Multiplicity := 1)
                         has_label An_Identifier (Where := Centered);
```

```
    node SYSTEMS              is Box
                              (Line := Solid;   Style := Thick;   Multiplicity := 2)
                              has_label An_Identifier (Where := Centered);
    -- Resources:
    node SPECIFICATICN        is Rectangle
                              (Line := Solid;   Style := Thin;   Multiplicity := 1)
                              divided_horizontally_into
                               subnode ATTRIBUTE_TYPES_AND_CONSTANT_ATTRIBUTES
                                has_list  Of_Attribute_Types      (Where := Centered)
                                has_list  Of_Constant_Attributes (Where := Centered)
                               subnode MESSAGES
                                has_list  Of_Messages             (Where := Centered)
                               subnode EXCEPTIONS
                                has_list  Of_Exceptions           (Where := Centered);
    node BODY                 is Rectangle
                              (Line := Dotted;   Style := Thin;   Multiplicity := 1)
                              divided_horizontally_into
                               subnode ATTRIBUTE_TYPES_AND_ATTRIBUTES
                                has_list  Of_Attribute_Types      (Where := Centered)
                                has_list  Of_Attributes           (Where := Centered)
                               subnode OPERATIONS
                                has_list  Of_Operations           (Where := Centered)
                               subnode OBJECTS
                                has_list  Of_Objects              (Where := Centered);
-- Arc definitions:
  -- INTERACTIONS must be labeled with the associated messages and may be labeled
  -- with the associated attribute types, constant attributes, and exceptions.

arc INTERACTION is Arrow (Line := Solid; Style := Thin)
                    has_label An_Identifier (Where := Centered);

-- Parenting rules:

  -- Objects:

  OBJECT := OBJECT(CONCURRENT) or OBJECT(SEQUENTIAL);

  may_nest     OBJECT               in OBJECT(C0NCURRENT);
  may_nest     OBJECT(SEQUENTIAL)   in OBJECT(SEQUENTIAL);
  may_nest     OBJECT               in SUBASSEMBLY;
  may_socket   OBJECT               to SUBASSEMBLY  (Where := Straddle);

  -- Classes:

  CLASS := CLASS(CONCURRENT) or CLASS(SEQUENTIAL);

  may_nest     CLASS                in SUBASSEMBLY;
  may_socket   CLASS                to SUBASSEMBLY  (Where := Straddle);

  -- Subassemblies:

  may_nest     SUBASSEMBLY          in ASSEMBLY;
  may_nest     SUBASSEMBLY          in SUBASSEMBLY;
```

```
may_socket  SUBASSEMBLY  to ASSEMBLY     (Where := Straddle);
may_socket  SUBASSEMBLY  to SUBASSEMBLY  (Where := Straddle);

-- Resources:

SPECIFICATION_PARENT  := OBJECT or CLASS;
BODY_PARENT           := OBJECT or CLASS or SPECIFICATION;

must_parent  SPECIFICATION;
must_parent  BODY;

may_socket  SPECIFICATION  to SPECIFICATION_PARENT  (Where := Outside);
may_socket  BODY           to BODY_PARENT           (Where := Outside);
```

```
-- Arc rules:
   TERMINATOR :=  DEVICE or DEVICES  or OBJECTBASE  or OBJECTBASES  or
                  PERSON or PERSONS  or SYSTEM      or SYSTEMS;

   START_NODE :=  OBJECT or CLASS or SUBASSEMBLY or ASSEMBLY or TERMINATOR;

   END_NODE   :=  OBJECT or CLASS;

   may_connect START_NODE with INTERACTION to END_NODE;

end INTERACTION_DIAGRAM;
```

## C.3.5    Composition Diagrams (CMDs)

Composition diagrams (CMDs) document an aggregation hierarchy consisting of an aggregate entity, its component entities, and the "has component" relationships between them. Figure C-14 documents the 7 valid nodes and 2 valid arcs of CMDs.

The following is the specification of the syntax and the semantics of composition diagrams (CMDs), which are part of the object model:

```
diagram COMPOSITION_DIAGRAM is

-- Node definitions:
-- Node icons must be labeled with the identifier of the corresponding entity.

   -- Object-Oriented nodes:

node OBJECT(CONCURRENT)   is Parallelogram
                          (Line := Solid;   Style := Thick;   Multiplicity := 1)
                          has_label An_Identifier (Where := Centered);
node OBJECT(SEQUENTIAL)   is Rectangle
                          (Line := Solid;   Style := Thick;   Multiplicity := 1)
                          has_label An_Identifier (Where := Centered);
node CLASS(CONCURRENT)    is Parallelogram
                          (Line := Solid;   Style := Thick;   Multiplicity := 2)
                          has_label An_Identifier (Where := Centered);
```

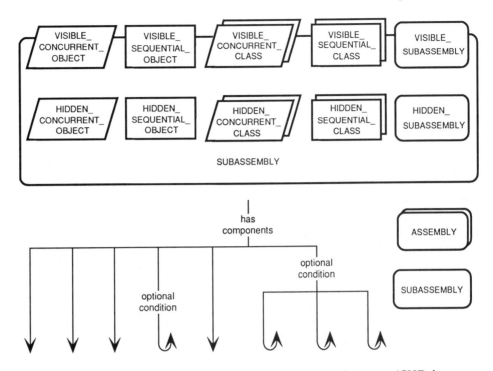

**Figure C-14: Valid Nodes and Arcs for Composition Diagrams (CMDs)**

```
    node CLASS(SEQUENTIAL)      is Rectangle
                               (Line := Solid;    Style := Thick;       Multiplicity := 2)
                               has_label An_Identifier (Where := Centered);
    node SUBASSEMBLY           is Rounded_Rectangle
                               (Line := Solid;    Style := Thick;       Multiplicity := 1)
                               has_label An_Identifier (Where := Centered);
    node ASSEMBLY             is Rounded_Rectangle
                               (Line := Solid;    Style := Thick;       Multiplicity := 2)
                               has_label An_Identifier (Where := Centered);

-- Arc definitions:

    arc HAS_COMPONENTS         is Arrow_Fork
                               (Line := Solid; Style := Thin; Constraints := X_Y_Axes)
                               has_label "has components" (Where := Centered);
    arc MAY_HAVE_COMPONENT     is Arrow_Bent
                               (Line := Solid; Style := Thin; Constraints := X_Y_Axes);

-- Arc rules:

    CLASS  := CLASS(CONCURRENT)  or CLASS(SEQUENTIAL);
    OBJECT := OBJECT(CONCURRENT) or OBJECT(SEQUENTIAL);
```

```
may_connect ASSEMBLY       with HAS_COMPONENTS      to SUBASSEMBLY;
may_connect ASSEMBLY       with MAY_HAVE_COMPONENT  to SUBASSEMBLY;

may_connect SUBASSEMBLY    with HAS_COMPONENTS      to SUBASSEMBLY;
may_connect SUBASSEMBLY    with MAY_HAVE_COMPONENT  to SUBASSEMBLY;
may_connect SUBASSEMBLY    with HAS_COMPONENTS      to CLASS;
may_connect SUBASSEMBLY    with MAY_HAVE_COMPONENT  to CLASS;
may_connect SUBASSEMBLY    with HAS_COMPONENTS      to OBJECT;
may_connect SUBASSEMBLY    with MAY_HAVE_COMPONENT  to OBJECT;

may_connect OBJECT         with HAS_COMPONENTS      to OBJECT;
may_connect OBJECT         with MAY_HAVE_COMPONENTS to OBJECT;

end COMPOSITION_DIAGRAM;
```

## C.3.6    Classification Diagrams (CLDs)

Classification diagrams (CLDs) document the classes, instances, the "has superclass" relationship between subclasses and superclasses, and the "has class" relationships between classes and their instances. Figure C-15 documents the 8 valid nodes and 2 valid arcs of CLDs.

The following is the specification of the syntax and the semantics of classification diagrams (CLDs), which are part of the class model:

```
diagram CLASSIFICATION_DIAGRAM is

-- Node definitions:
-- Node icons must be labeled with the identifier of the corresponding entity.

  -- Object-Oriented nodes:

  node OBJECT(CONCURRENT)    is Parallelogram
                             (Line := Solid;   Style := Thick;  Multiplicity := 1);
                             has_label An_Identifier (Where := Centered);
  node OBJECT(SEQUENTIAL)    is Rectangle
                             (Line := Solid;   Style := Thick;  Multiplicity := 1);
                             has_label An_Identifier (Where := Centered);
  node CLASS(CONCURRENT)     is Parallelogram
                             (Line := Solid;   Style := Thick;  Multiplicity := 2);
                             has_label An_Identifier (Where := Centered);
  node CLASS(SEQUENTIAL)     is Rectangle
                             (Line := Solid;   Style := Thick;  Multiplicity := 2);
                             has_label An_Identifier (Where := Centered);
  node SUBASSEMBLY           is Rounded_Rectangle
                             (Line := Solid;   Style := Thick;  Multiplicity := 1);
                             has_label An_Identifier (Where := Centered);
  -- Resources:

  node CLASS_PARAMETERS      is Rounded_Rectangle
                             (Line := Solid;   Style := Thin;   Multiplicity := 1);
                             has_list Of_Parameters (Where := Centered);
```

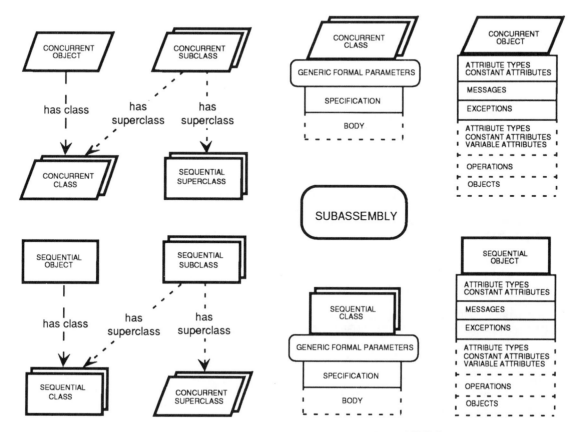

**Figure C-15: Valid Nodes and Arcs for Classification Diagrams (CLDs)**

```
node CLASS_SPECIFICATION    is Rectangle
                            (Line := Solid;   Style := Thin;  Multiplicity := 1)
                            divided_horizontally_into
                             subnode ATTRIBUTE_TYPES_AND_CONSTANT_ATTRIBUTES
                              has_list  Of_Attribute_Types      (Where := Centered)
                              has_list  Of_Constant_Attributes (Where := Centered)
                             subnode MESSAGES
                              has_list  Of_Messages             (Where := Centered)
                             subnode EXCEPTIONS
                              has_list  Of_Exceptions           (Where := Centered);
node CLASS_BODY             is Rectangle
                            (Line := Dot;     Style := Thin;  Multiplicity := 1)
                            divided_horizontally_into
                             subnode ATTRIBUTE_TYPES_AND_ATTRIBUTES
                              has_list  Of_Attribute_Types      (Where := Centered)
                              has_list  Of_Attributes          (Where := Centered)
                             subnode OPERATIONS
                              has_list  Of_Operations          (Where := Centered)
```

```
                                subnode OBJECTS
                                has_list Of_Objects                 (Where := Centered);
-- Arc definitions:

    arc HAS_SUPERCLASS        is Arrow (Line := Dot ;  Style  := Thin;
                              has_label "has_superclass" (Where := Centered);
    arc HAS_CLASS             is Arrow (Line := Dash; Style  := Thin;
                              has_label "has_class"      (Where := Centered);


-- Parenting rules:

  -- Objects:

  OBJECT := OBJECT(CONCURRENT) or OBJECT(SEQUENTIAL);

  may_nest      BJECT    in SUBASSEMBLY;
  may_socket    OBJECT   to SUBASSEMBLY (Where := Straddle);

  -- Classes:

  CLASS := CLASS(CONCURRENT) or CLASS(SEQUENTIAL);

  may_nest      CLASS   in SUBASSEMBLY;
  may_socket    CLASS   to SUBASSEMBLY (Where := Straddle);

  -- Resources:

  must_parent   CLASS_PARAMETERS;
  must_parent   CLASS_SPECIFICATION;
  must_parent   CLASS_BODY;

  may_socket    CLASS_PARAMETERS      to CLASS (Where := Outside);
  may_socket    CLASS_SPECIFICATION   to CLASS (Where := Outside);
  may_socket    CLASS_BODY            to CLASS (Where := Outside);

-- Arc rules:
  may_connect CLASS                  with HAS_SUPERCLASS to CLASS;
  may_connect CLASS_PARAMETERS       with HAS_SUPERCLASS to CLASS;
  may_connect CLASS_SPECIFICATION    with HAS_SUPERCLASS to CLASS;
  may_connect CLASS_BODY             with HAS_SUPERCLASS to CLASS;
  may_connect OBJECT                 with HAS_CLASS      to CLASS;

end CLASSIFICATION_DIAGRAM;
```

## C.3.7    State Transition Diagrams (STDs)

State transition diagrams (STDs) document the states of objects and classes. STDs also document the transitions between the states. Figure C-16 documents the 8 valid nodes and 5 valid arcs of STDs.

The following is the specification of the syntax and the semantics of state transition diagrams (STDs), which are part of the state model:

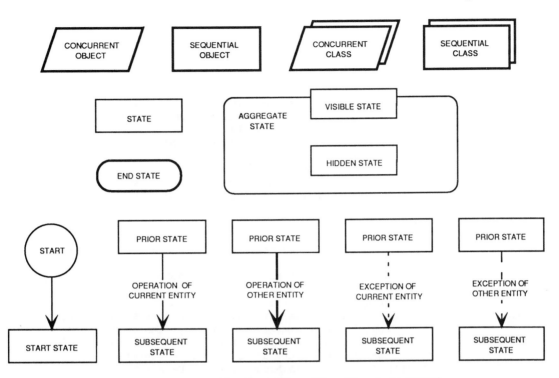

**Figure C-16: Valid Nodes and Arcs for State Transition Diagrams (STDs)**

```
diagram STATE_TRANSITION_DIAGRAM is

-- Node definitions:
-- Node icons must be labeled with the identifier of the corresponding entity.

  -- Object-Oriented nodes:

  node OBJECT(CONCURRENT)    is Parallelogram
                             (Line := Solid;   Style := Thick;  Multiplicity := 1)
                             has_label An_Identifier;
  node OBJECT(SEQUENTIAL)    is Rectangle
                             (Line := Solid;   Style := Thick;  Multiplicity := 1)
                             has_label An_Identifier;
  node CLASS(CONCURRENT)     is Parallelogram
                             (Line := Solid;   Style := Thick;  Multiplicity := 2)
                             has_label An_Identifier;
  node CLASS(SEQUENTIAL)     is Rectangle
                             (Line := Solid;   Style := Thick;  Multiplicity := 2)
                             has_label An_Identifier;
```

```
-- State nodes:

  node START                    is Circle
                                (Line := Solid;   Style := Thin;  Multiplicity := 1)
                                has_label "START" (Where := Centered);
  node STATE                    is Rectangle
                                (Line := Solid;   Style := Thin;  Multiplicity := 1)
                                has_label An_Identifier (Where := Centered);
  node AGGREGATE_STATE          is Rounded_Rectangle
                                (Line := Solid;   Style := Thin;  Multiplicity := 1)
                                has_label An_Identifier (Where := Centered);
  node END_STATE                is Rectangle
                                (Line := Solid;   Style := Thin;  Multiplicity := 1)
                                has_label An_Identifier (Where := Centered);

-- Arc definitions:
  -- INTERACTIONS must be labeled with the associated messages and may be labeled
  -- with the associated attribute types, constant attributes, and exceptions.

  arc START_ARC                          is Arrow (Line := Solid; Style := Thin);
  arc OPERATION_OF_CURRENT_COMPONENT is Arrow (Line := Solid; Style := Thin)
                    has_label An_Identifier (Where := Centered);
  arc OPERATION_OF_OTHER_ENTITY      is Arrow (Line := Solid; Style := Thick)
                    has_label An_Identifier (Where := Centered);
  arc EXCEPTION_OF_CURRENT_COMPONENT is Arrow (Line := Dot  ; Style := Thin)
                    has_label An_Identifier (Where := Centered);
  arc EXCEPTION_OF_OTHER_ENTITY      is Arrow (Line := Dash ; Style := Thin)
                    has_label An_Identifier (Where := Centered);

-- Parenting rules:

  must_parent  START;
  must_parent  STATE;
  must_parent  COMPOUND_STATE;
  must_parent  END_STATE;

  COMPONENT :=  OBJECT(CONCURRENT) or OBJECT(SEQUENTIAL) or
                CLASS(SEQUENTIAL)  or CLASS(SEQUENTIAL);

  may_nest    START       in COMPONENT;
  may_nest    START       in AGGREGATE_STATE;
  may_socket  START       to AGGREGATE_STATE (Where := Straddle);
  may_nest    STATE       in COMPONENT;
  may_nest    STATE       in AGGREGATE_STATE;
  may_socket  STATE       to AGGREGATE_STATE (Where := Straddle);
  may_nest    END_STATE   in COMPONENT;
  may_nest    END_STATE   in AGGREGATE_STATE;
  may_socket  END_STATE   to AGGREGATE_STATE (Where := Straddle);

-- Arc rules:

  may_connect START  with START_ARC                          to STATE;
```

```
may_connect STATE  with OPERATION_OF_CURRENT_COMPONENT  to STATE;
may_connect STATE  with OPERATION_OF_CURRENT_COMPONENT  to END_STATE;

may_connect STATE  with OPERATION_OF_OTHER_ENTITY       to STATE;
may_connect STATE  with OPERATION_OF_OTHER_ENTITY       to END_STATE;

may_connect STATE  with EXCEPTION_OF_CURRENT_COMPONENT  to STATE;
may_connect STATE  with EXCEPTION_OF_CURRENT_COMPONENT  to END_STATE;

may_connect STATE  with EXCEPTION_OF_OTHER_ENTITY       to STATE;
may_connect STATE  with EXCEPTION_OF_OTHER_ENTITY       to END_STATE;

end STATE_TRANSITION_DIAGRAM;
```

## C.3.8    Control Flow Diagrams (CFDs)

Object-oriented control flow diagrams (CFDs) document the control flow (and possibly data flow) relationships between and within objects, classes, and their terminators. Figure C-17 documents the 22 valid nodes and 6 valid arcs of CFDs.

The following is the specification of the syntax and the semantics of control flow diagrams (CFDs), which are part of the control model:

```
diagram CONTROL_FLOW_DIAGRAM is

-- Node definitions:
-- Node icons must be labeled with the identifier of the corresponding entity.

  -- Object-Oriented nodes:

  node OBJECT(CONCURRENT)    is Parallelogram
                             (Line := Solid;   Style := Thick;   Multiplicity := 1)
                             has_label An_Identifier;
  node OBJECT(SEQUENTIAL)    is Rectangle
                             (Line := Solid;   Style := Thick;   Multiplicity := 1)
                             has_label An_Identifier;
  node CLASS(CONCURRENT)                 is Parallelogram
                             (Line := Solid;   Style := Thick;   Multiplicity := 2)
                             has_label An_Identifier;
  node CLASS(SEQUENTIAL)                 is Rectangle
                             (Line := Solid;   Style := Thick;   Multiplicity := 2)
                             has_label An_Identifier;
  node SUBASSEMBLY                       is Rounded_Rectangle
                             (Line := Solid;   Style := Thick;   Multiplicity := 1)
                             has_label An_Identifier (Where := Centered);
  node ASSEMBLY                          is Rounded_Rectangle
                             (Line := Solid;   Style := Thick;   Multiplicity := 2)
                             has_label An_Identifier (Where := Centered);

  -- Terminators:
  node DEVICE                is Box
                             (Line := Solid;   Style := Thin;    Multiplicity := 1)
                             has_label An_Identifier (Where := Centered);
```

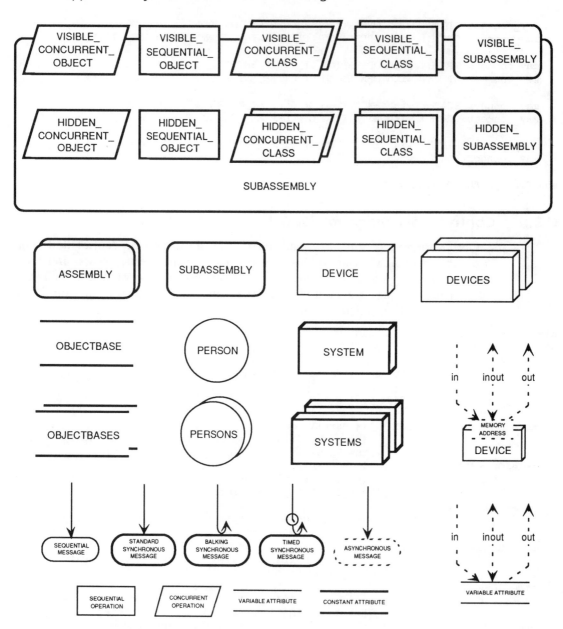

**Figure C-17: Valid Nodes and Arcs for Object-Oriented CFDs**

```
    node DEVICES                  is Box
                                  (Line := Solid;   Style := Thin;    Multiplicity := 2)
                                  has_label An_Identifier (Where := Centered);
    node OBJECTBASE               is Data_Store
                                  (Line := Solid;   Style := Thick;   Multiplicity := 1)
                                  has_label An_Identifier (Where := Centered);
    node OBJECTBASES              is Data_Store
                                  (Line := Solid;   Style := Thick;   Multiplicity := 2)
                                  has_label An_Identifier (Where := Centered);
    node PERSON                   is Circle
                                  (Line := Solid;   Style := Thin;    Multiplicity := 1)
                                  has_label An_Identifier (Where := Centered);
    node PERSONS                  is Circle
                                  (Line := Solid;   Style := Thin;    Multiplicity := 2)
                                  has_label An_Identifier (Where := Centered);
                                  node SYSTEM        is Box
                                  (Line := Solid;   Style := Thick;   Multiplicity := 1)
                                  has_label An_Identifier (Where := Centered);
    node SYSTEMS                  is Box
                                  (Line := Solid;   Style := Thick;   Multiplicity := 2)
                                  has_label An_Identifier (Where := Centered);
-- Resources:

    node ATTRIBUTE(CONSTANT)      is Data_Store
                                  (Line := Solid;  Style := Thick;    Multiplicity := 1)
                                  has_label An_Identifier (Where := Centered);
    node ATTRIBUTE(VARIABLE)      is Data_Store
                                  (Line := Solid;  Style := Thin;     Multiplicity := 1)
                                  has_label An_Identifier (Where := Centered);
    node MESSAGE(ASYNCHRONOUS) is Oval
                                  (Line := Dot;    Style := Thin;     Multiplicity := 1)
                                  has_label An_Identifier (Where := Centered);
    node MESSAGE(SEQUENTIAL)      is Oval
                                  (Line := Solid;  Style := Thick;    Multiplicity := 1)
                                  has_label An_Identifier (Where := Centered);
    node MESSAGE(SYNCHRONOUS)  is Oval
                                  (Line := Solid;  Style := Thin;     Multiplicity := 1)
                                  has_label An_Identifier (Where := Centered);
    node OPERATION(CONCURRENT) is Parallelogram
                                  (Line := Solid;  Style := Thin;     Multiplicity := 1)
                                  has_label An_Identifier (Where := Centered);
    node OPERATION(SEQUENTIAL) is Rectangle
                                  (Line := Solid;  Style := Thin;     Multiplicity := 1)
                                  has_label An_Identifier (Where := Centered);
    node MEMORY_ADDRESS           is Data_Store
                                  (Line := Dot;    Style := Thick;    Multiplicity := 1)
                                  has_label An_Identifier (Where := Centered);

-- Arc definitions:

    arc CONTROL_FLOW(BALKING)     is Arrow_Bent     (Line := Solid;  Style := Thin);
    arc CONTROL_FLOW(STANDARD)    is Arrow          (Line := Solid;  Style := Thin);
```

```
arc CONTROL_FLOW(TIMED)      is Arrow_Clock    (Line := Solid;  Style := Thin);
arc DATA_FLOW(IN)            is Arrow          (Line := Dot;    Style := Thin)
                             has_label "in"    (Where := Centered);
arc DATA_FLOW_FLOW(OUT)      is Arrow_Reverse  (Line := Dot;    Style := Thin)
                             has_label "out"   (Where := Centered);
arc DATA_FLOW_FLOW(INOUT)    is Arrow_Both     (Line := Dot;    Style := Thin)
                             has_label "inout" (Where := Centered);
```

```
-- Parenting rules:

  -- Objects:

  OBJECT := OBJECT(CONCURRENT) or OBJECT(SEQUENTIAL);

  may_nest    OBJECT               in OBJECT(CONCURRENT);
  may_nest    OBJECT(SEQUENTIAL)   in OBJECT(SEQUENTIAL);
  may_nest    OBJECT               in SUBASSEMBLY;
  may_socket  OBJECT               to SUBASSEMBLY  (Where := Straddle);

  -- Classes:

  CLASS := CLASS(CONCURRENT) or CLASS(SEQUENTIAL);

  may_nest    CLASS                in SUBASSEMBLY;
  may_socket  CLASS                to SUBASSEMBLY  (Where := Straddle);

  -- Subassemblies:

  may_nest    SUBASSEMBLY          in ASSEMBLY;
  may_nest    SUBASSEMBLY          in SUBASSEMBLY;
  may_socket  SUBASSEMBLY          to ASSEMBLY     (Where := Straddle);
  may_socket  SUBASSEMBLY          to SUBASSEMBLY  (Where := Straddle);

  -- Resources:

  must_parent ATTRIBUTE(CONSTANT);
  must_parent ATTRIBUTE(VARIABLE);
  must_parent MESSAGE(ASYNCHRONOUS);
  must_parent MESSAGE(SEQUENTIAL);
  must_parent MESSAGE(SYNCHRONOUS);
  must_parent OPERATION(CONCURRENT);
  must_parent OPERATION(SEQUENTIAL);

  COMPONENT := OBJECT or CLASS;

  may_nest ATTRIBUTE(CONSTANT)     in COMPONENT;
  may_nest ATTRIBUTE(VARIABLE)     in COMPONENT;
  may_nest OPERATION(CONCURRENT)   in COMPONENT;
  may_nest OPERATION(SEQUENTIAL)   in COMPONENT;
  may_socket MESSAGE(ASYNCHRONOUS) to COMPONENT (Where := Straddle);
  may_socket MESSAGE(SEQUENTIAL)   to COMPONENT (Where := Straddle);
  may_socket MESSAGE(SYNCHRONOUS)  to COMPONENT (Where := Straddle);
```

```
    -- Hardware:

    must_parent   MEMORY_ADDRESS;
    may_socket    MEMORY_ADDRESS to DEVICE (Where := Straddle);

-- Arc rules:

    OPERATION   :=  OPERATION(CONCURRENT) or OPERATION(SEQUENTIAL);

    MESSAGE     :=  MESSAGE(ASYNCHRONOUS) or MESSAGE(SEQUENTIAL) or
                    MESSAGE(SYNCHRONOUS);

    TERMINATOR :=   DEVICE or DEVICES  or OBJECTBASE  or OBJECTBASES  or
                    PERSON or PERSONS  or SYSTEM      or SYSTEMS;

    START_NODE :=   OBJECT or CLASS or SUBASSEMBLY or ASSEMBLY or TERMINATOR or
                    OPERATION;
    END_NODE   :=   OBJECT or CLASS or SUBASSEMBLY or ASSEMBLY or TERMINATOR or
                    MEMORY_ADDRESS or MESSAGE;

    may_connect START_NODE with CONTROL_FLOW to END_NODE;
    may_connect START_NODE with CONTROL_FLOW(BALKING) to MESSAGE(SYNCHRONOUS);
    may_connect START_NODE with CONTROL_FLOW(TIMED) to MESSAGE(SYNCHRONOUS);

    if
     parent(MESSAGE(ASYNCHRONOUS)) = parent(OPERATION(CONCURRENT))
    then
     may_connect MESSAGE(ASYNCHRONOUS) with CONTROL_FLOW to OPERATION(CONCURRENT);
    end if;

    if
     parent(MESSAGE(SEQUENTIAL)) = parent(OPERATION(SEQUENTIAL))
    then
     may_connect MESSAGE(SEQUENTIAL) with CONTROL_FLOW to OPERATION(SEQUENTIAL);
    end if;

    if
     parent(MESSAGE(SYNCHRONOUS)) = parent(OPERATION(CONCURRENT))
    then
     may_connect MESSAGE(SYNCHRONOUS) with CONTROL_FLOW to OPERATION(CONCURRENT);
    end if;

    START_NODE  :=  OPERATION;
    END_NODE    :=  OPERATION;

    if
     parent(START_NODE) = parent(END_NODE)
    then
     may_connect START_NODE with CONTROL_FLOW to END_NODE;
    end if;

    ATTRIBUTE   := ATTRIBUTE(CONSTANT) or ATTRIBUTE(VARIABLE);
    DATAFLOW    := DATAFLOW(IN) or DATAFLOW(INOUT) or DATAFLOW(OUT);
```

```
may_connect OPERATION with DATA_FLOW(IN)      to ATTRIBUTE(VARIABLE);
may_connect OPERATION with DATA_FLOW(INOUT)   to ATTRIBUTE(VARIABLE);
may_connect OPERATION with DATA_FLOW(OUT)     to ATTRIBUTE;
may_connect OPERATION with DATA_FLOW          to MEMORY_ADDRESS;
```

```
end CONTROL_FLOW_DIAGRAM;
```

## C.3.9    Timing Diagrams (TDs)

Timing diagrams (TDs) document the timing or sequence interactions between objects, classes, and their operations. Figure C-18 documents the 1 valid node and 3 valid arcs of TDs.

The following is the specification of the syntax and the semantics of timing diagrams (TDs), which are part of the timing model:

```
diagram TIMING_DIAGRAM is

-- Node definitions:
-- Node icons must be labeled with the identifier of the corresponding entity.

   node TIMING_BOX       is Rectangle
                         (Line := Solid; Style := Thin; Multiplicity := 1);

-- Arc definitions:
  -- INTERACTIONS must be labeled with the associated messages and may be labeled
  -- with the associated attribute types, constant attributes, and exceptions.

   --   ENTITY :=  OBJECT or CLASS or OPERATION;

   arc ENTITY            is Line_Segment
                         (Line := Solid; Style := Thick; Constraints := Y_Axis)
                         has_label An_Identifier (Where := Above,Outside)
                         [divided_horizontally_into
                          {subnode A_State
                           has_label Identifier (Where := Centered)}];
   arc INTERACTION       is Arrow
                         (Line := Solid; Style := Thin;  Constraints := X_Axis)
                         has_label An_Identifier (Where := Centered);
   arc END_OF_CYCLE      is Line_Segment
                         (Line := Dash;  Style := Thin;  Constraints := X_Axis);

-- Arc rules:

   may_connect TIMING_BOX  with ENTITY        to TIMING_BOX;
   may_connect TIMING_BOX  with END_OF_CYCLE  to TIMING_BOX;
   may_connect ENTITY      with INTERACTION   to ENTITY;

end TIMING_DIAGRAM;
```

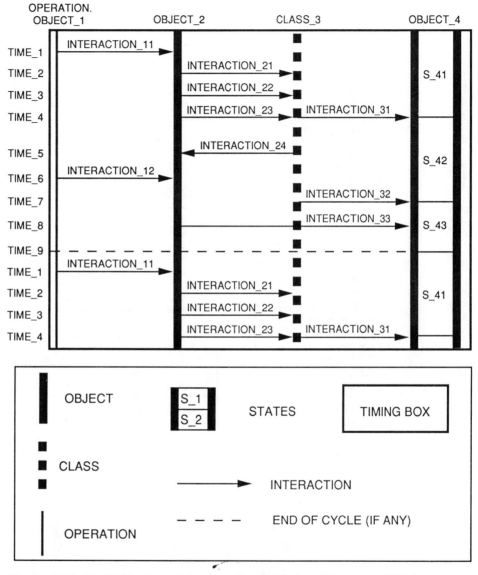

**Figure C-18: Valid Node and Arcs for Event Timing Diagrams (ETDs)**

## C.3.10  Module Diagrams (MDs)

Module Diagrams (MDs) document a subassembly, the existence and visibility of its component modules, and the dependencies between them. Figure C-19 documents the 6 valid nodes and 3 valid arcs of MDs.

The following is the specification of the syntax and the semantics of module diagrams (MDs), which are part of the implementation model:

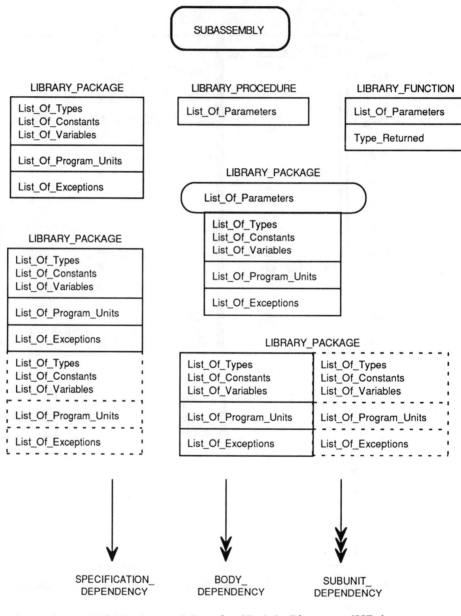

**Figure C-19: Valid Nodes and Arcs for Module Diagrams (MDs)**

```
diagram MODULE_DIAGRAM is

-- Node definitions:
-- Node icons must be labeled with the identifier of the corresponding entity.

-- Module nodes:

    node LIBRARY_PACKAGE    is Rectangle
                            (Line := Solid;   Style := Thin;   Multiplicity := 1)
                            has_label AN_IDENTIFIER              (Where := Above)
                            divided_horizontally_into
                             subnode EXPORTED_TYPES_AND_OBJECTS
                             has_list  Of_Types                 (Where := Centered)
                             has_list  Of_Constants             (Where := Centered)
                             has_list  Of_Variables             (Where := Centered)
                             subnode EXPORTED_PROGRAM_UNITS
                             has_list  Of_Program_Units          (Where := Centered)
                             subnode EXCEPTIONS
                             has_list  Of_Exceptions             (Where := Centered);
    node LIBRARY_PROCEDURE is Rectangle
                            (Line := Solid;   Style := Thin;   Multiplicity := 1)
                            has_label AN_IDENTIFIER              (Where := Above)
                            has_list Of_Parameters              (Where := Centered);
    node LIBRARY_FUNCTION   is Rectangle
                            (Line := Solid;   Style := Thin;   Multiplicity := 1)
                            has_label AN_IDENTIFIER              (Where :=    Above)
                            divided_horizontally_into
                             subnode PARAMETERS
                             has_list Of_Parameters             (Where := Centered)
                             subnode TYPE_RETURNED
                            has_label The_Type_Returned         (Where := Centered);
    node SUBASSEMBLY        is Rounded_Rectangle
                            (Line := Solid;   Style := Thick; Multiplicity := 1)
                            has_label An_Identifier (Where := Centered);
-- Resources:

    node PACKAGE_BODY       is Rectangle
                            (Line := Dot;     Style := Thin;   Multiplicity := 1)
                            divided_horizontally_into
                             subnode HIDDEN_TYPES_AND_OBJECTS
                             has_list  Of_Types                 (Where := Centered)
                             has_list  Of_Constants             (Where := Centered)
                             has_list  Of_Variables             (Where := Centered)
                             subnode HIDDEN_PROGRAM_UNITS
                             has_list  Of_Program_Units          (Where := Centered)
                             subnode EXCEPTIONS
                             has_list  Of_Exceptions             (Where := Centered);
    node PARAMETERS         is Rounded_Rectangle
                            (Line := Solid;   Style := Thin;   Multiplicity := 1)
                            has_list  Of_Parameters             (Where := Centered);
```

```
-- Arc definitions:

    arc SPECIFICATION_DEPENDENCY   is Arrow          (Line := Solid; Style := Thin);
    arc BODY_DEPENDENCY            is Arrow_Double    (Line := Solid; Style := Thin);
    arc SUBUNIT_DEPENDENCY         is Arrow_Triple    (Line := Solid; Style := Thin);

-- Parenting rules:

    must_parent PACKAGE_BODY;
    must_parent PARAMETERS;

    may_socket PACKAGE_BODY   to LIBRARY_PACKAGE    (Where := Outside,Below);
    may_socket PACKAGE_BODY   to LIBRARY_PACKAGE    (Where := Outside,Right);
    may_socket PARAMETERS     to LIBRARY_PACKAGE    (Where := Outside,Above);
    may_socket PARAMETERS     to LIBRARY_PROCEDURE  (Where := Outside,Above);
    may_socket PARAMETERS     to LIBRARY_FUNCTION   (Where := Outside,Above);

-- Arc rules:

    START_NODE := LIBRARY_PACKAGE or PACKAGE_BODY or LIBRARY_PROCEDURE or
                  LIBRARY_FUNCTION;

    DEPENDENCY := SPECIFICATION_DEPENDENCY or BODY_DEPENDENCY or
                  SUBUNIT_DEPENDENCY;

    END_NODE   := LIBRARY_PACKAGE or LIBRARY_PROCEDURE or LIBRARY_FUNCTION or
                  PARAMETERS;

    may_connect START_NODE with DEPENDENCY to END_NODE;

end MODULE_DIAGRAM;
```

# Appendix D

# Conferences and Publications

## D.1 CONFERENCES

### C++ World

C++ World is an annual conference in the United States sponsored by C++ *Report* and presented by SIGS Conferences. Call (212) 274-9135 or fax (212) 274-0899 for more information.

### ECOOP—European Conference on Object-Oriented Programming

ECOOP is an annual conference that was first held in 1987. ECOOP was organized to structure object-oriented activities taking place in European countries by providing a European forum for theorists and practitioners interested in the object-oriented paradigm. The ECOOP tradition has been to move the conference location each year from one country to another: ECOOP'87 in Paris, France; ECOOP'88 in Oslo, Norway; ECOOP' 89 in Nottingham, England; ECOOP'90 in Ottawa, Canada; and ECOOP'91 in Geneva, Switzerland. Call Gert Florijin at (31) 30-322640 for more information.

### ICOOMS—International Conference on Object-Oriented Manufacturing Systems

The ICOOMS Conference is sponsored by the University of Calgary and the Society for Computer Simulation.

### LOOK—Lectures and Object-Oriented Konference

LOOK is an annual conference sponsored by *The Journal of Object-Oriented Programming* and *Object Magazine*. It is presented by SIGs Conferences. Call (212) 274-9135 or fax (212) 274-00899 for more information.

### MacApp Conference

MacApp Conference is sponsored by the MacApp Developers' Association (MADA). MacApp is the object-oriented framework for developing Macintosh applications. Call (408) 253-2765 for more information.

### Object Expo

Object Expo is an annual conference sponsored by *The Hotline on Object-Oriented Technology*, *The Journal of Object-Oriented Programming*, and *Object Magazine*. It is presented by SIGS Conferences. Call (212) 274-9135 or fax (212) 274-0899 for more information.

### Object Expo Europe

Object Expo Europe is an annual conference sponsored by *C++ Report*, *The Journal of Object-Oriented Programming*, *Object Magazine*, and *Computing Magazine*. It is presented by SIGS Conferences. Call (212) 274-9135 or fax (212) 274-0899 for more information.

### Object-Oriented Analysis and Design (OOA&D) Seminar

OOA&D is a 2-3 day public seminar presented 3-4 times a year by Ed Yourdon. OOA&D is sponsored by Digital Consulting Inc. Call (508) 470-3880 for more information.

### Object World

Object World is a biannual conference sponsored by the Object Management Group (OMG) and managed by World Expo Corporation, P.O. Box 9107, Framingham, MA 01701-9107. Call (800) 225-4698 for more information.

### OOP (Objekt-Orientiertes Programmieren) and C++ World

An annual conference in Germany sponsored by *C++ Report*, *The Journal of Object-Oriented Programming*, and *Object Magazine*. It is presented by SIGS Conferences. Call (212) 274-9135 or fax (212) 274-0899 for more information.

### OOPSLA—Object-Oriented Programming, Systems, Languages, and Applications

OOPSLA is an annual conference that was first held in 1986. OOPSLA was organized to create a forum for researchers, practitioners, exhibitors, and novices interested in the object-oriented paradigm. OOPSLA is sponsored by the Association for Computing Machinery (ACM), and the proceedings are published as a special issue of SIGPLAN Notices by the Special Interest Group for Programming Languages (SIGPLAN) of the ACM. Call (407) 628-3602 for more information.

### OOSS—Object-Oriented Systems Symposium

The Object-Oriented Systems Symposium is an annual conference sponsored by Digital Consulting Inc., 6 Windsor Street, Andover, MA 01810. For more information, call (508) 470-3880.

### TOOLS—Technology of Object-Oriented Languages and Systems

The three annual TOOLS conferences (Europe, Pacific, and USA) are sposored by TOOLS, a subdivision of Interactive Software Engineering. The proceedings are published by Printice Hall. Call (805) 685-1006 or fax (805) 685-6869 for more information.

## D.2  PUBLICATIONS

### The C++ Journal

*The C++ Journal* is a quarterly publication of The C++ Journal Inc., 2 Haven Avenue, Port Washington, New York 11050. Call (516) 767-7107 for more information.

### The C++ Report: The International Magazine for C++ Programmers

*The C++ Report* is published 9 times a year The SIGS Publications Inc. Send subscription orders to *The C++ Report*, Subscriber Services, Department CPR, P.O. Box 3000, Denville, NJ 07834-9979. Call (212) 274-0640 or fax (212) 274-0646 for more information.

### FIRST CLASS

*FIRST CLASS* is a 28-page bimonthly newsletter of The Object Management Group, Inc. Send subscription orders to OMG Publications, 41730 Walnut, Suite 206, Boulder, CO 80301. Fax (303) 449-4009 for more information.

### HOOT—Hotline on Object-Oriented Technology

*HOOT* is a monthly publication of The SIGS Publications Inc. Send subscription orders to *HOOT*, Subscriber Services, Department HOT, P.O. Box 3000, Denville, NJ 07834-9979. Call (212) 274-0640 or fax (212) 274-0646 for more information.

### The International OOP Directory

*The International OOP Directory* is an annual directory of all OOP conferences, vendors, and publications. It is a publication of The SIGS Book Inc. Send orders to SIGS Publications, 588 Broadway, Suite 604, New York, NY 10012. Call (212) 274-0640 or fax (212) 274-0646 for more information.

### JOOP—Journal of Object-Oriented Programming

*JOOP* is published nine times a year by The SIGS Publications Inc. Send subscription orders to *Journal of Object-Oriented Programming*, Subscriber Services, Department OOP, P.O. Box 3000, Denville, NJ 07834-9970. Call (212) 274-0640 or fax (212) 274-0646 for more information.

### Object Magazine

*Object Magazine* is a bimonthly journal published by SIGS Publications Inc. Send subscription orders to *Object Magazine*, Subscriber Services, Department OBJ, P.O. Box 3000, Denville, NJ 07834-9876. Call (212) 274-0640 or fax (212) 274-0646 for more information.

### Object-Oriented Strategies

*Object-Oriented Strategies* is a monthly publication of Cutter Information Corporation, 37 Broadway, Arlington, MA 02174-5539. Call (617) 648-8700 for more information.

### OOPS Messenger

*OOPS Messenger* is a quarterly publication of the Special Interest Group on Programming Languages (SIGPLAN) of the Association for Computing Machinery (ACM). Call ACM Headquarters at (212) 869-7440 for more information

### The Smalltalk Report

*The Smalltalk Report* is a publication of The SIGS Publications Inc. Send subscription orders to *The Smalltalk Report*, Subscriber Services, Department SML, P.O. Box 3000, Denville, NJ 07834-9876. Call (212) 274-0640 or fax (212) 274-0646 for more information.

# Appendix E

# DOD-STD-2167A Documentation Guidelines

## E.1 INTRODUCTION

The object-oriented paradigm is currently recognized as the best general approach to requirements analysis and design of nontrivial software, especially the large, complex, long-lived, state-of-the-art software of the type often developed for the military in the avionics, C3, and electronic warfare domains. Unfortunately, a great deal of confusion and disagreement exists as to whether the use of an object-oriented development (OOD) method is encouraged, permitted, or even prohibited on military projects using current military software development standards, such as "Defense System Software Development" [DOD-STD-2167A] and "Technical Reviews and Audits for Systems, Equipments, and Computer Software" [MIL-STD-1521B]. Software developers are rarely experienced in both modern OOD and the intent and specific requirements of military policy and standards. This appendix discusses the military expectations and requirements with regard to (a) the documentation of software plans on projects using object technology, (b) the actual and perceived inconsistencies between the documentation of military and object-oriented requirements and designs, and (c) specific recommendations for documenting object-oriented requirements and designs on military projects using current military standards.

## E.2 MILITARY EXPECTATIONS AND REQUIREMENTS

Current military expectations and requirements with regard to the documentation of software requirements and designs are driven by federal law and by past and present military policy, standards, and actual and perceived experience. Although military experience, until recently, was primarily with procedural languages such as CMS-2, JOVIAL, and TACPOL, United States public law 101-511 [U.S. Congress 1990] and military policy [DODD 3405.1, DODD 5000.2] clearly mandate the use of the object-based language Ada83 [ANSI/MIL-STD-1815A-1983]. Although Ada will not fully support inheritance, polymorphism, and dynamic binding until approximately 1993, with Ada9X, OOD is clearly very popular (and even preferred and mandated by the military) and many military projects are currently using object-oriented requirements analysis (OORA) methods in order to improve analysis and the transition to an object-oriented design. Relevant military standards include "Defense System Software Development" [DOD-STD-2167A] and "Technical Reviews and Audits for Systems, Equipments, and Computer Software" [MIL-STD-1521B], both of which are currently under revision, whereby the issue of compatibility with object-oriented methods is a major topic of discussion. DOD-STD-2167A is organized in terms of software activities (reminiscent of the phases of the classic waterfall development cycle and written in terms of the software organizational entities of computer software configuration item (CSCI), computer software component (CSC), and computer software unit (CSU). DOD-STD-2167A also has several data item descriptions (DIDs) that mandate the format and content of deliverable documentation, the most important of which for this appendix being the software requirements specification (SRS), the interface requirements specification (IRS), the software design document (SDD), and the interface design document (IDD).

According to its foreword, DOD-STD-2167A, defense system software development "establishes uniform requirements for software development that are applicable throughout the system life cycle. The requirements of this standard provide the basis for Government insight into a contractor's software development, testing, and evaluation efforts." When DOD-STD-2167A replaced DOD-STD-2167 on 29 February 1986, several modifications where made specifically to better support both the mandated, object-based language Ada and the increasingly popular OOD paradigm.

Although the original standard clearly mandated the use of hierarchical functional-decomposition methods, these requirements were removed, and the foreword of the new standard states that "This standard is not intended to specify or discourage the use of any particular software development method. The contractor is responsible for selecting software development methods (for example, rapid prototyping) that best support the achievement of contract requirements." Furthermore, almost all references to the word function were removed to avoid promoting functional decomposition. CSUs need no longer perform a single function, an inappropriate and often impossible requirement if objects and classes are CSUs and have multiple operations (i.e., methods). Support for OORA methods was enhanced because requirements are now decomposed into capabilities instead of functions and subfunctions, and all mention of input-processing-output was removed from the SRS. At present, paragraph 4.2.1 of DOD-STD-2167A merely requires that the "contractor shall use systematic and well documented software development methods to perform requirements analysis, design, coding, integration, and testing of the deliverable software." The waterfall development cycle and its *phases* were replaced in DOD-STD-2167A by a generic software development *process* and *activities* "which may *overlap* and be applied *iteratively* or *recursively*" (emphasis mine). The word *recursively* was added specifically to allow the recursive development cycles common with object-oriented methods.

Unfortunately, what the government gives with one hand, it may inadvertently take away with the other. MIL-STD-1521B, "Formal Reviews and Audits" was not updated at the same time as DOD-STD-2167 and is both contractually and philosophically inconsistent with DOD-STD-2167A. DOD-STD-2167A states that "the contractor shall conduct one or more Software Specification Review(s) (SSR) in accordance with MIL-STD-1521. . . . The contractor shall conduct one or more preliminary design review(s) (PDR) in accordance with MIL-STD-1521. . . . The contractor shall conduct one or more Critical Design Review(s) (CDR) in accordance with MIL-STD-1521." Paragraph 4.2.1 of DOD-STD-2167A further states that "The contractor shall implement software development methods that support the formal reviews and audits required by the contract." Paragraph 40.1 of MIL-STD-1521B states that the Preliminary Design Review (PDR) "shall be held . . . prior to the start of detailed design," thus prohibits the overlap of the preliminary and detailed design activities. This is inconsistent with DOD-STD-2167A, which allows the activities to "overlap and be applied iteratively or recursively."

# E.3  OBJECT-ORIENTED DEVELOPMENT (OOD)

There are numerous OOD methods including but not limited to those indicated in the reference list [Booch 1991, Coad and Yourdon 1989, Colbert 1989, Firesmith 1989, Rumbaugh et al. 1991, and Shlaer and Mellor 1988]. Because these different methods use different models, graphics, and development cycles, the documentation approach should vary from method to method. However, a great many similarities unify these methods and differentiate them as a group from the older methods. First of all, they are based on the concept of an object, an abstraction or model of an application-domain entity that localizes and encapsulates both attributes (i.e., data) and operations (i.e., functions). Objects are not data, are in fact more that the sum of data and related operations, and do not exist in the older methods. Similar or identical objects are instantiated from (i.e., created by) classes, which are templates that exist in inheritance hierarchies of superclasses and subclasses. Classes, inheritance, and the related concepts of polymorphism and dynamic binding are also new to many in the military (and in civilian industry). OOD methods use new and modified models and graphics (see next section).

Most object-oriented methods employ an incremental, iterative, and recursive development process, the activities of which are different and exhibit massive overlap. Software engineers identify objects and classes and develop various object-oriented models. The concepts of preliminary and detailed design, if they exist at all, often have radically new meanings unrelated to the design of CSCs and CSUs. Object-oriented methods often incrementally develop assemblies (e.g., CSCI), one subassembly (e.g., CSC) at a time, using an "analyze a little, design a little, code a little, test a little" recursive development cycle. The concept of a single preliminary design review (PDR) separating the preliminary design phase from the detailed design phase (a la MIL-STD-1521B) is utterly foreign to many OOD methods that instead rely heavily on iteration and recursion and may instead employ in-process reviews (IPRs). In fact, many object-oriented methods use the same models and graphics for both software requirements analysis and design, and the distinction between the two is blurred, especially if significant iteration is employed. Thus, deliverable documents, such as SRSs and SDDs, are not developed during the phases of the traditional development cycles.

## E.4  ACTUAL AND PERCEIVED INCONSISTENCIES

Numerous inconsistencies, both real and perceived, exist between current military documentation requirements and the proper documentation of object-oriented requirements and designs. The military and object-oriented paradigms are based on different concepts, models, hierarchies, documentation formats, development cycles, and formal reviews. Some of these inconsistencies have critical contractual implications and require early tailoring. Other inconsistencies are merely perceived, represent misunderstandings, or result from human inertia. These inconsistencies are best treated with early and adequate training.

The military considers software to consist of CSCIs that are decomposed into CSCs and CSUs, the requirements of which are decomposed into capabilities, and the designs of which are primarily decomposed into data (e.g., input/output data elements, local data elements, data structures, local data files or database) and operations (e.g., algorithms, error handling, data conversion operations, logic flow). The software design document is organized by CSC (i.e., preliminary design) and CSU (i.e., detailed design). Object-oriented methods consider software to consist of subassemblies (a.k.a., clusters, subjects, "subsystems") of objects and classes, which primarily encapsulate attributes and operations. A successful mapping between the two sets of concepts is necessary in order to document the object-oriented entities according to the military standards.

The military is primarily used to older, functional-decomposition versions of methods such as Structured Analysis [DeMarco 1978], Structured Design [Yourdon and Constantine 1979], and Structured Development for Real-Time Systems [Ward and Mellor 1985]. Many military reviewers thus expect to see software-engineering models based on such graphics as data flow diagrams (DFDs), state transition diagrams (STDs), and structure charts. Object-oriented methods use other models. Object models consist of semantic nets (SNs), interaction diagrams (IDs), composition diagrams (CMDs), and the specifications and bodies of objects. Class models consist of classification diagrams (CLDs) and the specification and body of all classes. State models are similar, although the state transition diagrams are restricted to the state of individual objects or classes. Control models use object-oriented control flow diagrams (CFDs) and operation bodies rather than functional decomposition Data Flow Diagrams. Timing Models consist of timing diagrams and/or STDs and CFDs annotated with temporal information.

The military software organization is an aggregation hierarchy based on the hierarchical decomposition of CSCIs into CSCs and CSCs into lower-level CSCs and CSUs. Object-oriented methods use aggregation, dependency, inheritance, and message hierarchies based on objects, classes, and their important relationships.

The military expects, and sometimes requires, specific documentation formats (e.g., the DOD-STD-2167A SRS [DI-MCCR-80025A] and software design document [DI-MCCR-80012A]) without proper tailoring. Software engineers and methodologists naturally prefer appropriate document formats organized around (a) subassemblies, objects, and classes, (b) their important relationships, and (c) their attributes and operations. At best, these two formats are indirectly related because of the difference in fundamental concepts, and they therefore require proper mapping (e.g., from CSU to object and class). At worst, the two formats are fundamentally incompatible and require significant tailoring or replacement. For example, the DOD-STD-2167A SRS and SDD DIDs still emphasize the distinction between and separate the documentation of the data and the functions on that data, while attributes (i.e., data) and operations (i.e., functions) are encapsulated in objects under an object-oriented paradigm.

In spite of significant changes, many military personnel expect and military standards still partially mandate the use of the obsolete waterfall development cycle. However, most OOD methods use an incremental iterative and globally-recursive development cycle that is topologically inconsistent with the waterfall development cycle. This has profound impact on formal reviews, which tend to be in-process reviews (IPRs) rather than SSRs, PDRs, and CDRs.

## E.5  GENERAL RECOMMENDATIONS

First of all, software engineers on military projects should learn the documentation requirements and expectations of DOD-STD-2167A and MIL-STD-1521B. Software engineers on projects using OOD should learn how to use OOD effectively to properly document requirements and designs in terms of (a) objects, their resources (e.g., attributes, operations, exceptions, component objects), and their relationships, and (b) classes and their inheritance relationships. In accordance with professional ethics and current military policy, contractors should propose the best documentation solution for object-oriented specifications and designs. Software engineers on military projects using OOD should understand the inconsistencies between the traditional military project requirements and expectations and the object-oriented application requirements and design. Contractor technical experts should develop or acquire OOD-method-specific DID formats and contents standards and should provide a requirements trace to ensure that all relevant requirements of the military DIDs are met. Contractor technical experts should map the OOD entities to the DOD-STD-

2167A software organization entities (e.g., assembly or "system" => CSCI; subassembly, cluster, subject, or "subsystem" => CSC, object and class => CSU).

In addition, software engineers, technical managers, and proposal staffs should work with and educate their contracting agencies to get the standard and DIDs properly tailored and interpreted, using military policy, the recommendations of experts, and organizations such as the SIGAda Software Development Standards and Ada Working Group to provide objective rationale and guidance. They should ensure that the OOD experts they choose have experience with military policy and standards. All parties should understand that DOD-STD-2167A is intended to be method- and paradigm-independent; while some requirements inadvertently imply a partial waterfall development cycle, the body of the standard does not. Finally, contractors should evaluate CASE tools carefully to ensure that they properly support the project-specific OOD method (perhaps via customization) and that they relatively automatically generate deliverable documentation that properly documents object-oriented requirements and designs while meeting military documentation standards.

## E.6  SPECIFIC RECOMMENDATIONS

### E.6.1    DOD-STD-2167A

Several changes were incorporated into DOD-STD-2167A specifically to permit the use of recursive object-oriented methods:

"FOREWORD:
This standard is not intended to specify or discourage the use of any particular software development method. The contractor is responsible for selecting software development methods (for example, rapid prototyping) that best support the achievement of contract requirements.

4.1.1 Software development process. The contractor shall implement a *process* for managing the development of the deliverable software. The contractor's software development process for each CSCI shall be compatible with the contract schedule for formal reviews and audits. The software development process shall include the following major *activities*, which may *overlap* and may be applied *iteratively* or *recursively*:
a.  System Requirements Analysis/Design
b.  Software Requirements Analysis
c.  Preliminary Design
d.  Detailed Design
e.  Coding and CSU Testing
f.  CSC Integration and Testing
g.  CSCI Testing
h.  System Integration and Testing.

4.2.1 *Software development methods*. The contractor shall use systematic and well documented software development methods to perform requirements analysis, design, coding, integration, and testing of the deliverable software. The contractor shall implement software development methods that support the formal reviews and audits required by the contract."

The project-tailored version of the OOD method is formally documented in the software development plan (SDP). The products produced by the OOD method are formally documented in the software requirements specification (SRS) and the software design document (SDD).

### E.6.2    Software Development Files (SDFs)

According to DOD-STD-2167A:

> "4.2.9 *Software development files.* The contractor shall document the development of each Computer Software Unit (CSU), Computer Software Component (CSC), and CSCI in software development files (SDFs). The contractor shall establish a separate SDF for each CSU or logically related group of CSUs...."

SDFs are nondeliverable collections of working documents. In OOD terms, this means that the contractor shall document the development of each of the following:

*   Assembly (CSCI)
*   Subassembly (i.e., CSC)
*   Class and object of anonymous class (CSC)

SDFs should document these intermediate products of the project-tailored version of the OOD method and be organized according to the steps of this method. As a globally recursive OOD method, ADM3 produces deliverable and nondeliverable software and documentation incrementally, subassembly by subassembly. Subassembly-level (i.e., CSC-level) SDFs are the natural unit for collecting working documentation. Unless electronically maintained via a common database, classes and objects may be at too low a level to collect and maintain working documentation. Assembly-level SDFs should

*   Contain the assembly diagram (AD) and context diagram (CD)
*   Be used to control the development of the component subassemblies
*   Tie the subassembly SDFs together

### E.6.3    Software Development Plan (SDP)

The intent of DOD-STD-2167A is to be language- and method-independent. The SDP must therefore document the contractor's plans concerning the development method (i.e., ADM3) to be used in the development of the software. The SDP must provide the contracting agency with sufficient detail to properly evaluate what may be radically different proposed methods (e.g., ADM3, OOSD, and Structured Design). Traditional boilerplate SDPs that merely parrot back the requirements of DOD-STD-2167 are no longer adequate.

Because a draft SDP is often required as part of the proposal, the contractor must understand (and document in the SDP) the software development method earlier and in more detail than is traditional. The following paragraphs and subparagraphs of the untailored DOD-STD-2167A SDP and SDP DID (DI-MCCR-80030A) are affected by the use of an OOD method and require ADM3 or OOD-specific information. The following paragraphs in the SDP and its associated DID also require either ADM3 or OOD-specific tailoring or interpretations:

| SDP | SDP DID | Title |
|---|---|---|
| 3.2.1 | 10.2.5.2.1 | Activities |
| 3.2.2 | 10.2.5.2.2 | Activity network |
| 3.3 | 10.2.5.3 | Risk management |
| 3.8 | 10.2.5.8 | Formal reviews |
| 4.1.2 | 10.2.6.1.2 | Personnel—software engineering |
| 4.1.3 | 10.2.6.1.3 | Software engineering environment |
| 4.1.3.1 | 10.2.6.1.3.1 | Software items |
| 4.2 | 10.2.6.2 | Software standards and procedures |
| 4.2.1 | 10.2.6.2.1 | Software development techniques and methodologies |
| 4.2.2 | 10.2.6.2.2 | Software development files |
| 4.2.3 | 10.2.6.2.3 | Design standards |
| 4.2.4 | 10.2.6.2.4 | Coding standards |
| 4.3 | 10.2.6.3 | Non-developmental software |
| 6.5.X | 10.2.8.5.1 | Software products evaluation—(activity name) |
| 8 | 10.2.10 | Other software development functions |
| 8.X | 10.2.10.1 | (Function name) |

### E.6.3.1  Activities

The DOD-STD-2167A SDP DID currently states:

> "10.2.5.2.1 *Activities*. This subparagraph shall be numbered 3.2.1 and shall briefly describe each software development activity of the project and its associated schedule, based on the contract master schedule (if applicable). The development schedule shall indicate all significant events, such as reviews, audits, key meetings, etc. The schedule may be provided graphically. For each activity, the schedule shall indicate:
> a. Activity initiation
> b. Availability of draft and final copies of formal and informal documentation
> c. Activity completion
> d. Areas of high risk."

This SDP DID paragraph does not require tailoring, but it does require interpretation. The corresponding SDP paragraph should:

- Summarize the project-tailored version of OOD development process and development cycle on a DOD-STD-2167A activity by activity basis
- Make it clear that the DOD-STD-2167A activities greatly overlap and are performed both iteratively and recursively
- Summarize the method-specific relationship between the activities and the formal (in-process) reviews, including how those reviews are scheduled in accordance with the project OOD process, development cycle, and method
- Not attempt to schedule the development of individual CSCs (subassemblies) or

CSUs (classes or objects), but rather remain at the assembly (e.g., CSCI) and build level. This is because the software is incrementally analyzed, designed, coded, and tested on a subassembly by subassembly basis if a recursive development cycle is used
- Discuss the relationship between the incremental development of (a) the assemblies and subassemblies, and (b) the software development folders (SDFs), software requirements specifications (SRSs), and software design documents (SDDs)
- List the high risk aspects of assembly and build scheduling

### E.6.3.2  Activity Network

The DOD-STD-2167A SDP DID currently states:

> "10.2.5.2.2 *Activity network.* This subparagraph shall be numbered 3.2.2 and shall describe the *sequential* relationship among the activities of the project. This subparagraph shall include identification of those activities that impose the greatest time restrictions on project completion and those activities with an excess of time for completion. This information may be provided graphically."

This SDP DID subparagraph requires both modification and interpretation. The corresponding SDP paragraph should:

- Take into account that the OOD development activities greatly overlap, are applied recursively, and therefore do not occur *sequentially.* See Figure E-1: Overlap of Development Activities
- Remain at the assembly (e.g., CSCI) and build level
- Be tailored to replace the word sequen*tial* with *temporal*

Project management CASE tools that are used to graphically schedule projects do not typically handle recursive development approaches well and may therefore not be useful for developing the information required by this subparagraph.

### E.6.3.3  Risk Management

The DOD-STD-2167A SDP DID currently states:

> "10.2.5.3 *Risk management.* This paragraph shall be numbered 3.3 and shall describe the contractor's procedures for managing areas of risk to successful project completion. This paragraph shall:
> a. Identify the areas of risk to successful project completion and prioritize them.
> b. Identify the constituent risk factors that contribute to the potential occurrence of each risk.
> c. Document procedures for monitoring the risk factors and for reducing the potential occurrence of each risk.
> d. Identify contingency procedures for each area of risk, as appropriate."

This SDP DID paragraph does not require tailoring, but it does require interpretation. The corresponding SDP paragraph should identify and prioritize OOD-specific risks, such as lacks of, or inadequacies in, the following:

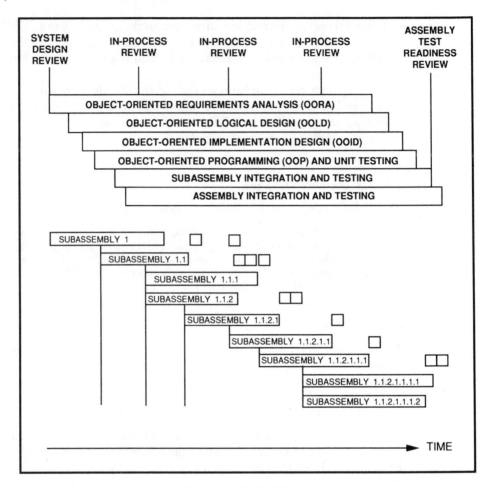

**Figure E-1: Overlap of Development Activities**

- Developer experience and training with OOD
- Developer experience and training in the project-tailored version of the OOD method
- Production-quality CASE tools to support OOD
- Proper tailoring of DOD-STD-2167A, the DIDs, MIL-STD-1521B, etc.

### E.6.3.4  Formal Reviews

The DOD-STD-2167A SDP DID currently states:

> "10.2.5.8 *Formal reviews.* This paragraph shall be numbered 3.8 and shall describe the contractor's internal procedures for preparing for and conducting formal reviews."

Different software development methods produce different intermediate products at different times, according to different development cycles. This is especially true of globally recursive OOD methods such as ADM3. The corresponding SDP paragraph should therefore:

- Document the impact of the project-specific OOD method on the formal reviews
- Document whether the reviews are to be held incrementally and simultaneously or are to be renamed and redefined.
- List the planned number and type of formal reviews
- Describe the products to be reviewed
- Document the contractor's proposed acceptance criteria

The preceding paragraph implies that this SDP DID paragraph requires the following requirements to be added:[1]

"This paragraph shall describe the relationship between the contractor's software development method(s), the method-specific development cycle, and the corresponding formal reviews. This paragraph shall describe the contractor's plans for the formal reviews including the *method-specific* : number of reviews, type of reviews, products to be reviewed, and the contractor's proposed acceptance criteria for passing the reviews."

### E.6.3.5  Personnel—Software Engineering

The DOD-STD-2167A SDP DID currently states:

"10.2.6.1.2 *Personnel—software engineering.* This subparagraph shall be numbered 4.1.2 and shall describe the number and skill levels of personnel who will perform the software engineering activities. The personnel shall be described by title and minimum qualifications for the position. In addition, this subparagraph shall specify any requirements unique to particular positions, such as geographic location, security level, extended hours, etc."

This SDP DID paragraph does not require tailoring, but it does requires interpretation. The corresponding SDP paragraph should document:

- The OOD-specific qualifications (e.g., software engineering, OOD, and Ada experience or training) required of the developers
- Whether the contractor plans to hire at least a minimum of one or two developers with prior OOD experience
- Whether the project methodologist (or OOD expert) is properly experienced with the project-specific OOD method
- The planned type and amount of training and schedule of training for each class of personnel

---

[1]Although tailoring is by deletion only, additional requirements can be added and modifications to existing requirements can be made via the project statement of work (SOW).

### E.6.3.6  Software Engineering Environment—Software Items

The DOD-STD-2167A SDP DID currently states:

> "10.2.6.1.3 *Software engineering environment.* This subparagraph shall be numbered 4.1.3 and shall be divided into the following subparagraphs to identify and describe the plans for establishing and maintaining the resources (software, firmware, and hardware) necessary to perform the software engineering activities."

> 10.2.6.1.3.1 *Software items.* This subparagraph shall be numbered 4.1.3.1 and shall identify the software items, such as operating systems, compilers, code auditors, dynamic path analyzers, test drivers, preprocessors, test data generators, post-processors, etc., necessary to perform the software engineering activities. This subparagraph shall describe the purpose of each item and shall identify any classified processing or security issues associated with the software items."

This SDP DID paragraph does not require tailoring, but it does requires interpretation. The corresponding SDP paragraph should document plans concerning the evaluation, selection, acquisition, and training concerning the following tools:

- Method-specific upper CASE tools (e.g., ObjectMaker) for analysis and design
- Class browsers
- Debuggers that understand the impacts of inheritance (e.g., that the definition of an object may be scattered among several classes in an inheritance hierarchy)
- Automatic code generators for object-based (e.g., Ada) and object-oriented (e.g., C++) languages
- Automatic document generation tools that understand both DOD-STD-2167A DID requirements and the proper content and format of documentation of object-oriented software
- Configuration management tools (e.g., the Rational R-1000 development environment's support for "subsystems")
- Requirements tracing tools that understand:
  —The impact of incremental, recursive development cycles
  —The building blocks of OOD (e.g., objects, classes, attributes, operations)
- Stub generators (because many recursive OOD methods are top-down, whereas Ada has bottom-up compilation order restrictions)

### E.6.3.7  Software Standards, Procedures, Development Techniques, and Methodologies

The DOD-STD-2167A SDP DID currently states:

> "10.2.6.2 *Software standards and procedures.* This paragraph shall be numbered 4.2 and shall be divided into the following subparagraphs to describe the software standards and procedures the contractor plans to use."

> "10.2.6.2.1 *Software development techniques and methodologies.* This subparagraph shall be numbered 4.2.1 and shall identify and describe the techniques and methodologies the contractor plans to use to perform:
> a. Software Requirements Analysis
> b. Preliminary Design

c. Detailed Design
d. Coding and CSU Testing
e. CSC Integration and Testing
f. CSCI Testing."

"10.2.6.2.3 *Design standards.* This subparagraph shall be numbered 4.2.3 and shall describe the design standards the contractor plans to use in developing the software."

"10.2.6.2.4 *Coding standards.* This subparagraph shall be numbered 4.2.4 and shall describe the coding standards the contractor plans to use in developing the software."

The current structure of this part of the SDP DID is illogical, incomplete, and inconsistent. Although the development process drives the development method(s) and the method(s) drive the standards and procedures, methods are currently documented as a subparagraph under standards and procedures. DOD-STD-2167A should require standards for requirements analysis, testing, and integration in addition to standards for design and coding. Because Ada is both a design language and an implementation language and because the OOD methods used in the Ada community are highly Ada-oriented, it is practically impossible to develop a credible Ada design standard that does not contain coding standards or credible Ada coding standards that contain no design standards. The SDP DID does not clearly require procedures at all! The terminology of DOD-STD-2167A is methods, not techniques and methodologies. The SDP should map well to the development process used, and many OOD methods have different and more detailed activities than DOD-STD-2167A.

These four SDP DID paragraphs require both significant modification and interpretation. Specifically, these DID paragraphs should be replaced with the following single paragraph:

"10.2.6.2 Software *development process, methods, standards, and procedures.* This paragraph shall be numbered 4.2 and shall identify and describe the contractor's planned software development process and associated development cycle. For each activity of the contractor's planned development process, this paragraph shall identify and document the contractor's planned software development method(s) including the associated standards and procedures."

This corresponding paragraph of the SDP should contain:

• Analysis and design standards for the object-oriented graphics (e.g., semantic nets, control flow diagrams), the subassemblies, the objects and classes, and the corresponding program design language (PDL) and code
• Coding standards for implementing the objects and classes in Ada

### E.6.3.8  Software Development Files (SDFs)

The DOD-STD-2167A SDP DID currently states:

"10.2.6.2.2 *Software development files.* This subparagraph shall be numbered 4.2.2 and shall define the contractor's plans, including the responsible organization(s), for the creation and maintenance of software development files (SDFs). This subparagraph shall define the format and contents of the SDFs and describe the procedures for maintaining SDFs."

Each OOD method produces (slightly) different intermediate products, according to (slightly) different development cycles. The SDFs should contain the working products (e.g., graphics, PDL, code, requirements traces, etc.) specific to the project-OOD method. SDFs should be created for each subassembly (CSC) and not necessarily for each object-class (CSU). This DID subparagraph also should be moved to be consistent with the rewriting and reorganization of its surrounding paragraphs.

This SDP DID paragraph therefore requires the following modifications to be made via the project statement of work (SOW):

> "10.2.6.2.1 *Software development files.* This subparagraph shall be numbered 4.2.1 and shall define the contractor's plans, including the responsible organization(s), for the creation and maintenance of software development files (SDFs). This subparagraph shall define the types and the *method-specific* format and contents of the SDFs and describe the procedures for maintaining SDFs."

### E.6.3.9  Nondevelopmental Software

The DOD-STD-2167A SDP DID currently states:

> "10.2.6.3 *Non-developmental software.* This paragraph shall be numbered 4.3 and shall identify and describe *each non-developmental software item*, such as commercially available, reusable, and Government furnished software, to be incorporated into the deliverable software. This subparagraph shall briefly describe the rationale for the use of each non-developmental software item."

Reusable software is a central tenet of any OOD method, and this is especially true of methods (e.g., ADM3), which have explicit steps for the searching and updating of the reuse repository.

This paragraph should be tailored to require documentation of the contractor's plans for reuse and documentation of how reuse fits into the contractor's proposed software development method(s). It is a mistake to attempt to list each reusable software item. This is inappropriate design information that is impossible to know at proposal time when the draft SDP should be due, and the number of reusable, software non-developmental items (NDIs) may run into the hundreds on a large project.

### E.6.3.10   Software Products Evaluation—(Activity Name)

The DOD-STD-2167A SDP DID currently states:

> "10.2.8.5.1 *Software products evaluation—(activity name).* This subparagraph shall be numbered 6.5.X (beginning with 6.5.1) and shall describe the contractor's plans for conducting evaluations of each of the products of the activity. The description shall identify the specific products to be evaluated. For each product to be evaluated, the evaluation criteria to be used and the evaluation procedures and tool to be employed shall be identified. For evaluations performed on items contained in SDFs, the method of selecting the sample and the percentage of the items to be evaluated shall be specified."

Each OOD method produces slightly different intermediate products that need to be evaluated for completeness, (internal and external) consistency, correctness, and conformance to the the OOD method. This SDP DID paragraph therefore requires tailoring. Object-oriented development methods should have specific product evaluation criteria associated with the method-specific intermediate products, and DOD-STD-2167A should require these criteria to be identified. Examples include graphic-specific quality criteria and criteria for determining whether they truly document object-oriented designs or violate complexity limits.

## E.6.4    Software Requirements Specification (SRS)

DOD-STD-2167A replaced "functions" with "capabilities" in order to permit the use of object-oriented software requirements analysis methods such as ADM3. Capabilities on OOD projects are requirements associated with the following:

1. Entire assemblies
2. Entire subassemblies
3. Classes
4. Objects
5. Attributes or attribute types
6. Messages
7. Operations
8. Exceptions
9. Scenarios

For additional guidance on how to use OOD methods on Ada projects using DOD-STD-2167A, see *Documentation Guidelines for Ada Object-Oriented Development using DOD-STD-2167A*, Report Number TR-L801-066, published 5 September 1989 by the US Army Communications-Electronics Command (CECOM) at Fort Monmouth, New Jersey [CECOM 89]. Unfortunately, this report is not as useful as its title might sound, as it is almost totally based on Shlaer and Mellor's Object-Oriented Systems Analysis method [Shlaer and Mellor 1988] and is *not* very applicable to other OOD methods, such as ADM3.

The following paragraphs and subparagraphs of the tailored DOD-STD-2167A SRS and SRS DID (DI-MCCR-80025A) are affected by the use of an OOD method and require ADM3 or OOD-specific information. These sections may also require, or would benefit from, either ADM3 or OOD-specific tailoring or interpretations:

| SRS DID | SRS | Title |
|---------|-----|-------|
| 7.6 | N/A | None |
| 10.1 b | N/A | Use of alternate presentation styles |
| 10.1.3.2 | 1.2 | CSCI overview |
| 10.1.3.3 | 1.3 | Document overview |
| 10.1.5.1 | 3.1 | CSCI external interface requirements |
| 10.1.5.2 | 3.2 | CSCI capability requirements |
| 10.1.5.2.1 | 3.2.X | (Assembly name and project-unique identifier) |
| 10.1.5.2.1.1 | 3.2.X.Y | (Class/Object name and project-unique identifier) |

| SRS DID | SRS | Title |
|---|---|---|
| 10.1.5.2.1.1.2 | 3.2.X.Y.Z+1 | Global data |
| 10.1.5.2.1.1.3 | 3.2.X.Y.Z+2 | Global operations |
| 10.1.5.3 | 3.3 | System states and modes |
| 10.1.5.6 | 3.6 | Sizing and timing requirements |
| 10.1.8 | 6 | Notes |

### E.6.4.1  Incremental Development

Because several globally recursive "Analyze a little, design a little, code a little" OOD methods (e.g., ADM3) develop the requirements incrementally, one subassembly at a time, the following paragraph should be added to the DOD-STD-2167A SRS DID:

> "7.6 A SRS may be developed incrementally in accordance with the contractor's software development method(s) described in the Software Development Plan (SDP)."

### E.6.4.2  Contractor-Internal Data Product Formats

The current format of the DOD-STD-2167A SRS DID is too general and inappropriate for adequately documenting object-oriented requirements. The DOD "Acquisition Streamlining Directive" [DODD 5043] explicitly allows, and the foreword of DOD-STD-2167A implicitly allows, the use of more appropriate formats to provide the necessary information. Therefore, add the following to paragraph 10.1-b. "Use of alternate presentation styles":

> "Method-specific formats are acceptable because DOD-STD-2167A is not intended to . . . discourage the use of any particular software development method (e.g., any object-oriented software requirements method) and because DODD 5000.43, Acquisition Streamlining, states that a contractor's . . . data product formats shall be used instead of specifying other approaches unless the acquisition activity determines that the contractor's approaches cannot satisfy the program needs."

### E.6.4.3  CSCI Partitioning into Assemblies

The primary entity of software decomposition within DOD-STD-2167A is the CSCI, whereas the primary entity of software decomposition within OOD is the assembly. A CSCI may contain multiple assemblies. Therefore, add the following requirement to 10.1.3.2 *CSCI overview*:

> "This paragraph shall briefly describe any partitioning of the CSCI into assemblies, identify each assembly by name and project-unique identifier, and briefly state the purpose and role, within the CSCI, of each assembly."

### E.6.4.4  Document Overview

The reader should understand how the new DID does (or does not) implement the requirements of the original DID and the rationale for the modifications. Therefore, add the following requirement to 10.1.3.3 *Document overview* :

"If a significantly-tailored/modified or contractor-internal version of this DID is used, this paragraph shall, directly or by reference, briefly describe the rationale for the modification and provide a mapping from this original DID to the modified version of this DID."

### E.6.4.5   CSCI External Interface Requirements

The information required by 10.1.5.1, *CSCI external interface requirements*, can be provided in part using a CSCI-level interaction diagram. Such a diagram would be useful because classes and objects primarily interact via messages. Interfaces should be briefly described in terms of:

- Visible attribute types and constant attributes
- Messages and their corresponding parameters
- Exceptions

### E.6.4.6   CSSI Capability Requirements

The current format of the DOD-STD-2167A SRS DID does not recognize the basic building blocks of and the structure produced by OOD: assemblies, subassemblies, classes, and objects. Because attributes, operations, and exceptions are encapsulated within classes and objects, capability requirements associated with attributes, operations, and exceptions should be organized along class and object lines. Therefore, replace the entire current subparagraph 10.1.5.2.1 (*Capability name and project-unique identifier*) with the format described in Chapter 7.

Because object-oriented capablilites may be associated with assemblies, subassemblies, classes, and objects, add the following to 10.1.5.2 "CSCI capability requirements":

"Capabilities may be decomposed and organized by assembly, subassembly, and class/object."

An object-oriented analysis method does not consider data in isolation, but only in the context of data encapsulated within classes and objects. Only a tiny amount of global data, if any, is developed and must be documented separately. Therefore, the current contents of 10.1.5.4 "CSCI data element requirements" should be incorporated into the new 10.1.5.2.1.1.1.1 "Exported data" and 10.1.5.2.1.1.2 "Global data."

Because the states and modes in terms of capabilities is only understandable once the capabilities have been analyzed and organized, move the last two sentences of 10.1.5.2 "CSCI capability requirements" to form a new 10.1.5.4 "System states and modes." These last two sentences are "If the system of which the CSCI is a part can exist in various system states and modes as documented in the system specification, this paragraph shall identify each such state and mode and shall correlate each CSCI capability to those states and modes. A table may be used to depict this correlation."

### E.6.4.6.1   Assembly Capabilities

Because a CSCI may contain multiple assemblies, add the following new subparagraph:

"10.1.5.2.1 (*Assembly name and project-unique identifier*). This subparagraph shall be numbered 3.2.X (beginning with 3.2.1), shall identify in the subparagraphs that follow all of the CSCI capability requirements that the assembly must satisfy, and shall briefly describe the partitioning of the assembly into logical subassemblies. Diagrams (e.g., assembly system semantic net, assembly diagram) may be used to aid in this description."

### E.6.4.6.2    Subassembly Capabilities

An assembly will typically contain numerous subassemblies which in turn consist of classes, objects, and a tiny amount of global data and operations. Object-oriented analysis methods (e.g., ADM) often recursively develop the requirements in increments of essential subassemblies. Therefore, add the following new subparagraph:

"10.1.5.2.1.1 (*Subassembly name and project-unique identifier*). This subparagraph shall be numbered 3.2.X.Y (beginning with 3.2.X.1), shall identify in the subparagraphs that follow all of the assembly capability requirements that the essential subassembly must satisfy, and shall briefly describe the partitioning of the essential subassembly into essential classes, objects, global data, and global operations, and the significant relationships (e.g., dependency) between them. Diagrams (e.g., subassembly general semantic net, subassembly interaction diagram, timing diagrams) may be used to aid in this description."

### E.6.4.6.3    Class and Object Capabilities

Object-oriented analysis methods (e.g., ADM3) typically identify and analyze requirements according to essential classes and objects. Therefore, add the following new subparagraph:

"10.1.5.2.1.1.1 (*Class or Object name and project-unique identifier*). This subparagraph shall be numbered 3.2.X.Y.Z (beginning with 3.X.Y.1), shall state the purpose of the essential class or object, shall identify in the subparagraphs that follow all of the subassembly capability requirements that the class/object must satisfy, and shall specify the behavior of the class/object in terms of attribute types, attributes, messages, exceptions, and operations. Diagrams (e.g., class- or object-level state transition diagram, control flow diagram) may be used to aid in this description."

### E.6.4.6.4    CSCI Internal Interfaces

Interfaces should be assembly to assembly interfaces. Interfaces below this level involve design decisions and belong in the Interface Design Document (IDD).

### E.6.4.7  Notes

In order to promote understandability, this section should include a standard "boilerplate" overview of the OORA method; describe the natural products and their organization into essential assemblies, essential subassemblies, essential classes, and essential objects; and contain a glossary of relevant method-specific terms.

## E.6.5    Software Design Document (SDD)

### E.6.5.1  Incremental Development

Most OOD methods rely on globally-recursive "analyze a little, design a little, code a little" approaches to develop the design incrementally, one subassembly at a time. Therefore, replace the following paragraph

> "7.3 An SDD is incrementally developed as follows:
> a.  Sections 1, 2, 3, 7, and 8 are produced during preliminary design and are presented at Preliminary Design Review (PDR).
> b.  Sections 4, 5, and 6 are produced during detailed design and all other sections are updated as applicable. The complete SDD is presented at Critical Design Review (CDR)."

with

> "7.3 A SDD may be incrementally developed and reviewed in accordance with the contractor's software development method(s), as described in the software development plan (SDP)."

### E.6.5.2  Contractor-Internal Data Product Formats

The current format of the DOD-STD-2167A SDD DID is too general and is therefore inappropriate for adequately documenting Ada- and object-oriented designs. The acquisition streamlining directive explicitly, and the foreword of DOD-STD-2167A implicitly, allow the use of more appropriate formats to provide the necessary information. Therefore, add the following to 10.1 b. "Use of alternate presentation styles":

> "Method-specific formats are acceptable because DOD-STD-2167A 'is not intended to . . . discourage the use of any particular software development method' (e.g., any object-oriented software requirements method) and because DODD 5000.43, Acquisition Streamlining, states that 'a contractor's ... data product formats shall be used instead of specifying other approaches unless the acquisition activity determines that the contractor's approaches cannot satisfy the program needs.'"

### E.6.5.3  Document Structure

The building blocks of object-oriented logical design are assemblies, subassemblies, classes, and objects. The building blocks of object-oriented implementation design using Ada are extended library units and program units. Therefore, replace paragraph 10.1 g. "Document structure" with:

> "g. *Document structure* This document shall consist of the following:
> (1)  Cover
> (2)  Title page
> (3)  Table of contents
> (4)  Scope
> (5)  Referenced documents
> (6)  Logical design

(7)   Implementation design
(8)   Scenario design
(9)   Requirements trace
(10)  Notes
(11)  Appendixes."

In order to promote the software engineering principle of uniformity, modify section 6 of the SDD to be consistent with the corresponding sections in the SRS as described in paragraphs E.6.4.6.1 through E.6.4.6.3 of this appendix.

## E.7 CONCLUSION

Current military standards and DIDs, though greatly improved over superseded ones, still require proper tailoring and reinterpretation when used to produce object-oriented software requirements specifications and design documents. This tailoring and reinterpretation is non-trivial and must be performed early during the development of the Request For Proposal (RFP) and the proposal which should include a draft Software Development Plan (SDP). The SDP also requires appropriate tailoring and reinterpretation. Adequate and timely training of both contractor and contracting agency personnel is essential if proper tailoring and interpretation is to occur. Hopefully, the updates to DOD-STD-2167A and MIL-STD-1521B will remove the remaining roadblocks to documenting object-oriented specifications and designs on military projects.

## E.8 APPENDIX REFERENCES

[ANSI/MIL-STD-1815A-1983] Ada Joint Program Office, *Reference Manual for the Ada Programming Language*, United States Government, 1983.

[Booch 1991] Grady Booch, *Object-Oriented Design with Applications*, Menlo Park, CA, Benjamin Cummings, 1991.

[CECOM 1989] U.S. Army Communications-Electronics Command, *Documentation Guidelines for Ada Object-Oriented Development using DOD-STD-2167A*, Report Number TR-L801-066, Fort Monmouth, NJ, 5 September 1989.

[Coad and Yourdon 1989] Peter Coad and Edward Yourdon, *OORA—Object-Oriented Requirements Analysis*, Englewood Cliffs, NJ, Prentice Hall, 1989.

[Colbert 1989] Ed Colbert, "The Object-Oriented Software Development Method: A Practical Approach to Object-Oriented Development," *Proceedings of TRI-Ada'89 — Ada Technology in Context: Application, Development, and Deployment*, 23-26 October 1989, Association for Computing Machinery, pages 400-415, 1989.

[DeMarco 1978] Tom DeMarco, *Structured Analysis and System Specification*, Yourdon Press/Prentice Hall, 1978.

[DI-MCCR-80012A] Joint Logistics Commanders Computer Software Management Subgroup, "Software Design Document", Department of Defense, 29 February 1986.

[DI-MCCR-80025A] Joint Logistics Commanders Computer Software Management Subgroup, "Software Requirements Specification", Department of Defense, 29 February 1986.

[DODD 3405.1] William H. Taft IV, "Computer Programming Language Policy", Department of Defense, 2 April 1987.

[DOD-STD-2167A] Joint Logistics Commanders Computer Software Management Subgroup, *Defense Systems Software Development*, Department of Defense, 29 February 1986.

[Firesmith 1989] "The Ada Development Method (ADM): An Object-Oriented Development Method for the Entire Development Cycle," *Summer 1989 SIGAda Conference Program and Abstracts,* pages xvii-xxvi, 8-11 August 1989.

[Rumbaugh et al. 1991] James Rumbaugh, Michael Blaha, William Premerlani, Frederick Eddy, and William Lorensen, *Object-Oriented Modeling and Design,* Englewood Cliffs, Prentice Hall, 1991.

[Shlaer and Mellor 1988] Sally Shlaer and Stephen J. Mellor, *Object-Oriented Systems Analysis, Modeling the World in Data,* Yourdon Press,1988.

[US Congress 1990] United States Congress, *Department of Defense (DOD) Appropriations Act 1991,* Public Law 101-511, Section 89092, United States Government, 5 November 1990.

[Ward and Mellor 1985] Paul Ward and Stephen J. Mellor, *Structured Development for Real-Time Systems, Volume 1: Introduction and Tools, Volume 2: Essential Modelling Techniques, Volume 3: Implementation Modelling Techniques,* Yourdon Press, 1985.

[Yourdon and Constantine 1979] Edward Yourdon and Larry Constantine, *Structured Design,* Englewood Cliffs, NJ, Prentice Hall, 1979.

## E.9  GENERAL BIBLIOGRAPHY OF RELATED DOCUMENTS

Anderson, John A., and Elaine S. Ward "Technology Transfer: Experiences in introducing Object-Oriented Methods to Government Projects," *Proceedings of the Eighth Washington Ada Symposium/Summer SIGAda Meeting,* pages 10-15, 17-21 June 1991.

Ellison, Dr. Karen S., and William J. Goulet, "A Practical Approach to Methodologies, Ada, and DOD-STD-2167A," *7th National Annual Conference on Ada Technology Proceedings,*pages 51-57, 13-16 March 1989.

Firesmith, Donald G. "Ada Community Concerns Regarding DOD-STD-2167,"*Defense Science and Electronics,* 6(4,7), April/July 1987. "Ada and DOD-STD-2167A," *National Institute for Software Quality and Productivity CASE Technology Conference,* 11-12 April 1988. "DOD-STD-2167 and the Classic Waterfall Life-Cycle," *Tactical Communications Conference—88,* 5 May 1988. "The Management Implications of the Recursive Nature of Object-Oriented Development", *1987 AdaEXPO/SIGAda Conference Proceedings,* 7-11 December 1987. "Resolution of Ada-related Concerns in DOD-STD-2167, Revision A," coauthored with 1Lt Colin Gilyeat USAF, *Ada Letters,* September/October 1986. "Software Development Standards and Ada Working Group Issues and Subissues Report,"SIGAda SDSAWG, "Structured Analysis and Object-Oriented Development Are Not Compatible," *Ada Letters,* November/December 1991.

Gray, Lewis "On Decomposing an Ada CSCI of a Large Command and Control System into TLCSCs, LLCSCs, and Units: With Suggestions for Using DOD-STD-2167A," *Proceedings of the Ninth Annual National Conference on Ada Technology,* pages 55-68, 4-7 March 1991.

Overmyer, Scott P. "The Impact of DOD-STD-2167A on Iterative Design Methodologies: Help or Hinder?," *Software Engineering Notes,* 15(5), pages 50-59, October 1990.

Sally Shlaer and Stephen J. Mellor *Object Lifecycles, Modeling the World in States,* Yourdon Press,1992.

Sodhi, Jag, Guy Daubenspeck, and Thomas Archer "Forward Entry Device Software Engineering and DOD-STD-2167A
Experiences," *8th Annual National Conference on Ada Technology Conference Proceedings*, pages 63-68, 5-8 March, 1990.

Ward, Elaine S. and John A. Anderson "Documenting Object-Oriented Requirements Analysis Understandably for DOD-STD-2167A," *Structured Development Forum XI Proceedings*, 30 April through 3 May 1990.

# Index